ELUSIVE DESTINY

ELUSIVE

THE POLITICAL VOCATION OF JOHN NAPIER TURNER

DESTINY

PAUL LITT

UBCPress · Vancouver · Toronto

20 19 18 17 16 15 14 13 12 11   5 4 3 2 1

Printed in Canada.

Library and Archives Canada Cataloguing in Publication

Litt, Paul
    Elusive destiny: the political vocation of John Napier Turner / Paul Litt.

Includes bibliographical references and index.
Issued also in electronic format.
ISBN 978-0-7748-2264-0

    1. Turner, John N., 1929-. 2. Liberal Party of Canada. 3. Prime ministers – Canada – Biography. 4. Politicians – Canada – Biography. 5. Canada – Politics and government – 1945-. I. Title.

FC626.T87L58 2011	971.064	C2011-905567-8

e-book ISBNs: 978-0-7748-2266-4 (epdf); 978-0-7748-2267-1 (epub)

Canadä

UBC Press gratefully acknowledges the financial support for our publishing program of the Government of Canada (through the Canada Book Fund), the Canada Council for the Arts, and the British Columbia Arts Council.

This book has been published with the help of a grant from the Canadian Federation for the Humanities and Social Sciences, through the Aid to Scholarly Publications Program, using funds provided by the Social Sciences and Humanities Research Council of Canada.

The C.D. Howe Foundation also provided financial support for this volume.

UBC Press
The University of British Columbia
2029 West Mall
Vancouver, BC V6T 1Z2
www.ubcpress.ca

CONTENTS

FOREWORD

By John English

John Turner came of political age in the 1950s when Canada's finest historians wrote great political biographies. Donald Creighton's biography of John A. Macdonald framed the central debates about Canadian identity at Canada's creation and in the confident 1950s. Creighton's Macdonald found its superb counterpart in J.M.S. Careless's brilliant biography of Macdonald's longtime liberal antagonist and brief collaborator George Brown. The two biographies express the spirit of their time, the fundamental debate about how individual character shapes the circumstances of national experience.

Academic historians moved suddenly away from political biography during the rebellions of the sixties. Political biographies were, after all, about "great men," as Thomas Carlyle had declared in the mid-nineteenth century. And like the Victorian age, they suddenly seemed fusty remnants, like wing-tipped collars, waistcoats, spats, and spittoons. History was to be written "from the bottom up," and the excluded became the proper study of the proper historical mind as social history became the dominant school for aspiring historians. Simultaneously, and not coincidentally, the celebrated French Annales School argued for the irrelevance of political leadership in the *longue durée* of historical change. Kings and courts were mere flotsam and jetsam on the endless oceans of history. Michel Foucault, more fashionable than Marx in the seventies, argued for resistance against the processes of the state, thereby steering historians toward madness, prisons, and rebellion. These intellectual arguments were cogent in a period when the women's movement found its voice, when the European colonies broke the chains of empire, and when students shunned academic gowns and glory.

John Turner is the George Brown of his political times – a giant. Unlike Brown, Turner did become prime minister, albeit briefly, and fortunately he has lived much longer than the murdered Brown. But, like Brown, Turner deeply affected the central debates of Canadian political life for more than a generation. Paul Litt's fine biography argues conclusively that Turner represented a well-defined current within Canadian Liberalism that left a deep imprint upon Canadian politics during the seventies and eighties.

For John Turner, the Liberalism of Mackenzie King and C.D. Howe was bred in the bone. His mother, Phyllis, was an outstanding public servant, an economist whose rare female voice was heard in the corridors of economic power during the challenges of depression and war, when Canadians turned to Ottawa for leadership. In his youth in Ottawa, Turner encountered Canadians dedicated to making the state an instrument for economic revival and, after September 1939, for fighting a world war. There were worthy and hard-won victories in both battles. King, Howe, Claxton, Martin, Ilsley, Pearson, and St. Laurent were more than names to Turner; they represented the best of a powerful political tradition of which he, because of his beliefs, exceptional ability, and personal charisma, became a distinguished part.

Elusive Destiny portrays an exceptional athlete, scholar, lawyer, businessman, and politician. Of these pursuits, John Turner would later argue that the last was the highest calling, one that was wrongly and dangerously depreciated in the second half of the twentieth century. As minister of justice, Turner knew that his reform of the Criminal Code profoundly affected the way Canadians lived their lives. As minister of finance, his careful stewardship of the nation's finances during the turbulent years of the OPEC oil embargo, the world food crisis, and the breakup of the Bretton Woods system maintained Canadian economic balance through the most difficult economic circumstances since the Great Depression.

Turner's political presence lingered after he returned to private life in 1975. Paul Litt has written a political biography that does not dwell upon

Turner's personal life but rather concentrates on Turner's public career. Still, Litt recognizes that an examination of Turner's beliefs and life before and beyond politics is essential to understanding political motivation. Through Litt's careful scholarship and perceptive prose we come to know John Turner and what "made him run," to use a cliché of his political times. When Pierre Trudeau resigned in 1984, as Canada stumbled out of a deep recession, Turner became Liberal leader and then, briefly, prime minister. Defeated badly in the 1984 general election, Turner stayed on to fight another campaign. It was his finest hour.

Leading a divided party, haunted by memories of old feuds, Turner confronted Brian Mulroney on the issue of free trade. He lost the election, but his evocative warning that Canadians had built a nation from sea to sea to sea, which Brian Mulroney weakened with the stroke of a pen, is an image that has lingered with Canadians. His powerful words drew upon his experience of the confident Canada of his youth as well as the wariness of a too close relationship with our great neighbour. A good friend of influential Americans such as George Schultz, Turner knew that American national interest would trump agreements and close the border. What happened after 9/11 was no surprise to Turner.

Elusive Destiny captures Turner's eloquence and passion in the historic political battles of the late eighties exceedingly well. He makes a strong case for Turner's hesitations about the trade agreement with the United States and shares Turner's view that the agreement was not "free trade" and that the United States Congress would never relinquish American sovereignty over trade or, as Canadians learned later, over security. More controversially, Litt takes Turner's side in the Meech Lake debate, strongly arguing that Pierre Trudeau was unfair to his successor in his vitriolic opposition to Meech. Many Liberals will disagree, but all readers will understand the basis of Turner's position and the depth of his convictions.

In a different time, John Turner's biography, with its profound relevance to contemporary debates about Liberalism, nationalism, and Canada in the world, would have been published earlier. Unfortunately, as Turner has eloquently warned, Canadians have become too indifferent to their political history and traditions. Ultimately, memory forms consciousness and provides the understanding that gives meaning to our common life. Biography particularly illuminates choices: how leaders developed, how differences festered, and how personal relationships influenced decisions. While historians still rightly shun Carlyle, events have persuaded many that the role of the individual in effecting historical change can be decisive. The end of the Cold War, for example, is difficult to explain without reference to Mikhail Gorbachev, an almost accidental successor to Soviet leadership after the deaths of others in power. Moreover, those historians who minimized the role of Stalin and emphasized local circumstances in the terror that transformed the Soviet Union were forced to revise their judgments when archives revealed his personal hand in thousands of executions. And for better and worse, all agree that Mao fundamentally changed China.

In Britain, after a brief pause, biography is flourishing again, even in academic circles. Martin Gilbert's monumental biography of Churchill has chugged on for decades, while major writers such as Antonia Fraser, the politician Roy Jenkins, and Robert Skidelsky have had great popular success. German and French bookstores are now crammed with outstanding biographies of major and minor political leaders. In the United States, the tide turned in the nineties as academics and others turned to the Founding Fathers and, especially, to Abraham Lincoln, while television has been especially kind with history and biography channels.

Canadians, however, have not been served as well. The major historical project of the Canadian Broadcasting Corporation was *Canada: A People's History,* whose title clearly and correctly indicates that the focus was on "ordinary" Canadians not on the political elites. As the general editor of the *Dictionary of Canadian Biography/Dictionnaire biographique du Canada,* I have discovered that it is often extremely difficult to find authors to write biographies of prominent political figures. The C.D. Howe Foundation gave a generous grant that permitted us to publish biographies of prominent Canadians, including C.D. Howe, but we are still trying to find appropriate writers for other important politicians.

This volume, written with the cooperation of John Turner and supported by the Howe Foundation, reveals how important academic biographies based upon scrupulous research on Canada's major political leaders can be. One hopes that the University of British Columbia Press will publish many future political biographies of this quality. When Lester Pearson read

Creighton's Macdonald in the early fifties, he wrote his former colleague in the History Department of the University of Toronto and told him that the biography illuminated what Macdonald meant and what Canada had become. John Turner's story similarly tells us so much about what we were and how his political generation shaped the nation we know today.

ELUSIVE DESTINY

THE RIGHT MAN AT THE WRONG TIME

T he studio was in a nondescript building in suburban Ottawa, but the stage was national. Three men in suits faced the cameras and the questions of journalists. In the middle was Brian Mulroney, the Progressive Conservative prime minister, looking sleek and smug; on the right, Ed Broadbent, the leader of the New Democratic Party, exuding earnest determination; and to the left, John Turner, the Liberal leader, keyed up and champing at the bit. It was the leaders' debate in the 1988 Canadian general election. The three had been sparring for over an hour, with some spirited exchanges but no decisive blows.

This was a critical moment for John Napier Turner. He had stumbled during the leaders' debate in 1984; some thought it had cost him the election. Now he was trying to rally a party disheartened by four years in opposition. The Liberals had started the 1988 election campaign riven by factionalism and intrigue, squabbling over major issues of the day and disheartened by the prospect of remaining out of power. In the opening weeks of the campaign, they fell to third place in the polls. Pundits were predicting they would soon follow the British Liberal Party into political oblivion.

Turner opposed the free-trade deal that Mulroney had signed with the United States, but his message had not been getting through to Canadians. Now came the wake-up call. Late in the debate Turner listed a number of flaws in the agreement and asked the prime minister why he had accepted them. Mulroney deflected the question. Turner went back at him. Ignoring the old adage that patriotism is the last refuge of a scoundrel, Mulroney launched into pious finger wagging about how his ancestors had helped build Canada. Turner again brought him back on topic and forced the issue in one eloquent outburst:

> We built a country east and west and north. We built it on an infrastructure that deliberately resisted the continental pressure of the United States. For 120 years we've done it. With one signature of a pen, you've reversed that, thrown us into the north-south influence of the United States and will reduce us, I am sure, to a colony of the United States, because when the economic levers go, the political independence is sure to follow.[1]

Turner had driven his point home vividly and passionately. He had done it in one memorable sound bite, and the media ran with it. The clip led on the television news, aired repeatedly on radio, and was printed verbatim in newspapers. Turner came across as forceful and driven by conviction, in marked contrast to the dissembling Mulroney. The polls showed the Liberals surging ahead of the Tories. John Turner was back.

But not for long. Having lost this round on the free-trade issue itself, the Tories retaliated by attacking the messenger. They impugned Turner's character; he wasn't a true patriot, really – he was just trying to save his own political skin. An advertising blitz by the Conservatives branded him a liar. Business interests poured money into commercials that predicted job losses and economic decline if the deal were rejected. The Canadian Chamber of Commerce mobilized its members nationwide, and prominent figures at home and abroad were recruited to undermine Turner's credibility. Under this assault, the Liberal rally faltered – and the Tories won their second consecutive majority government.

A few months later, Turner announced that he was stepping down as Liberal leader. Though electoral victory had eluded him, he could at least take some satisfaction that, after leading the Liberals to the brink of extinction, he had restored them as a viable species. In 1993 his party would return to power for another thirteen years.

Character, or rather, voters' perceptions of character – the target of the Tories' late campaign advertising blitz in 1988 – is critical to any politician's success. People want to be able to trust their leader. For voters disoriented by a swirling wash of issues and information, focusing on character has the virtue of simplicity. Since the mid-twentieth century, they have been able to decide whether they like and trust politicians from what they see of them on television.

John Turner's generation was the last to grow up before television. His middle-class upbringing in pre-war Ottawa was shaped by family, school, and the Catholic Church. They imbued residual Victorian values of duty, honour, and public service, then cast him into an exemplary role in a rapidly changing modern world. Turner played by the rules and excelled. He won a Rhodes Scholarship in the late 1940s, became a successful lawyer in Montreal in the 1950s, a rising star of national politics in the 1960s, and a powerful Cabinet minister in the 1970s. His resignation as minister of finance in 1975 was a serious blow to the Liberal government of Pierre Trudeau. Everyone said he was simply biding his time, waiting for the next step; some day, some day soon, he would be prime minister.

The prediction came true in 1984, when Turner won the Liberal leadership and succeeded Trudeau. Then fate played a cruel trick. It allowed him to live his dream for seventy-nine days before snatching it away and dangling it just beyond reach for four long years. The 1988 election was Turner's last chance at power. He came agonizingly close, but close doesn't count in politics. What had gone wrong?

You have to be lucky in politics, and luck, more often than not, means simply being the right person in the right place at the right time. Turner's timing was off in three critical ways. When he first went to Parliament in 1962, he seemed the perfect representative of the youthful, urban, bicultural, and cosmopolitan Canada that was emerging in the post-war period. Fluently bilingual, handsome, an Oxford graduate and Olympic-calibre athlete with connections in the West, the Maritimes, and Quebec, he was the model of a smart, contemporary politician in the mould of President John F. Kennedy. Then came the cultural revolution of the mid-1960s, which injected into mainstream politics a potent desire for change. Politicians responded by implementing social democratic policies and striving to appear in tune with the restive spirit of the era. Turner advocated reforms and tried to be hip, but the image of the man in the grey flannel suit lingered. He lost the 1968 Liberal leadership to Pierre Trudeau, whose nonconformist image played perfectly to the cultural moment.

Canada seemed to be coming of age during the heady days of the Centennial and Expo 67, and the social justice ethos of the sixties would remain influential long after the events of the decade faded in memory. Turner encountered it again when he returned to politics in 1984 and found his concerns about mounting government deficits interpreted as a mean-spirited moral failing. Fiscal responsibility would not again become a desirable trait in a Canadian politician until after he retired from public life in 1993.

The second case of bad timing, not unrelated to the first, was the concurrence of Turner's and Trudeau's careers. The effect of Trudeau's candidacy on Turner's leadership prospects in 1968 was bad enough, but Trudeau's political longevity was worse. John Turner was thought to be a bit young for the leadership in 1968, but in the 1970s he was in his political prime. If an older candidate had won in 1968, or if Trudeau had lost an election and resigned as leader in the early to mid-1970s, the timing would have been just right. As it was, by the time Turner inherited the leadership, the Liberals had been in power under Trudeau for so long that voters wanted a change. To make things worse, the longer Trudeau stayed in office, the more his leadership was questioned. As ever more pundits suggested he should resign in favour of Turner, Trudeau increasingly resented his rival. Eventually, he so loathed Turner that he actively sabotaged his leadership campaign and his short time as prime minister.

The rise of television was the third and decisive timing factor in Turner's career. Kennedy's ascension to the US presidency in 1961 and Trudeau's rapid political rise in 1968 both exemplified the power of charisma in the television age. Political leaders were now expected to project star quality, and politics became another arena of celebrity popular culture. John Turner was not a natural television performer. This weakness was not critical in his early political career, but when he returned to national politics in 1984, he was subjected to a new level of scrutiny. Now in late middle age, he was still photogenic: tall and well built, with silver hair and patrician looks. Yet on videotape he came across as too "hot" in a medium Marshall McLuhan famously described as "cool."[2] Viewers saw him as tense and uncomfortable, and they knew from their favourite television shows that characters who looked ill at ease were hiding dark secrets or unsavoury motives.

Journalist Ron Graham tried to delve into the Turner psyche to explain his image issues in a profile written during the 1984 Liberal leadership campaign:

> His personality is a methodically achieved balance between his obsessive fears of failing or making a mistake and his heroic conceits about his ability to influence people and get things done. His fears are tested constantly by his ambition, his assumption of superiority, and the expectations of others; but any arrogance is checked at once by his insecurity, his sensitivity to criticism, and the humility ingrained by his Roman Catholic faith.

Graham likened Turner to a circus performer executing "a high-wire act of balance, determination, and cautious progress above the abyss of conflict, failure, or eternal damnation."[3]

Despite its supercilious exaggeration, Graham's observation was revealing. John Turner had good reason to be tense. From a young age he had constantly been pushed ahead and pulled in different directions by the expectations and demands of others. He was eager to please and more than capable. He had been raised by a single mother who had high standards – and he had measured up. Teachers expected a lot from him – and he shone. His friends were awed by his accomplishments and predicted great things – and he obliged. Supporters in business and politics invested in his future – and he delivered. With every accomplishment, the bar was set higher. The *oblige* was part and parcel of the *noblesse*. He was public property, a national resource, his private self battened below the hatches, accessible only to God and, schedule permitting, John Turner himself.

Turner's leadership style reflected his accommodating personality. He emulated Mackenzie King and Lester Pearson, two of his political heroes, in practising a classic conciliatory style of Canadian politics. It involved consulting, communicating, consensus building, and compromising to continually balance competing interests. His political philosophy was also a product of tension, in this case between the claims of social conscience and fiscal responsibility. He believed that government had a role to play in promoting social justice through welfare programs, yet should do only as much as it could afford. This approach placed him squarely in the centre of the political spectrum – the place where the votes lay, in both the Liberal Party and the electorate as a whole. When Turner's position was at odds with that of the Liberal Party, it was usually because he believed that the party had veered too far right or left. Invariably, he steered back toward the centre.

Accommodation was not a style that came naturally to Pierre Trudeau. Famous for his independence and self-assurance – some called it arrogance – he was seen as a leader who would strike out boldly in the direction he wanted to go and expect the country to follow him. The differences between Turner and Trudeau offered an instructive study in contrasting leadership styles, yet working together, they proved remarkably effective. Trudeau inspired Canadians with his principled causes, but often it was Turner who made them work, whether by calming Western premiers' fears about the *Official Languages Act* or energy policy, representing Canada's interests to the White House, or trying to get labour and business to work together.

On one key issue, however, they were at odds. For Trudeau, Quebec had to be treated as a province like all the others. Making concessions to Quebec nationalism would sap the foundation of Canadian federalism, perhaps even destroy the country. For Turner, Quebec was obviously unique, and constitutional arrangements to accommodate its needs would strengthen rather than weaken Canada. This difference between them could not be reconciled, and it came to a head in 1987 over the Meech Lake Accord. The Liberal Party was torn apart over the issue and would not heal for decades.

The tension at Turner's core may have short-circuited his prime-time image, yet for most of his long political career it drove him from one success to another. He produced under pressure. More than any other Canadian politician, he translated the spirit of the 1960s into substantial changes to the laws of the land. He was a central player in the French-English issues that dominated the era, negotiating with the provinces to implement bilingualism and constitutional change. As minister of justice, he played a major role in the 1970 October Crisis. He went on to be minister of finance during the economic crises of the early 1970s that signalled the end of the

Keynesian consensus that had attended post-war prosperity. In subsequent years his economic thinking reflected how influential policy-makers responded to the flux of the postmodern economy.

Turner's glorious opposition to free trade during the 1988 election offered Canadians an alternative to wholesale continental integration. He lost that battle but won an enduring place in history by making the case for a more independent Canada. The leading anglophone Liberal of the late twentieth century, John Turner deserves to be remembered for more than the frustrations he encountered in the final chapter of his career. His destiny was elusive; his legacy, substantial.

PART 1
LIBERAL APPRENTICE, 1929-68

1

THE MAKING OF AN EXTROVERT

In the 1930s, Canada's national capital was still a work in progress. The Parliament Buildings presided majestically over the landscape from a bluff above the Ottawa River, surrounded by manicured lawns and statues of statesmen, yet signs of a rough lumber town intruded in the background. On Parliament Hill, muffled sounds could be heard from the mills upstream at the Chaudière Rapids, and chemical odours wafted on the riverside breeze. On their way home from work, politicians and public servants skirted the working-class enclaves of LeBreton Flats and Lower Town. A half century earlier, Ottawa had been dismissed as "a sub-arctic lumber village converted by royal mandate into a political cockpit."[1] There was still truth in the gibe.

In the fall of 1933, during the bleakest days of the Great Depression, a twenty-nine-year-old widow rented a small apartment in downtown Ottawa. Phyllis Turner had come to Ottawa for a trial position with the Tariff Board, a new government agency. Though a place wasn't guaranteed, she had four-year-old John and two-year-old Brenda in tow, all the way from British Columbia. Come what may, she was determined to succeed in Ottawa.

She got the job, and within a few months the Turners moved into a rented duplex at 132 Daly Avenue in the Sandy Hill neighbourhood where John would grow up. The area was popular with public servants because it was close to their offices downtown. Although working-class Ottawa had distinct Irish Catholic and French Canadian Catholic neighbourhoods, in Sandy Hill more prosperous citizens of differing religious and cultural backgrounds lived side by side. One of the city's older residential areas, it was bounded by the Rideau Canal to the west and the Rideau River to the east. There was a mix of housing, from small frame cottages and brick row houses to handsome stone mansions on large lots. A few low-rise apartment blocks had been built along Laurier and King Edward Avenues, its major thoroughfares. Only the spires of its churches – United, Presbyterian, Anglican, Lutheran, and Catholic – rose over the trees that lined the streets.

The Turners' new home was on the west side of Sandy Hill, around the corner from an Anglican church that had been attended by John A. Macdonald, Canada's first prime minister. A few blocks away stood Laurier House, once the residence of Prime Minister Wilfrid Laurier and occupied since by Liberal leader William Lyon Mackenzie King. He had been replaced as prime minister three years earlier by Conservative R.B. Bennett. Catholic landmarks were prominent in some of the choicest riverside locations – colleges, seminaries, and the University of Ottawa, where Irish and French Catholics jostled for control.

Ottawa's ethnic and religious divisions were also evident in its schools. There were English-language non-denominational public schools (effectively Protestant) and Catholic schools run in both English and French by separate school boards.[2] Phyllis Turner transcended these divisions by sending her son to the Ottawa Normal Model School. Staffed by able teachers who trained student teachers in their classrooms, it was considered to be a cut above the average public school. John quickly revealed himself to be an excellent student with a competitive bent. He consistently placed at the top of his class, so he was pushed ahead, skipping grade four.[3] His determination showed on the playing field as well. When he was in grade six, he entered the 100-, 220-, and 440-yard runs as well as the broad jump at his school track meet. He won each event and collected the boys' trophy for all-round athlete.

Phyllis Turner appreciated the importance of education. Born Phyllis Gregory, the daughter of a mining-hoist engineer in Rossland, British Columbia, she had made her own way in the world through academic ability. She was the only one of the four children in her family to go to university. In 1921 she enrolled in the Department of Economics, Sociology, and Political Science at the University of British Columbia, then located in downtown Vancouver. Unlike most educated women of her day, Phyllis Gregory did not choose one of the helping professions; nor did she accept a subordinate role, such as secretary, in the white-collar workforce. Instead, she went on to graduate school at Bryn Mawr, a prestigious women's college just outside Philadelphia, where she won a scholarship to study economics and politics.[4] After graduating with a master's degree in the spring of 1927, she entered the Bryn Mawr doctoral program, again on scholarship. She spent the first semester of the 1927-28 academic year in England, studying at the London School of Economics, then travelled to Germany to do research for her thesis.[5]

Back in England, she met Leonard Turner, a lanky, good-looking Englishman who, subsidized by proceeds from his family's import-export firm, styled himself a gentleman of "independent means." Phyllis left her studies to become a wife and mother, and the couple settled in the suburbs of southwest London. Their first child, John Napier Wyndham Turner, was born in Richmond, Surrey (now part of London), on June 7, 1929. A second son, Michael, followed, but died as an infant. Then a daughter, Brenda, was born on August 20, 1931. By this time Leonard was experiencing thyroid problems. Doctors performed a thyroidectomy, an experimental treatment that only made things worse. He died of acute broncho-pneumonia on November 18, 1932. He was only twenty-eight.[6]

Phyllis Turner was left widowed with no means of supporting her family. Not long before, she had been a promising young academic riding a string of accomplishments; now she was an unemployed single mother far from home in the middle of the Depression. She decided to return to Rossland, British Columbia, and stay with her parents. The ship and train journey became one of John's earliest memories. "Gosh, it was exciting," he recalled – "the train crews and the porters, and the dining-car waiters ... going across those trestles on the old Kettle Valley line."[7] For his mother it was an adventure fraught with anxiety. The experience of being left suddenly alone in the world, with pressing responsibilities and few resources, was seared into her consciousness. She endured months of uncertainty before she found her feet again in Ottawa. As time passed, she would volunteer only the scantest facts about her brief marriage. Some things just weren't talked about, and Leonard Turner became one of them. She put her past behind her and created a mystery.

Single mothers with professional careers were unusual in Ottawa in the 1930s. Many women had gone to work for the government during the First World War, but once the soldiers returned, policies changed to ensure that men were hired and promoted into the best jobs. Phyllis Turner was exempt only because society recognized that as head of a household she needed to work to support her family. She hired a Scottish housekeeper to manage domestic duties and supervise the children while she was away.[8]

Smart, charming, and attractive, she quickly became well known in Ottawa. She liked to entertain colleagues at home, playing the piano and leading singalongs. Walter Gordon, later finance minister under Lester Pearson, remembered her as "bright and very good-looking – everyone just swarmed about her."[9] Her circle of friends included Norman Robertson, a fellow student at UBC who, in 1941, would be appointed undersecretary of state in the Department of External Affairs; Graham Towers, governor of the Bank of Canada; and Hugh Keenleyside, a diplomat who became secretary to the Canadian section of the Permanent Joint Board of Defence during the war. "As we grew older we knew she was something special, because of the people who used to come home to dinner or to a cocktail party," Turner remembered.[10] One of her admirers was R.B. Bennett, who was prime minister until 1935, when King returned to power. The Turners had a Rhone springer spaniel named Blue. When John took him out to nearby Strathcona Park, he often ran into King, walking his dog, Pat, and both humans and canines would exchange greetings.

Phyllis Turner and her friends were absorbed by the great public issues of the day, including the challenge of the state's response to the Depression. In the Turner living room, the merits of the New Deal were debated and leading political figures dissected and lampooned. In retrospect, Turner recognized that "it certainly made me more at ease with public issues, because I had heard them discussed at home, and at a high level."[11] Canada's federal civil service was one of the best in the world in those years. "They shared a belief that public service was a civic virtue," Jack Granatstein observed of the Ottawa mandarins. "They felt a duty to serve their country and its people."[12] Senior public servants like Turner's mother had deep sympathies and close ties with the Liberals, who would remain in power until 1957, throughout John Turner's late childhood and young adulthood.

In 1938 the Turners moved to 434 Daly Avenue, a detached house at the east end of Sandy Hill. Here they lived for seven years – it was the house the Turner children would remember as their childhood home. Their mother worked long hours but spent much of her free time with them. On Sundays in good weather, they often went on a picnic.

A childhood friend of the Turner children remembered that their mother was nice but "quite a disciplinarian."[13] "She wasn't domineering or oppressive," Brenda explained, "but Mummy believed in striving for excellence. Not for fame or money or ambition – which is rather déclassé, isn't it – but for excellence."[14] "She had a thing about ... doing one's duty and she pushed him hard," recalled another friend.[15] If John got anything less than an A on his report card, she would want to know why.[16] "She knew John was bright and she always expected it of us," Brenda recalled. "If you've been given talents, given gifts, use them."[17]

Use them – and give thanks to God. The Turners attended 9:00 a.m. mass at the neighbourhood parish of St. Joseph's every Sunday except during Lent, when they went daily at 7:30 a.m.[18] The children grew up in a world where hard work and good conduct, plus a little luck, could bring comfort and security. But nothing was certain. Around town were many examples of less fortunate families that had fallen on hard times, and "there but for the grace of God go I" was often the message from the pulpit. It was a Snakes and Ladders moral universe in which industry and rectitude could elevate you to success, but indolence or immorality could send you sliding down into poverty or disgrace. You could get ahead if you made all the right moves, but disaster was always just a misstep away.

Because public service jobs were relatively secure, Ottawa's middle class was less affected by the Depression than its equivalent in other cities. Salaries remained stable while prices deflated. John was kept busy after school with figure-skating classes and piano lessons, but there was plenty of time left over to hang around with the neighbourhood kids and explore the city. Like others his age, he grew up listening to radio shows such as *Amos 'n' Andy*, following the Dionne quintuplets, and watching *The Wizard of Oz* and other Technicolor spectacles at the local movie theatre. The dime fiction of his youth featured gumshoes and cowboys, tough-guy role models personified by Humphrey Bogart on the big screen. Some summers the family took the train west to visit Phyllis's parents and siblings. From the age of seven, however, Turner enjoyed stints at Camp Temagami, a camp for boys run by outdoorsman A.L. Cochrane, the physical education instructor at Upper Canada College in Toronto.[19] There he learned canoeing, swimming, and wilderness survival. While John was at camp, his mother and sister holidayed in the Gatineau Hills, north of Ottawa. Norman Robertson introduced Phyllis Turner to his friend Lester Pearson, and she ended up renting a summer cottage next door to the Pearsons on the Gatineau River, near Wakefield.

Turner had plenty of male role models at camp, at church, and among his mother's colleagues in the public service.[20] None of them, however, could substitute for a father. Nor did his mother invoke the memory of the missing father as part of her parenting. With no paternal figure, real or imagined, in the household, Turner compensated by romanticizing masculine society. In time he would instinctively adopt a locker-room persona in male company, making more of being "one of the boys" than he might have if he had experienced the demystifying example of a father close at hand in his childhood.

The young John Turner learned to divide the world into distinct spheres in which he played different roles. There was the domestic sphere, a feminine realm characterized by its moral tone, where his mother held absolute sway and rules were strict. The same morality applied in the public sphere, which at this stage in his life consisted primarily of church and school. In this wider context, being from a single-parent household made him different. Those who grew up with their family status assured could afford to treat bourgeois pieties cavalierly, but John felt he had to measure up. He proved himself through outward action and accomplishment. The pressure to perform meant that the private sphere of what he really thought and felt was rarely displayed. Yet he developed an ironic awareness of the contingency of the social norms he was following. In this regard the masculine sphere took on even greater significance because it acknowledged the baser aspects of human nature and offered a realistic corrective to the hypocrisy of public morality.

By 1939 Phyllis Turner had worked her way up to the position of chief research economist for the Tariff Board. When the Second World War broke out, she was swept up in the war effort, putting in long hours, including weekends and holidays. She was seconded to the Wartime Prices and Trade Board (WPTB), which managed the supply and distribution of food, fuel, and other essentials. There she became the senior woman in the federal public service. Her title – "oils and fats administrator" – was hardly glamorous, but her job was critical to the war effort. Glycerine, a component of fat, was a key ingredient in explosives, and she often had to come up with substitutes for other products that were critical to wartime production but unavailable under wartime conditions. Her staff grew rapidly, and she was increasingly involved in negotiations with the Allies, travelling frequently to Washington.[21]

For her schoolboy son, the war was a distant concern of the adult world.[22] In 1940, when he turned eleven and was going into grade eight, the Normal School was taken over by the government for wartime purposes, so Phyllis Turner sent him to Ashbury College, a private boys' school in the fashionable suburban neighbourhood of Rockcliffe Park. He continued to excel and displayed a similar competitiveness in extracurricular activities. He won the junior debating cup, continued to run track, and played soccer, cricket, and hockey. When he was twelve he ran the 100-yard dash in just over eleven seconds. He also won the junior school's 220- and 440-yard race as well as the hurdles championship and was awarded the trophy for best all-round student.

At Ashbury, Turner was accelerated another grade, which made him two years younger than most of his classmates. As a result, he was finishing grade ten when he turned fourteen in June 1943. At that point his mother decided to send him to St. Patrick's College, a local Catholic high school. The parish priest at St. Joseph's, Father Joseph Birch, was a friend, and he convinced her that John should have a Catholic intellectual and spiritual formation.[23] He probably thought the Turner boy a good candidate for the priesthood. Birch's order, the Oblates, was always on the lookout for new recruits, and in John it saw a smart lad from a good family, spirited but tractable, with a keen sense of duty.

St. Patrick's occupied a five-storey collegiate Gothic building facing the Rideau Canal, south of Sandy Hill. Plucked from the private-school fraternity of Ashbury, John was thrown into a bear-pit of boys from up and down the Ottawa Valley. One of his classmates remembers him showing up the first day in a sports jacket, tie, and short flannel pants. The last item of apparel provoked the ridicule of the tougher kids. "Any pomposity was knocked out of anyone," Turner later recalled.[24] The St. Pat's boys got into the usual kinds of trouble. Dodging the prefect of discipline to sneak a smoke in the washroom was considered good sport. For those caught breaking the rules, the penalty was "visible, physical, and brief." John learned math both in class and from the poker and craps games one of the students ran in an unused corner of the building. "It was a typical boys' school," he remembered, "rough and it was hard but it was also fun. You had very firm guidelines. You knew what was expected of you. You knew what would happen if you didn't deliver. So you knew exactly where you stood."[25]

Turner adapted quickly to his new environment, his competitive streak as strong as ever. He was the smallest kid in his grade but held his own in schoolyard scuffles. His marks continued to be outstanding – he scored in the nineties, while the next best student had an average in the eighties. He became editor of the school newspaper, the *Patrician,* which the students nicknamed "the Perdition." He also joined the debating team. Public speaking came naturally to him – in fact, his self-confidence grew to the point where he became something of a showboat.[26] In athletics, the focus was on team sports. Turner played on the hockey team, which went to the Memorial Cup quarter-finals for three consecutive years.[27] He also played centre on the football team. In May 1945, his last year at St. Pat's, the school held a track-and-field meet. Running against seventeen-year-olds, Turner cleaned up in the 100-, 220-, 440-, and 880-yard races. He then won the broad jump and was on his way to run the mile when he collapsed from exhaustion. At the end of the year, he won the Governor General's Award for all-round excellence.

The Oblate priests who taught at St. Patrick's made a lasting impression on the boys. Sometimes called the "rural Jesuits," the Oblates were an intellectually rigorous teaching order.[28] Unlike Protestant clergy, whose role in children's lives was often limited to a weekly appearance in the pulpit, they presided daily over classroom and extracurricular activities. Most were Irish Catholics, but some had been educated in England and steeped in the tradition of English Catholicism. John Grace, one of Turner's classmates, recalled that they "nurtured us in a classical curriculum. They enlivened English and history and religion by connecting these subjects to contemporary political and religious controversies in England as well as Canada ... It was a big, exciting world they opened up for us."[29] Grace and Turner came to identify with the English Catholic tradition and its intellectual heroes Cardinal John Henry Newman, G.K. Chesterton, and Hilaire Belloc.[30] Given the need to know and explain their exceptional status as Catholics in a majority Protestant society, these defenders of the Catholic faith had particular relevance for them.[31] The young John Turner took seriously his responsibility to be a good representative of his faith.

In the economic dislocation following the Depression, the social justice teachings of the Catholic Church had special relevance. The priests taught Pope Leo XIII's 1891 encyclical *Rerum novarum* (On new things), in which he criticized the abuses of capitalism and emphasized the state's responsibility for the poor and the weak. They supplemented it with Pope Pius XI's 1931 encyclical *Quadragesimo Anno* (In the fortieth year), which aimed at "reconstruction of the social order," calling on Catholics to contribute to the common good by taking action locally and personally. These teachings made an impression on Turner. Concerned that their star pupil's accomplishments might go to his head, the priests drilled into him St. Augustine's dictum that man's gifts were given by the grace of God, and the scriptural injunction "For unto whomsoever much is given, of him shall be much required: and to whom men have committed much, of him they will ask the more."[32] He would continue to cite some variation of this guiding principle throughout his life.

When Turner was almost sixteen, his Ottawa childhood ended. His mother always had many male admirers in the capital, and during the war she began seeing businessman Frank Ross. He was a "dollar-a-year man," one of the captains of industry who had volunteered their services to their country during the wartime crisis. Most were recruited by C.D. Howe, the minister of munitions and supply, to help run the wartime economy. A Scot by birth, Ross had become wealthy through shipbuilding, metal fabricating, and manufacturing interests in New Brunswick and British Columbia. The couple put off marriage, waiting until their wartime services were no longer vital to their country, and finally wed in April 1945. They moved to Vancouver, where Ross had his head office, and settled into 4899 Belmont Avenue in the exclusive neighbourhood of West Point Grey. It was a sprawling mansion with an indoor swimming pool and extensive grounds. Located northeast of the endowment lands of UBC, which had relocated nearby in the mid-1920s, it commanded a stunning view over Burrard Inlet and across English Bay to downtown Vancouver.

Over that summer, Turner moved from Ottawa to Vancouver, from middle class to wealthy, and from man of the house to his stepfather's son. He was also a precocious sixteen-year-old who was moving out into the world. His new semi-independent status was reflected in his accommodation – a separate suite above the garage. He spent the academic year 1945-46 at the University of British Columbia, coping with his courses and acclimatizing to the new social scene. The number of students there exploded from three thousand to ten thousand after the war, and the university scrambled to absorb the unexpected growth. Once again Turner found himself among an older peer group – the first-year cohort of eighteen-year-olds was already being supplemented by veterans in their twenties, men and women mature beyond their years after the experience of military service.

Turner had his own motorcycle that he rode to campus. "I used to love really juicing that thing up along Marine Drive, just really opening her up," he recalled.[33] He was rushed by the Beta Theta Pi fraternity, which was dismissed by one outsider as a collection of "brains, squares and wimps."[34] Here he found companionship to replace faraway friends and the attentions of his mother, now a society matron preoccupied with charity work and entertaining.[35] The fraternity often held chapter meetings or hosted a sorority at his house. These get-togethers frequently featured a barbeque and dancing, or a singalong, with Turner at the piano.[36] His newfound affluence allowed him to build up a collection of jazz records, which he also played for his friends.

Frank Ross did not become the father John had never known. He did not presume to play that role; nor did Turner desire it. He always called him "Mr. Ross." Their relationship was correct and respectful, with the kinds of tensions to be expected when a teenager is tentatively asserting his independence within the ambit of a powerful older male. Ross nevertheless provided a model of a successful urbane businessman who worked and lived hard. He left for the office early each day, broke for lunch at his club, and, after handling routine administrative matters, returned home with friends or business associates for drinks, where they often killed the better part of a bottle of Scotch during the cocktail hour. Dinner, he theorized, absorbed the alcohol. Discussions at the supper table could get testy if John disagreed with his stepfather's point of view.

By the time he entered second year, Turner had decided to major in political science. His favourite professor was economist Henry Angus, who had dazzled him when he lectured in one of his classes as a last-minute replacement. In response to a student's question, Angus delivered an analysis of the 1945 United Nations Charter that climaxed with a compelling conclusion precisely as class time ran out. Then in his mid-fifties, Angus had taught Turner's mother twenty years earlier and was pleased to discover in her son "a good general attitude, intellectual ability, skill in sports, a sense of public service, and a commitment to his fellows."[37]

That year Turner also began to write for the sports section of the university newspaper, the *Ubyssey,* as "Chick," a nickname bestowed on him by a friend. One of his heroes was Pierre Berton, who had written for the same paper a few years before, and he thought he might follow in his footsteps. As associate sports editor, he reported on the fortunes of UBC's teams. He soon graduated to writing a column, "Chalk Talk with Chick." Inspired by Damon Runyon's streetwise writing style and aided by a handy thesaurus, Turner used obscure synonyms for everyday terms wherever possible, lurching between slang and mock high diction. His subjects did not merely put on their running shoes, they donned scampers; instead of walking, they ambled or strode; when they met, they exchanged felicitations. Swimming became "a torrid display of frenzied nautical muscular rhythm." Hemingway he was not. "It was all quite marvelous," his editor recalled, "though God knows if anyone actually understood it."[38] When his description of a pennant-seeking team being "out to cop the gonfalon" was challenged by other *Ubyssey* staff, Turner explained that a gonfalon was a banner suspended perpendicularly at medieval jousts, and the editor cleared the copy.

In his second year Turner also went out for the university track-and-field team. Daily training soon rounded him into form, and he began turning in some fast times: ten seconds flat in the 100-yard dash and twenty-two seconds in the 220. He was a powerful runner who exploded out of the blocks and burst down the track. "He was determined and ran almost the way he talked, sort of staccato," observed Robert Osborne, UBC's director of physical education.[39] His times made him the university's sprint star. In 1947 UBC captured the Pacific Northwest Conference title when the relay team he was on won the final event. The province funded a team to go to the Dominion Track and Field Championships in Edmonton that June, and Turner was appointed captain. He won the 100 and the 220, then entered the 440 but was talked out of it by Lloyd Percival, the coach of the Ontario team, on the pretext that he was pushing himself too hard.

In the summers, Frank Ross arranged jobs for his stepson at one of his plants. One day Ross went missing with a friend, department store magnate Colonel Victor Spencer, on a jaunt to Spencer's summer retreat near Lytton, at the northern end of the rugged Fraser Canyon. Turner, just eighteen, was dispatched to find them. He drove up and followed the cliffside road until he came to a spot where the guardrail had been broken, and from there he spotted their car. It had gone over the edge, careened down the embankment, and smashed into a large rock that prevented it from plunging into the river. Turner backtracked to the nearest service station and returned with two tow trucks. The rescuers scrambled down the mountainside on ropes. They found the two men inside the car, still drinking, and annoyed that they hadn't been rescued sooner. "What took you so god-damned long?" Ross demanded.[40]

Turner continued to go to Camp Temagami as a counsellor during his summer vacation. Sometimes he joined his family at Ross's farm near St. Andrews, New Brunswick. It had a stone farmhouse that overlooked the St. Croix River as it flowed into Passamaquoddy Bay. When Ross was there, he met with his cronies in the backroom of the local general store. Some of them were locals; others were summer residents, including the powerful federal Cabinet minister C.D. Howe and business magnates Sir James Dunn and E.P. Taylor. Turner would tag along as they drank coffee, smoked, and chatted about public affairs, solving the world's problems in their own informal parliament of common sense.

John Dobson, a summer friend, remembers that Turner got to know all the farmers, fishermen, and shopkeepers in the area.[41] He had a particularly valuable acquaintance in the bellboy at the local hotel, who informed him whenever eligible young ladies checked in. Girls – how to meet them, get a date, find the right one – were increasingly on his mind. Dating was relatively innocent and chaste among middle-class youth at the time.

Although it was possible to get serious and go steady, it was just as common to play the field. Turner worried about getting into a long-term relationship because he had yet to figure out what he wanted to do with his life. The Oblates had encouraged him to be a priest, and he still considered this a possibility. Like many other young Catholic men of his generation, he was attracted by the ascetic ideal of dedicating himself to a life of spirituality and service – but it remained a romantic notion rather than a deliberate course of action.

By his third year, Turner the sports columnist and track star cut quite a swath on campus. He was a public figure, and he liked it. His time was spent not in intimate soul-searching talks with kindred spirits but in purposeful action, be it social, athletic, or academic. The adolescent social imperative was to move with the crowd:

> On weekends there were parties at White Rock or Crescent Beach. Bogart and Spencer Tracy filled the drive-in screen. There were parties and dancing. The Vagabond Lover, Rudy Vallee, visited the campus to croon his big hit, Whiffenpoof. On weekends at the Commodore, the frenzied university crowd bopped to the rhythm of the Big Bands. The Duke, the Count, Louis Armstrong and Vancouver's Dal Richards were 1940s rock stars.[42]

Turner had the confidence to bridge the yawning divide between the young undergraduates and the veterans. The older group advertised their worldly experience by growing moustaches, smoking pipes, and wearing tweed jackets with elbow patches. They had an informal organization called the Joker Club that was generally hostile to fraternities and other establishment institutions. Turner, though an underage frat boy, managed to ingratiate himself with this older crowd. Classmates marvelled at the social dexterity this required.[43] "Chick always had the quip, the gag, that would break everybody up," explained one friend, "and he was good at introducing it when people were arguing over some kind of problem."[44] His skills were recognized when, the following year, he was elected to the position of Student Council coordinator of activities. It was a social position, but in winning it he learned that his social skills could be translated into elected office. "John Turner was something out of a Scott Fitzgerald novel," recalled a classmate. "He had a lightness of touch and style. He carried a gold glow around his head."[45]

Turner's athletic ability came to the attention of an eccentric character named Major H.B. Morris Kinley. At one time Kinley had been a political organizer, but he had always coached track and field as well. Under Kinley's tutelage, Turner learned how to improve his starts, how to run loose in the middle of the race, and how to finish. He began to sprint in world-class times, clocking 9.7 seconds for the 100-yard dash.[46] It looked as though he would win the Canadian championship in both the 100 and the 220 yards again that year. Just before the championships, however, he foolishly competed in a local meet that pitted his Point Grey parish against a downtown parish. That race may have cost him a record, because he ran only a 10-second 100. In the 220, however, he redeemed himself, winning in 22.5 seconds. With this victory, he won the right to attend the Canadian trials for the 1948 Olympics.

One night in February 1948, Turner was driving home from a football game in Bellingham, Washington, with his date and another couple. As they passed over a level crossing on Arbutus Street in Vancouver, a train appeared out of the heavy fog. "We were lucky we were only hit in the front of the car and not in midship," Turner recalled. "I saw this light coming out of nowhere and was able to turn and roll with the train as it hit us."[47] The train was not moving rapidly, but it still drove the car a hundred feet down the track. Turner's left knee was smashed. Surgeons were able to piece it back together, but his leg muscles atrophied as he waited for the bone to heal. By the time he could run again, it was too late to train for the Olympic trials in Vancouver that June. He showed up anyway and gave it a shot, but his knee gave way and he collapsed on the track.

In his fourth year, 1948-49, Turner continued his hectic schedule of sports, journalism, extracurricular activities, socializing, and academics. His position on the Student Council, which involved running orientation, made him the "czar of freshmen," reported the *Ubyssey,* "the man responsible for outlandish regalia for opening week."[48] The UBC track team competed in the Evergreen competition that year, a tougher test than the Pacific Northwest Conference. Despite his injury, Turner tied the meet record in the 100 yards and finished second in the 220.[49] To complete the requirements for his honours BA in political science, he chose to write his undergraduate thesis on the Senate of Canada. He pronounced the Senate an archaic embarrassment that should be reformed or abolished. It was an impressive piece of work for a nineteen-year-old, grounded in solid research and informed by analysis that appreciated both liberal democratic ideals and *realpolitik*.[50]

With fourth year winding down, the question of what to do next loomed large. The priesthood was still on his mind, but he remained uncertain. He applied to Dalhousie Law School and Harvard, hoping especially to get into the American university. Law school, he calculated, was a good interim plan. Even if he never became a lawyer, it would still be a sound grounding for other pursuits. Then Henry Angus suggested he stand for a Rhodes Scholarship. He was the type of well-rounded student that Cecil Rhodes had in mind when he endowed the award. "Turner really had everything in those days," recalled classmate Peter Worthington. "He was good look-ing. He was terribly clever. He was a great athlete."[51] There was one Rhodes scholar for each province, except for Ontario and Quebec, which had two each. Turner beat out the fifty other competitors in British Columbia in 1949. Acknowledging his achievement, the *Ubyssey* wrote that its departing sports columnist "rolls sportsmanship, scholarship and leadership, the three-fold Rhodes ideal, into a handsome package that has made him undoubtedly the university's most popular student."[52]

Turner had arrived at UBC with a lot going for him. He made the most of it and was rewarded handsomely. Some of his fellow students would later insinuate that he had always been on the make – dating the right girls but never getting into sexual or romantic entanglements, popularizing a rum concoction called Moose Milk but never letting partying interfere with his studies, putting together an impossible combination of popularity and achievement both in the classroom and on the sports field. Such as-sessments were not untainted by envy. A more generous classmate recalled, "The strange thing was he managed to beat everyone else ... and seem[ed] to have everything going for him, with rich parents and big home, and still be considered a good guy. That took some doing at university in those days. But he got away with it because he was just genuinely a nice person."[53]

Turner chose to attend Magdalen, one of the oldest and most distin-guished of Oxford colleges. There, for the first time, he found himself in a group where he wasn't the best scholar or even the top athlete. He was awed by the poise of the British students, especially by their spontaneous eloquence. His nationality and his education clearly relegated him to a second-tier starting position. He spent a good deal of his first year assessing whether he could achieve a first-class honours degree and, if so, whether it was worth it. That meant weighing the psychological cost of trying and perhaps failing against the enticing alternative of enjoying everything Oxford had to offer and expecting no more than a second.

The two principal figures on the academic side of the equation were his tutors, J.H.C. Morris and Rupert Cross. Turner studied jurisprudence with Morris, an expert in the conflict of law, a field concerned with reconciling differences between national legal regimes in international commerce. Cross, though blind since childhood, had become an authority on the law of evidence. While studying under these men, Turner was also expected to attend lectures on subjects related to his field to ensure that he would pass his exams.

While keeping his tutors happy, Turner was soon pursuing his usual smorgasbord of extracurricular activities. As a member of the Newman Society, a Catholic student organization, he often breakfasted after Sunday mass with the Reverend Ronald Knox. Like his friends G.K. Chesterton and Evelyn Waugh, Knox was a literary figure who had converted to Catholicism. A noted stylist, he had written extensively and brilliantly on apologetics and had recently published a book on the importance of tempering spiritual enthusiasm with the rigour of doctrine. At these breakfasts, Knox presided over an informal question and answer session on current church issues. He provided Turner and his friends with a role model rooted in a Catholic tradition at the university that went back more than a century to John Henry Newman and the Oxford Movement.

Turner played squash regularly, rugger occasionally, and captained the Magdalen College cross-country team. He also joined the Oxford Track and Field Club and won a blue in track. In his first year, the captain was Roger Bannister – later the first man to break the four-minute mile; in his third, it was Chris Chataway, another great distance runner. Turner became friends with both. He also chummed around with Malcolm Fraser, a future prime minister of Australia. Fraser owned an Aston Martin, and Turner became his co-driver at rallies. "I don't think we ever finished a race," he recalled. "We'd meet a couple of girls somewhere, and you know ..."[54] He went to shows in London and attended sports events, sometimes with dates and sometimes with groups of fellow students. He was "candid, brilliant, witty and sharp, a social animal, who loved people and put them at ease, often by poking fun at himself," recalled an acquaintance of the time.[55]

On school breaks, Turner travelled around northern Europe, spending most of his time in France because he knew more girls there and was trying to learn the language. His letters home to his sister featured romantic possibilities, complications, and intrigues above all else. By the end of his first year, his wide range of extracurricular activities, both social and athletic, indicated that he had decided to enjoy Oxford and settle for a second.

He still took his law studies seriously. He served as secretary of the Oxford Law Society and represented Oxford against Cambridge at the Moot Court, appearing in mock trials before some of the era's great judges, including Justice Denning ("the most radical lawyer on the Court of Appeal," he noted approvingly).[56] Turner passed his bachelor of arts in jurisprudence after two years at Oxford with a second, scoring high in that range because he performed strongly in the oral component of the exams. He then had his Rhodes Scholarship extended for the academic year 1951-52 so he could take his bachelor of civil law. As his exams approached, he joked to his sister, "I know all my examiners, which is not a bad start, and I may be able to float past on sherry."[57]

Canada's Amateur Athletic Union nominated Turner to run the 100- and 200-metre races at the 1952 Summer Olympic Games in Helsinki. He was led to believe that the times he posted in England would be accepted and that he would not need to return to run in the trials for the Canadian Olympic team in Hamilton, but the Canadian Olympic Association refused to recognize the English results. If it had, Turner would have been on the team. Although he did not get to run, he went to Helsinki anyway to watch his friends Bannister and Chataway perform.

He was, meanwhile, no closer to deciding on a career. He laid out his thoughts in a letter to his sister:

I have been worrying about the future lately, wondering just what to do with myself. I am singularly lacking in confidence in myself, and am almost afraid to meet the competition of the world ... I have the helpless feeling that after six years of university I am still a stark boor. What I'd like to do best would be to knock around Europe for a year or two and repair some of the more obvious gaps in my education: philosophy and literature. Then there's always the call of the priesthood, and I am going to have to make up my mind to give it a try within the next year or two ... I am thoroughly unsatisfied with myself.[58]

The young John Turner evidently felt the same trepidations as others in the same position in life. Yet he kept his self-doubt to himself and was never paralyzed by it. He continued to take comfort in the distractions of his social life; the same letter provided his sister with an annotated list of his fifteen favourite female companions. The next few months were a continuing social whirl, spiced with gossip about romance or the possibility of romance among a wide circle of friends and acquaintances. When his mother visited Oxford, "checking over some of my feminine friends," he noted that "the shrewder of them were immediately aware of Mom's own shrewdness."[59]

In the fall of 1952, Turner went to London to study for his bar exam. He moved to Paris in the spring of 1953 while awaiting the results and enrolled at the University of Paris to study under the renowned law professor Henri Battifol for a doctorate in private international law.[60] "He went to mass every morning," remembers an acquaintance, "then took some lovely girl out every night."[61] Brenda was also in Paris, ostensibly to get a master's degree but mainly to travel and learn some French. The siblings, close during childhood but separated for long periods through adolescence, now had a chance to spend time together. John took Brenda on a tour of France in the summer of 1953 with an itinerary organized around visiting all the French girls he knew. She later visited Oxford with him and dated some of his friends.[62]

In the late summer of 1953, Turner returned to London to be called to the bar at Gray's Inn. Back home, Frank Ross was beginning to worry that his stepson was becoming too fond of a sybaritic student lifestyle. He wrote, "You've had a good run, you know. When are you going to come back and get to work?"[63] Turner took the hint and booked passage home to Canada.

Whatever lay ahead, he seemed most likely to succeed. People looked up to him, told him he was gifted, and predicted great things. The more he accomplished, the more was expected. "If he can't be Prime Minister, he can always be Pope," his mother once joked to his sister.[64] It was funny because it was so preposterous, yet plausible.

2

CIRCLING HOME

O n his way back to Vancouver from Europe, Turner stopped off in Montreal to visit friends. It was a bustling cosmopolitan centre where the cultures of both French and English Canada co-existed, sometimes mingling, occasionally clashing, usually ignoring each other. The street life and the night life were livelier than anywhere else in Canada, and there was action in business too, with headquarters for most of the largest Canadian companies located downtown. Turner was captivated. Montreal was the centre of the action, a place where he could have fun and test his mettle. He wanted to stay.

He rented a room and began looking for a job with a law firm. Frank Ross's connections helped. Turner got an interview with Heward Stikeman, who, with his partner, Fraser Elliott, had recently set up a firm specializing in corporate tax. They were concerned that Turner's elite education might have spoiled him for the daily grind of legal practice, but they offered him $100 a week to start as a student lawyer. Turner had offers from two other firms, but he liked the ground-floor opportunity presented by Stikeman & Elliott. Assured of a regular paycheque, he rented a basement apartment at 1536 Summerhill Avenue, a short street that ran parallel to Sherbrooke Street at the base of Mount Royal, near McGill University. He painted his walls purple, a passionate colour for a cool bachelor pad. A twenty-minute walk took him to his office on Victoria Square in Old Montreal, close to the legal and financial district and a short walk from the courthouse.[1]

At first Turner handled some criminal cases and matrimonial law. As time passed, however, his practice increasingly focused on tax litigation along with some corporate law. With the tax work, he often represented clients in cases against the federal Department of Revenue. Stikeman and Elliott were pleased with his performance. He worked hard, quickly grasped the essential issues in cases, and had a knack for finding practical solutions.

Turner's credentials did not qualify him to practise in Quebec, where the civil law was derived from the French *ancien régime.* He took courses on the Quebec civil code at night school at McGill, planning to sit for the Quebec bar exams. When he heard of another lawyer who had bypassed this process by getting a private member's bill passed in the provincial legislature, he approached Daniel Johnson, a backbencher in the governing Union Nationale party, to sponsor one for him. Johnson agreed. When the bill came before the committee of the Legislative Assembly that reviewed private members' bills, Turner travelled to Quebec City to appear before it. At the last minute another MLA gave him an excellent piece of advice: address the committee, which included Premier Maurice Duplessis, in French. Turner did just that, with dramatic results. The premier, pleased to see an anglophone making the effort to speak in French to francophones, launched into a passionate speech about the contribution of bilingualism to the greatness of Canada, after which no one raised any objections to the bill. Duplessis then invited Turner and Johnson to have a sherry in his office before lunch. Turner acquired his accreditation, a lesson in bicultural politics, and some significant new contacts. (Johnson would become leader of the Union Nationale in 1961 and premier five years later.) Turner sent Johnson a forty-ounce bottle of Dewar's to thank him for his trouble and, in due course, was called to the bar of Quebec in 1954.

As Stikeman & Elliott prospered and expanded, Turner was involved in recruiting new talent for the firm. One of his first catches, in 1955, was Jim Robb, a native Quebecker who had attended McGill University. The firm's juniors were responsible for office morale, so Turner and Robb ran a lunch-time bridge game in an old vault that served as the file room. The legal community in Old Montreal was small, and all the young lawyers working in the same neighbourhood soon got to know one another. They met for lunch or for drinks after work. Robb introduced Turner to Mel Rothman, a friend of his at Phillips Vineberg, a nearby law firm. John Claxton, who was with Dixon, Claxton, Senecal & Stairs in the same building as Stikeman & Elliott, became another regular.

Though Turner was increasingly immersed in the legal community, he remained unsure that law was his life's work. His conscience still told him he should become a priest. "He was really serious about it," recalled Heward Stikeman, who didn't think his protege was cut out for the priesthood at all and did his best to talk him out of it.[2] The experience of his old St. Pat's friend John Grace also gave Turner pause. Grace had entered a seminary the year before but had recently left. In the end, Turner contented himself with being a warden at his parish church, St. Patrick's on Dorchester Boulevard, the oldest English-speaking congregation in the city. He eventually became chief warden and got to know Paul-Émile Léger, the archbishop of Montreal. They had dinner together every few weeks, and Léger asked Turner to do his personal legal work.[3]

On some tax cases, Turner and Heward Stikeman worked as a team and appeared before the Income Tax Appeal Board or, less frequently, the Exchequer Court of Canada or the Supreme Court. Over time Turner did fewer tax cases and more corporate law, which involved closer collaboration with Fraser Elliott. He also branched out into litigation, specializing in maritime and transportation work. As a member of Gray's Inn, Turner belonged to the bars of Jamaica, Barbados, and Trinidad. The partners encouraged him to keep up this membership because the ability to act in the Caribbean gave them a certain cachet.

Turner and Elliott, both bachelors, frequently dined together after work at local establishments such as Mother Martin's or the Maritime Bar in the Ritz-Carlton Hotel. On Friday nights Turner sometimes headed to his friend John Grace's family cottage on Roddick Lake in the Gatineau Hills north of Ottawa. He and Grace canoed the neighbouring lakes and rivers or just hung around the cottage, where Turner liked to relax by reading political biography or history.

Cottage life was a respite from the social whirl of the city, where Turner was part of a smart set enjoying the prosperity of the post-war years. The men were young professionals; the women expected to marry and stay home to raise a family. In the meantime, they were fun loving and impatient with the status quo, more in the manner of heirs apparent than rebels. They got together at restaurants and clubs or at various charity balls, where they danced to big-band music. At private parties the host wore a shirt and tie and mixed martinis, while "the girls," in cocktail dresses and pearls, offered dainty hors d'oeuvres from decorative plates.

Athletic clubs were another focus of social activity. Turner played squash at the Montreal Badminton and Squash Club, enjoyed tennis at the Mount Royal Club, and skied in the Laurentians. He arranged get-togethers for his friends and occasionally organized long-weekend excursions to his stepfather's place in St. Andrews. "I used to rent a whole Canadian Pacific railway car," he recalled, "with those twelve or fourteen little bedrooms and I'd knock two of them off for a bar and my pals would come and we'd take guys and gals from Montreal."[4] Turner's sister, Brenda, had a friend from McGill who worked for the Kennedys, so occasionally John, Brenda, and some friends would head off to Hyannisport on Cape Cod for a visit. Turner and Bobby Kennedy, four years his senior, became friends and kept in touch over the years. Turner also hosted his firm's Christmas party. As Stikeman & Elliott grew larger, it began to rent clubs for the event, so Turner's place became the venue for the after-the-Christmas-party party. Later in the decade he moved to a more opulent apartment up the street, a penthouse at 1520 McGregor.

Blended in with work and play was community service, and Turner did more than most. He served on the executive of the Quebec Red Cross and was a founding director, and later president, of Harterre House, a charity that cared for mentally and emotionally troubled children. He was also on the board of Newman House, the centre for Catholic students at McGill University. He sat on the junior committee of the Montreal Symphony, served as its president in 1956-57, and continued as the orchestra's honorary secretary and legal counsel. In this capacity he got many of his friends interested in the orchestra. For one gala fundraiser, he organized a ball aboard a ship in Montreal harbour. The carousing went on well into the morning, and Turner, having fallen asleep on board, awoke to find himself miles down the St. Lawrence en route to Quebec City. He returned by train, sheepish in his rumpled formal wear.

By the late 1950s, Turner was a high-profile young man about town. If he looked the junior executive, his saving grace was his ability to laugh at himself and the whole crazy Montreal scene. He wasn't ready to settle down and, as was common at the time, went out with a number of women simultaneously.[5] He moved easily between the French and English communities in the city. He dated French Canadian and English Canadian girls, and he worked as an English-speaking organizer for the reform-minded Jean Drapeau in his unsuccessful bid for re-election as mayor in 1957. His involvement with the symphony was remarkable because it was located on the east side of town, deep in French Canadian territory, and was supported mostly by the French Canadian and Jewish upper classes. No matter. Turner simply followed his passion for classical music and got involved. As a newcomer to the city, he was not hindered by local cultural boundaries.[6]

He also kept in touch with Maurice Duplessis, who would come to Montreal to see the Canadiens play at the Forum and occasionally invited Turner to join him for dinner and the game. Turner concluded that Duplessis liked having him around as a non-partisan sounding board. "I was one of the people he could talk to frankly about what was going on in the province," he recalled. "I wasn't a member of his party ... I was just a junior lawyer in Montreal."[7] Duplessis' way of operating made an impression on him. The premier spent entire mornings phoning friends and political contacts around the province – a hands-on style that reminded Turner of Mackenzie King's sensitivity to local politics.

As the decade wore on, Duplessis' Union Nationale regime became increasingly controversial. He appealed to voters with a traditional French Canadian nationalism based on an idealized farm life, church control of social institutions, and a division of power between the French sphere of provincial politics and the English world of business. As post-war prosperity continued and their province modernized, Québécois found it increasingly difficult to reconcile this old-style nationalism with urban industrial life. Turner fraternized with many French Canadians who were appalled by the corruption of the provincial government. The progressive anti-clerical journal *Cité libre* voiced this point of view, arguing that Duplessis used nationalism to distract French Canadians from the way the system exploited them economically and abused their democratic rights. Turner knew labour lawyer Pierre Trudeau, a co-editor of *Cité libre.* Though Trudeau was a decade older than Turner, their social circles intersected, and they sometimes dated the same women.[8]

34

The entire country was conspicuously modernizing in the 1950s. The extended prosperity of the post-war period, sustained by technological innovation, industrial growth, and expanding international trade, set in train myriad social changes that were widely accepted as both inevitable and beneficial. Happy to forget the Depression and the war, Canadians looked expectantly to the future. Consumer goods gilded in chrome and plastics were embraced as harbingers of an imminent techno-utopia, and every television antenna bristling from a suburban roof was seen as a sign of progress. Planners had ambitious expressways and public housing projects on their drafting boards. A restive "can-do" spirit challenged traditional ways, promising a bigger, better tomorrow.

The federal political scene seemed out of step with the times. Louis St. Laurent, the Liberal prime minister, was in his mid-seventies; C.D. Howe, the minister of trade and commerce, was not much younger. Liberal strategists put the best spin possible on their aged leadership, styling St. Laurent as "Uncle Louis," but this ploy could be no more than a temporary expedient. Turner and his lawyer friends were aware that their world was changing rapidly and believed that traditional ways of doing things needed updating. They had come of age in an era one historian has described as "a moment of high modernism, a belief in progress and reason" characterized by "a heady mix of liberalism and nationalism, a gospel of public service, and the faith in an interventionist state."[9] They were a vanguard of a "technocratic modernity" in which men mastered the world through "expertise, instrumental reason, and stoical self-control."[10] Given their profession, that meant deploying managerial rationalism to effect practical reforms to the justice system. Their vehicle would be the Montreal Junior Bar, to which Turner was elected a board member.

In 1955 Howe persuaded St. Laurent to appoint his friend Frank Ross as lieutenant governor of British Columbia. As the vice-regal couple, Frank and Phyllis Ross in due course became the hosts during the summer of 1958 for the west-coast tour of Princess Margaret, the younger sister of Queen Elizabeth. At that time, royal visits were significant events, with many English Canadians honouring the Crown as a symbol of Canada's British heritage. Princess Margaret's arrival attracted even more notice because she was a celebrity as well as a royal. The romantic life of the pretty twenty-seven-year-old fascinated the tabloid press. Under pressure from her family, she had recently broken up with Group Captain Peter Townsend, an RAF war hero many years her senior, because he was divorced. Now she was unattached and, the tabloids presumed, heartbroken.

Turner's mother suggested that he fly out to help them entertain their special guest. He was busy at work, so demurred. But then the pressure mounted: Brenda phoned to tell him his family needed him, and Frank Ross telegraphed, commanding his appearance. Turner relented and booked a flight. The royal occasion began with a dinner party at the Ross home in Point Grey (Government House in Victoria had recently been destroyed by fire), followed by a ball at HMCS *Discovery,* the navy's shore base in Vancouver harbour.

The princess was delighted to meet a handsome and sophisticated young man her own age.[11] She danced with Turner to the exclusion of other partners, banished her aides from their table, and discouraged all interruptions. The British tabloids loved it; here was a fairy-tale romance of a princess and a commoner who was not only a colonial but a Catholic to boot. Turner accompanied the princess during her tour of the BC Interior before heading back to Montreal. At a ball in Ottawa a few days later, the princess and Turner again danced and talked, though not as exclusively as they had in Vancouver. This second encounter sent headline writers around the Commonwealth into a tizzy and forced Stikeman & Elliott to hire extra switchboard operators to handle the calls flooding in.

The princess was scheduled to attend yet another ball in Montreal, but she cancelled. Rumour had it that Buckingham Palace had instructed her to cool things down. Turner denied there was anything to their relationship other than two young people hitting it off and becoming friends. They continued to correspond, and, a year later, he flew to England for a visit, sharing a room at Balmoral Castle with photographer Antony Armstrong-Jones, whom the princess would marry in 1960. Turner was the only unofficial guest from outside Britain invited to the ceremony. The friendship brought him into the public eye in Canada and made him, thereafter, "the man who danced with Princess Margaret."

In 1960 Turner was elected president of Montreal's Junior Bar – a coup for a lawyer from a small firm. He won a close-run contest against a conservative candidate with a power-base among English-speaking lawyers. Turner, however, was more popular with the French Canadians, many of whom he knew from his work with the symphony. He had also gained some scholarly cachet from lecturing on law at Sir George Williams University and having his senior undergraduate essay on the Senate published in a volume honouring Henry Angus.[12] The *Ottawa Journal,* for which his friend John Grace now worked, published excerpts on April 24 and 25, 1961. In his review of the Angus festschrift, historian Frank Underhill applauded Turner's dissection of the desiccated upper chamber. Turner sent a copy to friends and acquaintances, including Pierre Trudeau.[13]

When he took over the presidency, Turner inherited from his predecessor, Émile Colas, a reform crusade for legal aid. The junior bar had set up its own legal aid office, the Legal Aid Bureau of Montreal, which fielded public requests for legal representation and tried to find qualified volunteers.[14] This initiative appealed to Turner. As director of the bureau from 1960 to 1963, he worked to popularize and expand the scheme. He promoted it to lawyers by arguing that it was in their own self-interest. "Our view in the Junior Bar then was that legal aid was something that had to come, and that if we were smart we'd institute the plan and run it ourselves, rather than have the government run it," he later explained. "Lawyers got ahead of the doctors on that. We got a pretty good system of legal aid across the country run by the various provinces and professions, but we haven't got the government all over us."[15]

Meanwhile, Turner was being drawn into federal politics in various ways. Family connections from his childhood in Ottawa conspired to make him a Liberal. In 1957, at Howe's request, he went down to St. Andrews to help run the federal election campaign of the local Liberal candidate. When Howe himself was defeated, Turner wrote him a sympathetic note, commiserating that "our party had been swept from office." Howe replied, urging him to enter public life and saying he had found it a deeply satisfying career. Receiving such a letter from the fabled "Minister of Everything" was, to Turner, like being anointed. Howe subsequently entrusted him with his personal legal work. When Lester Pearson ran for the leadership of the Liberal Party in 1958, Turner, along with Liberal heavyweights Jack Pickersgill and Walter Gordon, became a trustee of a fund established to compensate him for the financial sacrifice he made in entering politics.

It was a tumultuous period to get into politics in Quebec. The election of Jean Lesage's Liberals in July 1960 brought an end to the Duplessis era and ushered in the Quiet Revolution, which recognized that Quebec was a modern urban industrial society and began building an activist, interventionist government. The Province of Quebec replaced the Catholic Church as the institutional buttress of French Canadian nationality, taking on new responsibilities in social programs, education, and culture. A new generation of nationalists debated whether a renegotiated federalism or even complete separation was necessary for French Canadians to fulfill their destiny as a people. With the threat of separatism hovering in the background, Quebec governments pressed Ottawa for new powers, creating tensions that would destabilize federalism and threaten national unity throughout the 1960s.

In September 1960 Turner was invited to the federal Liberal Party thinkers' conference at Queen's University in Kingston, a gathering organized at Pearson's suggestion by Mitchell Sharp, then deputy minister of trade and commerce. The conference was part of the Liberals' attempt to rebuild after Diefenbaker's massive majority win in 1958. Pearson had originally thought of a small gathering of some fifty people, but interest grew and Sharp eventually accommodated two hundred. Turner, who attended as president of Montreal's Junior Bar, delivered a short paper on legal aid and revelled in the experience. He was rubbing shoulders with some of the same people his mother had entertained when he was a boy, except now they took him seriously. Many of those present, including Sharp, Walter Gordon, Gérard Pelletier, Maurice and Jeanne Sauvé, Pauline Jewett, Gordon Blair, Jack Davis, Alastair Gillespie, Maurice Lamontagne, Jean Marchand, and Otto Lang, were destined to become Liberal candidates in future federal elections. Frank Underhill, one of the founders of the Co-operative Commonwealth Federation (CCF), was present, as was Tom Kent, an economist and journalist who would become Pearson's principal secretary, and Davidson Dunton, president of Carleton University and a former CBC president. The quality and diversity of attendees fostered substantial debate on issues rather than a staged display of partisan unity. Pearson hoped the conference would demonstrate that he was open to new ideas, and it clearly did: the clash of opinion generated positive publicity for the party by signalling that the Liberals were in intellectual ferment, open to criticism and making a fresh start.[16]

In the wake of his performance at Kingston, Liberal strategists began to view Turner as a possible candidate for their party in the next election. Paul Martin, who had been minister of national health and welfare in the St. Laurent government, came to Montreal, took Turner to dinner, and asked him to consider a career in politics. Allan MacEachen, a former Liberal MP who was now serving as Pearson's executive assistant, made a similar pilgrimage, encouraging Turner to run in the riding in which he lived: St. Lawrence–St. George. All this attention was very flattering for a young man disposed to hold Liberal politicians in high regard. He thought he could make a contribution. He knew for certain that he had a better understanding of Quebec than the Diefenbaker government did.

Turner turned to his family and friends for direction and got conflicting advice. His mother had no political ambitions for him.[17] Frank Ross told him that politics was "a mug's game." Heward Stikeman thought Turner was not cut out for politics, because he wanted too much to be liked and was too sensitive to criticism to make the tough decisions that confront politicians.[18] There were practical considerations as well. He had no guarantee he'd win: St. Lawrence–St. George had flipped back and forth between Liberals and Conservatives since its creation in 1917. The incumbent, Egan Chambers, scion of a Montreal establishment family, was a war hero, a past national president of the Progressive Conservative Party, and a popular MP. His wife, Gretta, was a well-known Montreal journalist. Running would require a considerable commitment. Even if he won he would lose in one sense, because he would make considerably less money as an MP than he could as a top-notch lawyer in Montreal. "He had to be talked into it," one Liberal insider recalled. "It wasn't nearly as easy as you might think."[19]

Turner's friends decided that politics was the natural course for him, given his love of people, inclination toward community service, and interest in public affairs. John Grace told him there were plenty of good lawyers, but, with his gifts, he could contribute something more.[20] Increasingly, Turner began to mention the Biblical passage from Luke that the Oblates at St. Pat's had drilled into him: "For unto whomsoever much is given, of him shall be much required." It took more than resolve, however, to prepare for an election campaign. He would also need money. John Dobson, his chum from summers in St. Andrews, and John Claxton began to raise funds from all the usual suspects in the riding. One evening Claxton was summoned to Senator Donat Raymond's greystone mansion and ushered into his study. "I like John," the senator announced, and proceeded to peel off ten $1,000 bills – enough to fund a quarter of the cost of a constituency campaign.[21] Turner's mother also made a substantial contribution.[22]

The election was called on April 19, 1962. Canadians would go to the polls on June 18. Turner's first challenge was to win nomination as the Liberal candidate for St. Lawrence–St. George. In the past, the affairs of the federal Liberals had been run autocratically in the province, with the party's Quebec lieutenant appointing candidates in most ridings. Following their defeat by Diefenbaker in 1958, however, the federal Liberals were pushing internal reforms in an effort to revitalize the party. Keith Davey, a Toronto radio station sales manager who had helped create a more open and democratic Liberal organization in Ontario, was named national director of the federal Liberal Party. Quebec Liberals were receptive to a democratic rebuilding initiative, and Quebec became one of the first provinces to hold open nominating conventions in every riding. St. Lawrence–St. George was a test case for the new process. Claude Richardson, who had been the riding's Liberal MP from 1954 to 1958, was backing William H. Pugsley, a professor of management and marketing at McGill University, but Liberal strategists thought Turner had a better chance of winning the riding. The nomination meeting was postponed from January to May to give him time to organize. Davey assured Turner that he would have Liberal organizers such as John de B. Payne, a Pearson aide, to work for him behind the scenes as much as they could, though he felt that Turner would have no problem winning the nomination in any case.[23]

The nomination contest became a matter of seeing who could sign up the most new members to the constituency association. Turner turned to his wide circle of friends and members of the junior bar for help. In the days leading up to the nomination meeting, his forces managed to sign up more than half of the new recruits. Payne chaired the meeting, which was held in the auditorium of Montreal High School on May 1. In his nomination speech, Turner described the previous four years of government as wasted and unproductive. He was disturbed by the Diefenbaker government's indifference to the forces of change in Quebec: "The real question," he declared, "is whether Canada can survive another four years of Diefenbaker."[24] He won the convention handily.

Since the nomination had come relatively late, the Turner campaign team had to swing into action – and fast. St. Lawrence–St. George, a downtown riding, was one of the most diverse in Montreal, if not the country. Roughly a third of the constituency's voters were English, another third were French, and the rest hailed from all corners of the earth. To the northwest was wealthy anglophone Westmount. The riding included McGill University and the downtown shopping district, with its elegant shops, hotels, and department stores, Montreal's Chinatown, the stone mansions of the Golden Mile along Sherbrooke Street, and dwellings on back alleys that still had dirt floors. It even contained establishments of ill repute on the south part of St. Lawrence Boulevard – "the Main" – a neighbourhood where successive waves of immigrants struggled to get a toehold in the local economy.

Turner was fortunate to get his friend John Claxton to act as his campaign manager. Claxton knew the riding well: his father, the prominent Liberal Cabinet minister Brooke Claxton, had been the incumbent from 1940 to 1954. John had learned the ropes running his father's last campaign. Jim Robb helped to organize, drawing on his experience with provincial and federal constituency campaigns over the previous decade. John de B. Payne, who had a background as a lobbyist and publicist, advised on policy and media relations. Turner's sister, now Mrs. Brenda Norris, chaired the social committee, and her circle, which intersected with Turner's friends in the young professional community, was a plentiful source of campaign workers.[25]

Turner's team approached his campaign like a business project, bringing its professional skills and management talent to bear. The first challenge was gathering information. He was fortunate to have three team members with the necessary expertise: James Davey, a management consultant; Dino Constantinou, a math and statistics whiz who did market research for the Steinberg grocery chain; and Geills Kilgour, a graduate of the Harvard Business School who worked for IBM. Davey compiled a demographic profile of the riding. Noting that the English in the riding tended to vote Conservative, with large voter turnout, whereas the French and ethnic vote tended to be Liberal, with lower turnout, he advised that they emphasize the candidate rather than the party with English Canadian voters and focus on getting out the French Canadian and ethnic voters.[26]

Constantinou devised a survey and deployed a team of campaign workers to gather information on constituents, their concerns, and their voting preferences. Kilgour wrote a computer program to process all the data and produce statistical overviews. The information was punched into cards and run on company computers at night. The results allowed campaign strategists to monitor residents' voting intentions on a poll-by-poll basis over the course of the campaign. The canvassers also collected information on issues raised by voters in different areas. The results were coded and run on computers as well, allowing advisers to brief Turner daily on policy positions that addressed the concerns of specific neighbourhoods.[27]

The first poll showed that Turner was running ahead of Chambers, with the NDP candidate a distant third. The disappointing performance of the Diefenbaker government was allowing the Liberals to win back much of their traditional electoral support after five years out of office. Pearson was making headway by criticizing the Tories for cancelling the Canadian-made Avro Arrow interceptor and for presiding over rising unemployment and a declining Canadian dollar. The Conservatives, Liberals argued, were running a weak and divided government; they, by contrast, were competent managers.

Because Turner had the early lead, his campaign organizers concentrated on shoring up shaky support and winning over lukewarm Conservative voters and the undecided. They found that the proportion of long-term anglophone residents had been dropping in the west end of the riding as more transient students, downtown office workers, and young couples moved into new apartment blocks along Sherbrooke Street. This was a potential area of growth for Turner, but the apartments presented a challenge for campaigning. His organizers devised a novel approach: an advance team would blitz the building, informing residents that John Turner would like to meet them. A small crowd would gather – refreshments would be served – and the babble would attract more residents. Turner would show up, give a short speech, and mix with the crowd. If he kept moving, he could squeeze in four buildings a night. Some upscale buildings were targeted for longer-lasting cocktail parties, hosted by friends of Brenda Norris.[28] Turner's campaign was fortunate to be able to draw on lots of young female volunteers. "Pretty girls," as they were described in the press, were considered an essential accoutrement of politicking in the 1960s.

St. Lawrence–St. George's role as a landing stage for immigrants gave it a mix of English, French, and new Canadians that anticipated the bilingual and multicultural Canada that would be celebrated in decades to come. Engaging recent immigrants who had little knowledge of Canadian politics was difficult. Turner's team translated campaign materials, liaised with community leaders, and struck committees to focus on various ethnic groups – one each for Chinese, Poles, Hungarians, Greeks, and Italians.[29] When Turner visited one of these communities, an attractive local girl would go ahead of him, knock on doors, and introduce him.

Turner was intrigued by the seamy side of life in the big city. He later liked to tell a campaign story in which he portrayed himself as a young innocent oblivious to the fact that he was knocking on doors in the red light district. He remarked to his guide on how many women seemed to be home alone during the day and was advised that this was a function of their line of work. He clued in when one woman greeted him clad only in a towel and cooed, "You come back after the election – I'll be dry and you'll have more time." On one level, anecdotes such as this intimated the worldly experience of the savvy politician, but their titillating intent spoke more eloquently of what the storyteller believed to be taboo.[30]

Inevitably, any group of young professionals involved in an election campaign in 1962 was influenced by John F. Kennedy's dramatic rise to the US presidency a year and a half earlier. Theodore H. White's *Making of the President* became essential reading for political junkies, but even casual observers knew the basics of the Kennedy formula: youth, sexiness, glamour, and the promise of change. Turner was a passable Canadian facsimile of Kennedy: young, handsome, well-to-do, sophisticated, and professional. His campaign team even sought the advice of Lou Harris, one of the public relations experts who had helped put Kennedy in the White House.[31] Its campaign strategy emerged from a reading of the public mood. Change was in the air: presenting Turner as a man of action who wanted reform would tap into this spirit. His speeches were crafted accordingly. "Politics," he declared, "needs the vigor and the impatience of younger men ... if it is to survive the second half of the 20th century."[32] The change promised did not involve remaking the status quo so much as repopulating it with younger people and their up-to-date thinking.

A journalist who saw Turner on the platform thought he displayed "that magic something."[33] He came across as youthful and dynamic, yet serious and trustworthy. He had a common touch, chatting easily with strangers while working the crowds. Despite being popular within his own social group, Turner wasn't well known throughout the riding. To generate a higher profile, his campaign team rigged up a large open tour bus with a band, a film projector and screen, and pretty girls. When it rolled into public spaces – school parking lots or streets in front of community centres – the band played, people gathered, and the organizers showed a film promoting the candidate. At the appropriate moment, Turner himself appeared to give a short stump speech touching on the "time for a change" theme and attacking Diefenbaker. His masculine good looks were enhanced even more by the young women arrayed around him, adding sizzle to the proceedings. He shook hands and mingled for a while, then jumped on the bus for a dramatic departure. The locals were impressed.

The two English-language Montreal dailies, the *Star* and the *Gazette,* were intrigued by Turner's new-look campaign and gave him extensive coverage. They characterized it as an "American Style Blitz" and picked up on the candidate's claim that the time had come for a younger generation in politics. The organizers bought extensive advertising in these papers but did not rely on print media alone. Turner did radio shows and got on television whenever possible – making seven appearances in a nine-day stretch between June 4 and 15. In early June, with the election little more than a week away, Montrealers woke up to find a large marquee on an empty lot at the northwest corner of Sherbrooke and Peel decked out with "Vote for Turner" signs and bunting in Liberal colours. In case the tent alone weren't conspicuous enough, the campaigners tethered overhead an army surplus barrage balloon with "Turner" on its sides. They staffed the tent with pretty girls. The entrance tunnel, dubbed the Chamber of Horrors in honour of the rival Conservative candidate, was lined with blown-up copies of editorial cartoons ridiculing Diefenbaker. The tent was a publicity coup that got people talking and generated substantial comment in the media.[34]

The Turner organizers pulled out all the stops when Liberal leader Lester (Mike) Pearson came to town on June 12 for a rally to support local Liberal candidates. They put a Dixieland band on their bus at the head of the motorcade and staged a rousing event beside the Turner tent.[35] There were convertibles filled with pretty girls, more girls handing out Liberal placards, and a bass drummer hammering out a rhythm for chants of "We Want Mike." Estimating the turnout at ten thousand people, national journalists travelling with Pearson thought it the best Liberal event of the entire campaign.

Claxton was able to report a week before the election that Turner was ahead of Chambers, with 50 per cent compared to 28 per cent. He was bound to win.[36] They had only to get the Liberal vote out. On election day the campaign sent workers with detailed instructions to those areas where they needed to encourage voters. When the polls closed, Turner had won 52 per cent of the vote, taking many of the riding's traditional Conservative polls in addition to the reliable Liberal ones. He was mobbed by enthusiastic supporters when he arrived at campaign headquarters. He was, he told a reporter, overjoyed and very proud of his workers.[37]

Turner had been helped by national trends: everywhere that year, the big-city vote went either Liberal or NDP. The Diefenbaker Tories barely retained power, winning 116 seats to 100 for the Liberals, 30 for Social Credit, and 19 for the NDP. Even though the tide was turning toward the Liberals, Turner had done well to beat a popular Conservative candidate. He had prevailed through a savvy publicity effort, superior organization, and his motivated friends and supporters. "Turner has burst on the political scene so impressively," wrote Peter Gzowski in *Maclean's*, "that he may have trouble topping his own debut."[38]

3

GETTING AHEAD
IN CANADIAN POLITICS

The 1962 election revitalized the federal Liberals, bringing to Ottawa promising young MPs such as Donald Macdonald, Maurice Sauvé, Herb Gray, Edgar Benson, and, of course, John Turner. His maiden speech showed he was determined to stand out from the pack. Traditionally, new MPs extol the virtues of their riding, but Turner attacked the government instead. During the balance of the parliamentary session, however, he spoke far less than his peers, and his interventions were relatively innocuous. "You don't get things done for your constituents by standing up and blowing off in the House," he explained. "Where you get the action is behind the scenes."[1] He was studying the flow of power on Parliament Hill and getting his feet wet.

He also began to build a national profile by making public appearances on behalf of the party. In a speech to the Alberta Liberal Association in November 1962, he laid out his political philosophy. As a Liberal, he prized individual freedom. He even advocated that a bill of rights be enshrined in the constitution.[2] But individualism had to be balanced by concern for the common good, he insisted. Political freedom was meaningless without a modicum of economic security, so government must provide social programs. State intervention was also necessary for fostering economic development where the private sector could not meet the need, though here too judicious balancing was necessary to ensure that government did not encroach unduly on free enterprise. Turner's outlook blended the liberal concern for individual freedom with the moral claims of social justice and a technocratic faith in rational planning. It also reflected an appreciation of the mood of the electorate and a partisan appropriation of the most popular positions of the newly minted New Democratic Party.

In this same speech, Turner also tackled foreign ownership, an issue pushed onto the political agenda by rising nationalist sentiment. Wartime victory and unprecedented influence in post-war international affairs had boosted national pride. Yet as English Canada finally began to slough off its attachment to Britain in favour of a more autonomous national status, it found itself locked in the gravitational pull of its southern neighbour. Harold Innis, the noted University of Toronto political economist, put the question succinctly: Had Canada gone from colony to nation to colony?[3] Throughout the 1950s, *Maclean's*, the *Toronto Star*, and other nationalist voices had resisted continentalism by asserting Canada's unique culture, history, and identity. Economic nationalism was added to the mix when the Royal Commission on Canada's Economic Prospects, chaired by Walter Gordon, released its report in 1957. It raised the spectre of a country perpetually indentured to a rich neighbour that owned its most lucrative resources and industries.

Prodded by a journalist from *McCall's* a few years later, Turner would demonstrate his appreciation of the value of the Canadian experiment with an alternative form of liberal democracy in the northern half of North America:

> We were not born in revolution as you were. We were born in a compromise which we imposed upon ourselves by legislative agreement with Great Britain. We have more consciously maintained the historic traditions from Europe, especially those of Britain and France ... We are not a "melting pot," but a "mosaic." Fundamentally, the difference between us results from the fact that we are officially and in reality a country of two languages and cultures: French and English, Anglo-Saxon and Gallic, re-enforced [sic] by one-third of the population who come from every corner of the world, particularly those countries in Western and Central Europe. The two languages and two cultures mean that we will never be as homogeneous in our attitudes as our American neighbours.[4]

Turner knew Canada better than most Canadians, having spent spans of time in Ontario, British Columbia, and New Brunswick before his political career took him all over the country. He loved the vastness of the land, its wild beauty, natural wonders, and diversity from coast to coast to coast.

Yet Turner was leery of the irrational and illiberal side of nationalism, particularly the peevish anti-American tone that often crept into its Canadian strain. He also feared that economic nationalism could do real damage to the Canadian economy, leaving ordinary Canadians to pay the price. In this sense he followed C.D. Howe, who had welcomed American investment as vital to Canadian economic development while expecting US companies to be good corporate citizens in Canada.[5] Turner's Alberta address acknowledged that foreign ownership was a problem and recognized the national interest as a legitimate qualification on free enterprise. But he went no further. He was speaking to a Western audience, and, historically, the West associated Canadian economic nationalism with special protection for Eastern interests. Instead, he changed the channel, declaring that he was more concerned about breaking economic oligarchy within Canada in order to spread the wealth around. With the region's demographics in mind, he also emphasized the need for upward mobility for members of the country's diverse ethnic groups.

None of the ideas Turner presented to the Alberta Liberal Association were particularly radical for the times. Delivered passionately by a dynamic young man, however, they made a forceful impression. Turner was soon much in demand as a speaker all across the country. He was seen as the "epitome of the smart young executive type which in recent years has cut such a swath in American politics."[6] Good looking, athletic, full of zeal for positive change – John Napier Turner was indeed Canada's answer to John Fitzgerald Kennedy.

His age was a particularly important political factor in the 1960s. The baby boomers were rapidly approaching maturity and would be an increasingly significant political force as the decade progressed. Turner told his audiences that a new generation was on the rise, questioning established ways. Confident that he understood young people's aspirations and hoping to harness their support, he positioned himself as a representative of youth.

Speechmaking gave Turner a chance to get publicity, test new ideas, and cultivate support across the country. He met local worthies and gained insights into grassroots party networks. He had the knack – handy for a politician – of being able to remember faces and attach names to them. Cam Avery, a constituency organizer for Ron Basford (MP for Vancouver-Burrard), recalled an election event in Vancouver in the early 1960s where Turner was mainstreeting. Although Turner had met him only once before, he spied him in the crowd and hailed him by name.[7]

Though conversant with issues and ideas, Turner also conceptualized the Canadian public sphere in terms of people, where they came from, and where they fit in. Politics was no dry academic exercise, but a matter of places and personalities with unique quirks, life stories, and interests. The Canadian political scene was a collection of fluid, democratically accessible regional meritocracies whose interests were brokered at the federal level. By getting to know the players, Turner learned how Canada was governed, an approach that was good politics in terms of both the national interest and his own career.

He had sage advice to assist him in developing his national profile. John de B. Payne became his main sounding board on matters of policy and political strategy. An Anglo-Montrealer, Payne had worked in Winnipeg as a CBC producer and as a manager for the Hudson's Bay Company before moving to Ottawa as one of Pearson's executive assistants. He was, at first, a hard person to like. Prone to pontificate, he came across as a know-it-all, earning the nickname "John de Bullshit Payne." But for Turner he was a connected insider, an older authority figure of the type he had always looked up to. He valued his experience, advice, and confidences. Behind the officiousness, he found in Payne a loyal ally with a love of political gossip, media management, and big-picture strategizing.[8] Payne in turn saw Turner as a promising protégé, a future star through whom he could continue to play a backroom role as a new generation rose to power.

There would be many opportunities to draw on Payne's talents through the shaky minority governments and frequent elections of the early 1960s. By February 1963 Diefenbaker's minority government had been torn apart by his indecisiveness over defence policy. An election was called for April 8. Less than a year had elapsed since his first campaign, so Turner was able to mobilize the same team and deploy the same tactics. The party had him campaign in other ridings too, a sign that St. Lawrence–St. George was now considered a safe constituency. He was presented as a symbol of Liberal youth, vigour, and competence in contrast to the fumbling and bumbling of the old Tory chief. Pearson promised "Sixty Days of Decision" and sketched out an ambitious program of social reforms, including medicare, a national system of old age pensions, and regional economic development. On election day the Liberals won a minority government with 129 seats, compared to 95 for the Conservatives, 24 for Social Credit, and 17 for the NDP. In his own riding, Turner improved on his previous victory, winning 58 per cent of the vote, more than twice that garnered by Chambers, his closest rival.

The day after the election, the *Montreal Gazette* ran a photograph of Turner at an election party at the Reform Club, flanked by "the most important ladies in his life" – his mother, his sister, and his fiancée.[9] The 1963 election was the last time that John Turner could use his bachelor status to enhance his electoral appeal. He and Geills Kilgour, the computer expert who had analyzed the riding data in his first election, were married in Winnipeg, her hometown, on May 11. Turner's old friend John Grace was best man, and numerous friends and associates from Montreal were on the guest list. The bride's father, David E. Kilgour, the president and CEO of Great West Life Assurance, gave her away. They took up residence in a new high-rise apartment building at 85 Range Road, overlooking the Rideau River on the east side of the Sandy Hill neighbourhood where Turner had grown up. Soon they would move to a house in Rockcliffe Park, an affluent Ottawa suburb, where they would begin to raise a family – their first child, Elizabeth, would be born the following March.

Turner was seen as an up-and-comer in the new government. In his optimistic moments, he hoped for a seat in Cabinet. But he had only one year's parliamentary experience. Pearson told him he needed more seasoning in the "kitchen of government" and appointed him parliamentary secretary to Arthur Laing, the minister of northern affairs and national resources. Turner felt that had Pearson not known him as a child he would have been taken more seriously. Nevertheless, he resigned himself to his fate. He respected Pearson, who epitomized the ideals and virtues of his mother's generation of public servants – a sense of duty, social conscience, diplomatic skill, and cosmopolitan outlook, all leavened by a knowing modesty and quiet patriotism. For idealistic young Liberals in the 1960s,

1 John Turner's father, Leonard Turner (c. 1930), who died in 1932 when John was three, prompting his wife, Phyllis, to return to British Columbia from England with her two young children.

2 The Turner family in Rossland, BC: John, mother Phyllis, and Brenda, c. 1933-34.

3 John Turner as a boy, c. 1939. He attended the Ottawa Normal School, then spent two years at Ashbury College before going to St. Patrick's College, a Catholic high school. Along the way he skipped two grades, so he was only sixteen when he started at the University of British Columbia in 1945.

4 Turner preparing to sprint at a US college track meet in 1948. He was a star on the UBC track team and won the 100 and 220 at the Canadian championships in 1947. A car accident sidelined him from the 1948 Summer Olympics in London and then red tape prevented him from representing Canada at the 1952 Olympics in Helsinki.

5   As a woman executive, John Turner's mother was a rare bird in 1940s Canada, rare enough to make the cover of the August 1, 1942 issue of *Maclean's*. Her job was to ensure that essential commodities were available for the war effort. She became the senior woman in the federal public service and later in life served as chancellor of the University of British Columbia.

6   John Turner at the 1952 Helsinki Olympics with Chris Chataway (left), who would later set a world record for the 1500 and help pace their mutual friend Roger Bannister when he broke the four-minute mile.

METRO EDITION

TORONTO DAILY STAR

THE WEATHER

INDEX

TUESDAY, AUGUST 5, 1958 —48 PAGES

10c Per Copy, 55c

Expect Margaret to Dance Third Time With Montreal Lawyer

PRINCESS MARGARET danced for the second time with handsome Montreal lawyer John Turner, 29, at the Governor-General's ball on Saturday. Margaret met Turner at a ball in Vancouver during her visit there last week and he turned up again 2,000 miles to the east at the dance in Government house at Ottawa given by Gov.-Gen. Vincent Massey. He is expected to attend a third dance for her in Montreal.

Keeps Margaret Gay John Turner To See Her Once More in Montreal

By ANGELA BURKE
Star Staff Correspondent
Montreal, Aug. 5—Princess Margaret's favorite Canadian escort — John Turner — is getting his white tie and tails ready for tonight's ball at the Queen Elizabeth hotel.

And his date will be—the Princess.

This will be the third ball in which the 29-year-old

When it stopped, it wasn't the Princess' request. As one informant said: "She would have danced until 5 or 6 a.m."

It was Gov.-Gen. Massey who finally—despite royal

protocol — grew desperate enough to call a halt.

As one guest put it: "The G.G. looked all in. His shoulder was suffering an inflammation and his right arm (Continued on Page 2, Col. 5)

49 Canadians Drown

Russian Warships Off Newfoundland Said 'Power Show'

Hamburg, Germany, Aug. 5— (UPI) — An authoritative West German naval intelligence report said today the Soviet Union recently moved forces of its strong Arctic fleet as far west as Newfoundland in an apparent demonstration of Soviet naval power.

Intelligence officers said the Soviet "show of strength" in waters of the western hemisphere coincided with Moscow's announcement of troop manoeuvres along the Iranian and

The officials also noted increased activity in movements of units of the Soviet Pacific fleet.

According to the intelligence reports, surface vessels of the Soviet Arctic fleet, presumably accompanied by submarines, were observed in Newfoundland waters carrying out manoeuvres usually held well within the range of the fleet's land-based aircover of 500 jet-fighter planes.

The sources said the Arctic fleet in normal manoeuvres con-

7 Rumours of a royal romance got Turner in the headlines in 1958. Then a young lawyer in Montreal, he was asked by his stepfather, Frank Ross, lieutenant governor of British Columbia, to help entertain the princess during her royal tour of Canada. The two hit it off, generating headlines that made Turner "the man who danced with Princess Margaret."

8 Turner, the eligible bachelor, Montreal, c. 1959. The social whirl included skiing in the Laurentians, racquet sports, charitable balls, and a vibrant night life. Unlike many of his anglophone contemporaries, Turner socialized outside the English Canadian community. He was active in the Montreal symphony, a cultural institution favoured by French Canadian and Jewish Montrealers.

9 Turner (centre) had a campaign tent and balloon at Peel and Sherbrooke Streets in Montreal that generated lots of publicity for his 1962 election campaign in the riding of St. Lawrence–St. George. The barrage balloon disappeared one night, and the air force later tried to bill the Turner campaign for the cost of scrambling fighters to intercept it.

10 During the 1962 election, Turner was described as "the epitome of the smart young executive type, which in recent years has cut such a swath in American politics." Here he and his campaign team greet Liberal leader Lester B. Pearson, who was in Montreal for a campaign rally.

11 Turner after his 1963 election victory with (left to right) his mother, Phyllis Ross, his fiancée, Geills Kilgour, and his sister, Brenda Norris. Turner and Kilgour, who met when she was at McGill in the late 1950s, were married in her hometown of Winnipeg in April 1963.

12 Diefenbaker and Turner chatting on the beach in Tobago, January 1964. When the Turners found themselves vacationing at the same Tobago resort as the Diefenbakers, Dief and Turner struck up a friendship. A couple of years later, when the two couples coincidentally vacationed at another resort, Diefenbaker might have drowned had Turner not swum out to pull him from the surf.

13 Turner was first named to Cabinet on December 18, 1965, as minister without portfolio. Here Prime Minister Pearson poses with his new ministers after the swearing-in ceremony. Left to right, Joe Greene (minister of agriculture), Jean Luc Pépin (minister of mines), Judy LaMarsh (secretary of state), Allan MacEachen (minister of national health and welfare), Pearson, Georges Vanier (governor general), Mitchell Sharp (minister of finance), Jean Marchand (minister of citizenship and immigration), Turner, and Jean Pierre Côté (postmaster general).

14 In 1967, Turner was made registrar general in the Pearson Cabinet. The other ministers brought into Cabinet for the first time were Pierre Trudeau, the new justice minister (far left) and Jean Chrétien (far right), who became minister without portfolio. All three newcomers to Cabinet would become prime ministers of Canada.

15 Turner in the eye of the camera as he woos delegates at the 1968 Liberal leadership convention in Ottawa. Two years earlier he had commented presciently: "Today, television is the great equalizer ... I think that today with a properly conceived campaign, an absolute unknown could be propelled from obscurity to national leadership within six months."

16 On the convention floor, Ottawa, April 6, 1968. In the manoeuvring prior to the last two ballots, Turner was trailing and under intense pressure to throw his support to one of the English Canadian candidates who had a chance to catch Pierre Trudeau. Having pledged an open campaign with no backroom deals, Turner stayed in until the final ballot, placing third with 195 votes.

"Mr. Pearson" had shown by personal example how the emerging Canadian nation should make its way in the world.

At first Turner and other new MPs followed the party's senior leadership unwaveringly. But it soon became apparent that the elders were not infallible – in fact, they sometimes stumbled badly. The foreign ownership provisions of the June budget, for example, drew so much criticism that Walter Gordon, the finance minister, was forced to gut them less than one month later. The younger members of caucus grew concerned that their political futures were in shaky hands. Encouraged by the impatience they sensed in their constituencies, they began to question authority in caucus. They even proposed that they be consulted on any plans for legislation. Senior Liberals replied that it was constitutionally impossible for Cabinet to consult backbenchers ahead of Parliament, but the rookies remained unappeased.

Turner was in the forefront of these protests and emerged as a leader of the reformers in caucus. He advocated expansion of the parliamentary committee system to allow information to circulate more freely and give MPs a constructive role in the legislative process. The party establishment found his criticisms irksome, but he was too valuable politically to be repudiated. Pearson responded by distributing significant parliamentary committee work to the young and restless – a substantial concession that effectively co-opted the dissent. "What is remarkable is not that Mr. Turner and the liberal Young Turks feel this way," wrote Christopher Young in the *Ottawa Citizen*. "What is remarkable is that the party leaders listened and acted."[10]

Pearson appointed Turner chairman of a caucus subcommittee on the role of the MP. Turner took up the cause and travelled around the country giving speeches on parliamentary reform. His analysis was accurate and important. The executive had too much control, he pointed out. Issues were resolved behind the scenes, never emerging before the public or its elected representatives for real debate. Democratic accountability was further subverted by a powerful but largely unaccountable bureaucracy. Finally, television exacerbated the problem by portraying the Canadian representative system of democracy in terms of "battles ... between supermen – the leaders."[11]

In "Democracy Is behind Closed Doors," a speech to the McGill Liberal Club, Turner bemoaned the fate of backbench MPs, decried their subordination to the party whip, and contrasted their present situation with their autonomy a century earlier:

> So this is your member of Parliament: whipped by the discipline of the party machines; starved for information by the mandarin class, dwarfed by the Cabinet and by bigness in industry, labour and communications, ignored in an age of summitry and of the leadership cult ... Insofar as a Member's relationship with his own party is concerned, my suggestion is that the government stop treating every vote as a vote of confidence ... Enormous life could be brought back to the House of Commons if the members could occasionally follow their own opinions regardless of the party stand.[12]

MPs needed resources – more staff, better facilities, and adequate research budgets – to enable them to do their jobs effectively. Asked by a reporter if he were a rebel backbencher, Turner responded, "If I am, there are thirty more like me in the backbenches who feel the same way."[13]

Turner consolidated his profile by networking with the media. The largely male members of parliament and the national press gallery enjoyed a non-partisan camaraderie, particularly after work. They played pick-up sports, shared meals and beers, and held raucous late-night poker games. Turner had always romanticized the masculine realm and revelled in being part of this scene – acknowledging the profane underbelly of life, lampooning the hypocrisies of polite society, swearing, telling off-colour jokes, and exchanging raw truths about personalities and power. Beneath the informality, certain unwritten professional rules applied. Journalists got information off the record that gave them valuable context, but this access came in return for discretion. When the status of information was in doubt, they asked for clarification rather than assuming they could print what they heard.[14] The relationship was symbiotic rather than adversarial. Journalists understood what politicians had to do to get re-elected, and politicians understood what journalists had to do to get a story. Turner treated the reporters he knew as valued colleagues and earned their respect. In the process he learned how political news was shaped and was assured that, all else being equal, journalists would give him the benefit of the doubt.

Unlike most politicians, Turner made friends across party lines. One of his pals was Erik Nielsen, the Conservative MP for the Yukon. In the fall of 1964, Nielsen levelled charges in the House that launched the Rivard affair, a scandal that accused some Liberals of helping a Mafioso with his legal troubles. In the ensuing partisan acrimony, Turner told Nielsen, "Erik, you did a good job. You went just far enough and not too far."[15]

Turner's most unlikely friendship was with John Diefenbaker. Their paths crossed coincidentally while both were vacationing with their wives at a small resort in Tobago during the 1963 Christmas holidays. The Diefenbakers invited the Turners to dinner, and a couple of nights later they celebrated New Year's Eve together. During the day, Diefenbaker and Turner sometimes bumped into each other on the beach, where they sat together and chatted. Two years later, again by coincidence, both couples found themselves at the Sandy Lane Hotel in Barbados. As the Turners sat on the beach one day, they watched Diefenbaker wade into the surf. Suddenly a big wave knocked him down, and he was sucked out by the undertow. Turner sprang up, swam out, and pulled him to shore. By that time, Diefenbaker was convulsing. Turner had just begun artificial respiration when the older man sat up. "Thanks John," he said. The incident was never again mentioned between them, though they continued to visit and kibitz regularly on Parliament Hill.[16]

Turner was also on good terms with the parliamentary staff, including the grounds crew. When the new Maple Leaf flag was proclaimed and hoisted over the Parliament Buildings in February 1965, the first flag raised went to the Speaker of the House. Turner had a word with a friend and got the second one, which he flew proudly at the Kilgour cottage on Lake of the Woods. He prided himself in being able to relate to Canadians from all walks of life. He was interested in people, and those who met him often commented, with amazement, that he listened to them and took their concerns seriously. The only jarring note was his lapses into profanity in male company, a trait disconcertingly at odds with his public persona. In these situations he was guilty of being too democratic, not realizing that the average person enjoyed rubbing elbows with celebrity but still wanted to look up to him.

Although the Liberals had only a minority government, they made substantial progress on the reform agenda Pearson outlined in his 1963 campaign. Continuing prosperity provided the revenue needed to fund new social programs, and the welfare state envisioned by post-war planners began to take shape. A deal had been made with the provinces that ensured interprovincial portability of old age pensions, creating a truly national system. National medicare was in the works, and regional development schemes were being launched. In an era of rising nationalist sentiment, such programs would soon be embraced as defining characteristics of modern Canada. Nationalists saw other hopeful signs that Canada was finally emerging as a distinctive independent nation. Pearson battled Diefenbaker over symbolic issues such as the new flag and dropping the royal coat of arms from the post office emblem.[17] Canadians generally welcomed these developments and looked forward to celebrating their centennial in 1967. With the United States embroiled in nasty controversies over civil rights, the Vietnam War, poverty, and urban decay, they flattered themselves that they were constructing in the northern half of North America a peaceable kingdom that would be more civil, tolerant, and just.

Quebec's continuing demands for greater power in the wake of the Quiet Revolution were an unsettling intrusion into such nationalist reveries. In response, Pearson had established the Royal Commission on Bilingualism and Biculturalism in 1963. As it studied the issue, federal politicians toyed with a "two nations" solution that would accord Quebec primacy in protecting and promoting French Canadian culture. As a fluently bilingual Montreal MP, Turner was well positioned to weigh in on the issue. On March 2, 1964, he gave a speech to the Canadian Club of Montreal in which he deplored the "dialectic of extremism in Quebec": French Canadian radicals scaring English Canadians into intemperate responses, which in turn generated an escalating cycle of acrimony. The moderate majority in each group should step up, he urged, and control the debate.

French Quebeckers, Turner argued, needed "equal opportunity for the development of language and culture, with access to federal services in French and the right to have their children educated in French in public schools where there were sufficient numbers."[18] Yet he believed that French Canadian ambitions were as much economic as cultural. Interpreting Quebec to a Vancouver audience later that year, he explained,

French-speaking Canadians are seeking a new climate of self-fulfilment ... They are Canadians in a hurry. The French-speaking Canadian, in economic terms, slept for generations ... He has a craving for education and for skills and competence of every kind. He has an urge for material improvement and wants to develop Quebec. He seeks to fulfill himself in his own language, whether for his bread and butter or for his leisure. He seeks a new tone of political maturity. For French-speaking Canadians the so-called Quiet Revolution is not a revolution against Canada; it is a revolution against themselves.[19]

At the same time, Turner defended the place of anglophones in Quebec: "This is our land. We too are Quebeckers ... We want a better life, more security and greater opportunities, here and together."[20] In tackling one of the country's most profound challenges, Turner characteristically displayed a determination to find solutions balanced by an appreciation of the sensitivities of the interests in play.

Turner had significant duties as parliamentary secretary to Arthur Laing. The North had always captured the Canadian imagination, and Diefenbaker's invocation of Canada's northern destiny in his 1957 and 1958 election campaigns had refreshed and heightened national dreams about the region. By the time the Liberals came to power in April 1963, northern development had not yet fulfilled the visionaries' promise, but significant progress had been made in constructing railways and hydro dams, and in prospecting for minerals, oil, and gas.

One of the reasons Turner was assigned to assist Laing was that the minister did not speak French or know much about Quebec – a serious deficiency at a time when Quebec and Ottawa were sparring about responsibility for the Inuit (or Eskimos, as they were still known) in northern Quebec.[21] After decades of decline, Native populations were growing, confounding long-standing predictions that they were doomed to extinction. René Lévesque, Quebec's minister of resources, thought Inuit living conditions deplorable. Their traditional way of life was no longer sustainable, but no substitute had yet been found. Lévesque demanded that Ottawa cede responsibility for the Inuit within Quebec's boundaries to the province. Only Quebec, he argued, could improve their lot because it had the power to impose conditions on resource companies operating in the area. In any event, Quebec could scarcely do a worse job than the federal government was doing.[22]

Inevitably the issue was coloured by the broader context of Quebec's struggle for greater power within the Canadian federation. Under the *British North America Act,* legislative authority over Indians rested with the federal government, but the Inuit were not mentioned. Quebec had referred this issue to the Supreme Court when it was trying to offload responsibilities during the Depression, and the court had ruled that the Inuit fell under federal jurisdiction. Initially, the federal Liberals were prepared to hand the Quebec Inuit over to the province, but when Laing made this position public, he was criticized for setting a dangerous precedent by surrendering a federal government prerogative to Quebec. He then announced that Ottawa would consult with the Inuit before making a decision.

Turner accompanied Laing on tours of the North in the summers of 1963 and 1964. There was disturbing evidence of cultural dislocation in some communities – dysfunctional families, alcohol abuse, juvenile delinquency, prostitution, unemployment, and abject poverty.[23] Yet Western medicine was saving lives and improving the general health of the population. The challenge was how to promote the welfare of a people whose traditional culture had been compromised by contact with white society. The assimilative policies of earlier eras were no longer in favour, but assimilative forces were increasing as economic development, schools, social programs, and mass communications penetrated the North.

Turner and Laing agreed that the best policy would be to promote Inuit initiative and mutual aid, which they hoped would allow them to adapt their traditional culture to new circumstances. They did not want to encourage a welfare culture and hoped instead to see the Inuit develop their own commercial enterprises. They saw great promise in an emerging cooperative movement exemplified by the Arctic char fishery at Port Burwell, logging operations at George River, and the soapstone carving business at Cape Dorset. Cooperatives were a means by which the Inuit could integrate into the broader Canadian market economy yet retain their distinctive cultural characteristics. Turner enthusiastically sang their praises.

Turner was irked by southerners who patronized the Inuit. He criticized those who acted like superior emissaries of the imperial power or built miniature bureaucratic empires. He also thought that government training programs were misguided because they ghettoized Natives in blue-collar jobs. If the Inuit were to build a self-sufficient society in their new cultural and economic milieu, they needed to run their own affairs, and that meant becoming their own teachers, administrators, technicians, and nurses. They also needed educational materials that reflected their way of life. Turner publicized these conclusions in speeches that reinforced his image as a thoughtful politician with progressive positions on important national issues.[24]

However much federal policy emphasized Inuit cooperatives and self-reliance, it was inevitable that large-scale resource extraction industries would be an important part of the North's future. Laing favoured private investment as the means by which the region could develop. Mining was the most promising sector. He continued the Conservatives' "Roads to Resources" agenda and looked for other ways to attract capital – which effectively meant American investment – into the area. This policy put him at loggerheads with Walter Gordon, the leader of the nationalist faction in the party, who continued to crusade against American ownership.

On this issue, Turner's reform impulses remained balanced by his pragmatism. In a perfect world he would have liked far less foreign ownership, but restricting capital inflows would hurt the economy, and not just in the North. As the conflict between these two positions divided the Pearson government, he tried to straddle the rift. He took the position that the best way to deal with the foreign investment issue was to encourage Canadian investment rather than to discourage American capital.[25] This search for a compromise solution to a seemingly intractable standoff exemplified his pragmatic, even-handed, and constructive approach to political issues.

In the spring of 1965, Turner had a rare opportunity to visit another North – that of the Soviet Union – along with Laing and Jack Austin, Laing's executive assistant. The Soviets hoped to overwhelm them with hospitality to distract them from any serious inquiries. They were chauffeured everywhere in limousines in the large cities, feted through endless dinners, and plied with Russian brandy. Though staggered by these tactics,

Turner managed to push their hosts to fulfill the itinerary. When they wanted to go to Siberia, they were told it was impossible because the only planes departed at three in the morning. Turner responded, "Tell us the way to the airport and we'll be there."[26] Peter Worthington, stationed in Moscow for the *Toronto Telegram,* reported that the trip would have been a failure without Turner. They became the first official Western delegation since the Russian Revolution to tour the area east of the Urals. Turner was fascinated by the Soviets' northern construction techniques. Near Bratsk they visited the world's largest power dam and an enormous pulp and paper mill. He was most impressed by Norilsk, a nickel and copper mining and smelting centre boasting a population of 100,000 and eight-storey buildings supported by steel and concrete pilings driven deep into the permafrost.

Turner kept extensive notes on the trip and, in a number of speeches over the next few months, reflected on the differences between the two countries' northern frontiers.[27] The USSR had a larger population and a more developed economic infrastructure in the North, and its command economy deployed labour and capital investment according to national priorities rather than market forces. He recognized that much of this infrastructure had been built by the forced labour of dissidents or prisoners of war. Nevertheless, the Soviet example showed that state intervention was necessary to establish the extra infrastructure needed in the North. Canada, he thought, should move quickly to inventory northern resources and improve north-south transportation links. Workers should be enticed northward with bonuses to cover the higher cost of living. Businesses could be lured with an accelerated capital depreciation allowance. He also floated the idea of establishing an Arctic Youth Corps, a Canadian variation on the US Peace Corps, which would expose young Canadians to the northern frontier. Laing supported the proposal, and it played well enough in Cabinet to be included in the 1965 Throne Speech before getting lost in the shuffle as the government prepared for yet another election that fall.

Turner's role as a parliamentary secretary also got him involved in the Columbia River Treaty, one of the most controversial resource issues of the era. The Columbia ran southward through the Rocky Mountains in British Columbia into Washington State. To engineering minds it called out for taming. By water volume it was the third-largest North American river, after the Mississippi and the St. Lawrence, and it carried three-quarters of its runoff in just half the year, with water levels a hundred times greater in spring than in winter. Its overflowing banks were a constant threat to people living on its floodplains south of the border. Damming would eliminate flooding, generate electricity, and divert water for irrigation into nearby farm regions.

The Americans had devised a comprehensive management scheme for the Columbia watershed that would distribute electricity and irrigation across Washington and into neighbouring states. The hydroelectric potential of the river could not be fully realized, however, if its upstream Canadian stretch remained untouched. American authorities proposed that if Canada built dams upstream, the United States would share the benefits of the resulting downstream gain in hydro power. Negotiations began in the late fifties, and on January 17, 1961, Prime Minister Diefenbaker and President Eisenhower signed the Columbia River Treaty.

The treaty quickly became a subject of federal-provincial wrangling. British Columbia premier W.A.C. Bennett favoured a hydro development scheme on the Peace River and wanted to sell the province's Columbia power entitlement back to the United States so he could use the revenue to develop the Peace project. This proposal led to a standoff with Ottawa, which wanted the Columbia electricity used in Canada. In early 1962 the Americans threatened to walk away from the table if the Canadians did not resolve their differences soon. Meanwhile, General Andrew McNaughton attacked the treaty as a sellout to American interests that failed to exploit the full potential of the Canadian section of the watershed or to compensate Canada sufficiently. McNaughton's opinion carried weight because he was a respected Canadian war hero and past president of the Canadian section of the International Joint Commission.

Nationalists feared that the Americans would take the Columbia deal as a precedent and expect that, in future, their needs should dictate what Canada did with its water. Capitalizing on voter queasiness about water issues, in 1962 Pearson pledged that, if elected, the Liberals would renegotiate the Columbia deal. Less than a month after winning power, he met with President Kennedy and got his agreement to renegotiate. Pearson settled with British Columbia, largely conceding to Bennett's demands, before signing a revised agreement with the Americans.

Wishing to keep close tabs on an issue that directly concerned both his portfolio and his home province, Laing proposed to Paul Martin, who was now secretary of state for external affairs, that Turner should steer the revised treaty through the House of Commons Committee on External Affairs. Martin agreed. Turner began his preparations with the help of Jack Austin, who had expertise in legal issues related to waterways.[28]

The parliamentary committee was expected to approve the amended treaty. The Conservatives were bound to support it because Diefenbaker had originally signed the agreement. The Social Credit members, though from Quebec, belonged to the same party as the BC premier. That left just the NDP offside. Nevertheless, Turner's assignment was delicate. The Columbia issue received extensive press coverage in the run-up to the committee's hearings in the spring of 1964, and most of the articles argued that Canada was being cheated out of a precious natural resource. Turner approached the task with his usual thoroughness. In keeping with his training as a lawyer, he wanted to be master of his brief when he went into the public forum. He covered every aspect of the issue – from the principles of international relations involved to the technical hydrological details – and studied the personalities of the witnesses he would be questioning.

The committee was constituted by the House on March 9. Turner had to defend both the treaty and the Liberals' changes to it in daily meetings from early April through to late May. He questioned several prominent witnesses, including Davie Fulton, the Diefenbaker Cabinet minister who had negotiated the initial deal. McNaughton was a particular challenge because Turner had to show esteem for a national hero while demonstrating that the general was not necessarily right on this issue. Turner was aware that he could win a battle by being aggressive but lose the war by appearing to be disrespectful. He succeeded in his mission by a skilful combination of tact, a mastery of the facts, and consistent invocation of the national interest. The committee approved the agreement and, on September 16, 1964, the treaty and its protocol were ratified.

Water issues became still more controversial when a continent-spanning water diversion scheme was proposed in the US Congress that year. The North American Water and Power Alliance hinged on diverting northern rivers southward to arid American lands. Reflecting on his experience with the Columbia treaty, Turner concluded that treaty provisions were no guarantee that Canada's sovereignty could be preserved in practice. The Americans might concede Canada's rights in principle, but deep down they believed they had a right to any water they needed. After downstream American communities became dependent on a regular flow of water from Canada, it would be hard to turn off the tap. And if they felt that way about water, how would they feel about other resources – oil and natural gas, for example? He wasn't anti-American, but the Columbia episode convinced him that the power disparity between the two countries made bilateral deals far riskier for Canada than for the United States.

On December 9, 1965, Turner addressed the National Water Conference of the Chamber of Commerce of the United States in Washington, DC. "North American water?" he asked his audience. "That sounds suspiciously like the suggestion that the waters of North America should be considered as a continental water supply and that is where we in Canada say – hold on a minute! We say there is *Canadian* water and there is *American* water."[29] Canada would provide for its current and future needs before it considered any water to be surplus, he told the Americans. Canadian newspapers gave the speech front-page coverage, and a number printed supportive editorials. Turner was inundated with appreciative letters from people across the country. Encouraged, he went even further. If the Americans wanted Canadian water, they could offer something substantial in return, such as guaranteed access to their markets for Canadian goods. The same went for other resources. "Continentalism is not in my vocabulary," he declared.[30]

In the fall of 1965, Pearson called an election on the advice of Walter Gordon, who thought the Liberals should exploit the fact that the Conservatives still had Diefenbaker at the helm and go to the polls in hopes of winning a majority. Turner was concerned because, as he told Pearson, "aside from medicare, we appear to have decided to run merely on our record and on the need for a strong federal majority."[31] Pearson asked for his advice on campaign issues, and Turner offered six policy ideas he had already proposed in his speeches: the Liberals should reform Parliament to make it more effective; strengthen Confederation by reasserting the role of the federal government against the decentralizing demands of the provinces; reconcile the two major cultural groups by making French Canadians more comfortable in their dealings with Ottawa and by strengthening minority rights; implement a national resource policy to guarantee that

Canada's interests came first; enhance social security by ensuring that every family had medicare and a pension; and provide skills training to help young people get into the workforce. Turner's speeches on these subjects became the basis for a party document used to prepare candidates and workers for the campaign.[32]

At Pearson's request, the governor general dissolved Parliament on September 8, 1965. The election would be held on November 8. Campaign strategists thought that having the prime minister make a statement on resource policy might be politically advantageous, so Pearson asked Turner for a full briefing on what such a policy might entail. Turner played an active role in the campaign, giving speeches, attending events, and campaigning for other Liberal candidates, even though his wife was expecting their second child. "Keith Davey has had me travelling all over the country," he reported.[33] He served as a bilingual emissary to Franco-Ontarians, did "hot-seat" sessions with university students, and campaigned through the Maritimes and the West. He was particularly active in Montreal, representing the Liberals at campaign events across the city.

As it turned out, Turner's policy ideas had little impact on the campaign. The two major parties emphasized each other's weaknesses rather than constructive programs. When the votes were counted, the Liberals' brushes with scandal over the previous months and Diefenbaker's effectiveness as a campaigner denied them a majority. They won 131 seats in the 265-seat Parliament. Turner easily won his own constituency, this time increasing his margin of victory to 60 per cent of the vote. He had served his time in the kitchen of government. As Pearson chose his new Cabinet, John Turner, though only thirty-six years old, was an obvious choice for a portfolio.

4

SHOALS OF CANDIDACY

A s the prime minister chose his ministers in November 1965, more than Cabinet posts were at stake. Pearson had led the Liberals for eight years, had failed to win a majority government, and was approaching seventy. Liberals suspected they would be choosing a new leader sooner rather than later. Turner was too young and inexperienced to contemplate a run for the leadership in the near term. But if Pearson stayed around for a few more years, he might have a shot, provided he got Cabinet experience in the interim.

Turner's hope for a prominent Cabinet post was fulfilled when Pearson promised him the Department of Mines and Technical Surveys, soon to be reorganized into a more significant portfolio, the Department of Energy, Mines, and Resources. His work on resource policy over the previous two years made him the natural choice for the job. Six hours before the announcement, however, Pearson told Turner he had bowed to pressure from the Quebec caucus and given the post to Jean-Luc Pepin. Turner was brought into Cabinet as a minister without portfolio to assist Jack Pickersgill, the minister of transport. Political observers thought he had been robbed.[1] Nevertheless, Peter Newman wrote that Turner's elevation to Cabinet might be the most significant aspect of the recent shuffle because it positioned him to win not the coming leadership race but the one after.[2]

Turner came to regard his new boss as a political genius. Pickersgill had been around Ottawa since the 1930s, first as a civil servant, then as a politician. He was now preoccupied with steering through Parliament a complex piece of legislation that rationalized the Canadian railways system. Turner helped by overseeing the day-to-day affairs of the department, receiving delegations, and attending meetings on Pickersgill's behalf. He also took the lead on certain projects. One of the most challenging involved negotiating with shipowners and seamen's unions to implement a traffic information system and other marine safety measures on the St. Lawrence Seaway.[3] Soon Pickersgill was entrusting him with political assignments such as liaising with Joey Smallwood, the premier of Newfoundland, where Pickersgill represented the riding of Bonavista-Twillingate.

Turner learned some new political tricks from his mentor. Pickersgill was careful always to canvass opinion on a proposal so people could get used to it before it came forward officially. He showed Turner that round-about ways could be the most effective. Memoranda fired directly at Pearson, for example, would often bounce off without making an impression. Better to have a proposal suggested to him casually, then kept in circulation until it grew familiar. He also advised Turner to attend only those meetings that were absolutely critical to his interests. And he passed on a ploy from King: do not write memos; rather, comment in the margins on memos sent to you and return them, thereby saving time and making it difficult for others to pin your political fortunes to a particular initiative.

Pickersgill also shared his extensive knowledge of parliamentary procedure and its partisan utility, enlarging Turner's appreciation for the House of Commons. Turner loved sitting in the House, in part because of the honour of the position and the significance of the work, but also for the ambience and camaraderie of the chamber. He saw there, personified, the politics of a nation. In one clubby setting, every name and face connected to a different complex of opinion shaped by region, interest, party, and personality. "Nowhere else in this nation does a man or woman gain the same sense of country," he wrote.[4]

Now that he was a minister, Turner could hire his own staff. He recruited Jerry Grafstein, a young Toronto lawyer, as his executive assistant. Grafstein had been active in the Liberal Party's rebuilding efforts and had impressed senior Liberals sufficiently to attract job offers from Keith Davey, Walter Gordon, and Paul Martin. He turned them all down and went with Turner, whom he regarded as a rising star. Turner's personal touch helped seal the deal. Other suitors had phoned, but he saw Grafstein at his office and also visited his wife.[5] Turner now had a direct line into the Toronto Liberal establishment in addition to his solid connections in Vancouver and Montreal.

Turner continued to accept speaking engagements all over Canada. He enjoyed meeting people and followed up with key figures, building political support one phone call at a time, hoping that his contacts could be mobilized into nationwide delegate support when the moment came for a leadership campaign. For speech material, he and Grafstein were constantly on the lookout for *the* current issue. They scoured the latest publications for topical social and political problems and policy solutions while mining the classics for enduring wisdom and fine sentiments. The results were stimulating, if eclectic. In one speech, Turner quoted the unlikely ensemble of Friedrich Nietzsche, St. Paul, Karl Marx, Marshall McLuhan, Sigmund Freud, and Damon Runyon.[6]

Turner continued to position himself as a progressive reformer. "We were all influenced by what Jack Kennedy and later Bobby Kennedy were doing," he recalled.[7] Many of his reform proposals appealed to the young, who were acquiring increasing political significance as the decade progressed. "Nearly half the country's electorate is under thirty-five," intoned the narrator of a CBC-TV public affairs show profiling Turner in 1967, "and now they want to take power."[8] Turner continued to hope that this rising generation would see itself represented in him. That possibility was thrown into doubt, however, as the times grew increasingly turbulent. Emergent youth subcultures presented an array of radical challenges to the mainstream. Long-haired hippies smoked pot, professed free love, and talked about dropping out of society. Crowds gathered in coffeehouses to applaud the utopian visions of folk singers. Strange new representations of sex, drugs, and rock and roll were shocking when they first appeared in living colour on television sets in suburban rec rooms, but continued to appear so regularly that they became a familiar backdrop to daily life. A climate of unrest spilled over the border from the United States, where the civil rights movement was succeeded by an anti-Vietnam War movement that generated violent confrontations that were featured regularly in the evening news. Soon Canadian campuses too were seething with sit-ins, boycotts, and rallies.

Turner's junior-executive style of youthful dynamism suddenly seemed dated. Although he didn't try to remake his image, he did radicalize his rhetoric. "You must exercise ... power to achieve the aspirations of our generation," he exhorted the Saskatchewan Young Liberals. "Don't be conned into routine work to get the older generation elected ... Mobilize your generation. Invade the ranks of the party and take over offices."[9] Rhetoric of this sort was not uncommon at the time. In its extreme forms, such as American counterculture seer Timothy Leary's famous 1966 injunction to "tune in, turn on, drop out," it represented a wholesale rejection of contemporary mores. Turner's exhortations sounded somewhat similar, but he was no Leary, and he was certainly not inciting Saskatchewan farm boys to embrace a hippie lifestyle, grow their hair long, drop acid, and stage a sit-in. He was challenging them to overhaul the system, not overthrow it.

At the same time, Turner worked to diversify and strengthen his reform agenda. Already on record as favouring the entrenchment of a bill of rights in the constitution, he now called for an economic bill of rights that would guarantee the right to good housing, legal counsel, and medical care. He proposed pragmatic remedies for a wide range of problems affecting parliamentary government, federal-provincial relations, the economy, education, the legal system, resource policy, foreign affairs, and even national identity. To give his program coherence he branded it "A Second Canada," a label that invoked his overarching argument that Canada could fulfill its potential in its second century by developing up-to-date solutions for modern issues.[10]

The most novel aspect of this program was its identification of the dangers of a modern mass society characterized by big bureaucracy, impersonal technology, and a bewildering pace of change. Turner pointed out the challenges that computer and communications technologies presented to individual freedom and privacy. The country's legal and political institutions required radical reform to cope with this brave new world.[11] Though he believed in the power of rational planning by teams of experts to solve humanity's problems, he cautioned against the narrowness of the technocratic vision and "the arrogance of assuming that people will accept the aristocracy of expertise."[12] In these aspects of "A Second Canada," there were echoes of the concerns voiced by George Grant in *Lament for a Nation* (1965), a tract that inspired a new strain of left-wing nationalism in late 1960s Canada. The moral critique underlying contemporary challenges to the status quo resonated with the concern for the common good instilled by Turner's Catholic faith. Reaching out to Canada's restless youth, he attributed their rebelliousness to "a search for values ... a quest for worthwhile goals."[13]

Turner's speeches got him noticed, but what he needed most to enhance his credibility as a leadership candidate was a portfolio of his own. He had hopes of getting the Justice portfolio, which would be a good launching pad for a leadership bid. He began to speak publicly about the need for law reform. In a speech to Osgoode Hall Law School in February 1967, he contended that there was one system of justice for the rich and another for the poor in matters such as bail and sentencing. He warned lawyers against being mere mercenaries for the wealthy and exhorted the students in his audience to pursue social justice – not just their clients' interests and their own careers. He called for the modernization of a stagnant, complacent justice system, a national legal aid plan, a national criminal law advisory council, and safeguards for privacy.[14]

A Cabinet post finally came in a backhanded fashion when the government decided to create the Department of the Registrar General to look after business-related matters such as trade restrictions, patents, bankruptcy, and copyrights and trademarks.[15] On October 1, 1966, legislation creating the new department was proclaimed, and Guy Favreau, president of the Privy Council, was given the post as an additional responsibility. Favreau's health was failing, however, and Turner was appointed acting registrar general pending his recovery.

Despite his many progressive policies, Turner's reform credentials would be called into question over two issues. The first cropped up in April 1966, when a free vote was held on a private member's bill that proposed a five-year moratorium on the use of the death penalty. Turner had thought seriously about this issue since his Oxford studies in criminal law. He knew that the majority of Canadians supported capital punishment, and he didn't like the fact that the alternative, a life sentence, could mean as little as ten years' imprisonment. He would have supported an amended bill that kept the death sentence for killers of police officers and prison guards – but the vote was held on straight-up abolition, so he voted against it. When another vote was held on the issue eighteen months later, this time with the police and guards proviso in place, he voted for it. His initial position, however, made the more lasting impression.

The second issue was foreign ownership – a topic that continued to divide the Liberals. It came to a head again during an October 1966 Liberal policy convention in Ottawa. Turner praised Walter Gordon as "a national conscience ... for my country – and my party," yet he maintained that the economic nationalism of Gordon's recent book *A Choice for Canada* did not represent mainstream political thinking in Canada.[16] For Turner, the mainstream flowed directly from C.D. Howe through to Mitchell Sharp, the minister of finance and the senior Liberal around whom resistance to Gordon's crusade now coalesced. He still considered foreign investment essential to Canada's continued economic development and prosperity. Yet he recognized that Gordon's concerns had merit and political potency, and he wanted to find a way to accommodate them. Consequently, he suggested that government foster an investment climate that would encourage Canadians to invest more in their own economy.[17] Tax incentives, for example, could be used to encourage Canadians to buy stock issued by Canadian subsidiaries of foreign companies. The following year he was appointed to a special Cabinet committee headed by Gordon that would preside over an inquiry into foreign ownership. University of Toronto economist Mel Watkins and a group of economists outside the government service were appointed to conduct the inquiry.

Capital punishment and foreign ownership were wedge issues that journalists used to categorize politicians as right or left, and Turner's stances on them jeopardized his reform image. Aware of this danger, he set out to solidify his progressive credentials at the Liberal policy convention. Under existing law, an employer could get a court order limiting pickets during a strike without the union being represented in court. When a motion on the convention floor favouring union representation was shelved, Turner objected and spoke in favour of it. Ultimately, the policy was approved. Though the government never followed through, Turner's intervention boosted his standing with left-wing Liberals.

When the next Cabinet shuffle came in the spring of 1967, Pierre Trudeau, elected two years earlier, was appointed minister of justice. Turner was confirmed as registrar general – he was "acting" no longer. Once again a French Canadian got preference, and Turner got a consolation prize. Pearson tried to soften the blow by promising that, within a few months, he would enhance Turner's portfolio with new responsibilities for consumer protection.

By this point, the radical spirit of the sixties was in full flower. Turner kept pace with the times. Soon after his appointment as registrar general, he got national television exposure when he was interviewed on CTV's *Pierre Berton Show*. He told Berton that the state should ensure that every Canadian had decent housing, that university tuition and medical services should be free, and that he favoured capital gains and inheritance taxes. The most controversial part of the interview was his declaration of support for a guaranteed annual income.[18] This idea had been circulating in policy circles, particularly in the United States. It appealed to some on the right as a way to rationalize an accumulated hodgepodge of social programs. Nevertheless, Conservative commentators were appalled by Turner's pronouncement and branded him "almost Communistic."[19] "Candidacy must precede election," US president Woodrow Wilson had once advised, "and the shoals of candidacy can be passed only by a light boat which carries little freight and can be turned readily about to suit the intricacies of the passage."[20] Turner, in contrast, had taken on some heavy freight and was listing left. "It is there," Bruce Hutchison concluded, "he evidently thinks that his own young generation is moving toward ultimate power."[21]

The year 1967 was Canada's Centennial, and Turner was caught up in the celebrations. As registrar general, he was centre stage for one of the highest-profile events – the visit of the queen and Prince Philip to Ottawa for Canada's one hundredth birthday on July 1, 1967. A reception was held on the grounds of Rideau Hall, following which, as Cabinet's unofficial representative of youth, he hosted a rock and roll party for teenagers. Expo 67, the world's fair hosted by Montreal, occupied two islands in the St. Lawrence River at the south end of his constituency, and he regularly attended ceremonies there over the summer as well. Expo was a spectacular success and attracted international acclaim. Canadians began to feel pretty good about themselves that summer.

Meanwhile, Turner was busy behind the scenes creating a new government department. The roots of Consumer and Corporate Affairs lay in a consumer protection movement that had been growing throughout the Western world over the previous decade. In the United States, consumer crusader Ralph Nader had grabbed headlines with his 1965 book, *Unsafe at Any Speed,* a damning indictment of car manufacturers' indifference to customer safety. On May 25, 1966, Pearson wrote to John Deutsch, the chairman of the Economic Council of Canada, asking whether the council would undertake a study to formulate "a general philosophy and perhaps some specific objectives" for consumer protection. Deutsch agreed.[22] The government also created a Joint Senate-House Committee on Consumer Credit and the Cost of Living, headed by Vancouver-Burrard MP Ron Basford and Senator David Croll, which began studying consumer issues. In December 1966 it produced a report that proposed a new department, with investigators who would handle consumer complaints, look into shady practices, and bring bad actors to justice.[23]

Some right wingers in Cabinet resisted the consumer dimension of the proposed department. They wanted it called Corporate Affairs and its mandate limited to rationalizing existing regulatory functions. At the start of the Cabinet meeting at which the issue was debated, Turner slipped Pearson a copy of the 1935 report of the Royal Commission on Price Spreads, which had exposed unfair corporate practices during the depths of the Depression. He had bookmarked its recommendation that the government establish a department of consumer affairs. The secretary of the commission was none other than Lester B. Pearson. That decided the matter.[24]

Turner had to extract pieces of other departments' bureaucracies and cobble them together to form his new department.[25] Inevitably, there were turf wars. He also had to fight the Public Service Commission so he could staff a new ministry in the middle of a government hiring freeze. At the same time he dealt with the media, carefully managing public expectations.[26] Consumer and Corporate Affairs, he told reporters, would not be able to protect consumers in every transaction; rather, it would give them the information they needed to protect themselves. Nor would the department get involved in regulating prices. A market economy, operating freely, should produce fair prices. The government's role was to ensure that it was functioning freely.

On October 13, 1967, Turner introduced into the House of Commons a bill to create the Department of Consumer and Corporate Affairs (Bill C-161).[27] It would have responsibility for trademarks, patents and copyright, food and drug inspection, and bankruptcy, combines, and security regulation. Passage of the bill was relatively smooth, setting the stage for John Turner to become minister of consumer and corporate affairs at the end of the year.

Turner made the most of his new responsibilities. Consumer protection fit with his concern for the rights of the average Canadian in the face of the impersonal bureaucracy and corporate autocracy of modern mass society. It was also a matter of social justice: the poor, he noted, commonly paid more because they lacked access to consumer choice and got stuck with the highest interest rates. "It's easy to cast Registrar-General John Turner in the role of television's White Knight, charging across the lawns of Parliament Hill, lance poised to strike the blow of freedom on behalf of the Canadian housewife," wrote the *Toronto Star*.[28] This image was all too clear to his leadership rivals, and they were not happy with it.

Just as they feared, Turner soon came up with some headline grabbers. The National Hockey League went through its first expansion in 1967, awarding franchises to six US cities while spurning an application from Vancouver. Under the *Combines Investigation Act,* Turner threatened to investigate this insult to west-coast pride. The issue was widely publicized, highlighting how he could use his new post effectively as a bully pulpit simply by putting miscreants on notice. He hinted that other potential targets were NHL player contracts and the control the draft system exercised over young players.

Turner continued his crusade for consumers with an attack on high drug prices. The government had already taken action on this front the previous June by removing the federal sales tax from prescription drugs. The main reason that drug companies could keep their prices high, Turner informed Cabinet in a memorandum on August 4, 1967, was that they enjoyed strong patent protection.[29] Lloyd Axworthy, a young Winnipegger Turner had recruited as his special assistant that summer, described how his boss prepared the ground for reform: "As a Minister should, he worked primarily with the departmental public servants in drafting the bill. But my instruction, as a political staffer, was to ensure that he receive alternative views from outside experts, soundings from MPs, public reaction and party opinion. This put him in a better position to choose the best policy ... It helped Turner achieve a successful legislative coup, against severe opposition from the drug companies."[30] On December 15 Turner introduced Bill C-190 to make prescription drugs more affordable by reducing patent-holders' protection against generic substitutes.[31]

He also announced plans for a variety of reforms on the corporate side of his portfolio. He promised a revision of the *Bankruptcy Act* that would tighten existing regulations, allow for federal intervention before a company collapsed, and make it mandatory for corporate directors to inform Ottawa if they suspected bankruptcy fraud. He planned to beef up the enforcement staff in combines, give the *Combines Investigation Act* more teeth, and extend it to cover service industries. He would make it possible for victims of price fixing to seek civil damages, as they could in the United States. On the securities front, he wanted to revise the *Canada Corporations Act* to tighten disclosure rules, improve reporting of insider trading, and increase the rights of minority shareholders. He even took a swipe at the advertising industry, deriding its skewed representations of society.[32]

Turner had set himself a formidable agenda, but it was unlikely that he would have to implement it. For one thing, the federal government's constitutional prerogatives in some of these fields were questionable, so he would have to consult with the provinces before moving ahead. His unilateral actions were necessarily limited. He set up a National Securities Investigation Squad within the RCMP to work with provincial police, and he established a small commission, modelled on the US Securities and Exchange Commission, that could deal nation-to-nation with the SEC in Washington. He also revamped federal bankruptcy regulation, which soon led to an increase in successful prosecutions for bankruptcy fraud.

The main impediment to Turner's implementing his program was Liberal Party politics. The long-anticipated Liberal leadership race was about to begin, and it was likely to be followed by a general election. Everything Turner needed to make a bid for the leadership had come together, if only at the last minute. He had worked feverishly, criss-crossing the country to cultivate a profile as a serious leadership contender with a reform agenda. He was the youngest prospective candidate at a time when youth appeal was vital and he was one of the few anglophones in Cabinet who could speak French fluently at a time when bilingualism was fast becoming a prerequisite of candidacy. With his Consumer and Corporate Affairs portfolio, he had gained the Cabinet experience necessary to qualify him for higher office. John Turner was ready, with a little luck, to become Canada's fifteenth prime minister.

Turner's name now came up regularly whenever journalists appraised the field of potential leadership candidates. The main criticism of him was that he was too perfect – there must be something phoney about him. Tim Creery of the *Edmonton Journal* took this line:

> At first glance, John Turner's well-tailored image has political sex appeal. He seems a real comer. Then it dawns on you that you've met the type before. The Big Man on Campus ... The winning handshake and the hi-guy-how-the-hell-are-you?
> ... Turner's speeches are generously sprinkled with labored borrowings from John F. Kennedy ... In John Turner's case, the put-on is too obvious ... The man's political stripes show through. He's Mackenzie King in a mod suit.[33]

When his progressive credentials were questioned, Turner bristled. "I'm a reformer," he declared. "I think that there has to be a willingness to upset applecarts, and that if this country isn't prepared to do this we won't be able to compete in the modern world."[34] Asked if he were ambitious, he responded that politicians had to be ambitious: "The plain facts are that, as in any other field, young people enter politics because they like it, enjoy dealing with people, and want to obtain power to implement their ideas."[35]

The extensive commentary on Turner's image demonstrated the increasing importance of the electronic media, especially television, in the political process. Political journalists were now treating image as a major stand-alone factor in electability. Yet they worried that, in doing so, they were being superficial. Their ambivalence put Turner in a no-win situation: he had to try to cultivate a good image but was suspect because he succeeded. Under these circumstances his physical appearance was a mixed blessing. With an athletic build, strong, regular features, a full head of hair, and, above all, striking blue eyes, he sadly lacked the type of flaw that signalled authenticity.

Yet careful observers questioned whether Turner was really as slick as he was made out to be. He was neither an effortless nor a spellbinding speaker. With a sympathetic crowd, he could get into a groove, but he often seemed self-conscious about how he was coming across. He responded to the glare of the television lights with determination. His eyes took on a watchful, hawkish glint, his jaw clenched, and his words came in rapid-fire, machine-gun bursts, with stiff karate-chops from his hands emphasizing important points. "The young minister's physical vibration and rather staccato gustiness in voice suit [his] popular mechanics kind of visionary line," observed the *Toronto Telegram*.[36] Turner's style worked well enough live because interaction with the audience softened the hard edges. A stage actor rather than small-screen idol, he came across even better in small groups, where he was relaxed and exhibited an endearing capacity to laugh at himself. Yet he was about to be thrust before the cameras on the national stage for one of the most memorable leadership races in Canadian political history.

5

CLOSE TO POWER

The Liberal leadership race kicked off when Prime Minister Lester Pearson announced his resignation on December 14, 1967. When a Gallup poll asked Canadians who was most likely to follow Pearson, John Turner was named by only 4 per cent of respondents.[1] His backers thought this number could be bumped up quickly. Of all the Liberal contenders, Turner offered the sharpest contrast to Robert Stanfield, the Tories' new leader. He should stick with his established themes of youth and change while signalling that, beneath his youthful dynamism, he was a man of substance with sensible views. To address the Quebec issue, he would emphasize his Montreal base and bilingualism. His team would target minority groups and youth (about 17 per cent of the delegates would be under thirty years of age) and try to generate momentum early on, hoping to create a bandwagon effect.

Turner expected to do well out west, particularly in British Columbia, where his closest rival would be Paul Hellyer. The Maritimes was a question mark. Ontario was fragmented among the different candidates, but Turner could pick up a lot of its delegates if rival candidates were knocked off the ballot.[2] In Quebec, delegates were up for grabs: French Canadians might see Turner as their man, provided no French Canadian were in the race. As for the youth vote, Turner had already locked up much of it earlier that fall by adding David Smith, who had recently been national president of the Young Liberals, to his political staff. Like Jerry Grafstein, Smith had his choice of politicians to work for but liked Turner best.[3]

In the second week of January 1968, the announcements of candidacy came in rapid succession: Eric Kierans, a former Quebec Liberal Cabinet minister, declared on January 9; Paul Hellyer, minister of transport, on January 11; and Allan MacEachen, minister of national health and welfare, on January 12. Turner declared his candidacy on January 10, a week after he officially became minister of the new Department of Consumer and Corporate Affairs. Recognizing that his age was one of his biggest liabilities, he tackled the issue head on, telling the press that "the profession of politics has to recognize there are generation gaps today. Men of my age are being appointed to senior positions in business and labour. The men who appoint them are looking not at their age, but at their judgment and potential."[4] He insisted that he was in the race to the bitter end. The Liberal delegates should decide the leadership in an open convention – he would make no backroom deals. He made such a good impression that veteran political reporters began to contemplate the possibility that he might actually win the race.

The crew that had run Turner's campaigns in Montreal came to Ottawa and soon had things up and running. John Claxton took on his usual role of campaign manager. Ron Basford was appointed campaign chairman, signalling Turner's BC connection. David Smith found office space on the south side of Sparks Street, and soon a staff of fifty was working there, a few of them salaried but most volunteers. The only decoration was a sign on the wall reading "There is no second prize."[5]

Turner's first move was to announce his policy positions. Most were familiar to those who had followed his speeches. He argued that foreign capital was needed to fuel the economy but should be subject to Canadian rules. He echoed the warning in the preliminary report of the Royal Commission on Bilingualism and Biculturalism about the seriousness of separatism in Quebec. He supported continued federal leadership in social welfare but said it should be delivered via a more rational system than the existing patchwork of programs – again suggesting a guaranteed annual income. He added a note of caution, however: in the future, government spending must be closely tied to revenue. The message was balanced: progressive on social policy yet fiscally prudent, John Turner was a bright young man who was sound on fundamentals.

On January 19 three more candidates joined the race: External Affairs Minister Paul Martin, Finance Minister Mitchell Sharp, and Agriculture Minister Joe Greene. Sharp, Hellyer, and Martin were the acknowledged frontrunners, but Tory organizer Dalton Camp, a shrewd political observer, gave even money on Turner and Sharp. The race soon developed into a free-for-all, and Pearson felt obliged to invoke the principle of Cabinet solidarity to keep his ministers from publicly eviscerating one another.

Press gallery reporters speculated that the Liberals needed a French Canadian to run in order to maintain their credibility in Quebec. Jean Marchand, the senior French Canadian in Cabinet, was the obvious choice, but soon attention focused on an intriguing alternative – Pierre Trudeau – a relative newcomer on the federal political scene. Elected in 1965 along with his friends Marchand and Gérard Pelletier, Trudeau had been named Pearson's parliamentary secretary in 1966 and justice minister in the spring of 1967, enjoying a rapid rise as Turner waited patiently for a significant Cabinet position.

On paper, Turner and Trudeau looked very similar. Both were bilingual lawyers from Montreal ridings who had lost their fathers at a young age, been educated at Catholic boys' schools and attended summer camps, excelled academically and athletically, and pursued graduate studies at elite European universities. But there were striking contrasts. Although he was bilingual, in cultural terms Turner was English Canadian. Trudeau's mother was English Canadian, but he identified as French Canadian. Turner was married with children; Trudeau was a bachelor who played the field. Turner was strikingly handsome in a conventional fashion; Trudeau had unconventional looks that were oddly beguiling. Turner was gregarious; Trudeau, a loner. As Keith Davey put it later, "Turner wanted to be loved. Trudeau just wanted to be left alone."[6] Even though Turner was a Rhodes scholar and Trudeau an unsuccessful applicant for the award, Turner came across as the jock, Trudeau as the intellectual. Turner's problem-solving style was to sit down with interested parties, have a few drinks, and hammer out a deal. Trudeau drank little and prided himself on his rational approach to problems. Had they been characters in the contemporary television series *Star Trek*, Turner would have been the outgoing Captain Kirk, and Trudeau the coldly logical Vulcan, Mr. Spock.

Turner told a reporter that Trudeau had great advantages in life – private wealth, freedom as a bachelor, and a bilingual, bicultural upbringing – all of which added up to "a rare kind of absolute individual freedom from normal concerns ... And he used this freedom and confidence to travel, kibitz, play, think, write, study, experiment – to get a kind of liberal education and a personal detachment possible to few men in any age."[7] Ironically, this was exactly the kind of privilege that people assumed Turner had enjoyed. But when he himself looked back to his childhood, he saw it in terms of "struggle, perseverance, proving himself, pushing, driving, always haunted by a lack of confidence, a wonder about himself – could he make it?" The reporter who noted this misperception concluded that one consequence of their contrasting childhood circumstances was that "Turner is less sure of himself than Trudeau, more highly strung, a 'quarter-horse,' almost febrile in energy and twitch."[8]

Marc Lalonde, then a policy adviser in the Prime Minister's Office (PMO), had been laying the groundwork for a Trudeau candidacy over the previous year, slowly building his friend's profile by arranging for him to appear at key party functions, particularly in Quebec. Pearson had mentored Trudeau throughout his time in Parliament and now encouraged him to stand for the leadership. With Quebec's future in Canada the most troubling issue facing the country, Pearson wanted his successor to be a francophone. When Marchand declined to run, Trudeau became the logical choice.[9]

Trudeau began to register with English Canadian voters when he spearheaded reforms to the Criminal Code in December 1967. A week after Pearson's resignation announcement, Trudeau introduced the *Criminal Law Amendment Act* into the House of Commons. It proposed to legalize abortion in cases where the mother's health was endangered, to decriminalize homosexuality, and to liberalize other aspects of the criminal law. Trudeau emerged as a harbinger of change just as the Liberal leadership contest was getting under way.

Pearson gave him another boost by holding a constitutional conference in February 1968 at which Trudeau, as justice minister, defended the federal government's position on the constitution. In the weeks leading up to the conference, Lalonde arranged for Trudeau to have preliminary discussions with the premiers. These excursions gave him national media exposure in capitals from coast to coast. When the constitutional conference convened,

Quebec premier Daniel Johnson demanded constitutional reform to recognize Quebec's special status as the homeland of French Canadians. Trudeau took a hard line against Johnson's arguments, turning in a bravura performance on national television as a champion of Canadian unity.

In the wake of the constitutional conference, support for a Trudeau candidacy spread quickly. Canadians were intrigued by the mix of diffidence, toughness, and intelligence he projected on camera. As a stylish bachelor, he personified the swinging spirit of the times; as a federalist French Canadian, he offered a simple solution to the national unity problem. The growing public excitement about Trudeau became evident when he travelled to Toronto to meet Liberal delegates at the Royal York Hotel on February 9, 1968. The room was packed, and he was mobbed by media and supporters as he arrived. On February 16 he announced his candidacy – and immediately became the man to beat.

Earlier, Trudeau had told Turner he was not going to run.[10] Though dismayed to see Trudeau's popularity snowball, Turner was not particularly surprised. "Today, television is the great equalizer," he had observed just months earlier. "I think that today with a properly conceived campaign, an absolute unknown could be propelled from obscurity to national leadership within six months."[11] The rapidly changing cultural landscape of the late sixties was another contributing factor. Turner's image as a junior version of the establishment man was now a negative stereotype, associated with the technocratic bureaucracies behind controversial modern projects ranging from expressways and urban renewal to US involvement in Vietnam. The counterculture gleefully vilified this conventional authority figure as "The Man," and popular culture was soon spoofing the type with shallow and dogmatic cartoon characters such as Dudley Do-Right (an earnest and ineffectual Mountie) and Roger Ramjet (an American air force pilot of fearsome resolve and vacuous cranium). Turner's image was similar enough that some wags in Ottawa began calling him Roger Ramjet.

Trudeau, in contrast, was a distinctly unconventional public figure. Even though he was ten years older than Turner, he seemed more youthful. His insouciant demeanour spoke more eloquently to the contemporary ethos than all Turner's rhetoric on modern technology, reform, and progress. Trudeau seemed a free spirit; Turner, conformist.[12] The Kennedy mystique that Turner had channelled had been superseded by the misanthropic anti-hero.[13] "What was handsome in the early 60s is dead," concluded one observer, looking back a few years later, "supplanted by the shaggier, acne-scarred machismo of the newer male."[14]

Turner had hoped to win the youth vote, attract strong support in French Canada as a bilingual Quebecker, and appeal to other delegates as a young man with fresh ideas who could manage Quebec and usher in a new era in an orderly fashion. It was a winning strategy. Unfortunately, Pierre Trudeau executed it better than he did. "Trudeau," Christopher Young noted, "not only comes from Montreal, but appeals to many of the same elements of the Liberal party that might favor Mr. Turner: the young, the sophisticated, the urban, the intellectual, the technocratic."[15] His entry into the race hurt Turner more than that of any other candidate. Turner retained the support of most Young Liberals because they had already committed to him, but his potential for growth was gravely curtailed. By the time the convention rolled around, his team estimated that he had about 45 delegates from Quebec, whereas Trudeau had more than 325, many of whom could have been Turner's had no French Canadian entered the race.

On February 19, three days after Trudeau announced his candidacy, the Liberals suffered an embarrassment in the House of Commons. A resolution calling for a 5 per cent surcharge on personal income tax over $100,000, part of the government's anti-inflation strategy, came up for third reading. Forty-three Liberals were absent from the House, many of them out electioneering, and the government lost the vote on the bill by a count of eighty-four to eighty-two. A defeat on a money bill is usually interpreted as a vote of non-confidence, so the Liberals were suddenly presented with the prospect of having to dissolve Parliament and call a general election in the middle of a leadership campaign. Pearson cut short a holiday and met with various members of Cabinet, including Turner, to try to find a solution. Allan MacEachen suggested they introduce a motion that the House did not consider the defeat a non-confidence vote. The Social Credit MPs, worried that they would be obliterated in an immediate election, supported the government, and an election was averted.

The episode damaged the candidacy of Mitchell Sharp, who, as finance minister, had been in charge of the bill in the House that evening. Trudeau was in the clear because he had been present for the vote. Turner had been away but had taken the precaution of pairing himself with an opposition

MP who also had to be away. Robert Winters, the minister of trade and commerce, who had been acting prime minister in Pearson's absence, somehow emerged unscathed and, on March 1, declared himself a candidate for the leadership.

As the minister of a new highly political department, Turner found it hard to get away from the House of Commons to campaign. Consumer and Corporate Affairs was a lightning rod for populist political gestures in the House. Whenever there was a price increase on a basic consumer product, he was besieged by opposition demands for government action. In 1967 price collusion among grocery chains had led the Prairie provinces to establish a royal commission to investigate. Turner took ownership of the issue, threatening a federal inquiry.[16] Ensuring passage of his generic drug bill also kept him tied down in Ottawa. The NDP supported it, but the Conservatives were opposed, claiming it didn't do enough to guarantee the safety of cheaper generic drugs.[17] When the bill bogged down in committee in February, Turner made amendments to address the criticisms and introduced it again. He pushed his case hard, noting that Canadian prescription drug prices ranged from two and a half to eight times the lowest prices available elsewhere.[18] He also made his crusade an issue on the campaign trail, threatening to go after the drug companies even harder if they didn't clean up their act.[19] To address the problem of having a candidate who could not travel, Turner's team dreamed up a novel solution: delegates who were unable to meet him personally could listen over the telephone to short taped interviews with him, and at the end of the call, after hearing him speak on a variety of subjects – education, labour, urban problems – they could leave their questions on an answering machine.[20]

In early March, Turner finally found time to fly out west for a weekend of campaigning. He landed in Calgary and was off on Saturday morning to Cranbrook to meet with delegates. When he arrived at the airport, he encountered the mayor of nearby Kimberley, the president of its Chamber of Commerce, and a half-dozen local Liberals. His spirits soared when he spied a crowd of over a hundred behind them but soon plummeted when he learned that it had gathered to see the local curling team off to a competition in Winnipeg. He shook hands with everyone anyway and posed with the curlers for photos. Later in the day he was greeted by more than a hundred people at a champagne reception in Kelowna. He told this crowd that Ottawa had been overspending and needed to clarify its budget priorities. Returning to Calgary after a fifteen-hour day, he was greeted by a banner hoisted over the entrance to his hotel: "Welcome, Pierre Elliott Trudeau."[21]

By March it looked as though Turner was running behind the leaders, Trudeau and Martin, and about even with Hellyer, Winters, and Sharp.[22] After his western swing, he was tied down in the Commons for a couple of weeks. On March 22 he headed out west again, accompanied this time by his wife, Geills, to a reception for delegates in Alberta. Inevitably, he was compared to Trudeau at every stop. "Turner hasn't got what Trudeau's got," concluded one young delegate.[23] Allan Fotheringham devoted a good chunk of his report on Turner's Vancouver visit to describing a teenybopper named Margaret who was unmoved by seeing Turner but had been crazy for Trudeau the previous week, despite the fact that her father, Jimmy Sinclair, was a Turner supporter.[24]

Turner's performances on the platform were inconsistent. At times he spoke too quickly, jumbling his words and raising doubts in delegates' minds. He was better when he didn't read from a script because he spoke more slowly, directly to the audience, and seemed more sincere. As usual he was most effective in small groups.[25] Just before the leadership convention, a friend sent him a depressing review of one of his public performances:

> You are glib. This is the result not only of the speed of your retort and your facial expression but also the kind of language you use ... Somehow or another you don't seem quite real to me ... While I know you are deadly serious about your role in this country, on occasion on Wednesday evening, because of the fast quip, you almost gave the impression that you didn't take Canada very seriously despite your statements to the contrary.[26]

Although he recognized that "the man in the grey flannel suit is dead," Turner was not prepared to act differently just to impress people.[27] "Your letter was brutal and frank," he replied to the friend, "but I appreciated it." He added,

> I do not think I am going to be able to remake myself, or to be remade. I am what I am ... What I really think is happening at the moment is that

Trudeau is setting a style of detachment with which I do not fit ... I do not think I am going to be able to change my appearance either – it may be a disadvantage but there it is.[28]

Turner's campaign team put a photo of him in the press and delegate kit for the convention that pictured him with a five o'clock shadow and loosened tie – but that was as far as the reimaging went.

The team tried to get the media to look beyond the image to appreciate his substance as a candidate. The *Ottawa Journal,* where his friend John Grace was assistant editor, published an interview with Turner in late March in which he laid out a variety of reform proposals.[29] The team also collected some of his speeches into a book, *Politics of Purpose,* and sent a copy to every delegate. Trudeau had a book out too, a collection of his essays published in English under the title *Federalism and the French Canadians.* Trudeau's essays read better than Turner's speeches because they had been written to be read rather than spoken. Their emphasis on Quebec gave them greater focus and topicality than Turner's speeches, which covered a wide range of issues. With sales fuelled by public curiosity about the author, Trudeau's volume sold nearly fifty thousand copies by the end of the summer, dwarfing the modest print run of *Politics of Purpose.*

Turner was frustrated by the media treatment of Trudeau as a winner who could do no wrong. If Trudeau said he did not know the answer to a question, he pointed out, journalists concluded he was an honest man. If Turner gave the same response, they said he was too young for the job. It wasn't fair, but that was beside the point. Trudeau had captured the imagination of Canadians. By promising to take care of the Quebec issue, he offered English Canada relief from a wearisome anxiety. That prospect – and his trendy image – made a potent combination.

Turner came to accept that he would have to fight things out on Trudeau's ground. He believed that his flexible approach to Quebec was superior to Trudeau's hard-line position. If he could engage Trudeau on the issue, the debate could have the effect of elevating him to Trudeau's level in the public eye. While taking care to mention that he greatly admired Trudeau personally, Turner underlined their policy differences by presenting himself as a strong federalist who was also willing and able to negotiate with Quebec. Trudeau's categorical grandstanding, in contrast, limited his ability to find a constructive solution. Turner also emphasized that Trudeau's rationalist approach to Quebec would not work, because it failed to take into account the passion that inspired nationalism. "He thinks the Justice Minister, whom he admires, is too coldly logical on the national unity question," the *Toronto Globe and Mail* reported. "The reasons for the crisis are partly emotional, he says, and must be taken into account in reaching a political solution."[30] In a speech in Hamilton on March 26, Turner asked Canadians to face facts:

> The overwhelming majority of French-speaking citizens of the province of Quebec share a distinctive philosophical and cultural background. They share a pride in their unique history of survival in North America. They share a sense of nationalism different from all the other provinces. Quebec is governed through a system of law different from both the British common law system and the French legal system. In reality, therefore, Quebec is different![31]

Le Devoir publisher Claude Ryan saw Trudeau as an embittered and radicalized veteran of internecine Quebec nationalist struggles and endorsed Turner's approach over Trudeau's.[32] But it was all for naught. Trudeau's strong stance against French Canadian nationalists offered the rest of Canada the comforting prospect of keeping both Quebec and the constitutional status quo.

The convention was held in Ottawa, at the new Civic Centre arena at Lansdowne Park. With 2,396 delegates and 795 alternates in town, plus over a thousand journalists, the city took on a carnival atmosphere. Proceedings commenced on Thursday, April 4, with policy workshops for the delegates. Turner delivered a hard-hitting speech on Quebec that won favourable notice. Then came the surprising news that Mitchell Sharp had decided to drop out of the running and throw his support behind Trudeau. Although strategists thought that some of Sharp's supporters would instead migrate to Turner or Winters, Turner publicly denounced this move as a violation of the open-race ideal he had been advocating throughout his campaign. Reporters dismissed the comment as sour grapes.

Pearson made his farewell speech that Thursday evening. On the following night, the eve of the balloting, came the candidates' speeches. The order was determined by lottery, and Turner drew the final slot. Trudeau would speak before him, second last. The delegates dutifully sat through the early speeches, but anticipation focused on the newly minted celebrity, Trudeau. He approached the stage meekly. Suddenly, banners unfurled, the arena exploded with music and cheering, and a deep thicket of signs and arms pumped the air. Trudeau remained subdued as he spoke at length about his passion for individual rights. It was not his best performance, but it nicely counterbalanced all the hoopla and hype surrounding his candidacy by conveying seriousness, substance, and a certain "I am not worthy" humility.

The long lead-up to Trudeau left Turner in an awkward position. He seemed like an afterthought – the functionary appearing at the end of the show to thank the organizers as the audience prepares to exit the auditorium. Somehow, he had to get the audience to focus back on the stage. He stepped up to the microphone, grabbed the lectern, and charged ahead. He tackled directly the perception that he was running only to position himself for some future leadership race. "I'm not bidding now for your consideration at some vague convention in 1984 when I've mellowed a bit," he declared. "My time is now, and now is not the time for mellow men!"[33]

He sounded his main themes: the need to give the disadvantaged an opportunity, to mobilize youth, to realize Canada's potential. Challenging Trudeau's rational chic, he declared,

> Canada is not an abstraction; Canada is not a theory; it is beyond logic. Our country is not solely a product of the mind, because in many ways it does not make sense ... Even today there are those who want to break our country up. My answer to them is not in logic, but in the heart. If you cast your vote for me, you will be choosing a Canada that believes in nationalism, has pride in our community, our political sovereignty, our economic integrity.[34]

"He bit into his monosyllabic words with an angry rhythm that evoked the Kennedys," wrote one observer. "Turner was ripping apart the politician to expose the man he really is, in private – a tough, sincere, honest fellow who has a passion about Canada."[35]

On Saturday, the Civic Centre was packed with delegates, workers, and the media. The drama ran high. Pundits had a rough idea of the amount of support already cornered by each candidate, but with so many contenders, many of them seemingly neck-and-neck, no one could predict how things would unfold from one ballot to the next. It was still anybody's race.

The candidates each had a portion of the arena seats staked out for themselves and their supporters. The Turner team had decked out its supporters in yellow jackets to make them stand out and topped them with white construction hard hats to indicate that they were rough and tough and ready to work. They chanted "We want Turner" and waved placards wildly, especially when the television cameras seemed to have them in their sights. Journalists roamed the floor and the stands in search of behind-the-scenes power-brokers, wheedled comments out of delegates, and swung boom mikes over the heads of candidates to eavesdrop on their conversations. Trudeau's organizers surrounded him with girls in Trudeau T-shirts waving Trudeau banners and chanting his name. He was the main focus for television producers – "the anointed of the television establishment."[36]

First ballot voting began around 1:00 p.m. on Saturday. Troubles with the vote-tabulating machines led to an hour's delay. The candidates waited it out, anxious to discover the results of their months of hard work. Finally, at 2:30 p.m., the results were announced:

Trudeau	752
Hellyer	330
Winters	293
Martin	277
Turner	277
Greene	169
MacEachen	165
Kierans	103

Turner hadn't enjoyed any spectacular breakthrough, but his support had held up in the midst of a crowded field. The big losers were Hellyer and Martin, both of whom were far lower than expected.

With the cards on the table, the game began. Kierans and Martin withdrew from the race and left their delegates free to vote for the candidate of their choice. MacEachen withdrew but too late to have his name taken off the second ballot. Turner was now alone in fourth place, and, if he could pick up enough of the dropouts to look as though he were building momentum, there was a chance he could come up the middle to win. Another two hours elapsed while the delegates voted again and the second ballot was counted:

Trudeau	964
Winters	473
Hellyer	465
Turner	347
Greene	104
MacEachen	11

This was a disappointing result for Turner. To have any chance of winning, he had to move up on this ballot and appear to have momentum leading into the next one. Obviously, delegates opposed to Trudeau saw Winters, an older establishment figure, as a better representative of their cause. The way things were stacking up, Trudeau would win unless Winters, Hellyer, and one other candidate joined forces. Both Winters and Hellyer met with Turner and tried to convince him to join them, but he continued to insist that the delegates should decide. "I'm staying," he declared, "I'm staying all the way."[37] Bill Lee, Hellyer's campaign manager, advised Hellyer to withdraw and support Turner. His instincts told him that Turner had more potential for growth than either Hellyer or Winters. Neither of them could beat Trudeau, but Turner had a shot. Hellyer, understandably, could see no reason to stand down in favour of someone with fewer votes.[38]

Then it was back to the stands for more cheerleading and placard waving. Turner's early supporters began to move to candidates they felt had a chance to win. The third ballot confirmed the trend already in place:

Trudeau	1,051
Winters	621
Hellyer	377
Turner	279
Greene	29

Hellyer's and Winters's support combined added up to 998 delegates. Hellyer made the move to Winters, and the two of them set out to find Turner, with dozens of supporters and journalists in their wake. They urged him to throw his support to Winters and put him over the top. Turner didn't hesitate a moment: "Gentlemen, I am staying in," he declared.[39] Moving through the crowd, he shook hands with his delegates. Some tearfully pledged to stay with him to the bitter end. Others had kind words but said they didn't know what to do. "That's a personal decision you'll have to come to yourself," he told one. "I'll understand if you don't stick."[40]

Turner couldn't win, but he didn't want to abandon his open-democracy pledge. Had he put his own leadership aspirations first, going to Winters would have made sense, for Winters was an older man who was unlikely to stay in power as long as Trudeau. But he probably could not have carried his Young Liberal supporters to Winters, and he didn't like the optics of two Anglos ganging up on the French Canadian.

The fourth ballot results were announced by Liberal Party president John Nichol at 8 p.m.:

Trudeau	1,202
Winters	954
Turner	195

Pierre Trudeau was the leader of the Liberal Party and the next prime minister of Canada.

With the victor declared, the candidates gathered onstage to demonstrate party solidarity and congratulate Trudeau. Gracious in defeat, Turner called him "the greatest Canadian of this generation."[41] Two of Turner's diehard supporters, British Columbians Cam Avery and Tex Enemark, headed back to Turner's hotel suite for the wake. When they got there, Enemark took his name tag out of its plastic sleeve, wrote on the back "195 Club," and pinned it to his lapel. Others followed his example, and a myth was born.[42] The 195 Club, conceived in rueful humour, would later be imagined by journalists as a covert network of Turner supporters working assiduously toward the day he would finally rise to power.

The morning after the convention, Turner realized that, however disappointed he was, others felt worse. He called Paul Martin and asked him, his wife, and his son, Paul Jr., over to lunch.[43] As time passed and he gained perspective, he was philosophical. "I personally feel we did the right thing and I have no regrets," he wrote to a friend:

> It was a great human experience. The reaction of most people from all parts of the country indicates that we did the right thing by staying to the final ballot. I had run a campaign based upon ensuring my supporters that there were no deals or arrangements and that the delegates themselves had the final choice. We kept faith with those supporters. Moreover I am convinced that had I opted for either Trudeau or Winters I would have contributed to a schism in the Party – East vs. West, left vs. right, French vs. English.[44]

Meanwhile, the political pundits puzzled over the significance of Turner's role in the final ballot. By staying in, he emerged from the convention with more credibility and stature than any of the other losing candidates. He had demonstrated that he was an independent power within the party, and he became the next logical alternative to Trudeau as leader. "It was a crucible. He saw how the deals were made, how power was traded. It was a toughening experience," John de B. Payne concluded. "That convention was the last glance anyone ever had of a young John Turner."[45] It would be a long time before journalists would again write about him as a superficial politician-on-the-make.

In the new Cabinet, sworn in on April 20, 1968, John Turner continued as minister of consumer and corporate affairs and took on the additional post of solicitor general. But not for long. On April 23 Trudeau called a June election. The Liberals were hoping to capitalize on a boost in the polls from their leadership contest and the popularity of their new leader. The press coined the term "Trudeaumania" to describe the adulation and excitement Trudeau generated that spring. He ran on his charisma, on the trendy slogans "participatory democracy" and the "Just Society," and on the implicit message that he, a federalist French Canadian, would parry the Quebec threat to national unity.

John Turner's riding of St. Lawrence–St. George had been wiped out by electoral redistribution, and no likely seats were free elsewhere in Montreal. He decided to run in a new constituency, Ottawa-Carleton, which encompassed the eastern parts of the city of Ottawa and adjacent rural areas. Ottawa-Carleton included the neighbourhood where he had grown up, so he had a legitimate connection to the riding. Best of all, he and his family were already living there; no longer would he have to travel to visit his riding. Yet it was a curious choice for a politician with leadership aspirations. The Quebec problem dominated federal politics, and he had symbolic currency by being a bilingual Anglo from a Quebec riding. A British Columbia riding would have provided an equally valuable regional power-base. Turner had put his family first.

Although the areas making up the new riding tended to vote Liberal, the Conservative candidate, Ken Binks, was well known and had run before in Russell, one of the old ridings partly subsumed by Ottawa-Carleton. Turner's prospects were favourable, but nothing could be taken for granted. He ran with the same intensity and élan as he had in his earlier campaigns, supported by eight hundred volunteers, most of them young and enthusiastic students who were attracted to politics by idealism and the sex appeal of both the candidate and the new prime minister. Despite taking a week off to be at home following the birth of his third child, Turner played a more active role in the party's national campaign than any Liberal except Trudeau. He travelled to the Maritimes, Newfoundland, the Prairies, and southern Ontario to mainstreet with local candidates and speak at campaign rallies.

Late in May he flew out to British Columbia to campaign in Vancouver Centre for his friend Ron Basford, whose Conservative opponent, David Kilgour, was Geills Turner's younger brother. At a Liberal go-go dance, Turner was photographed doing the frug. "I'm sorry Pierre isn't here," he told the crowd. "He'd have enjoyed this swinging party ... This has got to be the swingingest riding in Canada."[46] Knowing Turner had widespread appeal, the campaign strategists showcased him in motorcades and rallies the same way they did Trudeau. By the end of the campaign, he was deeply tanned – and deeply exhausted. "Outside we all look great," he told a reporter, "but inside it's mush."[47]

On election night, June 25, Turner awaited the results from his riding at his campaign headquarters. The first two polls reported that he was ahead with 166 votes compared to 112 for Binks and 16 for Wilson, the NDP candidate. Ten minutes later, seventeen polls had reported, and Turner had

1,890 votes to 714 for Binks. These early indicators were borne out in the final result. Turner won with 28,941 votes, compared to 11,712 for the Conservative candidate and 3,116 for the NDP. He attended his campaign's post-election party in the gym at St. Patrick's, his old high school, and celebrated with his campaign workers.

Later that night, Turner joined Trudeau at the Château Laurier to monitor the national results. At first the news was mixed. Newfoundlanders and Maritimers elected more Tories than in the previous election, whereas rural Quebeckers elected more Social Credit MPs than they had in 1965. But after that, things looked up. The Liberals got their usual level of support in rural Quebec and Ontario, and swept the cities in central Canada, drawing support from young, urban, well-educated, and middle-class voters. They also did well in the West, where they picked up nineteen seats. Here too the Liberal gains came mainly in urban areas. In the country as a whole, they won over 45 per cent of the popular vote, an increase of more than 5 per cent from the previous election, and raised their total from 131 to 154 seats in the 264-seat House of Commons. The result was the majority government that had eluded them under Pearson's leadership.

Trudeau recognized Turner's new prominence in the party by offering him the Justice portfolio.[48] His only concern with making the appointment was that the minister of justice was traditionally the lead on constitutional matters. The constitution was Trudeau's main area of interest and expertise, and Turner's position on Quebec differed from his, so he stipulated that he would retain responsibility for constitutional negotiations.

On the sunny Saturday afternoon of July 6, 1968, Turner and his fellow Cabinet nominees followed Pierre Trudeau up the driveway of Rideau Hall to meet the governor general to be sworn into office. A new era had begun in Canadian politics, and John Turner was positioned to play a major role in it.

PART 2
MASTER POLITICIAN, 1968-79

6

DRIVING THE OMNIBUS

Justice had always been a prestigious portfolio, a Cabinet post often held by future prime ministers – most recently, Pierre Trudeau. It was something of an anomaly in the Canadian government because it was more like an in-house law firm than an operational department. The department's main responsibilities were providing legal advice and recommendations on the appointment of judges to the government, criminal law reform, the drafting of legislation for matters under federal jurisdiction, representing the Crown in court, and overseeing those parts of the justice system not administered by the provinces. Its status derived from the majesty of the law and the quality of its ministers rather than any track record of public policy innovation and leadership. The department tended to mind its knitting, focusing on its pressing day-to-day responsibilities rather than big-picture strategizing.

When Pierre Trudeau was justice minister, he had expressed frustration with the department's limitations. "Justice should be regarded more and more as a department planning for the society of tomorrow," he told Peter Newman, "not merely the government's legal advisor ... Society is throwing up problems all the time ... It's no longer enough to review our statutes every 20 years."[1] When he was charged with preparing the government's position for the federal-provincial constitutional conference in February 1968, Trudeau decided that the Justice Department did not have the capacity and expertise he needed, so he set up an independent committee to advise him.[2]

By the time Turner inherited the portfolio, the department had two hundred in-house lawyers, a twenty-fold increase over the previous thirty years. Turner's deputy minister was Donald Maxwell, appointed by Trudeau the year before. He was an imposing figure: tall, solidly built, energetic, self-confident. Like most previous deputies in the department, he had risen through the ranks. He and Turner got along well. They were roughly the same age, and Maxwell was the kind of man's man Turner liked. The department's associate deputy minister posts reflected Canada's bijural character. Rodrigue Bédard, formerly a municipal judge in Hull and dean of the University of Ottawa Law School, had taken over the civil law section in 1960. On the English common law side, the associate was Donald Thorson, who, like Maxwell, had been hired from Osgoode Hall in 1951. Thorson's expertise was legislative drafting. He would succeed Maxwell as deputy and go on to play a key role in constitutional reform and the patriation of the constitution in the late 1970s and early 1980s. The third level of management was composed of assistant deputy ministers and assistant deputy attorneys general, who oversaw departments for tax, criminal law, civil litigation, and departmental administration. The criminal law section, responsible for the Criminal Code reforms that Trudeau had introduced the year before, was headed by yet another "Don" – the serious-minded, meticulous Donald Christie, originally from Saskatchewan, who had been with the department since 1953.

The biggest priority on Turner's agenda when he took over from Trudeau as minister of justice was the *Criminal Law Amendment Act* that Trudeau had introduced the previous December. Known as the omnibus bill, it had died on the order paper when the 1968 election was called. Although its most notable measures dealt with abortion and homosexuality, it was a wide-ranging package of 120 clauses that also covered issues such as gun control, lotteries, and drunk driving. Its various proposals prompted public responses ranging from indifference to constructive critiques to outrage.

The most controversial aspects of the omnibus bill were those that proposed to remove various forms of moral regulation from the Criminal Code. Viewed in its broadest context, this deregulation impulse reflected a continuing trend toward secularization in the Western world. Yet the process was far from complete in 1960s Canada. The principle of separation of church and state, operative in English Canada since the nineteenth century, was intended to transcend squabbles between sects, not to purge Christianity from public life. In 1968 it was still hard to imagine a Canada in which mainline churches, Catholic and Protestant, were not influential voices in public affairs. Traditionally, it was assumed that the law and the churches defended the same standards of public morality. With public piety in decline, however, the liberal proposition that morality should be a matter of individual conscience was gaining greater credence.[3]

Although formal legal ties with the United Kingdom had been severed with the abolition of appeals to the Judicial Committee of the Privy Council in 1949, Canadian law still tended to follow English precedents and trends.[4] The debate in Canada over the death penalty, for example, followed a movement to abolish capital punishment in Britain in the 1960s. For many progressive thinkers, one of the leading legal lights in Britain was the eminent jurist Lord Denning, the "people's judge," who was both lionized and pilloried for his penchant to override aspects of common law that he deemed inhumane in light of contemporary values. Turner had long admired Denning; back in his Oxford days, he had been thrilled to appear before him in moot court at Cambridge. In 1957 Britain's Wolfenden Committee focused public discussion on the relationship of law and morality when it recommended the decriminalization of homosexuality. The highly publicized *Lady Chatterley* case, in which British courts deliberated whether D.H. Lawrence's 1928 novel were pornographic, was another bellwether. *Lady Chatterley's Lover* was judged redeemable for its literary merit in 1960, and the forces of moral deregulation prevailed on other fronts as well, leading to the decriminalization of abortion, homosexuality, and gambling in Britain as the decade progressed.

The ripple effects were soon evident in Canada. In the early 1960s, Ontario sponsored a review of laws regarding lotteries, gambling, and sports betting, which concluded that attempts to enforce morality in these areas were futile, encouraged underground criminality, and undermined respect for the law.[5] The reform of Canada's divorce law was another sign of the times. Before the 1960s, there was no federal divorce statute in Canada. Divorce laws varied widely from one province to the next, with adultery the most common grounds. Couples whose marriages had broken down had either to commit adultery or perjure themselves in court to get a divorce. In provinces that had no such laws, divorce could be granted only by act of

Parliament. Every year, Ottawa witnessed a salacious circus in which politicians acted in lieu of judges to grant relief to desperate couples. Pressure for change had been building for years, and Pearson finally set up a Parliamentary Committee on Divorce in February 1967. A new law was drafted that included permanent marriage breakdown along with adultery, cruelty, and desertion as grounds for divorce. Trudeau had overseen the progress of the *Divorce Act* through the House of Commons and its passage into law in December 1967.[6]

When Turner took over from Trudeau as minister of justice, the omnibus bill became his most pressing priority. He supported its reform thrust, but he would have preferred to take a more incremental approach. Aware that Canadians' attitudes were changing at variable rates, he thought that bundling a large number of contentious issues in a single bill was asking for trouble. If changes were instead introduced on a serial, piecemeal basis, opponents to any one measure would be isolated in an ineffectual minority position. The omnibus approach turned this "divide and conquer" adage on its head by combining a host of changes, each of which could generate opposition to the bill as a whole.

Fortunately, as Turner saw it, there was a solution. The previous March, several Catholic Liberal MPs had asked for free votes on individual parts of the bill to allow them to avoid voting for particular policies about which they had conscientious objections. During the election, Conservative leader Robert Stanfield tried to exploit this issue by announcing that, if his party won, he would permit a free vote on abortion and homosexuality. Turner liked this idea: it was consistent with his long-standing interest in empowering MPs, and it conceded something to his Catholic conscience and the Catholic constituency. Like Mackenzie King, he believed that any stratagem that avoided dividing Canadians on a matter of principle was worth trying.

In July Turner told the press that the omnibus bill would be reintroduced, and he mused about having separate votes. "I want to make sure that an MP who is against abortion but for ... a tougher firearms law doesn't lose his vote," he explained.[7] He was deluding himself. Trudeau had campaigned on a single omnibus bill and had no interest in flip-flopping. On July 18 the prime minister told a reporter that he still considered the bill a single item but added that, if Turner "has grave reasons for changing it, I suppose we'd consider them."[8] Turner's reasons proved insufficiently grave to carry the day. There would be no division of the bill and no free votes. Turner was exposed to a barrage of abuse in the House, and as the debate on the omnibus bill heated up, Diefenbaker repeatedly taunted him as a man supporting it against his own best judgment.

While Turner was overseeing the redrafting of the bill that summer, Pope Paul VI issued an encyclical, *Humanae Vitae,* which reiterated the Catholic Church's ban on abortion and contraception. Suddenly, abortion was transformed from being a treacherous political issue into an unstable and explosive one. The reform contemplated in the omnibus bill had been intended as a way to find a middle ground between pro-choice and anti-abortion forces by clarifying the prohibition against abortion in the Criminal Code. Section 209 of the code made it a crime to kill an unborn child. Any woman who had an abortion could go to jail for two years, and any doctor who performed an abortion could be imprisoned for life. However, subsection 209(a) exempted anyone who "by means that, in good faith, he considers necessary to preserve the life of the mother of a child that has not become a human being, causes the death of the child."[9]

The meaning was ambiguous; the result, confusion. Some doctors refused to perform abortions for fear of prosecution; others performed them on the grounds that they were protecting the health of the mother. Access to abortion varied wildly from one community to the next. Some women travelled to countries where abortion was legal, but this option was available only to the affluent. Many others sought an illegal abortion at a significantly higher risk of injury or death. The Humanist Association of Canada claimed that 100,000 criminal abortions were performed every year in Canada, with eight hundred associated maternal deaths.[10]

The omnibus reform proposed that therapeutic abortion committees made up of three doctors in accredited hospitals could certify that the continuation of a pregnancy would be likely to endanger the life or health of the mother. It effectively medicalized and downloaded the issue to doctors, rendering it a case-by-case judgment. Pro-choice groups thought this reform did not go nearly far enough, but at least it was a step in the right direction. Anti-abortion groups objected strenuously. They thought the mother's health proviso would open the door to abortion on demand and, in effect, legalize abortion. Catholic groups launched a concerted lobbying campaign against the proposed change. The Justice Department received thousands of letters on the issue in 1968, the vast majority opposed, and thousands more anti-abortion petitions with varying numbers of signatures.

The abortion issue challenged Turner to reconcile his private religious beliefs with his public duty as a politician. As an engaged member of the Catholic laity, he had given considerable thought to such problems. In general he favoured liberalization of church practices, many of which he regarded as antiquated.[11] In 1967 he had gone to Toronto for the Congress on the Theology of the Renewal of the Church, which featured leading thinkers such as German theologian Karl Rahner and Protestant philosopher Paul Ricoeur. For over a decade, Turner had been deputy head of Michaelmas, an annual conference at St. Michael's College in Toronto, where lay Catholics discussed contemporary theological and church issues. The Second Vatican Council was a major focus of interest in those years, and the Michaelmas attendees were encouraged by its reform spirit and emphasis on the importance of lay involvement in the church and society.

In thinking through the abortion issue, Turner reduced it to two basic questions – one a matter of politics; the other, of conscience. In the first, he judged the points of view of the anti-abortion and pro-choice groups to be irreconcilable. Because it was impossible to find a solution that pleased everyone, the best that could be achieved was a way forward that least offended the polarized factions. This reasoning was reflected in his position that the proposed changes to the abortion law did not legalize abortion but merely codified and clarified established practice. He would reiterate this position as he dealt with hard-liners on both sides of the issue. He solicited endorsements of his position from prominent Catholic lawyers across the country. They were all in basic agreement with his argument that the courts already allowed abortion when the mother's health was jeopardized.[12]

When it came to the abortion issue as a matter of conscience, Turner wrestled with his duty as a Catholic legislator. Catholic politicians were plentiful and uncontroversial in Canada's history, but John F. Kennedy's run for the presidency earlier in the decade in the United States, which had never before had a Catholic president, had made topical the question of whether Catholics' obligations to their church might compromise their duty to the state. *Humanae Vitae* had recently stoked the issue to a full boil.

Conscious of the delicacy of his position, Turner again sought expert opinion. That August he discussed the issue with members of the theological faculty of St. Michael's College. The Reverend Robert W. Crooker, an expert in church law at the Pontifical Institute of Mediaeval Studies, provided him with his written opinion that a good Catholic should oppose the abortion proposal. As a minister of the Crown, however, Turner had other responsibilities, and the abortion change, which "does not, strictly speaking, authorize the taking of foetal life," was insufficient grounds for him to break ranks with his government.[13] He also solicited the opinion of a Dominican theologian at Université Laval, who echoed the Kennedy position that, in governing a diverse society, Catholic legislators could not impose their personal consciences on the whole polity. The duty of a Catholic legislator in a pluralistic society was to serve the common good by finding a peaceable reconciliation of diverse views.[14]

These opinions did not conflict with those of the hierarchy of the Canadian Catholic Church. Canada's bishops were uncompromising on the question of abortion itself. On February 7, 1968, the Canadian Conference of Catholic Bishops had publicly reiterated the Catholic Church's position that abortion was wrong, even if the mother's health were at risk.[15] Yet the issue of a Catholic legislator's duties was something else again. Canada's bishops were at that time more liberal than many other national hierarchies and were largely sympathetic to the influence of the Second Vatican Council, which in their interpretation required them to respect the status and position, properly understood, of the laity, including Catholic legislators. As bishops, they would interpret church doctrine for the faithful and the wider public, but they would not presume to impose a Catholic view of issues on society at large, let alone tell a particular politician how to do his job.

As the abortion debate heated up, Turner wanted to be absolutely sure that he and the bishops understood one another. He invited the executive of the Canadian Conference of Catholic Bishops for dinner at the Cercle Universitaire, a private club in an old mansion on Laurier Avenue in Ottawa. There he laid out the government's case along with his perception of his duty as a Catholic and a minister of the Crown. He told the bishops that the compromise position represented by the omnibus bill was the best they could hope to get. This was, for Turner, a moment of high drama – he dreaded being forced to choose between personal faith and public duty. He would always remember the happy moment when Bishop Alexander Carter, president of the conference, concluded, "Gentlemen, I think John has convinced us. Let's have a drink."[16] It was not quite that simple. The bishops did not abandon their opposition to abortion, but a truce had been struck. They respected the fact that Turner was acting responsibly in a sphere that was not their area of competence and understood that a public servant in a pluralistic society should not impose his religious beliefs on his fellow citizens.[17]

Opposition from other major denominations on the issue ranged from muted to non-existent. The United Church strongly supported the reform, and protests came only from Baptists, Pentecostals, and some evangelical sects. Turner visited with Pentecostals in Newfoundland and evangelicals in the West to try to allay their concerns. Ultimately, they failed to galvanize significant opposition to the bill. In the short term the only apparent political damage he suffered from the abortion issue was the loss of the president of his riding association in Ottawa-Carleton, Dalton J. McGuinty, an English professor at the University of Ottawa, devout Roman Catholic, and father of eight (including a future Ontario premier), who resigned as a matter of conscience over Turner's sponsorship of the legislation.

The other contentious provision of the bill was the proposal to remove the section of the Criminal Code that made homosexual acts punishable by up to fourteen years in prison. Its presence on the books gave state sanction to discrimination on the basis of sexual orientation. Although this law wasn't commonly used, homosexuals had in the past been imprisoned or committed to mental institutions, and, just the previous year, the Supreme Court of Canada had ruled that, under the existing law, a homosexual could be imprisoned indefinitely as a "dangerous criminal offender."[18] Turner was less comfortable with the decriminalization of homosexuality than with the changes to the abortion law. In 1960s Canada, homosexuals of either sex faced social stigma and religious condemnation as well as legal sanction. Most Canadians viewed this as a natural and proper state of affairs, and those who objected dared not make a public issue of it. Consequently, Turner tried to present decriminalization as merely a practical administrative matter. The criminal law, he argued, should not be concerned with subjects beyond the maintenance of public order. Unenforceable laws brought the administration of justice into disrepute.[19]

This ignoble defence of the change was influenced by the geographically based representation of public opinion in the House of Commons. Especially in rural regions and Quebec, anything deviating from heterosexuality was simply beyond the pale. In the boys-club context of the House of Commons, debate about homosexuality inspired snickering and snide comment. When Diefenbaker asked rhetorically, "What has the government done for the people of Canada since December 13 last?" one MP yelled out, "Made them all homos!" Social Credit leader Réal Caouette took to saying that "being homosexual is now okay, as long as it is in private between consenting Liberals," and Créditistes even suggested it was a "communist plot to prevent us from reproducing ourselves so as to be able to seize the country without any trouble."[20] In this climate of opinion, Turner let it be known that, personally, he was not enthusiastic about homosexuality. He told the House, "When acts are committed in private between two consenting adults, those acts, however indecent or repugnant or immoral, should remain a matter for their private consciences and not be a matter bringing into play the Criminal Code of Canada. The conduct contemplated in this clause, homosexual acts between consenting adults in private, is repugnant ... to the great majority of the people of Canada."[21] Turner's rhetoric would change in later years as more enlightened views pervaded society, but at the time it epitomized contemporary attitudes.[22]

Tighter firearms regulation was another controversial component of the omnibus bill. Compared to those of the United States, Canada's controls on handguns were already strict. Existing law required the registration of handguns and automatic weapons, and it stipulated that permits were required for certain specified uses. But the government now went further because it needed a trade-off for police acquiescence with the abolition of capital punishment. The reform called the registered types of firearms "restricted weapons" and created a new class, "prohibited weapons," that included sawed-off shotguns or rifles, silencers, and switch- or spring-bladed knives.[23] A new provision made it an offence to use, carry, or possess any firearm or ammunition in a dangerous manner. A new official registrar of weapons would be appointed to oversee these regulations.

When Trudeau first presented these changes there had been little public opposition, but in the intervening months a gun lobby had developed. The Justice Department began to receive letters objecting to the reforms. Soon they numbered in the thousands – more than on any issue except abortion. Hunters fretted that one day a federal Cabinet might arbitrarily place sporting firearms on the restricted list. Youth groups such as the Boy Scouts complained that the proposed law would make it impossible to continue giving firearms training as part of their programming. To placate these interests, Turner eliminated the possibility that Cabinet could add shotguns or hunting rifles to the prohibited list and dropped the proposal for a registrar of weapons.[24]

Two other parts of the omnibus bill also generated controversy. One concerned lotteries, which had been on the government's agenda since at least 1953, when the St. Laurent administration had considered assigning the issue to a royal commission.[25] The proposed changes loosened Criminal Code restrictions on lotteries, allowing them to be run by federal and provincial governments or, under provincial licence, by organizations such as churches, charities, and agricultural fairs. The Protestant churches were opposed to any such liberalization. Turner received letters, petitions, and, on September 9, 1968, a brief from the Canadian Council of Churches to this effect.[26] Despite these objections, he not only proceeded with the reform but enhanced it by removing a $10,000 annual limit on revenue that had been in Trudeau's bill.

The omnibus bill also included tougher penalties for drunk driving and made roadside breathalyzer tests compulsory for suspected drunk drivers. The breathalyzer, a recent invention that had yet to be used by Canadian police, offered the first means of proving scientifically that a driver was impaired. In collaboration with the Department of Transport, Turner launched a national public education campaign to reinforce the initiative.[27] Moral earnestness did not preclude occasional humour. "If we drink we shouldn't drive, and if we drive we shouldn't drink," he would tell an audience sternly. After pausing for effect, he'd continue: "I have exercised my choice. I have given up driving."[28]

When Parliament convened in the fall of 1968, Turner announced that he would introduce the revised bill by the end of October, but it took until December to complete all the changes. In the interim, the Association for the Modernization of Canadian Abortion Laws demonstrated on Parliament Hill, attracting press attention with a gruesome display of the instruments used for illegal abortions.[29] Turner introduced the omnibus bill for first reading on December 19, 1968. When it came up for second reading on January 23, abortion remained the most controversial issue. "There are those on the one hand who abhor abortion for any cause or any reason whatsoever," Turner told the House. "There are those on the other hand who would make abortion wholly permissive or at the personal option of the woman. We have not reached a consensus between those views in this bill. We have reached only what I might call an accommodation."[30] Recently introduced rules gave MPs more involvement in the legislative process, and, at committee, several minor amendments were considered and approved. In the end, MPs across party lines felt they had ownership of the bill, and, on May 14, 1969, Bill C-150 passed its third and final reading by a vote of 149 to 55.

Turner hadn't seen the last of the omnibus issues. Abortion remained contentious, with pro-life and anti-abortion supporters demonstrating regularly on Parliament Hill and hundreds of letters flooding into his office every week.[31] Trying to cool things off, he and Trudeau issued a joint statement in June 1970, saying they had no intention of revisiting the law in the foreseeable future. Turner was also to be plagued by an irksome loose string from the new Criminal Code strictures on impaired driving. They had included a provision that a subject who was asked to blow into a breathalyzer had the right to have a breath sample saved in a separate container for independent testing. Unfortunately, such a container had yet to be invented. Turner delayed implementing the breathalyzer provisions of the omnibus bill until December 1, 1969, in hopes of finding a solution, but to no avail. When breathalyzer cases began to come before the courts, many were dismissed on technicalities. Then a lawyer defending a drunk driver in British Columbia challenged his client's conviction because the breathalyzer law was incomplete and had not been properly proclaimed. The case went to the Supreme Court of British Columbia, which supported this defence in a ruling brought down on April 6, 1970.

Turner decided to try to salvage the legislation by having it referred to the Supreme Court of Canada.[32] Confident in his knowledge of the Supreme Court justices, John Diefenbaker bet Turner that the government would lose the case. Turner took the bet. Diefenbaker's arithmetic was based on Saskatchewan's Justice Emmett Hall ruling against the government, but Turner recalled that Hall's favourite nephew had been killed by a drunk driver. On June 26, 1970, the Supreme Court upheld the legislation by a five to four ruling.[33]

Steering the omnibus bill through Parliament was a huge job that took up much of Turner's energy during his first year as minister of justice. It required all his political skill and experience. In a way, it was a thankless task. No matter how much he had to do with its implementation, in the public mind it would always be associated with Pierre Trudeau. Once it was passed, however, Turner was able to turn his attention to his own agenda and put his stamp on the Justice Department. To this end, his focus shifted from moral deregulation to an issue that was a better fit with his own long-standing reform agenda: the rights of the individual against the state.

7

IMPLEMENTING THE
JUST SOCIETY

Exactly what Trudeau meant by the "Just Society" he had promised in the 1968 election was never clear, but the pledge opened the door for Turner to pursue his own reform program once the omnibus bill had passed. He already had an agenda from when he had been angling for the Justice appointment – to protect the individual from the increasingly arbitrary power of the state in modern society. He was determined to show that the law could be an agent of positive change.[1]

Turner laid out his plans the day he was sworn in as minister. They included bail reform, protection of privacy from wiretaps, compensation for victims of crime, and a process to appeal the rulings of federal tribunals. He later sent Trudeau the same list with several additions, including amendment of the *Expropriations Act,* reforms to the federal superior courts, and a review of the federal role in legal aid.[2] Implementing this reform program would not be easy. The Department of Justice was a traditional organization hard pressed to keep up with an ever-expanding workload, let alone tackle systemic reform. Moreover, the justice system it oversaw had relatively autonomous institutions, a traditional culture, and a quotidian focus that made it resistant to change. The legal system's hidebound nature raised a strategic issue: How could it be made more responsive to contemporary society on an ongoing basis? In addressing this issue, Turner would make his most significant reforms.

The Canadian system harboured a vague notion of "British liberty" that was at odds with an equally strong legacy of parliamentary supremacy. The two values were reconciled on an ad hoc basis in accord with shifting social values and particular circumstances. In the aftermath of the Second World War there was growing concern about the potential excesses of untrammelled state power. With long-entrenched racist ideas discredited by the Holocaust, Canada's treatment of minorities, including its recent wartime internment of Japanese Canadians, would attract a new critical scrutiny. The United Nations issued its Universal Declaration of Human Rights in 1948, but another decade elapsed before rights discourse rose clearly to the fore in Canadian politics. Diefenbaker's 1960 Canadian Bill of Rights was a significant start, but wide public acceptance came only with the dramatic television coverage of the civil rights movement in the United States.[3] Canadian viewers felt compelled to side with the underdogs and congratulated themselves on being more enlightened and tolerant than their American neighbours.

The development of the welfare state added an interesting wrinkle to the rights revolution. Its origins were rooted in the recognition that, in practice, individuals required at least some equality of opportunity if they were to exercise their rights. Turner had often made this point in his speeches as he expounded his understanding of twentieth-century liberalism. Ironically, insofar as the emerging welfare state was more bureaucratically cumbersome and interventionist than its predecessor, it was also more prone to abusing individual rights – a point Turner recognized as well. His rights crusade could therefore be sold simultaneously to progressives as a social justice measure and to conservatives as a means of constraining big government.

One of the most significant services offered by the state was education. The rapidly expanding universities of the post-war era provided employment for social scientists and legal scholars, many of whom turned their critical gaze on the modern state. Progressive legal ideas flourished at the Osgoode Hall and new University of Toronto law schools, and faculty members packaged and promoted them in the public sphere.[4]

Turner was aware of these intellectual currents and was directly plugged in to some of the leading players through his friend and former assistant Jerry Grafstein, who had returned to legal practice in Toronto. The minister of justice symbolized the values of the administration, Grafstein told Turner, advising him to develop a progressive image in sympathy with the public mood. He went so far as to speculate that Trudeau might be a one-term prime minister. As a reaction against the excesses of Trudeaumania, he mused, voters would opt for substance over style and would look to Turner to provide it. "Any collateral ancillary objectives," Grafstein wrote, referring obliquely to Turner's political ambitions, "will only be advanced in direct relation to your success as a unique and outstanding Minister of Justice."[5]

Ontario had been the first Canadian jurisdiction to embrace a rights-based approach to law reform. In 1964 Premier John Robarts appointed Judge James McRuer to head the Ontario Royal Commission Inquiry into Civil Rights, a monumental undertaking that, in three reports between 1968 and 1971, reviewed statutes and regulations, sampled public opinion, and revised thousands of provincial laws and regulations.[6] In the course of the next few years, the bulk of its recommendations were implemented.

Practical political considerations would help Turner secure support for a similar reform agenda in Ottawa. The government wanted to keep Parliament busy, but revenue was tight. Turner's proposals would make it look like an activist administration, but unlike expensive social programs, they were relatively cheap and did not involve long-term spending commitments. Trudeau was happy to give Turner the green light.

The first item on Turner's agenda was bail reform. In existing practice, the onus was on the accused to prove that bail was warranted, and most people who were arrested were detained before trial. Impressed by critiques of the bail system in the United States, Osgoode Hall law professor Martin Friedland had conducted a study in Toronto. He concluded not only that it was mostly the poor who were jailed before trial but that their detention prejudiced the presumption of innocence in subsequent court proceedings.[7] In 1964 Turner's friend Robert Kennedy, the US attorney general, hosted a conference on the topic. Friedland's study received extensive media coverage when it was published in 1965. The John Howard Society issued a pamphlet, based on a talk given by Friedland, which circulated among MPs and got mention in the House of Commons. A private member's bill was introduced and later referred for study to the Standing Committee on Justice and Legal Affairs. The Canadian Committee on Corrections (known as the Ouimet Committee after its chair, Mr. Justice Roger Ouimet of the Quebec Superior Court), established in 1965 to study the prison reform system, subsequently recommended changes to the bail system in its March 1968 report. That spring, the McRuer Commission made a similar recommendation. Here, clearly, was a reform whose time had come.

Turner had considered including bail reform in the omnibus bill, but he abandoned the idea when he realized that completing the necessary research would hold back passage of the larger reform package. Although based on the recommendations of the Ouimet Report, his bail reform bill, Bill C-220, went further than Ouimet had recommended.[8] It directed police officers not to detain a suspect charged with a minor crime if the offender posed no threat to society and would probably appear in court. The bill also stipulated that people who had been arrested and jailed must be taken before a justice as soon as possible. In addition, it placed the onus on the Crown to show that bail should not be granted.

Editorials applauded the law's humanitarianism: no longer could the rich buy their freedom while the poor languished behind bars. The practical payoff of easing overcrowding in jails also attracted praise.[9] But some police chiefs, ignoring the principle of presumption of innocence, grumbled about criminals being allowed to walk the streets. Turner set out to win them over. He made positive public statements about the police and attended the Canadian Association of Chiefs of Police annual convention in London, Ontario, in September 1970, where he tried to convince members he was saving them work and giving them more on-the-spot discretion. Then he temporarily withdrew the bill, revised it with some of the police criticism in mind, and brought it back to Parliament as Bill C-218. As another concession, he delayed its proclamation to give police forces the time they needed to adjust to the new measures.

Expropriation was another area in which the state often trampled on individual rights. Under existing law, nothing prevented governments from taking property arbitrarily, paying whatever they wanted, and leaving owners without any legal recourse. Ontario's McRuer Commission had tackled the issue, recommending measures to ensure due process and fair market value as compensation, and the Province of Ontario was in the process of passing legislation that implemented these recommendations. In May 1969 Turner introduced into the House a federal expropriation act that contained similar provisions.[10] Critics warned that if the pendulum swung too far the other way, property owners could hold governments hostage and unfairly subvert the public interest, but the initiative was well received in both the press and the House, and was passed into law the following year.

Wilbur Jackett, a judge on the Exchequer Court of Canada (and former deputy minister of justice), came to Turner with yet another reform idea: wholesale restructuring of his court. Founded in 1875 to adjudicate legal disputes over matters in which the Canadian government was involved, the Exchequer Court also served as Canada's admiralty court, administering maritime law, and had acquired a variety of other responsibilities over the years. Unchanged since 1887, it was ill-equipped to handle the myriad demands placed on it in the modern world.

Jackett envisioned a single national court that would deal with all claims against the Crown as well as other matters of federal jurisdiction, including patents, trademarks, and admiralty law, plus appeals against decisions of federal tribunals and regulatory agencies. It would have a trial division and an appeal division, both of which would be bilingual and travel across Canada to make their services more accessible. Turner gave the initiative his wholehearted support, brought the Canadian Bar Association onside, cleared it through Cabinet, and shepherded the legislation through the House. Because the proposals had gone through an extensive consultative process before being introduced, the bill passed with relative ease. The new Federal Court began sitting on June 1, 1971.

Like Turner's other reforms, the *Federal Court Act* enhanced individual rights. It gave citizens the right to sue the federal government and to appeal rulings of government tribunals, boards, and commissions – thereby empowering them in the face of some of the least accountable manifestations of state power. It made it easier to gain access to government documents as evidence, provided for local registries where litigants could initiate proceedings without travelling to Ottawa, and streamlined administrative procedures to speed up the litigation process. "A giant step towards putting the citizen and the government on a more equal footing," concluded the *Montreal Gazette*.[11]

For years Turner had fretted publicly about the threat that modern bureaucracy and technology posed to individual privacy. In a September 2, 1969, speech entitled "Twin Freedoms: The Right to Privacy and the Right to Know," he argued that invasion of privacy could stifle legitimate democratic dissent.[12] New information technologies were contributing to the problem. "National data banks, commercial reporting agencies, computerized transactions and the like are making us the greatest data-gathering, privacy-invading society ever known," he warned.[13] He commissioned a Computers and Privacy Task Force to look into the issue. He also put his officials to work on the related issue of electronic eavesdropping. They drew up legislation that he brought to the House in June 1971. It banned eavesdropping by anyone except police with judicial approval or by the police or armed forces in cases where national security was at risk.[14] Turner then attacked government secrecy with the *Statutory Instrument Act,* which required disclosure of the thousands of rules, orders-in-council, and regulations passed by Cabinet. It was based on the principle that the arbitrary powers possessed by the executive should not be exercised without public scrutiny. Turner practised what he preached by making sure that the Justice Department was open and accountable. "I don't have an information office in my department," he boasted. "I run an open government, and ... the senior members of my department have been told to answer all calls from the press."[15] He was far ahead of public opinion on these issues. Comprehensive federal legislation on access to information and protection of privacy would not come for another fifteen years.

As minister of justice, Turner was finally in a position to do something about legal aid, a cause he had advocated since his days on the junior bar in Montreal.[16] Soon after taking office, he had the Justice Department research the patchwork of provincial legal aid systems to estimate the feasibility of implementing a system nationwide. He tried to prepare the ground for the reform by stating publicly, whenever he got the chance, that every Canadian should have the right to legal representation. In March 1970 he announced that he would be negotiating with the provincial attorneys general the establishment of a coast-to-coast federally funded legal aid system that would cover both civil and criminal cases. His plan was modelled on medicare, with federal money to be provided to the provinces if they met certain standards. He won the Canadian Bar Association's endorsement for it that September.

The provinces, already struggling to fund medicare, baulked at the prospect of having another expensive and cumbersome federal scheme foisted on them. The potential cost went beyond hiring defence counsel: having a lawyer encouraged a defendant to plead not guilty, which made trials more expensive. In addition, the inevitable jurisdictional issues arose. Jérôme Choquette, Quebec's justice minister, protested that a national legal aid scheme represented unwarranted federal interference in an area of provincial jurisdiction. Eventually, all the provinces said they were willing at least to discuss the prospect provided it would be federally funded.[17]

Turner proposed inserting a right to counsel into the charter of rights that was being considered as part of the ongoing constitutional negotiations, but the provinces would not agree. He contemplated acting unilaterally by putting the right to representation into the Criminal Code – an arrangement that would guarantee legal aid in criminal proceedings but not in civil cases. Eventually, he decided that comprehensive coverage achieved through provincial cooperation would be better than an imposed half-measure, so he continued negotiating. The proposal then got side-tracked into ongoing federal-provincial negotiations. Only in the territories, where the administration of justice was solely a federal responsibility, was a scheme implemented.[18]

Turner also pursued a clutch of other minor reforms, some of which came to fruition.[19] He knew from his days in private practice that appeals of government tax rulings were costly bureaucratic processes that only the wealthy could afford. To address this problem, he instituted a tax review board that would allow the average taxpayer to appeal a federal tax ruling without a lawyer. This system also provided that, in cases involving $1,000 or less, the government would pay the legal costs incurred by taxpayers who won a judgment. This initiative was yet another example of his concern for the rights of the individual against the system.

There were limits to Turner's reform ethos. After a rash of student demonstrations on university campuses, most notably destructive riots at Sir George Williams University in Montreal, he denounced violence as a means of political protest. On other occasions he mused publicly about introducing tougher laws against violent crime. He was also reluctant to change the law to accommodate the drug culture of the era. Gerald Le Dain, dean of Osgoode Hall Law School, had been appointed in 1969 to head a five-man federal inquiry into the non-medical use of drugs. Its interim report recommending liberalization of marijuana laws was submitted to the government in April 1970. Turner and most of Cabinet were opposed.[20]

Assessments of marijuana were still in progress, and Canada was bound by international agreements on illegal drugs. Still, he had no wish to see young people getting criminal records for experimenting with pot. To this end, he had already recommended lighter sentences for possession. "No one wants a society where we are going to send a generation to jail," he explained.[21]

Turner was conflicted on other reform measures as well. A House of Commons committee on hate literature recommended legislation that would make it a crime to advocate or promote genocide or to publicly promote hatred against any distinctive social group. Maxwell Cohen, dean of law at McGill, had written the report that underpinned the bill. It argued that the Holocaust had begun with hate-mongering and that hateful rhetoric was the means by which prejudice was fomented. Turner had relied on Cohen for advice in handling the Columbia River Treaty and had great respect for his views, but in this case he had misgivings about limiting freedom of speech. When he introduced the anti-hate bill into the House, he took pains to emphasize that it would restrict free speech only when such action was clearly justified. Critics decried the bill as thought control and portrayed it as government pandering to a particular ethnic community. Nevertheless, it passed third reading on April 13, 1970, and became law later that spring.

The minister's activism impressed the lawyers in the Department of Justice. They regarded Turner as one of their own because he had previously practised law. They appreciated his intelligence, his diligence, and his democratic habit of wandering into their offices to talk shop. When Turner had an important meeting on one of his reform proposals with his high-ranking officials, he often asked the junior lawyers who had worked on the file to join them. This was a big change for a department accustomed to a hierarchical protocol in which only senior managers dealt with the minister. Turner unfailingly recognized the efforts of his staff by singling them out for praise in front of their peers. He gave them a crusading slogan, "Society is our client," and assigned them challenging, meaningful work. A good judge of talent, he delegated responsibility effectively. "He is probably the most demanding minister in the cabinet to work for and he exhorts his frazzled aides like the coach of a ball team," wrote one reporter. "He was always urging us to get down to the 'nitty-gritty' of a problem," an aide commented. "He's happiest when he's hip-deep in a fight and ... there's 'lots of action.'"[22]

Turner was in his office every morning by eight-thirty and often worked until ten at night. He kept up with the mounds of paper shoved his way and absorbed briefs effortlessly, remembering the salient facts, the points that required his political attention, and the line to take with the press. His office in the West Block of the Parliament Buildings, once occupied by John A. Macdonald, was "abustle with youthful activity," noted one observer. "Aides and assistants, none of whom appeared to be over 30, kept wandering in 'to have a few words with John.'"[23] Turner, his executive assistant Richard Hayes, and his special assistant Ernest Hébert got along well with Don Maxwell and his assistant deputy ministers, forging a strong management team with a shared sense of mission.[24]

The reform ethos in Justice was bolstered further when Turner acquired the services of a new speechwriter in the fall of 1968. Irwin Cotler, a graduate student in law at Yale University, had written to Turner, urging him to use the law to attack social injustice. Cotler had studied law at McGill University, so Turner asked his friends in Montreal about him. Receiving favourable reports, he hired Cotler to help him with a speech he was scheduled to deliver. Cotler found that he and Turner were on the same wavelength, and he soon became a permanent fixture in Turner's office. Justice staff would draft speeches that covered the technical aspects of a reform, then Cotler would infuse them with reform rhetoric that drew attention to their substantial social implications. With his long hair and granny glasses, Cotler looked every bit the contemporary student radical. He functioned as a kind of departmental hippie mascot, living proof of the minister's commitment to change. His presence went over better in some quarters than others. When Turner made a two-day visit to Washington on March 22, 1969, he paid a courtesy call on his US counterpart, Attorney General John Mitchell. "You let people like that work for you?" Mitchell asked. "He's my in-house radical," Turner explained.[25]

Turner established an informal think-tank on legal reform by convening a small annual gathering at Montebello – a conference facility fifty miles east of Ottawa, on the north side of the Ottawa River. It was an appropriate venue for radical thought, the property having been the seigneury of Louis-Joseph Papineau, leader of the Patriotes in the Lower Canadian Rebellion of 1837. A select group of practising lawyers, judges, and reform-minded legal scholars was invited, including luminaries such as Maxwell Cohen, Gerald Le Dain, Gérard La Forest, F.R. Scott, and Cotler's American friend Alan Dershowitz.[26] The discussions had a ripple effect, influencing not only the Justice Department but each participant's legal circles as well.

Turner was not shy about publicizing his efforts. He maintained his tactic of using speeches to get his message out, delivering a public address every few weeks. A stream of press releases announcing new initiatives also flowed from his office, providing newspapers with ready copy. In October 1968 he appeared on the front cover of *Maclean's,* the subject of a feature interview. "I think the fabric of our laws must be such that everyone must be guaranteed equal access to the courts and to redress of grievances," he declared, then laid out the specific reforms he was planning.[27] On the Ottawa front, Turner consulted with caucus, bounced ideas off the opposition, held talks with interest groups, and floated trial balloons with the press. He also communicated with his provincial counterparts more than any of his predecessors.[28] By the time a Turner bill hit the Commons, awareness was raised, criticisms accommodated, and opposition members disinclined to object strenuously. As a result, he passed more legislation than any other Cabinet minister during Trudeau's first term.[29]

Turner's greatest contribution to law reform was still to come. The omnibus bill had been an overdue yet onerous process, but he recognized that, when it and his subsequent reforms were added together, they made only a slight dent in the system. If the reform momentum were to be continued, the system had to change. He developed a three-pronged strategy to make this happen: a strategic planning capability in the Department of Justice, ongoing professional education for judges and lawyers, and a law reform commission to institutionalize continual reform of the legal system.

The first step involved a full-frontal assault on the traditional methods and temperament of the Justice Department. Over the years it had coped, barely, with its increasing day-to-day legal workload, but it had failed to develop any capacity to step back from its duties and strategize about big-picture issues. Le Dain once dismissed it as a "200 man law firm which couldn't think about law reform."[30] Canada needed a Justice Department that could discern the legal dimensions of social issues and respond with effective policy solutions based on hard data and incisive analysis.

Turner's solution was to establish a Legal Research and Planning section in the department. Its mandate was to collect information on the operation of the law in society as the basis for new legislation. In this way he established a review and reform function at the core of the department's operations, making it more responsive to social change. He set up liaisons between the new section's lawyers and their specialist counterparts in private practice across the country. He also introduced a computer network that would keep track of cases before the courts and provide ready access to case law and legal precedents.[31] Then he gave the section clout by appointing Gérard La Forest, the dean of law at the University of Alberta, to head it up as an assistant deputy attorney general.

Turner also launched a campaign to improve the quality of the judiciary. Patronage was one of his first targets. He set out to change the old pork-barrel system in which allegiance to the governing party was the key criterion for appointing judges. He became the first minister of justice to seek an opinion from the Canadian Bar Association's National Council on the Judiciary before making a judicial appointment. He ignored party affiliations when he appointed John Osler and Thomas Berger, both prominent supporters of the NDP. Lloyd Houlden, a Stanfield supporter, was named a judge because of his expertise in commercial and bankruptcy law. Half the judges Turner appointed during his first six months in office had no Liberal connections.[32]

Turner took a lot of heat in Cabinet and caucus from colleagues who coveted these appointments for their friends and supporters. In time he institutionalized a non-partisan appointment process wherein the minister of justice sent a list of possible candidates to the Canadian Bar Association, which categorized the names as well qualified, qualified, and unqualified. After more consultation, the minister made the appointment from the top two sections.[33] With this simple but bold step, Turner significantly improved the quality of the Canadian judiciary.

His appointments were trail blazing in other ways as well. On March 20, 1970, he appointed Bora Laskin to the Supreme Court, the first Jewish judge to sit on that body.[34] He admonished the Canadian Bar Association for not having women on its executive. During a meeting of Cabinet with the National Council of Women on January 27, 1969, he announced that the federal government was considering appointing women judges to all provincial superior courts.[35] The expanded grounds for divorce under the new 1968 law made such appointments imperative. Réjane Laberge-Colas, who became a puisne judge of the Superior Court for the District of Montreal on February 22, 1969, was the first woman to sit on a superior court in Canada. On November 10, 1971, Turner appointed Mabel Van Camp to the Supreme Court of Ontario.

Turner then helped implement the Canadian Judicial Council. The council was a national forum in which senior judges from across Canada would discuss common issues and was a peer review disciplinary authority to deal with complaints about judges, issue warnings and suspensions, and, in the most serious cases, prepare recommendations for their removal. In January 1969 he also announced plans for continuing education for judges. For more than a decade, Canadian judges had been going to the United States for refresher courses on contemporary issues – an unsatisfactory practice given the differences between the two countries' legal systems. Judges, Turner pointed out, played the most important role in the administration of justice, and ensuring they were on top of the issues was fundamental to a fair justice system.

Lawyers were also a target of Turner's improving ethos. He launched a forum, the National Conference on the Law, to foster dialogue between lawyers and non-lawyers about legal issues and their relationship to society. The first conference was planned for February 1972.[36] The legal profession was getting used to Turner haranguing it about its selfish ways. He told the graduating class at Osgoode Hall in October 1968,

> Just as the shaping and sharing of all democratic values in the Just Society must not be the exclusive privilege of the few, but the inclusive right of all ... so the law must not be the exclusive prerogative of the privileged, but the privileged right of all ... If therefore the right to bail is the prerogative of the rich, and preventive detention the plight of the poor; if privacy is the right only of those who with counsel can claim it, and invasion the deprivation of those who unwittingly suffer it ... if, in short, there is justice for some of us, but not social justice for all of us, we dare not speak of the Just Society for any of us.[37]

He was once again challenging members of his profession to be more than hired guns, appealing to their conscience so they would see themselves as critical agents for positive social change.[38]

The Law Reform Commission of Canada was the capstone of Turner's plan to institutionalize reform in the Canadian system of justice. There were precedents for such a body in Ontario (1964), Britain (1965), and elsewhere. The Ouimet Report had recommended a law reform commission to replace the various royal commissions and special committees that reviewed the law on an ad hoc basis. Turner wanted a commission that would encompass all federal statutes within its purview and operate at arm's length from government, one that would "review and reform ... the law and the administration of justice in this country ... to keep it alive and moving in a changing society."[39] He introduced a bill to establish the Law Reform Commission of Canada on February 16, 1970.[40] It passed on May 12 and received royal assent in June. Turner told reporters that he would make the commission effective by recruiting "young tigers, between 35 and 45, young enough to have some juice, old enough to have made their mark."[41] It was the crowning achievement of his reform crusade.

Turner's record in Justice did not go unrecognized. By the summer of 1970, with the Trudeau government halfway through its mandate, journalists began to take stock of its accomplishments. It was generally acknowledged that Turner was one of the few standouts in Cabinet. In an article otherwise very critical of the government, one of Turner's friends and admirers, W.A. Wilson of the *Montreal Star,* wrote that he was "emerging as an outstanding and possibly great minister of justice."[42] And, when the *Toronto Star* commissioned a public opinion poll on the performance of Cabinet ministers, John Turner came out far ahead of his colleagues, earning an approval rating of 58 per cent.[43]

The reforms Turner introduced as minister of justice were not attributable to his efforts and ideas alone, but he orchestrated the necessary political support, framed the legislation, and got them passed. They reflected the concerns he had articulated in his speeches over the years and were consistent with his previous record in public life. As president of the Montreal Junior Bar he had championed legal aid, and as a young MP he had campaigned for more autonomy for members of parliament. He had called for a bill of rights to be enshrined in the constitution, paired with an economic bill of rights. At Consumer and Corporate Affairs, he had worked for the rights of the consumer against big business and had taken on the monopoly pricing policies of grocery chains and the big drug companies. He had run for the Liberal leadership on a social justice platform. Along the way he had lambasted the advertising industry, the legal profession, and other privileged groups for their lack of social responsibility. At Justice, Turner showed what he could do when given the chance to take on a significant portfolio. He prevailed over institutional inertia and entrenched interests to deliver on his promises and fulfill the public's high expectations of the first Trudeau government. Under his direction, the reform impulse of the 1960s had a more extensive impact on the system of justice than on any other sector of Canadian public life.

8

APPREHENDED INSURRECTION

The "peace and love" mantra of the hippies proved elusive in the late 1960s. Throughout the Western world, student demonstrations, protest marches, violent strikes, police brutality, hijackings, and underground guerrilla groups were in the news. In Canada the epicentre of social unrest was Montreal. Since 1963 a group calling itself the Front de Libération du Québec (FLQ) had been setting off bombs, rattling everyone's nerves, and occasionally killing an innocent person. The unrest increased as the decade wore on. When the nationalist journalist Pierre Vallières was jailed in 1966 for his role in the FLQ violence, supporters marched in protest, clashed with police, and vented their anger in a property-destroying rampage. In 1968 the monopoly enjoyed by an airport limousine company became the target of a similar protest by a group with the unlikely name of Le Mouvement de libération du taxi. Again the fallout was bashed heads, broken bones, and bad blood. The cab liberators marched again the following year when the Montreal police were out on an illegal strike. Security guards fired on the crowd, killing an undercover policeman and wounding others. Quebec's solicitor general invoked the *National Defence Act* to call in the army to preserve public order.[1] In February 1969 a bomb went off at the Montreal Stock Exchange, injuring twenty-seven people. When the Union Nationale government of Premier Jean-Jacques Bertrand passed a language law later that year, a Front du Québec français sprang up to organize protests, leading to more mayhem, injuries, and arrests. The year closed with a campaign for Vallières' release that involved the fire bombing of city hall, police headquarters, and several banks.

Late the following year, radical lawlessness escalated to a whole new level. On October 5, 1970, British trade commissioner James Cross was kidnapped at gunpoint from his home in Montreal. Later that day an FLQ cell claimed responsibility and set out terms for Cross' freedom. They included a $500,000 ransom and the release of a number of "political prisoners" – persons convicted or charged in connection with FLQ bombings and robberies. The kidnappers threatened to kill Cross if their conditions were not met by Wednesday, October 7.

At first, Quebec premier Robert Bourassa stalled for time. When the federal Cabinet met on October 7, it debated whether to reject the FLQ demands categorically, offering only safe passage out of the country, or to leave open some possibility for negotiation. Because Cross was a diplomat, Mitchell Sharp, the secretary of state for external affairs, became the federal government's spokesperson.[2] He announced that the FLQ demands would not be met but indicated a willingness to negotiate. One of the demands was publication of the FLQ manifesto, a diatribe against Quebec elites that called for a French Canadian workers' *coup d'état*.[3] It was broadcast on a private radio station in Montreal, and then by Radio-Canada TV. The FLQ extended its deadline to 6:00 p.m. on October 10, the Saturday of the Thanksgiving weekend.

John Turner was in Canberra, Australia, that week, attending a Commonwealth Parliamentary Conference. Sharp asked him to stay on in the South Pacific, where he was scheduled to visit Fiji as Canada's representative at ceremonies celebrating its independence. In the meantime, the crisis deepened. Shortly before the FLQ's Saturday deadline, Quebec justice minister Jérôme Choquette spoke on the radio, refusing most of the FLQ demands but offering safe passage abroad to the kidnappers in return for the release of their hostage. Cross had been kidnapped by the Liberation cell of the FLQ. Now another cell calling itself Chénier got into the act. Within minutes of Choquette's broadcast, it snatched Pierre Laporte, Quebec's minister of labour and immigration, from outside his house in Montreal.

Turner returned to Ottawa on Monday, October 12. Earlier that day the federal government had called in the army to guard federal officials and buildings in Ottawa, and he arrived home to find soldiers trampling the rose bushes around his house in Rockcliffe Park.[4] On Tuesday, newspapers printed excerpts of a letter from Laporte begging Bourassa to meet the terrorists' demands and save his life. The Quebec Cabinet agonized over its response. Many of Laporte's colleagues were close friends who did not want to abandon him, yet neither could they yield to terrorist extortion.

Meanwhile, saturation media coverage stoked by incessant news bulletins was heightening anxiety in Montreal. Radical agitators staged demonstrations sympathetic to the FLQ. On October 14 sixteen "eminent personalities" – including prominent labour leaders, Parti Québécois leader René Lévesque, and Le Devoir editor Claude Ryan – held a news conference and called on Bourassa to free the "political prisoners" to save Laporte. Rumours were circulating about discussions Ryan had engaged in the previous Sunday, first with colleagues and later with Lucien Saulnier, the chair of the Montreal Urban Community, about whether the provincial government needed to be bolstered to deal with the crisis – presumably by augmenting it with some eminent personalities.[5]

The Montreal and Quebec governments decided they should round up suspected FLQ members and sympathizers. To do so, they wanted special powers that would suspend habeas corpus so police could arrest suspects without a warrant and detain them without laying charges. The two levels of government asked Ottawa unofficially whether it would authorize such powers if they made a formal request.

Turner was a member of the Cabinet Committee on Security and Intelligence, which met on the morning of Wednesday, October 14, to discuss the government's response. Don Christie, his assistant deputy minister, had talked to Julien Chouinard, Quebec's deputy attorney general, the day before. Don Maxwell, the deputy minister of justice, described the meeting as "unsatisfactory," adding that "he was not aware of any *facts* indicating that special powers were required." RCMP Commissioner William Higgitt thought provincial authorities wanted "action for the sake of action" to "hit at revolutionaries in general." Turner told the committee that he "did not feel on the basis of information from Quebec through Mr. Christie that additional legislation was needed." Charges of treason or seditious conspiracy could be prosecuted successfully under existing laws.

In short, the committee saw no compelling case for granting special powers. Invoking such powers, Trudeau noted, could backfire by shifting public opinion against the government. "The population was already being excited" by agitators, Trudeau noted, and "there would be a real danger of the movement gaining many converts, resulting in the creation of a popular movement."

The prime minister's concern prompted Turner to comment that they were fighting a "psychological war." Bud Drury agreed, observing that the terrorists were becoming "folk heroes." The best way to deal with this situation, Turner thought, was to place a time limit on negotiations and make it clear that any harm that befell the kidnap victims thereafter would be the fault of the FLQ. When the deadline passed, the government could consider instituting special legislation if there was a provincial request for it. Even then it should only be in force for a limited period of time. The committee agreed with this approach and adjourned until Turner could report back on the options available for implementing special powers of arrest and detention.[6]

When the committee met again that evening, Turner presented three alternatives: proclamation, without amendment, of the *War Measures Act,* legislation passed in 1914 to give the federal government the power to govern by decree in an emergency; special legislation to amend the *War Measures Act* for the situation at hand; or an entirely new piece of purpose-built legislation. After Turner explained the advantages and disadvantages of each, Trudeau announced that he favoured new legislation and asked Turner to have Justice prepare it for Cabinet consideration on the morrow.[7]

The next morning, the Quebec government called in the army to protect public buildings, explaining that it needed to free up police officers to pursue the FLQ investigation. By afternoon, a thousand soldiers from the Valcartier military base would be on the streets of Montreal. When Cabinet convened that morning, Marchand reported on meetings he had had in Montreal the day before with Bourassa and Saulnier. He was convinced the situation was dire. Marchand now told his colleagues that "what actually looked like an abduction was really more than that; it was a big organized plan." His police contacts in Montreal had told him that more FLQ cells were waiting to act on coded messages in the speeches of sympathizers. They were planning to detonate radio-controlled truck bombs to blow up buildings in Montreal – in fact, one such attack had been attempted the day before, thwarted only by a technical malfunction. The Montreal police had been infiltrated by the terrorists, and "the FLQ was a state within a state that must be disorganized now."[8] Marc Lalonde, Trudeau's principal secretary, was on the phone with Choquette during the meeting and periodically issued grim reports that reinforced Marchand's portrayal of the situation.[9]

Many Cabinet ministers remained skeptical. Nothing in the police reports supported Marchand's claims. Turner warned against "overkill" and asked whether apprehension alone were enough to justify overriding civil liberties. He reiterated that police action at this point was premature. At the prime minister's request, he then presented *An Act to Provide Emergency Powers for the Preservation of Public Order in Canada,* the special legislation he had been asked to draw up the previous day.[10]

As the discussion wore on, Marchand's alarming claims had more effect than Turner's counsel of caution. The FLQ had tapped into a uniquely Canadian paranoia, triggering dark imaginings of revolution afoot in a vast terrorist underground in Quebec. Bombings had increased over the years. The FLQ had now moved on to kidnapping and threats that selective assassination of politicians would follow. No one really knew its strength, but it was easy to imagine there was more to it than met the eye. In Montreal a crisis atmosphere was building to a fever pitch. Quebec labour leaders were publicly expressing their sympathy for the FLQ. The Parti Québécois had pointedly refused to denounce the terrorists' tactics. Leading citizens wanted to yield to terrorist extortion and were allegedly scheming to undermine duly constituted authority.[11] Students had passed resolutions supporting the FLQ, occupied campus buildings, and swarmed to rallies where radicals declared support for the terrorist cause. Perhaps it was just all froth whipped up by the kidnappings, perhaps not. In any case, media sensationalism fed on the dramatic developments, generating an enveloping anxiety that intensified with each passing day.

Marchand's take on the situation spooked the prime minister, who now began to worry that events were spinning out of control. Using violence to provoke a repressive response that would legitimate, publicize, and attract support to a cause was a well-known revolutionary tactic.[12] Take an atmosphere of crisis, add a few thousand protesters looking for trouble, mix in a nervous, strung-out police force and a media willing to depict idealistic youth martyred by oppressive authority – it was easy to picture street protests in Montreal cascading into widespread civil unrest. Gérard Pelletier would later recall genuine concern that "a gathering of all the protest factions would develop in a sudden conflagration."[13] If agitators precipitated a clash that polarized Quebec society, the FLQ would be successful beyond its wildest dreams.

That very evening a pro-FLQ rally was to be held at Paul Sauvé Arena in Montreal. It was just the type of radical protest that might precipitate violence in the streets. Marchand and Trudeau wanted to give the police the go-ahead to make arrests that night so that any fallout from the rally at the Paul Sauvé Arena could be contained. There was not enough time to pass special legislation before then, so Cabinet considered the option of passing it the next day and making it retroactive to cover police activities of the night before. Turner baulked at this suggestion. "If a bill was to be introduced after illegal seizures had taken place the night before," he argued, "the government would have put itself in a bad posture." However, "if the legislation didn't go into effect the next day, they'd have to be let go and the gov't would lose face."[14]

Marchand was impatient with such legal niceties. He warned that if they delayed they ran the risk of "losing Quebec." Trudeau agreed: "The longer we [give] opinion makers in Quebec," he declared, "the more we stand to lose."[15] Trudeau polled Cabinet on whether the raids should be staged that night. The FLQ might boast up to a thousand hard-core members, Trudeau told Cabinet, and "if that should be the case and the government did not react and there were an insurrection, where would the government stand?" It was best to anticipate the worst, because "one only got to know after the fact whether one was facing an insurrection or not."[16] Turner and the other skeptics went along with their alarmed colleagues. If there was anything close to the danger of insurrection they feared, the situation warranted immediate and decisive action.

For Turner, that meant the *War Measures Act* – nothing else would be legal. Special legislation was incompatible with immediate action. The *War Measures Act* was the off-the-shelf solution: it could be proclaimed immediately, declare the FLQ an unlawful organization, and authorize arrests without charges.[17] He qualified his support at the Cabinet table that afternoon, however, by saying that the government should subsequently pass less draconian substitute legislation in Parliament. When Trudeau asked him why, he explained: "If the War Measures Act were used to prevent a feared insurrection, and then, if it were withdrawn and replaced by more moderate legislation, we would be regarded as having used the War Measures Act as a protective and temporary measure. If, on the other hand, what was apprehended in Quebec really was insurrection, then we could keep the War Measures Act in force; if it is not, we should not abuse that very restrictive Act."[18]

The full powers of the *War Measures Act* were not required, but Ottawa needed the legal authority it provided to invoke regulations that would give the Quebec and Montreal governments the powers they had requested. Turner gave his colleagues a draft of the regulations to be adopted under the act to declare the FLQ an illegal organization and allow police to search premises, arrest without a warrant, and detain without laying charges. Pelletier and Marchand were entrusted with reviewing the police list of suspects to see if they could spot any anomalies before the roundup began.

The night of October 15-16 was an eventful one in Montreal. The army was already on the streets. At 9:00 p.m. the Quebec government issued an ultimatum giving the FLQ six hours to surrender its hostages. At Paul Sauvé Arena, a crowd of three thousand, roused by FLQ sympathizers, began chanting "FLQ! FLQ! FLQ!" After receiving a formal letter of request from Bourassa at 2:25 a.m., the federal government brought the *War Measures Act* and the case-specific regulations it had formulated into effect at 4:00 a.m. that Friday morning, October 16.[19]

While Trudeau went on television to speak to the nation, Turner explained the government's action to the House of Commons. The government had acted reluctantly because it had no other choice, he said. The government of Quebec and the civic administration of Montreal had sent written requests for assistance. He was devoted to civil rights, but government compliance with the FLQ demand to release convicted criminals would have been "nothing less than the first installment in a program of continuing blackmail."[20] Turner assured the House that the *War Measures Act* would be in force only temporarily. Meanwhile, the police were busy rounding up suspects. More than 200 arrests were made, 140 of them in Montreal.

On Saturday, October 17, Pierre Laporte was strangled to death. His body was found in the trunk of a car at St. Hubert airport soon after midnight on October 18. Turner was in the midst of the continuing House of Commons debate on the crisis when, just before 1:00 a.m., he heard of Laporte's death. Trudeau, who had been at home, arrived on Parliament Hill an hour later. With Turner present, he spoke to the media, expressing the shock of the nation and extending sympathy to Laporte's family. The following day, the House of Commons passed a motion supporting the government's introduction of the *War Measures Act.*

The dramatic invocation of the act and the shock of Laporte's death had a sobering effect in Montreal. No restrictions had been put on the media, yet the incessant radio and television updates tapered off. Agitations and demonstrations likewise ceased, and the mounting sense of crisis dissipated. The government's actions were very popular with a public that was spooked by the kidnappings, fearful for the remaining hostage, and worried about public order.[21] Still, the possibility that the government had overreacted began to get a public airing and emboldened opposition parties' questioning in the House of Commons.[22] On October 28 Turner reported that 397 persons had been arrested under the *War Measures Act,* of whom 259 had since been released. No charges had been laid against the 138 who were still detained.[23] This revelation provoked indignant protests in the House and the press.

On November 2 Turner introduced the *Public Order (Temporary Measures) Act* into the Commons as a replacement for the *War Measures Act.* The new legislation was aimed specifically against the FLQ and was framed to give the government means unavailable in the Criminal Code for dealing with "a well-organized group of criminal revolutionaries."[24] "A single revolutionary spark may kindle a fire that, smouldering for a time, may burst into a sweeping and destructive conflagration," Turner declared, quoting US Supreme Court justice Edward T. Sanford.[25] His choice of words reflected the government's continuing uncertainty about the extent of the FLQ's organization, capabilities, and popularity. Confident that he had public opinion on his side, he pushed the new act through the House quickly, ignoring opposition amendments. The *Public Order Act* passed the House of Commons on December 1 and, after a quick passage through the Senate, came into effect on December 3. The new legislation had a built-in sunset clause of April 30, 1971.

On November 6 police arrested FLQ member Bernard Lortie. The next day he admitted to being one of the kidnappers of Pierre Laporte. By late November, police concluded that another suspected FLQ member, Jacques Cossette-Trudel, was involved in the Cross kidnapping. They located and began to follow him, which led them to 10945 Des Recollets Street in Montreal. On December 2 police decided to arrest anyone they caught leaving the house. They subsequently detained Cossette-Trudel and his wife, Louise, who were initially uncooperative. Eventually, however, Cossette-Trudel indicated that Cross was at the Des Recollets address and claimed that the premises were booby-trapped with dynamite. Police cordoned off the area and, around 3 a.m. on December 3, a piece of iron pipe was thrown from the house. It contained a message naming acceptable negotiators. Talks began.

Turner was acting solicitor general in place of an ailing George McIlraith, so while Trudeau fielded questions in the House, he oversaw negotiations with the Cross kidnappers behind the scenes.[26] The government agreed to give them free passage to Cuba once they released their hostage. Turner told the press that, had the police lacked the special powers given to them by the *War Measures Act,* Cross might not have been saved.[27] The connection may have been debatable, but it showed that he was already thinking of how the invocation of the act could be justified after the passions of the moment had cooled.

Just before New Year's Eve, Laporte's murderers were arrested, bringing the October Crisis to a close. It had been a searing experience for the government. Turner worked closely with Trudeau throughout the crisis. "That's the closest I ever felt to him," he recalled later. "We were like buddies in combat. I mean, when you stand beside a guy who's eyeball-to-eyeball with danger and he doesn't blink, you can't help but feel admiration."[28] As an acknowledgement of their shared experience, Trudeau gave Turner a signed copy of a photograph showing the two of them emerging grim yet resolute from his office at 3 a.m. on the night of Laporte's murder.

As it gradually became apparent that the forces arrayed against the state had been two rag-tag gangs of radical misfits, suggestions that the *War Measures Act* had been unjustified and the insurrection overly apprehended gained credibility.[29] Although Turner initially proposed alternative emergency measures and pushed for speedy implementation of the *Public Order Act,* he had, nevertheless, supported the Cabinet decision to invoke the *War Measures Act.* Moreover, as attorney general and then as acting solicitor general, he had overseen and defended its implementation. Certainly, as the leading anglophone Liberal, he was one of the most prominent apologists for the government's actions.

The episode distressed him. "You can appreciate how difficult it is for me as a strong advocate of civil rights over the years to share some responsibility for this stern emergency posture," he wrote to a friend. "But ... a threat to the very structure of society can only be met sometimes by a temporary suspension of some of the ordinary rights to which we are accustomed."[30] He acknowledged that the *War Measures Act* was "too blunt an instrument" but pointed out that only those regulations made under it by Cabinet had the force of law and that most of its powers had not been used.[31] He discussed the dilemma at the Montebello gathering that December. In the months that followed, he continued to turn it over in his mind, analyzing all the factors that had led to the decision, and discussed them in public. "It involved an erosion of public will, escalating calls to violence and the tenseness of a city beleaguered," he explained. "I am convinced that to have let matters run for more hours or more days might have been disastrous."[32]

As security concerns melted away, critics of the government felt more free to express outrage about its assault on civil liberties. Turner became a target of protests regarding his role in the affair and was sometimes heckled during public appearances. The worst incident came on March 6, 1971, when he visited his alma mater, UBC, to give a speech to the Vancouver Institute. Protesters, including "women's liberationists, hippies, Yippies ... assorted street people," and a man in a gorilla suit, showed up in force, chanting "No free speech for the Québécois; no free speech for Turner."[33] They shouted him down when he tried to speak, and after a half-hour he had to give up and leave.

The termination of the *Public Order Act* at the end of April 1971 brought the civil liberties issue back to the fore. Robert Bourassa, the Quebec police, and most Quebec members of the federal Liberal caucus either wanted the act extended or replaced with permanent legislation providing similar powers. Turner would not hear of it. During a vigorous debate in Cabinet, he argued that normal laws were now sufficient to maintain law and order:

> In his opinion the War Measures Act had been invoked in October, because the government did not have enough knowledge about the extent of the threat to public order posed by the F.L.Q. In retrospect it was evident that there had been "substantial overkill" in its application since approximately 495 people had been arrested and only 62 people charged. In any future crisis he was confident that the police and governments had learned a great deal from their experience in October and it would probably not be necessary to invoke the War Measures Act on another such occasion. He himself now doubted that there had been an "apprehended insurrection" and believed that the current Criminal Code was adequate for dealing with most aspects of civil disorder associated with terrorist activity.[34]

"He beat his boss to the draw in a cabinet shootout," wrote *Toronto Star* reporter Rae Corelli, "and now the boss, called Pierre Elliott Trudeau, is angry because no law materialized in time."[35] Newspapers reported that Turner threatened to resign over the issue. He denied it, but in any case his position prevailed, and the act self-destructed as scheduled. Bourassa publicly denounced Turner's "softness, lack of logic and inconsistency."[36] But Turner had both a more realistic assessment of the terrorist threat and greater respect for the principle of civil rights. He also sensed that retrospective concern about the *War Measures Act*'s incursion on civil liberties could be aroused into strong opposition to any special legislation introduced by the government, especially if there were no demonstrable need for it. Sensitive to criticisms that the government had veered right the previous fall, Turner steered back toward the centre.

During the debate on the implementation of the *War Measures Act*, he had told the House, "It is my hope that someday the intelligence upon which the government acted can be made public because until that day comes, the people of Canada will not be able to fully appraise the course of action which has been taken by the government."[37] This pronouncement was odd, because the ambiguity and agitation that precipitated the decision would not be evident in the police intelligence, such as it was, available at the time. Turner was speaking in the heat of a moment when spectral apprehensions beset a confused government under intense pressure.

What Turner actually said and did during the October Crisis told a different story. He had resisted using the *War Measures Act,* consented to it reluctantly, then maintained Cabinet solidarity through the crisis. Once the crisis eased, he led efforts to mitigate the restriction of civil liberties and then restore them fully. "Some of the measures we have had to adopt in the short run and for a short term are philosophically abhorrent to us," he told the Canadian Club of Ottawa on November 12, 1970. "We intend as soon as we can to turn once more to the road of law reform and the continuing enhancement and protection of civil liberties."[38] He followed through on this pledge, ensuring that the October Crisis would represent a temporary rather than a permanent breach of civil rights in Canada.

9

INTRANATIONAL DIPLOMACY

When Turner was appointed minister of justice, political pundits made much of the fact that Trudeau held on to the constitutional file that traditionally went with the portfolio. Turner accepted this condition because he knew that the constitution was Trudeau's special interest and that they had different views on Quebec. It would not be long, however, before Trudeau turned to Turner for help. Together, the two would provide formidable federal leadership during a tumultuous period in federal-provincial relations.

The Trudeau government inherited from the Pearson regime the vexed issue of how to accommodate the feisty French Canadian nationalism of the era. Canada had traditionally taken a hybrid, ambiguous approach to French Canadian rights. Confederation had created two bilingual jurisdictions, the Dominion Government and the Province of Quebec, and had given the provinces those powers deemed essential to enable Quebec to protect French Canadian culture. At the same time, measures were put in place to safeguard the English minority in Quebec and Catholic schools in particular jurisdictions outside Quebec. Later, guarantees for the French language were part of the agreement that brought Manitoba into Confederation in 1870.

French Canadians were influential in federal politics, and they used this power to protect their minority interests. Yet the French fact was not reflected in the public service. Despite its substantial French population, Ottawa was largely run by anglophones. In federal offices it was common to see French Canadian elevator operators, office cleaners, and secretaries but uncommon to find them in senior management. The same pattern prevailed across the country. In the decades after Confederation, English Canadian majorities outside Quebec rode roughshod over guarantees for the French language and Catholic religion. The hanging of Louis Riel, provincial abuses of minority schools and language rights, and wartime conscription crises offered French Canadian nationalists proof that, when the interests of the "two founding nations" came into direct conflict, they would always be vulnerable to the will of the English Canadian majority.

Traditional French Canadian nationalist dogma, which portrayed French Canadians as a Catholic people with a timeless rural way of life antithetical to the godless materialism in the wider commercial world of *les anglais,* had been eclipsed by the Quiet Revolution in 1960. The province took over education, health care, and other social services from the Catholic Church, then went on to nationalize all electrical utilities under Hydro-Québec, giving it cheap electrical power with which to plan and develop the economy. Quebec suddenly had an activist, interventionist government and a new self-image. The transformation was rapid and accompanied by intellectual ferment, including debate about why modernization had been so long delayed in Quebec.

The answer to this question had profound political implications. One school of thought held that nationalism was to blame: French Canadians should shake off their self-imposed fetters and find new freedom and prosperity within the broader context of a renewed Canadian federalism. For others, Confederation and *les anglais* were responsible for French Canadians' past subordination. Nationalism was not the problem but the solution. Only the Quebec state could protect French Canada, and to do so it needed considerable new powers, if not complete autonomy. Pierre Trudeau became the most articulate exponent of the former school of thought, whereas René Lévesque emerged as the champion of the latter when he left the provincial Liberal Party to form the Parti Québécois in 1967.

Turner's attitude toward French Canadian nationalism was not as uncompromising as Trudeau's. He regarded nationalism as a natural part of the human condition and, in moderation, not necessarily a bad thing. He had distinguished himself from Trudeau in the 1968 leadership contest by calling the Quebec issue a matter of the "heart and gut" rather than one of logic and reason. Both men believed in a strong central government. But while Trudeau imagined the nation within an intellectual framework resting on fundamental principles, Turner perceived it as a complex, constantly changing admixture of regions, interests, and cultures that demanded flexible ongoing management.

With Catholicism and agrarianism increasingly relegated to French Canada's past, language issues now loomed all the larger, becoming the single most important marker of French Canadian identity. It was here that the battle for Quebec would be joined. Pearson had appointed the Royal Commission on Bilingualism and Biculturalism soon after coming to power in 1963. Even before its work was completed, he announced a plan to make French Canadians more comfortable with their federal government by promoting bilingualism in the public service. In April 1966 he had assured the House that implementation of bilingualism would be gradual and would not hurt the careers of unilingual public servants.' The cause of Canadian unity would not be helped simply by replacing injustice to French Canadians with injustice to English Canadians.

Trudeau put implementation of bilingualism at the top of his agenda. His close friend, Secretary of State Gérard Pelletier, introduced the *Official Languages Act* (Bill C-120) into the House of Commons for first reading on October 17, 1968. It proposed to make Parliament and the federal government bilingual. Bilingual districts would be established where at least 10 per cent of the population used the minority official language. In these districts and in the National Capital Region, government services would be available in both official languages. Moreover, the courts would have to ensure that anyone appearing or giving evidence before them could do so in either French or English without disadvantage.

Immediately, there was stiff opposition to the bill in English Canada. On one level, resistance stemmed from the chauvinistic assumption that Canada was basically an English-speaking country where, embarrassingly, an odd French minority had somehow persisted. Criticism of this sort tended to stir up opposition by caricaturing the policy as autocratic compulsion: anglophones would have French "forced down their throats" by a government dominated by French Canadians. Confusion fed this apprehension. At one point Turner fielded an inquiry from Joey Smallwood, who wanted to know whether the official bilingualism meant that all Newfoundlanders would have to learn French.

A milder, more credible resistance emanated from Canadians who came from neither French nor English backgrounds and wondered where they fit into the "two founding nations" conception of Canada. From the perspective of Western Canada, where many of these Canadians lived, it was difficult not to view the Quebec issue as central Canada's problem – indeed, as one of those perverse central Canadian obsessions that contributed to Ottawa's pathological neglect of the West. Criticisms from the "third force," Canadians whose ethnocultural identity was neither English nor French, had already scuppered the bicultural premise of the Royal Commission on Bilingualism and Biculturalism, and now threatened to sink its language recommendations as well.

The proposed policy also provoked practical concerns about its implementation. Premiers, particularly in the West, wondered how they were going to transform their unilingual court systems into functionally bilingual operations, especially when there were so few bilingual professionals in their workforces.[2] They worried that, as they scrambled to meet the bill's requirements, sharp lawyers would use the new legislation to frustrate the course of justice. They were also uncomfortable with French-language requirements in the federal bureaucracy, fearing that their citizens, who were overwhelmingly anglophone, would be at a disadvantage in competing for jobs there.

The government's initial response to these criticisms fed anglophone paranoia about "French power" by creating the impression that a French Canadian clique was ramming the policy through Parliament. Although Trudeau and Pelletier had spent their lives wrestling with Quebec issues, they had never been sensitized to how they played in the West. Convinced of the righteousness of their cause and its indispensability to national unity, they displayed an unfortunate tendency to regard its critics as crypto-racist, intellectually challenged, or some combination of the two. Pelletier had little experience steering legislation through the House of Commons. When Western opposition MPs expressed their concerns about the bill, he was uncompromising, even dismissive. But opposition was not so easily repulsed. Turner was approached by Jimmy Walker, a popular MP from York Centre who chaired the Liberal caucus. The feedback from the constituencies was alarming, Walker told him, and a caucus revolt was brewing. Walker said he was going to ask Trudeau to bring Turner in to salvage the legislation.

Turner was the obvious man for the job. He had a background in Quebec and the credibility of being bilingual. He knew and was trusted by many of the leading politicians in the West. Moreover, he had the parliamentary expertise to finesse the legislation through the House. By bringing in an English Canadian to champion the bill, the government could pre-empt simplistic French versus English, East versus West readings of the standoff. Trudeau took Walker's advice and asked Turner to help out.[3] Despite being in the middle of managing the omnibus bill and developing his legal reform agenda, Turner signed on. He thought official bilingualism was a just policy that was vital to national unity, and he feared English Canadian indifference to issues that the Québécois regarded as vital. He believed that the *Official Languages Act* would be a bulwark of national unity, but he also understood the practical problems it presented for the provinces and for unilingual Canadians, especially in Western Canada. Most importantly, his political instincts told him that, if bilingualism were to work, people would have to agree with it in principle and cooperate willingly.

The bilingualism issue intersected with ongoing federal-provincial constitutional negotiations. Pearson's 1968 constitutional summit had revitalized talks that had proceeded sporadically since the Second World War. A follow-up conference was now slated to convene in early February 1969. Canadian constitutional talks had a predictable pattern. The federal government wanted to patriate the Canadian constitution, which continued to be a statute of the British Parliament at Westminster. Ottawa consulted the provinces before doing anything because it was politically preferable, if not legally imperative, to have their agreement to patriation and the terms on which the constitution would reside in Canada. The most contentious issue was how the constitution would be amended. The federal government wanted a practical arrangement that would make changes politically possible; each province wanted a formula that would maximize its own influence on the process. In exchange for agreeing to patriation and an amending formula, the provinces invariably demanded more powers. Trudeau had expressed an interest in having a charter of rights added to the constitution when it was patriated, and the provinces felt they could extract even more concessions in return for agreeing to this request. Finally, constitutional negotiations offered Quebec a vehicle to advance its claims for special status as the government representing the French Canadian homeland. It wanted more powers than the other provinces, but Trudeau was determined to treat them all the same way.

As if these issues were not enough, it now looked as though there might be a nasty confrontation over the *Official Languages Act* at the upcoming conference in February. The week before it began, the premiers of the Prairie provinces sent a telegram to the prime minister questioning the constitutionality of certain parts of the bill and threatening to test its validity before the Supreme Court. Trudeau hinted at apocalyptic consequences, telling reporters that such a challenge would "confirm the belief of some Quebecers that a bilingual country is impossible" and that that would be "the end of the ball game."[4] Turner, for his part, declared stoutly that, if it came to that, he would personally represent the government before the Supreme Court. Yet the government did not really want to go to court. Whatever their outcome, legal proceedings would damage the very national unity that the *Official Languages Act* was intended to repair.

With a crisis looming, Turner went on the road to talk to the provinces about constitutional matters generally and the *Official Languages Act* in particular. At each stop he sat down with the premier and key officials, heard their side of the issue, presented matters from his perspective, and explored common ground. He was already on good terms with W.A.C. Bennett, who was a friend of his stepfather, Frank Ross. Bennett dealt with the issue efficiently. "John," he asked, "is bilingualism and biculturalism good for the unity of the country? If you say so, that's fine with me." Turner said so. Bennett asked that, in return for his support, the federal government would make its next justice appointment to the Supreme Court from British Columbia. Trudeau agreed. Turner and Bennett sealed the deal with a handshake.[5]

Alberta premier Harry Strom had just come to office, so Turner's discussions with him were inconclusive. In Saskatchewan he dealt with Liberal premier Ross Thatcher, who months earlier had responded to Turner's reforms at Consumer and Corporate Affairs by calling him a communist. Later, however, Diefenbaker had taken Thatcher and Turner fishing when they were all vacationing in Barbados, and the two had gotten along, so

Thatcher was prepared to give Turner a hearing. Their relationship warmed through the negotiations. Thatcher had no time for Trudeau or Otto Lang, the leading federal Liberal from the province, so Turner became the federal ambassador to Saskatchewan on this and subsequent issues.

In Manitoba Turner met with Premier Walter Weir and Attorney General Sterling Lyon. He also defended the *Official Languages Act* before the local press.[6] It was not just for French Canadians from Quebec, he stressed, but for French Canadians outside Quebec and for English Canadians within Quebec too. And it would not cost any jobs. Federal employees in positions designated French speaking would get plenty of opportunity to learn the language.

Trudeau had his principal secretary, Marc Lalonde, accompany Turner on his trip to Quebec City to meet Premier Jean-Jacques Bertrand. The Quebec premier was more concerned with constitutional issues than the language bill but strongly objected to the establishment of bilingual districts – which, in the Quebec case, meant providing services in English. He was not in good health, however, and his political mandate was precarious. Turner advised Trudeau to take these factors into account and play for time.[7]

Throughout these negotiations, Turner looked for ways to change the legislation to assuage the provinces' fears without compromising its effectiveness. He was willing to work with them to define more precisely the conditions under which court proceedings should be conducted in a minority language. The premiers also wanted to be consulted about the establishment of bilingual districts – a reasonable request, Turner thought. To quiet fears that unilingual anglophones would face discrimination in the federal public service, he emphasized that the criterion for employment would not be the ability to speak French, but the willingness to learn to speak French.

As the constitutional conference approached, there was a sense that everything was up for grabs. Quebec was talking about renaming the country "the Canadian Union," and British Columbia's Bennett promised to bring a map – in colour, for the television cameras – showing how Canada could be consolidated into five provinces. The two-day conference opened on February 10, 1969. Whereas the previous year Trudeau had sat beside Pearson at the head of the conference table, now it was Turner beside

Trudeau. Trudeau's main objectives were to get acceptance in principle of the official languages policy and a charter of rights. First, the federal side had to endure a barrage of provincial complaints about how Ottawa dominated taxation and abused its spending power while saddling the provinces with expensive social programs such as health care. Once the premiers had unburdened themselves, Trudeau made his pitch for the charter. Most provinces were more receptive to the idea than they had been the year before, but British Columbia, Alberta, and Manitoba remained opposed. The balance of the conference was spent discussing redistribution of powers, without much apparent progress. Quebec continued to be aggressive in its demands, with Bertrand arguing that Canada consisted of two communities and that, because Quebec spoke for one of them, it deserved special status in any constitutional renewal. Commentators doubted that the gap between Quebec's and Ottawa's positions could ever be bridged.

When discussion turned to the *Official Languages Act,* Turner's diplomatic mission paid off. The premiers were restrained in their criticisms, saying that their opposition to the act rested on concerns that some of its sections trespassed on provincial jurisdiction over the courts. Alberta's Harry Strom went so far as to say that he understood French Canadians' linguistic concerns and that the provinces had a responsibility to accommodate them. The parties agreed to continue to negotiate and, to this end, Turner committed to follow-up meetings with the provincial attorneys general. Meanwhile, the federal government would go ahead with second reading of the act. After that, the act would be discussed in a parliamentary committee, where the provinces could testify if they wished. On the whole the conference was more positive and productive than the previous one. Federal-provincial committees were created to continue work on outstanding issues. With this stratagem, the conference ended cordially. Turner's part in the positive outcome was acknowledged in the press.[8]

Turner met with Attorneys General Sterling Lyon of Manitoba, Darrel Heald of Saskatchewan, Edgar Gerhart of Alberta, and Leslie Peterson of British Columbia in Victoria the following week. They went over the *Official Languages Act* clause by clause, discussing its implications and potential changes. Turner told reporters that the meeting had been "very constructive" and praised his provincial counterparts for being open-minded.[9] Over the next four months, he travelled west several times to negotiate details with provincial officials. He stoutly defended the principle behind the bill and its constitutionality, while showing himself to be flexible about ways and means.[10] Here again he was avoiding confrontations over principles – which reasonable people could disagree about – in favour of practical negotiations through which reasonable people could find common ground and workable solutions. As talks progressed, the terms of the debate shifted subtly but significantly from whether the *Official Languages Act* were acceptable to how it would be implemented.

Turner's negotiating technique blended bravado, male bonding, and horse trading. "I said 'Come on, you guys,'" he told a reporter, "and once I had a few drinks with the guys and we gave them a few amendments, so the thing got through."[11] He also deployed his usual sales technique, the speech sortie, to allay fears about official bilingualism in the West. On one of these forays that April in Edmonton, he again defended the *Official Languages Act* as essential to the future of the country while dismissing the wild rumours about its implications. Bilingualism would not mean that everyone would be forced to speak French, he assured his audience – it was simply intended to provide equality of access to government services. He addressed the criticism that those who were not of French or English stock would be second-class citizens by declaring unequivocally that there was only one class of citizen in Canada. He appealed to tolerance, fair play, and selfless patriotism. The fact that he went west in person to deliver the message contributed to its favourable reception.

Turner outlined his thinking on amendments to the *Official Languages Act* in memoranda to Cabinet on March 19 and May 6, 1969. After summarizing his talks with the four Western attorneys general and reminding his colleagues of those provinces' threat to take the legislation to court, he outlined some concessions that would allay the premiers' concerns without compromising the bill's basic principles.[12] The provinces would not challenge the bill if they were given more say about what bilingual services to offer in the courts, and how soon, as well as the right to be consulted on the designation of bilingual districts. Pelletier and a few others thought Turner was caving in to bigotry, but Cabinet as a whole sided with Turner.

"The cost of bilingualism is part of the price of being Canadian," Turner told the House of Commons during the debate following introduction of the *Official Languages Act* for second reading on May 16, 1969.[13] He promised

amendments to meet provincial concerns about some of its details, especially regarding the courts. On July 3 he assured the House that public
servants would not suffer career setbacks for being unilingual without first
being given adequate opportunity to learn the second official language.[14]
Although Diefenbaker and sixteen other Conservatives, mostly from
Western Canada, opposed the act on second reading, it was approved
without a formal vote on third reading on July 7 and came into effect on
September 7, 1969. Turner had played a critical role in getting it through
Parliament and avoiding a damaging confrontation with the Western
provinces.

The government hoped to have the civil service functionally bilingual
by 1975. Turner advised Trudeau not to push too hard at first. Anglophone
public servants – who comprised a substantial portion of his constituents
in Ottawa-Carleton – were worried about their jobs. Their careers depended
on how many positions would be designated bilingual, how soon, and what
level of bilingualism would be required. Turner heard from friends that
the English community in Montreal was even more agitated about the bill
than his constituents. He continued to address such fears in his public
remarks on the bill, assuring anglophones they would get the French training they needed.

Soon Turner was hearing complaints that the Public Service Commission
was pushing bilingualism without regard for the government's pledges to
anglophones. In October 1969 a tax auditor in Montreal wrote that he had
been rejected from a job competition because he was not bilingual.[15] He
appealed his rejection, quoting Pearson's and Turner's assurances about
job security for anglophones. The appeal board stated that it was bound
only by acts of Parliament, not politicians' pronouncements, yet overturned
the competition on technical grounds. In the new competition, however,
the French-language requirements were raised. When the auditor entered
a competition for a lower-level position, he was told he did not meet its
language requirements. He appealed again, this time unsuccessfully.[16] The
board ruled that because he had lived in Quebec for a decade, he'd had
plenty of time to learn French – a decision that suggested the *Official
Languages Act* applied retroactively.

Turner wrote to John Carson, chairman of the Public Service Commission.
"No meaningful opportunity has been provided to the English speaking

auditors in the Montreal Department to improve their French," he said. "Accordingly, I am deeply disturbed by the attitude being shown in this situation." Carson was uncooperative. Turner sent letters to Pelletier and Trudeau, expressing his worry that the policy was being applied zealously, risking an explosive backlash in English Canada.[17]

The auditor talked to a journalist, William Morris, and asked for permission to publish his correspondence with Turner. A Turner aide told him "to use his judgment."[18] Morris published articles about the case in the *Toronto Globe and Mail* on July 15 and 16, 1970, generating outrage in the English-language media nationwide.[19] Turner had considered raising the case in Cabinet, but now there was no need. The political implications of a ham-handed implementation were clear. Still, he felt that Trudeau and Pelletier failed to recognize and appreciate both the English-speaking public servants' fears and their efforts to learn French. He rued their failure to make any sort of gesture to ease the political pressure bilingualism placed on English-speaking Liberals.

There was a small but sour and foreboding footnote to Turner's crusade for bilingualism. When a Supreme Court position came open in 1973, Trudeau ignored Turner's promise to Bennett that a BC bencher would get the nod and, instead, appointed a Manitoba judge, Brian Dickson. Turner heard about this ahead of time and stalled the appointment for a week. When it went through regardless, he flew out to Vancouver to apologize to Bennett in person. Turner retained his confidence, but Bennett never trusted Trudeau again. Turner, for his part, did not break ranks over the incident. But it was an episode he would remember.[20]

While the implementation of the *Official Languages Act* was being sorted out, talks on the constitution continued. On June 11 and 12, 1969, the prime minister and the premiers had met in Ottawa to review the division of powers, taxing and spending, regional disparity, and shared-cost programs. Their discussions continued at conferences in Ottawa in December 1969 and February 1970.[21]

The negotiations over the *Official Languages Act* had proved Turner's effectiveness as an ambassador to the provinces, and he now resumed his shuttle diplomacy to help conclude a constitutional agreement. Aside from Quebec, the provinces were not very motivated or informed about constitutional reform. It became clear that a comprehensive reform package would be too complicated and politically treacherous to negotiate. Still, all parties recognized that some constructive result was desirable for the sake of national unity. In the end, they agreed to patriate the constitution, combine it with a manageable package of reforms, and leave other issues to be resolved through future negotiations.[22] The federal government worked out a package with Quebec, and it then fell to Turner to secure the English Canadian premiers' agreement. In Newfoundland he discussed the state of the world, particularly Newfoundland politics, with Premier Joey Smallwood. Almost as an afterthought, Smallwood then asked, "So what do you need constitutionally?"[23] In Saskatchewan, Thatcher accorded Turner the honour of speaking from the floor of the legislature – the first time someone not a member of the legislature had been allowed this privilege. In British Columbia, Bennett, who would host the June 1971 constitutional conference in Victoria, sent his limousine to the airport for Turner and was waiting for him on the steps of the legislature when he arrived. He also asked Turner to speak from the floor of the BC legislature. Later, Turner was accorded a similar honour in Prince Edward Island. These symbolic gestures recognized his growing political stature and signalled that a historic agreement was imminent.

At the Third Working Session of the Constitutional Conference, convened in Ottawa in February 1971, the prime minister and the premiers agreed in principle to patriate the constitution. It seemed that a full agreement would be possible at the Victoria conference that June. Turner flew to England in late May to discuss with British officials how the *British North America Act* could be transferred to Canada. He was careful to make it clear that he was not prejudging the outcome of the June conference, but it was necessary to give the British a heads-up in case the issue did arise in the coming months.

Before he left, Quebec threw a wrench into the works. It was having second thoughts, belatedly recognizing that the negotiations leading up to an agreement in Victoria might be its last chance to gain full control over social policy. Administrative arrangements had previously been agreed on for family allowances and manpower training, but now Quebec wanted its prerogative in these areas included in section 94A of the *BNA Act,* a clause that gave the provinces primacy over old age pensions and associated benefits. In effect, it wanted to be able to opt out of all federal programs and be compensated financially by Ottawa for the money it would have spent in Quebec on the equivalent national programs. When Turner met with his provincial counterparts after his return from Britain, he diplomatically allowed that he was "surprised" by this new demand but downplayed the issue for fear of jeopardizing the success of the conference, now just two weeks away.[24]

When the conference convened in Victoria on June 14, negotiations were complex and exhausting. On the fourth and last day, thirteen hours were devoted to meetings – some were closed sessions of the full conference chaired by Trudeau, whereas others, chaired by Turner, were committee deliberations on the Supreme Court, which was now to be enshrined in the constitution for the first time. The first ministers agreed to a charter of rights. There would be an amending formula that effectively gave Quebec a constitutional veto. Equalization payments were to be embedded in the new constitution as well. English and French would be confirmed as Canada's two official languages, and citizens would be able to use either language in their dealings with Ottawa. In addition, legislatures were to become bilingual in all provinces except the three most westerly (British Columbia, Alberta, and Saskatchewan), and courts would be bilingual in New Brunswick and Newfoundland (the legislature and courts were already bilingual in Quebec). Three Supreme Court judges were to be from Quebec.

The other provinces were reluctant to give Quebec the extra powers it had recently demanded on social policy, and the federal government fretted about ceding to the provinces all direct contact with its citizens. Eventually "family, youth and occupational training allowances" were added to section 94A, along with a clause preventing federal legislation from overriding present or future provincial law – a concession of the federal powers of reservation and disallowance that had symbolized federal supremacy since Confederation. Turner felt the final package gave Quebec what it needed to protect its French Canadian majority. But Bourassa wasn't certain it was enough, and he asked to consult with his Cabinet before confirming the deal.[25] Whether he would expend the political capital necessary to get agreement back home remained to be seen. The separatist Parti Québécois was gaining support and would undoubtedly accuse him of selling out. On his return to Quebec, Bourassa was indeed met with harsh accusations that he had failed to secure the powers Quebec needed to protect its distinctiveness.

A blistering attack by Claude Ryan, the influential editor of *Le Devoir,* was particularly devastating. On June 23 Quebec announced its rejection of the draft agreement – the Victoria Charter was dead.

"We are all a little shell shocked," Turner admitted.[26] Though not entirely unexpected, this outcome was a cruel disappointment. The prize – a solution to the Quebec question that had been plaguing national affairs for a decade – had been tantalizingly within grasp. In the wake of the October Crisis violence, it had been especially tempting to demonstrate that "sunny ways" and established institutions could produce a just and lasting accommodation. "We have never been closer to our own home-made constitution," Turner wrote in his notes. "Sharp setback for constitutional review. Missed opportunity [to] bring constitution to Canada. Process will undoubtedly be shelved for some time."[27] The federal negotiators were disappointed with Bourassa, who had jilted them after they had gone to the wall for him. All the good will Turner had helped generate toward Quebec among the other provinces suddenly disappeared. "A unique opportunity has been missed to modernize our constitution," he told the *Ottawa Citizen.*[28]

Turner had now been minister of justice for more than three years. When *Toronto Star* reporter Rae Corelli interviewed him that year, he noted "a new bluntness. There is more grey in the hair. The eyes are harder, less compromising. There is less apparent concern with image and more with objectives."[29] A member of the Liberal caucus enumerated Turner's accomplishments with a note of awe: "He carried the can for the whole War Measures Act almost from the beginning. They stuck him with selling that Official Languages Act in the West and he sold it. He's got a wad of legislation through or pending in the Commons that would choke a goat."[30]

Turner's relations with Trudeau remained cordial. When Trudeau was single, the Turners occasionally had him over for dinner at their house on Prospect Avenue in Rockcliffe Park. Turner's wife, Geills, helped Margaret Trudeau adjust to Ottawa after the Trudeaus' surprise marriage in March 1971. On Christmas Eve later that year, Margaret Trudeau wanted to attend an English church service, so Trudeau phoned Turner and asked if they could join them for midnight mass. Turner called his parish priest at Our Lady of Mount Carmel to let him know that the prime minister and his very pregnant wife would be in the congregation that night. The next morning, Margaret gave birth to the Trudeaus' first child, Justin.[31]

17 On July 6, 1968, Turner (third from right) joined other Cabinet nominees walking up the drive at Rideau Hall to be sworn into office. Pierre Trudeau, fourth from the right, takes the lead. On the far left is James Richardson (minister without portfolio), and, partially hidden behind Trudeau, Don Jamieson (minister without portfolio). Second from the right is Jean Marchand (minister of forestry and rural development), while on the far right is Gérard Pelletier (secretary of state).

18 Along with measures pertaining to abortion and homosexuality, the omnibus bill of reforms to the Criminal Code, which Turner oversaw as minister of justice, aimed to combat drunk driving with a novel piece of technology, the breathalyzer (pictured here with Turner at a press conference in Ottawa, November 14, 1969). At the same time, Turner launched a publicity campaign against drinking and driving.

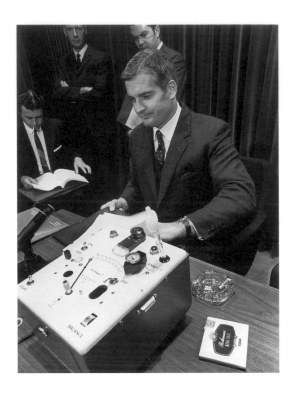

19 Trudeau and Turner emerge from Trudeau's office on Parliament Hill in the early hours of the morning on October 18, 1970, the night that Pierre Laporte's body was discovered. "That's the closest I ever felt to him," Turner later recalled. "We were like buddies in combat. I mean, when you stand beside a guy who's eyeball-to-eyeball with danger and he doesn't blink, you can't help but feel admiration."

20 Turner walking to Parliament Hill, November 11, 1970, guarded by one of the soldiers called out to protect prominent officials during the October Crisis. At Turner's house in Rockcliffe Park, soldiers trampled the rose bushes while his wife and children went about their daily routines unattended. "You can appreciate how difficult it is for me as a strong advocate of civil rights over the years to share some responsibility for this stern emergency posture," he wrote a friend, referring to the *War Measures Act,* "but ... a threat to the very structure of society can only be met sometimes by a temporary suspension of some of the ordinary rights to which we are accustomed."

21 The Turner family in 1972. In front of John, left to right, Elizabeth (born March 8, 1964), David (born May 14, 1968), and Michael (born October 28, 1965). Geills Turner is holding Andrew (born October 7, 1971). Turner's growing family was a large factor in his ongoing internal debate about retiring from politics in the early 1970s. Early in 1975, he would outline the factors affecting his decision on an index card: "New career (1). PM set for duration (2). No other challenges (3). Lack of stimulus at Cabinet table (4). Family (5). Finances (6). Am[?] right for new start (7). Uncertainty of Quebec (8)."

23 *(facing page, bottom)* Turner, with Trudeau steps behind, heads to the House of Commons to present his first budget, May 8, 1972. "It is the one event where Parliament and the country focus completely," he observed. "There's a countdown ... like opening night for an actor with an overwhelming role."

22 At the Victoria Conference in June of 1971, Turner, Trudeau, and Marchand confer with Ontario premier John Robarts (second from left). "We have never been closer to our own home-made constitution," wrote Turner ruefully when the Victoria deal fell through, "Sharp setback for constitutional review. Missed opportunity [to] bring constitution to Canada. Process will undoubtedly be shelved for some time."

24 After talking through trade problems and other economic issues at the White House, Turner and US secretary of the treasury George Shultz would often repair to the tennis courts for a quick game, sometimes followed by dinner with the president. This photograph, taken in 1973, was inscribed from Shultz, "To John Turner, a great partner on and off the court, with my great admiration and very best wishes."

26 When the energy crisis put Ottawa and Alberta at loggerheads over oil resources, it was Turner – the government's most effective emissary and negotiator – who got the job of dealing with Premier Peter Lougheed. This photograph was taken in July 1973 at the Western Economic Opportunities Conference in Calgary.

25 *(facing page, bottom)* Simon Reisman, deputy minister of finance, with Turner at a parliamentary committee in the early 1970s. Although they were allies in the struggle to control government spending, Reisman could be difficult to manage. He told Turner he was a poker player who won nineteen out of twenty times. "You haven't played me," was Turner's reply. Reisman would later be Canada's chief negotiator for the Canada–US Free Trade Agreement and denounce Turner as a "traitor" for opposing the deal.

27 "Jumping Ship," *Toronto Star* political cartoonist Duncan Macpherson's take on the Turner resignation. Citing the tradition of successful French-English leadership duos in Canadian politics, veteran journalist Bruce Hutchison saw dire consequences from Turner's departure. "When no other English-speaking member of the government enjoys or is likely ever to win anything like Mr. Turner's almost bi-partisan influence," he wrote, "Mr. Trudeau lacks the partner essential to his own success and the nation's welfare."

28 On December 10, 1979, Turner met the press in Toronto to announce that he would not be entering the race to replace retired Liberal leader Pierre Trudeau. Geills Turner is in the left foreground. In passing on the opportunity, he confounded observers who saw him as a prince in exile itching for an opportune moment to reclaim power.

Despite such friendly encounters, politics conspired against a close and trusting relationship. Turner was being hailed as "the best Justice Minister since Confederation."[32] His status in the party, the government, and the nation at large was now unrivalled by any politician but Trudeau himself. Although Turner was scrupulously loyal and did nothing to challenge Trudeau's authority, he did hope to succeed him as prime minister one day. Trudeau justifiably had apprehensions about a once and future leadership rival.

The different political styles of Turner and Trudeau were becoming more apparent as the Liberals' term of office progressed. Hoping to rationalize decision making and make it more efficient, Trudeau had created an elaborate system of Cabinet committees. Some ministers enjoyed the cut and thrust of debate at these meetings, but critics likened them to academic seminars in which eager beavers competed to win the gold star as the brightest student. Turner found them time consuming and largely pointless. He believed that the system generated unnecessary intrigue as Cabinet ministers negotiated support for each other's proposals. Public servants learned how to manipulate the system and wielded undue power. Captured by bureaucratic process, the politicians lost touch with their constituencies and the way political winds were blowing. "The collegiality system destroyed the integrity, accountability and responsibility of the line depart ments," he later complained. "[It] made the business of government burdensome, slow, cumbersome, ineffective and expensive. It crippled the strong ministers and protected the weak ministers. And it crippled the strong departments and the strong deputies, and protected the weak ones."[33] He eventually grew openly contemptuous of the entire regime. Unless he had an item on the agenda, he would send a representative to Cabinet committee meetings. If he did have an item on the agenda, as soon as it was disposed of, he would claim some urgent appointment and leave. Trudeau rather admired Turner for this behaviour. "I often suspect the only appointment John Turner has to keep is a tennis game, but he gets away with it," he told another minister.[34]

The *Official Languages Act* episode pointed up other differences between Trudeau and Turner. Many Canadians responded positively to Trudeau as a leader who knew his own mind and would resolutely see his vision realized. Yet his fearless, principled leadership antagonized powerful constituencies, particularly the West and the business community. Turner, in contrast, saw himself as having been schooled in a pragmatic apprenticeship in the trenches of the party. Canada was not the logical construct that Trudeau seemed to expect, but rather, a jury-rigged contraption best coaxed along by a sensitive operator with an ear for any change of pitch in its internal workings. Personal relationships and diplomacy were the duct tape and WD-40 of Canadian politics. Turner was the kind of operator who was in tune with the particularities and vagaries of the Canadian body politic and had a realistic appreciation of how hard the machinery could be pushed. "One of the major differences between John Napier Turner and Pierre Elliott Trudeau [is that] the former has always thought a politician can get farther with honey than with vinegar," one political journalist concluded. "Turner likes to avoid confrontation. He'd rather talk than knock political heads. He believes that verbal brawls and put-downs are unproductive, that you don't always look good by making your opponent look bad."[35]

In contrast to the self-contained and self-controlled Trudeau, Turner was always looking for feedback and approval.[36] While serving as justice minister, he continued to cultivate his network of friends and supporters in the Liberal Party. A Turner supporter had buttons reading "195 Club" made up, and hundreds were distributed across the country. It reinforced the myth of the 195 Club that, in its most exaggerated form, imagined that Turner's fourth-ballot supporters from 1968 endured as a kind of secret organization still busily working underground to win their man the top prize. Diehard Turner delegates did indeed meet for annual reunions for a few years after the 1968 leadership, but only in an ad hoc fashion, and no formal organization developed.[37] The 195 Club wasn't a club at all, but rather a loose-knit bunch of loyal supporters Turner stayed in touch with who might support him in the future.

Turner's network also encompassed key figures in the public service and the media in Ottawa. *Toronto Star* journalist Jack Cahill was just one of many he cultivated. As Cahill recalled,

> In the early 1970's, when I was Ottawa bureau chief for *The Toronto Star* and Turner was Justice Minister, I came to know him fairly well, as most senior journalists did, both as a contact and as a friendly acquaintance.

Frequently, when other cabinet ministers were lunching in the opulent Parliamentary Restaurant or the expensive Chateau Grill, Turner and I would lunch at his favourite haunt, the old Belvedere Hotel on Albert Street, where the members of the Ottawa Rough Riders football team hung out and which turned itself into a cheap jazz joint at night. Turner liked the jock atmosphere of the place and probably liked the bills, which we always shared, because he was not a rich man. Our lunch was usually a hamburger and a beer, which cost about $1.50 for each of us. He would talk political philosophy and personalities with surprising frankness for a cabinet minister, but never once, as far as I can remember, did he tip me to an actual story, and certainly not to a cabinet secret.[38]

Turner and Trudeau had different political styles that generated contrasting public images. This wasn't necessarily a bad thing: their strengths could complement one another for the benefit of the party and the nation. Whereas Trudeau's intellect and will commanded the respect of the electorate, Turner humanized the party's image by being down-to-earth, approachable, and accommodating. Turner would have been a formidable asset to any party, but the way in which his strengths compensated for the leader's shortcomings gave him particular value. As minister of justice, he was on an equal footing in Cabinet with established heavyweights such as Mitchell Sharp and Allan MacEachen, and his standing in the party generally had by now eclipsed that of any other anglophone. Through hard work, political smarts, resilience, and sheer talent, John Turner had emerged as the leading English Canadian Liberal of his time.

10

SHOKKU

By the summer of 1971, John Turner was seriously considering whether he should leave politics. On August 13 he jotted down a brief political calculus of pros and cons. On the one hand, he liked being at the centre of the action and acknowledged the claims of "duty to country" – his shorthand phrase for serving Canada. On the other hand, he was making far less money than he could in the private sector, a factor made increasingly relevant by his growing family – he now had three children, with another on the way. He added, intriguingly, "incompatibility with Trudeau gov't" but did not elaborate. The fact that he had a lot invested in his political career and had a chance of becoming prime minister also weighed into the equation. Yet the prospect of replacing Trudeau was uncertain: no matter how deserving he was, political fortune was capricious. Turner also saw his image as a liability. Despite his reform record, there was something about his appearance and manner that came across as establishment, privileged, and, compared to Trudeau, staid. Despite these misgivings, for the time being he leaned toward staying in politics. But he was ready for a new challenge. He thought it would be good to gain some experience in an economic portfolio dealing with "hot" issues.[1]

Economic issues were hot because the economy was experiencing its most serious troubles since the war. In the late 1960s, the cost of living began to rise faster than normal. The Canadian government promised to "wrestle inflation to the ground," only to find itself grappling for a firm grip on a slippery opponent. By tightening the money supply and raising interest rates, it reduced the inflation rate to 3.3 per cent in 1970, the lowest in any industrialized country, but caused unemployment to rise to around 6 per cent. Higher interest rates also attracted foreign capital and put upward pressure on the Canadian dollar, which had been pegged at US92.5 cents. To ease the pressure, the government had to increase the money supply so it could buy foreign currencies, but this response only fuelled inflation. To escape this bind, in May 1970 the government let the Canadian dollar float. Thereafter, Canada's high interest rates caused its dollar to appreciate higher than the American dollar, and that hurt exports. These problems might not seem serious in comparison with the economic disruptions of subsequent decades, but at the time, relative to the untroubled growth and prosperity of the preceding quarter century, they were both grave and perplexing.

While wrestling with these economic woes, the Trudeau government had also tackled tax reform. The Royal Commission on Taxation, headed by the respected accountant Kenneth Carter, had been appointed by Diefenbaker in 1962 to suggest reforms to Canada's tax system. The Carter Report, published in 1966, recommended a simpler, more equitable taxation policy that would treat all income the same and abolish many loopholes. The Trudeau government largely ignored the radical single-tax idea but suggested some reforms in a 1969 white paper on taxation. Wealthy Canadians and corporations that stood to pay more tax lobbied ferociously against these proposals. Finance Minister Edgar Benson eventually introduced some changes, including a capital gains tax, but he failed to prepare the ground politically – so much so that opposition to his reforms was spearheaded by a Liberal, Izzy Asper, a Manitoba businessman and former provincial party leader. While Turner was merrily reforming the justice system, Benson was eviscerated by business for changes to the tax system. Money evidently mattered more than morality or rights in Canadian politics.

On August 15, 1971, just two days after Turner jotted down his reflections on leaving politics, US president Richard Nixon announced his New Economic Policy (NEP). The United States had enjoyed economic preeminence in the years following the Second World War and had indulgently umpired global trade by, among other things, underwriting the international currency exchange system. But now it was incurring a worrisome trade deficit. Rival trading nations such as Germany and Japan had rebuilt their industrial capacity with newer, more efficient technologies and equipment, and were not burdened, as the United States was, with defence expenditures.[2] With the competition heating up, the States could no longer afford to subsidize its commercial adversaries.

The Nixon *shokku,* as the Japanese called it, was, on one level, a series of economic measures, including wage and price controls and a 10 per cent surtax on imports, aimed at boosting America's international competitiveness and righting its trade deficit. Symbolically, however, it was much more than that. It signalled that the United States had changed from everyone's indulgent rich uncle into the hard-nosed neighbourhood bully. This new attitude was personified by the irascible secretary of the treasury, John Connally, who immediately began strong-arming trading partners into line. "My basic approach," he declared, "is that the foreigners are out to screw us. Our job is to screw them first."[3]

At first the Canadian government thought that the Americans had targeted Canada along with other nations by mistake. Canadians surely were not "foreigners." Didn't the two countries have a special relationship? When Benson and other officials trekked to Washington to straighten things out, they had a rude shock. Connally's sights were firmly trained north of the border. In his view, there was no sense in trying to rectify the US trade deficit without dealing with its top trading partner, which was currently enjoying a trade surplus from the relationship. Canada had special privileges that could no longer be justified. Connally wanted changes to the Auto Pact, the 1965 bilateral trade deal for car manufacturing, which was responsible for thousands of auto worker jobs in central Canada, and to the Defence Production Sharing Agreement, which guaranteed Canadian suppliers access to US military contracts.

By late 1971, then, Trudeau had a finance minister who had been battered for his management of domestic economic policy, tax reform, and, most recently, the trade crisis. Benson asked for less onerous duties. Looking for a competent replacement who could inspire public confidence, Trudeau turned to Turner. They discussed terms over dinner. Turner opposed introducing protectionist measures in response to the Gray Report on foreign investment, which Cabinet was then considering, and Trudeau agreed – Cabinet was too spooked by recent economic developments to risk scaring off capital investment. He assured Turner that he would respect the prerogative of the Department of Finance to set economic policy, and they agreed that it would be important for the minister of finance to reach out to the business community. On the basis of these understandings, Turner accepted the offer.[4] At forty-two years of age, he would be the youngest minister of finance in the twentieth century.[5] On top of that, he was taking on the most difficult portfolio in Cabinet at one of the most challenging moments in post-war economic history.

On November 18, 1971, with his new appointment still under wraps, Turner raised his profile on economic issues with an address to the Empire Club of Toronto. He discussed economic growth, unemployment, and inflation, and zeroed in on the Nixon shocks, advocating a constructive response rather than the immediate gratification of sniping or retaliation. The same cautious approach characterized his stance on foreign investment. Finally, he explicitly rejected the idea of trying to eliminate economic irritants with the United States by negotiating a free-trade deal. "The political consequences would be irreversible and would dilute or even destroy any claim we had to our own sovereignty," he declared.[6]

Turner's new portfolio was announced as part of a Cabinet shuffle in January 1972. In discussing the appointment, Trudeau told reporters that he was "not one to make shuffles just for the heck of it." As he explained, "I find it hard work. Management of men – or women for that matter – is not my strong suit."[7] The economy would be a major issue in the coming election, he explained, so he had decided to put a strong minister in place to deal with it. "No one will suggest that Turner is a weak minister," he noted. "One characteristic of Turner is that he likes to succeed."[8] The press interpreted Turner's appointment as an attempt to reassure the private sector, the major source of campaign funding, in the run-up to the next election. Business required some hand holding, and Trudeau had given it the government's most effective emissary and negotiator.

The in-joke in Ottawa was that Trudeau's hidden agenda was to destroy the career of his main political rival. "I recalled the day Turner was sworn into that job, on a cold January 28, 1972, when I met him in the washroom at Government House where he was taking off his overshoes, and asked whatever possessed him to take it," wrote national columnist Charles Lynch. "He smacked his lips the way he does and said that when his leader asked him to do something, he did it. Did it not seem a trap set for him by Trudeau? He paused, smiled that non-smile of his where the eyes stayed cold, and said it was just his duty. Just that."⁹ Turner was well aware of the potential pitfalls of the job, but the upside was just as great. Finance could boost his national political profile still higher and, given recent developments, offer him a chance to prove himself on the international stage. The trajectory of his career had always been onward and upward, meeting challenges and moving on to bigger things. This was just the latest step and, with any luck, the penultimate one.

Nevertheless, the fate of his predecessor was enough to give any ambitious politician pause. Turner thought Benson had been treated unfairly, but there was no reason for both of them to be martyred. As soon as he took over, he signalled that he would implement Benson's tax reforms "carefully." He also took pains to win the public's trust. When he gave his first address in the House of Commons as minister of finance during the debate on the Throne Speech on February 24, 1972, humility was the order of the day. There were, he admitted, "significant limits on the manoeuvrability of a minister of finance and his ability to exercise precise control over the course of the economy. Anyone in my position who yields to the pretence of sounding omniscient is either a charlatan or a fool."¹⁰ Current economic knowledge could not explain the type of inflation Canada had been encountering or how to deal with it.¹¹ Having lowered expectations, he proceeded to show empathy for what ordinary Canadians were experiencing. Citing the human cost of joblessness, he changed the government's policy direction 180 degrees by identifying unemployment rather than inflation as the main economic challenge facing the country. Finally, he sounded a note of optimism, saying he expected stronger economic growth in 1972.

It was a promising start, but he would soon face a far more stringent test. The Trudeau government was then in the fourth year of its mandate and trailing in the polls. In early April, Trudeau ruled out a spring or summer election. (One Liberal MP, when asked why going to the polls later would be better, replied sensibly, "Because if it's now, I'm going to be defeated.")¹² Turner would have to deliver a budget that spring. It needed to be something more substantial than a traditional pre-election sunshine budget and, at the same time, placate the interests that had savaged his predecessor.

He had some money to play with. The economy was still growing, as were tax revenues, and the government balance sheet was in the black. He listened to his finance officials, but, wary of becoming captive to their views, also talked informally to Cabinet colleagues and to friends and associates in his network of connections across the country.[13] Some wanted a stimulative budget that would kick the economy along and put a big dent in unemployment, whereas others argued for a more moderate expansionary strategy that would keep the lid on inflation.

The budget Turner devised addressed Canada's economic problems with solutions qualified by the dictates of politics in an election year. He attributed the unemployment problem to structural changes caused by the arrival of baby boomers and more women in the job market. Inflation was being driven partially by rising world prices for food and commodities, and partially by government spending. One option would have been to cut back on spending to rein in inflation and then provide some short-term programs for the unemployed until the labour market could absorb them. But that risked alienating both the unemployed and the interests affected by cutbacks. Another political consideration was the need to reach out to business. Consequently, he crafted a budget that would support continued expansion and target unemployment at the risk of exacerbating inflation.

As Turner delivered his budget speech on May 8, the usual harassment arose from the opposition benches, but he was calm and in control, playing his audience with patience and guile. The chief stimuli in the budget were a reduction in corporate income tax (from 49 per cent to 40 per cent) and a reduction in the period over which industrial equipment could be written off (from five to two years). The latter would help job-intensive manufacturing, where employment had been declining relative to the workforce as a whole, and mining, a sector particularly incensed by tax increases from Benson's reforms.

Turner cleverly offset these bonuses for business with equally significant measures that had a human face. In the future, he announced, old age and veterans' pensions would be indexed to the cost of living. This change would help some 2 million pensioners whose incomes were being ravaged by inflation. He told the House of Commons that he wished he could do more – offer more tax breaks, alleviate more inequities – but he couldn't do "everything at once." The inflationary risk remained high.[14] It was a politically astute budget that targeted a few key areas for significant change rather than indiscriminately dispensing pre-election goodies.

Bringing down a budget was different from any other experience Turner had ever had in politics. "It is the one event where Parliament and the country focus completely," he observed. "There's a countdown ... like opening night for an actor with an overwhelming role." Now that the budget was presented, all he could do was wait for its reception – "just as the actor waits up for the reviews in the morning papers."[15] The response was favourable. The press thought him well cast in the role of minister of finance. His humble-yet-competent-and-concerned act worked wonders. Liberal ministers reported a jump in party morale. Among "men deeply involved in pre-election organizational work," observed W.A. Wilson, one of Turner's biggest cheerleaders in the press, "Mr. Turner's stock in the party is high these days."[16]

Although the budget had gone well enough, Turner was having less success tackling trade issues with the United States. When President Nixon made an official visit to Ottawa in April 1972, he and Trudeau agreed not to talk about trade because there was little hope of any progress on the issue. In any case, with a general election imminent in Canada and a presidential election coming up in the States, it seemed that progress would have to wait until there were renewed mandates or new leaders. Nixon's visit was significant primarily for the new tone it introduced in Canada-US relations. He downplayed the usual pieties about the two countries' special relationship and emphasized that each one had its own interests and the right to pursue them. "The Canada-US partnership is ended; we're now foreign like the others," Charles Lynch concluded wryly.[17]

The United States was moving ahead with measures that gave concrete form to Nixon's rhetoric. Its new Domestic International Sales Corporation (DISC) plan encouraged US multinationals to invest at home, particularly in manufacturing, by allowing them to defer taxes on profits earned by exports. DISC threatened to limit US capital investment in Canada more effectively than any measure proposed to date by Canadian economic nationalists. At the same time, disturbing signs indicated that the United States was considering new trade sanctions, with a Michelin tire plant in Nova Scotia rumoured to be a prime target on the grounds that Department of Regional Economic Expansion grants toward building it constituted an unfair trade subsidy.

Meanwhile, Connally continued to make ominous noises about the Auto Pact. For a government struggling with unemployment, this was a grave threat. Since the signing of the pact in 1965, automotive manufacturers had invested in new production facilities in Ontario, which had generated economic spinoffs in related sectors such as parts manufacturing and many well-paying blue-collar jobs. Auto manufacturing was now Canada's single most important industry, symbolic of a resource-based economy's modernization into one founded on manufacturing. Although the 5.2 per cent rate of unemployment in Ontario was among the lowest in Canada (bested only by the Prairie provinces, at 4.5 per cent, with the coasts and Quebec all much higher), no government wanted to campaign for reelection in vote-rich Ontario as auto workers were being laid off.[18]

Turner tried his best to arrange a meeting with Connally. He believed that they could start to solve their problems if only they sat down and got to know each other. He included some laudatory remarks about his American counterpart in a speech to the Canadian Club of Toronto in April, arranged for a copy to go to the American embassy, then followed up with the ambassador to say that he wanted a "quiet private" meeting with Connally. The International Monetary Conference of the American Bankers Association in Montreal that spring would be a convenient occasion, he suggested. They could get together for lunch or breakfast. He had no particular negotiations in mind or any preconceived ideas – he just thought a "frank and informal 'get acquainted' meeting" would be useful. "We have got to get this thing back on the tracks," he told his contact at the embassy. "I want to solve the problem eventually, but it will take a little time."[19] Connally ended up cancelling his visit to Montreal, and Turner had to field questions in the House suggesting he had been stood up. Behind the scenes he kept trying to buttonhole his US counterpart, to no avail. What Turner didn't know was that Connally was submitting his resignation as treasury secretary and therefore had different priorities.

In the meantime, Turner had to content himself with pursuing the time-honoured Canadian strategy of multilateralism. He had noted in his budget speech that, in the wake of the Nixon shokku, stabilizing the international trading system was the most important multilateral issue of the day. The currency exchange system that Nixon had ended dated back to the Bretton Woods Agreements that had created the World Bank and the International Monetary Fund (IMF) in 1944. National currencies had been pegged at relative values that could be adjusted only with IMF approval and were valued in terms of the US dollar, which served as the benchmark and reserve currency in the system. (The value of the US dollar was in turn tied to a specified amount of gold, so, theoretically at least, it was convertible into gold on demand.) This system had sustained freer and fairer trade by preventing countries from devaluing their currencies to increase exports, a stratagem that invariably led to retaliatory sanctions and trade wars.[20]

When the United States began to run trade deficits in the late 1960s, it blamed the system for keeping the currencies of its trading partners unfairly low. After the Nixon shokku, leading industrialized countries (known collectively as the Group of Ten, or G10) had cobbled together a temporary currency regime, the Smithsonian Agreement, in Washington in December 1971. They revalued their currencies in return for the Americans lifting their 10 per cent import surtax.[21] Canada did not have to revalue along with the rest because it had already let its dollar float.

In July 1972 the IMF established a Committee of Twenty (or C20) to develop a permanent replacement for the Smithsonian Agreement. Turner became Canada's representative on the new committee. Much of its discussion revolved around whether Special Drawing Rights (SDRs), a financial instrument created by the IMF in 1969 in response to concerns about a shortage of global liquidity, could be used in place of the American dollar as the foundation of a new currency-exchange system.[22] At the same time, developing countries, which Canada engaged primarily through the Commonwealth, were lobbying to be given SDRs as a form of foreign aid.[23] Turner thought that using them for this purpose would skew efforts to stabilize the international trading system, but he promised developing countries that the C20 would find other ways to help them with their economic challenges.

Prospects for progress on the US front brightened when George Shultz replaced John Connally as US treasury secretary in May 1972. Shultz, who had been secretary of labor and director of the powerful Office of Management and Budget, was a more urbane breed of Washington power-broker than Connally. He was also a trained economist with considerable business experience. He would not openly repudiate Connally's positions but was known to be far more reasonable. Turner put out feelers and secured a meeting. When they got together on September 18, Shultz insisted that the United States had to find ways to address its balance of payments problem, but he was willing to consider each item on the list of trade irritants on its own merits.[24] The two men did not resolve any issues immediately, but the visit was a success because Turner was able to establish a rapport. "It is time we stopped cussing each other," Shultz later wrote to Turner, "and started once again to emphasize the many ways in which we benefit by our basically good relationships."[25] Turner could not have agreed more. As a sign of Canada's willingness to cooperate, he initiated some tariff reductions on American imports, which he could sell domestically as inflation-fighting measures.

The first tangible payoff came on October 16, when Shultz phoned to let Turner know that nothing would be done about Michelin until after the election in Canada. When the long-threatened countervailing duties on Michelin tires were imposed in January 1973, Shultz gave Turner advance warning that the decision was coming and apologized for being powerless to stop it. The Michelin duties had been unavoidable, but Turner credited his relationship with Shultz for limiting them to only 6-8 per cent rather than an anticipated 15-20 per cent.

Thereafter, Turner flew down to Washington regularly to discuss trade.[26] He and Shultz would go over the outstanding bilateral issues and talk through any that seemed to be resolvable, then pass the decision on to their officials. Turner discovered that Shultz played tennis, and they got into the habit of stealing away for a quick game on the White House grounds. On more than one occasion, drinks after the game were followed by dinner with the president, whom Turner found to be well briefed on Canadian issues. Turner also developed a good relationship with Bill Simon, the deputy secretary of the treasury, who succeeded Shultz in 1974. In the end, the Americans did not follow through on their threats to the Auto Pact and the Defence Production Agreement. Turner was not the only contact between the two nations on trade issues, but he had helped gain Canada a sympathetic ear in Washington. Without his personal diplomacy, things could have been much worse.

Larger issues raised by the Nixon shocks would continue to play out for years to come. The Americans' unilateral abdication of responsibility for the international trading regime threw into question the conventional wisdom that economic issues were amenable to astute management by experts. This conceit had informed not just international trade relations but post-war domestic economic policy in Western countries as well. According to the Keynesian common sense of the day, steady economic growth and high stable levels of employment could be achieved through judicious intervention in the economy. The state was responsible for counteracting cyclical downturns with expenditures that could be taxed back during periods of prosperity, a role that dovetailed nicely with the post-war political project of building the welfare state through new and expanded social programs. The problems that developed countries were now having with inflation and unemployment, however, were slowly sapping the belief that economic prosperity could be astutely orchestrated by experts. The "managed" prosperity of the 1950s and 1960s had been nice while it lasted. In comparison, the way ahead was murky and uncertain.

The collapse of economic institutions and ideas that had underpinned the immediate post-war decades ushered in a period of uncertainty and instability. One fact was clear: the prosperous times that had funded a succession of significant new social programs were gone, at least for the immediate future, and an era of consolidation, if not retrenchment, had begun. An early casualty of the shifting climate of opinion was the idea of an economic bill of rights, a measure once advocated by Turner and discussed as a possible feature of constitutional reform in the late 1960s. In the talks leading up to the Victoria Charter in 1971, the notion dropped off the table, never to be heard of again. The Trudeau administration's last significant social program enhancement was Labour Minister Bryce Mackasey's 1971 revision of unemployment insurance, which raised benefits and relaxed requirements for eligibility. The government would be roundly criticized during the 1972 election for both the reform's cost and its corrosive effect on the work ethic. The political centre, which in the late sixties had migrated further left than ever before, was now correcting rightward.

Business took advantage of the uncertainty of the times to promote its interests. It had chafed under welfare-state liberalism because social programs were funded by higher taxes, which cut into its profits, and because the social justice ethic shifted power and moral authority to the public sector at the expense of its accustomed prestige and influence. Now private-sector ideologues launched a counter-offensive. Corporations sponsored public-relations initiatives and think-tanks that spouted nineteenth-century free-market nostrums. The mainstream media, happy to find all-purpose answers to big-picture questions beyond its competence, began parroting the logic and slogans of the corporate apologists.[27]

Turner did not buy into these arguments. He saw inflation and unemployment as products of factors that were largely beyond his control but likely to be of limited duration. In the interim he focused on keeping things on an even keel, preventing expenditures from outstripping revenues, protecting the vulnerable from the worst ravages of inflation, and ensuring that unemployment was managed compassionately until economic growth caught up with the labour supply. Nevertheless, Turner became the figure business identified with in government. The minister of finance was expected to be fiscally conservative compared to his Cabinet colleagues. Moreover, his pilgrimages to the United States reassured business that he was looking out for its interests.[28] Increasingly, he was seen in business quarters as an economic realist, one of the few sound men in Cabinet, a paragon of stability in uncertain times. To win the support of the business constituency, he did not have to adopt its neo-liberal doctrine. It was enough to be just discernibly to the right of his colleagues and, most symbolically, the prime minister. This is not to say that the right wingers' views had no effect on him. As a pragmatic politician, a centrist always seeking equilibrium, he factored them into the political equation that he ceaselessly tried to balance.

In the summer of 1972, the *Toronto Star* published the results of an informal survey it had conducted of Ottawa "power brokers." It concluded that, after the prime minister, the most powerful man in Ottawa was John Turner. "Unlike most cabinet ministers who gauged their success by their abilities to influence Trudeau and by the respect he showed them personally," the *Star* explained, "Turner has remained his own man – often expressing impatience in private or even dislike of the Trudeau administration and some of its policies."[29] Surveys showed that Turner and Trudeau were both identified in the public mind as strong figures, but, unlike Trudeau, Turner was not seen as arrogant. "There is something in his bearing and manner that 'WASP' Canada identifies with its own best characteristics," one commentator noted. "The obvious Turner stamp on the record of the Trudeau government, particularly this year, appears to many English-speaking Canadians to be a sign that their influence in the cabinet would not diminish during a second Trudeau term."[30] Turner's habit of cultivating the press no doubt contributed to such positive assessments. It stood in marked contrast to Trudeau's attitude toward the media, which ranged unpredictably from standoffish to contemptuous.

On September 1 the prime minister announced an election, to be held October 30. The Liberal Party wasn't as prepared as it had been for the previous contest; nor would it be able to run on its leader and little else, as it had in 1968. This time out, Liberal strategists thought it wise to run as a team, with the prime minister and the most prominent Cabinet ministers playing national roles while others focused regionally or locally, according to the length of their coattails. Next to the prime minister, the most visible candidate would be John Turner, the only leading Liberal who had a following across the country. "Turner is the one member of the cabinet whom we can use anywhere, anytime," observed a senior Liberal strategist.[31]

Equipped with a flimsy slogan, "The Land Is Strong," Cabinet ministers fanned out across the country to make promises, announce programs, and defend the government's record. Bill Lee, the former Hellyer aide who had served as Trudeau's campaign manager for the general election in 1968, was again brought in to run the campaign. This time, however, he found his efforts frustrated by Trudeau and his advisers. The prime minister decided that, rather than running a traditional campaign, he would have a rational dialogue with the people. Liberals soon grew concerned about his conduct on the hustings. He seemed detached and philosophical, projecting a "take me or leave me" insouciance instead of the type of earnest appeal for approval electorates expected of campaigning politicians. He was travelling around the country in a cocoon of aides who told him he was doing well, when in fact he was bombing.

Instead of rekindling Trudeaumania, the campaign reminded Canadians of how few of their expectations Trudeau had fulfilled. Determined not to be seduced again, journalists compensated by being hypercritical and disparaged Trudeau for his content-free campaign. When he got into some unseemly fuddle-duddling out west, George Bain of the *Toronto Globe and Mail* concluded that he had "piqued too soon."[32] W.A. Wilson of the *Montreal Star* saw a silver lining in the philosopher king's impervious cloak. "If this election produces a minority government, there is serious doubt among the Liberals that Mr. Trudeau possesses the temperament that could handle a 1960s type of House of Commons," he opined. "If that were the case, Mr. Turner is now the man to whom the party would be most likely to turn as an alternative."[33]

Turner campaigned hard. Every candidate wanted his help, and, despite being away for ten days fulfilling international obligations, he visited fifty-three ridings – far more than Trudeau.[34] He was also kept busy parrying opposition attacks on the national stage. NDP leader David Lewis picked on Turner's tax breaks for business, arguing that they "amount to giving giant corporations interest-free loans at the expense of the average Canadian taxpayer." Lewis coined the phrase "corporate welfare bums" to describe the beneficiaries of Turner's largesse and deployed it effectively throughout the campaign. Turner countered that the tax measures were necessary to keep the economy healthy. He told an audience in Timmins that Lewis' policies would turn their city into a ghost town: "If Mr. Lewis had his way, all of the residents of Timmins would be trapping, fishing, hunting or living in southern Ontario ... He'd turn Timmins into a municipal welfare bum."[35]

Economic issues came to define the campaign. In early October the Liberals were buffeted by a Statistics Canada report that unemployment had hit a new high of 7.1 per cent and that the consumer price index had risen 5.3 per cent over the previous year – the greatest increase in twenty years. Asked to comment by reporters, Trudeau called the results "puzzling." That wasn't good enough for political commentators, who thought he should have a constructive response, if not a strategy for dealing with the issue. Turner picked up the slack. Canada's economic performance was stronger than that of most of its competitors, he explained, but demographic changes had brought so many new entrants into the labour force that even a booming economy could not absorb them all. It was a temporary aberration that would be worked through over the next few years.

Conservative leader Robert Stanfield again came across as a man of integrity and did his best to tag the prime minister with responsibility for the country's economic woes. He held the Liberals to account for unemployment, and he proposed indexing tax brackets to the cost of living so inflation alone wouldn't expose taxpayers to a higher tax rate. Turner noted that these measures would cost the government between $1.5 and $2.0 billion a year in lost revenue. "For Robert Stanfield this isn't an election, it's an auction," he quipped.[36]

Nevertheless, the opposition parties' attacks on the government's economic management were effective, and the Liberals found themselves fighting a rearguard action. Polls revealed that, from September through to the third week in October, Liberal support had dropped from 42 per cent to 37 per cent of voters. The drop was also attributable to Trudeau's conduct of the campaign, which made the Liberals seem "aloof, unconcerned, even arrogant," as if they took re-election for granted.[37] The result on election day was a dead heat. At first it appeared that the Conservatives had won 109 seats (with 35.0 per cent of the popular vote) to the Liberals' 108 (38.5 per cent), with 30 for the NDP (17.7 per cent) and 15 for Social Credit (7.6 per cent). Turner was re-elected easily in Ottawa-Carleton, although his margin of victory was cut in half. Results in many other ridings were so close that judicial recounts were required to determine the final tally of seats for each party.

While awaiting the outcome, Turner considered how the Liberals should conduct themselves in this situation. Giving the appearance of desperately clinging to power might provoke resentment and reinforce the perception that the country was being ruled by an autocratic French Canadian cabal. In the long term, he thought, it would be better for the Liberals to surrender power gracefully and turn their attention to rebuilding the party for the next election. If they resigned, however, they would hand the initiative to Stanfield, and Quebec would feel abandoned. Their interim strategy, he concluded, should be to wait for recounts and consult with caucus and with Stanfield while waiting to see what happened. "No deals (with N.D.P.)," he wrote, somewhat hopefully, on a note to himself.[38]

Many Liberals thought Trudeau had blown the campaign. The day after the election, Liberal MP Ralph Whicher suggested publicly that Trudeau should resign to make way for Turner.[39] When Bill Lee met Robert Andras, the minister of state for urban affairs, to consider the results, he offered the same advice. "He [Trudeau] caused this political crisis through his philosophical musings throughout the campaign, against our advice," he said. "Tell him to call a press conference, accept the responsibility, and announce he is resigning and will ask the Governor General to call on John Turner to see if he can form a government that would gain support for a period in the commons."[40] Not surprisingly, Trudeau was unreceptive to the idea. He decided instead that, if the Liberals were ahead after the recounts, he would make a deal with the NDP. A recount in the riding of Ontario, just east of Toronto, reversed the original results: this time Liberal incumbent Norm Cafik came out ahead of the Conservative candidate by four votes. Another riding thought to have been won by the Tories ended up going to the NDP. When the election results were finalized in the second week of November, the totals stood at Liberals, 109; Conservatives, 107; NDP, 31; and Créditistes, 15.

The result added poignancy to Turner's reflections the previous summer about retiring. Had he left then, it is possible to imagine that a weakened Liberal Party would have lost the election, precipitating a leadership race during the spring of 1973 in which he would have been the principal candidate. With a fresh face at the helm, the Liberals would have been well positioned to defeat a Stanfield minority government. Once again John Turner had come very close to being prime minister of Canada.

A few weeks after the election, Turner saw Lester Pearson for the last time. "Mrs. Pearson called me up and said Mr. Pearson would like to see you," he recalled. "We poured ourselves a couple of scotches. He knew he was dying. For the first half hour he talked about his life and our government. He was very, very distressed about Trudeau's foreign policy and attitude to the alliances ... and he talked about what I should do and where I would go. He said that someday I would be Prime Minister and that I should be patient and just wait it out."[41]

This was a memorable moment for Turner. He had always looked up to his political elders. He had dreamed of being Pearson's successor, but Pearson hadn't favoured him, and the timing had been wrong. Now Pearson seemed to be telling him that he had made a mistake – or so Turner could interpret their encounter if he wanted to feel sorry for himself. But the next day he was back in harness, loyal to his leader and party. Now in a bit of a bind, they needed him more than ever.

11

THE PRICE OF GAS

Barbara Frum, co-host of CBC Radio's *As It Happens,* interviewed John Turner for *Maclean's* in 1973. In the style of the times, Turner's hair was a little longer and shaggier than it had been in his younger days. He had grown sideburns, and his suits, though still navy or grey, sported wide lapels offset by fat, brightly coloured ties – mainstream fashion's concession to flower power. When Frum asked him how he handled the pressures of office, he related some of his secrets for executive efficiency. He had learned the importance of saying no, he said, and saying it quickly and forcefully. He also liked to keep his desk clean – otherwise some things would get overlooked and sneak back to bite him. Matters of trivial or middling importance he handed off to his staff, who had a system for tracking items and bringing them forward at the right moment. And he had one unorthodox practice: he always carried blank index cards on which he jotted down ideas and reminders. He kept one set in his jacket side pocket for notes on official matters – speeches, subjects to raise with the prime minister or in Cabinet – and another set in his inside breast pocket for personal matters. Given the amount of time he spent in the House, in meetings, or on the road, this system made sense in the days before the personal digital assistant. He had transformed himself into an ambulatory office.

Turner's chauffeured sedan dropped him off on Parliament Hill every morning at 8:10 a.m. The first order of business was correspondence, which he liked to get done early, clearing the way for phone calls and meetings.

"I get on the phone with people to find out what they're thinking every morning," he explained, "how they're reaching out to what the government is doing and what Parliament is doing."[1] His secretary had a phone list with hundreds of names, and, when she reached someone, Turner would get on the line for a chat.[2] His style was jocular and profane to show he was a regular guy, with an undercurrent of solemnity that showed he took his contact's views seriously. Superior knowledge, intelligence, and power were, for Turner, best hid under a bushel. Regulars on the list were phoned every six months or so; closer friends and more powerful contacts received special calls on their birthdays. Everyone was sent a card from the Turner family at Christmas.

In defiance of the technocratic code of contemporary Ottawa, Turner refused to write memos. "It's a time-wasting, protect-your-ass technique," he explained.[3] Instead, he phoned people or went to see them in person. "Hey man, there's this problem I need your help with," he'd say, before talking things through and making a deal.[4] His most significant time-saving tactic continued to be skipping Cabinet committee meetings. His presence was essential at very few. As for his colleagues who diligently attended them all, he could only conclude that they must be insecure.

Turner prided himself on his planning and efficiency. His staff kept elaborate project-management charts setting out the critical path for the completion of key tasks, interwoven with his hectic schedule months into the future. Like any successful executive, he assessed potential dangers that lay ahead and developed risk-management strategies to contain them. He kept a list of ten "time wasters" under the glass on his desk and made sure his staff followed his rules: never touch a piece of paper twice; never ask a question twice; make a decision and move on. He expected hard work and integrity. Don't lie or mislead the media, he said. If you can't tell the truth, don't say anything.

Turner was wary of trying to solve problems by brute effort. When things became overwhelming, or if he was feeling burnt out, his solution was to walk away for a while – get a change of scenery, play a game of squash, maybe go to a movie. "You've got to ... get rid of the anxiety and frustration so you can concentrate on the really innovative things," he noted – "the people things, the imaginative things, the new and lively things."[5] He prided himself on working flat out during the day but never taking work home, except for letterbooks – he didn't consider signing off on correspondence to be real work. If he got home at a decent hour, he liked to fit in a game of tennis at the club in Rockcliffe Park. When necessary he would put in eighteen-hour days, but he tried to be with his family at least three evenings a week.

Turner's problem-solving style had always been to immerse himself in an issue in all its detail. Once he felt he knew it well, he became comfortable and quite effective in managing it. Officials in Finance were impressed by his ability to absorb complex files and liked the fact that he actually read and understood the materials they prepared for him.[6] He had the work ethic, brainpower, and analytical skill necessary to process the masses of information that the department generated and cut to the heart of issues.

Ron Graham of *Saturday Night* magazine likened Turner's mind to a filing cabinet. He filed subjects away in his memory, called one up when necessary, devoted his entire attention to it, and, when he was finished, filed it away again and moved on to something different with the same singular concentration and efficiency.[7] One of his staff felt that the first time they met, Turner scanned his face, assessing but also memorizing it. He was a student of human nature, genuinely fascinated by what made people tick. "He was friendly, but he was always in charge," said a staff member. "He seemed to have an unerring instinct for knowing what matters could be left to subordinates, and what ones he had to seize for himself. He was a quick learner and a good listener."[8] On business trips, Turner always invited his team in for drinks in his hotel room. "We know it's an act," one admitted, "but even bureaucrats enjoy the chance to talk on even terms with the great."[9] One senior public servant, initially skeptical about his new boss, soon concluded that he was dealing with a superior mind. "He's quicker than Trudeau; in fact, he's almost as quick as Jack Pickersgill," he told a journalist acquaintance. In Ottawa, Pickersgill was the gold standard.[10]

The same qualities made Turner an influential figure in the House of Commons. One of the fundamental differences between Trudeau and Turner, wrote one observer, was that "the latter has developed into a first-rate Commons man" with a real feel for the House.[11] One of Turner's most effective tactics was to pay careful attention to what opposition members said in their speeches, thereby gathering information he could use later to deflect criticism by pointing out inconsistencies in his opponents' positions. Diefenbaker's former aide Sean O'Sullivan, who later became an MP, observed that Turner earned respect by treating his peers generously:

> He had no inhibitions about letting an opposition member look good, either by helping out with a problem or taking a question seriously in the House. At committee hearings, he'd arrive early, shake every member's hand and make everyone feel important. If a difficult bill was going before a committee, he'd have all the members involved over to his office a few days before his anticipated appearance, pour a few drinks, give us a little jock talk and try to sound out our views. Everyone was made to feel like a confidant.[12]

For O'Sullivan, Turner's approachability stood in marked contrast to that of his own party's leader, Robert Stanfield, whom he saw as a self-styled patrician who lacked the personal touch. Sometimes Stanfield didn't even seem to know his MPs' names. Turner, in contrast, "never failed to stop to chat it up with MPs, shake hands with their constituents, or answer their queries."[13] Richard Gwyn wrote of a Conservative front-bencher who, upon being hospitalized, found that his first get-well card came from John Turner.[14]

Turner did not have to restructure Finance as he had Justice. "Our Department of Finance really was as good as anything in the world in those days," he would later recall.[15] His deputy minister, Simon Reisman, stood apart in a public service culture that generally valued urbanity over profanity. Aggressive and opinionated, he was used to getting things done – his way. He was jealous of his department's role as the government's economic policy-maker, a role he often conflated with himself. Reisman was, nevertheless, a shrewd and effective deputy minister. He had bolstered the ranks of senior management at Finance with new talent, bringing in from the University of Toronto economists William Hood (assistant deputy minister for policy analysis and international finance) and Ed Neufeld (director of international finance under Hood). Both adapted well to a world in which economics was practised rather than theorized. From the private sector he recruited Marshall (Mickey) Cohen, a Toronto tax lawyer (assistant deputy minister for tax policy). The assistant deputy minister handling federal-provincial relations was the courtly Tommy Shoyama, whose early career had been in Saskatchewan under the CCF government of Tommy Douglas.

It took Reisman a while to get used to Turner. He liked to control the flow of information and, thereby, his minister. In the summer of 1973, Michael Hunter, Turner's executive assistant, sent his boss a memo warning that his political staff had to be better informed by the department about breaking developments so they could prepare him for possible questions in the House and from the press. When Turner passed the memo on to his deputy minister, Reisman exploded.[16] He phoned Hunter and upbraided him, shouting profanities. This incident was not out of character. Reisman was known to play power games, even to the extent of refusing to pick up the phone for a call with Turner until Turner was already on the line.[17]

John Turner had a great respect for public servants, a legacy of his upbringing, and he tended to rely more on them and less on political staff than most of his Cabinet colleagues did. He was not one to be pushed around, however. He came into Finance half expecting that he would need to get rid of Reisman. As it turned out, he didn't have to. He set the tone for their working relationship early on. Half an hour after being sworn in as minister of finance in January 1972, he phoned Reisman, who was at a conference at Montebello, an hour's drive away. He told Reisman he wanted a briefing for a federal-provincial conference of finance ministers in Jasper that was coming up in three days. Reisman suggested they do it during the flight to Alberta that Sunday night. Turner made it clear he wanted a briefing *now*. Reisman hurried back to Ottawa and arrived at Turner's house at nine that night accompanied by his senior officials.[18] Thereafter, Turner managed Reisman's bluff macho swagger with more of the same. When Reisman boasted he was a poker player and won nineteen out of twenty times, Turner retorted, "You haven't played me."[19] This kind of bluster earned Reisman's respect.

Turner would discuss issues with Reisman, drawing on information and analysis generated by the finance department, but invariably he mixed in feedback from other sources as well. As one journalist described it, "The Turner approach to politics and government is essentially one of energetic consultation and judicious balancing of advice. He has never relied on his departmental experts alone. He had to get their confidence but, also, he had to find outside advice as a counterbalance."[20] In defiance of Reisman's controlling instincts, Turner continued his practice of consulting directly with lower-level staff. If he were reading Cabinet submissions or briefing notes, he would phone the authors to discuss the issues or compliment them on their work. Often he asked them to join him in his office with Reisman to discuss some point.

The morale of the department rested on its self-image as a team of experts with a long tradition of giving the government tough-minded advice on the most important yet complex of its responsibilities. It was a point of corporate pride that this advice had never been contested in times past. Though exaggerated, this perception was significant because unrivalled influence over economic policy became increasingly difficult to exercise in the changing bureaucratic environment of the 1970s. The importance of the economy ensured that other departments, Cabinet committees, and the prime minister's inner circle would all try to shape policy. Trudeau may have promised Turner free rein on economic policy, but what that meant was open to interpretation, and, in the flow of events, proved a principle much honoured in the breach. Treasury Board had been separated from Finance and now administered the "spending envelopes" associated with Trudeau's Cabinet committee system. The prime minister was an independent thinker who was no more likely to rely solely on the views of Finance than Turner himself relied on any one source of advice. Inevitably, the question of Finance's prerogatives in economic policy would become intertwined with the political rivalry between Trudeau and Turner.

During his first few weeks in the job, Turner had corresponded with the prime minister to clarify his role. Trudeau emphasized the need for better economic forecasting and "a liaison between all the departments of government whose mandates include matters of economic concern."[21] He recognized that decentralization had hampered the government's ability to develop and apply economic policy consistently. When Reisman saw Trudeau's letter, his territorial instincts bristled. "I am persuaded that the Prime Minister wishes you to assume a strong and positive leadership on economic matters, but I am not so sure that this is shared by everyone around him," he warned.[22] Reisman, like Turner, was annoyed by the PMO's drive for self-sufficiency, the diffusion of ministerial power under the Cabinet committee system, and the cost of these developments to his executive authority. He resented the fact that the advice offered by Finance was polluted by the independent opinions Trudeau sought from economist Albert Breton, a comrade-in-arms from battles against separatism in Quebec. For Turner's reply, Reisman suggested a rewording that would require other branches of government to consult with Finance before making announcements with economic implications.[23] Turner could use his chairmanship of the Economic Policy Committee of Cabinet to keep tabs on what was in the works.

Minority government put additional pressure on the finance minister. The Liberals would quibble with the opposition about what represented a vote of confidence that could bring down the government, but parliamentary tradition dictated that all money bills qualified. Thus, the fate of the government rested with any legislation Turner brought forward. In the immediate aftermath of the 1972 election, the Conservatives were particularly eager to defeat the government because constitutional convention would then require the governor general to ask them to form a government rather than call an election. The NDP, for its part, had decided to get what it could out of the Liberals until it saw some likelihood of picking up more seats in another election. The Liberal strategy was to keep NDP support without letting it appear that the NDP was dictating policy.

Trudeau had drawn lessons from his near defeat, which changed his approach to governing and facilitated cooperation with the NDP. He decided that he had let his government get bogged down in debate and process in the misguided belief that Canadians would appreciate the rational deliberations behind important decisions. Instead, he had come off as unproductive, self-absorbed, and out of touch. Now he resolved to be activist, progressive, and, above all, more political in his approach in order to win back his majority.[24] All these elements were displayed in the Speech from the Throne that opened Parliament in January 1973.

During the debate on the speech, Trudeau came close to squandering this promising start when he blamed the Liberals' election setback on anti-French bigotry. He claimed that the Conservatives had "tried to divide Canada" by alleging that the government played favourites with Quebec. This allegation provoked jeers from the opposition that escalated into shouting matches between the prime minister and Tory backbenchers. Turner took it on himself to heal the breach. Referring to the preponderance of Liberal seats in Quebec, he told the House on January 9 that this majority placed "a special burden on every member of the House of both languages ... that anything we say enhances the unity of this country. I do not believe that any political party has a monopoly on national unity."[25] Diplomatically yet emphatically, Turner calmed the waters, in the process displaying how his leadership style differed from Trudeau's.

Allan MacEachen, the Liberal House leader, had the delicate job of managing a fluid entente with the NDP. No measure could be put before the House unless he was assured of the NDP's support, so he met regularly with NDP leader David Lewis to negotiate. Out of this relationship came the introduction in January of legislation on foreign ownership. The Foreign Investment Review Agency would assess transfers of ownership to foreign interests to determine whether they were of "significant benefit" to Canada. The bill was tougher than what the Liberals had proposed in their previous majority government, a development for which Lewis claimed credit.

The priority item on Turner's agenda was a budget that would win NDP support. The implications of this exercise for his career were intriguing. If his budget were a success, he would prolong the life of the government and Trudeau's tenure as prime minister. If his budget brought down the government, however, it could lead to Trudeau's resignation as head of the party – and give him a shot at the leadership. But then he would be the author of his party's misfortune, which could easily take him out of contention in a leadership race.

Turner was determined to follow through on the tax cuts and fast write-offs for corporations he had promised the year before and wanted them reintroduced in the new budget. They were a tough sell in Cabinet. He took the position that the cuts were required to show that the Liberals were more business-friendly than the NDP. His colleagues acknowledged that the government had "given firm commitments," but they were more concerned about losing NDP support and falling from power.[26] Lewis, after all, had structured his entire election campaign around the "corporate welfare bums" theme. MacEachen thought the NDP might accept the cuts if they came with a firm terminal date, but to be safe he wanted them introduced separately from the budget. As the debate heated up, Trudeau played Turner off against MacEachen, saying that substance was Turner's responsibility, but the parliamentary strategy was up to MacEachen. Turner refused to play along. "You can't separate the smile from the cat," he told

Trudeau. Only two other ministers, Don Jamieson and Hugh Faulkner, supported Turner. Herb Gray later explained that he didn't jump in because he would "rather be a live coward than a dead hero."[27] Turner lost the fight.

Reisman said he had never seen a finance minister take such a pounding in Cabinet without the prime minister coming to his rescue. Incensed by the outcome, Turner told Hunter that most of his ministerial colleagues were not fit to make a living in the real world. As for Trudeau, he said, his judgment of Parliament was poor, and besides, how could you trust someone who did not drink, or at least drank only the odd beer or sherry? On one of his index cards, he jotted, "Disconcerting to feel that before presenting the most important budget in many years, I didn't have the full support of PM. I'd put myself on line for him but I wasn't receiving support in return."[28]

The most notable aspect of the episode was Turner's recklessness. His case was weak, yet he put his prestige on the line, daring Cabinet to reject him. If it did, it would only reinforce his status as an independent and somewhat alienated locus of power within the Liberal regime. Though temporarily rebuffed, he resolved to "play it hard and tough" to get the cuts through after the budget and, "if necessary, resign."[29] Along with his repudiation of Trudeau's anti-French accusations in the House the previous January, the episode showed he was now prepared to challenge the prime minister when it suited him. Their relationship, which had always been correct, if cool, had now degenerated toward mutual wariness and distrust.

The budget Turner brought down on February 19, 1973, was written against a backdrop of continuing economic expansion and another healthy government surplus. Nevertheless, unemployment remained high and inflation continued to increase. In keeping with his previous budget and the need to keep the NDP onside, unemployment remained his main target. The budget provided further stimulus to the economy, with an income-tax reduction and cuts to sales tax on items such as children's clothing, shoes, candy, and pop. Old age pensions were enhanced and inflation targeted by lowering tariffs on food and a few other products. Overall, the result would be more money in the hands of consumers.

As a centrepiece, Turner stole one of Stanfield's campaign planks – the indexing of tax brackets to the rate of inflation. No longer would Canadians be lifted into a higher tax bracket by inflation alone. The Liberals considered this measure to be a major inducement for the NDP to support the budget. Cabinet recognized that, as a result, "future government expenditure plans might be unnecessarily inhibited" but decided to go ahead regardless because the measure would ease the impact of inflation on taxpayers and, moreover, "the political advantages outweighed the disadvantages."[30] The downside was that government expenditures would continue to rise with inflation. With revenues now decoupled from expenditures, the government would have far more difficulty in balancing its books from this point on.

Turner used the platform of his budget speech to discuss the use of wage and price controls to rein in inflation. Britain and the United States had been experimenting with such controls, with dubious results, and discussion about their applicability in the Canadian context had increased over the previous year. Turner doubted they could work. "Controls would demand a far wider public consensus and more evidence of an emergency situation than is now the case," he explained.[31] As an alternative, he called on Canadians to exercise restraint in their wage demands.

The NDP supported the budget, and the Liberal government lived to fight another day. As time passed and its legislative program took shape, the likelihood of a non-confidence vote leading to the Conservatives being asked to form a government diminished. The prime minister could now advise the governor general to call an election instead. The Liberals felt they were in a position to hold office for at least another year.

Turner remained committed to getting the corporate tax cuts passed, but opposition in Cabinet remained strong. When he left Ottawa to attend International Monetary Fund (IMF) meetings in Paris in mid-March, the gossip mill kicked into high gear. His opponents in Liberal ranks let it be known that in insisting on the cuts he was catering to business interests for his own personal advancement at the expense of the party. On March 21 Robert Stanfield announced that the Conservatives would support the cuts because business had assumed they were coming, but only for the balance of the year. The time limit was questionable economics as the measures would not generate jobs until years later, but politically it drove a wedge into the emerging crack in Liberal unity.

The tension had escalated by the time Turner returned. He came up with a scheme for implementing the corporate tax measures that would fulfill his 1972 budget pledge yet be close enough to what the Conservatives wanted for the business community that they would feel obliged to support it. In the bill introducing the cuts, he included a provision that, upon the request of sixty members, they could be reviewed by the House after a year. Given that the NDP had only thirty-five members and the Liberals were unlikely to want a review, this ploy effectively gave the Conservatives an annual veto on the measures. A deafening chorus of hoots and catcalls resounded in the House on May 29 when opposition members caught on to what Turner was up to, but his scheme worked. The Conservative House leader told him that the Tories wanted changes in committee but would support the bill.[32]

Turner had got his way, displaying, in the process, both cunning and clout. Journalists noted that he had now been at the centre of government business for most of the new Parliament, his profile overshadowing Trudeau's as economic issues eclipsed national unity concerns. "Attention is heaped upon Mr. Turner because he is talking about issues that many people feel lie at the heart of the nation's life," explained the *Toronto Globe and Mail* – "about jobs and prosperity, about the work ethic, about the distribution of income."[33]

In some parts of the country, Turner was far more popular than the prime minister. The Liberals won only seven seats west of the Lakehead in 1972, four of them in British Columbia. The government tried to reach out to the West with a Western Economic Opportunities Conference in July 1973. There was talk of a new national policy that included the West, but Trudeau showed up with little concrete to offer. The provinces concluded that he had planned to divide the NDP governments in Saskatchewan, Manitoba, and British Columbia from the Conservative government in Alberta, only to be surprised when they offered a common front. When Transport Minister Jean Marchand arrived, the premiers raised traditional Western grievances about the costs of east-west transportation. Marchand came off badly because he was unprepared; the premiers ended up looking like Anglo thugs bullying a French Canadian. As he banged down the gavel to end the desultory proceedings, Trudeau declared, "Well, thus ends the first and only Western Economic Opportunities Conference" – a conclusion many westerners interpreted to mean that he was fed up with trying to please the West.[34] Turner hung around with a bunch of disappointed Western Liberals that evening as they downed drinks and nursed resentments late into the night. His friend and fellow minister Ron Basford, who held a seat in Vancouver, ranted that the party establishment didn't understand the West and, worse, didn't seem to care that it didn't. Turner presented himself as equally at odds with the Trudeau regime. "They treat me like a choirboy," he told Basford's friend Cam Avery. The next morning when they were waiting to be picked up outside the hotel, Turner spied Avery and came over. "Cam," he declared, "I meant what I said last night!"[35] As the breach widened between Turner and Trudeau, he was reaching out to disenchanted elements that might one day be cobbled together into a viable coalition within the party.

Ottawa's relations with the West would soon be further aggravated by a new set of issues. Following the Second World War, the western oil industry had struggled to find a dependable market. The most obvious customer, the United States, had a quota on imports. To subsidize Alberta, Diefenbaker's Conservative government had introduced an energy policy that dictated that a great swath of Canada, from the Rocky Mountains to the Ottawa River, would buy Alberta crude at a higher than world price. Canada had an oil pipeline connecting the West with Ontario, but it didn't extend past the Ottawa Valley to eastern seaports because the government wanted to maintain a protected market for western oil producers. Since the early 1960s, Alberta oil had sold for about $3.00 a barrel compared to imported oil at $2.50 a barrel.

This scheme began to unravel in early 1973 when demand for oil spiked in the United States and the Americans dropped their import quotas. Suddenly, Alberta oil was fetching $3.80 a barrel south of the border. The Liberal government responded by freezing the domestic price at $4.00. Foreseeing a time when Canada would have an insufficient supply of oil, in March 1973 the federal government introduced oil export controls. At the same time, the Organization of Petroleum Exporting Countries (OPEC) – an association of oil-producing nations – began to raise its prices, making oil imports to eastern Canada more expensive. The price of a barrel of oil arriving in Montreal jumped 50 per cent to around $6.00 in the first nine months of 1973. The government was obliged to lift its $4.00-a-barrel freeze. It then cobbled together a new policy aimed at national energy self-sufficiency. On September 4, 1973, Trudeau announced that the government would extend the western oil pipeline to Montreal by the end of 1975, petroleum prices would be frozen until January 31, 1974, and a control mechanism would be devised to keep domestic oil prices from escalating with each new surge in world prices.

Worse was yet to come. On October 6 the Yom Kippur war broke out when Egypt and Syria attacked Israel. Arab countries, led by the Saudis, unilaterally raised oil prices by 70 per cent, reduced production, and embargoed shipments to the United States and other countries sympathetic to Israel.[36] Oil climbed to $7.50 a barrel by November, then to $10.00 a barrel by year's end. Every $1.00 increase in its price added half a percentage point to the Consumer Price Index and eventually pushed Canada's annual inflation rate over 10 per cent – a level unheard of in the modern era.

Energy issues pitted Western Canada against Eastern Canada, adding new strains to long-standing regional tensions. The oil industry and the Alberta government wanted to reap the benefits of windfall profits and resented the federal government's attempts to set prices or to restrict and tax exports for the benefit of the country as a whole. Meanwhile, the Maritimes and Quebec, a Liberal stronghold, wanted cheaper fuel from the West to free them from OPEC extortion. Natural resources belonged to the provinces, but Ottawa had an obligation to ensure energy supply and could use its taxing and spending powers to shape a national energy policy. Moreover, the Liberals were dependent on the support of the NDP, which opposed market pricing and believed that multinational oil companies were reaping huge profits from resources that rightly belonged to the people of Canada.[37]

Buffeted by these opposing interests, the Liberals hastily devised a new energy policy in the fall of 1973. "Self-sufficiency" was still the byword. On December 6 Trudeau announced that the government would set up a national petroleum company that would have a mandate to conduct exploration, develop the tar sands in northern Alberta, and import oil and gas. Work on the Montreal pipeline would be expedited. A new pipeline along the Mackenzie Valley was proposed to tap natural gas resources in the Beaufort Sea. Finally, the government imposed export taxes on Alberta oil, promising to use the revenue to subsidize more expensive eastern oil imports.

The export tax did not go over well with Alberta premier Peter Lougheed. After an acrimonious encounter between Lougheed and Energy Minister

THE PRICE OF GAS

Donald Macdonald, Turner was once again tapped to be the government's emissary to the West. This mission would be more difficult than selling bilingualism had been five years earlier, especially because it was Turner's job as finance minister to bring in the export tax legislation. That measure touched off a heated debate in the House of Commons over the size of the tax, the level of subsidy, the division of revenues, and the effects of all these changes on federal-provincial fiscal relations. To sugar-coat the pill, Turner promised on January 4, 1974, that the provinces would get all the revenues from the export tax for the first four months.

Ottawa was also on the hook for additional millions in equalization payments because oil revenues had broadened the gap between have and have-not provinces. Turner told the House of Commons that, if only half the benefits of increasing prices to world levels went to the producing provinces, their treasuries would receive $2.5 billion in additional royalties, and Ottawa would end up having to pay another $800 million in equalization.

The federal government continued to negotiate with the oil-producing provinces through the early months of 1974.[38] At a meeting in March, they reached an agreement that only the portion of oil and gas revenues that went into provincial general revenues would be included in calculations of equalization payments. Tax revenues that were set aside to fund future exploration would be exempt. At the insistence of the NDP, the price of oil would remain frozen at $4.00 for an interim period, but it was slated to go to $6.50 in April 1974 and no doubt rise again soon after. Alberta and Saskatchewan accepted $6.50 temporarily, only after the federal government offered them cash compensation.[39]

Yet another dispute followed when, in his May 1974 budget, Turner removed the tax exemption oil companies had enjoyed for royalties paid to the provinces. Lougheed characterized this change as an illegitimate infringement on provincial control over resources. He also claimed that it threatened Alberta's economic future by stealing profits that would otherwise be reinvested in exploration and new production. Turner refused to cave in on the federal government's right to tax. He told Lougheed to weigh the implications of reaping windfall profits that crippled its economic partners against the long-term benefits of participation in a strong national economy. The talks would eventually come down to bargaining over the level of federal taxation. Once again Turner transformed a clash of principle into a straightforward issue of how best to divide up the pie.[40]

One silver lining of the energy crisis was that it prompted the United States to think in strategic terms about energy. Because Canada was a friendly neighbour with much-needed oil, the American government realized that bullying Canada over trade issues such as the Auto Pact or the Defence Production Sharing Agreement would be unwise. Canada could take some comfort in this adjustment in attitude. Moreover, because Canada had its own supply of oil, its domestic economy was insulated from the worst effects of the energy crisis.[41] It had to import oil at higher prices, but it also had higher receipts from its exports to offset this cost.

Other countries were not so lucky. When Turner first got involved with the IMF's Committee of Twenty (C20), restructuring the international currency exchange system had been the priority. Subsequently, the world had moved to a free market in currencies.[42] Now there was a new crisis as oil-importing countries incurred substantial trade deficits caused by skyrocketing oil prices. Economists feared that countries suffering from the oil shock would resort to competitive currency devaluations or a beggar-thy-neighbour protectionism that would sabotage international trade. To address this problem, the IMF established an "oil facility," a fund that members could draw on to support their currencies while their economies adjusted to the new post-OPEC world.

With the immediate crisis in hand, the C20 turned its attention to related longer-term questions. What should happen to the money that oil-importing countries were spending on more expensive oil? Was it to be continuously siphoned off, sapping their trade balances? Western leaders hoped instead for a reinvestment of Arab oil profits into enterprises in other countries that would help to keep their economies going and integrate the Arab oil-producers into the Western economic system. Encouraging such a "recycling" of petrodollars became a major IMF objective in 1974. One obvious short-term use for the OPEC cash was the IMF oil facility. The profits of oil-producers could be lent back to oil-consuming countries that, because of the debt they had incurred from importing expensive oil, needed help in protecting their currencies.

An upcoming transition period in IMF governance complicated matters. With the currency exchange system settled, the C20 no longer had a mandate. Yet there was a need for an interim body to manage world trade issues while the amendments to the IMF Articles of Agreement recommended by the C20 were being approved by member countries. Denis Healey, Great Britain's chancellor of the exchequer, asked Turner if he would be prepared to accept the chairmanship of the interim committee. William Simon, who had replaced George Shultz as secretary of the treasury, backed his candidacy. Turner was interested. There was only so much he could do at home, and international affairs offered an alternative outlet for his energy and ambition. At the same time, Canada's interests would be well served by having him play a key role in a central multilateral institution.

Turner had the confidence of the major powers and the developing countries, and at the IMF meetings in Washington in early October 1974, his candidacy prevailed. His first priority was to address the needs of developing countries rocked by the energy crisis. Although oil-producers' profits were now being recycled, they tended to be invested in stronger economies where they were least needed. Developing countries were again agitating for special access to Special Drawing Rights (SDRs), this time to shore up their currencies, whereas developed nations remained reluctant to re-purpose them. As Turner saw it, his immediate challenge was to ensure that the IMF oil facility would address the needs of the developing world.[43]

With this goal in mind, Turner embarked on a tour of the Middle East in April 1975, visiting Saudi Arabia, Iran, Kuwait, and Algeria in an effort to persuade them to recycle their petrodollars.[44] On April 21 he was in Iran for an audience with the shah. The IMF needed to be restructured to deal with the economic realities of the new post-OPEC world order, he explained, and middle powers such as Iran and Canada should be taking leadership roles in their spheres of influence by building bridges between the major economic powers and the developing world. "Only by such a bridge building group composed perhaps of Canada, Iran, Brazil, Mexico and maybe one or two others could [we reconcile the] impatience of [the] developing world with [the] dignity of those great powers whose economic influence is clearly on the wane," Turner told his host.[45] The shah cooperated by cutting a substantial cheque for the IMF oil facility. "I did the same thing in Kuwait and Saudi Arabia," Turner later recalled. "I met the kings and princes in their big tents and persuaded those fellows to start loosening up the money and get it back into circulation."[46]

The IMF's oil facility succeeded in its goal of easing the stress on the international trading system caused by the oil-price shock. It was the type of accomplishment that got scant attention because it was preventative. The average Canadian had little appreciation that a beggar-thy-neighbour trade war of the kind that had deepened the Great Depression had again been a real possibility. Turner's international work benefited Canada as a trading nation but was little understood on the domestic front.

The domestic political scene was, in any case, sufficiently eventful to preoccupy all but the most avid political junkie. The spring of 1974 brought signs that the Liberal minority government would not be around much longer. The NDP was making combative noises, and the Liberals were less inclined to dance to its tune because polls showed they had enough support to win a majority. As finance minister, Turner would play a leading role in finessing the government's complicity in its own demise. On April 26 he delivered a speech in Winnipeg that strongly defended corporate profits as necessary for the health of the economy. It was calculated to provoke NDP leader David Lewis – and succeeded admirably. Soon the NDP leader broached four non-negotiable demands for the government. He wanted a commodity (read oil) pricing system with two levels, one for export and one for domestic consumption; a prices review board; and a 6 per cent ceiling on residential mortgages. He also targeted the windfall profits of multinational oil companies by proposing an excess profits tax.[47]

Turner's challenge was to trigger an election with his budget without appearing to intend to do so. To this end, it had to offer some items for the NDP but not enough to make it happy with the overall package. "Lewis had put out his shopping list," Turner later recalled. "I had to have something good enough to make him hesitate: at least the NDP had to think about the budget's economic points."[48] Turner, Trudeau, and MacEachen held a war council over lunch at Cercle Universitaire and developed proposals that the NDP could not support but would look churlish in opposing.[49]

Turner's budget, delivered on May 6, included a Registered Home Ownership Savings Plan and a mix of general tax increases and targeted tax decreases. Turner made only a token gesture in response to the NDP demand for an excess profits tax by imposing a one-year, 10 per cent sur-charge on a limited set of business sectors that did not include oil companies. On May 8, 1974, the government was defeated in the House in the vote on the budget. This marked only the third time since Confederation that a government had been brought down by a confidence motion in the House, and the first time it had been over a budget.

Trudeau advised the governor general to dissolve the House, and an election was set for July 8, 1974. The Liberals were much better organized, aggressive, and opportunistic in 1974 than they had been in 1972. They had prepared for this election for months, analyzing polling data and devising strategy accordingly. Pierre Trudeau's wife, Margaret, hit the hustings, and her husband's image benefited from the freshness her youth and sincerity brought to the campaign.

For Turner, the campaign was bittersweet. If Trudeau won a majority, his hopes for the leadership would be on ice for at least another half-decade. Yet he was philosophical, recognizing that leadership opportunities were hugely dependent on timing. Senator Keith Davey, who co-chaired the Liberal campaign with Jean Marchand, told Turner that a successful campaign would make him "this generation's Paul Martin." Turner was unfazed. "Give it all you've got! I'm with you all the way," he replied. And he was. Once again he played a role second only to Trudeau on the hustings nationwide.[50] He campaigned extensively in Ontario and toured the West, even braving a meeting sponsored by the Calgary Chamber of Commerce to explain the government's oil policy.

The central plank in the Conservatives' platform was wage and price controls. Stanfield campaigned on the promise that he would introduce a ninety-day freeze to break the upward inflationary spiral. Liberal polling had found that there was widespread support for freezing prices but not wages, so Turner and Trudeau both attacked Stanfield's proposal, arguing it would reduce the supply of goods and aggravate inflation. Turner told audiences dramatically that the Tories would freeze prices high (he put one hand up above his head) and wages low (his other hand dropped to his knees). But Trudeau's characterization of the Tory plan was the most memorable. He ridiculed Stanfield's proposal by pointing a finger at his audience and declaring, "Zap, you're frozen."

The Conservatives did well in Newfoundland, the Maritimes, and the West. Overall, they increased their popular vote by half a percentage point, but the vote split translated this gain into a loss of 11 seats, leaving them with 95 members in the House. The New Democrats dropped only 2.5 per cent in the popular vote but lost half their seats in the process. Social Credit was reduced to 11 seats, one short of the total needed for official party status. The Liberals, in contrast, made huge gains in Quebec and Ontario, securing a majority government by winning an additional 32 seats, for a total of 141 seats in the 264-seat Parliament. Turner was worried about his own riding because the Conservatives had a good candidate, Bill Neville, who had run a strong campaign. On election night, Turner had one speech in his pocket in case he lost and another in case he won. As it turned out, the Conservatives gained votes in Ottawa-Carleton, but NDP support dropped. Turner ended up winning 54 per cent of the vote.

Pierre Trudeau had another majority government, and John Turner had been instrumental in his comeback. "We owed this one to Margaret [Trudeau] and John," said a senior Liberal strategist. "He worked like a son-of-a-bitch in that campaign, brought us maybe 20 seats ... but he never got any credit."[51] During the election night celebrations at the Château Laurier Hotel, Trudeau singled Turner out for thanks, bringing him onstage to share the spotlight in the moment of victory.[52]

The political potency of the Trudeau-Turner combination was reminiscent of other bicultural teams that had underpinned successful Canadian governments going back to the Union of the Canadas: Baldwin and Lafontaine, Macdonald and Cartier, Laurier and Fielding, King and Lapointe, St. Laurent and Howe. There was, however, a less distinguished alternative tradition of prime ministerial paranoia about leadership rivals that included Alexander Mackenzie and Edward Blake, Arthur Meighen and Richard Bennett, and, in the case of King, both Vincent Massey and Mitchell Hepburn. In 1974 it was unclear which pattern would come to distinguish the Trudeau-Turner relationship, but signs indicated that the latter would prevail. Turner was becoming increasingly restive and confrontational, and Trudeau's circle began to interpret everything he did in terms of his leadership ambitions.[53] On the night of the election, Turner went to 24 Sussex Drive, mingled for a while, and had a few drinks, half hoping that Trudeau would seek him out and they could bond a little. It didn't happen. Trudeau's failure to follow up the public recognition with some personal acknowledgment bothered him. "Those guys," he told his friends, "just think of me as a jock with political charm."[54] Mutual suspicion was fostering an atmosphere of distrust that bode ill for the future.

12

STALKING STAGFLATION

During his early years in Finance, Turner had to deal with inflation and unemployment, but at least the economy was growing. The period from 1962 to 1973 was an extended boom, with GNP increasing between 5.2 and 7.7 per cent each year – Canada's longest sustained period of economic growth in modern times. Then, at the end of 1973, the oil shock hit Western economies. In Canada, real economic growth, which had risen by 6-7 per cent in 1972-73, fell during the second half of 1974 and continued to decline in the first half of 1975. This decrease drove unemployment, already high because of the numbers of baby boomers entering the workforce, to levels not seen since the 1930s. Although Canada's economy wasn't doing badly compared to those of other Western countries, its performance in 1974 in relation to previous years was abysmal.

Worse, an unsettling new phenomenon was evident in the bleak economic landscape. Even though economic growth slowed and unemployment rose, inflation did not ease. This combination of factors marked the beginning of stagflation, a hitherto unheard-of predicament in which economic stagnation was accompanied by inflation. Stagflation confounded economists and generated a cacophony of debate and contradictory expert opinion. It was just the latest in a series of economic crises that threw into question the post-war belief, derived from British economist John Maynard Keynes, that governments could manage their economies and world trade through judicious intervention to ensure ongoing prosperity and high employment.

Business interests continued to peddle their market-oriented alternatives to the crumbling Keynesian consensus. According to their critique, government spending was the root of stagflation. It had led to massive borrowing that bumped up interest rates, fuelled inflation, and overstimulated the economy to the point where it no longer responded to the usual macroeconomic controls. This analysis was underpinned by the moral critique that social programs had skewed incentives at the lower end of the labour market, undermining the work ethic by making it more attractive to collect unemployment or welfare.

This interpretation had a certain appeal for policy-makers frustrated with the ineffectiveness of their usual array of economic tools. It was cathartic simply to clear the decks and start again with the basics. Simon Reisman, Turner's deputy minister, reacted this way. He soon converted to the fundamentalism of University of Chicago economist Milton Friedman, who preached a radical reduction in the size of governments, a return to a laissez-faire reliance on unfettered markets, and a rigorous anti-inflationary monetary policy.

Pierre Trudeau responded by exploring his options and seeking alternative perspectives. In the summer of 1974, when Turner was on vacation, Trudeau set up a PMO advisory committee on economic policy under the chairmanship of his principal secretary, Jack Austin, formalizing his practice of seeking independent economic advice.[1] Trudeau had long been interested in the writings of economist John Kenneth Galbraith, whose response to the crisis was to urge more rather than less government intervention. In Galbraith's neo-corporatist vision, big business and big unions were the critical players in modern Western economies. They were impervious to normal market pressures and had to be regulated in the public interest by big government through measures such as wage and price controls.

In the wake of the Liberal election victory of 1974, Turner found himself for the first time in a position to formulate economic policy free of the political exigencies of a looming election or a minority government. His economic ideas had been formed during the era of Keynesian consensus, and his Catholic social conscience, Liberal heritage, and political apprenticeship disposed him to regard the social programs of the post-war era as his party's greatest accomplishments. A pragmatist with an innate intellectual aversion to grand theories, Turner thought that the problem with the economy was not Keynesianism, the welfare state, or even the neo-corporatism depicted by Galbraith, but an unfortunate conjunction of short-term factors. As he'd noted previously, unemployment was largely attributable to structural changes in the labour force.[2] As for the inflationary effects of spending on social programs, he was willing to accept that the economy was having problems circulating wealth in new ways, but he thought it would adjust in time. Besides, inflation was only partly due to government spending. International food and commodity prices, spiked by the oil shock, were the real culprits. Their combined impact had temporarily dampened economic growth.

"I have always believed fundamentally in equalizing opportunity and redistributing wealth. If not, why get into politics?" Turner wrote in response to a question about his economic philosophy. "But the social thrust of any government depends on a strong growing economy. Human priorities must be advanced within the ability of any economy to sustain them."[3] An unrepentant believer in welfare-state liberalism made possible by the productivity of private enterprise, Turner wanted to balance the books to preserve social programs and save the Keynesian system from itself. "I think there always has to be a proper balance between equity and incentive and between growth and re-distribution," he maintained. "I'm concerned to see that we have sufficient growth in order to discharge our social responsibilities."[4]

Balancing the budget was a challenge because the government had little fiscal manoeuvring room. Most of its expanding expenditures were non-discretionary commitments to social programs that it was bound to fund through agreements with the provinces. These deals made it difficult to control the costs of the programs, which were increasing annually. Turner concluded that the federal government had to rethink the open-ended nature of these commitments. Social programs had to be rationalized "in tune with the ability of the country to absorb the additional costs without any basic changes to the tax system."[5] Health care and post-secondary education were the major areas of spending in which costs were accelerating out of control. In 1971 Ottawa had imposed a ceiling on its contributions to educational spending, promising in return to continue its funding until March 1974. Throughout his tenure as finance minister, Turner engaged the provinces on the possibility of further reductions. Quebec and

Ontario suggested that Ottawa simply allow the provinces to opt out of the federal funding arrangements and give them the tax room necessary to finance the programs, but many have-not provinces preferred the existing arrangements.

Turner was not willing to concede Ottawa's primacy in taxation. He offered the provinces some new taxing powers plus some cash to explore lower-cost programs, while slowing the rate of escalation of matching funds for health care. For post-secondary education, he proposed changing from a system based on a percentage of tax revenues to one geared to each province's number of university-age residents. Ontario's Bill Davis rejected this approach and again demanded compensation for opting out. The wrangling continued – indeed, it would be an ongoing feature of federal-provincial relations for decades to come.

Turner also fought a running battle against new spending initiatives. Chief among them was a proposal for a guaranteed annual income (GAI) that Marc Lalonde, the minister of health and welfare, had developed at Trudeau's behest. A GAI plan had been circulating since 1973 in various drafts of the Working Paper on Social Security in Canada (the Orange Paper). This initiative put Turner in an awkward position: he, along with other candidates, had endorsed a GAI during the 1968 leadership race. Back then, it had appealed to progressives as a guarantee of social equity and to conservatives as a way to replace multiple social programs with a single income-support program. However, the proposal Lalonde brought forward constituted an additional social program rather than a rationalization of the welfare state. Turner believed that a major new social program was simply unaffordable under current economic conditions.[6]

When the government was preparing to make its final decision on the GAI early in 1975, Turner pronounced himself sympathetic to the plan's goals but warned that "the economy was in a precarious state ... and announcing new expenditure commitments ... could have a dangerous psychological impact."[7] He told Cabinet that the new program would have to wait until real economic growth had generated higher government revenues. Cabinet decided that Lalonde could talk to the provinces about the income-support portion of his plan but not its central component – a much more expensive income supplement. In the ensuing months, the plan would die the death of a thousand evasions, qualifications, negotiations, and delays. Other countries that had been considering a guaranteed annual income and had encountered a similarly rocky economy came to the same conclusion in this period.

Later commentators would accuse Turner of deliberately pre-empting the guaranteed income initiative by curtailing government revenues with his previous tax reductions, but such analyses overlook the contingent, ad hoc nature of each of Turner's budgets. Moreover, the GAI had been under consideration for most of the period in question, with the attendant revenue/expenditure equation in plain view of Cabinet at large.[8] "Any holder of the portfolio of Finance inevitably finds himself locked into this corner," Turner later explained apologetically. "It is his job to say 'no' and to attempt to reconcile and orchestrate the legitimate priorities advanced by his colleagues. This role puts him in a position of appearing to frustrate his colleagues' ambitions, both at a personal and political level."[9]

Discretionary spending was a relatively small part of the government's budget, but it was the one area that was wholly within its control. In the summer of 1974, Turner implemented a strict spending control policy. He had a stout ally in Jean Chrétien at Treasury Board. Chrétien had been directed to keep increases in spending under 15 per cent, but he wanted to do better than that and worked closely with Turner to that end. Turner preached his restraint message directly to Cabinet.

Even as he pursued this crusade, Turner found himself assessing his career progress and options. Should he now be moving to another portfolio, perhaps External Affairs? On the whole he thought himself better off in Finance. What about Transport? He would like the practical challenges and the chance to work on Western issues, but initiatives took a long time to come to fruition in that portfolio. He decided to stick it out in Finance for another couple of years. It didn't challenge him as it once had, but if he left politics from Finance, he would be going out on top – unless, of course, the economy tanked and took his reputation down with it.[10]

Just such a decline was a real possibility in an economy gripped by stagflation. Informed opinion increasingly saw wage settlements as the most significant factor contributing to inflation. Organized labour was militantly keeping its members' pay in step with the cost of living, and collective agreements were being negotiated for increases ranging from 20 per cent up to a stratospheric 80 per cent. Limiting such increases was difficult because about 35 per cent of Canada's workforce belonged to unions. Governments paid a high political price when they intervened in collective bargaining disputes and were reluctant to take the risk.

Higher wages led to higher prices, and vice versa, each bidding the other up in an incessantly escalating cycle. Controlling prices was just as difficult as controlling wages. More than half of Canada's manufacturing industry was under foreign ownership, much of it owned by multinational corporations operating beyond the control of any national government. The public, meanwhile, was increasingly sensitive to the ravages of inflation and alarmed at news of double-digit wage settlements and rising prices. The conventional wisdom in policy circles was that government intervention was necessary, at least temporarily, to break the inflationary spiral. This line of reasoning led back to the Conservative plank from the previous election – wage and price controls.

Despite its contemptuous rejection of Stanfield's proposal for controls during the 1974 election campaign, the Trudeau government had been flirting with them in various ways since it first came to power. In 1968 it had appointed a Prices and Incomes Commission, which conducted a publicity campaign for voluntary restraint. When that proved ineffective, the commission called for mandatory controls in its 1972 report. The government had ignored its advice. In 1973, when international food shortages caused food prices to rise rapidly, Turner introduced measures to restrict the export of meat and to subsidize the domestic consumption of wheat. The government then created a Food Prices Review Board under economist Beryl Plumptre to manage the problem.

Any plan for controls would be plagued by logistical difficulties. How could the government possibly intervene effectively in an economy as complex as Canada's? Another problem was how to implement controls equitably. Any talk of controls encouraged groups to demand increases for themselves before they were frozen, which would cause inflation to spike in the near term. And no one knew what kind of economic reforms were required during the period when controls capped inflation. In light of his mother's job in the wartime economy, it was ironic that Turner should now find himself faced with the issue of wage and price controls. During the 1974 election campaign, he had declared, "They won't work. I think the

United States threw itself into a Depression with wage and price controls."[11] He remained skeptical about their usefulness. Yet a post-election opinion poll showed that a majority of Canadians now favoured controls, even though they had voted against Stanfield.

Turner began to think that a one-time, temporary imposition of controls might break the inflationary spiral and allow a fresh start. But to avoid the challenge of administering such a scheme and the embarrassment of going back on a campaign promise, he was adamant that the government should first try to broker a voluntary controls scheme. If the situation grew so dire that mandatory controls were required, they would be easier to justify if voluntary controls had already been tried and failed. He convinced Trudeau to give him a chance to coordinate a voluntary system of wage and price controls. Organized labour would be the main stumbling block. For union leaders, getting in bed with big business and big government would be politically risky. Yet Turner received tentative support from labour. Encouraged, he decided to press ahead.

Before this initiative could be launched, however, there was another budget to bring down. It was Turner's fourth, or rather, a re-presentation of his third budget, which had led to the defeat of the Liberals' previous minority government. He explained his budget-making process to journalist Douglas Fisher:

> I begin by trying to get a fix on where the world is going in the next year or two and the effects this will likely have on Canada. The overwhelming political aspect of this budget ... relates to federal-provincial affairs. I had to wrestle with whether what I was doing was the right thing ... getting a fair share for all Canadians from the resource field while treating the provinces fairly ... I also had to live with my responsibility to redistribute and share the benefits.
>
> As a social document, I had to analyze who had to be helped most urgently in the inflationary phase ... [and] decide how far up the scale of income I would go in giving tax relief to individuals. Then I had to ask: Who has to be stimulated?
>
> Here we get into the psychological thing. The most vital component of expansionism is confidence. Businessmen have to see both some

prospect for return and some leeway from government. On labor's side I had the bargaining table in mind. That's why I framed the tax cuts in terms of personal disposable income, which is literally better than "take-home" pay.[12]

The economy had deteriorated significantly under the impact of the oil shocks since the Liberals' re-election. Turner felt obligated to apply some stimulus to avoid a recession. Consequently, the budget he presented to the House on November 18 reduced taxes to encourage consumer spending. At the same time, it restrained the growth of government spending and, in keeping with previous budgets, provided targeted measures to mitigate the effects of inflation on vulnerable members of society. Turner predicted a deficit of about $1.5 billion, much of it attributable to energy-related expenditures, in contrast to the surplus of $275 million anticipated for 1974-75.

He also unveiled his campaign for voluntary wage and price controls. He had already worked out a timetable for reaching an agreement between government, business, and labour. He would brief the provincial finance ministers when they met in Ottawa in early December, then hold private meetings with business and labour leaders over the winter, anticipating a decision about whether to proceed by spring. The dialogue that ensued involved Turner, officers of the Canadian Labour Congress (CLC), and representatives of various business sectors, supported by detailed negotiations at the staff level.

Turner began the talks by seeking a common understanding of Canada's economic situation as a foundation for agreement on appropriate measures of restraint. The feedback he got from business was sobering. It blamed big government for the economy's woes and suggested that the first step in any restraint program should be for government to control its spending and limit wage increases to public-sector unions. After all, governments were the largest employers in the country, with 1.2 million of 9.5 million employed Canadians on their payrolls. (If para-governmental organizations were included – schools, universities, social agencies – the number jumped to 2.5 million.) This message strengthened Turner's resolve to control government spending so he could lead by example on his voluntary controls campaign.

That winter Turner and Trudeau coincidentally vacationed in the same part of Jamaica at the same time. On the flight home, Turner was discouraged to see Trudeau reading Galbraith's *Economics and the Public Purpose*. Trudeau, he feared, was too easily beguiled by Galbraith's "big-picture" structural analysis and failed to appreciate how entrepreneurs and dynamic new businesses generated prosperity in a free-market economy. It bothered him that, as he pursued his campaign for voluntary controls, the prime minister already seemed to be thinking about a mandatory scheme.

Although Turner and Trudeau did not argue face to face about their differences on economic policy, they did fight proxy battles. The economic advisory committee that Trudeau had set up in the PMO under Jack Austin became a bone of contention. Its very existence was an affront to the Department of Finance's prerogative in economic planning. When Turner found out that it had been briefed on the 1974 budget prior to its delivery, he "turned purple," a senior bureaucrat reported. There had been no leaks, but Turner regarded the briefing as a breach of budget secrecy that challenged the finance minister's control of the budget process. Was the prime minister relying on his finance minister for economic advice, or his own office? The line had to be drawn somewhere, and the budget consultation issue seemed to be as good a place as any. Turner protested strongly to Trudeau, who told him he was making too much of it. "I don't care," Turner told him. "You break it up."[13] Trudeau disbanded the committee and simply reverted to his old practice of informally consulting Albert Breton and others of its members.

When Turner jotted down the pros and cons regarding retirement on one of his index cards that winter, the cons – the lack of new challenges within government, the lack of time with his family, the relatively low pay – carried more weight than ever before.[14] He was dismayed that Trudeau had appointed his friend Michael Pitfield as clerk of the privy council that January. He saw the appointment as a dangerous sign of the politicization of the public service and a further centralization of power around the prime minister that would undermine the already diminished independence of Cabinet ministers. Meanwhile, the economy was not getting any better. Trying to contain government spending was an impossible task. Trudeau had been somewhat supportive, but overall there was insufficient political will within Cabinet to make the necessary sacrifices.

As for the top job, there was no sign of it coming open any time soon. ("What are we going to do?" his mother asked an acquaintance during a visit to Ottawa. "This man [Trudeau] is staying far too long. If he doesn't go soon, John will never be prime minister.")[15] Turner felt that he had done all he could in Finance. He could leave now with his political reputation largely intact and live to fight another day. If he stayed, things might end badly, and all his hard-earned political capital would be squandered. Mike Hunter, his former executive assistant, advised him, "There was no question ... you should leave now ... You are spending your credibility quickly for others and will be, if you take another portfolio ... another professional liberal politician like Drury or Martin."[16]

A job in the private sector was an alluring alternative. It couldn't be any more difficult, and it would certainly pay far better. He had four children and wanted them to have a good education. His wife was from a well-to-do family, and he felt he owed her a better standard of living. His Cabinet minister's salary was $54,600 – a good upper-middle-class income for the time – but he spent a lot on entertaining, which was not covered by any expense account. He still had a substantial mortgage on his house in Rockcliffe Park.

Some of Turner's press contacts had direct access to his thoughts on this issue, and they circulated in the press.[17] Journalists were also aware that Turner had been contacted regarding whether he was interested in being considered for the presidency of the World Bank.[18] This leak provided grist for the Ottawa gossip mill for months, but nothing ever came of it.

Before Turner could retire, his deputy minister beat him to it. After twenty-nine years of public service, Simon Reisman announced his imminent retirement in December 1974. He was fed up with the Trudeau way of doing things, angered by Pitfield's appointment, and looking for a new challenge after serving in the top finance post for four years. He thought Turner's work for the International Monetary Fund a useless diversion and his pursuit of voluntary controls a waste of time that merely delayed the inevitable day of reckoning with government spending.[19] Reisman was only fifty-five, and his enemies in government had a field day speculating derisively about the reasons for his departure. In a gesture rare for a Cabinet minister, Turner countered with an article in the *Ottawa Journal* praising Reisman and cataloguing his accomplishments in the public service. The subtext was that Finance, under Reisman's replacement, Tommy Shoyama, would not be easing up on its crusade to control government spending.[20]

Out of the country on IMF business in early April, Turner returned to find that the talks on voluntary controls had reached an impasse. He had invited the unions to accept a 12 per cent limit on wage increases. This amount may have seemed like a generous ceiling, but so far that year, wage increases had been running at 18.0 per cent in the private sector, twice as high as in the United States, and 19.6 per cent in the public sector. At the annual meeting of the Canadian Labour Congress in April, Turner's voluntary wage and price controls proposal was debated for only five minutes before being summarily rejected. Joe Morris, the president of the CLC, had been unable to sell the idea to member unions, and the CLC lacked the authority to impose it. Turner was shaken by this setback and bitterly described the unions as "lemmings" rushing to their own destruction.[21]

At this juncture, he might easily have abandoned his campaign for voluntary controls. He had yet to invest a huge amount of political capital in it and could simply have walked away. Once again he paused to consider the possibility of resigning but decided he wasn't yet finished and plunged ahead.[22] The quest for voluntary controls was difficult for him to resist because it played directly to his political strengths and self-conceits. Although many industrialized countries had some institutionalized form of cooperation between business, labour, and government, Canada lacked any such mechanism. When these sectors had last joined together in a common cause, during the Second World War, informal networks of elites in various sectors had coordinated economic production. Turner remembered those days and the people, such as his mother and C.D. Howe, who had orchestrated a national war effort. He saw himself as their direct heir. He also believed that he was the only politician in the country capable of playing such a role. It was a reprise of his corporate tax cuts initiative: he would go all in and take his chances. If he lost, he had an excuse to leave politics. If he won, he would garner a suitable crowning achievement, a political tour de force, his departing gift to his country.

Turner deployed the time-honoured tactic of manufacturing a sense of crisis to spur the adoption of voluntary controls. He began to exaggerate the bleakness of current economic conditions and the need for immediate action.[23] In ratcheting up the rhetoric, however, he also raised the political stakes and created the perception that an expeditious solution was imperative. Over the next month, he devoted himself to his controls crusade. Endless arm twisting, pleading, and deal making occurred behind the scenes, but it was all for naught.

Turner would later say that Trudeau should have pitched in at this point. This issue was the biggest one confronting the nation, he reasoned, and he had expected the government to throw its full weight behind him.[24] Trudeau should have invited the corporate and labour leaders in for drinks, deployed some of his famous charisma, made them feel important, and solicited their support with a heartfelt appeal to their sense of national duty. But this was Turner's style, not Trudeau's. Trudeau may have been happy to see Turner secure an agreement. On the other hand, perhaps he was not unhappy to see his rival twist in the wind. In any event, from Trudeau's standpoint, there was no good reason for both of them to sacrifice their influence in a lost cause.

The voluntary controls imbroglio was soon subsumed by budget preparations. The country was facing its worst economic conditions since Turner had become finance minister. Inflation had now hit double digits. Real GDP growth had fallen from 7.7 per cent in 1973 to 4.4 per cent in 1974 and was down to 2.6 per cent in 1975. Turner wrote to Trudeau on June 6, 1975, to lay out policy options for the budget. Unemployment was higher, he reported, and inflation rising, bolstered by wage settlements that continued to escalate.[25] He told Cabinet that "he was operating in an economic strait jacket" with "little manoeuvrability to produce a politically popular Budget."[26] The result was a neutral plan that would stay the course in its macro elements, leaving the economy to work through many of its problems itself.

In presenting the budget on June 23, 1975, Turner admitted that, in the current situation, "the traditional instruments of demand management policy" could no longer keep the economy on course. "When inflation reaches a certain point, the stimulation of spending may simply lead to higher prices rather than more jobs." But he was unwilling to use severe measures of fiscal and monetary restraint to rein in inflation while unemployment rose uncontrollably. "The cost would be too high," he said. "The hard-won sense of security in our society would be replaced by a sense of fear and anxiety."[27] He was again trying to steer a middle course.

He told the Commons that he regretted the failure to reach a voluntary agreement on wage and price controls, and that Cabinet had considered mandatory controls but had rejected the idea.

There was another fix they would try first. Business had told government to practise the voluntary controls it preached, and that was what Turner hoped to do. To save money, he raised unemployment insurance premiums and extended the waiting period for unemployment insurance from three weeks to six. He warned of a coming clampdown on federal spending on health care. Tight controls would be implemented to restrain other expenditures, and wage settlements in the public sector could only follow, not lead, those in other sectors. He asked Cabinet for $1.5 billion in spending cuts, got Chrétien's support, and together they won Trudeau's acquiescence. Ultimately, Cabinet agreed to $1.0 billion in cuts. These measures may have seemed impressive, but all they did was reduce the increase in government spending to 15 per cent instead of the 20 per cent originally projected. To help finance this increase, Turner raised income taxes on those making more than $27,000 a year. That still left a projected deficit of $3.675 billion. Despite all his efforts, he was fighting a losing battle.

Media commentary on the budget was mixed. Some were unimpressed by the size of the promised cutbacks, whereas others applauded them as a step in the right direction.[28] Journalists did not want to dwell on the budget, however, because they had exciting gossip to spread. The budget would be Turner's last, they announced. He had had enough of Finance, enough of the Trudeau government, and enough of politics. He would be gone, they reported, before the end of the year.

Again, the national press gallery proved remarkably well informed. In early July Turner met with the prime minister to talk about his political future. He told Trudeau that it was time for him to leave Finance. Trudeau wasn't particularly happy at this prospect and asked him to stay one more year. They talked about the possibility of Turner taking another Cabinet post. External Affairs was the only ministry as prestigious as Finance, but Allan MacEachen had assumed that portfolio just the previous summer. Transport, another option, was already taken. That left Trade and Commerce. It would be a step downward, but it was the best post available. If Turner stayed another year, however, more options could open up. The meeting ended indecisively, and Turner and Trudeau agreed to talk again in a few weeks. In the interim, Turner stewed over the fact that Trudeau had mentioned Marc Lalonde as his possible successor at Finance. He knew that no one was irreplaceable but was annoyed that the prime minister had a ready substitute in mind.[29]

The failure of his campaign for voluntary wage and price controls and the frustration of his efforts to curb spending left Turner without any compelling reason to stay. While holidaying that August at the family cottage on the Lake of the Woods, he thought through the decision from every angle. There was no chance of becoming leader soon. He felt the government was oriented "dreamily left" and had an unrealistic assessment of both economic issues and the public mood. The prime minister wasn't providing effective leadership and hadn't given him sufficient support on voluntary controls or expenditure restraint. If he stayed, his personal position would deteriorate.[30] This time, the cons decisively outweighed the pros. He summoned friends and advisers to Ottawa to help him manage his exit.

Turner made an appointment to see Trudeau on Thursday, September 10, 1975, at 2:15 p.m. He would request that the PMO make the announcement of his departure in a press release – there would be no press conference and no leaks before then. He would not get into an in-depth discussion with Trudeau of the issues behind his decision. A resignation letter was typed up. Key aides were to be informed and sworn to secrecy.[31] He also told friends such as Supreme Court Justice Douglas Abbott and *Montreal Star* columnist W.A. Wilson. Just before seeing Trudeau, he lunched with his deputy minister, Tommy Shoyama, and broke the news. Then he left for Trudeau's office in the East Block.

Trudeau and Turner had already talked the issue over in their previous meeting, so they did not go into as much depth this time. Turner reported that he had thought the matter through and had decided to resign. Even as he made this announcement, the part of him that loved politics was inwardly protesting against the rational side of him that said it was time to go. The prime minister took Turner at his word and did not try to change his mind. Because they had reviewed the dearth of suitable Cabinet posts at their earlier meeting, Trudeau merely mentioned that Turner was of course welcome to have a seat in the Senate or an appointment to the bench. In his conflicted and emotional state, Turner chose to take this comment as a slight, a response that had the attendant moral and psychological benefits of enabling him to present himself as a wronged party rather than as a deserter. He returned to his office and directed that his letter of resignation be sent to the PMO.[32]

Turner's resignation meeting with Trudeau has since been dissected by numerous commentators, most of whom have concluded that Trudeau could and should have talked Turner out of resigning. Perhaps that was possible, but that interpretation also reflects how Turner spun the meeting afterward.[33] In truth, he had been on his way out for at least a couple of years. As Trudeau well knew, it wasn't in Turner's interest to stay any longer. He had done everything he could do in federal politics, short of being prime minister, and that job wasn't available.

Immediately after Turner resigned, the PMO was abuzz in crisis mode. Trudeau and his aides debated whether he should ask Turner to reconsider. But before they could decide, Keith Davey deliberately leaked news of Turner's resignation to the press. The cat was out of the bag, and there was no stuffing it back in.[34] The next day Turner attended a previously scheduled constituency event in Orléans. What would otherwise have been a low-key local affair was now a national media story, with reporters and cameras swarming the scene. He spent Friday at his office on Parliament Hill but left early. His friend John Grace picked him up at a back door of the Parliament Buildings, and they escaped to Grace's cottage on Thirty-One Mile Lake for the weekend.[35] Meanwhile, Trudeau sent a "Dear John" letter accepting Turner's resignation.[36] It was full of praise and regret, but buried within it was the highly political claim that Turner's resignation did not spring from any policy disagreement.

That was true in the strictest sense of the term. Turner hadn't used policy disagreement as an excuse for resigning, and the underlying cause of his departure was his own political self-interest. Yet the PMO's pushiness on this point betrayed its awareness that the real policy differences between Turner and Trudeau could be politically damaging if they were publicized. "It wasn't any one particular thing," explained his executive assistant, John Swift. "It was the whole drift of government policies."[37] If the government had been wholeheartedly pursuing Turner's agenda of voluntary controls and spending restraint, he might have continued on. In the event he was annoyed by Trudeau's "no policy disagreement" ploy. The PMO heightened his aggravation by sending Jim Coutts to ask him to clarify to the press that his resignation had not been for policy reasons.[38] He considered writing a reply to put his concerns on record but decided it was best to remain silent.

Trudeau's supporters predictably portrayed Turner's departure as disloyal. Ontario Liberal leader Robert Nixon was particularly angered by the timing. He was coming to the end of an election campaign that many thought he could win, but on September 18 the Conservatives under Bill Davis won a minority government. There were many possible reasons for why the Ontario Liberals fell short, but the temptation to externalize blame by claiming that Turner's resignation damaged the Liberal brand at a critical moment was irresistible.

From a national unity standpoint, Turner's departure made a government that was already accused of being too French Canadian appear still more so. It also highlighted another of the party's traditional rifts. Turner represented a pragmatic Liberal tradition in the spirit of King, St. Laurent, and Howe, whereas Trudeau and the bulk of Cabinet fell into a more idealistic left-liberal stream.

The press had a field day with the resignation. It was front-page news on September 11, and opinion pieces, op-ed articles, and letters to the editor reverberated for days afterward. Turner was praised for his work on the *Official Languages Act,* his reforms as justice minister, and his brilliant manoeuvring around the 1973 budget. But what dominated commentary was the message his resignation sent about the government's economic policies. He had left, most agreed, because he couldn't get his colleagues to rein in spending and make the country live within its means.[39] In this context, Trudeau's claim that there had been no policy differences seemed patently incongruous.[40]

In Tory circles the news raised an enticing possibility. Could John Turner be recruited to lead the Progressive Conservatives? Stanfield was preparing to resign. If they could draft Turner, they would have the most popular politician in the country running against a struggling government. Victory would be a sure thing.[41] Ten days after his resignation, Turner and his wife attended John Diefenbaker's eightieth birthday party in Saskatoon. The press swarmed him, asking whether this gesture indicated he was changing his political stripes. He was there purely because of his friendship with

Diefenbaker, he replied, and he was a Liberal "by conviction, friendship and loyalty."[42] Despite this disavowal, in a poll asking for ratings of fifteen potential Conservative leadership candidates in Toronto that October, Turner came out on top.[43] He also had to turn down a delegation of Ontario Liberals sounding out his interest in the leadership of their party.

Turner's resignation forced the government to confront the problems facing the Canadian economy. In the press as in business and policy circles, the pressure for dramatic action escalated into an insistent clamour. At the same time, the departure of the leading advocate of voluntary controls cleared the way toward a mandatory system. Recent polls showed that the public would support such drastic intervention.[44] On October 13 Trudeau announced in the House that the government would introduce mandatory price and wage controls after all. He rationalized his about-face by saying that he had campaigned against a wage and price freeze, not controls.

If Turner were held personally responsible for the Canadian economy during his time as minister of finance, his record would have been dismal. When he took office, inflation was 2.9 per cent, unemployment was 6.4 per cent, and the economy was growing at 5.65 per cent annually. In 1975 inflation was 10 per cent, unemployment was over 7.1 per cent, and economic growth had slowed to 2.6 per cent. His record in balancing the books wasn't much better. During these same years, federal expenditures rose from $15.75 billion to $32.43 billion – a 106 per cent increase. The government incurred a deficit in 1974 and would continue to do so in the years to come, in marked contrast to the decades preceding his tenure.

In his defence, he was operating in economic conditions that were not of his making and largely beyond any politician's control. He inherited an inflation problem that the government had been wrestling with unsuccessfully for years. Then unemployment became an issue. The former was attributable to international conditions and the latter to temporary demographic phenomena. Just as he was grappling with these problems, the energy crisis rocked industrialized economies. In 1974 economic growth slowed throughout the West, and Canada faced the novel problem of stagflation. All Western industrialized nations experienced similar conditions – and few managed better.

In Turner's early budgets, political exigencies trumped economic strategy. He made unemployment his main target while using tax reductions and indexing to shelter those Canadians who were most vulnerable to inflation. The consequent reduction in government revenues was not accompanied by proportionate reductions in spending. The political conditions required to initiate spending cuts were not in place until the Liberals won a majority in 1974. Although in his final budgets he was able only to diminish the rate of increase in government spending, it was a step in the right direction.

Indexing income-tax brackets was the most significant of Turner's budget measures because it uncoupled revenues from inflation while leaving expenditures subject to inflationary pressures. Indeed, in retrospect, Canada's subsequent two decades of deficits originated with Turner's 1973 budget. From that point on, the trend lines of revenues and expenditures diverged.[45] Some commentators have interpreted the indexing as part of a hidden agenda inspired by ideological opposition to big government – a pre-emptive strike that made new or enhanced social programs impossible by undermining the government's capacity to fund them.[46] In fact, it was just one of a number of responses – partisan, ad hoc, and short-sighted – to the political and economic exigencies of the moment. Indexing was intended to protect Canadians from the ravages of inflation. The alternative – leaving revenues to rise along with inflation – was less palatable, for it allowed increased taxation without taxpayer's consent. The disconnect between the revenue and expenditure sides of the equation is obvious in hindsight. Raising tax rates for income brackets would thereafter require a deliberate government action that would be politically unpopular. At the time, however, the long-term implications of the indexing measure were unanticipated.

The consistency in Turner's economic record lay in his mix of socially progressive and fiscally conservative instincts. He supported social programs but not beyond the government's fiscal capacity to fund them. A healthy economy with continuing economic growth into the future was a necessary precondition for the government revenues required to fund existing social programs and develop new ones. Always the pragmatic politician, he resisted neo-liberal nostrums and panaceas, hoping to ride out the passing economic storms and consolidate the existing foundations of the welfare state before building anew.

Whatever his record of economic management, Turner excelled in the qualitative side of the job. Canadians knew things were bad but believed they would have been far worse had John Turner not been minister of finance. He emerged from Finance with his reputation enhanced, despite his failure to right the economy.[47] This was a strange yet wonderful phenomenon that could be explained only by his ability to project stability in unstable times. It was a quality eminently desirable in a finance minister. As the gap between revenues and spending continued to widen and government debt mounted in ensuing years, Turner's tenure in finance came to look like a Golden Age of prudence, stability, and balanced budgets, and his image would be burnished by nostalgic longing for the good old days.[48]

Yet Turner symbolized something more important still. In the eyes of the Canadian public, he was playing a historic role as the Anglo partner in the English and French Canadian alliance that traditionally governed Canada. Bruce Hutchison saw his departure in terms of the overriding significance of this role:

> One fact should be clear ... the sudden breakdown of what we may call the inward political structure of a dual nation. As history has demonstrated over and over again since the original partnership of Macdonald and Cartier, the nation can be governed successfully by a coalition of an English-speaking and a French-speaking leader and not otherwise. Until the last few days that kind of unwritten coalition existed in the persons of Mr. Trudeau, who held the confidence of Quebec, and Mr. Turner, who held a broad constituency among the other provinces. When no other English-speaking member of the government enjoys or is likely ever to win anything like Mr. Turner's almost bi-partisan influence, Mr. Trudeau lacks the partner essential to his own success and the nation's welfare.[49]

At a Rough Rider versus Eskimos football game a week after he resigned, Turner was spied entering Lansdowne Park. A murmur ran through the stadium. When he came into clear view, the crowd of twenty-nine thousand rose and cheered. He was overwhelmed. Of all the tributes – the farewell dinners, the media testimonials, the speeches in the House – this was the one that really hit home. In the emotion of the moment, tears filled his eyes. As he noted, with more candour than grace, "They wouldn't have done that for Trudeau."[50]

13
CITIZEN TURNER

John Turner had an advantage most job-seekers lacked: the marquee value of his name. Whatever firm hired him would gain status and credibility that would help attract business and get deals done. He received a number of attractive offers. Brascan offered to appoint him president, with the promise that the CEO position would be his when it came open. Turner's old partners at Stikeman & Elliott wanted him back, so long as he was done with politics. He wouldn't go for that, as he explained: "Whatever I decide to do I hope to do for the rest of my life. Except for one thing. If a situation arose where there was a demand from the country for my services ... then I would want to consider it."[1]

Pressure to run for the leadership of the Progressive Conservative Party continued to mount. Everyone agreed that, with Turner at the helm, the Tories would be guaranteed to win a majority in the coming election. But he simply couldn't bring himself to do it. His sense of loyalty prevented him: he would not abandon his friends and supporters or the party in which he had made his career. The decision was also ideological: the Liberal Party represented ideals he believed in. And in part it had to do with ethics. Although he had always been both ambitious and flexible, he wasn't an unprincipled opportunist. So he turned down the Tory offers. At the Progressive Conservative convention in February 1976, Joe Clark, a relative unknown, surprised everyone by winning the leadership.

That winter Turner joined the Toronto law firm of McMillan Binch as a senior partner. The firm had blue-chip clients such as the Royal Bank and

Algoma Steel, but with some thirty lawyers, it wasn't a large practice. Bill Macdonald, the firm's managing partner, had ambitious growth plans, however, and Turner was just the person to spearhead expansion. He bought a substantial home in Forest Hill, a wealthy Toronto enclave. His new workaday routine began with a walk south to St. Clair Avenue, where he caught a streetcar to the subway. A few months after he started, McMillan Binch moved into the new Royal Bank Plaza, a twin-towered complex sheathed in sparkling gold glass.

Turner's work differed from that of his early law practice. His new partners had invested in his reputation and contacts, betting that his prestige and influence would make things happen. He would be, in effect, executive account manager for big business clients – dealing directly with the CEOs of corporations, heading up teams of lawyers on important files, and offering strategic advice as well as legal opinions on deals, negotiations, tax issues, and regulatory frameworks. His forte in politics had been to analyze a situation, factor in the personalities and interests involved, devise a solution, and orchestrate its implementation. As a business impresario he was just as valuable.

Turner was not quite finished with federal politics. In March 1976, just a month after submitting his resignation as an MP, he gave a speech to the Ontario Economic Council that laid out the views of Citizen Turner on the economy.[2] During an end-of-year interview the previous Christmas, Trudeau had ruminated about how the Canadian economy's recent problems raised doubts about the efficiency of markets. His remarks had been seized on by the right and distorted to give the impression that the prime minister did not believe in free enterprise. The controversy resurrected Turner's long-standing worries about Trudeau's flirtation with Galbraith. "The Prime Minister warns us that we must change our attitudes," he observed. "I doubt that we can change men's motives, including the drive for material betterment." His main point, however, was that government had to discipline its spending. "Clearly some ... programs are out of control," he explained. "I mean the open-ended programs of medicare, hospitalization and post-secondary education. These programs are essential. But they can be redesigned so that the costs do not continue to rise at a rate well above that of the gross national product."[3]

These comments were nothing new: he had made the same points consistently as finance minister. Now, however, he also argued for a tighter fiscal policy, including restrictions on the money supply. Throughout his time at Finance, he had shunned such measures because of the human and political costs involved. Now he decided that unemployment could never be solved unless inflation was dealt with first. Though a departure for Turner, this was hardly a radical position for the times. The Bank of Canada had already adopted it the previous September. Like other policy-makers, Turner was casting around for any kind of economic management tool that would have an appreciable effect on the economy. The desperate times of stagflation and oil shocks called for desperate measures.[4]

Citizen Turner's economic views put him to the right of the Trudeau Liberals, but again, only marginally so. There was vastly more political ground further to his right than there was between him and Trudeau, and in his new job he was working in that terrain on a daily basis. The venerable family firms of stockbrokers, accountants, bankers, and lawyers on Bay Street had always been run by a parochial old boys' network. In an earlier era its privilege had been attended by a sense of social obligation. The generation now passing from the scene had lived through the Great Depression, when Christian charity was taken seriously, and had subscribed voluntarily to the social contract of the post-war reconstruction era. The generation now on the rise was, in contrast, reverting to laissez-faire doctrines that rationalized business privilege. C.D. Howe would have been hard put to recruit many dollar-a-year men from its ranks. Many of its leading spokesmen were unreconstructed nineteenth-century laissez-faire liberals who embraced a mono-causal free-market model of how things worked and blamed big government for all the world's woes. As the government's ability to direct the economy seemed to slip, they grew more confident in the correctness of their unenlightened self-interest.

Though Turner was of the same vintage as the rising generation on Bay Street, his values were closer to those of its parents. He remained a C.D. Howe Liberal who believed that government had an important role to play, especially if it were run by good men who could handle the big issues. His faith in rational management dovetailed with the social justice injunctions of his Catholicism, underpinning his support for the welfare state and a mixed economy. "I've been influenced by the encyclicals of Pope Leo XIII, which favour the working man, one's duty to one's employee, and one's duty to the weaker elements of society, so my religion has a lot to do with

my liberalism," he told a journalist.[5] That Turner wasn't quite ideologically aligned with many of his followers was illustrated by an incident at a
November 1977 Liberal fundraising dinner he hosted in Toronto. When
he began his remarks in French, a heckler yelled, "We're in Toronto, John!"
– followed by much guffawing. Turner snapped back, "We're also in Canada."
There was a pause, followed by a warm ovation.

Bill Lee, Trudeau's one-time campaign manager and head of the Ottawa
lobbying firm Executive Consultants, kept Turner up to date with what
was happening in the capital. Turner dispensed this insider information
to his business contacts, demonstrating that he was still knowledgeable
about the federal scene.[6] Such information was valued by corporations.
Soon after leaving politics, Turner was offered, and accepted, two corporate directorships. By the next spring he had three more. In the boardroom
he rubbed shoulders with many directors of great wealth or power, but
few could match his reputation. He had an aura of influence from having
moved in the corridors of power around the world. Rumours circulated
that he would be the next head of the International Monetary Fund. Whenever a foreign statesman he knew came to town, Turner invited him for
lunch at the firm, along with McMillan Binch's biggest clients. The visitor
would give a short address with an insider's analysis of an issue of the day,
then take questions. Everyone would leave sated with fine food, good drink,
and the satisfaction of being plugged in.

Turner soon fell into the habit of lunching at Winston's, a pricey restaurant
a few blocks from his office. He had a regular table where he conducted
business or talked politics over a martini or two before the food arrived.
Lunch was steak and salad accompanied by red wine, followed by his ha-
bitual Monte Cristo cigar. Winston's was a favourite haunt of Bay Street
power-mongers, and a parade of acquaintances and admirers stopped by
his table to pay homage. Business people thought that Turner, by resigning
and coming to work with them, had endorsed their world view. Those who
opposed Trudeau, but respected the Liberals' long association with power,
looked to him as the one who could bring the natural governing party back
to its senses – and back to them.

On a day-to-day basis it was impossible for Turner to avoid commenting
on federal politics. At work, at lunch, and on the cocktail circuit, he was
constantly solicited for his opinions. He enjoyed speaking with a freedom

he had not had while in office. The list of the government's failings was long, and, for the sake of simplicity, he laid the blame at the feet of the prime minister: Trudeau demoralized and politicized the public service; his government had no control over spending; his fixation with a symmetrical, centralized federalism provoked needless confrontations with the provinces; he had queered relations with Canada's allies, particularly the United States and members of NATO. And that was just for starters. Turner's main objections to the Trudeau government stemmed from his brokerage approach to politics. He felt that Trudeau had allowed a breakdown in communications with key constituencies. He had centralized power in his office and the Privy Council Office, thereby weakening critical departments and their ministers. He ignored the party rank and file and was hostage to an insular clique of Machiavellian advisers. Canada instead needed the type of leader who would unite it by reaching out to all its disparate parts.

Turner's critiques of Trudeau were also based on his understanding of the Liberal Party's historical role in the country. Over the years the Trudeau government's leftist, interventionist bias had solidified support for it among Quebeckers, immigrants, women, youth, and low-income Canadians. Deeper loyalties from these groups had come at the expense of support in the middle and upper-middle classes and the West. These divisions concerned Turner, who saw the Liberal Party as a pan-Canadian institution through which regions, classes, minority groups, and other interests should all be reconciled. "The country is being divided," he told Richard Gwyn. "We are seeing rigidities on all sides; the provinces at Ottawa's throat, labor hostile, business suspicious, bilingual antagonisms."[7] Turner's Liberal Party was an accommodating yet progressive instrument of national unity rather than an opportunistic cabal that cynically divided Canadians for the sake of short-term electoral advantage.

Though Turner had firm opinions and a constituency in the Liberal Party, he was not campaigning to replace Trudeau. In the fall of 1976, Richard Gwyn asked him point-blank if he were still hoping to become prime minister. The answer was candid. "I am not looking for it," Turner told him. "I'm a realist about politics, about a time and a place and so on ... There is no party in exile. There is no cabal ... I am not biding my time." Still, in the same breath he repeated his "call of duty" proviso, adding, "If the opportunity came to serve the country in that position, no, I wouldn't turn my back on it."[8]

Such a prospect alternately brightened and dimmed throughout the late 1970s. Trudeau's popularity sagged in the year following Turner's resignation. Then the election of the Parti Québécois in November 1976 raised fears that Quebec would separate. Trudeau seemed the only hope for keeping the country together, and his popularity climbed. In 1977 his marital problems generated public fascination and sympathy that further boosted his popularity. His advisers urged him unsuccessfully to call an election in the fall, only three years into his mandate, when they saw an opportunity to win another majority. The moment soon passed, and Trudeau's popularity nose-dived again, after which talk of Turner's return to save the Liberals resumed once more.[9]

Turner had to walk a fine and wavering line to keep his political currency without appearing to be advancing his personal agenda at the expense of his party. There were always critics ready to call him offside. One such occasion came when he addressed the Primrose Club, a Jewish social club in Toronto, just after the Parti Québécois victory. Convinced the country faced a grave crisis, he reiterated his long-standing position that Quebec had legitimate aspirations that could be accommodated without compromising the integrity of Confederation and that the federal government should be more flexible in its constitutional stance. A *Toronto Star* reporter was one of the five hundred people in the audience for these "off-the-record" remarks. They appeared in the *Star* the next day, spun, for human interest value, as evidence of the rivalry between Liberal titans Turner and Trudeau.[10] The Trudeauites responded immediately with renewed accusations of disloyalty. Turner wrote to the *Star* to protest that he had not once mentioned Trudeau's name, but, given that he had directly assaulted Trudeau's policies, this objection was disingenuous – as was his defence that he was speaking in a private setting. Although he had every right to comment on issues, his remarks were bound to become public.[11]

Trudeau was a proud man who resented Turner's comments and bristled at suggestions he should step aside for his former finance minister. There were other reasons for his bitterness. In 1977 his wife, Margaret, left him in the full glare of the international media spotlight, decamping to New York to become a party-girl and serial groupie to the Rolling Stones and others in the passing celebrity parade. In the warm-up to Margaret's melt-down, Trudeau had suspected that details of his private life were passing from her friend Gro Southam to Geills Turner and from there to the Toronto cocktail circuit.[12] Liberal organizers were informed that they should not expect to have both Trudeau and Turner attend the same event. Trudeau's murderous state of mind was evident in his response to a reporter's question about his leadership. "If I found in my own ranks that a certain number of guys wanted to cut my throat," Trudeau replied, "I'd make sure I cut their throats first."[13]

The Trudeauites' resentment of Turner did not diminish their appreciation of his political value. In June 1977 they sent emissaries to Toronto with a peace offering: he could have the Toronto riding of Eglinton, soon to be vacated by Mitchell Sharp, and rejoin the government as minister of external affairs – the post that had not been available when he resigned. The talks went nowhere. The governing faction's fallback strategy was to use patronage to cherry-pick Turner supporters, many of whom were successfully recruited into party or government positions.[14]

Turner should have learned from the Primrose episode that he could not criticize the government and expect his comments to be treated like those of an ordinary citizen venturing his opinions in private, but he did not. His law partner, Bill Macdonald, was an enterprising power-broker with decided right-wing views. Some remembered him as the author of Hellyer's nomination acceptance speech at the 1968 Liberal leadership convention, a turgid address widely credited with sending dozens of delegates scurrying to support other candidates. While building McMillan Binch into a leading Bay Street law firm, Macdonald satisfied his appetite for politics by circulating his commentary on current events at Queen's Park and Ottawa to friends and colleagues. In 1977 he proposed to Turner that they publish a restricted-circulation newsletter that would offer information on and analysis of current events in business and government. It would be part of the firm's package of services to clients, generating some revenue (a subscription would cost $15,000 a year) while simultaneously boosting the McMillan Binch brand. Turner agreed.

The newsletters were relatively innocuous. They contained concise evaluations of the economy, the political prospects of governments, and speculation about election calls – the type of incisive, informed insider's commentary that a busy executive could retail at the club to show he was "in the know." Occasionally, the newsletters made passing comments on particular politicians. Referring to Minister of Finance Jean Chrétien, the March 31, 1978, issue claimed that "the Minister's optimism (some of which is admittedly professional) is leaving him with a growing credibility gap."[15] The edition on July 14 said Chrétien had been "hurt" by "the sales tax brawl" and now had "much less leverage," portraying him generally as a lame duck. The next issue catalogued "weakness in some key economic ministries of the federal government." One of the weak links named was Turner's long-time friend and supporter Alastair Gillespie, the minister of energy, mines, and resources. "The Minister is generally perceived to lack the confidence of the Prime Minister," it asserted. "He is dedicated to a mixture of very strong economic nationalism and an apocalyptic obsession about physic-ally running out of Canadian oil and gas all of a sudden one morning."[16]

If Turner thought these slighting remarks would remain under wraps, he was deluding himself. Copies of the newsletters found their way into the hands of eager reporters, and Global television and the *Toronto Star* ran stories on them in early September. Their criticisms of the Trudeau administration were again interpreted as evidence of tensions between the prime minister and his heir apparent. The personal comments caused the most serious damage. Although he had never been close to Turner, Keith Davey was stung by comments about him and would recall the slight in his memoirs years later. The effect was worse on those who thought they were Turner's friends. Gillespie was hurt, and Turner apologized, explain-ing that his remarks had been taken out of context.[17] When they next met, he explained that he hadn't written the offending remarks. That wasn't good enough for Gillespie, since Turner was, after all, billed as the co-author of the newsletters. Gillespie decided that Turner was suffering from a form of the Stockholm syndrome: now a hostage of the business community, he had begun to block out his former life and identify with his captors.[18]

Jean Chrétien was also angered by the comments about him.[19] His par-liamentary secretary, Ed Lumley, phoned Turner and told him the damage he had done. Turner wrote to those he had offended in Ottawa to explain his criticisms, and he and Chrétien ostensibly made up in September 1978. Later, however, another newsletter criticized a Chrétien budget, provoking Chrétien once again. He was sensitive about his reputation and remembered slights for years. Turner didn't realize the severity of the wound – and it would come back to haunt him.[20]

The whole affair was probably nothing more than a case of bad judgment on a minor project that Turner had ill-advisedly approved but was too busy to keep tabs on. Whatever the cause, his failure to repair the damage was more troubling. As a politician he had been consistently adroit in his personal relations. In this case he had been ham-handed. He dismissed the negative reaction to the newsletters as overblown and never fully comprehended the severity of the damage they caused. Had he lost his touch?

A more likely explanation was that he was distracted. During this period Turner was emerging as one of the country's best-connected and most influential businessmen. Edgar and Charles Bronfman had retained him as the legal counsel for Cemp Investments, their holding company, which controlled (besides Seagram's) Cadillac Fairview, Bow Valley Resources, and other firms. He sat on the boards of Canadian Pacific and MacMillan Bloedel. He was also a director of a clutch of lesser-known firms: Sandoz Canada (a subsidiary of a Swiss-owned pharmaceutical firm), Crédit Foncier (a Quebec trust company), Marathon Realty (CP's real estate arm), and two mutual funds – the Montreal-based Canadian Investment Fund and the New York-based Canadian Fund. As he had back in his Montreal days as a lawyer, Turner also dedicated time to volunteer service, sitting on the boards of an array of charities and public-sector institutions.[21] "He's a splendid fellow, a good director," said Toronto financier Hal Jackman. "I like him because we like the same brand of cigars, Monte Cristo #3. We sit at the same end of the boardroom table and smoke our six dollar cigars together."[22]

A constant stream of business deals commanded Turner's attention. In 1979 his friendship with George Shultz led to a position on the board of Bechtel, an American multinational engineering firm. Turner's connections were useful for a company that was involved in the Alberta oil-sands and the James Bay hydroelectric development in northern Quebec.[23] As a Bay Street colleague put it, "big corporations, especially big U.S. corporations ... can go to their boards and justify having hired the former finance minister of Canada."[24] His international experience also helped. "He had the ability and knowledge of world financing which helps clients find the money to fund overseas projects," explained Robert Paul, president of Bechtel

Canada.[25] In one case, he arranged $700 million in loans from Canadian chartered banks and the federal Export Development Corporation to build a natural gas processing plant in Algeria. Bechtel had done $20 million worth of preparatory work when the president of Algeria died and the project was shelved. Turner helped get the Algerians to pay the bill.

Turner dealt with businessmen the same way he had dealt with premiers, American secretaries of state, and IMF officials. He did his homework, sized up the issues and the players, established a rapport, and then got everyone to sit down and coaxed them toward a deal. A little socializing went a long way. When he was in Toronto, there was a constant whirl of dinner parties, corporate events, and charity fundraisers where business and pleasure were so intermingled that it was difficult to distinguish between the two. "I drink a bit," Turner explained as he tried to describe one of the hazards of this life. "Scotch now and then. But if I'm drinking with some guy I don't know and he stops, I stop too. He's after something."[26]

After three years in the private sector, Turner was fully immersed in his new life. "People think there is something going on with Turner and his gang and nothing could be further from the truth," David Smith told a reporter. "Turner ... sees the question of whether he goes back into politics as something determined by factors outside his control."[27] That did not prevent the press from touting him as the leader-in-waiting.[28] Trudeau's spectacular rise to power back in 1968 had a lasting effect on public expectations of leaders, and the press yearned for the emergence of a new storybook personality to advance the plot of the national narrative. Turner-as-leader-in-exile was an appropriate confection. "Wherever Turner goes he exudes that unmistakable star quality," proclaimed one national affairs columnist.[29] Turner was imagined into mythic proportions to serve political commentators' need for a viable alternative to Pierre Trudeau. The myth grew as Trudeau's popularity declined, keeping Turner's political future alive even as it grotesquely inflated and distorted his image.

Speculation about Turner's return referred reverentially to the 195 Club as if it were an omnipotent secret cult. Although there was no formal organization based on Turner's 1968 delegates, he did have an extensive network of contacts and supporters. Many would benefit by becoming part of the new plugged-in elite if he became leader, and they could be expected to respond to a call-to-arms. Taking a long-term view, they manoeuvred for influence within riding associations so they could determine the selection of delegates should a leadership convention be called. They had staked their political fortunes on Turner. For the moment, however, they could do little more than urge him to run and pepper him with advice on how to position himself and when to make his move.

Meanwhile, Trudeau's popularity continued its steady decline. Burdened with a decade of accumulated grievances, his government was fighting a losing battle against the economy and sliding in the polls even as an election loomed. Fifteen by-elections were held in six provinces on October 16, 1978, and the Liberals lost all but two of them, including Donald Macdonald's old seat of Rosedale (Macdonald, like Turner, had resigned as finance minister and MP). The logical alternative to Trudeau should have been Conservative leader Joe Clark, but "Joe Who?" came across as plodding and ineffectual. In December 1978 the *Toronto Star* published a poll showing that Clark's eight-point lead in the current polls would turn into a four-point deficit if Turner were Liberal leader instead of Trudeau.[30]

When Turner had been in government, Trudeau's closest confidants had regarded him as a threat and had circled the wagons instead of reaching out to him. Now their siege mentality deepened. They saw Turner and his legendary network as an enemy force massing without, and they slipped into a paranoia that blamed all their travails on Turner's treachery. With an election call imminent and the results anticipated to be unpleasant, government loyalists portrayed Turner's 1975 resignation as the defection of a traitor. More astute players hedged their bets. When Keith Davey found himself on the same flight as Turner en route to a Liberal gathering in 1978, he passed him a note that read simply, "John – The great ones always return. Welcome back."[31]

Trudeau postponed calling an election for as long as possible. Finally, on March 26, 1979, he asked the governor general for a dissolution and set the election date for May 22. As it turned out, Clark's Progressive Conservatives won a minority government. Everyone predicted that Trudeau would resign within a few months. At first he was adamant he would not leave. Some speculated this refusal was a dog-in-the-manger stance to deny the party leadership to Turner. After contemplating his limited options and his low approval ratings, Trudeau announced his resignation as Liberal leader on November 21, 1979. The race was on.

Most political pundits were predicting the triumphal return of John Turner, followed, in due course, by an election that would bring another Liberal majority government. Letters had been streaming into Turner's office for months, pleading with him to run to save the country. Some were from friends and party workers, but others represented a cross-section of Canadians, from an elderly lady in Halifax to a restaurant owner in Montreal to CEOs of major corporations. "Much afraid of Trudeau and his henchmen!" declared Mrs. S.W. Proudfoot of New Glasgow, Nova Scotia.[32]

In the week following Trudeau's resignation, senior Turner supporters gathered to plan his campaign.[33] They commissioned a national poll to assess who would do better in an election against Clark, Turner or Donald Macdonald. John de B. Payne and Bill Macdonald coached Turner on how to handle the press. Turner talked to his friends and supporters in Ottawa and across the country, assessing who was likely to run and how the forces were lining up. Then he sketched out the pros and cons of running on his index cards.

He didn't like the odds. The rivalry between him and Trudeau had deepened into bitter antagonism over the previous four years. The newsletters, his private-public comments, his putative alliance with Bay Street, and media hyping of him as the heir apparent had all created a schism in the Liberal Party. His detractors resented his perceived acts of disloyalty. He might be able to neutralize the damage with an apology, but he had no appetite for eating humble pie. The Trudeau forces had used the months between the election and Trudeau's resignation to do everything they could to block a Turner succession. Keith Davey and Jim Coutts were cajoling and pulling in IOUs in senior party ranks to line up support for Donald Macdonald, their favoured candidate, and most of the caucus was likely to go along. Meanwhile, Marc Lalonde was busy working to deliver Quebec delegates to Macdonald. The "fix was in," Turner concluded.[34] His advisers suggested that the establishment's push for Macdonald could backfire and that Turner should run as the candidate of open democratic process in the party. Perhaps, but it would still be a close-run campaign that he could easily lose. And what would be the prize if he won? An exhausted and divided party, and quite possibly, a lengthy spell in opposition.[35]

Turner also had to consider what he would be giving up for a run at the leadership. He was fully engaged in a lucrative and gratifying business career. He was being considered for the position of CEO of Canadian Pacific. His children were still living at home, benefiting from having a father who came home after work most days. His wife was lukewarm about his returning to politics. They were living the good life: a house in Forest Hill, private schools for the children, a ski chalet in Collingwood, summer vacations at Lake of the Woods, memberships in private clubs, winter holidays in the Caribbean, and wilderness canoe expeditions on remote northern rivers. All these luxuries took more money than a prime minister earned. His supporters suggested a trust fund to compensate him for his financial sacrifices, similar to the one he had once overseen for Lester Pearson, but he knew that wouldn't wash in the modern political environment.

None of these considerations would have stopped Turner had he felt compelled to run. However, he liked and respected Macdonald and thought he would do a good job. There was no clarion call to duty. He arranged a press conference on December 10, three weeks after Trudeau's resignation, and told the assembled scribes that he would not be a candidate for the leadership of the Liberal Party. There was surprise, some consternation, a brief speculation that he was playing hard to get, and then everyone forgot about it and concentrated on those who were in the race.

The episode was revealing. Months before, a friend had noted that Turner's "political adrenalin isn't flowing any more."[36] If he truly lusted after power, this was his moment to jump in, fight for the prize, and seize his destiny. Instead, he was ambivalent and hesitant – not the qualities required for the cutthroat competition of national politics. Citizen Turner returned to private life and, had events unfolded as expected, might well have disappeared forever from the pages of Canadian political history.

PART 3
LEADERSHIP, 1979-88

14

A MYTH AND A MUDDLE

Turner's abstention proved propitious. No sooner had he announced his decision than a bizarre chain of events resurrected Trudeau's political career. On December 13, 1979, the Conservatives lost a vote of confidence on a budget that would have raised the excise tax on gasoline by eighteen cents a gallon, and their minority government fell. The Liberals found themselves facing the prospect of an election without a leader. Senior politicians and party officials consulted frenetically. Trudeau began to consider returning, Macdonald's supporters tried to dissuade him, and others tried to convince Turner to step forward. Allan MacEachen argued that there was no time for a divisive leadership contest: their only option was to bring Trudeau back to fight another campaign. Ed Lumley agreed and phoned Turner, who concurred.[1] Trudeau agreed to return as leader, leaving putative leadership candidates Donald Macdonald, Lloyd Axworthy, and Jean Chrétien in the lurch. On February 18, 1980, the Liberals won a majority government. It was as though Canadians had wished to discipline Trudeau, but, having done so, did not want to see themselves represented by Joe Clark, and so restored Trudeau, hoping he would behave himself this time.

Trudeau's last government presided over one of the more eventful periods in Canadian politics. Quebec held a referendum on separation. The economy slid into the worst recession since the Dirty Thirties. Alberta clashed with Ottawa over its National Energy Program. Then the federal government faced off against a majority of the provinces and forced through patriation and reform of the constitution. This last momentous development came from a rare alignment of the stars. First, Trudeau interpreted his return to power as a gift of the fates to allow him to fulfill his life's great work. He was back just in time to fight for federalism in the referendum on sovereignty-association that Quebec premier René Lévesque had called for May 20, 1980. During that campaign, Trudeau promised Quebeckers a new deal in Confederation. When the federalist side won with 58.6 per cent of the vote, he renewed efforts to patriate the Canadian constitution and fuse a charter of rights to it. After several plot twists and turns, including a confrontation with Margaret Thatcher, references to senior courts, and high-tension negotiations with the provinces, a deal was struck late one night during constitutional talks in Ottawa. At a ceremony in Ottawa on April 17, 1982, Queen Elizabeth II signed the proclamation of the new Canadian constitution.

Trudeau had previously been something of a disappointment as prime minister. Now that he had ensured himself a lasting place in Canadian history, expectations grew that he would arrange a succession and retire gracefully from office. The future of the party could be assured by an early and orderly leadership transition that would give his successor time to put his stamp on the government and choose an appropriate moment for an election. When these expectations went unfulfilled, the Liberal Party began to seethe with discontent. A steady flow of letters poured into Turner's office, imploring him to return to public life and offering support and financial assistance. The Liberals grew so unpopular that polls showed they would lose no matter who was at the helm, but under Turner they did better than with any other leader. Given that he had been out of politics for over seven years, this support raised the hope that he would poll even better were he back in the public eye.

Trudeau's new claim on posterity piqued Turner's own sense of destiny. His situation differed from what it had been in 1979 in several respects. McMillan Binch was now one of the country's major law firms. By 1982 it had tripled in size to ninety lawyers, and billings had quintupled to over $20 million. Turner was a major reason for the firm's success. His income was reputed to be around $350,000 annually, and his career was more successful with each passing year. The Bronfmans had appointed him to the board of Seagram's in 1980. He had joined the board of Massey Ferguson the same year, and was named to the board of Holt Renfrew in 1982.[2]

These prestigious corporate directorships were laurels symbolizing his status as a senior statesman of the business community rather than new challenges. He had proven himself in business and had sufficient financial resources to revisit his old political ambitions. In terms of his career, Turner felt much the same as he had toward the end of his time as finance minister in 1975: restless and ready for a change. Now that his youngest child was twelve, his family commitments were easing. He could afford to revisit old dreams. "I remember once when I was on the phone with him from my office on Parliament Hill and he was in his law office in Toronto," David Smith recalled. "I said I had to go because the bells were ringing to call in the MPs for a vote. He asked me if I could just hold the phone up – he wanted to hear the bells again."[3] For most of Turner's life, people had expected that one day he would be prime minister. He had come to expect it himself. As journalist Walter Stewart observed, politics was in his blood: "Economic power is pleasurable, but political power is addictive. As a businessman, Turner can do well, become rich and have a lot of fun; as a politician, he has the potential to change the nation."[4]

Trudeau's constitutional coup did not translate into enduring political popularity. The National Energy Program – the Liberals' new strategy for splitting oil and gas revenues with the producing provinces, directing exploration and development, and achieving greater energy self-sufficiency – was reviled in the West. The government's economic management soon made it unpopular elsewhere in the country as well. Finance Minister Allan MacEachen's 1981 budget attacked business tax breaks, arousing the ire of powerful vested interests. The government had counted on rising oil prices to boost the economy and fund federal spending. Instead, worldwide supply increased, prices plateaued, and projected revenues failed to materialize. Following the lead of the United States, where Federal Reserve chairman Paul Volcker had set out to strangle inflation with high interest rates, the Bank of Canada eventually raised interest rates to more than 18 per cent. In time inflation did drop back to marginal levels, whether as a result of government monetary policy, falling oil prices, or both, but in the interim this stiff fiscal discipline precipitated a sharp recession in 1981. As a result, more demands were made on social programs, and the government's expenditures rose just as hoped-for revenues dwindled. In 1983 the deficit reached $30 billion, an increase to 6.2 per cent of GNP from 3.5 per cent in 1980.

Rather than having to apologize for his criticism of the Trudeau government, Turner was now benefiting by his distance from it. The worse the Liberals did in the polls, the more they needed Turner. He offered both fiscal competence and a clean break with the ruling regime. Yet he did nothing to put together an organization to mount a leadership bid. In his mind, to do so would be to violate the Liberal tradition of loyalty to the leader. In any event, opposition to the Trudeau regime was coalescing without his help. Rank-and-file Liberals were angered by the concentration of power in Trudeau's inner circle, most notably around Jim Coutts and Keith Davey, and the withering of the Liberal Party as a democratic national organization. When Coutts got himself nominated as the Liberal candidate for the Toronto riding of Spadina for a 1981 by-election, many saw it as a shameless abuse of insider influence and were happy to see him lose.

The Young Liberals traditionally took the lead in demanding reform, and so it was on this occasion. At the November 1982 Liberal policy convention in Ottawa, a motion was introduced proposing that the rules of the convention be changed to provide for a review of the leadership. Dissidents were still unwilling to attack Trudeau directly, so the motion failed, but the youth group found an indirect way to get the point across. It drafted Resolution 40, a bluntly worded denunciation of the manipulative practices of backroom oligarchs, which passed with strong support.

Turner went to the policy convention for just one day, Saturday, November 6, missing Trudeau's speech on the Friday night. He was mobbed wherever he went. "It was like a coronation parade, a royal walkabout," reported the *Montreal Gazette*, and described Turner "blue eyes ablaze above an even-toothed smile, pausing every few steps to pump another out-stretched hand among the throngs of Liberals who pressed enthusiastically around him."[5] Turner did not openly challenge Trudeau, but he let it be known that he agreed with Resolution 40. The two were at pains to avoid running into each other, which led to some Keystone Cops turns as their aides manoeuvred frantically in the hallways to keep them apart.

In January 1983 another Gallup poll suggested that, although Clark would defeat Trudeau, he would lose to Turner.[6] The poll was commissioned privately, probably by a Progressive Conservative power-broker with an interest in ousting Clark through a leadership review vote coming up at the Tory convention later that month. As it happened, Clark received 66.9 per cent support at the convention, but declared it an insufficient endorsement and called a leadership convention in Ottawa that June. There he was replaced as Conservative leader by Montreal lawyer and business-man Brian Mulroney.

Turner was unimpressed with the Tories' choice. The party's best – men he trusted and admired such as Peter Lougheed, Bill Davis, and former Ontario treasurer Darcy McKeough – had stayed out of the race. He re-garded Mulroney as "a charming intellectual lightweight whose business experience consisted largely of running errands for his bosses at Iron Ore Co."[7] The new Conservative leader was portrayed in the press as glib, not up to speed on the issues, and, worse, a bit of a shyster. "He's cunning, shallow, and untrustworthy," wrote Douglas Fisher. "Overfull of ambition, and a hypersensitive ego."[8] Mulroney's arrival on the scene arguably im-proved Turner's prospects for the Liberal leadership. Mulroney was a businessman offering a rightward correction to the politics of the Trudeau era. So was Turner. By electing a bilingual Quebecker, the Conservatives were hoping to make inroads on the Liberals' enduring bloc of MPs from Quebec. But Turner was also bilingual and had a background in Quebec, not to mention the West. By electing him leader, the Liberals would be able to fight fire with fire, with the bonus that Turner had stronger private-sector credentials and more political experience than Mulroney.

Meanwhile, the media continued to pump out stories suggesting that Turner was waiting in the wings. The previous fall, Christina McCall-Newman had published *Grits: An Intimate Portrait of the Liberal Party*, which included a long section portraying Turner as a glamorous but shallow political animal on the make. It became the standard background piece for journalists rushing to cobble together a story on the Liberal heir ap-parent. Another influential article appeared in the June 1983 edition of *Toronto Life* magazine. Penned by veteran political journalist Walter Stewart, its title, "The Natural," nicely summarized the sense of inevitability surrounding Turner's candidacy. Stewart had talked to long-time Turner supporters as well as those who were jumping on the bandwagon. He concluded,

> There comes a time in every leadership campaign – even the undeclared ones – when everything seems to click into place for one candidate ... It doesn't mean the campaign is over, by a long shot, but it means that, barring calamity, one candidate stands head and shoulders above the rest. In Ottawa, today ... there is a strong whiff of Turner in the air ... as the party regulars swing into position behind the corporation lawyer from McMillan Binch, who says he is not yet willing even to consider whether he will run.[9]

This edition of *Toronto Life,* with Turner's face on the cover, could be seen everywhere in southern Ontario throughout the summer of 1983. Stewart's profile was not uncritical, yet the amount of media space accorded Turner perpetuated the myth of the imminent return of the saviour.

Turner asked some trusted friends what he should do if and when Trudeau did resign. They assured him that the buzz was real; he had an excellent chance of winning the leadership. In August he left for his annual holiday at the family cottage on Lake of the Woods. These vacations usually gave him the time and perspective he needed to think things through, but this time he returned home undecided. Later that fall he began to meet for private discussions about his candidacy with a group of advisers that included John de B. Payne; lawyer John Swift, his former executive assistant in finance; Bill Lee, the Ottawa lobbyist; Rick Alway, warden of Hart House at the University of Toronto and a friend from the annual Michaelmas Conference at St. Michael's College; and Bob Foulkes, a Petro-Canada executive based in Calgary who had once been Judd Buchanan's executive assistant. Irene Robinson, a veteran Toronto Liberal organizer, was later drafted as a concession to gender equity. The "Group of Seven," as they came to call themselves, met in the Newfoundland Room on the mezzanine level of Toronto's Royal York Hotel, a short walk from Turner's office.

Their discussions included a review of factors that might trip up a Turner candidacy. In 1981 he had been questioned by the McDonald Commission regarding the RCMP's illegal actions against Quebec separatists during the early 1970s while he was minister of justice, but he had emerged from the affair with his reputation unsullied.[10] The only other potential embarrassment was his involvement with CFI Investments, a company that had tried to take advantage of tax laws intended to stimulate investment in Canadian filmmaking but was now going through bankruptcy. Turner had been showcased as chairman of the enterprise to give it credibility with investors who had now lost their money.[11] The group concluded that although this incident was unfortunate, it was unlikely to become more than a minor issue.

The main thing holding him back, Turner told his advisers, was that he didn't feel compelled to run. The drive that had spurred him to Ottawa as a young man simply wasn't there. He appreciated his comfortable life and hesitated to give it up. He needed to hear the clarion call, to feel that he was answering a summons to duty. For the time being, the group decided to hire Angus Reid, a pollster and University of Manitoba academic Turner had met at Lake of the Woods that summer, to do some preliminary polling to determine his potential delegate appeal. Turner insisted that no one but those around the table should know what was going on, but the press soon got wind of the stirrings in the Turner camp and began reporting that he was in the race.

Winning the leadership was one thing; winning the subsequent general election was something else again. The rise of Margaret Thatcher in Britain and Ronald Reagan in the United States suggested that the political centre was shifting right. With the exception of the short Clark interlude, the Liberals had been in power since 1963. Their electoral defeat was long overdue. Indeed, Trudeau was leaving because they seemed doomed to lose. A poll conducted that fall by the Carleton School of Journalism reported that, although Turner would do better against Mulroney than any other potential Liberal leader, the Tories had the support of 56 per cent of the electorate, compared to 26 per cent for the Liberals.[12] Veteran journalist Bruce Hutchison provided a glum assessment of Turner's prospects: "Is Mr. Turner willing to risk his future on a pretty desperate, perhaps hopeless, gamble? Is he prepared, in fact, to lead a forlorn hope and, most likely, a parliamentary opposition for at least four and possibly eight years, depending on the uncertain tides of politics?"[13]

Hutchison's prognosis was realistic. In the wake of the Young Liberal revolt against backroom influence, the new party president, Iona

Campagnolo, had created a reform committee. Its report concluded that the party had serious financial troubles, haphazard fundraising, chaotic communications with riding organizations, and that it even lacked a comprehensive membership list. Commenting on the report, Richard Gwyn observed, "It mounts a case that Trudeau has effectively destroyed the Liberal party as a political movement. The party, it states, has 'slipped into the role of simply an electoral machine, cranked up every four years but largely dormant and ineffective.' It has 'the most anaemic fund-raising campaigns of all three parties, the smallest number of donors ... the most underfunded national headquarters.'"[14]

Grim warnings indeed, but if Turner were ever to be prime minister, he could not afford to sit this one out. By the time the next leadership contest came around, he could well be in his early sixties and out of the game for more than fifteen years – an eternity in politics. If another anglophone won this time, in the subsequent race he would be up against the Liberal tradition of alternating French and English Canadian leaders. So it was now or never. Privately, he decided he probably would run – there was a chance that his leadership would restore enough public confidence in the Liberals to win the next election. If not, he was prepared to sit in opposition.[15] There he would be positioned to become prime minister when the Liberals reclaimed their customary hold on power in the subsequent election. Turner's musings were unattended by any action. If he were to have any hope of electoral victory, the news that Liberal Party organization was in total disarray should have prompted him to begin organizing a professional political team immediately. Instead he held back, waiting for Trudeau to officially resign, citing his party's tradition of loyalty to the leader. This principle, however admirable, was a throwback to his early career, when gentleman politicians had behaved honourably. Canadian politics had become far more cutthroat in the eight years Turner had been away.

The prospect that the Liberals might still form the next government dimmed with each passing month. In the fall and early winter, Trudeau was touring foreign capitals on a crusade for international peace and disarmament. Some thought it a ploy to resuscitate his popularity at home; others read it as a legacy project, the type of high-minded statesmanship politicians indulged in when they were close to quitting. Either way, it meant that Trudeau stayed on, seemingly unconcerned about leaving his successor no room to manoeuvre before an election. Turner's former law partner at Stikeman & Elliott, Jim Robb, told a reporter that Turner was trying to keep a low profile "because every time a survey shows him to be more popular than Trudeau, it spurs Trudeau into staying on an extra three months."[16] Nevertheless, the leadership contest would now almost certainly come in 1984. Ironically, this was the very year Turner had invoked, arbitrarily, in his 1968 leadership convention speech when he declared, "I'm not bidding now for your consideration at some vague convention in 1984 when I've mellowed a bit."

Turner's advisors made discreet calls across the country to plumb the extent of support for their candidate. The responses were positive. By December they were preparing policy materials so Turner could be brought up to speed on current issues.[17] Angus Reid told him that he had more potential than the results of the Carleton University poll suggested.[18] By Christmas the talk at the advisers' meetings shifted from discussions about whether Turner should run to how he should run. Other assumptions gelled. If Turner became prime minister, John Swift would be appointed his principal secretary and Bob Foulkes his senior policy adviser.[19] The group agreed that Bill Lee should run the leadership campaign, but he begged off, suggesting instead Heather Peterson, who was young, energetic, female, bilingual, and had good contacts from working in Trudeau's PMO, not to mention Queen's Park, where her brother-in-law was Liberal leader.

On January 3 Henry Karpus, the head of the Toronto ad agency Ronalds-Reynolds, sent Turner a memo with his analysis of polling the group had commissioned from US pollster Peter Hart the previous month. It pegged Conservative support at around 47 per cent of the electorate, with the Liberals trailing badly at 22 per cent and the NDP at 12 per cent. A total of 18 per cent of voters were undecided.[20] Turner was not as well known as Mulroney, but considering the greater exposure Mulroney enjoyed as Conservative leader, Turner's profile was quite high. He also scored higher by far than two potential leadership rivals, Macdonald and Chrétien. Karpus concluded that Canadians wanted leadership and that Turner should develop solid positions on issues and stick to them, in contrast to Mulroney's waffling. Voters' anger with the Liberal Party might then be assuaged after Trudeau's departure.

Turner remained uncommitted. Although he let his advisory group gather information quietly and discuss prospects, he still refused to organize. "He wouldn't allow us to put pen to paper," said John de B. Payne. "No policy, no skeletal organization, nothing. We weren't set up for anything. We knew we were going to pay one hell of a price for a standing start."[21] Other potential candidates were already signing up support, but Turner would go no further as long as Trudeau remained leader. "We were so frustrated," said Alf Apps, one of the Young Liberals who was fed up with Trudeau. "We knew the Prime Minister was going to resign, and all January and February we were trying to get out and organize, but couldn't get the go-ahead."[22]

In late February Turner and his wife left for a holiday in Jamaica. On the 28th, Pierre Trudeau finally decided to resign. He announced his decision the next day, a leap-year day. On Turner's behalf, Bill Lee issued a press release that opened with an appreciation of Trudeau's leadership and continued with the statement that Turner would be considering his options in consultation with family, friends, and fellow Liberals. He would make an announcement on March 16. That night the CBC ran a retrospective on Trudeau's career on its news show *The National.* The Trudeau piece was followed immediately by a profile of John Turner. In similar fashion, newspaper reports on Trudeau's resignation were run in tandem with speculation about Turner's candidacy. The inference was clear: Turner was the natural successor. "It is an extraordinary political phenomenon that Mr. Turner should be so widely perceived within the party as a political savior," wrote Jeffrey Simpson. "He has said next to nothing about policy for nearly a decade ... His appearances at Liberal gatherings have been perfunctory. He even signed newsletters to legal clients containing highly critical comments about the Government."[23]

Turner was staying at the Jamaica Inn, outside Ocho Rios, in a deluxe one-bedroom suite. He was relaxing on the beach, reading and playing tennis every day. He had planned to raise the prospect of his candidacy with his wife during their holiday, and now Trudeau's resignation forced the issue. She proved less than enamoured of a return to political life. When they arrived back in Toronto, however, they were greeted at the airport by an enthusiastic throng of supporters.[24] Geills Turner began to think that maybe he should give it a shot.

Aside from Turner, three men were considered to be legitimate contenders for the leadership: Jean Chrétien (minister of energy, mines, and resources), Marc Lalonde (minister of finance), and Lloyd Axworthy (minister of transport). Allan MacEachen was no longer on the list because he had fizzled in Finance. Donald Macdonald had effectively taken himself out of the race by accepting the chairmanship of the Royal Commission on the Economic Union and Development Prospects for Canada, appointed in 1982. He had negotiated a fee of $800 a day, a figure that stuck in people's minds and would have crippled his candidacy had he run. Lalonde was hampered by the fact that he was seen as "Trudeau without charisma."[25] Chrétien had been quietly organizing a leadership bid for two years and was now busy soliciting the support of fellow MPs. No one yet knew what Axworthy would do.

In the weeks following Trudeau's announcement, Donald Johnston (minister of state for economic and regional development), Mark MacGuigan (minister of justice), and John Roberts (minister of employment and Immigration) announced their candidacies. By this point, Turner's confidants told reporters, there was "about a 1% chance" that Turner would *not* be a candidate.[26] He was under enormous pressure not to let his party down. "Look, I'm going to be perfectly frank with you," a Cabinet minister who supported his candidacy would later tell a reporter. "I went with Turner because he can win. With Turner we've got a shot at it. I think with Turner in there we can win this mother. He can put us back into office again, it's as simple as that. And I just don't want to ever be in opposition again. I had nine months of it when Clark won."[27] Even though he had done virtually nothing to organize a leadership bid, simply by entertaining the possibility of running Turner had unleashed a train of events that had gained an irreversible momentum. For years he had been perceived as the heir apparent – the time had come to put up or shut up. It was a challenge and an obligation. Still, he wasn't sure. It was stressful, and his lunches at Winston's grew longer as he stewed.

Payne had established a makeshift office in a room on the eleventh floor of the Royal York Hotel. In the wake of Trudeau's resignation, hundreds of supporters called to offer their services to a Turner campaign. "We didn't have enough people to get back to them to tell them how to plug in," reported one Turner insider. "There were a lot of noses out of joint."[28] By the second week of March, however, Payne and Swift were in Toronto to begin organizing. Henry Karpus was doing more polling. Heather Peterson left her job in the PMO to help set up a Turner team.

Even so, Turner was still bogged down in the ambivalence that had held him back in 1979 and once again prevented him from running early and running hard. "Not lusting," he wrote on one of his index cards. Still, he believed in the dignity of politics and had a desire to serve – and, in effect, it was now too late to turn back.[29] "I hope you guys realize the sacrifice I'm making," he told reporters, "and I hope the country realizes it."[30]

Turner's half-hearted return to politics was enabled by the media, which had maintained his political currency even though he had been a private citizen for close on nine years, isolated within insular upper-class Toronto business and social circles. The Turner the media had created was a fiction, a perfect alternative to Trudeau, the answer to all Canada's leadership needs. Over time, political cultures change in ways that can be deadly to the unwary. Between Turner's uncertainty and the media's confidence in the Turner myth lay a welter of misapprehensions that would be treacherous political terrain to negotiate in the months ahead. Turner knew that his political skills were rusty and worried that he would be unable to live up to expectations. "People have an image of me that may not be right," he warned. "I'm older now and hopefully I'm wiser. But I'm not the blue-eyed boy of the image anymore."[31] There was a real risk that, as Tory David Crombie put it, "When he comes out of his attic, he will look like Howard Hughes."[32]

15

OILING THE TINMAN

The Liberal leadership convention was scheduled for June 14-17 in Ottawa, a mere three months away. Turner's refusal to organize as long as Trudeau was at the helm left him scrambling to mount a leadership bid from scratch. He had one enormous advantage: the widespread notion that he was the natural successor. He would win because people said he would win. This belief was also his biggest disadvantage: he could enter the race unprepared amid expectations that he would perform superbly. Encumbered by muddle and myth, the Turner campaign would lurch from its head start toward the finish line as a better-prepared candidate gained ground from behind.

Once he decided to run, Turner and his advisers debated how to manage both the optics and the substance of regime change. If the Liberals were to have any hope of getting re-elected, they had to signal that Turner represented a decisive departure from the Trudeau years. At the same time, he needed the backing of former Trudeau supporters if he were to win the convention and the general election that followed. The advisory group decided to play it safe, signalling change and accommodation simultaneously, at the risk of blurring his image. Turner would not criticize Trudeau directly, but the differences between them would be obvious in his policies. On fiscal management, he would urge deficit and debt reduction. For trade, better relations with the United States. In government, less bureaucracy and more efficiency. In federal-provincial relations, harmony and co-operation. For language policy, the status quo, with a new note of respect for provincial prerogatives. For the West, an influential voice in Liberal councils. Turner promised open government. "No elites! No rainmakers!" he declared, appealing to those who felt they had been long shut out of the party's inner councils.[1] That meant he would eschew behind-the-scenes deals with other Liberal politicians to get their support for the leadership.

In short order, one of these goals had to be sacrificed in pursuit of another. Turner wanted a westerner on his team to give him credibility in the region, and he hoped to convince Lloyd Axworthy, the minister of transport, to join his campaign instead of running for the leadership himself. They met for dinner in Toronto, and Turner made his pitch. Axworthy agreed – with conditions. He wanted Trudeau's peace initiative continued, job creation programs protected, reformers Judy Erola and Monique Bégin kept in Cabinet, and the West given a prominent place in decision making. All but the last represented continuity rather than change. Turner nevertheless agreed. He appointed Axworthy co-chair of his campaign, along with Lise Saint-Martin Tremblay, a vice-president of the national Liberal Party from Quebec.

Turner's March 16 press conference was held at the Château Laurier in Ottawa. Journalists gathered to see the myth revealed in the flesh. He stepped to the podium in front of a room bristling with cameras, microphones, and tape recorders. "Today I return to public life," he declared. After running through his rationale (duty, public service, experience), he laid out some of his objectives (openness, accessibility, accountability, Parliament as the focus of national life). He went on to extol the virtues of the Liberals ("the party of reform in Canada"), vowed to "fight Tories, not Grits," and promised to restore the Liberals' national base by increasing representation from the West and Atlantic Canada. He would continue Trudeau's peace initiative, be inclusive of women, fight youth unemployment, and make Canada a "learning and earning" society again. He challenged Canadians to help him solve the country's problems. "I have no instant solutions," he cautioned. "But I do make a pledge. I will make whatever sacrifices are necessary. I will devote myself to my country. I will not flinch from the tough decisions. You will know where I stand."[2]

The reaction to Turner's announcement was mixed. Some believed they had seen the myth incarnate. "He quipped his way through the political minefields laid by reporters with an ease that belied that 8½ years out of public life," reported the *Globe and Mail*.[3] Such approval was to be expected, at least initially. By entering the leadership contest, Turner was doing exactly what the media had asked him to do. Yet there was also a vague sense of disappointment. The real Turner, live and in person, turned out to be something less than expected. Rather than the easy manner of the aristocrat bred to rule, there was a tenseness and self-consciousness. Instead of speaking in smooth, flowing cadences, he had a rapid-fire delivery. The "total package" appeared to be under a lot of internal pressure.[4]

One reporter asked Turner about French-language rights in Manitoba. The issue could be traced back to 1870, when the province had been established with special constitutional protection for both English and French. Over time the anglophone majority had abolished French-language rights, but recently unilingual provincial practices had been challenged in the courts. The Trudeau Liberals had endorsed the court challenge and promoted new French language services in the province as well. The question was complicated for Turner because he wanted to signal that he would be more flexible with the provinces than Trudeau had been. From his work on the *Official Languages Act* a decade and a half earlier, he remembered the difficulties the Western provinces had faced in implementing the use of French in the courts. Moreover, as a lawyer, he analyzed the issue from a legal perspective: constitutionally protected language rights were one thing – the federal government had an obligation to protect them – but any extension of minority-language services was a provincial prerogative. "We have to recognize that what is at issue here is a provincial initiative," he told the reporter, "and that a solution will have to be provincial."[5]

The next day, the Saturday edition of *La Presse* claimed that Turner had said the Manitoba situation was a provincial matter and failed to recognize a threat to the fundamental duality of Canada. Lise Bissonnette, the editor of *Le Devoir*, was even more scathing: "The more he talks about the Manitoba affair, the more he demonstrates that he does not know the issue well."[6] These editorialists ignored the potential benefits for Quebec's constitutional aspirations inherent in Turner's emphasis on provincial rights, but Quebec anglophones were alive to that angle. They interpreted Turner's message to mean that he would do less to protect their minority rights against incursions by a Parti Québécois government.

Alerted by the criticism in the Quebec press, the anglophone media began to run with the issue. It started from the premise that the Trudeau legacy on language was an unassailable orthodoxy. Consequently, Turner's position could only be a sign of incompetence. He had committed an "ill-advised blunder" and "shocked many Liberals by seeming to back off from the firm defence of minority language rights that had characterized the Trudeau era," wrote *Maclean's*.[7] Turner's critical role in promoting official bilingualism by winning acceptance for the *Official Languages Act* in 1968 was long forgotten.

Jean Chrétien exploited the issue when he declared his candidacy for the Liberal leadership. "Constitutionally protected minority language rights in every province have become a Canadian responsibility," he declared in French. "This achievement is the proud heritage of all Liberals."[8] Conservative leader Brian Mulroney jumped on Turner as well, claiming he was motivated by "political greed" to undercut his party's principles. For Quebec's 700,000 anglophones, he said, it meant, "I am hereby delivering you into the hands of René Lévesque."[9]

Turner's Quebec supporters worried that his remarks would cut into his support in the province. By the following Tuesday, Turner and his aides recognized that the issue was mutating out of control. They began working the phones, urgently canvassing supporters for advice. "He is kicking himself for not being more specific. And we are all upset about the amount of emotion the issue has generated," said one of his senior officials.[10] On Thursday Turner issued a statement: the federal government had a duty to intervene, if necessary, to protect minority-language rights. He hoped for a political solution at the provincial level in this case because the extension of language services within a province was a provincial responsibility – unless the courts ended up ruling otherwise.[11] He also set up a meeting with Franco-Manitoban leaders to quiet the fears his remarks had raised.

The lasting effects of the incident were difficult to gauge. It showed that Turner and his advisers had misjudged the situation. They had been out of politics for years and were no longer sensitive to how issues could be distorted by the media. Turner lost the support of five MPs – three who had previously been committed to him and two who were leaning his way. John de B. Payne thought the episode would make it harder for Turner to win delegates in Quebec, but that they would eventually come around when they recognized Turner's lead elsewhere in the country. There was also speculation that Turner's position had won him support in the West. The political pundits on Peter Gzowski's *Morningside* concluded that he hadn't been hurt at all by the affair.[12]

The most disturbing aspect of the incident was the way the media had turned on Turner. They relished attacking him, and several pundits exhibited a knowing superiority and condescending tone while doing so. "The national press corps have wanted a race and have now created the impression that there is one," Payne explained. "Having built you up as a myth and a crown prince for eight years ... they now want to bring you down a peg or two or three."[13] Chrétien had seen it coming. "I ... figured that the press had been too good to him," he recalled. "It would start to feel guilty within a month, and what had built him would destroy him."[14]

By early April, two more candidates had entered the race: Eugene Whelan (minister of agriculture) and John Munro (minister of Indian affairs and northern development). Some suspected that the only reason both were running was as part of an "Anyone but Turner" scheme in which their role was to collect delegates they could throw to the second-place candidate in the second ballot. With their entry, the field was now complete at seven leadership candidates: Chrétien, Johnston, MacGuigan, Munro, Roberts, Turner, and Whelan.

Turner was still struggling to get his campaign off the ground. "He had to come from Ground Zero," reported Henry Karpus, the campaign's communications guru. "The big myth of it all being wound up like a mainspring ready to spring into orbit just wasn't so."[15] Before the operation was properly up and running, Turner was sucked into an endless whirl of campaign events and duties. He would fly into a town one morning for a round of receptions, speeches, and interviews, fly off in the afternoon to another community for a similar routine, then do it all again the next day in a different part of the country. In between events, he tried to deal with all the local people who wanted to see him, digest the briefing notes in his overstuffed briefcase in preparation for the candidate policy forums, and manage his campaign from afar.

In his absence, the chain of command at the College Park headquarters in Toronto broke down. Many of his senior officials were former aides who were accustomed to having direct access to him rather than reporting through an intermediary, and they continued to do so. As a result, the left hand didn't know what the right was doing. Conflicting orders were issued and arrangements botched.[16] Some of the consequences were farcical. To decide on campaign colours, Angus Reid was commissioned to poll people on the streets of Winnipeg about their reactions to various colour combinations. Not surprisingly, no clear direction emerged. When Turner found things in disarray, he got frustrated, lost his temper, and then afterward felt guilty. It was, as one worker put it, "amateur night at the bingo."[17] Precious time was being lost. There was still no system in place for putting volunteers to work, and that left them feeling unwanted. Some significant power-brokers in the party went looking for another candidate. "The assumption was that we had a great organization," said Shaun Sullivan, a Turner organizer in British Columbia. "You know, 10 years in the waiting, slick, professional, perfect. So what happens? Nothing ... Just a mad goddam scramble."[18] By the first week of April, riding association presidents in Quebec had all received personal phone calls from Chrétien but had yet to hear from Turner.

Finally, Senator Al Graham buttonholed Turner and told him bluntly that his campaign was a circus. Conceding the point, Turner called Bill Lee, who had left for Florida the day after Turner announced his candidacy. Lee agreed to come back and help out on condition he had full authority to run things. He arrived in Toronto on April 4. After talking to key members of the team, Lee quickly made decisions that had been delayed. He chose campaign colours and a slogan, "Win with Turner" – not particularly catchy, but effective at least in exploiting his main strength as front-runner. Most importantly, he imposed an organizational structure that clarified responsibilities and reporting relationships, and got the campaign workers functioning together productively. Every decision would now flow through him. Except for Lee, only Payne had direct access to Turner.[19]

Despite these early stumbles, Turner was running well ahead of the pack, even in Quebec. By early April it was clear that Jean Chrétien was his only serious competition. Chrétien was bitterly disappointed when colleagues and friends whose support he had counted on opted to back Turner. His former parliamentary secretary, Ed Lumley, was one. So was André Ouellet, the party's powerful Quebec organizer, whom Chrétien had regarded as a close friend. Chrétien was up against the tradition of alternation between francophone and anglophone leaders in the Liberal Party, the perception that the best candidate would be one who represented a fresh departure from the unpopular Trudeau regime, and the myth of Turner as prince in exile. Everyone wanted to go with the candidate most likely to win the next election. "You know what it is?" Chrétien complained. "They're saving their own asses. They don't love the man. They love power."[20]

In early April the media dutifully reported on a Turner campaign swing through Manitoba and Saskatchewan, but most remained fixated with the discrepancy between their expectations and the real John Turner. "After eight years as a corporate lawyer in Toronto, Turner's as rusty as a graveyard gate," wrote Val Sears in the *Toronto Star*. "On his first campaign tour of the West last week," he continued, "he creaked and scraped and stumbled like the Tin Man waking up in Oz and looking for an oil can."[21] Worse was another negative tag – "yesterday's man" – that began to appear around the same time. A piece by Frances Russell in the *Winnipeg Free Press* took this line: "Turner so far seems to be a man in a time warp, frozen in the political style and idiom of the late 1960s. In 1984, it sounds off, even insincere."[22]

Turner met these challenges head on, again emphasizing what distinguished him from Trudeau. "Leadership is less a Cartesian master plan than a human procedure," he declared. "The technocrat is an impatient type, but we mustn't forget consulting, communicating, winning people onside ... My skills are people skills, and those are the skills required to put a human face on technology and government."[23] But his open, people-friendly, consultative style didn't come across on television. "You can be a great communicator if the graceful wordsmith called John Turner that I used to know emerges from the legalistic banker bullshit that seems to encrust you at present," Jerry Grafstein told him.[24] Trudeau's remoteness had been deliberate, calculated to create an aura around him as leader. He had been contemptuous of the media, yet they perversely respected him for it. Turner had more democratic instincts. He wanted to be liked and tried to reach out but came across as stilted and self-conscious, and the press made fun of him for it.

On April 11 Turner was in Montreal to launch his campaign in Quebec. Advance publicity promised a jam-packed "Wonderful Wednesday" that would include a news conference with Premier Robert Bourassa in the morning; an afternoon meeting with the leaders of Alliance Quebec, the leading anglophone rights group; and a rally in the evening. But instead of spending the day in pleasant politicking with positive sound bites for the evening news, Turner ran smack into another language controversy.

This time the issue was Quebec's Bill 101. Passed by the Parti Québécois in 1977, the bill made French the official language of the province for the legislature and the courts, civil administration, commerce and business, and education (except for anglophones currently residing in Quebec). French Canadian Quebeckers regarded it as a bulwark of protection for their language and culture; for Trudeau, it was a retrograde nationalist infringement on individual rights. In 1980 the Supreme Court of Canada had upheld a judgment of the Quebec Superior Court that struck down the section that declared French the exclusive language of the legislature and the courts. Bill 101 was back in the news in 1984 because the Supreme Court was deliberating whether its provisions regarding education and public signage violated the Charter of Rights and Freedoms.

Before his afternoon meeting, Turner was rushed by journalists in a hotel lobby. "What's your position on Bill 101?" one reporter demanded. Speaking in French, Turner said he supported it "in principle ... But perhaps there are sections ... which should be tested before the courts." Later that day, he spoke of the need to balance the various interests involved. Some parts of Bill 101 "may well be beyond provincial jurisdiction and offend the Charter ... It is within the rights of the anglophone minority in Quebec or other minorities to have that law tested," he cautioned. He added that the federal government should protect the rights of minorities across the country.[25] That evening, Turner promised to defend language rights. However, journalists again seized on his support for the bill "in principle" and spun it as another blunder. "Turner Lands in Hot Water in Quebec," declared a typical headline.[26] The episode cost him more anglophone delegates from Quebec.

"The Bill 101 controversy was the result of a wolfpack-type of journalism that's now in vogue," Derek Hodgson of the *Toronto Sun* commented. "Its practitioners take part in 'scrums' ... surrounding a politician's warm body and prodding it with electronic recorders until he or she says something. Turner can't handle them."[27] Accustomed to the old camaraderie between politicians and the national press gallery gang, Turner was taken aback by the aggressiveness of the new crop of journalists. They had no compunction about eavesdropping on his private conversations, and every drink he took during a flight could be mentioned in a "campaign notebook" column. He tried to get to know the new crowd, but there was a yawning cultural gap between them. As Christopher Walmsley, a veteran CBC national news reporter, explained, "Few [journalists] had a decent, fundamental grounding in political science, economics, or history."[28] But they were well schooled in cynicism and could not accept Turner's pieties about public service at face value. They discounted the strengths of his old-school values while cringing at the anachronisms.

For his part, Turner hadn't adjusted to the feminist sensibilities in the contemporary journalistic workforce. He would tell jokes off the record that would have been well received in the old days but now violated the strictures of political correctness. He referred to the media as "gentlemen of the press" or "the boys." When a female *Maclean's* editor questioned him aggressively, he quipped "Down girl!," an attempt at humour that, given the sensibilities of the times, simply fell flat.[29] The cultural gap was exacerbated by technological change. Back in the seventies, political coverage on television consisted of set-piece interviews in which gentlemen journalists and politicians chatted in front of a stationary camera. Now television crews had lightweight equipment that made them mobile, and journalists used palm-sized tape recorders that captured every remark for later verification. They wanted five-second clips, not the forty-second quotations that were the norm a decade earlier.

Turner struggled to adapt to being covered on the fly, often intrusively, frequently confrontationally. Bill Lee coached him to spin platitudes to the cameras rather than offering extended analyses of complex issues, but this stratagem went against his instincts. One day a pack of journalists swarmed around him as he waited for an elevator, looking for a quick clip about his plan to cut the deficit by 50 per cent over three to seven years. "I spent fifteen minutes in Quebec City with the national media describing exactly what I have in mind," he told them, "and I'm not able to shorten that to two minutes."[30] The journalists were not pleased, and their dissatisfaction showed in their reporting.

As time went on, Turner got better at spouting evasive nothings. After his campaign was launched with appearances on the major television public affairs shows, he turned down interview requests from national networks, happy to rely instead on local television, which usually provided lengthier and more sympathetic coverage. Otherwise, his campaign became a carefully scripted affair that concentrated on getting him into personal contact with as many delegates as possible at private functions. When he met delegates, he was warm, charming, and solicitous. He looked them straight in the eye, clasped their hands, memorized their names, and established a rapport.[31] He liked to describe his campaign style using the Spanish phrase "*mano a mano*," which gave his up-close-and-personal approach macho overtones of hand-to-hand combat.[32]

Although it was possible to win a leadership race by the serial seduction of individual delegates, Turner wouldn't be able to do the same with every voter in the general election that lay ahead. His team worked with him to eradicate the rapid-fire delivery and other traits that grated on camera. Henry Karpus took him down to New York for media coaching, but there was only so much the consultants could do in a few hours. Karpus had to reinforce their advice while Turner was on the job. "You have to loosen up!" he told him after one appearance. "The audience is with you, John ... So, why do you seem to almost scowl at them?"[33] Turner was a quick learner, and his public performances improved greatly over the course of the campaign. Yet his initial failure to measure up to expectations stuck in people's minds. "Turner was OK for television 10 years ago when television was stiff itself," an experienced broadcaster observed, "but now you've got to be natural, and John just can't be natural."[34]

Turner's business connections created another headache for his image polishers. He sat on the boards of seventeen Canadian corporations and derived a six-digit income from directors' fees alone. The optics of these connections didn't play well in left-leaning circles of the party where he would be seeking political support. His friend Richard Alway tried to persuade him to give up his directorships before he ran, but Turner saw no reason to do so until he was actually elected to office.[35] He was not arrogant enough to assume that he would win, he said, and if he didn't, he still had to support his family. He did not expect his rivals to give up their Cabinet posts.[36]

By mid-April the race was clearly a two-man contest, with Jean Chrétien in hot pursuit of Turner. Donald Johnston was running third but seemed unlikely to generate enough support to come up the middle or to play kingmaker. In contrast to Turner's Bay Street image, Chrétien presented himself as "le petit gars de Shawinigan," deployed self-deprecating humour, and made emotional declarations of his love for Canada. Another thing he had going for him was, paradoxically, his association with the outgoing regime, for although the Liberals under Trudeau had become unpopular, their positions on issues such as language rights and the sanctity of social programs had become deeply entrenched. Canadians were weary of Trudeau and his style more than his policies, and Chrétien's folksy shtick offered a marked change of style. His daughter had married business tycoon Paul Desmarais' son, so he too had money behind his campaign, yet the media portrayed him as the underdog and gave him an easier ride. As the campaign wore on and he gathered support, he began to think of himself as the candidate of the people.

In defending the Trudeau government's record, Chrétien appeared to be on the left of the party, at least in relation to Turner, and their policies polarized into offsetting positions. Turner advocated cutting the deficit; Chrétien insisted on supporting the poor and unemployed. Turner emphasized the provincial prerogative in language issues; Chrétien countered that protecting language rights was a federal responsibility. Turner made friendly gestures to the provinces; Chrétien championed strong central government. A poll of Liberal riding association presidents released in early April reported that they saw unemployment and economic growth as the major issues in the campaign. Turner had an edge among this group because they thought he was the best man to solve these problems.

At the candidates' policy forum in Halifax on May 6, Turner's opponents attacked his pledge to eliminate the deficit in seven years, claiming he couldn't do it without cutting social programs. He countered that his emphasis on deficit reduction was inspired by his commitment to social programs, which could be sustained only by a prosperous economy.[37] The rank and file of the Liberal Party wasn't ready to accept this argument. As with language issues, Turner discovered that there was a price to pay for deviating from the Trudeau legacy. He decided to trim his sails and emphasize the positive side of the equation – righting the economy – rather than the bitter medicine of spending cuts. On social policy, he had highlighted the issue of youth unemployment since the start of his campaign.

Now he also worked hard to exhibit his empathy with multiculturalism and women's issues, both of which mattered to delegates on the left of the party.

Although the Liberals were determined to avoid accusations of dirty tricks during the delegate selection process, many of the ridings were hotly contested. It was possible to sign up party members just days before the selection and stack the nomination meetings with new Liberals. In urban ridings, batches of these instant Liberals were culled from tight-knit immigrant communities. Chrétien's campaign, much better organized than Turner's, gleefully launched pre-emptive strikes into riding associations thought to be predisposed to Turner, winning dozens of delegates in the process.

The press took a particular interest in the battles between the Turner and Chrétien forces in Quebec. Chrétien would need substantial support from his home province to win, but many Quebec delegates, including most of the riding association presidents, had committed to Turner early because he looked like a winner. As Chrétien's campaign gained momentum and the Bill 101 issue hit the press, Turner's lead slipped to the point where he and Chrétien seemed to be running in a dead heat. On the prairies it was also a two-candidate race, but there Turner was solidly ahead of Chrétien. As Don Braid reported in the *Montreal Gazette*, "Chrétien gets the affection [in the West] while Turner gets the delegate votes."[38] In British Columbia, Turner and Chrétien were again neck and neck. Ontario, with its large bloc of delegates, was also a hotly contested arena. Turner was well ahead, but his opponents continued to gain. When delegate selection wound up on May 10, about a third of those chosen weren't committed to any one candidate.

In all these contests, Turner's trump card was the promise that he was the Liberals' best bet to win the coming election. Whether he could in fact beat Mulroney was another question. "No one with real marbles expects Turner and the Liberals to overcome the vastly deserved contempt the voters hold for the present government," wrote Allan Fotheringham.[39] A *Globe and Mail* CROP poll on April 11 projected the Liberals under Turner losing to the Conservatives under Mulroney, 50 per cent to 38 per cent. The numbers were the same when no leaders were specified. But on May 1 the results of a Gallup poll conducted at the end of March suggested that the Liberals, profiting from the free publicity accorded their leadership campaign, were leading the Conservatives in popularity. It showed them with the support of 46 per cent of the electorate, the Tories at 40 per cent, and the NDP with 13 per cent. Many experts didn't believe the poll because it indicated an unprecedented drop of 14 per cent in support for the Tories in just one month.

As his campaign bus was heading along Highway 401 on the afternoon of May 10, returning from a rally in Trenton, Ontario, Turner ventured down the aisle to visit with the journalists at the back. Things went well at first. One asked him what he thought of current interest rates. He said they should be lowered, but he trusted the Bank of Canada to do the right thing. The conversation wound its way back to his resignation nine years earlier. It must have been difficult as minister of finance, suggested one journalist, to be caught between a business community calling for govern-ment restraint and political pressures to increase spending. That went with the job, Turner replied – he had resigned not for that reason but because his boss didn't support him. Asked to elaborate, he gave the example of his inability to close a voluntary deal on wage and price controls. After that there was little point in staying on, he said, and Trudeau had offered him only a Senate seat or a judgeship.

The next morning the front page of the *Globe and Mail* announced that Turner had resigned in 1975 because Trudeau had failed to back him up on controls. Trudeau's long-standing resentment of Turner exploded in anger. He wanted to call a press conference to repudiate Turner, using his "no policy differences" letter in reply to Turner's resignation as proof of the arriviste's perfidy. Instead, Trudeau's assistant, Joyce Fairbairn, phoned Turner aide Mike Hunter and asked if Turner could call Trudeau. Turner obliged, and Trudeau reiterated his assertion that no policy disagreement had lain behind the resignation. Turner was embarrassed that his remarks had been published. He felt he had violated his pledge on Cabinet confi-dentiality as well as his campaign strategy of leaving Trudeau alone. He told Trudeau he was sorry his comments had become public. That wasn't enough for Trudeau. He issued a press release later that day, claiming that Turner had "misrepresented the facts" – had lied – and had apologized for doing so. It was an astounding intervention into a leadership campaign.[40] Payne told Turner he had been too nice. "The dumbest thing you have done in the campaign is phone the Prime Minister," he wrote. "You have nothing to apologize for."[41]

Whose representation of the facts was correct? Trudeau originally made the "no policy differences" point in his letter, but Turner never confirmed it. Turner was looking for sympathy when he said he was offered only the Senate or the bench – that offer had come at his final meeting with Trudeau after they had discussed the dearth of suitable Cabinet posts available at the time. Moreover, Turner's strategic calculations of his own career interests were the main reason for his resignation in 1975. Yet the policy differences were undeniable. Trudeau had not been as committed as Turner to spending cuts. On voluntary wage and price controls, Trudeau had decided to preserve his political capital and let his finance minister and leadership rival hang out to dry.[42]

In the wake of this fiasco, Turner redoubled his resolve to give the press nothing of substance to riff on. In formal interviews, he stuck to his file cards so he wouldn't wander off-script. In media scrums he spouted sweet nothings. When critics questioned his pledge of an "open, accessible and accountable government," he replied that Liberal delegates were his focus during the leadership campaign, and, moreover, the media provoked this kind of response with its irresponsibility. "If I have one mission on this campaign," he told reporters, "it's to make you guys at least a bit less cynical."[43] The media resented this attitude, and Turner's relationship with the press took another slide downhill.

Turner travelled to his mother's hometown of Rossland, BC, in late May to set up some flattering photo ops. The memories were bittersweet because his mother was now in a nursing home, a victim of Alzheimer's disease and oblivious to her son's arduous political comeback. When he unexpectedly encountered a portrait of her in the town museum, tears came to his eyes, but he recovered by telling journalists an anecdote about the hat she was wearing. "The following day in the plane," one of the journalists wrote,

> the crack in the casing remains ... Turner plays with the cigar, a drink and his more private thoughts. "Next to the ministry," he says "public

life is the best vocation. God gives you gifts ... and they must be used for the furtherance of man, your neighbour. One has a duty to fulfill those gifts, to live up to one's own personal perfection and they are not to be wasted.[44]

The leadership campaign had been a wild rollercoaster ride. Turner had first been idolized, then pilloried, frustrated by the way he was portrayed in the press, yet reassured by the support of delegates he met. After a rocky start, he felt his old political skills coming back and rediscovered a taste for the cut and thrust of political combat. "In this last week on the road before the convention," reported Val Sears, "Turner is booming along. He's got The Speech down pat, his skin has thickened so he no longer reacts to press jibes, he's toned down his barking laugh. 'Finally,' says executive assistant Mike Hunter, 'he sounds like a politician and not a lawyer.'"[45] Turner's leadership campaign wound up in Peterborough, Ontario, on June 7, his fifty-fifth birthday.

A few days before the convention, Turner got a call from Finance Minister Marc Lalonde, offering his support. This was his most remarkable endorsement to date. Some of Turner's advisers thought they would be better off without Lalonde. What would the West think about one of the *bêtes noires* from the Trudeau years jumping aboard the Turner bandwagon? Turner, however, was glad to have one of the party's major power-brokers in his camp. Soon after, Allan MacEachen offered his backing. Turner's campaign strategists decided to announce this endorsement at the convention to maximize its impact on the delegates.

Turner and Chrétien were roughly even in constituency delegates, who accounted for about two-thirds of the total. But Turner was thought to have carried the thousand or so ex-officio delegates by a margin of three to one. It was a strange situation: while spurning Chrétien, who defended its legacy, the party establishment was supporting the candidate who challenged its record. This odd configuration of support complicated Turner's aspiration to symbolize change.

Sixteen years after their previous leadership convention, Liberals once again streamed into the capital city from ridings across the country. Again, the setting would be the Ottawa Civic Centre. The policy-minded delegates attended workshops where the candidates discussed issues, while the partiers gathered in the candidates' hospitality tents to drink, gossip, and enjoy free steaks and seafood. Well financed by donations from the business community, the Turner campaign entertained lavishly. It hired double-decker buses and ran tour boats on the Rideau Canal. The Chrétien organization offered every taxi driver in Ottawa a free lunch, hoping to get their support when delegates asked them for a "man-in-the-street" opinion.

The Turner campaign recruited Marc Pouliot, a Montrealer with experience organizing Olympic spectacles, to choreograph Turner's entrance into the arena for speech night. Operations on the convention floor would be coordinated by Sandra Severn from the "bunker," a communications trailer parked outside the centre. Staff developed about twenty scenarios of how the voting might go. They put seven hundred one-way radios in the hands of campaign workers so they could direct them regarding what to do next, depending on which scenario unfolded.

The big question was whether Chrétien had caught up sufficiently to be within striking distance on the first ballot. Would he be close enough to win if he picked up the bulk of the delegates released by candidates who bowed out of the race? Some pundits predicted just this situation, speculating that Chrétien could prevail on the second or third ballot.

Thursday night was the party's farewell to Pierre Trudeau. An audience of some seven thousand watched a ninety-minute tribute featuring Maureen Forester, Paul Anka, and Rich Little. There was a fast-paced film recounting the high points of Trudeau's career. The prime minister delivered a speech extolling the virtues of the Liberal Party and its great leaders in the past, but he stayed scrupulously neutral about the leadership decision ahead. Whoever won, Trudeau promised his support. "You will find me here, following him," he promised, "because we have much more building to do."[46]

Friday night brought the candidates' speeches – their last chance to change delegates' minds before voting began the next day. The speaking order, drawn by lot, was Whelan first, followed by MacGuigan, Munro, Roberts, Johnston, Turner, and Chrétien. The first five candidates' speeches became lead-ins to the main event between the two heavyweights.

Just before Turner took the stage, his supporters flooded into the arena in a thunderous demonstration, waving flags as the theme music from

Chariots of Fire resounded through the arena. It was a display of force designed to show that Turner's supporters far outnumbered those of any other candidate. When Turner walked out with Geills and their children, he was greeted with deafening cheers. He mounted the stage and launched into his speech, leading with the warmest tribute to Pierre Trudeau offered by any of the candidates. "I have said on several occasions but never face-to-face with him," he declared, looking straight at Trudeau, "that he has surely been the most remarkable Canadian of his generation." Trudeau smiled modestly and acknowledged the compliment with a slight nod.

Having negotiated this tricky business, Turner turned to the future of the party under his leadership. "I have listened and I have learned," he declared, acknowledging the trials of his re-entry into politics. Although he read from his text, he read well, with conviction and passion, switching easily between English and French. Commenting on the need for a strong economy, he did not mention deficit reduction. "Whatever we do, it will never be done at the expense of the unemployed, the aged, the poor, the sick or the disabled," he pledged. "Our economic and social objectives are complementary, not contradictory." He touched on the environment, multiculturalism, and women's issues. Then he took a swipe at Brian Mulroney, denouncing him as a "let's pretend Liberal." Canadians, he trumpeted, would rather have a real Liberal.[47] His address was forceful and confident. Turner was peaking at just the right moment.

Next came Chrétien. He seemed tired at first but warmed up, exuding the kind of earthy charm his supporters loved. He hit on all his customary points, but he did not light the place on fire. Turner's prospects for victory looked bright, though the numbers suggested it would not come on the first ballot. With 3,437 delegates in attendance, 1,719 votes were needed to win. Chrétien, the strategists predicted, would get about 1,100 votes on the first ballot, Turner 1,600. That would leave about 750 votes up for grabs as the other candidates dropped out. The race would be a close one only if Donald Johnston went to Chrétien and took all his delegates with him.

The balloting began on Saturday afternoon. An aide to Ronald Reagan put a call in to the bunker to say that the president wanted to congratulate Mr. Turner, but Sandra Severn told him he would have to call back. Party president Iona Campagnolo announced the first ballot results at 5:15 p.m.:

Turner	1,593	(46 per cent)
Chrétien	1,067	(31 per cent)
Johnston	278	(8 per cent)
Roberts	185	(5 per cent)
MacGuigan	135	(4 per cent)
Munro	93	(3 per cent)
Whelan	84	(2 per cent)
Total	3,435	

"That's it," Bill Lee told Turner. "You've won." Chrétien was too far behind to make up the gap. Turner didn't believe him. Lee asked John Rae, Chrétien's campaign manager, whether they wanted to go to a second ballot, and Rae said yes, Chrétien wished to see it through. And so another round of favour trading and intrigues began on the convention floor, as all the candidates except Johnston withdrew and visibly joined either Turner or Chrétien in their boxes. Their delegates, however, did not necessarily follow through with their votes. Chrétien pleaded with Johnston to throw his support to him, but Johnston turned away. He would go down fighting as Turner had done in 1968. That sealed Chrétien's fate.

The results of the second ballot were announced at 8:30 p.m.:

Turner	1,862	(54 per cent)
Chrétien	1,368	(40 per cent)
Johnston	192	(6 per cent)
Total	3,422	

John Turner was the new leader of the Liberal Party, and soon to be the next prime minister of Canada.

It is customary for defeated candidates to rally behind the winner and unite the party for the battles ahead, and Iona Campagnolo came to the podium to call all the candidates to the stage. Struck by the bitter disappointment among Chrétien's supporters, she proclaimed that, though Chrétien may have been "second on the ballot," he was "first in our hearts." The delegates roared with approval. For Turner supporters, it seemed an odd pronouncement. Was she saying that Turner didn't deserve to win? But worse was to follow when Chrétien graciously called on the delegates to make the vote for Turner unanimous. By this point all the defeated candidates were at the back of the stage in a wide semi-circle. Pierre Trudeau joined them, and when the delegates recognized him, he took a single step forward, gave a half-hearted wave, and stepped back. The roar of the crowd built in anticipation, then died away in confusion. Turner invited Trudeau forward so they could raise their hands together in the traditional gesture of continuity between leaders. Trudeau, smiling enigmatically, refused to budge.

16

PRIME MINISTER FOR A DAY

After the leadership convention, Turner would have liked to relax for a while, but now he was confronted with a higher order of chaos. The tasks facing him were both critical and complex: taking over the government, uniting the party, choosing a Cabinet. Every move he made had implications for one overriding issue: when to call an election. Should he stay in office for a few months or go to the polls immediately? As long as he put off this decision, every other choice was compromised because, ideally, they all had to fit into a strategy based on the timing of the election. The longer he took to decide, the worse the consequences for the campaign, particularly if the ultimate call were to go to the polls early.

The election decision was framed by some tight parameters. The Liberals' mandate ran out within the year, and there were a limited number of places in the calendar to schedule a fifty-day-long election campaign. The queen was coming to Canada from July 14 to 27 to attend bicentennial celebrations in New Brunswick and Ontario, and the pope was scheduled to visit from September 9 to 20. There were three choices: an immediate call, with the election in early fall (which would entail postponing the queen's visit), a fall election while the pope was in Canada, or an election the following spring.

Other than the election call, Turner's main concern was the same as it had been during the leadership race. How could he signal that his leadership represented a new era in Canadian politics without alienating those from the Trudeau regime whose support he needed to win the looming election? To strike the right balance in this shifting political context, he would have to be both daring and sure-footed.

On the Sunday evening after the convention, Turner met with Trudeau at 24 Sussex Drive to discuss arrangements for transferring power. He got Trudeau's permission to receive briefings from senior bureaucrats, and the next morning he met with Gordon Osbaldeston, the clerk of the privy council, to plan the process. John Swift was in charge of the transition, with assistance from Simon Reisman and James Grandy, former deputy ministers to Turner (at Finance and Consumer and Corporate Affairs, respectively), who were working now as consultants. Under their direction, Turner's aides began the grinding work of poring over briefing books and absorbing lectures from Privy Council officers on the structure and processes of the government.

The next day Turner made a symbolic appearance in the gallery of the House of Commons. He was recognized from the benches below with a generous round of applause. Trudeau wasn't one of those clapping, having pre-arranged to be called away to Montreal on urgent business concerning renovation of his recently purchased house. Billboards appeared in major cities across the country bearing Turner's picture, the Liberal Party logo, and the slogan "Today We Celebrate Our Future."

Meanwhile, a steady stream of advisers, Cabinet ministers, former leadership rivals, and office seekers flowed through Turner's rooms at the Château Laurier, where he was staying until Trudeau vacated 24 Sussex Drive. As the afternoons wore on, the suite grew thick with cigar smoke. Seeking privacy or fresh air, Turner often took visitors for a stroll in the park behind the hotel and sat on a bench to talk. Many of the discussions involved party solidarity. Leadership contests are emotional affairs in which campaign teams develop close relationships in a common cause. Tellingly, Mark MacGuigan had been the only rival to come to Turner at the convention. Turner knew he had to make some gestures of accommodation to unravel and reknit all these ties.

Most of the issues were resolved amicably enough, but soon it became clear that Jean Chrétien would not easily be placated. He was bitter. He believed that he had been the better candidate in the leadership race but had been denied the support he deserved by the party establishment's perverse conviction that Turner could win the next election. The media had loved Chrétien during the race, and he was deeply disappointed when he lost.[1]

Turner was prepared to recognize Chrétien's standing in the party by giving him what he wanted, within reason, but Chrétien demanded too much. He wanted the role of deputy prime minister. No problem, said Turner. He wanted his choice of Cabinet portfolios. Again, no problem – he had earned that. He wanted his key campaign supporters given safe havens: those who were ministers should be reappointed to Cabinet; those who were not should get either a Cabinet post or a plum patronage appointment. This demand was difficult because, to signal that his government would be leaner and more efficient than Trudeau's, Turner was committed to reducing the size of Cabinet. But after some protests, he acquiesced. It was worth it for the sake of party unity, he thought.

Yet another demand followed. Chrétien wanted to be the party's Quebec lieutenant, the chief organizer and patronage czar for the province. The billions spent by the federal government in Quebec created patronage opportunities galore, and influencing them would allow him to build his Quebec support for a future leadership bid. The problem was that Turner had earmarked this role for André Ouellet, the veteran Liberal Cabinet minister who had run his leadership campaign in Quebec. Chrétien knew that only too well. Indeed, part of the reason he wanted the appointment was because it would position him to wreak revenge on all the senior Quebec Liberals – Ouellet, Marc Lalonde, Monique Bégin, and Serge Joyal, among others – who hadn't supported him for the leadership.

Turner was reluctant to offend Chrétien. He feared he might resign, which would hurt the government's credibility. Polls reported that Chrétien was now the most popular Liberal in the country. Still, Turner could hardly tell his Quebec organizers that, after they had won, he was taking power away from them and giving it to Chrétien. He also knew that Chrétien had alienated many Quebec Liberals during the leadership campaign by threatening them with dire consequences if they did not support him.[2] Emotions were running high on both sides. When Marc Lalonde got wind of Chrétien's demands, his response was blunt: "Why doesn't he [Turner] step in and slug the son of a bitch?"[3]

The entire standoff was well reported in the press. Southam Press columnist Allan Fotheringham noted that Chrétien had the reputation among fellow ministers of being an intellectual lightweight with a short attention span. He wouldn't stay in a meeting longer than a quarter-hour and wouldn't read any memo over a page in length. His French Canadian colleagues found his habitant act embarrassing. Now, however, warmed by the media spotlight, Chrétien believed his own press and overplayed his hand. Serge Joyal told reporters he doubted whether Chrétien could be trusted: he was still smarting from the leadership contest, an indication that he was "too 'emotional' to handle the job."[4] Beyond the immediate issue, all this wrangling was an ominous sign that the power vacuum in Quebec left by Trudeau's departure would be filled by turmoil.

While negotiations with Chrétien dragged on, Turner wrestled with the election issue. Bill Lee had given him a comprehensive analysis in a twelve-page memo ten days before the convention. The main advantage of going to the polls early was to capitalize on the momentum built up by the leadership race and to limit the danger of governing for long with the "same old gang" the caucus and Cabinet elected under Trudeau. It also eliminated the need to get Turner a seat in the House through a by-election. On the con side, Lee pointed out that a summer election would give the Liberals little time to recover from the leadership race, conduct polls, sign up new candidates, and organize the myriad details required to run an effective campaign. They would also have to be prepared to offend monarchists by postponing the queen's visit.

A fall election, in contrast, had a lot going for it. Turner would have the opportunity to host the queen and the pope, do a turn or two as a statesman on the international stage, stake out some policy positions, and get Canadians used to the idea that someone other than Pierre Trudeau was prime minister. He could still avoid seeking a seat through a by-election because Parliament would sit for only a few days in September before it was time to call the election. That parliamentary session could include a Speech from the Throne and a budget that could be used as a launching pad for a campaign. There would be time to organize and seek out good candidates for office. The only downside to this scenario was that November was a depressing time of year when seasonal unemployment began to rise, and Turner would have to govern until then with the Trudeau team.

The third option, spring 1985, had certain attractions: the season made people more optimistic, the budget should by then be having an effect, and there would be ample time to recruit first-rate candidates. Turner could not avoid running in a by-election before then, however, and he would be stuck with the old gang for an uncomfortably long period. The media would criticize him for not having a mandate and for holding on as long as possible out of desperation. For these reasons, Lee did not recommend this choice.

How to decide, then, between spring and fall? Lee presented polling and election returns data from the eight previous general elections. In all but one, Liberal support had dropped between the time of the election call and election day by an average of 4 per cent. There were regional voting patterns to be taken into account as well, of course, but Lee's general recommendation was to poll and to go for an early election if the Liberals had a 6 per cent advantage. Between 3 and 5 per cent would be a judgment call. Anything under 3 per cent, he advised, and it would be safer to wait for the fall.[5]

Turner was inclined to wait. He was exhausted from the leadership campaign and needed time to acclimatize to his responsibilities as prime minister. The pope's visit need not be an impediment to a fall election. If he called it just before the pope's arrival, the pontiff would be gone by the time the campaign really got going. For the moment he suspended judgment until he got a read on public opinion. They commissioned polls from both Angus Reid, the favoured pollster of Turner's new regime, and from Martin Goldfarb, Trudeau's pollster, then sat back to await the results.

In the meantime, Lee tried to find someone to run the election campaign. He proposed Jerry Grafstein, Royce Frith, Sandra Severn, Al Graham, Alf Apps, and even Keith Davey. "Christ, I can't do that," Turner replied indignantly at the mention of Davey, citing his promise to banish rainmakers. Lee had raised the idea earlier with Davey, who dismissed it just as summarily, saying "the optics would be all wrong."[6] Lee also tried to get some of the preliminary arrangements in place for the campaign. Looking into the organization bequeathed by the previous regime, he found that the party reform committee's report of the previous January was all too true. "The Liberal Party of Canada Headquarters ... is a disaster area," he informed Turner.[7] During the Trudeau years, the Prime Minister's Office had taken over many party responsibilities, including running elections.[8] Marc Lalonde and Tom Axworthy had been heading up the election preparedness committee, but their work had been premised on Trudeau running again.[9] The news that the party's electoral capability resided in the PMO came too late. Turner's team had dismissed a few people as part of its renewal efforts. Many more, anticipating that a wholesale changeover was both inevitable and imminent, had simply quit. Turner had relieved Keith Davey of his duties as national campaign chair and had discharged several campaign officials at the provincial level. There were few people left who had up-to-date experience running a campaign. Money was also a problem. Much of the Liberals' war chest had been spent staging the leadership convention. Following instructions from the Trudeau PMO, Iona Campagnolo had used the balance of party funds to clear old debts rather than to build up an election fund. All these factors militated against calling an early election.

Yet another reason to put off an election emerged in the days following Turner's convention victory. Trudeau had been paying off his loyal supporters in a blitz of patronage. He had warned all the leadership candidates at a meeting on April 12 that he planned to make these appointments, offering them the option of doing so themselves if they preferred. Then he announced hundreds of appointments. This was unprecedented behaviour for Trudeau, who previously had taken little interest in party matters. The scale and cynicism of the exercise threatened to sully the Liberal brand and hurt his successor's electoral chances.

With the election call still up in the air, Turner worked on putting together his Cabinet. It was a critical exercise, for Cabinet would present the public face of the new government. One way to signal renewal was to reduce its size. Turner did so by cutting the number of ministers from thirty-seven to twenty-nine. He also tackled the elaborate system of decision making Trudeau had created. He reduced the number of Cabinet committees from thirteen to ten, simplified their procedures, eliminated all the shadow committees of deputy ministers, and reduced the number of spending envelopes within which budget decisions were negotiated. His most symbolic move was to eliminate two ministries of state: Social Development and Economic and Regional Development. Both were planning ministries that coordinated policy and spending priorities for clusters of departments within their areas. He was indicating that he would give back authority – and responsibility – to his ministers. Core features of the Trudeau "rational government" were gone, to be replaced by a leaner, faster, more efficient, and politically responsive decision-making process. That was just a start, Turner said. He would await a mandate from the voters to go further.

Meanwhile, the patronage issue was mutating dangerously. Before the leadership convention, Trudeau had appointed six MPs to patronage posts, leaving the Liberals with a slim majority in the House of Commons. Tom Axworthy, Trudeau's principal secretary, met with John Swift and Turner the day after the convention to inform them that Trudeau planned appointments for another half dozen or more MPs – meaning the Liberals would lose their majority. That raised a constitutional issue: Could the governor general call on Turner to form a government if he did not command a majority in the House? Turner turned to Gordon Osbaldeston for advice. Osbaldeston told him it was the governor general's responsibility to ensure that whomever she called to form a government had the confidence of the House of Commons. If the Liberals had a majority, there would be no issue, but if they were in a minority position, she would probably expect them to win a confidence vote very soon after taking office. Given this advice, Turner opted to make these remaining patronage appointments himself later and so preserve his majority until he had formed his government.

When Turner emerged from the meeting at which Trudeau gave him this final list of appointments, he told a waiting aide, "Turn away when I tell you this because you are going to vomit."[10] The list included the appointment of Bryce Mackasey as ambassador to Portugal. That was bound to generate unflattering headlines. Mackasey's reputation was in tatters following influence-peddling allegations, even though he had been acquitted of related charges in court. He was already collecting a parliamentary pension and a pension from his earlier appointment as chairman of the board of Air Canada. Yet another reward for this Liberal warhorse epitomized Liberal Party corruption – and, inevitably, Turner was now associated with it.

As these issues swirled around him, Turner continued to search for a way out of the Chrétien imbroglio. On Thursday, June 28, he issued Chrétien a combined compromise and ultimatum. There would be no Quebec lieutenant. Instead, he was establishing a committee of three – Ouellet, Chrétien, and Charles Lapointe, a Chrétien supporter – to oversee Quebec and advise him on political affairs in the province. Chrétien would nominally be the senior member of the triumvirate, and, as compensation, Ouellet would get greater Cabinet responsibilities. Chrétien reluctantly acquiesced.[11] "It's a more serious rift than anything we have ever had in the Liberal party before," one Cabinet minister told *Maclean's* magazine.[12]

With the Chrétien breach papered over, a day or so remained to finalize the Cabinet appointments. Here again Turner struggled to balance the countervailing demands of renewal and party unity. He had promised Axworthy to keep Judy Erola and Monique Bégin, and, besides, he wanted women in Cabinet. He had to reward those who had supported his leadership bid, so Marc Lalonde kept his Finance portfolio. He was obliged to retain others in the interests of party unity. These included the three ministers he couldn't drop, because Chrétien had protected them – Supply and Services Minister Charles Lapointe, Multiculturalism Minister David Collenette, and Employment Minister John Roberts. And still others, such as Charles Caccia, a Chrétien supporter from the Italian Canadian community in Toronto, represented constituencies that Turner did not want to alienate with an election coming up.

Turner managed to nudge a few bodies out. The three senators who had provided Western representation were dropped, and Mark MacGuigan was made a federal court judge. Turner kept sixteen ministers in the twenty-nine-member Cabinet in their old positions. Key posts were dominated by old faces: Marc Lalonde, Jean Chrétien, André Ouellet, Herb Gray, John Roberts, Robert Kaplan, Lloyd Axworthy, Gerald Regan, and Allan MacEachen (now government leader in the Senate). It took careful scrutiny to discern that power had shifted. Ed Lumley and Lloyd Axworthy emerged as the most powerful ministers. Lumley kept his Industry portfolio, and Axworthy stayed in Transport, but also headed the party's new Western and Northern Advisory Council. Turner was counting on Axworthy to help him bring the West back to the Liberal Party. Gerald Regan was another beneficiary, promoted to the high-profile post of Energy. Donald Johnston, who had hoped for an economic portfolio, had to be content with Justice. He was, however, the logical successor if and when Lalonde left Finance. With so many interests in play and commitments to fulfill, Turner ended up with just five new faces in Cabinet: Doug Frith (Indian Affairs and Northern Development), Jean Lapierre (Youth and Sport), Herb Breau (Fisheries), Remi Bujold (Regional Development), and Ralph

Ferguson (Agriculture). At least the new appointees' relative youth did something to signal change: Frith, Breau, and Bujold were under forty, and Lapierre, just twenty-eight, was the youngest Cabinet minister ever.

Turner was keeping tabs on all these details by taping index cards on a lampshade in his hotel suite. He had no secretariat, no gatekeeper, not even an executive secretary to keep track of things. His chief aides had been assigned big jobs related to the transition and reported back to him, and he tried to juggle everything else. It was a dangerous way to operate. Although the transition interlude was brief, it was also a critical period in which key decisions were being made. Once again he was suffering the consequences of his refusal to organize before Trudeau's departure. He had no experience managing a chaotic enterprise in a period of flux. What he really needed was a strong chief of staff to manage the five-ringed circus of the government, Cabinet, caucus, party, and the media while he deliberated on strategy. As it was, he could only hope to survive until his regime settled into office and he could establish the planning and project-management systems that had always been a hallmark of his administrative style.

The patronage issue continued to plague relations between the incoming and outgoing prime ministers. At the last meeting of his Cabinet on Thursday, June 28, 1984, Trudeau challenged Osbaldeston on the advice he had given to Turner. Later that day, Osbaldeston provided Trudeau with a letter detailing what he had said and why:

> At today's Cabinet you asked about the situation that would arise if you were to make enough appointments that the Government's majority would be lost in the House of Commons. (Current standings in the House are 145 Liberals [including the Speaker], 100 Progressive Conservatives, 31 New Democrats and 1 Independent – taking account of the Speaker, 12 appointments, resignations or withdrawals of support by Government members would be required for the Government to lose its working majority.)
>
> In our view the starting point is the Governor General's responsibility to have a Government that can command the support of Parliament. She would ordinarily turn to Mr. Turner as the leader of the party with the majority in the House and would expect him to confirm his standing,

within a reasonable time, either by winning a vote of confidence in the House or by calling a general election.

The situation would become more complicated, however, if the Government were to be reduced to a minority situation before Mr. Turner was sworn. In most circumstances we would anticipate she would call on Mr. Turner in view of the Government's plurality, but she would undoubtedly want some demonstration of confidence as soon as possible, especially if there were a substantial question of whether that would be forthcoming. In the extreme case of the Governor General becoming aware that the NDP had indicated it would not support the Government or even that it would support Mr. Mulroney she would be placed in an unprecedented and constitutionally very difficult situation.

It is difficult to predict how the Governor General would act in such circumstances, but clearly it is a situation to be avoided if at all possible. Should a minority occur after the new Government had been sworn to office but before dissolution, the Governor General might want to discuss the situation with her first Minister, but once a government was in place, even if it were a minority, she would be under less obligation to request an immediate test of confidence than she would be at the point she is choosing whom to call upon to form a Government. The critical point is at the moment the Governor General is to exercise her prerogative to install a new Government, and our advice to Mr. Turner was based on the desirability of avoiding the potentially very difficult situation described above.[13]

Acting on this advice, Turner had agreed to make the patronage appointments Trudeau had demanded. Had he made a decision to call an election that summer, he need not have worried about preserving a majority. As it was, he was still undecided and trying to keep his options open.

Trudeau demanded that Turner put his commitment to making these appointments in writing. Turner reluctantly agreed, and Trudeau sent him a letter setting out the patronage appointments he expected him to make:

> In every case these are individuals who have served the government and the Party well, and I am committed to promoting their future careers.

> Our desire to assist our colleagues, however, must be balanced with the
> need to maintain a majority in the House of Commons. Therefore, I will
> not exercise my prerogative to submit all of my proposed appointments
> to the Governor General, but I ask you to make an undertaking to follow
> through with the remaining appointments prior to any dissolution.[14]

Turner wrote back the same day, saying, "I am in agreement with the terms
of the letter, and I undertake to you that I will make the appointments on
your list prior to any dissolution."[15] On Friday, June 29, Parliament recessed.
Turner would be sworn in the next day.

On the morning of Saturday, June 30, Pierre Trudeau arrived at Rideau
Hall sporting an ascot, the trademark rose in his lapel. He submitted his
resignation to Governor General Jeanne Sauvé. His armour-plated black
limousine drove him back down the Rideau Hall driveway and across the
street to 24 Sussex Drive, where he climbed into his Mercedes convertible
and motored off the political scene. A half-hour later, Turner and his
Cabinet arrived to be sworn in. His family came along to watch the ceremony, including his sister, Brenda Norris, her family, and a swarm of RCMP
plainclothes officers and aides.

Turner was criticized for making the ceremony off-limits to reporters
after having promised open government, but he held a long press conference afterward to make up for it. He told reporters that he would be seeking
a seat in British Columbia. He also announced that he would not have a
Quebec lieutenant. "I intend to deal directly with the Quebec population,
without an interpreter," he said. In addition, he emphasized his plans to
revamp government: "I felt for some time that the cabinet, the cabinet
committee system, and indeed the entire decision-making process were
too elaborate, too complex, too slow, and too expensive. Because of this
system, the responsibility of the ministers and of their departments has
become diffused and eroded and blurred. Decisions are difficult to arrive
at in an efficient and timely fashion."[16] One reporter asked why it had been
necessary for Trudeau to get a pledge in writing that Turner would implement his remaining patronage appointments. Offering his word, Turner
said, "would have been satisfactory to me. Perhaps he felt he had to assure
those members of his caucus to whom he'd made commitments."[17]

Turner tried to head off criticism of his Cabinet choices by underlining that it was a "phase one Cabinet re-organization only." Down the road he would shake up Cabinet and government organization to an extent un-rivalled in recent history. In the meantime, he had to make do with the materials at hand. He wanted to recruit more women, westerners, and minorities into the House of Commons. "Everyone in the present Cabinet will have to fight to keep that job," he assured reporters.[18]

Turner's performance for the cameras left much to be desired. His answers were punctuated by lengthy pauses in which he collected his thoughts, and as he paused, he looked upward and raised his eyebrows, causing his eyes to bulge briefly. Editorial cartoonists had by now picked up on this trait and would make it a feature of their Turner caricatures. Nevertheless, the press conference was well received. The journalists in attendance were pleased that he had asked them to give him their "suggestions as to how [they] would like our relationship to proceed."[19] His decision to run in British Columbia, said one columnist, displayed "a little class, a little prin-ciple, and willingness to put his head on the block for political principle."[20] *La Presse* praised Turner lavishly for his decision not to have a Quebec lieutenant, a post it considered a patronizing anachronism.

When it came to the new Cabinet, however, reviews ranged from bemused to highly critical, with disappointment the dominant note. Turner may have made significant changes to the structure of Cabinet and redistributed power within it, but these were subtleties overshadowed by the many familiar faces from the Trudeau years. The general conclusion was that he had failed to deliver on his promise of change. The Liberal establishment had first colonized Turner's leadership campaign and now his government. "What has happened," Tory leader Brian Mulroney joked, "is that the old bunch went out one door and came right back in the other."[21]

On Sunday, July 1, after just one day in office, Turner participated in the Canada Day ceremonies on Parliament Hill. There was much colourful pomp: the changing of the guard, a royal salute and a twenty-one-gun salute for the governor general, choirs singing patriotic anthems, and a flypast by air force jets. He gave a brief address that struck sentimental notes of national pride and resolve in the face of future challenges, then accompanied Governor General Sauvé on a walkabout to greet members of the crowd. It was a moment to bask in the glory of being the country's leader.

For the following week, Turner lay low, planning his next move. The results from the polling by Angus Reid and Martin Goldfarb had come in late the previous week. They reported a Liberal lead in the 4-6 per cent range – an indecisive level of support, according to Lee's memo on when to announce an election – so the decision was a judgment call. When it came to a choice between the leaders of the two parties, Reid reported that Turner led Mulroney by a seven-point margin. Although Canadians found Mulroney more likeable than Turner, they thought Turner more competent. Recalling how Mulroney had publicly supported Joe Clark while organizing against him, voters were also concerned about his ethics. Liberal popularity was also up in Quebec – a reassuring report because the Conservative base there had been growing since Mulroney was elected leader. "The new Turner government has achieved considerable forward momentum," Reid stated, "and [Canadians] are even more likely to choose a Liberal government led by John Turner."[22]

Turner had to act quickly if he were to call an election: the queen was scheduled to arrive in Canada within two weeks, and the royal yacht *Britannia* would set sail for Canada any day. Although the Liberal lead reported by pollsters Reid and Goldfarb wasn't quite what Lee had recommended as the trigger for an early election, Turner and his advisers were feeling confident. Their ascension to power had been intoxicating. The Liberal caucus was about 70 per cent in favour of trying to capitalize immediately on their lead in the polls, and senior party strategists agreed. Everyone remembered 1968, when Trudeau had followed his spring convention victory with a summer election call that delivered a Liberal majority. The opportunists convinced themselves that history was repeating itself.

As Turner considered his decision, his long-term concern about federal spending and accumulating deficits influenced him most. When he left Finance, the federal debt had stood at 17 per cent of gross national product. By 1983 it had risen to 28 per cent of GNP, and Lalonde's budget the previous February projected it ballooning to 47 per cent by 1985-86.[23] Turner believed that this debt level was unsustainable. Yet when he mentioned the issue publicly, he was accused of being reactionary. His compromise had been to talk about bringing down the debt gradually with minimal effect on the disadvantaged – a plausible strategy for an economy that seemed to be recovering from a deep recession.

Now, suddenly, there was disturbing economic news. Lalonde came to Turner's suite on July 3 to brief him on the economic forecast he would be presenting to the Cabinet Committee on Priorities and Planning the following day. Canada's economy was hitched to a hot US economy that was pulling out of the recession. This link created a healthy demand for Canadian exports – natural resources and especially automobiles, where continental demand for models manufactured in Canada was strong. As a downside, it kept interest rates high in the United States and attracted speculative investment in the US dollar. The Canadian dollar was holding its own against every international currency except the US dollar, and the Bank of Canada was trying to keep it from slipping relatively lower by raising interest rates. Meanwhile, Canada, like other industrial nations, was still dealing with some of the fallout of the recession, most significantly unemployment. Although new jobs were being created, so many workers were entering, or re-entering, the economy that the unemployment rate remained high. That kept federal spending on social programs high and exacerbated the deficit, thereby putting more pressure on interest rates.

The upshot was that Finance was now predicting a weaker economy than had been foreseen in Lalonde's February budget. Unemployment could rise to 15 per cent by the fall, interest rates were headed in the same direction, and the dollar could drop as low as sixty-five cents US. Growth would be slower than predicted, meaning that revenues would be lower and the deficit higher. There was even concern that inflation, knocked back to 4 per cent by the tough monetarism inspired by US Federal Reserve chief Paul Volcker, was set to climb again. "Events have clearly driven us off the February budget track and a number of very tough decisions will be required simply to get back to that track, let alone to make the further progress in managing the deficit that the investment community demands," Lalonde reported.[24]

The forecast was alarming, and Turner took it very seriously. Voters were still smarting from the recent recession, and now runaway inflation and high interest rates seemed about to make a comeback. Middle-class voters with progressive sensibilities who were usually partial to the Liberals tended to take refuge with the Conservatives when their pocketbooks were threatened. If the economy were tanking, going to the polls in the fall would be suicidal.

On Wednesday, July 4, a report surfaced that Turner had phoned the queen's private secretary. Rumours flew around Ottawa. On July 6 Gallup released the results of a national poll, conducted between June 21 and 23, which put the Liberals eleven points ahead of the Tories, with 49 per cent of the vote compared to 38 per cent, and the NDP trailing at 11 per cent. Insiders were skeptical of its reliability because it had been conducted less than a week after Turner's election, when the convention bounce was at its apex. That Saturday Turner and his wife flew to England to tell the queen that he had decided to call an election and that, though she was welcome to come to Canada, he would respect any decision she made. In an age of instantaneous communications, he had no real need to go to England, but he had a relationship with the royal family stretching back to his famous fling with Princess Margaret, and he wanted to show the queen respect by breaking the news in person.[25]

While Turner was winging his way back to Canada the next day, his government announced the patronage appointments to the Senate, the judiciary, the diplomatic corps, and other posts that he had promised Trudeau he would make. The list had now inflated to nineteen in total, eighteen of them Liberals, including seventeen sitting MPs. On Monday morning Turner met with his Cabinet. At 12:30 p.m. he arrived at Rideau Hall and asked Governor General Jeanne Sauvé to dissolve Parliament. A press conference was called for the National Press Building at 2:00 p.m. Turner told the assembled scribes that he needed a fresh mandate to deal with the economic challenges facing Canada. "This Parliament has run its course, and I sense that the people of Canada want and should have a choice and an opportunity to clear the air," he said.[26] The election would be on September 4, the Tuesday following the Labour Day holiday weekend – fifty-six days away.

A mere three weeks had passed since Turner had been elected Liberal leader and just nine days since he had become prime minister. Following his announcement, the leaders of the other major parties held news conferences. Mulroney focused on the economy, whereas Broadbent emphasized that only his party offered an alternative to Turner and Mulroney, the ideological "Bobbsey Twins of Bay St." Senior strategists on both sides told reporters they were hoping for a majority, but a minority was possible. "Lucky breaks and bad blunders could swing the result either way," Richard Gwyn opined, "and also swing it all the way from a small Conservative minority to a sizable Liberal majority, and vice versa."[27]

Most proponents of the early election call favoured the politics of image and believed that the post-convention bump in popularity was substantial enough to win the Liberals re-election. Turner felt some obligation to them: they had supported him for the leadership because they thought him the only candidate who could win the next election. He also felt uncomfortable about governing for long without a mandate from the electorate. Those who saw election campaigns primarily as organizational challenges were dismayed. Turner had been disorganized from the start of his leadership campaign, and things had not improved. His refusal to begin organizing before Trudeau's resignation was still plaguing him.

In the past, Turner had always erred on the side of caution and prepared-ness. However, in this instance his concern that the economy was about to sour was decisive. He opted to launch a logistically complex campaign in the full glare of the national spotlight, even though he was still readjusting to politics and his party was disorganized. He had muddled through his leadership bid that way. But would it do for a national election campaign?

The night before Turner flew to England, Jim Robb was buttonholed by John de B. Payne while they were attending a reception on a cruise boat out of Montreal. Payne pulled him over to the stern railing to tell him the news. Robb nodded as he took it all in, then jokingly asked Payne, "Should we throw ourselves off right now?"[28]

17

THINGS FALL APART

Turner was more popular than his party, so the Liberals planned to build their election campaign around him. They certainly couldn't rely on their campaign organization – they had none. Bill Lee hadn't even managed to find a campaign manager, so, days before the election call, he agreed to do the job himself.[1] After that, a mad scramble ensued to get things going.

The Conservatives, in contrast, had been preparing for months under the direction of Norm Atkins, an advertising executive and key organizer of the Ontario Conservative Party's "Big Blue Machine." Discontent with the Liberals and anticipation that the Tories would form the next federal government had bolstered their campaign coffers. In 1983 they had raised $14 million, compared to the NDP's $8 million and the Liberals' $6 million. Their candidates had been equipped with personal computers linked to headquarters. While waiting for the election call, they had refined their candidate training, tour planning, and media relations. Their polling firm, Decima Research, could track voter opinion on particular issues across the country or by individual neighbourhood, and it had a direct mail system that could target swing voters with personalized letters. Taking a cue from Ronald Reagan, the Conservatives even had a portable stage for their leader's tour. Before every Mulroney speech, five roadies assembled a blue plastic podium and backdrop replete with the party logo, sound system, and lighting. Its appearance highlighted how campaigning was geared now to television. The Tories' election machine was fully assembled and ready to roll. The Liberals were still sourcing parts.[2]

Election laws prohibited television advertising until four weeks before election day. In the interim, parties relied on the leader's tour to generate television coverage and get their messages across. That, at least, was the conventional strategy. But Turner, exhausted by his exertions since March and feeling obliged to attend to his responsibilities as prime minister, decided not to campaign hard for the first couple of weeks. He wanted a proper leader's tour organized before he started. With a substantial lead in the polls, he hoped to get by for now by making a few appearances and projecting prime ministerial gravitas.

Negative reviews of Turner's Cabinet and patronage appointments dominated coverage of the first week of the campaign. Eugene Forsey, a constitutional expert and Liberal senator, announced that whoever had advised Turner that he might not be asked to form a government if he lacked a majority was a "jackass bonehead." "I don't know what kind of fairytales he's been fed," he declared. "It's all rubbish."[3] Although patronage had long been a fixture in Canadian political life, the press, especially the conservative press, was increasingly treating it as a form of corruption. "Blackmail is what Pierre Trudeau pulled on John Turner," concluded the *Toronto Sun*. "No outgoing prime minister ever so offensively and publicly hamstrung his successor. It was a parting kick at the man Trudeau least wanted in the job." Turner told reporters that the appointments he made at Trudeau's behest should be seen as "concluding an era" and that he should be judged on his "own appointments from now on." For a sign of things to come, he said, they should assess the appointment process for judges he had introduced when he was minister of justice.[4] No one bothered, of course – that was all ancient history.

Turner's ability to distance himself from the patronage issue was compromised because, along with the appointments he had promised to Trudeau, he had layered in another six, most of them at Chrétien's behest. They included the very noticeable figure of Eugene Whelan, the former minister of agriculture, who was rewarded with a berth at the World Food and Agricultural Organization in Rome. Turner further complicated the issue at the press conference announcing the election when he told the media, "All of these appointments except one were in furtherance to my commitment to ... Trudeau ... or had been discussed and agreed to at cabinet meetings of the previous administration."[5] He was thinking that he had made only one appointment for his own purposes – a posting for an incumbent MP that opened up his riding for a female candidate. All the others were associated with the outgoing government. He left the impression, however, that he had added only one appointment to Trudeau's list, when in fact he had added six.[6]

Trudeau, who had made hundreds of patronage appointments, now took offence at being held responsible for an additional half dozen associated with the end of his regime. One of his aides contacted Turner and threatened to release the letter specifying his patronage list to the press. That would have embarrassed Turner by contradicting his statement and showing that he, not Trudeau, was responsible for the Whelan appointment, which was becoming almost as controversial as the Mackasey posting. Once again Trudeau was playing hardball with his successor at the expense of the party. Turner took care not to make the same claim again, but he was left without an effective way to distance himself from Trudeau's patronage orgy.

This was an ominous start to the campaign. Mulroney could use the patronage issue to dramatize the need for change, and he made the most of it. He called the recent appointments "something right out of an Edward G. Robinson movie. You know, the boys cutting up the cash."[7] If he were prime minister, he solemnly vowed, the public would be impressed by the quality and impartiality of his appointments. "Patronage is killing us," Senator Philippe Gigantès reported from the hustings a few days later.[8]

The patronage issue was offset by a Tory stumble in the opening days of the campaign. Finance critic John Crosbie had estimated the cost of the party's election promises at $6 billion. On July 12 it was reported that he had a document suggesting that the real price tag would be $20 billion over five years. At this rate, the Tories would have to increase the deficit, the very thing they had been vociferously criticizing the Liberals for doing. Mulroney was thrown on the defensive but managed the issue by denying the $20 billion figure and promising to reveal the cost of his promises by the end of the campaign.

That weekend brought a second Tory blunder. Chatting to a bunch of reporters on his campaign plane, Mulroney admitted that he had told his partisans one thing about patronage and the Canadian public another. Regarding Mackasey's appointment, he remarked, "There's no whore like an old whore," adding that, if he were Mackasey, he'd have had his nose in the trough too.[9] Mulroney thought his comments were off the record, but they appeared in the *Ottawa Citizen* the next day. Aside from undermining all his carefully cultivated indignation about Liberal patronage, they exemplified the moral dodginess that Canadians suspected of him. The Tories moved quickly to limit the damage – within two days Mulroney had apologized, saying he should not have made light of something that was not a joking matter.

These early problems heartened the Liberals. The Tories' traditional gift for self-destruction seemed undiminished. If they kept on this way, maybe no one would notice that the Liberals were not prepared for the campaign. The disparity in election readiness between the two main parties was, however, all too obvious to the press. The Conservatives had a platform, whereas the Liberals were still working on one. Every day Mulroney was provided with briefing notes on his schedule, the people he was going to meet, and local issues. Turner relied on memory and whatever he could pick up along the way. The lack of a strong right hand was now becoming apparent – there was no one to advise, no one to guard the leader's time. The Tories had leased a Boeing 727 to fly Mulroney, his entourage, and reporters to campaign stops around the country, and the NDP had chartered a smaller plane. The Liberals, in contrast, began their campaign by booking commercial flights for Turner. Instead of being coddled in a party plane, journalists had to scramble to book airplane tickets to catch up with him. They were annoyed, and it affected their coverage. No matter how well Turner performed or how smoothly an event went off, reporters began to use the word "gaffe" to characterize glitches in his campaign.[10] It would become a dominant motif in their coverage.

The Liberals had suspended nominations during the leadership race and now had candidates in only 40 of the 281 ridings, whereas the Conservatives and the NDP both had more than 200 in place. About one in five Liberal incumbents had decided not to run again. It would be challenging to ensure that there were Liberal candidates for every riding, let alone people with name recognition and credibility. Turner had some high-profile nominees in mind, and he asked Monique Bégin to help him recruit female candidates in Quebec. André Ouellet wanted Turner to appoint some Quebec MPs to patronage positions in order to open Liberal nominations for women, but the growing controversy over patronage left him reluctant to use this customary stratagem.[11]

Gaffes were inevitable because the Liberals were divided as well as disorganized. Turner hadn't had time to nurture working relationships between party factions, and he was overseeing a mélange of Liberal interests that had yet to learn how to communicate, let alone cooperate. The group loyalties that had formed around leadership candidates persisted, most significantly in the case of Chrétien. Relations with the executive of the national party organization were still being sorted out. Now that Turner was prime minister, the Liberal caucus and Cabinet also had his ear. Some were defenders of the Trudeau legacy, some were disappointed Chrétien supporters, and all felt entitled to direct access to him. Turner's aides from his leadership campaign had, for the most part, been out of active politics for over a decade and had weak connections with the Trudeauites, who, by dint of their greater and more recent experience, felt themselves entitled to lead the way.

Polling was one of many areas where factionalism caused trouble. Turner continued to use both Angus Reid and Martin Goldfarb. Reid emphasized the need to signal change, Goldfarb warned of the dangers of alienating Trudeau's traditional constituency, and Turner ended up with conflicting advice.[12] The most critical breakdown in relations, however, was between the PMO and the national campaign committee. At first senior officials from both organizations consulted every evening, but tensions soon developed. The PMO suspected that Bill Lee was withholding polling information and blamed him for producing unsuitable or unreliable campaign materials. Lee, for his part, resented being second-guessed.[13]

According to the textbook approach to campaigning, the party leader should entrust subordinates with all but the most urgent or strategic decisions so he can concentrate on being the candidate and performing for television. Instead, everyone was reporting to Turner, who had little more than his sense of obligation to guide him in sorting things out. That led to more gaffes. On one occasion Turner and his advisers decided that the position of national campaign chair would be shared by three fresh faces: Lise Saint-Martin Tremblay from Quebec, Doug Frith from Ontario, and

Izzy Asper from Manitoba. Turner was supposed to phone Marc Lalonde and tell him that the Quebec position would not be his, but he forgot. The day before the election call, word came that Lalonde had assumed he had the job and had plunged into it. Pulling the rug out from under him would be insulting, so Turner contacted Tremblay and rescinded his offer. In order to get female representation on the committee, he then had to bump Doug Frith and put in Judy Erola for Ontario.

The Liberals' disorganization prevented them from taking the initiative and setting the agenda for the campaign. Long-suffering Liberal candidates got their policy positions from reading the pronouncements of their leader as reported in the press. When Turner visited Calgary, for instance, they learned that he planned to reform the National Energy Program, a major focus of Western resentment during Trudeau's last term in power. Turner also reiterated his concern about the deficit, but, wary of alienating the left, again promised to do so without harming social programs. How he could work this miracle was not clear, but Mulroney was equally vague on the point, so greater precision was not required.

On Monday, July 16, Turner was in Vancouver to announce that he would stand for election in Vancouver Quadra, a riding just south of the downtown area that included his alma mater, the University of British Columbia. The Tories had arranged to have Mulroney run in the Quebec riding of Manicouagan, which included his hometown of Baie Comeau. Turner also had a background in Quebec, where the polls told him he had a bigger lead than anywhere else in the country. He hoped that the Liberals could hold their traditional support in central Canada while storming the Conservatives' western strongholds. The point wasn't just to win seats, since, proportionately, populous central Canada was far more important. For Turner, it was a case of rebuilding the Liberals as a national party that represented all the regions of Canada.

The Liberal hold on Quebec could not be taken for granted. Trudeau had been seen as a native son, and the Québécois were happy to have French power in Ottawa and nationalist, or even separatist, governments in Quebec City. They saw no inconsistency and, in fact, much to gain from playing the two off against each other. The Quebec electorate was divided roughly in three: a third was federalist, something less than a third favoured an independent Quebec nation-state, and another third was ambivalent but capable of swinging one way or the other depending on the circumstances. Many federalists were nationalists insofar as they believed in the existence of a French Canadian nation and the need for a strong Quebec government to protect it. Where separatists and other nationalists split was over the desirability of an independent Quebec state, given the possible economic costs involved. Thus, a constitutional deal that would give Quebec additional powers without disrupting the Canadian economic commonwealth had a broad political appeal in Quebec. Mulroney had devised his Quebec strategy accordingly: he would appeal to nationalism by sympathizing with Quebec's constitutional aspirations while assuming Trudeau's mantle as the native son.

Quebec issues provoked some sparring between Turner and Mulroney in the early weeks of the campaign. On July 19 Turner held a press conference in Montreal to introduce seven new Liberal candidates in Quebec, including Raymond Garneau, his star recruit. Garneau, Turner's provincial counterpart when both were finance ministers in the early seventies, had run for the provincial Liberal leadership and lost, and like Turner, had spent time out of politics in business. By recruiting Garneau, Turner was signalling that he too was prepared to make a constitutional deal to accommodate Quebec. Garneau even threw out the possibility of Quebec recovering the constitutional veto Lévesque had given up in the constitutional negotiations during the early 1980s, with the proviso that talks would have to be conducted with a Quebec government that believed in Confederation. The Parti Québécois government was coming to the end of its term, and an election was in the offing. Mulroney had taken the same hard line against the PQ the year before, but now, hoping to attract soft nationalists, he expressed indignation at the Liberals' caveat. This posture pleased René Lévesque, and PQ supporters began to work for the Conservatives.

Turner might reasonably have expected to have the PQ's efforts offset by the influence of the provincial Liberal Party, but the federal Liberals exercised no direct control over the provincial organization. The relationship between the federal and provincial Liberals in Quebec was by no means straightforward. Membership aand key officials overlapped, but the overall composition of each organization differed significantly, as did their orientation and goals. As the Créditistes and the Union Nationale had declined in recent decades, the provincial party found itself inheriting their supporters and occupying the centre-right and federalist position in opposition to the left-wing and separatist Parti Québécois. Whereas conservatives had no choice but the Liberals at the provincial level, such was not the case at the federal level.

Liberal leader Robert Bourassa publicly proclaimed neutrality, but in practice many provincial Liberals were working for the Conservatives. Mulroney and Bourassa were on good terms, whereas Bourassa had a history of rocky relations with the federal Liberals. Trudeau had been openly contemptuous of Bourassa after he backed away from the Victoria Charter and subsequently deviated from him on language policy. Nor did Bourassa have any particular fondness for Garneau, despite Garneau's service in his Cabinet in the 1970s. Bourassa calculated that a change of regime in Ottawa would improve his electoral chances against the PQ in the next provincial election. Moreover, he thought he could get more for Quebec from Mulroney than from Turner.[14]

The provincial party's lack of support was all the more significant given developments in the federal organization in Quebec. Under Trudeau, Marc Lalonde and André Ouellet had run what appeared to be an awesome political machine in the province, but the gears were no longer meshing. Many of Trudeau's patronage appointments had been intended to win support for Chrétien's leadership bid. Lalonde had never been a Chrétien fan, and Chrétien was furious with his former friend Ouellet over his support for Turner. Garneau's arrival further splintered the Quebec wing of the federal party into factions beholden to a variety of rival power-brokers. Turner had to umpire the resulting disputes. Chrétien, for example, complained to Bill Lee that he and his supporters were being frozen out of Ouellet's and Lalonde's election planning. Lalonde responded, "Screw [Chrétien], he lost ... We will deliver 74 seats." Turner told Lee to let Lalonde do his thing.[15]

While on his way to Vancouver to announce that he would run in Vancouver Quadra, Turner stopped off to campaign in ridings that the Liberals felt they had a chance to win in Calgary and Edmonton. In Edmonton on the evening of Friday, July 13, he attended the meeting of the party's new Western and Northern Council. Managers at CTV in Toronto debated what to do with footage taken by one of their film crews during that event. It showed Turner arriving onstage and throwing an arm around party president Iona Campagnolo's shoulder, kissing her on the cheek, and patting her posterior. Campagnolo promptly returned the greeting, striking a blow for gender equality but drawing more attention to his cheekiness. Then they moved off to work the room. The audio feed picked up the words "a perfect ass," seemingly from the prime minister, but it was not clear whose character or buttocks were being assessed.[16]

At first CTV did not air the clip. Management hesitated to focus on a triviality that had little to do with the issues facing the country. Word about the footage got around, however, and other journalists wanted to see it. Then, the following Thursday, CTV cameras filmed Turner patting Lise Saint-Martin Tremblay's bottom at a campaign event in Montreal. CTV aired both scenes the next day.

Turner had been warned about patting bums during the leadership race.[17] The warning didn't register, because he thought he needed no advice on gender relations. There were a number of strong women in his life, and he treated them with respect. He encouraged women to enter politics and strongly endorsed women's causes. When asked about the CTV clip, he remained unrepentant. "I'm a hugger ... I'm a tactile politician. I'm slapping people all over the place. That's my style," he explained. "People are reaching out to me and I'm reaching out to them."[18] And so he let the issue live on, in contrast to Mulroney, who, by apologizing for his coarse remarks about patronage, had quickly snuffed out that controversy. The media continued to broadcast the clips, generating editorials, cartoons, opinion pieces, and sly allusions in headlines. Feminists created a cardboard "Turner Bum Shield" that got more media coverage than anything Turner said or did over the next few days.

Week one of the campaign had been patronage. Week two was bum patting. Week three would be dominated by the television debates. The opposition parties had demanded a leaders' debate as soon as the election was called. Turner worried about the way he came across on camera. He was still getting up to speed on all the issues and, as the frontrunner, had the most to lose from a debate. Still, having debates early on would cover his absence from the campaign trail and give him more time to get organized. If they were held relatively soon, whatever transpired would presumably be ancient history by the critical closing weeks of the campaign. On

LOOKING AHEAD TO THE TURNER ERA

TORONTO LIFE

While the Tories choose their man and revel in the polls, the Liberal future is not so bleak—not with Old Blue Eyes as ace-in-the-hole

JUNE 1983 $2

PLUS:
our guide to the tops in take-out and barbecuing as a black-tie affair
Peter Gzowski gets inside the Queen's Plate
Alexander Ross on how not to run a gold rush

METRO'S FINEST ENTERTAINMENT LISTINGS
Toronto Calendar

29　When Trudeau returned to lead the Liberals to a majority government in February 1980, the myth of Turner as heir apparent was soon restored as well. Press expectations that Turner would return to lead the Liberal party back from its decline in popularity under Trudeau were exemplified by a story by Walter Stewart in this June 1983 edition of *Toronto Life*. Turner knew it would be impossible to live up to all the press hype. "People have an image of me that may not be right," he warned. "I'm older now and hopefully I'm wiser. But I'm not the blue-eyed boy of the image anymore."

31 Turner and his wife Geills embrace at the moment of victory in the 1984 leadership convention. In the left foreground is Bill Lee, Turner's campaign manager, while between Lee and Turner is Minister of Justice Mark McGuigan, the only other leadership candidate to throw his support to Turner. Moments later, Iona Campagnolo would tell delegates that although Turner had won, runner-up Chrétien was "first in our hearts."

30 *(facing page, top)* Turner surrounded by supporters on Parliament Hill during a campaign event leading up to the leadership convention in June 1984. "Whatever we do, it will never be done at the expense of the unemployed, the aged, the poor, the sick or the disabled," he pledged. "Our economic and social objectives are complementary, not contradictory."

32 Accusations of media bias followed Turner's loss in the 1984 federal election. "We always went after him as a group. We smelled blood, and we attacked," one journalist recalled. One example cited was this *Globe and Mail* front page photo from late August, which used forks on a poster in the background to demonize the prime minister.

33 By early August Turner knew the 1984 election was lost, yet he had weeks of campaigning to go. The strain is evident in this photo at a campaign event later that month where he announced a new youth employment program. Such policy announcements changed little – incessant polling made the Tory surge into the lead the story that defined the campaign.

34 "Turner was OK for television ten years ago when television was stiff itself," observed a television producer, "but now you've got to be natural, and John just can't be natural."

35 Turner with the "Rat Pack." Left to right, Brian Tobin, Don Boudria, Sheila Copps, and John Nunziata, in his Parliament Hill office, May 8, 1985. Turner, whose code of ethics forbade personal attacks on political opponents, found the Rat Pack's tactics troubling, but was loath to curb the crusading spirit of his young caucus members.

36 Turner consults with Raymond Garneau prior to a national caucus meeting in September 1986, when the Liberals' new resolution on Quebec and the constitution was fracturing caucus. Garneau felt that Trudeau had promised Quebec a new constitutional deal during the 1980 referendum campaign and that the Liberals had an obligation to deliver on that promise.

37 Waiting for the results of the leadership review vote at the November 1986 Liberal policy convention: (left to right) Doug Richardson, Geills Turner, John Turner, Brenda Norris, and the Turner children Elizabeth, David, Andrew, and Michael.

38 Celebrating the leadership review victory with Doug Frith (left) and Lise Thibault (right). "I've waited a long time to tell you this, John," Doug Frith said at the podium, "But you're first in our hearts!"

39 The *Toronto Sun* political cartoonist Donato thought Turner was being jerked around by former and future Liberal leaders. "Turner tried to give the party back to its members," one of his supporters explained. "But all they did with their new freedom for three years was mourn their dismal 1984 results, criticize his leadership, [and] hatch conspiracies."

40   "It is difficult for me, sometimes, to reduce the complexity of the problems facing Canada into a 30-second clip, into blacks and whites when there are so many shadings, and yet, obviously, one has to do that," said Turner, reflecting on the importance of television in modern politics, "Perhaps I should perform more as an actor."

41   "With one signature of a pen," Turner told Mulroney during the 1988 leaders' debate, "you … will reduce us … to a colony of the United States." Canadians turned against free trade, then changed their minds again when Mulroney's Conservatives launched a television ad campaign that effectively branded Turner a liar.

the basis of this reasoning, the Liberals agreed to one debate in each official language before the end of July.

Since the Conservatives had to make inroads in Quebec to have any hope of forming a majority government, they saw the French debate on Tuesday, July 24, as particularly important. Tory strategists wanted to get their candidate on camera with Turner so the French Canadian audience would recognize that Mulroney was one of them. There were no decisive exchanges, but Broadbent spoke French like the late learner he was, and Turner's French proved less nuanced and colloquial than Mulroney's. As for content, Mulroney displayed a fine sense of how to play issues in tune with Québécois sensibilities.[19] His stock in Quebec was on the rise.

The Liberals' organizational chaos afflicted Turner's preparation for the debates. Too many advisers from different factions produced a cacophony of contradictory advice. Before the English debate on July 25, Bill Lee told Turner to play it safe because he had more to lose than Mulroney, but Keith Davey told him that, if he got the chance, he should go for a knock out blow. Turner went into the debate uncertain about which approach to take. He held his own initially on questions regarding patronage, the Senate, bum patting, the economy, the deficit, and foreign policy. In the closing minutes, he sensed that proceedings had been deadly dull. Recalling Davey's advice, he decided to chastise Mulroney for his comments on patronage. "He [Mulroney] told his party last year that every available job would be made available to every living, breathing Conservative," Turner declared. "I would say, Mr. Mulroney that on the basis of what you've talked about – getting your nose in the public trough – that you wouldn't offer Canadians any newness in the style of government. The style that you have been preaching to your own party reminds me of the old Union Nationale, it reminds me of patronage at its best. Frankly, on the basis of your performance, I can't see freshness coming out of your choice."

Mulroney immediately recognized that he could assume the moral high ground. He turned the tables, declaring that Turner was complicit in an indecent orgy of Liberal patronage. He challenged him to produce his letter of agreement with Trudeau to prove that he had had no alternative but to make appointments on Trudeau's behalf.

Turner was taken aback. Mulroney's sanctimonious tut-tutting somehow struck a chord in his Catholic conscience. He hadn't felt comfortable with the whole patronage affair. Then he had mistakenly claimed to have added only one name to Trudeau's list. He seemed transfixed for a moment, like a deer in the headlights. "I told you and the Canadian people, Mr. Mulroney, that I had no option," he replied. His response was honest but feeble, and Mulroney, smelling blood, closed in for the kill. Stabbing his finger at Turner like a stern schoolmaster, he continued:

> You had an option, sir. You could have said I'm not going to do it. This is wrong for Canada, and I'm not going to ask Canadians to pay the price. You had an option, sir, to say no, and you chose to say yes to the old attitudes and the old stories of the Liberal party. That, sir, if I may say respectfully, that is not good enough for Canadians.

Turner knew he had blundered and struggled to recover. "I had no option. I was able ..." he stammered. Mulroney cut him off: "That is an avowal of failure. That is a confession of non-leadership, and this country needs leadership. You had an option, sir. You could have done better." By this point Turner had collected himself sufficiently to mount a defence:

> Mr. Trudeau had every right to make those appointments before he resigned. In order that he not do so, yes, I had to make a commitment to him, otherwise I was advised that, with serious consequence to the Canadian people, I could not have been granted the opportunity of forming a government.[20]

This exchange was the liveliest part of the debate, and Turner had gotten the worst of it. Michael Hunter had never seen him as depressed as he was during the ride home. "I fucked up," he said. Hunter assured him that he hadn't, but Turner did not believe him. "I fucked up," he kept repeating.[21] Would it make any difference? They crossed their fingers and waited for the reviews.

Initially, the press commentary was inconclusive. Some papers called it a draw, and others simply noted that Turner had been bested in the patronage exchange. The Liberals could find comfort in the publication of the latest Gallup poll, taken just before the election call, which showed them with a nine-point lead on the Conservatives. The new numbers included only one unsettling statistic: the percentage of undecided voters was up by ten points, to 38 per cent, from 28 per cent in the previous poll conducted after the convention in June.

Immediately after the debates, Turner took a two-day swing through the Maritimes, which was intended to serve as the shakedown cruise for his leader's tour, now finally readying for launch. Over the weekend he campaigned in Toronto and Hamilton. The gaffes continued, mainly because of errors in his briefing notes. The press recalled that, during the debate, he had claimed that the population of Manitoba was in decline, whereas, for the previous two years, it had been increasing. Turner admitted his mistake and apologized. Then, on the Saturday, speaking to Liberal candidates in Toronto, he accused Mulroney of planning to fire 600,000 civil servants, when the entire civil service numbered only 500,000 employees. Once again he apologized. These errors, coming so close together, reinforced the journalists' theme of Liberal incompetence. They also spooked Turner, confirming his suspicions that he could not trust the information he was getting from his campaign organization.

"I must tell you quite frankly that I am very uneasy about the way the campaign is developing," Marc Lalonde wrote to Turner on July 27. "This concern is shared by a good number of our mutual friends." Lalonde was having problems in Quebec, but they paled in comparison to what he heard about the campaign in Ontario. "Bill Lee tells me that you wish to remain the 'Chief Executive Officer' of the campaign," he said. "With all that you have to do, it seems to me neither realistic nor wise to think that you can stay on top of all aspects of the campaign."[22] Lack of direction and policies left the Liberals on the defensive and at the mercy of the Conservatives, Lalonde argued. They must take the offensive without delay.

Turner wasn't unduly alarmed, because he had yet to launch his leader's tour and start campaigning in earnest. More than five weeks remained until the election. Liberal campaign headquarters was finally up and running, equipped with a computer system. The organizers had leased a DC-9, which Turner had first used on his Maritimes swing. Campaign literature, buttons, posters, and brochures were starting to move out the door.

Needing another campaign co-chair for Ontario, Turner decided to recruit Keith Davey. He knew his stuff, and the urgency of plugging a gaping organizational hole outweighed the embarrassment of reneging on the "no rainmakers" pledge he had made during his leadership campaign. Davey said he would come aboard on condition that he got the title of national co-chair. Turner agreed, rationalizing that the title would be a symbolic one. He also let Davey retain control of Red Leaf Communications, the advertising group that was mobilized at election time to make political commercials for the Liberals in English Canada. According to the campaign organization chart, Red Leaf was supposed to report to the campaign's director of communications, who reported to Lee, but in the confusion surrounding the campaign start-up, this arrangement had been overlooked. Subsequently, Lee had ended up at loggerheads with Jerry Grafstein, one of the key players in Red Leaf, over the way its expenses were documented – or, more precisely, not documented. Lee also discovered that, in defiance of his earlier instructions, Red Leaf had produced some negative attack ads. Here again, conflict between Turner's new guard and the Trudeau old guard was undermining the Liberal campaign.

The leader's tour finally began on Monday, July 30. Turner flew out west, stopping in The Pas, Manitoba, en route to a three-day swing through British Columbia. He was in Vancouver for his July 31 nomination meeting in Vancouver Quadra, and later the same day visited Prince Rupert. While on the ferry between the airport and Prince Rupert, Turner visited the pilot house. He looked down to see an excited gaggle of reporters, backed by television crews, blocking his exit and demanding that he answer their questions about why "the rainmaker" was back in charge of the Liberal campaign. Eager for their gaffe of the day, they doubted his assurances that Davey's responsibilities were for Ontario only. On Thursday, Turner blitzed Prince Albert, Saskatchewan, then flew on to Toronto to make his first major policy announcement of the campaign – a $2 billion a year job-training program for young Canadians. On Friday he was in Orillia, an hour north of Toronto, for a large regional rally, and ended the day in Ottawa so he could attend Lloyd Axworthy's wedding.

This was his first full week of campaigning, and problems still needed to be ironed out. Turner had to run both the government and the campaign, even when he was on the road. He had his campaign organization, the PMO, Cabinet, and his tour staff reporting directly to him, with no effective communications or coordinating mechanisms among them other than himself. His wife, an intelligent woman with strong views, was travelling with him, and she also had his ear. Meanwhile, relations between the PMO and the campaign team continued to deteriorate. Turner had two competing briefing books, one from each.[23] According to the *Toronto Star*, "There were signs of a hastily patched together tour ... Turner is travelling in a smaller plane, a DC-9, with half the support staff, fewer flacks, no roadies to set up portable backdrops and lecterns ... He works against a locally provided backdrop of plywood and posters with a sometimes poor sound system."[24] Nevertheless, Turner was regaining his old form as a stump speaker. He lost some of his nervous tics, honed his delivery of his standard campaign speech, and revived his ability to rouse crowds. One reporter even ventured the term "Chickmania" to describe a Turner appearance.[25]

But it was too late. A CTV poll released on August 3 reported that the Conservatives were in front of the Liberals with 45 per cent of decided voters. Liberal support had plummeted to 36 per cent, with the New Democrats at 17 per cent. The undecideds were still high, at 33 per cent, but they were trending away from the Liberals. A month earlier, a Liberal majority had seemed possible; now a Conservative majority looked like a sure thing.

What had happened? To begin with, the Liberals had failed to appreciate the softness of their lead in the June polls. Turner had initially benefited from the publicity generated by the Liberal leadership race and the sense of renewal that accompanied the swearing in of a new government, but the effect quickly wore off, and voters' intentions began to shift even before the election call, when his "old look" Cabinet was revealed. Immediately following the call, patronage dominated the news. Both developments undermined Turner's claim to be a decisive leader and agent of change. Polls conducted during the first week of the campaign showed that the Liberals' lead had evaporated, leaving them effectively tied with the Conservatives. There followed a week of incessant media coverage of bum patting, which confirmed voters' fears that Turner was indeed "yesterday's man."[26] Then coverage moved on to the dramatic scene in the English debate during which Mulroney wagged his finger at Turner, and Turner failed to muster an adequate response. The latest poll had been conducted just after the debate.

Facing electoral catastrophe, the Liberals panicked and began to self-destruct. While Turner was on his western swing, Herb Gray chaired the

Wednesday Cabinet meeting. Cabinet, dominated by holdovers from the Trudeau era, instinctively blamed Bill Lee for the mess and sought solace in the methods of the past. That meant replacing Lee with Keith Davey as national campaign director. On Thursday Marc Lalonde briefed John de B. Payne, who then agreed to meet Cabinet later that day. Payne tried to arrange a compromise that would see a Cabinet nominee put in place alongside Lee with a subordinate title, but the ministers wanted Lee's head. Payne finally concluded that if Lee lacked the confidence of Cabinet, he could no longer be effective as campaign director, and he resolved to raise the issue with Turner when he was back in Ottawa that weekend.

Lee too was concerned about the reports he was receiving.[27] He penned a memo outlining what had gone wrong and what must be done to turn things around. Among other things, Turner needed a gatekeeper: "Far too many people have direct access to you to give you advice, views, and comments on strategy, policy, campaign tactics, whatever," he wrote. He recommended that Mike Hunter be given the role on tour and that he himself would play it in Ottawa. Attaching the latest grim polling data, he concluded, "If we continue to operate in this manner, you will become the Prime Minister with the shortest reign in Canada's history."[28]

At Lloyd Axworthy's wedding in Ottawa that Friday night, Izzy Asper asked Turner if he had read Lee's memo. Turner said he had not. Asper told him that Lee was being too kind: the situation was actually far worse. Turner read the memo and jotted down his own summary of its contents on a back page: "1) no communication; 2) no strategy; 3) lost confidence of cabinet and close advisors and the troops ... candidates."[29] He was shocked to realize how quickly the situation had deteriorated. His election campaign was over before it had properly begun.

When Turner learned about Cabinet's resolve to dump Bill Lee, he initially refused. Lee was a friend who had made great sacrifices on his behalf, he protested. Finally, facing a united front, he relented, called Keith Davey, and arranged a meeting with Lee the next day at Harrington Lake. Lee found the prime minister distressed at the latest polls. "I've screwed it up," he lamented. Lee, he said, had enemies in Cabinet. Then he stated baldly that he could not accept the demands Lee had laid out in his memo. They agreed to part ways. Turner had been advised that, to project an image of decisiveness, he should fire Lee, not just let him resign, but the two gave different versions of that day's events, providing the press with further evidence of Liberal confusion.[30] That was small potatoes, however, compared to the news that the Liberals were changing their national campaign director in midstream. Turner was, in effect, announcing to the country that his campaign was a shambles.

Polls were the story of the second half of the campaign. News organizations commissioned more than a dozen national polls that summer. Ceaseless reporting on the parties' relative standing in public opinion produced "horse-race" style coverage in which the Tories were shown coming from behind and surging into the lead. Uncommitted voters began to follow the trend reported in the polls, creating a bandwagon effect that made polling results a self-fulfilling prophecy.[31] It was difficult to turn things around with policy announcements or promises because they got far less attention.

In Quebec, Liberal support had begun to slide in late July. The Conservatives had organized effectively across the province, moving into areas where they had previously had no grassroots presence. They were aided by political operatives from both the provincial Liberals and the Parti Québécois, rivals united only in their antipathy to the federal Liberals. Allan Gregg, head of the Tories' polling firm Decima Research, had formerly thought that polls did not influence voting patterns, but the 1984 campaign changed his mind. "They [Quebeckers] changed their vote to correspond with what they thought was going to be a winning situation," he concluded. "It was strategic voting."[32]

By early August the Liberals' polls indicated that they had fallen behind the NDP in popular support. In Ontario many Liberal candidates were in danger of losing their deposits. Lalonde reported that the Liberals might be lucky to win fifteen seats in the whole of Quebec, some sixty less than he had promised the previous month. With four weeks left in the campaign, Richard Gwyn concluded that "all that remains to be determined ... is whether Mulroney will win by a minority or by a majority, as is probable, or by a sweep ... as is entirely possible if Quebeckers realize what is happening across the rest of the country and abandon the sinking Liberal ship."[33]

Turner shared the cramped cabin of the Liberals' twin-engine DC-9 with his campaign retinue and the media. Now dubbed the "DerriAir" by the press, it was a relatively small jet with no private compartment for the leader's entourage. The journalists collectively indulged in a gleeful egalitarian *schadenfreude* at the spectacle of the great man being cut down to size. On August 9 the press reported that a nervous waiter in a Trois-Rivières restaurant had spilled coffee on Turner and that he had had to wait in the men's washroom while his wife scrubbed his pants in the ladies' washroom down the hall. Back on the plane, one wit devised new lyrics to John Lennon's "Give Peace a Chance," and soon a lusty chorus was singing,

> All we are saying
> Is give Chick a chance
> All we are saying
> Is give Chick his pants.[34]

Now that Turner was vulnerable, journalists regarded him as fair game for their lampoons. "His speeches – the bark of his throat-clearing, the tongue flicking out like a hungry adder – were parodied everywhere," Val Sears recalled.[35] On August 25 the *Globe and Mail* published a front-page photo of Turner composed to make two forks that were part of an illustration behind him appear to protrude from his head like horns.

As the Liberals' new national campaign director, Keith Davey applied his old Trudeau-era credo that Liberals won elections by positioning themselves centre-left and appealing to the young, the poor, women, and minorities. From his perspective, Turner's critical error had been to allow Mulroney to outflank them on this ground. The Liberal campaign now veered off in a new direction, forsaking any notion that the electorate wanted change, let alone consistency.[36] Turner also tried to don Trudeau's international statesman mantle by pledging to continue his predecessor's peace initiative. But even on this issue, the Liberals found a way to self-destruct. After a Gallup poll reported that 85 per cent of Canadians favoured a nuclear freeze, Iona Campagnolo and other prominent Liberals tried to take this promise a step further by calling for a ban on cruise missile testing. Turner was more circumspect. The party's last policy convention had endorsed cruise testing by a two-to-one margin, and he was loath to reverse party-approved policy on the fly. "I cannot play politics with peace," he said. "We cannot, in effect, simply go it alone and walk away from our

NATO allies."[37] The confusion was compounded when Geills Turner, now campaigning on her own, declared her support for a freeze.

A special televised debate on women's issues was held on August 15. Turner was poised and knowledgeable, and in the closing moments, launched an attack that made Mulroney look like a hypocrite. His form as a campaigner continued to improve on the hustings. He revived his leadership campaign line that Mulroney was a "let's pretend Liberal," warned that he had a hidden agenda to cut social programs, and accused him of hiding the true cost of his campaign promises. The Liberals' policy machinery had at last started to produce, and a hodgepodge of initiatives was issued in quick succession: grants for young entrepreneurs, a new agency to co-ordinate support programs for small entrepreneurs, twice the write-off of capital losses for businesses, a tax credit for living in the North, a minimum tax on the wealthy, and a variety of measures for women. Turner dutifully announced each one, but no one was paying attention. In light of the polls, every move the Liberals made was now seen as an act of desperation.

Nevertheless, Turner soldiered on. He was determined to be a graceful loser. He had been honest with Canadians, he said, and he refused to lay the blame elsewhere. There was, however, one indignity he was not prepared to accept. Late in the campaign, a desperate Marc Lalonde tried to arrange for Pierre Trudeau to appear with Turner on the same platform. For Turner, who could trace so many of his problems directly back to his predecessor, the thought that he should now be trotted out as his saviour was simply too much. He vetoed the idea.

On the evening of September 4, Turner watched the election results in a Vancouver hotel room with his family. Early on, in the Atlantic provinces, the Liberals held their own. But as the results came in from central Canada, things quickly went downhill. The Liberals lost 58 of their 74 seats in Quebec and 38 of their 52 in Ontario. They made no gains in the West. Altogether, the Conservatives won a grand total of 211 of the 282 seats in the House of Commons, one of the largest parliamentary majorities in Canadian history.[38] The NDP took 30 seats, whereas the Liberals, with just 28 per cent of the popular vote, ended up with 40, their fewest ever – only three more MPs than had been in Trudeau's last Cabinet.

It remained to be seen whether Turner would win the riding of Vancouver Quadra. If he lost, he probably wouldn't be able to continue as party leader.

The riding had gone Conservative the previous four elections, and for weeks pundits had been issuing dire predictions about his prospects there. They didn't realize that his riding association was well organized and financed and running an effective campaign. Turner himself could make only occasional appearances, but his family had campaigned actively in the riding. In the end, he won with 44 per cent of the vote, a solid 6 per cent more than the incumbent.

When the results became clear, Turner went to the lobby of the Bayshore Inn and faced the press. He congratulated Mulroney and the Conservatives, and to console Liberal supporters, invoked the example of Lester Pearson, who, after he was defeated by Diefenbaker's record majority in 1958, had hung in and made a comeback. He then went to his riding campaign headquarters and thanked the people of Vancouver Quadra for "having resisted the national trend."[39]

The pundits immediately began dissecting the Liberal disaster. They favoured single all-encompassing explanations. Many, taking a cue from Davey, said Turner had erred by moving the Liberals to the right, and Mulroney had taken advantage by moving to the centre, stealing traditional Liberal territory in the middle of the political spectrum. This analysis would later be refuted by a scholarly evaluation that found that Canadians had "low ideological commitment" at the time and had responded to "short-term forces." As another commentator noted, the campaign had been dominated by television, and the "media generally were obsessed with personality items and public opinion polls to the detriment of the full airing of the policies at issue."[40]

Another school of thought saw the 1984 election as unwinnable for the Liberals under any circumstances. According to this argument, a decade and a half of Trudeau had turned the electorate against them. Turner suffered the punishment intended for his predecessor. In the forty years during which polling had been conducted, elections tended to confirm trends established in the polls over the previous few months, and in the ten months before the 1984 election call, the Liberals had been, on average, ten points behind the Conservatives. The federal Liberals, who had recently presided over the worst economic times since the Depression, were ripe for a fall. The only problem with this line of argument was that Turner had led the polls after he became prime minister. The support was, admittedly, soft and contingent on his performance, but with luck and good management, it might have been solidified. Neither quality was present, however, and in their absence support quickly dissolved.[41]

Others saw Turner as a victim of media mugging. On CBC-TV's *The Journal* on September 6, Izzy Asper suggested that "the journalists of Canada have got to do a little soul searching" about their role in Turner's defeat. Douglas Creighton, the publisher of the *Toronto Sun,* a Conservative paper, wrote that Turner was the victim of "cheap-shot journalism."[42] The media had exhibited a pack mentality, "hyena journalism," ganging up on Turner when he was down.[43] As Bob Hepburn, Ottawa bureau chief for the *Toronto Star,* put it, "We always went after him as a group. We smelled blood, and we attacked."[44]

Although it is fashionable to blame the media for a variety of modern ills, politicians recognize that contemporary political journalism is a blood sport – and they must be prepared for it. In the election aftermath, the Centre for Investigative Journalism organized conferences in Ottawa and Montreal on the question "Who Shot J.T.?" a play on the "Who Shot J.R.?" episode of the hit soap opera *Dallas.* The consensus was that Turner shot himself with his ineptness as a campaigner.

Each of these explanations for the Liberal debacle contain some truth, but none serve as a stand-alone explanation or even a root cause. Turner's campaign problems could all be traced back to the Liberals' lack of election readiness. Poor organization had cascading effects. It meant that Turner didn't have a platform to set the agenda for the campaign. In the absence of defining issues or policies, the leader's image became even more important. Yet the disorganized Liberals were ill-prepared to manage his image.

Here some of the blame must be laid on Turner. The organizational problems originated with his refusal to be seen as grasping for power during his time away from politics. He would come back if he were called, he said, and refused to organize a leadership bid until Trudeau announced his resignation. Then a misplaced sense of responsibility prompted him to run his own campaign. Less principled stoicism and more ruthless cunning might have made a difference. He was, for example, far too deferential to Trudeau and his followers on both patronage and his Cabinet appointments. Here some refusals would have been justified, politically expedient, and image enhancing.

Yet not all the organizational problems were Turner's fault. He was the victim of circumstances and an unhelpful predecessor. He was spurred to call a summer election by fears of a souring economy that turned out to be unjustified.[45] The decision was made under pressure in chaotic conditions because Trudeau had clung too long to the leadership, denying his successor both the time required to put his own stamp on the party and the room to manoeuvre in the lead-up to a looming election. Rather than remaining neutral during the leadership race, Trudeau had attacked Turner publicly. He left Turner a gutted party with no election machinery, saddled him with a patronage scandal, and then made extortionate threats about releasing his patronage letter.

Certainly, Turner was guilty of being human and making mistakes, most notably with respect to bum patting and his "no option" debate defence. Yet these missteps might have been incidental under different circumstances. Their magnification, together with the enormity of the Liberals' loss, points to the critical role that the politics of image played in the 1984 election. The "gaffes" motif of media coverage was devastating because it undermined those crucial perceptions of experience and competence that were Turner's main competitive advantage over Mulroney at the start of the campaign. This media focus on public errors and embarrassments reflected the disarray journalists knew existed behind the scenes in the Liberal camp. It also symbolized their general disappointment with the much-ballyhooed Turner candidacy. The man who emerged from retirement was not the Turner the media had imagined, particularly on television. "John Turner's got Paul Newman looks in still photos, but on camera not at all," explained a Toronto ad executive. "Small mannerisms stick out and people distrust him. He's been done in by television."[46] The journalists who had built up the Turner myth were among those most disappointed by this discovery. One of the ironies of the process was that, in cynically exploding the myth, they failed to recognize that they were attacking their own handiwork.

Though weary of the Liberals, Canadians were prepared to like Turner, as indicated by the polls in June. Wanting to believe in the myth, they were willing to overlook his initial rustiness and give him a chance to prove himself. When he failed to perform as expected, they quickly gave up on him. The Liberals' long-standing electoral hegemony was flattened in an eye-opening display of the fragility of political power in a democracy. Canadians ended up with a prime minister they didn't really like or trust because, compared with his rival, he seemed a less embarrassing representative of the nation.

18

THE ROAD BACK

The Liberals' defeat had been so decisive that some thought it spelled the end of the party on the national scene. Everyone cited the example of the British Liberal Party, which had dwindled into insignificance as national politics polarized between parties on the left and the right earlier in the century. *Toronto Globe and Mail* columnist Jeffrey Simpson proclaimed that the fate of the Liberals would be the biggest political story of 1985.[1] Would John Turner preside over the death of a political institution older than the country itself? Would the natural governing party ever govern again?

Turner's future as party leader was another subject of lively speculation. Those who thought him an opportunist predicted that he would soon be scurrying back to his lucrative law practice. This kind of comment got Turner's back up. He did not like losing, but he would not turn tail and run, even if he had suffered a spectacular defeat. "The last four weeks of the election were the toughest of my life," he wrote to his sister. "I think I proved something to myself in having to reach deeply into my personal strength and faith. Now I am committed to the task of rebuilding the Party."[2]

Turner's resolve was stiffened by friends and partisans who wrote to express sympathy and support. Walter Gordon fingered Trudeau as the "one who is responsible for our eclipse."[3] L.C. Audette, an Ottawa acquaintance, reached a similar conclusion:

The election results were foreseeable ... You were the victim of the incredible indignity of Trudeau's last moments, of the media, of polls, of a few stumbles of your own and, above all, of the sheer bad luck of being in the wrong place at the wrong time ... The last few years of Trudeau's prime-ministership have left you and the Liberal party with a burden which will probably take as much as two elections to shake: the alienation of the West ... the indignities such as "fuddle-duddle," as "mangez de la merde," as the raised finger from an expensive private railway car and all such like, the dilettantish and short-lived enthusiasms, the unwise Senate appointments ... above all, the very real divorce from contact with all strata of the Canadian people.[4]

"No thinking Liberal blames you," Senator Richard Stanbury assured Turner, begging the question of just how many party members that represented.[5]

Others thought Turner should make way for a new leader. They saw him as damaged goods that had to be jettisoned if the party were to have any hope of surviving, let alone winning the next election. So argued the Chrétien faction, which contended simply that their man could win and Turner could not. Had Turner lost his riding it would have been difficult to disagree. But he had just won a seat in the House, his mandate as Liberal leader was less than six months old, and he had duties as leader of Her Majesty's Loyal Opposition. He would stay.

Later that fall Turner would tell *Maclean's* that his defeat had been partly attributable to inheriting a party "without policy, without preparation, without recruitment." "The party was really run out of the Prime Minister's Office for the past number of years," he explained, "and ... was only held together by a loyalty to Trudeau."[6] Pierre Trudeau responded by summoning a friendly CTV reporter and telling him that the party had been in fine shape when he left and that, had he still been leader, the Liberals would have won the election. This bit of bravado was an ominous sign that Trudeau had not let go. Once again, it was Turner who smoothed things over, telling a television interviewer that he might have been "a little brutal and negative" in his evaluation.[7]

Turner resigned as prime minister just before the new government was sworn in at Rideau Hall on September 17, officially ending his term as prime minister at seventy-nine days – the shortest in Canadian history aside from that of Sir Charles Tupper in 1896. Mulroney distributed ministerial posts liberally in an effort to reward as many members of his bloated caucus as possible, boosting the size of Cabinet to forty ministers. His first few days in office focused on symbolic gestures. He flew to Washington to meet with President Ronald Reagan. He also rescinded the patronage appointments of Mackasey, Whelan, and others, and to appear non-partisan, appointed former Ontario NDP leader Stephen Lewis as Canadian ambassador to the United Nations.

Turner announced his shadow cabinet at a press conference on October 11, matching his forty-member caucus one for one with the forty-member Mulroney Cabinet. Chrétien would handle external affairs; Donald Johnston, finance; Lloyd Axworthy, regional industrial expansion; Warren Allmand, employment; Robert Kaplan, justice; and Raymond Garneau, Treasury Board. Herb Gray was made House leader, and Allan MacEachen became the Liberal leader in the Senate.[8] Turner vowed to hold the Conservatives to their election promises, especially job creation, and warned Mulroney not to get too cozy with the Americans. He was putting on a brave front. The Liberals would be stretched thin, given their numbers, especially since only a dozen or so of their MPs were accomplished performers in the House or in the media spotlight.

When the Speech from the Throne was read on November 5, the 211 Conservative MPs occupied three-quarters of the desks in the House, up one side and along both ends of the other, crowding the opposition. The government offered something for everyone, with a contradictory mélange of proposals for enhancing social programs and reducing the deficit. On the national unity front, it promised "reconciliation," which meant doing something to get Quebec's signature on the 1982 constitution. Turner led off the debate on the Speech from the Throne two days later by promising "a strong and vigilant opposition."[9] Yet Liberal morale was low. The NDP was styling itself as the "real opposition," and the Conservatives were playing along, both parties liking their chances in a political landscape devoid of Liberals.

A Liberal caucus retreat to plan strategy was booked for January at Montebello. Before it convened, Angus Reid reported Turner's approval level in the single digits. When caucus chair Doug Frith told Turner in person, he recalled that his leader was visibly staggered, like a cow stunned in a slaughterhouse. Frith couldn't bear the thought of him going home depressed to an empty house (his wife was in Toronto), so that night he picked up a bottle of Scotch and took a taxi to Stornoway, where he and Turner talked far into the night.[10] To make things worse, Frith had assumed that the poll would be kept confidential, but Reid announced the numbers at the Montebello retreat, then chatted openly about them with the media. That episode led to an acrimonious parting of the ways between the Liberals and their new pollster.

The Liberal caucus that gathered at Montebello may have been small, but it was big enough to encompass all the factions that beset the party as a whole. Turner went back a long way with some of its members. Herb Gray had come into Parliament with him in 1962, and Lloyd Axworthy, a former executive assistant, had put aside his own leadership aspirations to support him. Donald Johnston, whom Turner had hired at Stikeman & Elliott in the 1950s, was a natural ally because they shared a concern for fiscal restraint. Doug Frith, a charming Ontario MP, was a like-minded pragmatist. Raymond Garneau, Turner's most prominent recruit from Quebec, shared their fiscal views, although he had come to Ottawa primarily to work for a constitutional accommodation for Quebec. Garneau felt that Trudeau had promised Quebec a new deal during the 1980 referendum campaign, and the Liberal Party had yet to deliver. Most of the caucus was, however, left leaning, including Gray and Axworthy, who now had second thoughts about having backed Turner. Many suspected that Turner had a hidden right-wing agenda; he thought them obtuse about fundamental economic realities.

Many other fault lines ran through the caucus, particularly its Quebec wing. The senators, who outnumbered the MPs two to one, were largely Trudeau appointees inclined to defend his legacy, including his constitutional settlement. That put them at loggerheads with Garneau. Garneau didn't get along with André Ouellet. Jean Lapierre, the young Quebec MP Turner had appointed to his Cabinet, shared Garneau's constitutional views, but they came from different generations and political circles and had yet to get comfortable with each other. More significantly, fifteen of the forty Liberal MPs were diehard Chrétien supporters. Most were from Quebec, but they included anglophones such as David Dingwall, Ron Irwin, Sergio Marchi, and Charles Caccia.

Many caucus members blamed Turner for the election debacle, and he, in turn, felt guilty about it, ensuring that tension and alienation bedevilled their relations from the start. This wasn't what any of them had signed up for. A disproportionate number of the elected caucus members had escaped the recent slaughter because they were good constituency MPs rather than prominent figures in national affairs. They had been elected despite, not because of the leader, and they owed him nothing. Yet another split differentiated veterans, who were reluctant to criticize the government for policies they had followed when they were in power, and rookies who had no such scruples. The latter included a handful of newly elected English Canadian MPs – John Nunziata, Sheila Copps, Don Boudria, and Brian Tobin – who were eager to make their mark in national politics. Things were complicated further by the presence of "loose fish" such as Warren Allmand and Len Hopkins, who were prone to choosing principled independence over team play.

The main topic at Montebello was Liberal strategy in opposition. Some wanted to attack Mulroney immediately and generate headlines. Others demanded that the Liberals work up a set of policy positions to distinguish them from the government. Turner resisted. He argued that, as a duly elected prime minister, Mulroney had to be given a chance to govern. In time he would make mistakes, and the Liberals could go on the offensive. As for putting forward a platform, any policies rolled out by the Liberals would be commitments they might find themselves unable to fulfill when in power. In the interim they could either be stolen by the government or give the Tories a target to shoot at, distracting attention from the government's policies – which, for the moment, were the ones that mattered. Turner thought his MPs' determination to frame policy showed how accustomed they were to being in power. The opposition's role was different: it was supposed to keep the government honest by exposing its actions to public scrutiny.[11] If they acted instead as though they should still be in power, they might well be accused of arrogance – the very mistake Pearson had made in the wake of Diefenbaker's victory in 1957.

The approach Turner advocated would also help maintain party unity. The caucus members who wanted to stake out policy positions immediately tended to be left wingers anxious to distinguish themselves ideologically from the Conservatives. Turner was sympathetic to their goals, but most involved new spending, and he had not forgotten the country's fiscal predicament. At any rate, there was no point in aggravating caucus factionalism by bringing divisive issues to a head when the Liberals were in no position to do anything about them. Instead, Turner told his MPs it was time to get over their election defeat and start earning their keep as the official opposition. They could discuss issues freely and vigorously in caucus and in party circles, but once they established a consensus, they would have to stand united behind it in public.

Since the election, Turner had been planning how to lead the Liberals back to power. As his concession speech had suggested, he equated his situation with that of Pearson following Diefenbaker's massive majority in 1958 – having paid the price for the arrogance of the preceding Liberal regime, he faced an arduous passage to prove his mettle and earn the right to reclaim power. The first stage was to rebuild the party. He would visit constituencies across the country and listen to the grassroots, honouring the pledge for openness and accountability he had made during his leadership campaign. Then he would recruit new party workers and candidates to re-energize the rank and file – "progressive, moderate, concerned, compassionate people who share the historic centre-ground of the Liberal party."[12] He would give the grassroots responsibility for developing new policies for the party, breaking the backroom boys' cynical monopoly of policy as merely a form of election tactic. At the same time he would rebuild the national party executive and headquarters, restore relations with the party's provincial wings, and ramp up fundraising.

In year one, his efforts would dovetail nicely with the party's agenda, which included a special conference to be held on November 7-10 in Halifax to consider the report of the President's Committee on Reform. Turner had identified himself with the Young Liberals and other advocates of change in the party ever since they had mounted their reform drive in 1982. His efforts to regenerate the party would solidify this coalition. For the year ahead, then, the main order of business would be party renewal.

Turner calculated that, by the end of 1985, the Mulroney government's honeymoon with the electorate would be winding down. In year two, he would begin to attack the government more aggressively and raise his profile on the national stage. At this point he would also initiate a process to evaluate, refine, and develop consensus on the policies put forward by the grassroots. This exercise would culminate with the party's national policy convention scheduled for November 1986.

In year three, Turner planned to give special attention to reviving the Liberals' fortunes in their former stronghold of Quebec. In the country as a whole, the party would start developing the policies passed at the convention into a platform that would come together during year four, just in time for the next election. By then the party would be rejuvenated coast to coast, with money flowing into its coffers, provincial wings cooperating with the federal party, constituencies organized down to the poll level, and the whole coordinated from an updated national party headquarters. A full slate of impressive new candidates would be nominated and ready to run. At the front of the parade would be John Turner, the leader of a resurgent Liberal machine.[13]

One aspect of this plan that was not openly discussed concerned Turner's own political redemption. The party constitution called for a leadership review vote at the November 1986 policy convention. That was the only way to trigger a leadership convention before the next election. Rebuilding the party from the bottom up fit nicely with Turner's need to confirm his leadership. In doing so, he could make the party his own. Developing support within the broad party membership would also lessen his dependence on his MPs, who had been elected despite of, not because of, his leadership.

Phase one, rebuilding from the grassroots, was a challenge that appealed to Turner's heroic instincts. It involved the kind of "mano a mano" politics he enjoyed and required visiting all the different parts of the country he loved. He began immediately after the Montebello caucus, travelling to Winnipeg, Calgary, and Edmonton to give speeches, attend fundraisers, and appear at constituency meetings before returning to Ottawa for the re-opening of Parliament on January 21, 1985. For the next two years he would spend roughly half his time criss-crossing the country to revitalize the Liberal rank and file. This involved, as he put it, "a lot of travel, a lot of small towns, a lot of chicken dinners, a lot of therapy, a lot of morale-boosting, a lot of intellectual leadership, a lot of emotional leadership."[14] In his early forays he was something of a travelling one-man truth and reconciliation commission dedicated to hearing grievances, frustrations, and humiliations that lingered from the election. He met with defeated candidates to sympathize and consider their advice, and he encouraged no-holds-barred debate. When he felt that people had got the recent past off their chests, he nudged them toward the future.

This kind of party building involved different means and a different conception of party than that which had prevailed in the previous Liberal regime. Being in opposition meant having limited resources, a circumstance that was completely foreign to the Ottawa cadre of party operatives from the Trudeau years, who'd known only the boundless bounty of being in power. The difference between government and opposition still hadn't sunk in for most of them. They were prepared to get less gravy but still expected the gravy train to run on time. Many would be left waiting expectantly on the platform.[15]

Turner had to build the Office of the Leader of the Opposition from scratch, doing what he could with the little he had available. John Swift took the job of principal secretary. Intelligent, well educated, experienced, personable, and resilient, he was nevertheless unqualified for the task because no career path existed to prepare anyone for a job no Liberal had filled for more than a few months during the previous twenty years. Ottawa had changed greatly since he had worked with Turner in Finance. The only constant throughout those years had been that the Liberals had held power, and now that too had changed.

Turner's office was in the Centre Block, but most of his staff was housed across the street in the Wellington Block, including units for speech writing, parliamentary strategy, correspondence, and Vancouver Quadra constituency matters. There were also staffers for regional political desks. Key positions in the Office of the Leader of the Opposition were distributed to supporters of leadership rivals to continue the party-healing process. Brigitte Fortier, from the Roberts camp, was made press secretary. Stuart Langford, a Chrétienite, became Turner's executive assistant. David Miller, a Turner supporter, and Sharon Schollar, another Roberts supporter, were appointed as regional assistants for the West and Ontario, respectively. On the recommendation of Ouellet, and with the support of Garneau and Lapierre, Michèle Tremblay, a former journalist for the *Journal de Montréal*, was named director of communications. Later it became evident that her appointment had the effect of exacerbating rather than mending divisions because she was known in Quebec as a harsh critic of Chrétien.[16]

Turner trusted Swift and respected his advice, but he had always relied heavily on the counsel of men who were either senior to him or at least his contemporaries. Now he was the only one of his generation in an office staffed primarily by energetic, enthusiastic, but inexperienced twenty-somethings. It was lonely at the top. A few of his contemporaries were in caucus, but only one or two could be considered his supporters. He still looked to friends such as John de B. Payne, John Grace, and Richard Alway for advice, but their input was not captured by any formal process in his office. An uneasy co-existence of unofficial and official channels of influence increased the potential for miscommunication and misunderstanding.[17]

The entrance to the opposition leader's offices in the Centre Block led down a long corridor past a conference room where strategy meetings for the daily Question Period were held while Parliament was in session. Turner had a corner office on the left at the end of the corridor. On one side was his executive assistant's office, on the other, his secretary's, each with ad-joining doors that allowed Turner access to either without stepping into the corridor. The only problem with this set-up was that visitors could walk straight into his office, without his secretary or his executive assistant knowing. When they did, confusion resulted. Unaware of what was com-municated or promised, Turner's staff found it difficult to stay on top of things or follow up. Often the leader's position changed at the last minute because someone got to him and bent his ear.

When the House was in session, Turner was also distracted by his par-liamentary responsibilities. The daily Question Period was the main means by which the opposition attracted attention to its criticisms of the govern-ment. Since Turner had last sat in the House, Question Period had been televised. He regretted the change because, as he put it, it "forces members of parliament to be outrageous to get that 30-second clip."[18] Trumped-up charges and angry rebuttals created bad feelings in the House and sullied the reputation of Parliament. For years Turner had been denouncing the deterioration of conduct in the House. Now his most effective forum as leader of the opposition was an unruly bear-pit session. The House of Commons, an institution he cherished, had been bastardized by television, the medium that was his nemesis. He recognized that he had to learn how to use television to his advantage, yet he couldn't see how anyone could take its distorted presentation of politics seriously.[19]

Every morning that the House was in session, Liberal House leader Herb Gray presided over a tactics committee meeting in the boardroom adjacent to Turner's office. Its regular members were deputy House leader Jacques Guilbault, party whip Jean-Robert Gauthier, Senators Allan MacEachen and Joyce Fairbairn, and the five MPs who headed caucus policy committees: Jean Chrétien (external affairs and national defence), Donald Johnston (finance), Douglas Frith (social policy), Raymond Garneau (government operations), and Lloyd Axworthy (economic and regional development). The committee's job was to review the overnight news and the previous day's business in Parliament to identify targets for Question Period. Turner would attend if something extraordinary were afoot or a dispute needed to be settled. Otherwise, Scott Sheppard, his legislative aide, brought the committee's questions to him for review. Turner chose his issues carefully, trying to retain some dignity for himself, his office, and the institution of Parliament. If the tactics committee gave him questions that attacked individuals, he would reject them. He much preferred participating in debates in the House and delivering well-thought-out speeches on issues, even if they attracted less publicity.

The only problem with this approach was that he had "a lot of young tigers in the House who want me coming out of the gate like crazy every day."[20] Caucus needed its pound of flesh, preferably heated under the television lights. If Turner would not carve it out, the younger, newly elected Liberal MPs – Don Boudria, Sheila Copps, John Nunziata, and Brian Tobin – were happy to do so. They plotted ways in which they could hound the government and soon gained a reputation for their aggressive partisan attacks. *Toronto Star* reporter Bob Hepburn labelled them the Rat Pack, suggesting that they fought with the fierceness, and ethics, of marauding rodents. Delighted with the nickname, they staged a Rat Pack dinner, sold Rat Pack T-shirts, and promoted a rodent bill of rights. Turner was troubled by their tactics, which involved playing to television during Question Period in a way he found distasteful, yet he felt he had to give them their head or risk demoralizing the youngest and most spirited members of caucus.

As a compromise, he tried to set some boundaries on their conduct. "I've got to lecture the Rat Pack a lot," he explained:

I have to say to them ... remember you have ... a responsibility for people's reputations ... That's number one. Number two, you're like a trial lawyer: never ask a question unless you know the answer. And number three, you do your homework. And if you do all three of those things, you'll get backed by me as a leader. If you don't ... we'll have to walk away from you.[21]

The tension between Turner and the Rat Pack reflected a generational split in perceptions of the locus of power. For Turner, it was the House of Commons, an institution legitimized by the constitution, history, and its representation of the country as a whole. The younger generation, in contrast, saw the media as the centre of the action. The fact that the media representation of what went on in Parliament was shallow and distorted was irrelevant because they constituted the central forum of national politics.

Part of the reason the Rat Pack was so effective was that Brian Mulroney proved to be thin-skinned and oversensitive to criticism. By early 1985 his government was offering its critics fat targets. The Shamrock Summit in Quebec City in March 1985, at which the Mulroneys and the Reagans cavorted onstage like a vaudeville act, made many Canadians uncomfortable about the cost to national dignity of their leader's social climbing. The Tories also proved to be scandal-prone. Solicitor General Elmer MacKay admitted to an inappropriate meeting with Richard Hatfield before charges were laid against the New Brunswick premier for marijuana possession. Defence Minister Robert Coates was forced to resign when he created a security risk by leaving his briefcase behind at a strip bar during an official visit to Germany.

More significant was a policy rift between the prime minister and Michael Wilson, the minister of finance. Wilson hoped to attack the deficit by abandoning the principle of universality in social programs, but during the election campaign, Mulroney had famously described social programs as a "sacred trust." In the fall session of Parliament, Turner pressured the government to clarify its position until Mulroney came out in favour of universality. In Wilson's first budget, presented on May 23, 1985, he tried a different approach by de-indexing old age pensions from inflation. Soon senior citizens were up in arms. Chartered buses arrived in Ottawa and disgorged a small army of grey-haired protesters who converged on

Parliament Hill. Turner, who as finance minister had originally indexed the pensions, backed them up with questions in the House and the headline speech at a highly publicized seniors' rally in Toronto on June 25. The optics of little old ladies berating him for chiselling their pensions held little charm for Mulroney, and he vetoed Wilson's proposal. Turner's handling of the issue was a model of effective opposition.[22]

Turner continued to bring a thoughtfulness and personal touch to the practice of politics. He remembered people's birthdays and wrote notes of thanks and congratulations. Sheila Copps regarded him as unique among politicians in his ability to listen and empathize.[23] Journalists were impressed when he quietly attended the funerals of colleagues whose careers had intertwined with his back in the sixties and seventies. On June 20, 1985, he threw a dinner at the Château Laurier to celebrate Jack Pickersgill's eightieth birthday. A hundred guests attended, including Pierre Trudeau and both Paul Martins, father and son. When Paul Martin Sr. asked Turner why he hadn't been given a party when he turned eighty, Turner pointed out that Trudeau had been the leader then.[24]

Meanwhile, Turner continued his missionary work at the party grassroots. "There is a constant tug-of-war," he noted, "between the need to be in Ottawa all the time for Question Period because of the leadership cult the media has created and the national requirement out in the country."[25] When the House was in session, he dealt with this conflict by travelling on weekends. After meeting with local officials and party members, he would often give a speech or appear on a hot-line radio show. He wanted to renew the party by attracting a new generation into its ranks, and young people were responding.

Journalists who followed Turner into the hinterland thought he performed better there than in the national media spotlight. "The Liberal leader seems more confident," wrote one. "His speaking style is sharper and more effective than it is in Ottawa, and Turner clearly enjoys meeting people on their home ground." Moreover, as a British Columbia party worker put it after getting a chance to meet Turner for the first time, "He looks younger, and his eyes don't bug out like they do on TV."[26] A local Liberal who had supported another candidate for the leadership agreed. "Liberals are beginning to change their image of Turner," he said. "He may not be the kind of slick, sharp guy you expect to see in the 1980s. But he's coming across as someone with an honesty and integrity about Parliament and government. And people are beginning to understand he's ready to share the agenda."[27]

Reports such as these showed journalists going through the contortions required to reverse their bias against Turner. They had pulled him down and trampled his reputation during the election, but now their main target was the new government. To that end, they needed to remake Turner into a viable alternative to Mulroney. The media's cycling of Turner's reputation was back on the upswing, and numerous stories would appear about the "new" John Turner in the months to come.

Still, Turner had to become a better television performer if he were to salvage his public image. He retained the services of media coach Gabor Apor, known in the business as "Mr. Dress Up." Apor was the image-maker who had taken a nondescript Ontario Liberal MPP who wore baggy suits and big glasses, put him in power suits with a red tie, got him contact lenses, and created Premier David Peterson. He picked up where Hank Karpus had left off the previous year, working to eliminate Turner's cue cards, throat clearing, and unsettling intensity. Changing habits while constantly in the camera's eye was challenging, but Turner made progress. He "is returning to the form he displayed before quitting the federal cabinet a decade ago," wrote one reporter. He "has already all but eliminated the hoarse, nervous laugh that punctuated newscasts throughout the campaign. He is more relaxed in front of crowds and he banters with interviewers."[28]

After spending most of July tramping about the country on party business, Turner went on a canoe trip, then spent August at his family's cottage on Lake of the Woods. The Gallup poll that month brought good news: his approval rating was 39 per cent, closing in on Mulroney's 43 per cent, though still short of Broadbent's 56 per cent. Since his comeback plan called for ramping up his attacks on the government in year two, he was well positioned to improve this number in the months ahead.

When Turner returned to Ottawa for the opening of Parliament in September, he had plenty of new opportunities to make headlines at the government's expense. The Tories had recently presided over the first failure of a retail bank in Canada in six decades when the Canadian Commercial Bank collapsed. Their financial stewardship was called into question again when the Northland Bank of Calgary ran into trouble and was placed under government supervision. September also saw the eruption of the "tunagate" scandal, which led to the resignation of Fisheries Minister John Fraser for approving the sale of fish that federal inspectors had deemed unfit for human consumption. Turner was reluctant to be too hard on Fraser, an old parliamentary comrade, but he exploited the Conservatives' troubles sufficiently to reap favourable publicity for delivering vigilant and principled opposition in the House.

Things were unfolding as scripted in Turner's recovery plan – until Jean Chrétien unexpectedly upstaged him. That September Chrétien released a memoir, *Straight from the Heart,* which played up his folksy persona. As it climbed the bestseller lists, Chrétien toured the country, autographing copies in bookstores. Hundreds of people lined up to greet him. Turner attended the official book launch on October 15 in the ballroom of Montreal's Grand Hotel. Pierre Trudeau showed up as well, heading immediately for the corner furthest from Turner. When Chrétien mounted the stage, he began, "I am here to launch my campaign," paused, then concluded, "for my book." Turner laughed politely through clenched teeth. Chrétien, Jeffrey Simpson observed, "was a man having an affair with his own popularity."[29]

The Chrétien forces had decided that the leadership review vote, now little more than a year away, was their last best chance to replace Turner with their man as Liberal leader. His supporters stepped up their efforts behind the scenes, feeling out support, calling in IOUs, and seeding the media with anti-Turner stories. The media now cast Chrétien in the heir apparent role they had assigned Turner during the Trudeau years, but he played the part more actively and ambitiously than Turner ever had. In response to questions about the leadership, he was less than subtle. "I can't stop the press from writing about my ambition," he claimed. Protesting faintly that "the job [as leader] is not open," he nevertheless added the democratic caveat that "the party will decide ... The delegates will address that situation."[30]

The emerging storylines about the new John Turner and the Liberals' effectiveness in opposition were suddenly old news. Dissension in the Liberal ranks was again the hot topic, with reports invariably reflecting poorly on Turner's leadership. Two Quebec tabloids conducted a poll that showed voters would prefer Chrétien over Turner as prime minister by a margin of 51 per cent to 24 per cent. Journalists reported negative comments from Chrétien supporters: "Turner's dead," "He's absolutely finished," "It's embarrassing, but it [the leadership challenge] is already happening."[31] Chrétien's ambitions were presenting a serious challenge to Turner's comeback plan.

Yet another potential wrench in the works surfaced that fall. In the midst of the Volcker recession three years earlier, Trudeau had appointed Donald Macdonald to chair the Royal Commission on the Economic Union and Development Prospects for Canada. The commission's report, released on September 5, held that, if Canada were to prosper, it needed to be more flexible in adapting to rapidly changing technologies and international economic conditions. Its major recommendation was that Canada should seek a free-trade agreement with the United States. Free-trade proposals had been bruited in government policy circles since the 1981-82 recession, but the Macdonald Report put the proposal squarely before the public.

Despite being on record as opposing free trade, Mulroney now embraced it. The economic case for free trade rested primarily on fears that US protectionism was on the rise, but for Mulroney its primary attraction was political. He saw it as an initiative big enough to eclipse all his government's failings and set the agenda going into the next election.[32] He decided to begin talks with the United States that fall and appointed Simon Reisman, Turner's former deputy at Finance, as Canada's chief negotiator.

The NDP was against free trade in principle and had no quibbles about opposing Mulroney's new project. Turner's situation was not so straightforward. He supported free trade in principle but doubted that Mulroney could strike a deal with the United States in which the benefits would outweigh the risks. In his mind, Canada was the product of a nation-building process in which transportation, communications, commerce, governance, and culture had been constructed deliberately on an east-west axis to resist continentalism. He had grown up during the golden age of Canadian diplomacy, with its commitment to multilateralism; he had served under Pearson, one of the heroes of the era; and he had worked extensively with the International Monetary Fund, a key multilateral institution of the post-war period. Although he appreciated the benefits Canada derived from sectoral free-trade deals such as the Auto Pact, he thought that, given the power disparity between Canada and the United

States, a multilateral approach to trade liberalization was wiser than a comprehensive bilateral pact.[33]

Turner had been wary of bilateral agreements with the United States ever since his experience with the Columbia River Treaty over twenty years earlier. In 1971 he had explicitly rejected free trade as a solution to Canada's economic problems. "The political consequences would be irreversible and would dilute or even destroy any claim we had to our own sovereignty," he had concluded then.[34] Nothing had changed his opinion since. A bilateral deal would bind Canada into a two-way relationship with a much larger partner, and there would be no disinterested referee, whereas under the existing trade regime, the General Agreement on Tariffs and Trade (GATT), Canada could always challenge American trade law in Geneva. He pointed out that American tariffs against Canadian goods averaged between 4 and 5 per cent, and the next GATT round would probably reduce them to around 3 per cent. At these levels, fluctuations in the value of the Canadian dollar had far more effect on trade than tariff reductions did. If Canadian industries had to adjust to a free-trade environment, steep short-term costs would inevitably follow. He saw little to be gained and much at risk in Mulroney's initiative.

Although Turner's comeback plan required Liberals to avoid policy commitments before the next election, not having a position on free trade was politically impossible. Still, taking an unequivocal stand would divide the party and the caucus along left-right lines and exacerbate his leadership woes. The Liberals had been the party of free trade for Canada's first half century, yet they now had a strong economic nationalist wing rooted in Walter Gordon's 1960s crusade against foreign ownership.[35] Varied regional responses to free trade added further complications. In the West, the Conservatives sold free trade as a dismantling of Eastern economic privileges that dated back to the National Policy. English Canadian nationalist opposition was strongest in Ontario but so was the influence of manufacturers, who wanted unfettered access to the American market. In Atlantic Canada, where industries and jobs were created and protected by federal programs, selling the market logic and Darwinian morality of trade liberalization was harder. Given its high proportion of inefficient industries, Quebec was at first expected to oppose free trade, but, surprisingly, a new generation of entrepreneurs who supported it was able to overturn conventional wisdom.

Prodded by its urgings and fears of US protectionism affecting resource exports, the Quebec government had come to embrace the initiative. Protected by language, French Canadians did not share English Canadian nationalists' fears of continentalism. Indeed, from the French Canadian nationalist perspective, a trade deal with the United States would mitigate the negative economic consequences of separation. Even if separation never came, a deal appealed to nationalist sentiment to the extent that it undermined federal sovereignty.

Turner needed to gauge the depth and variety of party opinion and develop a consensus, so in the short term he stalled for time. The Macdonald Commission had asked Canadians to take a "leap of faith" on free trade. His initial response was cautious: "That's too big a jump ... We must know what we are trying to accomplish."[36] He demanded, before talks commenced, that Canada's negotiating position be outlined in detail and fully debated, both in Parliament and between the federal and provincial governments.

Free trade dominated the political news for the remainder of the fall and was a contentious issue at the Liberal reform convention that November in Halifax. Donald Macdonald attended to explain and defend his commission's position. Donald Johnston and Lloyd Axworthy clashed over the issue at one session, with Johnston in favour and Axworthy opposed. The nominal reform focus of the gathering got lost amid all the fuss over trade, and few reform measures were passed. The press subsequently depicted Johnston and Axworthy as heads of opposing camps in a Liberal Party that had no clear vision of the country's future.

For the media, however, the real business of the convention was neither free trade nor party reform but Turner's leadership. His supporters accordingly treated the conference as a dry run for the leadership review that would follow the year after. They tracked delegates, organized demonstrations of support, and planned dissent management. On the eve of the convention, Turner's office leaked a poll showing that his approval rating had drawn even with Mulroney's.[37] They were relieved when an anxiously awaited Gallup poll, released on the first day of the convention, showed the Liberals with the support of 35 per cent of decided voters – a 7 per cent recovery from election day (the Tories had fallen from 50 to 43 per cent, and the NDP was up to 22 per cent from 18 per cent).

When Chrétien arrived on Friday morning, cameras surrounded him as reporters peppered him with questions about his leadership aspirations. Worried that he had overplayed his hand, opening himself up to accusations of disloyalty that could hurt his leadership chances, he tried to dampen the speculation.

Attention then shifted to Turner. Anticipation ran high as delegates waited for his keynote speech on Saturday evening. He took the stage in rare form. "This conference represents phase one of the comeback of the Liberal Party," he declared. He defined and extolled liberalism, then roused the partisan crowd with attacks on Mulroney. The Tories, he declared, offered "a cosmetic, photo-opportunity style of government" that was "dictated to by the vagaries of public-opinion polls taken every night from Toronto." He attacked them for caving in to pressure from special interests, for lacking compassion for the poor, for toadying to Ronald Reagan. He aired his concerns about free trade, declaring that "the price of being Canadian is a price worth paying."[38] Then he shifted gears and spoke solemnly of his commitment to reform, to rebuilding the party, and, in the process, reinvigorating the nation. Canada's future was at stake, and Liberals had an obligation to fight for it. It was a barn-burner of an address that stirred the crowd with its persuasiveness and passion.

As Turner concluded, his supporters led the applause, but it soon took on a life of its own, swelling in a powerful wave, ebbing, then swelling again. The delegates, relieved and delighted to see that their leader could be so impressive and inspiring, waved red napkins and banged spoons against glasses. Chrétien made his way to the stage with the other Liberal MPs, shook Turner's hand, and sat at his table. The cheering redoubled. Some delegates broke into tears. Others sang "O Canada." Then they swarmed the stage, hoisted Turner onto their shoulders, and carried him out to the floor. They grabbed his wife, Geills, and did the same. When Turner was deposited back at his table, the crowd gathered round and sang "For He's a Jolly Good Fellow." A half-hour elapsed before the applause died down.

"I think the party for a long time needed a hug," a Vancouver delegate explained. "Turner did that by going around to every riding in the country and last night we just hugged him back."[39] Turner pronounced himself "delighted, then astonished, then quite overwhelmed." When asked the next day about Chrétien's challenge to his leadership, he replied, "I think he sensed the mood last night." "It was a resolution, a healing of our wounds, a sign that those who had been hurt had forgiven Turner," said former Kitchener MP Peter Lang.[40]

The spectacle signalled significant support for Turner in a party that was reinvigorated under his leadership. Given time to get his act together, he was exhibiting his fabled political talents. The triumph of the Halifax convention was topped off by the December Gallup poll, which showed that the Liberals had edged ahead of the Tories, 38 per cent to 37 per cent. Under John Turner the Liberals had not died after all, but were back as a formidable national political force.

Turner's comeback plan was back on track, but hazards loomed in the future. The biggest factor working against him, he believed, was the economy. The recovery from the recession was complete, times were good, and the Mulroney Conservatives would take the credit. There were other worrisome omens. Although he was connecting with live audiences in Liberal venues across the land, he had yet to master television. The impetus driving the poll numbers was no doubt more anti-Mulroney than pro-Turner sentiment. The Chrétien challenge was a reminder that, in his ministrations to the grassroots, Turner had yet to deal with Quebec, the traditional bastion of Liberal support he had lost to Mulroney. He believed the key to Quebec would be finding a constitutional settlement that would get the province's signature on the constitution without selling out the national interest. Finally, the appearance of free trade on the political agenda gave pause. To win his way back to power, he would have to grapple with both national unity and continentalism, two classic issues of Canadian politics that were as treacherous as they were intractable.

19

PARTICIPATORY DEMOCRACY

Turner's challenge in the wake of the reform convention was to translate the party's new energy and enthusiasm into electoral success. In 1986 he launched the policy development stage of his comeback plan. Ideas would be generated from the grassroots through discussion papers, seminars, and task forces, then sent on to policy conventions in each province and territory. By the end of June, the process would produce resolutions on party members' top priorities for debate at the November policy and leadership review conference in Ottawa.[1]

While waiting for the process to unfold, Turner endured criticism for having no vision and for not taking stands on issues. Through force of habit, the press, like the old guard in caucus, expected the Liberals to have an elaborate policy platform, as though they were the governing party. While defending "Liberalism in ferment," as he described it, Turner decided that he had to counter this criticism, so he began to play a more active role in the policy process.[2]

Free trade dwarfed all the other issues on the policy agenda. As the Canadian and American negotiating teams began their talks in May 1986, the prospect of a deal suddenly became much more real. Turner did not want to take a stand that would prejudice the party's grassroots policy process or predetermine its response to whatever specific deal the government eventually managed to negotiate. Caucus agreed on a two-part interim position. First, the Liberals supported multilateral trade over a bilateral deal and warned that Canada's other trading partners would feel frozen out if it made a special deal with the United States. They were not anti-American, but it was unwise for Canada to play favourites. Second, they cautioned that a bilateral trade agreement with a partner ten times Canada's size would have serious implications for sovereignty. After Mulroney appeared on national television in June to promote the negotiations, Turner reiterated the Liberal position in a televised address of his own, then tipped his hand. "We Canadians have built a unique community in North America," he declared. "We like our system of government, our spirit of tolerance, safety on our streets, our way of doing things. We do not intend to become the 51st state of the American Union. Sure, it may cost more to live here ... but I believe that the price of being a Canadian is a price worth paying."[3]

It was impossible to predict how free trade would play out with voters. To win the next election, however, the Liberals would need more than policy. They needed organization – and its essential prerequisite, money. The Liberals had emerged from the 1984 election $3.5 million in debt. The Trudeau regime had not taken advantage of changes to the *Election Expenses Act* in 1974 that had made individuals' contributions to political parties up to 75 per cent tax deductible. The NDP and the Tories, in contrast, had exploited this opportunity by building direct mail operations to solicit donations from the middle class to supplement those from the big donors on whom the national parties traditionally relied. Whereas the Liberals had 18,000 names on their mailing list, the Conservatives were estimated to have 180,000. "I could not believe how bad it was," said a Saskatchewan Liberal. "There were people on the list who not only supported the PCs but actually ran for the Tories."[4] To improve their list, the Liberals would have to acquire names and current addresses from their constituency organizations and keep them up to date. Part of Turner's continuing mission to the grassroots was to build the trust needed to elicit cooperation on this front. He assigned former Cabinet minister Judd Buchanan to negotiate a deal that would give the provincial wings and riding associations a cut of the take in return for passing on names and letting the national party solicit these Liberal supporters on their behalf.

There was no lack of ways to spend the money. The most tangible sign of party renewal would be a new $1.2 million four-storey national headquarters being constructed on land the party owned in downtown Ottawa. A search for a party director was under way, and in the spring of 1986, former Cabinet minister David Collenette was hired for that position. "We're 10 years behind the other parties in fund-raising, in computers, in all the mechanisms of modern politics," Turner admitted late in 1986, "but if we do as well in the next two years as we've done in the last two, we'll be in a good position for the next election."[5]

Although these steps were promising, relations between the major institutions that comprised the federal party – Turner's office, caucus, the research bureau, and the national executive – demonstrated that fractiousness still beset the senior ranks. Working out roles and responsibilities always took time, but in this case certain individuals didn't want these relationships to work. Positions had gone to representatives of various party factions with the idea that everyone would close ranks and move on, yet some appointees used their positions as anti-Turner power bases. The disparate loyalties of caucus were replicated in all quarters, even within the leader's office. Turner's resolve to run an open party exacerbated the problem: in the previous regime, the power of the leader's clique, however arbitrary and undemocratic, had curbed expansive egos and conflicting agendas. Disputes festered because Turner was often away rebuilding the party, visiting his riding or his declining mother, or on vacation.[6] He did what he could to smooth things out but believed, ultimately, that the only real cure for internal factionalism was power. He would stride for the finish line and pray that all the nipping at his heels did not trip him up en route.

The Liberals' resurgence in the polls made for a rancorous year in federal politics. The Commons was often in uproar as the Rat Pack baited the hordes of underemployed government backbenchers. The tone of political discourse also suffered from the Tories' hypocrisy on patronage. Far from shunning partisan appointments, as he had promised, Mulroney refined their dispensation into a science. He created a special branch in the Prime Minister's Office that liaised with senior Cabinet members and provincial advisory committees for regional input. Boards of government agencies and institutions that had traditionally had non-partisan directors were fired to make way for Conservative appointees. During his first eight months in power, Mulroney made a thousand appointments, 90 per cent of them Tories. The most notorious was the elevation of Denyse Patry, his former secretary at Iron Ore Canada, to the board of the Canada Council.

The Conservatives seemed to be operating on the premise that, because the Liberals usually had a monopoly on the fruits of office, they had better take full advantage of their once-in-a-lifetime opportunity. Accusations of nepotism were lodged against senior ministers Michael Wilson, Joe Clark, and John Crosbie. Questions were raised about Frank Moores, a friend of Mulroney whose lobbying firm enjoyed a remarkably successful track record with the government. Mulroney promised to introduce stronger conflict-of-interest guidelines for his Cabinet members and a bill to register lobbyists, but the revelations continued. Industry Minister Sinclair Stevens, Communications Minister Marcel Masse, and Transport Minister of State Suzanne Blais-Grenier all had to resign after being accused of abuses of office. Numerous backbenchers used their government connections and privileges in creative but ethically questionable ways. Their poster boy was MP Michel Gravel, who was charged for soliciting kickbacks on government leases and contracts. Then it came out that Mulroney himself had intervened to relocate a federal prison to his riding, even though $1 million had already been spent on preparations for a facility in Drummondville.

"There are so many birds in the air, we hardly know which way to shoot," said Turner happily.[7] Yet he chose his targets carefully, reluctant to trash a reputation for short-term partisan advantage. Character assassination, he knew, could cut both ways. When a Tory MP regularly appeared drunk in the House, for example, he tipped off the government benches that the Rat Packers were about to launch an attack and allowed them to deal with the problem themselves.[8] The pack thought its leader's scruples quaint but did not protest because there was an abundance of quarry at hand. The Liberals benefited greatly from the Tory scandals. The Rat Pack's heated pursuit of Tory malfeasance made headlines and boosted its members' public profiles. Sheila Copps, a progressive and nationalist MP from Hamilton, became the most notorious of the bunch because her spirited attacks on the Tories provoked sexist responses. "Just quiet down, baby," John Crosbie admonished her during one heated debate. Turner distanced himself from the Rat Pact's tactics but benefited strategically from their attacks. He may not have been as slick as Mulroney, but he was looking like a man of character in comparison, and the Liberal lead in the polls widened.

Whenever things were going well for Turner, however, Chrétien emerged to cut him down at the knees. This time, the occasion was the election of a new president for the Quebec wing of the Liberal Party in February 1986. The value of this prize was questionable. It was now quite clear that the Liberal electoral successes in the province in the 1970s and 1980s had been based not on an entrenched organization but on leadership and patronage. Trudeau and Marc Lalonde, two native sons, had gratified nationalist sentiment with their prominence and power. Both were gone. With the Liberals out of office, André Ouellet, the party's impresario of patronage in Quebec, found himself without any goodies to hand out. Raymond Garneau had some support, but it was based on old associations in the provincial rather than the federal wing of the party. Even there he had lost ground to Bourassa, who was now consolidating his base. Liberal power-brokers in the federal wing resented Garneau's ascension under Turner and did not rush to his aid. Chrétien had salvaged what he could of the Trudeau-era organization, and his supporters, concentrated in ridings on the South Shore and the Eastern Townships, constituted the most coherent federal Liberal network in Quebec.

The controversy over the presidency revealed that the resulting power vacuum was being filled by chaos. Former Trudeau Cabinet minister Francis Fox had considered running for the Quebec party presidency, and Turner had been supportive. When Fox vacillated, however, Turner backed Paul Routhier, a young Quebec City lawyer. Then Fox announced he would run. Chrétien backed him, turning the race into a contest of the old guard against the new "open-party" generation and, effectively, a battle between Chrétien and Turner forces. On February 12 Turner tried to contact Fox to ask him to withdraw and also had Chrétien for dinner at Stornoway to work something out, but Fox was away, and he and Chrétien failed to reach an understanding. Later that night Turner did get Fox on the phone, and Fox agreed to his request. Chrétien, enraged that Turner had outflanked him, informed the press that the Liberal Party in Quebec was suffering from a "malaise." The diagnosis was accurate; the irony was that he was a large part of the problem. Marcel Lessard, the outgoing president in Quebec, called on Chrétien to stop dividing the party with his "insidious campaign" against Turner.[9] The partisan flailing continued, further muddying the waters, until an already murky issue was totally unfathomable.

This spat gave Chrétien a pretext for leaving politics. After resigning his seat on February 27, he worked for a Bay Street law firm, Lang Michener, and eventually became a director of numerous corporations as well as an adviser to an investment firm – the type of career he had disparaged Turner for during the leadership race. Turner had tried to talk him out of leaving because, as he told the press, "You can't lose Jean Chrétien and not be the weaker for it."[10] But Chrétien's efforts to control Quebec demonstrated that he would never reconcile himself to the legitimacy of Turner's leadership. For the second time in a decade, the Liberal Party had failed to cement an alliance of its leading anglophone and francophone figures.

No one thought Chrétien was really gone for good. Indeed, quitting freed him to pursue his leadership ambitions unhindered by the niceties of caucus solidarity. Over the ensuing months he stayed in the public eye by campaigning for Manitoba Liberal leader Sharon Carstairs, visiting Edmonton to discuss energy issues with Premier Don Getty, and intervening to help end Senator Jacques Hébert's hunger strike protest over the cancellation of the Katimavik youth program. When Turner toured Quebec, making appearances and trying to build relationships, Chrétien often showed up in the same places a little later to upstage him. Meanwhile, Chrétien's long-time aide Eddie Goldenberg began organizing support for a leadership review by talking to key riding executives who had backed Chrétien in 1984. In private, Chrétien badmouthed Turner, calling him lazy and suggesting he drank too much.[11] In public, he announced that Turner could make no major electoral inroads in Quebec, in contrast to him, and that Turner would be lucky to get 50 per cent in the leadership review that November.

Quebec Liberals who were not Chrétien supporters were appalled at his audacity. "Chrétien must go ... He's causing nothing but trouble," said one. "Mr. Turner is catching on in Quebec but this could spoil everything. This quarrelling must stop." Party president Iona Campagnolo also weighed in, publicly warning that "Mr. Chrétien must follow the example of Mr. Turner when Pierre Trudeau won the leadership."[12] The internecine warfare in Quebec was particularly troubling because Turner's comeback plan had called for him to make Quebec a priority in 1986-87. The Liberals were now polling ahead of the Tories in the province. Turner had been taking four hours of language lessons a week to give his French a more Québécois nuance and was conducting an increasing portion of his day-to-day work in the language.

Chrétien's departure cleared the way for Turner to appoint Garneau as finance critic and chair of the Quebec Liberal caucus. After a decent interval, he would make him his Quebec lieutenant charged with rejuvenating the party's fortunes in the province.

Turner's Quebec strategy included developing a position on the province and the constitution. Mulroney had promised Quebec a new deal and was working on something behind the scenes. That winter Turner had Garneau assemble a team to develop a Liberal position.[13] Sure enough, the issue re-appeared on the national political agenda in the spring, when Gil Rémillard, the intergovernmental affairs minister in Robert Bourassa's new government, announced five conditions essential to Quebec before it would sign the constitution. It wanted recognition as a distinct society, increased control over immigration, limitations on federal spending power (including the right to opt out of any new shared-cost program, with full monetary compensation), the return of Quebec's constitutional veto, and input into the selection of Supreme Court judges. When the federal government responded with positive noises but no concrete commitments, Turner saw an opportunity to steal a march on the Tories. He had always viewed Quebec as a unique province with a special place in Canada. He had reservations about some of its new demands, but he thought he could accommodate the most important ones in a new Liberal policy that would solidify his leadership and underpin his campaign in Quebec during the next election.

Turner knew he would encounter resistance within the ranks of his own party. Quebec's conditions conflicted with the Trudeau constitutional legacy. In Trudeau's vision of Canada, individual rights always trumped collective rights and were protected by constitutional guarantees, enforced by a strong central government and by the Charter of Rights and Freedoms. Trudeau had developed his position as a way of containing French Canadian nationalism in Quebec, but it had, ironically, become a sacred credo of English Canadian nationalists. They idealized Trudeau as the gunslinger who had battled Quebec separatism and bested its champion, René Lévesque, in the constitutional showdown of 1982. They had forgotten about Trudeau the compromiser, who had negotiated the Victoria Charter in 1971. Victoria showed that he had once been prepared to make significant concessions to achieve a constitutional settlement. Only later did he conclude that no permanent "settlement" would ever be possible, because the provinces, Quebec in particular, would always come back looking for more powers, making constitutional negotiations a mug's game that the federal government could only lose. Trudeau particularly distrusted Bourassa, whom he thought had no interest in Canada other than as a source of subsidy cheques. He feared that restoring Quebec's veto would strengthen its position in any future constitutional negotiations, providing leverage to seek, and get, even more powers.

In contrast to Trudeau, Turner had always thought some realignment of powers was necessary to accommodate the aspirations of modern Quebec. He had been saying so ever since he entered politics in the early 1960s, and he had made a point of emphasizing how his Quebec policy differed from Trudeau's during the 1968 leadership race. He was ready, with the support of the party's new guard in Quebec, to take up the challenge again. Turner had been out of government during the federal-provincial negotiations leading up to the 1982 patriation and so lacked Trudeau's recent bitter experience of provincial cupidity. He remained an optimist when it came to Quebec and its demands, believing that agreement now could conclude Canada's long constitutional saga.

Turner asked Serge Joyal to outline his plans to Trudeau in the hope of neutralizing opposition from that quarter. Joyal reported that, though Trudeau had reservations, he would not intervene publicly. The Quebec wing of the Liberal Party was to meet on the weekend of June 14-15 in Ste-Hyacinthe, Quebec. Turner announced the new Liberal position in an interview with *Le Devoir* published the day before the meeting. He explained that the policy included the first two of Quebec's five conditions – recognition as a distinct society (with mention as well of the multicultural character of Canada) and control over immigration. It offered Quebec a constitutional veto over changes to federal institutions, the essence of its fourth condition. Turner expressed reservations about condition number three, limiting the federal spending power, and was mute on the fifth condition – input into Supreme Court appointments. There was more to his proposal, however, than new powers for Quebec. It suggested a constitutional amendment to give minority-language groups control over schools, compensation to provinces for transferring powers to the federal government, and the repeal of the notwithstanding clause.

"Yes to Quebec's Conditions" trumpeted the headline in *Le Devoir*.[14] The accompanying commentary said the Liberals' position represented a promising new departure. Garneau had already run it by Jean-Claude Rivest, Bourassa's chief constitutional adviser, who told him that Quebec would probably look very favourably on an offer of this sort. A resolution supporting the position was unanimously adopted by the Quebec Liberals at Ste-Hyacinthe that weekend.

Turner and Garneau returned to Ottawa to explain the position to caucus, assuring Liberal MPs that Trudeau had known about it ahead of time. The caucus split in response. One group consisted of Quebec MPs, led by Garneau and Lapierre, who felt that Trudeau had promised Quebec a new deal in the 1980 referendum and that Canada was obliged to deliver. Opposed to them were numerous Trudeauites who were suspicious of any devolution of federal power that would diminish their idol's constitutional legacy. This group included Toronto MPs with multicultural roots and constituencies such as Charles Caccia, Sergio Marchi, and John Nunziata, who resented the two-founding-peoples concept of Canada, and Montreal MPs such as Donald Johnston and David Berger, who saw themselves as representatives of the interests of the 800,000-strong Quebec anglophone community. Some who opposed a new constitutional position did so because they saw the issue as a lever they could use to propel Turner out of the leadership and replace him with Chrétien.

The Trudeauites' suspicions soon developed into consternation. Trudeau, they learned, had "hit the roof" when he read *Le Devoir*. He had been "sucked in" by Joyal, he claimed, and he now perceived what Turner had said as "crapping on everything" he had entered public life to achieve.[15] The Quebec resolution was debated at a stormy caucus meeting that took on an ugly French Canadian versus English Canadian dimension.[16] Trudeau loyalists in caucus, chief among them Donald Johnston, spoke in defence of his constitutional legacy. Turner responded with a speech stressing unity, tolerance, and accommodation, and eventually persuaded the antagonists to paper over their differences for the time being. To make peace he set up a new committee, chaired by Robert Kaplan and Lucie Pépin, which would work on a resolution that could be presented to the policy convention in November. Trudeau had claimed there was no good reason to raise the constitutional issue because separatism was quiescent and Quebec was bound by the constitution whether or not it had signed it. Turner directly challenged this notion. The issue was, he pointed out, already in play. Quebec had presented its conditions, and the government was working on the file, so the Liberals had to take a position. Rumour had it that Trudeau had intended to be at the caucus meeting until Turner's office exerted pressure to disinvite him. Subsequently, gossip had it that he would instead attend the convention and raise hell.

Another cankerworm of dissent was hatched in August, when Turner appointed Senator Michael Kirby as co-chair, with Garneau, of the Liberals' election readiness committee. Kirby was a former academic who had risen to prominence as a political adviser in Nova Scotia before joining Trudeau's office and playing a key role in the patriation of the constitution. He had a reputation for getting things done and, as an employee of Martin Goldfarb, access to polling data that the party could not otherwise afford. His new appointment effectively put him in charge of the next election campaign in English Canada. Keith Davey was still sitting in on Liberal strategy meetings, and, though he and Kirby were friends, Davey felt jilted. He sought revenge by spreading word that Turner was headed for trouble in the leadership review and could not win the next election.

That summer also saw major changes in Turner's office, as press secretary Brigitte Fortier, executive assistant Stuart Langford, and principal secretary John Swift all left. It was unreasonable to expect professionals to work forever for paltry salaries with no power and no resources with which to do things. Swift was the most serious loss, but Turner recognized that he had to get on with his career. Saskatoon lawyer Doug Richardson, who had organized his leadership campaign in Saskatchewan, had been working with Swift for months and was ready to take over the job. Richardson was a dedicated Turner supporter, but unlike Swift, he was not a comrade-in-arms from past political wars. He would find it challenging to get Turner to trust him and listen to his advice. Fortier had travelled with Turner across the country as he rebuilt the party, and he would miss her. Langford, a Chrétien supporter hired to help heal post-leadership wounds, did not get along with Richardson and left disgruntled.

These summer intrigues set the stage for an eventful run-up to the November leadership review. Turner tried to manage expectations by maintaining that he needed a simple majority of only 50 per cent plus 1 to affirm his leadership, but his rating would inevitably be compared to the results of the Conservatives' leadership review in 1982, when Tory leader Joe Clark had resigned after receiving the approval of 66 per cent of delegates. If Turner got less or even just slightly more support than Clark, putting the leadership issue behind him would be difficult.

A group of party activists rallied to Turner's assistance. The English Canadian wing of the "Friends of John Turner," as they came to be known, had begun organizing in Toronto the previous winter under the leadership of two young Liberals, Terry Popowich and John Webster. Its French Canadian wing was headed by MP Jean Lapierre and Senator Pietro Rizzuto. Doug Richardson liaised with the Friends, coordinating their efforts with those of the leader's office. Prominent in their ranks were Young Liberals with backgrounds on the Hill who hoped to rise to positions of influence as the party elite changed under Turner's leadership. The Friends estimated that their man had the backing of thirty-six of the forty Liberal MPs and fifty of the sixty-eight Liberal senators. The issue would be decided, however, by delegates to be selected by the 282 Liberal riding associations from June through October. Turner may have been tripped up by a lack of organization in the 1984 election campaign, but it was not about to happen again. John Addison, a friend and former Liberal MP who ran a Cadillac dealership on Toronto's Bay Street, raised money for a special fund to finance their efforts.[17] They equipped themselves with the latest in technology, including a computer system and phone banks, then evaluated potential delegates' sympathies and worked to get Turner supporters elected.

Meanwhile, the anti-Turner forces – dubbed the "contras" – were waging a similar campaign. At a Liberal picnic in western Metropolitan Toronto's Etobicoke in early July, a small plane droned overhead during Turner's speech, trailing a banner that read, "You have an option – review!" A button proclaiming "I'm Turnered Off" was in circulation, and anonymous contra sources were constantly being quoted in the press. Someone financed a new poll affirming that Chrétien was more popular with the Canadian public than Turner. Rumours that Turner had a drinking problem circulated, and Keith Davey even went so far as to suggest that, like his mother, Turner suffered from Alzheimer's. It was a "black campaign," Popowich told reporters, "spreading lies about Turner having personal problems which is simply not true."[18] Meanwhile, both sides recruited new party members to swing delegate selection meetings. "We did what we had to do to win," Popowich said. "I'm not saying it was pretty. It got nasty, nasty, nasty. It was a dogfight. Let's face it, what we did was stack the place."[19] Turner didn't know, or want to know, some of the things his Friends were up to.

Inevitably the controversy over the Quebec resolution fed into the leadership issue. A contra in Turner's office leaked word to the press of Trudeau's unhappiness about the party's Quebec resolution. Though Turner had announced the party's Quebec policy three months earlier, it suddenly became highly controversial. Davey jumped into the fray, telling a Liberal barbecue in York-Peel that, "in the tradition of Mike Pearson and Pierre Trudeau, we believe in one Canada – no special status – ONE Canada."[20] A journalist wrote about a discussion with a Liberal delegate on the issue:

> She said she was so upset about Turner's constitutional stand that she intended to challenge him on it at the November convention.
>
> "What's wrong with his position?" I asked.
>
> "He believes in special status for Quebec," the outraged delegate replied.
>
> "What does special status mean?" I asked.
>
> There was an awkward pause. "I don't know," she replied. "I'll have to look into it."[21]

Turner told reporters he remained committed to a new deal for Quebec but was willing to work on the Quebec resolution to see if its wording could be made more broadly acceptable. He had Kaplan and Pépin seek out Trudeau in Montreal to solicit his views on the issue. Later in September, he made the pilgrimage himself. He and Trudeau discussed the issue over lunch but failed to resolve their differences. Ultimately, Trudeau decided to keep his objections to himself.

In mid-September Keith Davey published his autobiography, *The Rainmaker,* which rehashed the horrors of the 1984 election campaign, relating anecdotes that reflected poorly on Turner. Davey's memory was demonstrably inaccurate on key points, suggesting that the book had been rushed to press so it could have an impact on the leadership review. As he promoted it, Davey shared his opinion that the party would benefit if Turner made way for Chrétien. On the day of the Confederation Dinner, the Liberals' big annual fundraiser in Toronto, he told a reporter, "As long as we have the review mechanism in our constitution, it's pretty unfair to criticize anyone as disloyal who votes for a review." This renunciation of the principle of loyalty by one of its staunchest advocates sent shock waves through party ranks. "He has given a new legitimacy to the subterranean anti-Turner movement," noted one observer.[22] In October the *Toronto Globe and Mail* reported that Davey and his friends were trying to recruit Trudeau to return and replace Turner as leader.

The president of the Young Liberals, David Herle, condemned Davey as a "son of a bitch" who was doing "very serious damage to the party."[23] Outgoing party president Iona Campagnolo also came to Turner's defence, suggesting that Davey should leave caucus if he could not be loyal to the leader. The contras replied with a public letter to Campagnolo, asking her to reverse her position. "This leadership review mechanism," they maintained, "would not be part of our Constitution if it were disloyal to use it."[24] Campagnolo responded that the upcoming convention was not a leadership convention and that triggering a review could cause serious damage to the party.

Turner met with Quebec Liberals throughout the fall to massage the wording of the Quebec resolution. Eventually, he engineered a compromise acceptable to all. Whereas the original resolution recommended that a preamble be added to the constitution recognizing "the distinct character of Quebec as the francophone homeland of Canada," the revised version called for one recognizing "the distinctive character of Quebec as the principal but not the exclusive source of the French language and culture in Canada."[25] It included an amending formula that accommodated Quebec's demand for a constitutional veto. The resolution was also broadened to recognize the aboriginal, regional, and economic dimensions of Confederation. Turner tried to pre-empt criticism of the resolution from Trudeau disciples by stressing that it "recognizes the pan-Canadianism of Pierre Trudeau" and "would not mean 'special status' for Quebec." Moreover, its veto was "perfectly consistent with Trudeau's policy that came out of the 1971 constitutional conference in Victoria."[26]

Tensions escalated in the weeks leading up to the convention. Though the contras were active in Liberal circles right across the country, they were most active in Quebec, where Chrétien supporters had set up telephone banks to solicit delegates and were calling publicly for a review vote. The most audacious assault on Turner came from an unexpected quarter. On November 11 Marc Lalonde mailed a letter to all thirty-five hundred Liberal delegates advocating a leadership review "for the good of the party." "One can deplore the fact that a leader's popularity plays such a large role in contemporary politics," he wrote. "Deplore it if you will, but ignore it at your peril."[27] At a subsequent news conference, Lalonde said that Turner must get 65 per cent support in order to have a solid mandate. On November 22 the *Toronto Star* joined the chorus calling for a leadership review. These defections reflected the Liberal establishment's addiction to power. It had made Turner leader because he promised power; now, when there was a chance to opt for a different leader who seemed to offer a better prospect of office, Turner was disposable. The problem with such cynical opportunism was that it was patently obvious to the public and tainted the party's image. The old Liberal tradition of loyalty to the leader had been not only more ethical but better for the Liberal brand.

Turner was hurt by this latest wave of attacks and grew depressed about his chances in the review vote. Then, miraculously, it became clear that the contras had gone too far. Rank-and-file Liberals truly believed themselves to be part of a newly democratized party in a post-Trudeau era. They saw those who questioned Turner's leadership as disgruntled representatives of an old guard reluctant to surrender its customary privilege. A party official in British Columbia told a reporter that this type of politics, not Turner, had been responsible for the Liberals' defeat in 1984. More good news surfaced just before the convention. Donald Johnston issued a press release saying he would vote against a leadership review.[28] Then Ontario premier David Peterson publicly endorsed Turner as leader. Turner headed into the review with momentum on his side, reaping rewards from his grassroots efforts to rebuild the party over the previous two years.

He also had the backing of a strong, well-oiled organization. In the days leading up to the convention, the Friends of John Turner set up operations at the Westin and Chateau Laurier Hotels close by the convention centre. They had computers and printing presses to coordinate operations and

provide quick turnaround for Turner propaganda. No detail was overlooked. Addison's fund paid the expenses of pro-Turner Young Liberals
who otherwise might not have been able to afford to attend. Delegates were
greeted at the airport or train station, given a lift to their hotel, and toured
around the party's recently opened national headquarters building. The
Friends of Turner kept a hospitality suite going in the Westin and held pep
rallies every morning across the street at the Chateau Laurier. Every night
they threw a party at a different venue. Delegates' thoughts on a possible
leadership review were collected and fed into a database.

Every delegate was presented with a folder bearing the slogan "The Turner
Vision." Inside was the *John Turner News,* headed by an article entitled "My
Vision of Our Future: Opportunities and Growth," which highlighted their
leader's commitment to jobs, bilingualism, national unity, world peace,
free enterprise with a heart, and opportunities for women. "We want an
open party, a party with no closed lists, no cosy groups, no backroom boys
or girls," the leader declared." Included was a pitch for Turner from prominent MPs:

> Over the past two years, Mr. Turner has led our party in renewing itself.
> The process has not been easy ... but we have stood our ground, and
> struggle has made us stronger ... The changes within our party have been
> nothing short of revolutionary ... For the first time in many years we can
> truly say that the Liberal party is a democratic institution accountable to
> its membership ... At the convention the struggle over reform will crystal-
> lize in the leadership review vote. We believe that the few who want a
> return to the old ways and old arrangements will vote for a review.[30]

A missive from past presidents of the party pointed out that it was currently
ahead in the polls, noted that Turner had "logged several hundred thousand
kilometres to listen, to consult, to rebuild the party," and reminded delegates
that the Pearson comeback had been based on party solidarity.[31]

The Friends waded into the fray in the convention centre armed with
walkie-talkies, Turner scarves, buttons, and smiles that belied their seriousness of purpose. Whenever a speaker used the term "backroom boys,"
Friends in the audience would erupt with boos and hisses. They monopol-
ized the microphones at the policy workshops, populated the viewing field

of television cameras, and besieged delegates with literature, phone calls, and in-your-face persuasion.

The convention was covered live by more than eight hundred reporters, analysts, photographers, and technicians working for the major networks and local stations. At its Thursday evening opening, Turner delivered a rip-roaring attack on both Tories and contras, winning enthusiastic applause. In the days to come he would also speak to the Young Liberals and the National Liberal Women's Commission, but his most important speech would be the conference keynote address on Saturday at noon. When that speech was over, voting on the leadership review would commence, continuing until Sunday morning.

He tried not to come on too strong. Speaking in tribute to past party president Iona Campagnolo on the Wednesday night, he joked, "If I were a Tory Prime Minister, I would give you an outrageous patronage appointment. If I were a football player, I would give you a pat on the extreme lower back. Fortunately I am neither – so I'd never consider doing either."[32] When his microphone went dead during his speech to the women's commission, he won more delegates by smiling wryly and quipping, "If a woman had set this thing up, it would have worked." The audience cheered.[33]

On Friday Turner breezed through an "accountability session" at which he answered delegates' questions. When Keith Davey came in to watch, he was treated as a pariah by Friends in the crowd and exited sheepishly. The leaders of the Friends had told their foot soldiers to play nice, but some, especially Young Liberals, were overzealous. A phalanx of Friends broke up a small pro-review demonstration in the convention centre. A contra who raised the leadership issue at a Young Liberals' luncheon was doused with glasses of water. When Chrétien arrived at the conference, a scuffle ensued as his supporters jostled for position with Turner forces, an unfortunate encounter that dramatized the leadership issue for the television cameras.

The other business of the convention was consideration of the policies produced by the party's grassroots policy development process. Delegates passed resolutions on women's issues, the economy, social programs, youth unemployment, and foreign affairs. Divisions over free trade were reflected in contradictory resolutions, one of which endorsed negotiating with the United States toward "freer" bilateral and sectoral trade agreements, whereas the other called for multilateral trade liberalization through the General Agreement on Tariffs and Trade. The debate over the Quebec resolution pitted Chrétienites and Trudeauites defending the equality of the provinces against Turnerites favouring pragmatic accommodation. Turner's pre-convention management of the issue proved effective: the resolution passed after just twenty minutes of debate.

Turner's major speech on Saturday touched on many of the issues the delegates had been confronting over the previous three days and reiterated the point that Canadian sovereignty was more important than a free-trade agreement. "We will not," he declared, "bargain away our independence."[34] It was a solid performance – not as rousing as his Halifax outing but in keeping with the relaxed competence he had projected throughout the convention. Voting on the leadership review question commenced immediately afterward.

Early Sunday afternoon, when the results were expected, Turner was sitting in the audience at the convention centre flanked by his wife, sister, and children, listening to the newly elected party president, Michel Robert. At 1:38 p.m. an aide came down the aisle and handed him a folded slip of paper. He looked at it and handed it to Geills. Neither betrayed any reaction. The tension in the hall mounted. Then convention co-chair Lise Thibault went to the podium to announce the results of the leadership review. The vote against a review, she announced, was 76.3 per cent. The hall burst into cheers.

This was a decisive victory for Turner, enough to resolve the leadership issue once and for all. Out in the convention floor, Marc Lalonde and Keith Davey donned white and red Turner scarves and pledged renewed loyalty to the leader. "Thank you for the clear, strong, unequivocal mandate you have given me," Turner told his cheering, flag-waving followers. "Today and together, you and I move forward to gain the same strong unequivocal mandate from the Canadian people." "I want to lead a grassroots government," he declared, "where each of you is a part of the decision making process." As Turner's family gathered around him on the stage, Doug Frith took the microphone. "I've been waiting a long time to say this to you, John," he declared, "You're first in our hearts!"[35]

20

CREATURE FROM
THE BLACK LAGOON

At its halfway point, Turner's four-year plan for a Liberal comeback was on track. He had ministered to the party grassroots and shepherded a bottom-up policy development process. The Liberals' performance as the official opposition in the House had made them the credible alternative to the government. They had been ahead in the polls for months and, at the end of 1986, held a ten-point lead on the Tories. Turner's victory in the review vote had seemingly resolved the leadership issue. His challenge now was to consolidate and build on these gains. The Mulroney regime had been dogged by scandal, and Canadians' distrust of the prime minister was deep. If Turner could come across as the strong leader of a united party, odds were good that he could find himself moving back into 24 Sussex Drive within the next two years.

Normally, maintaining party unity would be no problem. That was what Liberals did. But the late 1980s were not normal times. The Liberals were not used to being out of power, and the two issues that dominated national politics, free trade and the long-simmering dispute over Quebec and the constitution, raised fundamental issues about Canada that provoked emotional responses. Then there was the lurking threat of Jean Chrétien. "Fractious internal combat wasn't something that normally plagued the Liberals," Chrétien's biographer would observe, "but the ascent of the forever-combative Chrétien to the leadership circle brought to the party a new culture of conflict."[1] Turner had a mandate, but he faced a minefield.

The immediate question arising from the convention was how its resolutions would be translated into a party platform. Here the ideal of participatory democracy encountered the practical realities of politics. Initially, two members of caucus, Warren Allmand and John Nunziata, insisted that the convention resolutions were binding on the leader. One obvious problem with this position was that some of the resolutions were contradictory. Moreover, if the leader were bound by the resolutions, his ability to react to events or manoeuvre for electoral advantage would be lost. After the convention, Turner told reporters that the resolutions were "highly persuasive" – he took them seriously and recognized that he would pay a political price for deviating from them. It was possible, however, that political exigencies would demand paying that price. He still hoped to avoid committing himself to a platform until an election was nigh, and there would be more policy conferences, consultations, and committees to heed in the months to come.

Although the party was now in far better shape than it had been in 1984, important tasks remained to ready it for an election. Turner had to recruit candidates, build a campaign organization, and raise money. In early March, Michel Robert, the new party president, announced ambitious plans to raise $23 million to pay off the existing $5 million debt, finance ongoing operations, and build a $10 million election war chest. Nominations had been frozen while the renewal and policy development processes were under way, but now nomination meetings were scheduled to start in mid-May. Turner asked Paul Martin Jr., a Montreal businessman who was a rising star in the party, to handle candidate recruitment. He wanted more representation from ethnic groups, women, youth, and business. Although the rancour in Parliament made it more difficult to sell prospective candidates on life as an MP, there was some interest in Liberal nominations now that the Liberals had pulled ahead in the polls, particularly in ridings where they had a good track record.

His hand strengthened by the convention endorsement, Turner moved to make changes in some key party roles. Leo Kolber, the party's chief bagman, had been unhappy with the parallel fundraising of the Friends of Turner. He was replaced by Gerry Schwartz, a Toronto financier. David Collenette, a Chrétienite and the party's executive director, was suspected by overly partisan Turner supporters of working against their interests. He would be gone by spring.[2] Turner was relying increasingly on the strategic advice of Senator Michael Kirby, whom he had appointed co-chair of the party's election readiness committee the previous summer. Some leading figures of the Friends of John Turner had calculated that their contribution would see them elevated instantly to positions of power and influence by the leader's side. They were miffed when Turner continued to consult Kirby and old comrades such as Jack Austin (another senator appointed by Trudeau) and John de B. Payne. Feeling betrayed, they grew indifferent to Turner's fate as leader.[3]

Turner could have been forgiven for thinking he had left the leadership issue behind him, but a row over defence policy soon proved him wrong. The convention had passed conflicting resolutions, one that supported NATO and another that opposed cruise missile testing. Turner had subsequently appointed Doug Frith as defence critic and asked him to devise a policy on defence. Caucus committee meetings in January and February proposed that the Canadian Arctic be demilitarized as a step toward demilitarizing the entire circumpolar region. The issue came to a head in late February because, just as the latest series of cruise tests was ending, the United States asked for a five-year renewal. Turner was holidaying in Florida at the time, so Frith and external affairs critic Donald Johnston informed the press that it might be time to end the testing. When Turner got back, he responded with his usual caveat that all such decisions would emerge as the policy development process matured.[4]

The NDP seized the opportunity to expose an incipient split in the Liberal ranks and, on March 6, introduced a motion calling on the government to terminate the testing. The Liberal caucus almost unanimously favoured the NDP resolution, but Turner had the same reservations about this position that he'd had about calling for a nuclear freeze during the 1984 election campaign: it ignored Canada's obligations to its NATO allies. The United States and the USSR were then engaged in disarmament negotiations covering intermediate-range missiles, and he did not want to undermine Canada's ally by taking a bargaining chip off the table. He decided that the Liberals should move an amendment to end the testing in a manner consistent with Canada's NATO and bilateral commitments, and Johnston and Frith agreed. Thinking the issue was settled, Turner headed to Toronto to attend to some private business. When the vote came in the House, however,

Lloyd Axworthy, Charles Caccia, John Nunziata, and Warren Allmand broke with the party line and voted with the NDP.

The incident resurrected all the recently interred questions about Turner's leadership. The Liberals were displaying the same crippling pathology that had plagued the Conservatives during their endless years in opposition. In a classic Catch-22 dilemma, they were fractious because they were not in power, and seemed unlikely to achieve power because they were fractious.[5] Turner read the riot act to caucus members, telling them they could hang together or be hanged separately. Votes of conscience would henceforth be limited to moral issues such as capital punishment and abortion. Unfortunately, as opposition leader he had few incentives or penalties to enforce his ultimatum. Governing parties were able to dangle Cabinet posts, positions on parliamentary committees, or patronage appointments to keep order in the ranks, but Turner could offer only positions in his shadow cabinet and the promise of rewards when power was regained. The latter had little effect on those who thought they could never regain power under his leadership.

Compounding the predicament of being in opposition was the vexed relationship between the leader and his caucus. Here Turner's former talent for cultivating consensus was sadly lacking. Perhaps he felt that he now deserved a certain deference and shouldn't have to work for it. Although the 1984 election had left the Liberals with a raft of MPs who owed nothing to the leader, Turner should have been actively cultivating them regardless – lunching, stroking, seeking their sage advice and counsel. Yet they weren't his people. He knew it and instinctively shied away from dealing with them. As a result he failed to build a reservoir of good feeling that he could draw upon in a crisis.

Some of caucus members' hostility to Turner was sublimated through criticism of his office. It was "incapable of crisp decision making on policy and strategy," according to one of the "anonymous sources" quoted ceaselessly in the press.[6] It was blamed for cutting Turner off from caucus, the executive, and the rest of the party – particularly the grassroots reformers he had been allied with since 1982. Critics denounced his advisers as inexperienced and inept, or autocratic and manipulative. For some, Douglas Richardson, who had replaced John Swift as Turner's principal secretary in 1986, was too hard-nosed; for others, he was a milquetoast. "That office is a bloody mess," claimed another anonymous Liberal. "They don't know a crisis till it hits them in the face, and ultimately [Turner's] responsible for it."⁷ There were stories of policy documents getting lost en route to Turner's desk or making it there never to be heard of again. Turner's supporters countered that some disorganization was the price of running an open party. The top-down administration of the backroom boys under Trudeau had been efficient but hardly democratic.

During the early months of 1987, Liberal internal intrigues were eclipsed in the news by the government's continuing ethical misadventures. Tory scandals followed one another like inter-coastal ferries, one barely disappearing over the horizon before another hove into view. First came the escapades of an adviser to Public Works Minister Roch LaSalle who had partnered in a stripper-booking agency with a Mafia hit man from Montreal. Then André Bissonnette, the junior minister of transport, flipped land in his riding to a company that won a major contract from his department. The Tories' proclivity to play politics with government procurements backfired when Cabinet awarded a $1.3 billion maintenance contract for McDonnell Douglas CF-18 fighter jets to Canadair of Montreal rather than to the low bidder, Bristol Aerospace of Winnipeg. Westerners were outraged. Having tried and failed to find fair representation at the centre through the Progressive Conservatives, many began to explore other options such as Preston Manning's nascent Reform Party.

Then Mulroney transcended his government's trials with one dramatic stroke. On April 30, 1987, he met with the provincial premiers at the prime minister's retreat at Meech Lake to discuss the five points Quebec had earlier proposed as a basis for constitutional change. After one extended negotiating session, the first ministers reached an agreement in principle on what would become known as the Meech Lake Accord. The deal met all five of Quebec's conditions. It declared that the federal government agreed to preserve and promote the "distinct society" of Quebec, gave Quebec greater direction over immigration, restored its veto over constitutional change, reined in the federal spending power, offered provincial governments a role in appointing senators, and agreed to appoint Supreme Court justices from lists submitted by the provinces.⁸ It maintained constitutional symmetry by offering all the other provinces the same as Quebec except for recognition as distinct societies.

Expecting the first ministers' talks to fail, Turner had travelled to Montreal with Raymond Garneau so they would be in Quebec to criticize the government on a Quebec issue. They were taken by surprise when the deal was struck so quickly. Speaking to reporters the next morning, Turner allowed that it was a significant accomplishment. As he and Garneau headed back to Ottawa, he considered how he would handle the issue. He had always appreciated Quebec's distinctiveness and been prepared to recognize it both symbolically and in reasonable constitutional accommodations, so for him, the question was not one of principle. Meech wasn't the deal he would have made, but nothing is ever perfect, and he was inclined to live with its deficiencies for the greater purpose of getting Quebec to reaffirm its place in Canada.

Given the strength of the Trudeau legacy in his party and the customary role of the leader of the opposition, Turner could easily have opposed the accord. To placate Quebec provincial Liberals, he could have agreed with the notion of a constitutional accommodation in principle but criticized the specifics of this particular deal. He decided not to take this route because he believed that the Meech Lake Accord would be good for national unity. He saw it as another instalment in an ongoing adjustment of jurisdictional powers in the evolving Canadian federation. Its provisions would decentralize power to the provinces, but not radically. In return, the nation would be reaffirmed symbolically by having Quebec sign its constitution. As he saw it, Quebec had said "yes" to Canada by rejecting separatism in the 1980 referendum; it was now time for Canada to say "yes" to Quebec. Only rarely did particular conjunctures of circumstances offer an opportunity for constitutional accommodation. Just such an opportunity had been missed in Victoria in 1971 and now presented itself again. In Turner's view, Meech Lake was not radically different from the Victoria Charter. Although he had reservations about how some of its provisions would work, on the whole he judged that its symbolism – both the spectacle of English Canada trying to accommodate Quebec and the value of having Quebec respond by signing the constitution – outweighed its technical shortcomings. It was important that the federal Liberals join in welcoming Quebec into the 1982 constitutional settlement.

With Québécois public opinion strongly favouring the deal, supporting Meech would be good politics. To oppose it with reservations would be to risk being tarred in broad strokes as anti-Quebec. Premier Robert Bourassa, a fellow Liberal, promised Turner that he would reap the reward for his support for the deal in Quebec in the next election. The position of Ontario Liberal premier David Peterson also figured in Turner's political calculus. Peterson, like his Tory predecessors, believed he had a role to play in sustaining national unity by maintaining a *bonne entente* with his Quebec counterpart. Although he had reservations about Meech Lake, he too thought the deal worth doing to accommodate Quebec. Peterson spent a great deal of political capital convincing skeptical premiers such as Don Getty and Bill Vander Zalm to sign on.[9] It would be awkward for Turner to break with the Liberal premiers of the two big central Canadian provinces, Bourassa and Peterson, on such a critical issue.

In the House later that day, Turner congratulated the first ministers and called the signing of the accord a "happy day for Canada and Quebec." Recognition of linguistic duality and Quebec's distinctiveness was "a sound foundation on which to build the future."[10] Having signalled to Quebec that the Liberals were sympathetic to its aspirations, he went on to put his reservations about the deal on the record. Would the phrase "distinct society" be in the preamble to the agreement or embedded in the main text? Would Ottawa's ability to launch new social programs remain unaffected by the restrictions Meech placed on the federal spending power? Would the provision for unanimity for changes in federal institutions preclude further reform in this area? Did the federal government get any powers in exchange for those it had given up? With regard to this last point, the Liberals' policy resolution on the constitution had at least demanded repeal of the notwithstanding clause or an expansion of minority-language rights as a trade-off for Quebec's demands.

Ignoring Turner's caveats in favour of the stronger visual message of a photo op, Mulroney crossed the floor of the House and, much to Turner's embarrassment, vigorously shook his hand – a gesture caught on television and broadcast across the nation. "The next time you see Mulroney moving, let me know," Turner told Robert Kaplan. "I'm getting out."[11]

The Meech Lake Accord was an instant media sensation. Newspapers were full of commentary on how the deal was done and prognostications about its profound implications. Panels of pundits convened on public affairs shows to ponder the meaning of it all. The field was open for speculation because the accord dealt with aspects of federal-provincial relations where its impact would become evident only after its changes had been operating for some time. Since most of the accord's provisions were too dull, arcane, and complex for their implications to be grasped by the general public, attention focused on the distinct society clause. Like the "distinctive character" phrase in the Liberals' Quebec resolution, it signalled a departure from the prevailing Trudeau legacy. For adherents of Trudeau's equality of the provinces doctrine, asymmetry reared its ugly head. What did the distinct society clause entail? Was it just token recognition? Or was it an opening that could be exploited incrementally to build an independent Quebec? Would it allow Quebec to override charter guarantees of individual rights? Given the province's track record on language policy, this last possibility seemed all too likely.

Transcending all these imponderables was a larger strategic question. Would Meech Lake bring "peace in our time," or was it merely a naive and temporary exercise in appeasement? Bourassa provided no reassurance. Indeed, when playing to nationalists in Quebec, he presented Meech as the beginning of a process rather than a pact through which Quebec fully committed itself to a renewed federalism.[12]

Meech Lake was a cruel challenge for Turner. He had been working to dispel an unfair perception that the Liberals were unable to take a stand on issues, only to be presented with one that truly divided the party. "You are facing the toughest issue that any Liberal Leader faces," Michael Kirby pointed out, "the need to balance sensitivity to Quebec with English Canada's overwhelming belief in, and support for, a strong national government."[13] Meech again exposed the fundamental fault line in the Liberal Party between Turner's and Trudeau's constitutional positions. The same controversy that had attended the Liberals' constitutional resolution the previous year was playing out once more, this time in deadly earnest because a real deal was on the table.

Caucus again fractured into opposing camps. Supporters of Meech such as Raymond Garneau and Jean Lapierre had always regarded Trudeau's constitutional position as idiosyncratic and extremist. They represented a strain of Liberal opinion that was strong in Quebec but underrepresented in caucus. They were reinforced by veterans of Ottawa politics who viewed the accord as part of a long tradition in which national issues were managed through incremental adjustments brokered by elite accommodation. The majority in caucus, however, jealously defended the Trudeau legacy. Their Canada was defined by Trudeau's great works: official bilingualism, patriation of the constitution, the Charter of Rights and Freedoms, protection of minorities, and vigilant defence of a strong federal government against the forces of sectionalism. In this light, Meech was not just another political deal but a betrayal of the Canadian nation, and Turner's accommodating style a throwback to some dark era before Canada came of age under Trudeau. The Chrétien supporters in caucus generally held Trudeau's constitutional views while seeing Meech as a way to use an issue of principle to precipitate and rationalize a *coup d'état.* Turner and his staff, on the other hand, at first misread the principled opposition to Meech as nothing more than continued trouble making by Chrétienites.

While these fundamental divisions lurked in the background, the discontented restricted their criticisms to issues of process. Turner, they complained, had been hijacked by Garneau and had not consulted caucus before staking out his position. Douglas Richardson reminded them that, previously, they had complained that Turner would not take firm policy stands – and now they were carping because he had.[14] Turner, for his part, dismissed these complaints as groundless. The party had recently produced a resolution on Quebec and the constitution that was not unlike Meech Lake, he argued, so his positive response to the deal in the House was in keeping with the party's official position. At the same time, he had noted reservations that would give them room to manoeuvre. On Monday, May 4, he reiterated his concerns about the deal to a television reporter. The universal veto, he maintained, represented a "constitutional straitjacket" because it gave each of the eleven governments the ability to block reforms.[15] He also raised concerns about aboriginal rights.

Donald Johnston again emerged as the most vocal defender of the Trudeau legacy. He took the position that a constitutionally entrenched recognition of Quebec as a distinct society could sanctify laws giving Quebec the power to take away anglophone language and education rights, overriding the Charter of Rights and Freedoms. Late Monday, at a meeting with Turner and other senior Liberal MPs, Garneau and Johnston got into a shouting match. Another clash blew up at the Quebec caucus the next morning, with Garneau and André Ouellet facing off against Johnston.

The encounter ended with Ouellet denouncing Johnston as a "Westmount Rhodesian" – an epithet popularized by René Lévesque. Turner ordered him to apologize.

A rancorous caucus meeting later that day eventually ended in agreement on three points that supported Turner's position on the accord. First, the Liberals were pleased that Quebec would be signing the constitution. Second, they questioned certain aspects of the accord, particularly its spending-power provisions. Third, they would wait for the legal text to appear before making a final decision on whether they could support it.[16] Johnston's fellow MPs urged him not to break ranks, but to wait and see whether Meech could be amended or if its framers' consensus would fall apart when the first ministers met on June 2 to finalize the text.

Despite this truce, caucus members had different ideas about where the Liberals would eventually come down on the accord. Some thought they might ultimately withdraw their support if the concerns embodied in their proposed amendments were not addressed. Turner and Garneau, however, thought it was clear that they were supporting the accord while putting their concerns about it on the record. Mulroney, after all, had a huge majority and was referring to the accord as a "seamless web" that could not be altered.

To exploit the division in the Liberal ranks, the Conservatives announced that they would be introducing a motion asking for the support of the House in principle for the accord. Johnston, who had just lunched with Trudeau, now pronounced the accord a two-nation charter that would replace the dream of a bilingual nation with a French Quebec sequestered within an English Canada. While visiting his mother at her nursing home on Saltspring Island that Friday, May 8, Turner got a call from Johnston, saying he could not support the accord and had decided to resign as external affairs critic. Turner asked him to wait until he got back so they could discuss the matter, but Johnston did not want to be talked out of his decision. He released a resignation letter and began speaking to the media.[17]

During the debate on the government's resolution the following Monday, Turner laid out the Liberals' reservations. His main points were that entrenching two first ministers' conferences per year would create a new level of government, that the accord's limitations on the federal spending power jeopardized social programs, and that the distinct society clause should be expanded to embrace multicultural groups and aboriginals. Still, he did not object in principle to the deal. Meech was flawed, but the Liberals would support it because it fulfilled the higher goal of bringing Quebec back into Confederation.

Johnston's defection emboldened other Liberals who were uncomfortable with Meech. The most public gesture of dissent came from Toronto MP Charles Caccia, who distributed a newsletter in his riding criticizing the accord. In a caucus meeting on Wednesday, Turner laid down the law, telling his MPs that, from now on, there would be only one Liberal position and no public deviations. The next day Johnston again spoke out against Meech, and Montreal MP David Berger echoed his comments. Turner dismissed Berger from the shadow cabinet as science and technology critic. Caccia too would lose his post as environment critic.

Initial media coverage of the Meech Lake Accord was reverential, with journalists seemingly overawed by the responsibility of bearing witness to history in the making. Liberal infighting, with its raucous cast of flawed characters behaving badly, was, in comparison, an irresistible sideshow. Half of CBC-TV's Meech Lake coverage in May and early June focused on Liberal dissension and its consequences for Turner's leadership. The media's fixation with celebrity scandal put Turner in the hot seat, obscuring more significant dimensions of the issue. Women's, aboriginal, and ethnic groups laboured to get their concerns on record but, by comparison, received scant coverage.

The celebrity quotient escalated further when Pierre Trudeau entered the fray publicly with an anti-Meech diatribe published in *La Presse* and the *Toronto Star* on Wednesday, May 27.[18] Supporting Meech meant opposing Canada, he wrote, because it paved the way for the "balkanization" of the nation. "Those Canadians who fought for a single Canada, bilingual and multicultural, can say goodbye to their dream," he declared melodramatically. "There are henceforth two Canadas, each defined in terms of its language." Quebec nationalists were "snivellers" and "losers"; the accord's framers, cowards; and Mulroney, a weakling. Trudeau followed up with appearances on English and French television in the days that followed.[19] Although he had not attacked his successor directly, the reappearance of the philosopher king on the national stage badly hurt Turner.

"By going public, Trudeau has legitimized opposition to the Meech Lake Accord within the Liberal Party," Kirby warned Turner, and the result was "almost universal rejection of the Meech Lake Accord among English speaking Party members and ... a severe risk that the party would split along linguistic lines."[20]

On June 2-3, the premiers and the prime minister met in Ottawa to hammer out the final wording of the agreement. The session was tense, with Manitoba and Ontario pushing for language that would limit the distinct society clause and restrictions on the federal spending power. Bourassa refused to concede anything, and negotiations that were supposed to conclude by the end of the work day went all night, with Manitoba and Ontario finally agreeing to the original deal with no significant qualifications.[21] The Liberal caucus then met that afternoon to discuss the result. Whereas most of the francophone MPs from Quebec supported the accord, most of the Trudeau appointees in the Senate and several anglophone MPs opposed it, citing the usual litany of objections. After five hours of discussion, it was time for Turner to sum up. He told his caucus that the party had to accept the deal. It was the right thing to do for Quebec. If caucus would not fall into line, he was prepared to go over its head and appeal to the party rank and file. Anti Meech caucus members accused him of reading a prepared speech, revealing the consultative premise of the gathering to be a sham. In the end, caucus agreed to stay the course. It would accept the accord in principle but press for amendments to protect the federal spending power, recognize aboriginal rights and multiculturalism, weaken the unanimity clause, and strengthen minority-language rights.

The next day, June 4, Turner went on national television to explain the Liberals' position. "In June of 1986 I presented a constitutional proposal which became a resolution at our November Convention," he explained. "That resolution recognized the distinct character of Quebec, the need to entrench its role in immigration, Senate reform, a strengthening of the Charter of Rights and Freedoms, and a commitment to study the spending power. That resolution was endorsed by 90% of our delegates. The spirit of our resolution was reflected in the Meech Lake Accord. That is why I supported it."[22] The message to caucus was that, regardless of its bitter divisions, Turner was acting in accord with the democratically expressed wishes of the party.

Turner grounded his position in lessons from the long history of French-English relations in Canada. He referred to the numerous occasions in the past when francophones' aspirations had encountered indifference or hostility from the English-speaking majority. He spoke of the Riel affair, the conscription crises, and Quebec premiers' historic battles for provincial autonomy. The Royal Commission on Bilingualism and Biculturalism, Turner reminded reporters, had clearly stated that unless profound reforms were forthcoming, Canada would probably break up. Recalling the Trudeau government's response to this warning, he drew parallels between the Meech Lake Accord and the Victoria Charter of 1971. Although the two deals differed, he was trying to explode the romantic notion of Trudeau as a constitutional purist who had never been willing to negotiate and compromise.

Mentioning the Victoria Charter had the additional merit of allowing Turner to share in the credit for the Meech Lake Accord. "Since I was there at the beginning of the process," he had explained to journalists the day before, "I want to be there for a successful end of the process and to ensure that Quebec is brought into our Constitution."[23] Had Turner wished to demonstrate the full extent of his involvement with the issue, he could have told reporters to look up his speeches from the 1960s in which he had explained Quebec to English Canadians as a unique centuries-old society that, with understanding and tolerance from the rest of the country, could remain a major contributor to a strong, united Canada.

Turner's defence of his position was both erudite and eloquent, yet it failed to halt Liberal infighting. Over the next few days, the party slid toward anarchy. Small groups of caucus members met furtively as rumours of sinister plots and incipient mutiny swirled around Ottawa. Doug Frith, returning from a visit to constituency organizations, reported that he'd encountered "a whole generation of riding presidents out there with the Trudeau vision."[24] Rumour had it that Marc Lalonde, Tom Axworthy, and Gérard Pelletier were working with Trudeau on a series of speeches he would use to further sway public opinion. Chrétien jumped into the fray the following week, giving a speech in Edmonton that criticized Meech for its limitation on the federal spending power. Then Quebec intergovernmental affairs minister Gil Rémillard declared on June 19 that Quebec would be able to use the distinct society clause in the courts to override the Charter of Rights and Freedoms, thereby confirming the accord opponents' worst fears.[25]

Turner had long wanted to hold a "thinkers' conference" modelled on the 1960 Liberal conclave in Kingston that had first engaged him in politics and laid the foundation for Pearson's political comeback. As part of the party's ongoing policy formulation process, arrangements had been made for a series of such gatherings. One was to be held at Trinity College School in Port Hope that month. When Turner spoke there on June 20, he delivered another passionate and principled defence of his position, backed by a detailed account of the history of constitutional negotiations over the previous half century: "I exercise my responsibility on your behalf and in the best traditions of our party [by supporting an accord that includes] the recognition of French- and English-speaking elements of the Canadian community ... We are on the right side of history and we're doing the right thing as Canadians."[26] Turner admitted that the issue had caused strains but attributed them to the fact that the Liberals were an open party, unlike the Conservatives and the NDP. Trudeau, he reminded them, had promised a "renewed federalism" in the thick of the 1980 referendum debate, and that promise had to be fulfilled. "When it goes to the unity of the country, when it goes to the future of Canada, and it reflects the historic position of the Liberal Party, I believe my course is clear," he declared.[27]

The resolution approving the Meech Lake Accord came before the House for second reading on June 22. Turner dutifully introduced the Liberals' amendments to improve the accord, but the government of course wanted no part of them. The Quebec legislature ratified Meech Lake the following day. That started the clock ticking: other provinces had to ratify it within three years – by June 23, 1990 – otherwise the agreement would expire. This extended ratification period was odd and, given how fast circumstances can change in politics, inexplicable. With nine provinces and thirty-six months left to go, the Meech Lake Accord was destined to become a political soap opera to be played out in successive dramatic instalments on the national stage.

The next episode saw the accord referred for study to a parliamentary committee, the Special Joint Committee on the Constitution, before returning to the Commons for a final vote. Mulroney made it known before the committee's first meeting on August 4 that no part of the accord could be changed unless some "egregious error" were identified. André Ouellet and Robert Kaplan, the Liberal members, nevertheless used the committee to publicize their party's proposed amendments. When their concerns were ignored, they submitted their own dissenting minority report.

Turner meanwhile tried to heal the breach in the party with personal diplomacy, taking members of caucus out to lunch to plead for solidarity. But it was tough sledding. Dissent over Meech had affected public perceptions of the Liberals' competence, particularly that of their leader, with negative effects on the party's electoral prospects. The NDP had been catching up to the Liberals in the polls during the early months of 1987 and, boosted by the continuing reports of dissension in Liberal ranks, pulled ahead in May. On August 13 faint-hearted Liberals were spooked by an Angus Reid poll showing the NDP at 44 per cent, the Liberals at 29 per cent, and the Conservatives at 25 per cent. Reid also polled on leadership options and reported that, under Chrétien, the Liberals would be in first place. Turner supporters claimed that Reid's polls were biased by his lingering bitterness over their vexed relationship, pointing to a Gallup poll taken at the same time that had the Liberals and NDP virtually tied, with 36 per cent and 37 per cent support, respectively. The apparent surge in NDP fortunes nevertheless revived fears that the Liberals would dwindle into insignificance in a new binary partisan landscape that pitched socialists against conservatives. "This fear of the demise of the institution of the Liberal Party is extremely dangerous for the Leader because it enables people to oppose the leader while still being loyal to the Party," Michael Kirby told Turner. "Indeed, it is their concern about the Party which they use to justify their concern about the leader."[28]

A test of the Liberals' electoral appeal was coming with by-elections slated for July 22 in ridings in St. John's, Hamilton, and the Yukon. The Liberals had not held these seats for years. Only in the Yukon might they stand a chance, so they decided to concentrate their resources there. The Liberal candidates ran strongly, but the NDP won all three seats, adding to the speculation that the Liberals had been replaced by the NDP as the voters' preferred alternative to an unpopular government.

Back at the office, Turner was again dealing with staff turnover. Michèle Tremblay, his Quebec adviser, and Sharon Schollar, the party's national campaign director, both left that summer. The most significant loss came on August 12, when Douglas Richardson resigned as principal secretary. Turner was reluctant to see him go but recognized that he had to get on with his career – there was only so much benefit to be derived from working for a party in opposition. Richardson's departure had been anticipated for months, but in the context of that troubled summer, it was inevitably interpreted as more evidence of Turner's leadership troubles. Many disaffected Liberals had wanted Richardson gone because he had become a proxy for their discontent with the leader. Now that he was going, they interpreted his departure as a crisis. In a sense it was. Richardson had helped keep a lid on the Meech issue through careful management of individual caucus members. With his departure, MPs who had kept quiet out of respect for him felt freer to express their dissent.[29]

In a final memo to Turner, Richardson reiterated his views on how Turner could improve his performance as leader. He asked him to make more of an effort to understand and support his staff's efforts with caucus so they were not working at cross-purposes. He recommended that Turner do more to cultivate caucus dissidents to keep them onside. He had the right to make decisions, but his MPs had to feel they were part of the process. More troubling than these procedural deficiencies was the portrait Richardson painted of an embattled leader who, weary of the constant sniping and no longer certain whom to trust, had pulled up the drawbridge. Even his own staff were left on the outside, uninformed of his decisions and the reasoning behind them. This John Turner was a stark contrast to the man who had once been the consummate networker, always communicating, consulting, conciliating, and compromising.[30]

Meech had taken a sad toll on a leader who, nine months earlier, had enjoyed a resounding leadership endorsement at the head of a revitalized party that seemed poised for a return to power. Turner's continuing image problems and desultory poll numbers that summer made Liberal MPs fear for their seats in the next election. "There is no cabal to get Turner, or plot to unseat him," concluded Marjorie Nichols, his most loyal supporter among the press corps. "There is simply a sad consensus among the Liberals on Parliament Hill that no amount of patching and vulcanizing is going to bring this party back together in victory under John Turner's stewardship ... The lack of confidence in Turner is too fundamental to be fixed."[31]

While dimming prospects of power fuelled dissent, Meech Lake offered a principled excuse for it. Chrétien supporters fed off the dissatisfaction in caucus, chatting up old-guard Trudeauites and disillusioned Friends now looking to their futures in a post-Turner era. The support Turner had painstakingly cultivated among the party rank and file across the country was not impervious to continuous negative publicity about the goings-on in Ottawa. All the old complaints about Turner began to appear in the press once more. Liberals needed to believe in a cause, but Turner lacked conviction, vision, decisiveness. He was accused of not being a true Liberal – for some, this meant that he had supported Meech; for others, that he did not advocate left-wing reforms and had given lip service to progressive policies just to get elected. These accusations were followed by a litany of lesser sins. Turner was an absentee leader, away from Ottawa during such crises as the cruise vote, Johnston's resignation, and the publication of Trudeau's rant against Meech. He took long lunches, played tennis in the afternoon, and holidayed too frequently. He mistreated his office staff. Some complained that his advisers were incompetent, others that he didn't listen to his advisers. Each criticism could be explained or excused individually, but they were damning when melded en masse in the heat of the moment.

Turner didn't quite know how to respond. He attributed the onslaught in part to impatience with the slow development of policy under his open-party system. "There's always that delicate balance between an open, democratic party and a party where you impose cohesion," he explained. "We're now moving into the cohesive period."[32] He questioned the journalists' reliance on anonymous sources and attributed much of the griping to malcontents with unrealistic expectations. "If I walked on water," he remarked, "people would say I couldn't swim."[33]

Destroying the leader's reputation was one thing; removing him from office was another. Here the neo-contras faced a procedural dilemma. With the leadership review long past, there was no mechanism for unseating Turner before the next election. Some chose to abandon anonymity to exert public pressure on him to step down. The president of the Young Liberals of Canada and the president of the party's Ontario wing both told journalists that Turner had to shape up by offering clear policy positions and going out to sell them. Other dissidents remained anonymous but ramped up the barrage of negative press in the hope that it would convince him to depart. There was even talk that a delegation would go to Turner, suggest that he leave for the good of the party, and offer him $2 million to ease his transition back to private life. If he were forced to face facts, the reasoning went, he would see that he had to go.

Things came to a head when, on August 25, party president Michel Robert told a reporter that Turner had to turn things around quickly or else face an "open rebellion." Robert advised Turner to reorganize his office, define lines of authority and roles, and take firm stands on the issues. He stopped short of saying that Turner should resign, but, coming from the party president, this was an extraordinary public declaration, particularly since six weeks earlier Robert had said that caucus members who did not support Turner on Meech should quit. Turner told reporters that, if Robert had any suggestions, he should have kept them in-house. Then Lise Saint-Martin Tremblay, the national vice-president for Quebec, publicly echoed Robert's comments.

In the middle of the ensuing brouhaha, Pierre Trudeau appeared before the Special Joint Committee on the Constitution that was reviewing Meech Lake. Canada, he told the committee, had to be more than the sum of its provinces. Did the distinct society clause mean something or not? If it did, the charter was compromised. If it didn't, why have it? The proceedings were televised, and in the excerpts shown on the news and recycled through public affairs shows in the days that followed, Trudeau appeared passionate, principled, and eloquent. In the context of Turner's troubles, Trudeau's dismal approval ratings when he left office were forgotten in a wave of nostalgia for a lost Golden Age under the Great Leader. For Quebec nationalists, the resurrection of Trudeau and the support he received had a different meaning: the federal Liberals were standing in the way of Quebec's aspirations. All the political sacrifices Turner had made to show that the Liberals were sympathetic to Quebec were negated by Trudeau's intervention. Rebuilding the party in Quebec suddenly became far more of a challenge.

By late August, journalists were reporting plots to replace Turner. "He'll be gone in September," one anonymous source predicted confidently.[34] "Every dinner involving two or three high-profile Liberals at a posh Toronto or Ottawa restaurant is assumed to be an anti-Turner conspiracy," wrote

Carol Goar as August came to a close.[35] Three Liberal MPs were plotting mutiny by soliciting from their colleagues signed letters asking Turner to resign. They expected to collect thirteen letters to present to Turner, who, they presumed, would have no choice but to submit to a demand for his resignation from a third of his caucus.[36] Meanwhile, Alain Tardif, a back-bench MP who had supported Chrétien in 1984, called publicly for Turner to resign, and Denis Coderre, president of the Quebec Young Liberals (and previously one of the Friends of Turner), told reporters that his organization would be calling for Turner's resignation.

With their party in the process of tearing itself apart, senior Liberals intervened. On Sunday, August 30, dozens of MPs, senators, provincial party presidents, national executive members, and party officials convened on Ottawa for an emergency meeting. Turner absented himself so they could speak freely. They began with a griping session. The problems with Turner's office were rehashed. Then he himself was targeted with complaints about "everything from his reluctance to make tough decisions to his drinking habits and frequent afternoon tennis games."[37] The aggrieved unburdened themselves until mid-afternoon, after which the talk shifted to what to do about the situation. Support for Turner was strongest among the Quebec new guard, who feared that his departure would lead to Chrétien becoming leader and a reversal of the Liberals' support for Meech. The likelihood that Chrétien would replace Turner if an immediate changeover occurred gave pause to other potential leadership candidates who needed more time to prepare their bids. Eventually, all sides agreed to stop back-stabbing the leader and give him a chance to turn things around.

The Liberal campaign co-chairmen, Senators Al Graham and Pietro Rizzuto, Liberal House leader Herb Gray, and party president Michel Robert met with Turner to present him with the meeting's resolutions: he had to communicate better, concentrate on articulating a Liberal vision for Canada, maintain discipline in caucus, and mount a more active opposition in the House. Turner didn't take issue with most of them. "The only question that really annoyed me was on my working habits," he said. "I have travelled 600,000 km across this country. My lunch hour consists of 12:25 to 1:30 – I have to be back for Question Period. Every lunch is a business lunch with a member of a caucus or somebody who wants to see me. As for the tennis, I try to get in two games a week, three if I can. I believe it is my duty to stay healthy, to reduce the stress. It has always been part of my routine."[38] He told reporters that he would get new staff, work on tax reform policy and an alternative to the Tory trade initiative, and try to improve his personal style. "I try to get better," he said, "but my main urgency in the next few weeks is to maintain my sense of perspective and my sense of humour."[39]

Turner plunged back into his job and quickly found ways to satisfy his critics. On September 10 he spoke to a Liberal internationalist conference in Ottawa and signalled Liberal values by calling for the severing of diplomatic and economic ties with South Africa unless it took steps to end apartheid. Then, on October 2, he called in the House of Commons for a halt to cruise missile testing. He had a good reason for his reversal on the issue. The previous winter, he had argued that it would be irresponsible to end the testing while negotiations that encompassed the missile were under way between the superpowers, but now the United States and the USSR had reached a tentative agreement to ban intermediate-range mis siles. The tests were no longer needed, he declared. It was a dramatic an-nouncement, executed with faultless footwork and impeccable timing. Surprised and delighted, his MPs jumped to their feet to applaud him, and the NDP joined in.

Meech Lake remained a concern. After two days of meetings in early September, the Liberal caucus agreed to emphasize that the Charter of Rights should take precedence over the accord. The unanimity was short-lived, however. In the debate on the accord that began on September 29, Cochrane-Superior MP Keith Penner spoke out in opposition, saying it ceded too much to the provinces. In so doing, he joined the Liberal MPs already committed to voting against it, a group that by now included Donald Johnston, Charles Caccia, John Nunziata, Sergio Marchi, and David Dingwall. By this time, however, some NDP members were breaking ranks with their party position and announcing that they would vote against Meech Lake as well. That eased the pressure on Turner – no longer was he the only leader unable to keep his caucus united. The Liberals again pro-posed amendments to the accord, but to no avail. Those who had continued to hope that Turner would oppose the accord if and when the Liberals' amendments were rejected realized that he would not change his position. When the final vote on Meech Lake came on October 26, eleven Liberal MPs voted against it, with Mulroney's huge majority again carrying the day.

Turner had survived the Meech-inspired August putsch, but at tremendous cost. The headway in public opinion the Liberals had made from Tory scandals and the morale boost they had received from their policy convention the previous November had been completely squandered. Turner's image was as savaged as it had been in the wake of the 1984 election.

Some of his problems were attributable to his management style. In his previous career, he had held executive positions and had a deputy minister or managing partner to serve as chief operating officer, so his skill set did not include setting up or running the day-to-day operations of a large organization. Encouraging openness and dissent made management still more of a challenge. In this regard Turner was, not for the first time, the victim of his own political ideals. Furthermore, his commitment to a bottom-up policy process and his attempts to avoid divisions in caucus on issues of the day played into his critics' claim that he was indecisive. "Turner tried to give the party back to its members," one of his supporters explained. "But all they did with their new freedom for three years was mourn their dismal 1984 results, criticize his leadership, hatch conspiracies, and concentrate on marginal tasks such as amending the party constitution and setting up a bewildering array of committees and conferences."[40]

The media interpreted Turner's tolerance as weakness. It seems that what they really wanted was a little ruthlessness, however much it conflicted with liberal democratic principles. When Trudeau returned to the public stage to fight Meech Lake – aloof, arrogant, and doctrinaire – he was lauded as a principled statesman. "They seem to forget," noted a former Trudeau staffer, "that when Mr. Turner took over as leader in 1984, the Liberal Party of Canada was not exactly a thriving institution manned by enthusiastic Liberals from coast to coast and basking in national esteem."[41] Forgetting their recent disillusionment with Trudeau, the media, not to mention many Liberals, seemed to harbour a vestigial longing for an iron-fisted strongman.

Yet if Turner was not Pierre Trudeau, neither was he John Turner – at least not the Turner he had once been. His failure to co-opt dissent in caucus was troubling. Perhaps the leadership review victory deluded him into believing that he had the authority to lead boldly on Meech Lake and expect that his party would follow. If so, he was wrong. The mud slung at Turner during the summer of 1987 did contain some grains of truth. The Turner of the 1980s was not as shrewd and energetic as he had been in the 1960s and 1970s. Noblesse oblige was now accompanied by a certain *noblesse privilège,* a feeling that he had paid his dues, knew what he was doing, and deserved respect. This change was augmented by a middle-aged hardening of habit and attitude accompanied by an aversion to conflict that left problems to fester. He could be prodded into action and perform magnificently, but magnificence was no longer his default mode.

A bigger reason for Turner's troubles, however, was the extraordinary nature of the issues that faced Canada in the late 1980s. Cruise missile testing and free trade aroused emotions that trumped the traditional party values of solidarity and loyalty to the leader. Meech Lake had unleashed the fiercest passions of all. In the past, Turner had negotiated solutions by finding common ground on goals and negotiating the means of attaining them. Now he was confronted by issues of principle that invoked fundamental beliefs about the nature of Canada and had profound implications for its future. When he tried to accommodate everyone, he encountered intransigence grounded in moral rectitude, with suspicious observers on both sides interpreting his ministrations to the other side as indecisiveness or, worse, betrayal. "It would be better for Canada if the Meech Lake monster went back and drowned itself in the watery depths from which it should never have raised its hideous head," Trudeau would later write.[42] Despite having been on the opposite side of the issue, in retrospect Turner could sympathize with this sentiment.

Meech Lake was devastating for Turner because the constitutional issues it raised inevitably became entangled with questions of his leadership and Liberal prospects of power. Had Liberals believed that he could return them to office, the Meech fallout could probably have been contained. Trudeau's legacy was still potent because he had given Liberals what they most wanted for a decade and a half. If Turner had delivered the goods in 1984, he would have bonded the party to him. If he had seemed like a winner since then, he would have had less trouble with party factionalism over

Meech and other divisive issues. In a situation in which a party's fortunes depended so much on its leader, and the leader's image depended so much on the camera, Liberals had only to watch television to foresee their future. Turner's misfortunes, concluded one observer, were "the price a bad actor pays for living in an era when style and image count for so much."[43]

21

IMAGE, SUBSTANCE, AND SUBVERSION

The Meech Lake Accord revealed that Turner was not master of his party and almost sank his leadership. For all its deliberate, step-by-step practicality, his comeback plan had left one major factor unaddressed: Could he lead the Liberal Party back into power? He had self-destructed in full view of the voting public during the 1984 election campaign, so the key political question facing him and the party now was whether his image could ever be rehabilitated. If he looked like a winner, there was hope the party would win again. Could he change his media persona and come across well on television? If he managed this minor miracle, would it be enough to overcome voters' memories of 1984?

In the middle of the Meech Lake crisis, Michael Kirby, who styled himself a cold-eyed source of unflinching advice, informed Turner that a big part of his problem was that he did not "project warmth ... appear relaxed, and ... appear emotional on television."[1] Turner was well aware of his challenges in the medium. "It is difficult for me, sometimes, to reduce the complexity of the problems facing Canada into a 30-second clip, into blacks and whites when there are so many shadings," he confessed, "and yet, obviously, one has to do that."[2]

The afterthought betrayed the fact that he had never integrated television into his core operating philosophy. He listened to the advice of his media coach, then got back to what he considered his real job – dealing with political issues. "Perhaps I should perform more as an actor," he admitted. In his heart, however, he thought that Canadians were "entitled to have substance and frankness."³ Nice sentiments, but image *was* substance. In a political culture where the leader's image carried elections, competence in playing the image game was a basic political skill. Power came from the tube. Trudeau had that kind of power; Turner did not.

Turner's attitude was difficult to understand given that he had been following the effect of television on politics for three decades. He had observed the election of 1957, when Diefenbaker had used the medium to his advantage, while St. Laurent came across on television as a tired old man. He had been an active politician in the Pearson and Trudeau years, and witnessed the former's trials before the camera lens and the latter's effective exploitation of it. He had given speeches in the mid-sixties heralding the political changes wrought by television. So he knew, yet he was constitutionally incapable of exploiting his insight by transforming himself into a television personality. He made sporadic attempts to master television, first with Henry Karpus during his leadership run and later with Gabor Apor. After working with Turner, Apor came to the telling conclusion that "television can reinforce an image, but it's not very good at changing one."⁴

Now came yet another media coach, Henry Comor, who had earned the sinister nickname "Dr. Death" through his association with medical television shows. Roughly the same age as Turner, he was calm, erudite, and self-possessed. Turner respected him, and Comor's presence seemed to have a calming effect on him. Studying Turner on tape, Comor discerned that, when he answered a question, he concentrated so hard that he forgot to breathe. Comor also noticed that, in media scrums, Turner always focused intently on his questioner, which came across on camera as a hawkish glare "capable of scaring the bejeepers out of a television audience." He prescribed breathing exercises to get Turner to relax while speaking and worked on moderating his mannerisms to fit "into the frame of the TV box."⁵ Comor coached Turner to treat every media encounter like a relaxed conversation by imagining that the camera was a friend. Television was an intimate medium, he emphasized, and Turner should approach it using the same social skills he displayed in small-group interactions.

By 1988, however, Turner's image had been a problem for so long that he was battling not just an acting challenge but an entire storyline of factionalism under weak leadership in the Liberal Party. Polls consistently showed him trailing his party in popularity, and too many Liberals had concluded that they could never regain power under his leadership. Chrétien would not have challenged Turner's leadership had he not thought it possible that Liberals might oust Turner and bring him in to win the next election. He routinely called his supporters in caucus, fulminated about Turner, and got them worried about losing their seats – unless, of course, he replaced Turner as leader. The media found it more interesting to report on intrigue and insurrection than on Turner's supporters. Media organizations stoked the story by including questions about Turner's leadership qualities in polls. The Liberals' internal politics became a staple of political news, with anonymous sources providing story after story of backroom skulduggery. Turner was trapped in a vicious circle in which his image problems encouraged challenges to his leadership, which in turn further undermined his image.

The most damaging accusation – that he had a drinking problem – did not appear in the newspapers but burbled along underground, insidiously eroding his reputation. The charge was difficult to disprove. Drinking was part of his social life – indeed, part of his working life, in that getting people to sit down together over a couple of drinks had always been one of his negotiating techniques. He came from a "hard-drinking generation," as he put it, whereas the 1980s was a time of increasing cultural preoccupation with health and fitness issues in which habits once accepted, even admired, took on negative moral associations.[6] Mulroney had dealt with this kind of gossip by quitting altogether. Turner, in contrast, still met people around town for drinks and entertained at Stornoway with cocktails and dinner parties where the wine flowed freely. Sometimes, in the judgment of guests, he crossed the wavering, culturally contingent line between acceptable social lubrication and having one too many. Such judgments, however sanctimonious and hypocritical, had social currency.

Those who worked most closely with Turner didn't think that drinking affected his work, but it gave his enemies a potent avenue of attack. A veteran observer of the Ottawa scene later recalled "the rising chorus of whispered accusations of alcohol-induced untrustworthiness."[7] It wasn't just that Turner drank but what he drank. His taste for Scotch and cigars suggested dimly lit private clubs, the old boys' network, and Bay Street, all of which fed into the "yesterday's man" stereotype. John A. Macdonald had once turned his dipsomania to political advantage by declaring, "I know enough of the feeling of this meeting to know that you would rather have John A. Macdonald drunk than George Brown sober."[8] But times had changed. Whatever the physical effects of Turner's drinking on his performance as leader, it sapped his moral authority.

To give the ongoing narrative of "Turner's troubled leadership" some substance beyond mere character assassination, critics added a policy dimension: the Liberal Party did not stand for anything because its leader had no vision. Turner wanted to keep to his comeback plan – to wait for the grassroots policy process to unfold and to hold off until the next election campaign before presenting specifics about his "vision." But when the Liberals rose in the polls, they gained the status of a government-in-waiting, making it impossible to sustain this strategy. And all the while the various factions spoke anonymously to the press, fuelling more stories about Liberals in disarray under indecisive leadership. The "no policy" critique was exacerbated by journalists' tendency to see television as the central forum of national politics, whereas for Turner the House of Commons played that role. He was schooled in a parliamentary tradition that extended back to the beginnings of Canada and centuries earlier in Britain. "I believe in Parliament," he protested. "A lot of the policy vacuum I get accused of is in those debates."[9] No matter: few journalists paid any attention to his speeches in the House. A good example arose during a debate in April 1987 on reinstating capital punishment, abolished since 1976. Mulroney had promised a free vote on the issue, and, although all three party leaders opposed reinstatement, it appeared that a majority of MPs might vote in favour. Turner delivered a powerful speech that convinced three of the five Liberal MPs who had been in favour to change their minds.

"People forget what a compelling orator John Turner can be when he cares deeply about an issue," wrote Carol Goar. "He ... spoke with the eloquence of a man who knows where he stands and the passion of one who wants everybody else to know. It was one of his finest hours."[10] Turner's curse was to be forever forging compromises over complex issues in an ideologically divided caucus. What he needed, Goar believed, was a cause he could call his own, a black-and-white issue that he could really sink his teeth into. If he could find one, perhaps his image problems could be resolved.

The accusation that Turner was incapable of taking clear policy stands continued to be most damaging when it was applied to the Liberals' position on free trade with the United States. Here Turner had been consistent in his public pronouncements: the Liberals preferred multilateral arrangements, saw grave dangers to Canadian sovereignty in a bilateral deal, and doubted that the United States would ever surrender any significant power over its trade relations. Privately, Turner did not think that Mulroney would ever be able to strike a satisfactory deal. He often mentioned a conversation he had had with Senator Lloyd Bentsen, the chairman of the Senate Finance Committee, and three other US senators who had come to Ottawa to meet with the government about the trade deal in December 1986. He had asked Bentsen point-blank whether Congress would ever yield its authority over trade.[11] "Never," the senator replied. If Bentsen were right, and Turner believed he was, Canada could not get the guaranteed access to the US market that was its chief justification for free trade. Publicly, he continued to bide his time, insisting that the Liberals would have to see the terms of the final deal. In the meantime, he continued to criticize the process, focusing on the government's failure to consult with and inform the public about its intentions and the progress of the talks.

Turner reiterated the party's position during a parliamentary debate on free trade in March, but its subtleties and contingencies were lost on the media. Even the relatively simple distinction that he favoured free trade in principle but had grave reservations about the prospects for this particular agreement was ignored by journalists, who accused him of flip-flopping between pro- and anti-free-trade positions. They continually invoked the clash between Donald Johnston and Lloyd Axworthy at the 1985 reform conference in Halifax to illustrate the division in Liberal ranks. Party factionalism was dramatic, their awareness of it showed they were "in the know," and it fit with their established narrative framework of conflict and leadership woes in the Liberal Party.

Not until late 1987 did free trade finally mature into an issue on which Turner could take a definite and dramatic stand. Late that summer, Paul Martin Jr. reported that "Mulroney has completely messed up the trade negotiations."[12] Martin's report was borne out when the prime minister issued a press release on September 23 saying that the talks had been suspended. Turner noted publicly that their failure left Canada worse off than if they had never been proposed. By drawing attention to its trade surplus with the United States, Canada had invited the full wrath of American protectionism.[13]

As it turned out, Canada's withdrawal escalated the issue in Washington, and the White House decided on a last-ditch effort to save the talks. A team of Canadian negotiators travelled to the American capital, obstructions were swept aside, and, on Saturday, October 3, 1987, Mulroney announced that Canada and the United States had reached agreement in principle on a free-trade deal.

Now that an agreement was struck, Turner's training as a lawyer kicked in. He homed in on the terms of the deal. After a weekend poring over whatever reports he could get his hands on, he concluded it was more than a trade deal. It didn't just lower tariffs but included clauses that gave the United States substantial influence over energy, investment, and culture in Canada. Most critically, although the agreement included a dispute resolution mechanism, it was not binding on the US Congress, which retained its authority to set trade policy. That was the point he had quizzed Senator Bentsen on months earlier. His fears were now confirmed by the terms of the negotiated agreement. Mulroney had surrendered Canadian sovereignty for conditional access – he had given up too much for too little.

"The Prime Minister has put Canada up for sale," Turner announced in the House on Monday. He condemned the deal as an "absolute fraud" that failed to exempt Canada from US trade law.[14] Turner's passionate assault wowed his caucus. "A little more of that and he's out of the woods," remarked Brian Tobin.[15] It also stole the issue from the NDP. Turner had found the type of black-and-white issue on which he could let out all the stops.

He continued to attack the deal at public appearances in the weeks that followed. On October 26 he told the House that, if he were prime minister, he would tear up the agreement. The chattering classes fussed at his extreme rhetoric, but it caught the public's attention. When the legal text of the agreement was tabled in the House in early December, Turner challenged Mulroney to call an election on free trade. Mulroney promised only a debate in the House before he and Reagan signed the treaty in January.[16] Turner took a copy of the free-trade agreement home with him for the Christmas holiday. When he returned to Ottawa, it was ragged and dog-eared, with tabs and sticky notes protruding from it.[17] He knew it inside out – and liked it even less than before.

Cynics suggested that he had come down hard on the trade issue to project leadership qualities and distract attention from the Liberals' continuing infighting over Meech Lake. In fact, he was truly appalled by the agreement. As a lawyer with extensive experience in international trade issues, he judged it an unbalanced contract. As a patriot who knew his country's history and was proud of its distinctive character, he was deeply concerned about the treaty's implications for Canadian sovereignty.

Turner soon discovered that his former business associates did not share his sense of altruistic civic stewardship. While on a ski weekend over the holiday period with some of them at Collingwood, on Georgian Bay, he was astounded to learn that they were uniformly in favour of the agreement. The "dollar-a-year" men who had rallied to C.D. Howe in Ottawa during the wartime crisis had been succeeded by a corporate generation with a continental mindset. His Bay Street pals lacked the sense of Canada he had from his upbringing, education, and public service, and were instead bedazzled by the prospect of vast US markets opening before them. On his return to Ottawa, Turner bumped into Axworthy. "Jesus, Lloyd, I have just come back from Collingwood," he exclaimed. "They don't believe in Canada anymore!"[18]

Meanwhile, opposition to free trade was coalescing outside the business community. Churches, farmers' associations, trade unions, aboriginal groups, the women's movement, and ethnic, cultural, and environmental organizations formed anti free-trade alliances and, in April 1987, created a national umbrella organization, the Pro-Canada Network, to lobby against the deal. In addition to Turner's initial criticisms of the specific provisions of the agreement, a "harmonization" critique of free trade developed that highlighted the long-term effects of closer integration of the Canadian and US economies. It argued that the need to compete with US firms would lead Canadian businesses to pressure governments to lower their taxes and deregulate their industries to levels commensurate with those in the United States. This harmonization process would threaten Canada's unique civil society – particularly programs such as medicare – which made it a more compassionate and humane country than the United States.

Turner was able to carry most of the caucus and party with him on free trade. The main exception was Donald Johnston, who now found himself disagreeing with Turner on both critical issues of the day. On January 15 Johnston left caucus to sit as an independent Liberal. Opposing free trade also put Turner at odds with Robert Bourassa. Turner and Garneau travelled to Quebec City for René Lévesque's funeral in early November 1987. While having a coffee in the legislature cafeteria, they were approached by one of Bourassa's aides, who invited them to come to the premier's office nearby. The talk there turned to Meech Lake and free trade. The premier observed that, of the two, Meech was far more critical to Quebec's future. Bourassa had previously intimated that, if Turner backed Meech, he would be rewarded in Quebec when the next election came up. Turner and Garneau left his office with the impression that, in gratitude for federal Liberal support of Meech, Bourassa would at least stay neutral on the trade issue.[19]

They were soon disabused of this belief. When Mulroney went to Montreal to speak at a Chamber of Commerce luncheon on January 29, 1988, Bourassa introduced him and did so in glowing terms. Later the two appeared on a popular lunchtime radio show and lavished praise on each other. Turner had supported Meech Lake at great political cost; now the favour was not being reciprocated. Garneau was embarrassed and humiliated. "I don't like playing the role of happy cuckold," he said on province-wide radio.[20] The prospect of a handsome payoff for supporting Meech – a Liberal comeback in Quebec – had proved a mirage. Clearly, Bourassa had decided he could gain more from Mulroney's pandering to nationalist sentiment than he could from his federal brethren. Clearly, too, Turner had no leverage in Quebec. Years had passed since he held a riding there, and even then he was an anglophone Montrealer on the fringes of French Canadian politics. He had thought he was inheriting insight and influence in the persons of Marc Lalonde and André Ouellet, but their empire had crashed along with other grand Liberal illusions in 1984. He had also pinned his hopes on Garneau, but now it was obvious that his influence counted little against a determined and powerful premier. The only federal Liberal organization with any clout in the province was Jean Chrétien's.

Free trade wasn't the only issue that hurt the Liberals in Quebec. In 1987 the government had introduced Bill C-22 to win support for free trade from US pharmaceutical interests. It gave new drugs ten years of patent protection, effectively reversing the generic-drug legislation Turner had introduced when he was minister of consumer and corporate affairs. The legislation was popular around Montreal because it promised to invigorate the pharmaceutical industry centred there. When the Liberal-dominated Senate repeatedly waylaid the bill, its intransigence sparked great resentment in the province.

In addition, Pierre Trudeau's opposition to Meech Lake left many Quebeckers with the impression that the Liberals opposed the deal. On March 30 Trudeau made another appearance on Parliament Hill to denounce the accord. He told the Senate Committee on Meech Lake that it "should be put in the dustbin."[21] The provinces would always be back for more, he declared. Trudeau's certainty and eloquence fed growing opposition to the accord in English Canada while increasing anxiety about its fate in Quebec and further undermining the federal party's prospects there.

Bourassa's public support for Mulroney weakened Garneau's position in struggles for control of the Quebec wing of the party. Garneau was increasingly at odds with Senator Pietro Rizzuto, who headed the federal Liberals' election commission in Quebec, the body responsible for recruiting candidates and supporting campaign organizing in the ridings. Rizzuto, who came to Canada from Italy at the age of twenty and built a lucrative paving business in Montreal, had raised millions for the party. He wanted Garneau to play a figurehead role while he took care of business behind the scenes. In 1987, when Rizzuto made a bid to control fundraising at the riding level, Garneau blocked it because he was worried about the ethical implications of putting both fundraising and control over nominations in the same hands. Turner backed Garneau. In July that year, he made Garneau his Quebec lieutenant and appointed him to replace Rizzuto as head of the provincial electoral commission. He tried to promote Rizzuto out of the picture by naming him co-chairman of the National Election Readiness Committee, but the senator did not give up so easily. Rizzuto regularly entertained party officials and politicians at his resort properties in Mexico. At New Year's, he invited several senior Liberals to one of his new hotels near Puerto Vallarta, hoping to influence those who could help him in his continuing struggle with Garneau. These ongoing intrigues did not bode well for the party's electoral prospects in a province that had always been essential to its federal success.

Turner wasn't oblivious to the party's problems in Quebec, but they were just one concern among many that vied for his attention as he prepared for the election that had to come within the next few months. After Douglas Richardson's departure in August, he needed a new chief of staff. A search committee – headed by Herb Gray to appease ongoing caucus complaints about Turner's office – hired Peter Connolly, the son of Liberal senator John Connolly. Now forty-five, Connolly had served as chief of staff to seven ministers, including Gray, and was most recently an executive at Lavalin, the Montreal engineering firm. He differed from Swift and Richardson in that he was an Ottawa political operator who came with off-the-shelf knowledge of how the town and the party worked. Doug Kirkpatrick, another former Gray aide who also had experience at Queen's Park, was brought on board as Connolly's assistant, journalist Ray Heard became the new communications director, and John Webster, one of the leading Friends of Turner, was appointed campaign director for the next federal election.[22]

Connolly was surprised to find that Turner had an open-door policy and was accessible to anyone at any time. In the interest of efficiency, and to free up time for Turner to concentrate on preparing for the coming campaign, he instituted more structure and protocols. Staff were instructed to schedule appointments, disclose the reason for them so Turner could be prepared, and follow up if any commitments were made.[23] Unfortunately, MPs and party officials who formerly came freely now felt they were being shut out. "It was as if an Iron Curtain had been thrown up around his office," whined one MP.[24]

Turner's comeback plan had always called for production of a party platform when an election loomed in year four. He now directed the platform committee to review the resolutions from the national policy development process and begin preparing policy positions. Candidate recruitment was going slowly, but experience suggested it would improve as the election neared. The grassroots democratic revitalization that Turner had encouraged had taken hold in many constituencies. In urban ridings with large populations of recent immigrants, leaders of ethnocultural communities were able to sign up new Liberals in numbers sufficient to determine nominations. Chaotic confrontations at nomination meetings appeared on the evening news. Turner thought they demonstrated the vitality and openness of the party he had rebuilt. Inevitably, however, some journalists saw them as further evidence that the Liberals were in chaos under his leadership. They also discouraged some establishment candidates who were leery of investing time and money in pursuit of a nomination that might be snatched from them at the last moment.

Besides policy and candidates, the other key ingredient for an election campaign was money. Gerry Schwartz was successfully harvesting corporate donations despite predictions that the party's stance on free trade would dry up business sources. However, other types of fundraising were disappointing. The revenue-splitting deal orchestrated by Judd Buchanan a year earlier had the unintended consequence of leaving the provincial wings of the party without much incentive to fundraise. The direct mail operation was more than paying its way but was not yet as lucrative as that of other parties. Overall, the Liberals were raising more money than ever before, but they were also spending more. Getting the new national office up and running had been costly, as were the party renewal and policy development exercises. The party was almost $7.0 million in debt and owed $4.2 million to its banks, which now refused to lend it any more money. These financial woes were well publicized in the press and, not surprisingly, presented as further evidence of problems with Turner's leadership.

When the party's finances became news, the usual anonymous sources circulated accusations that Turner was spending party funds unethically. The main piece of evidence was a Toronto apartment the party rented for the Turners at a cost of $33,000 a year. It provided a home base for Geills Turner, and it also served as a *pied-à-terre* for Turner. Since he was often in Toronto for family reasons and party business, part of the cost could be justified by savings on hotel bills. Other accusations cropped up, including free clothes for Turner (the suits his media consultant bought to tweak his image), a maid for the apartment (it had none), and luxurious furnishings and accessories for Stornoway (a long story, but Turner had followed government rules). All were exaggerated.

Turner's character was further impugned when he was accused on national television of having a drinking problem. On CTV's *Question Period* of January 17, 1988, host Pamela Wallin commented, "There have been suggestions, I guess, is the best way to put it ... that you have, or potentially have, a drinking problem."[25] The mere fact that the question was posed was damning. "Yeah, I like a good party, and I've had some fun over the years," Turner replied, "but I have never allowed any pleasure or distraction to interfere with doing the job."[26] The press debated whether such a question were fair ball, but the public was left with another nagging doubt about Turner. The accusation stuck in his craw. "I tell you I didn't like some of that stuff over the last few years," he would later remark to a reporter. "Do I have a drinking problem? What the hell. Have you ever seen me not perform?"[27]

Once again Chrétien took advantage of Turner's misfortune to further his own interests. "People want to vote for the Liberals, but they don't want to vote for Turner," he confided publicly.[28] In mid-April, Carol Goar reported in the *Toronto Star* that a new leadership plot was hatching based on the calculation that, "if the Liberals get rid of Turner and plug in a popular new leader, just before the election, they might win a majority."[29] A couple of weeks earlier, at an Ontario Liberal conference in Windsor, Turner had sparkled, onstage and off, but his performance was undercut by a letter slipped under delegates' doors that ran him down, portraying him as a loser and calling for his resignation. Goar identified the principal agitators as Keith Davey, former Trudeau aide and Chrétien leadership supporter Dennis Mills, and former Trudeau Cabinet minister and leadership candidate John Roberts. Mills and Roberts denied any involvement.

As if he did not have enough afflictions, that winter Turner began to suffer back problems. Identifying the cause took some time, but eventually doctors concluded that bone was growing into the nerves in his spinal cord. The pain was severe. The capstone to what had been a difficult year came with the death of his mother, Phyllis Ross, at the age of eighty-five on April 18. Turner flew to Vancouver with his sister and their families to attend her funeral on Wednesday, April 20.

While he was gone, treachery was afoot in Ottawa. The Senate had recently sent the Meech legislation back to the Commons, with amendments, resurrecting that divisive issue once again. Liberal MPs had been shaken by the revelation of the party's financial distress and its spending on quasi-personal expenses for the leader. Even more unsettling were new polls showing the Liberals neck and neck with the other two major parties. As usual, the Angus Reid results were the worst: according to his numbers, the Liberals had fallen to 30 per cent support, and their two rival parties were tied with 34 per cent. The leadership crisis of the previous August had followed polls showing the NDP ahead, and now that doomsday scenario was resurrected.

Chrétien supporters decided that this moment was their last best chance to unseat Turner and have their man installed as leader before the next election. They circulated a letter among members of caucus that fretted about the party's debt, criticized Turner's support for Meech Lake, questioned his ability to win the election, and concluded that he should step down from the leadership. When MPs were approached to sign the letter, the recent accusations about Turner's personal profligacy with party funds were highlighted. Many were told that he was on the brink of resigning and needed only a gentle push to help him on his way. The plan was to confront him with the letters at the caucus meeting on Wednesday, April 27. He would then presumably acquiesce and trundle off into the sunset.

Soon there was a sheaf of twenty-two signed letters. "I knew I could be seen as a traitor," explained MP Sergio Marchi, "but I was convinced deep down that, if John was to step aside, the party would be saved and we would be able to turn the country around. Meech Lake was my reason."[30] On Monday, April 25, at 5:00 p.m., Brian Tobin, the Liberal caucus chair, heard rumours of a plot. He tipped off Turner, who called his aides to Stornoway. Fed up and humiliated, Turner was at first prepared to throw in the towel. "How can I go on?" he asked.[31] But the more they discussed it, the more he became convinced he should fight back. He was, after all, the democratically elected and reaffirmed leader of the party. If a clutch of MPs were arrogated the power to topple him, how would any leader be able to control caucus in the future? Senator Pietro Rizzuto was in possession of the letters. Brian Tobin and Doug Kirkpatrick tracked him down in his suite at the Château Laurier late that night and told him the plot was exposed. Many of the letter signers were roused in the wee hours of the morning and asked blunt questions. Caught off guard and confronted individually, most backpedalled.

The counter-insurgency action continued next day. Turner's office leaked news of the coup attempt, which had the intended effect of sending signatories scurrying for cover. Then his staff and caucus supporters hit the phones, talking to the dissidents and managing opinion elsewhere in party circles. Turner met Rizzuto and told him categorically that he was not going to resign. At 3:00 p.m. party president Michel Robert arrived at Turner's office and publicly announced his support for him.[32]

When Turner faced caucus that Wednesday, the stakes were high. If just a few of his MPs quit the party, Ed Broadbent could end up as leader of the opposition going into the next election. Throughout the morning, members vented their grievances. Turner was criticized harshly but stood his ground and made it clear he was not stepping down. After lunch they would have to adjourn for Question Period, following which Turner had a speaking engagement. Before the break, therefore, Brian Tobin, the caucus chairman, suggested that they put the whole affair behind them. Turner refused, insisting that they carry on as soon as he returned that afternoon. The interlude broke the critics' momentum and gave Turner time to consider his counterattack. When they reconvened, he reminded the caucus that it didn't elect the leader, the party did, and that he had won the leadership at an open party convention and been endorsed decisively at a subsequent convention. Prospects for forming the next government had never been better. If caucus members had complaints, they should discuss them openly with him rather than conducting themselves like army colonels in a banana republic. Turner concluded by inviting his MPs to come and see him privately if they had any issues.

He met one-on-one with a few of the rebels the next day. Some apologized, believing now that they had been manipulated in the service of someone else's leadership ambitions. Turner then met with members of the press and assured them he would remain as leader. In an interview on CBC-TV with Peter Mansbridge, he claimed that the conspiracy originated outside of caucus and reflected continuing resistance to change in the direction of the Liberal Party as well as the inability of certain people in the party to accept his leadership, despite the democratic verdicts of the leadership campaign and review.[33]

The caucus revolt prompted sympathetic insurgencies in a number of Quebec riding associations. Garneau called a meeting of riding association presidents and asked for a show of support for Turner's leadership, but the response was embarrassingly tepid. Then ten Quebec riding presidents announced that they thought Turner should step down. Another five were in agreement, Pierre Dalphond, a vice-president of the Quebec wing, told the media. Most represented ridings in the Chrétien camp. Elsewhere,

Liberals rallied to Turner's defence. Provincial wings unanimously declared their support for his leadership. Ontario premier David Peterson called the dissidents "politically stupid" for perpetuating the image of a divided party.[34] Liberal premiers Joe Ghiz of PEI and Frank McKenna of New Brunswick made statements supporting Turner. Even Robert Bourassa spoke out on his behalf. Meech Lake was now under assault in English Canada, and he had no wish to see Jean Chrétien, an opponent of the accord, succeed Turner. Better too that Turner should stay on and lose the next election – and so ensure that free trade would be passed.

Turner was hurt by the disloyalty and puzzled by the sheer stupidity of reigniting party infighting during the run-up to an election. Going into a campaign with people he couldn't trust was impossible, so he ditched Rizzuto from his position as national campaign co-chairman.[35] A few days later he relieved Michel Robert of his job as the party's chief financial officer, though he remained in his elected position as party president.

The uprising, like the one the summer before, showed just how dysfunctional Turner's relationship with caucus had become. The continual spouting of leaks and cutting press commentary based on anonymous sources had inculcated a siege mentality in him and his office, which in turn only exacerbated the complaints of the malcontents. More recently, caucus members – Turner supporters included – felt they had been shut out by Connolly's tighter management. In truth, Turner had become frustrated, concluding that caucus would continue to be a problem as long as the party was out of power. Instead of wading back in and grappling with the issues and the personalities, he had elected to try to float along above it all. His comeback plan involved biding his time patiently, waiting until the next election. That was when he would assert his leadership and take the party back to the promised land, leaving all the dissension and bickering behind. As it turned out, this was a miscalculation. He had no reason to expect an outright caucus mutiny – there was no precedent for it in his lifelong experience in the party. Yet treason flowered. It probably could have been prevented had he made more of an effort. The caucus might be "undisciplined and largely incompetent," but his disregard of the danger it posed had once again gravely damaged his leadership and the party's electoral prospects.[36]

A friend phoned Turner at Stornoway one night in early May to find him alone, working on his speech for the upcoming press gallery dinner, busily spinning his leadership travails into comedy. When it was his turn to speak at the dinner, he walked to the podium pouring himself a glass of milk. "I promised my caucus I'd only take one drink a day," he said. "This is the one for July 12, 1996." This was just the first of a series of self-deprecating one-liners. "The latest poll shows sixty per cent of Canadians think the Liberals will win the next election," he said, pausing for effect. "The other 40 per cent are Liberals." Mulroney, he continued, had promised patronage jobs to his steadfast and loyal supporters. He, John Turner, could never do that – he had no steadfast and loyal supporters. "Why are so many people after my job?" he asked in conclusion. "Because it's tough to find subsidized housing in Toronto."[37] These remarks brought down the house.

On a tour of the Maritimes the following month, Turner found that his support among the party rank and file was firm. He was greeted by endorsements from local politicians and supporters with placards reading "We don't backstab our leader." He continued to make light of the coup attempt. The day after the next election, he told one audience, the headline would read, "Turner wins majority. Caucus demands recount."[38]

Yet his trials were far from over. Ottawa insiders knew that Greg Weston, a journalist for the *Ottawa Citizen,* was working on a behind-the-scenes exposé of Turner's leadership. Weston had interviewed Bill Lee, former Turner executive assistant Stuart Langford, and other disgruntled Liberals. Published in early September, *Reign of Error* was a damning portrait of a Turner by turns incompetent and tyrannical, bumbling and bumptious. It described temper tantrums by the leader in his office, related unflattering anecdotes about his wife, Geills, and revealed that Turner supporters had set up a trust fund to pay for his children's education when he ran for the leadership. Excerpted in newspapers across the country, it generated a procession of unflattering headlines.

One reviewer's assessment was succinct: "Some of it is old news. Some of it is petty ... Some of it comes from former associates of Turner with axes to grind. Some of it is subject to varying interpretation."[39] The Turner forces did what they could to minimize the damage, but *Reign of Error* sold well and kept doubts about Turner's leadership qualities in circulation. Yet when Mike Duffy asked Turner how he felt about the book, he refused the invitation to wallow in self-pity. "What are you anyway, Duffy, some kinda' half-assed pop-psychologist?" he joked.[40]

The Weston book was just the latest in a long series of blows to Turner's reputation. He had tried repeatedly over the previous four years to rehabilitate his image, yet whenever he seemed to make progress, he was upstaged by Chrétien, blindsided by a revelatory book, a divisive issue, or a coup attempt. This time, however, things were different. An election was imminent, and he no longer had to stick to the incremental approach of his comeback plan. He had survived one of the roughest rides ever experienced by a Canadian opposition leader. The final test lay ahead. In his opposition to the Mulroney trade deal, he had a cause he believed in. Canadians were about to tune in to a different John Turner.

22

MAD DOG AND BUSINESSMEN

O n May 24, 1988, International Trade Minister John Crosbie tabled legislation ratifying the Canada-US Free Trade Agreement in the House of Commons. It was only a matter of time before the Conservative majority passed the bill. Turner was increasingly frustrated by this prospect. He knew he was right about the deficiencies in the deal and felt that, if he could get through to Canadians, they would agree with him. But he could not attract the public's attention.

One evening in early May, as he returned to Ottawa after delivering a speech, Turner bounced an idea off Peter Connolly, his principal secretary. What if he instructed the Liberal majority in the Senate to block the deal until the government called an election on the issue? Connolly thought it might work, so Turner asked the Liberal strategy committee, chaired by Senator Michael Kirby, to consider it. The committee endorsed the proposal while underlining the risk that the Conservatives might make the Senate's abuse of its power, rather than free trade, the election issue. The Liberals would have to stress the rationale for the Senate embargo: the Mulroney government had not included free trade in its platform during the previous election, and the issue was too important to the future of the country to be adopted without a mandate from the Canadian public.[1]

An election seemed imminent because the Tories were in pre-campaign mode. Mulroney was making high-profile trips around the country. He hosted a G7 Summit meeting in Toronto in June and visited Washington. Official visits from Ronald Reagan and Margaret Thatcher were calculated to make him look statesmanlike. Thatcher gave a speech to the House of Commons that applauded free trade and warned of the dangers of squelching the deal. Turner was appalled at her meddling in the internal politics of a foreign country. "We are no longer a colony of Great Britain," he pointed out, "and we do not want to become a colony of the United States."[2]

On June 20 the House voted to extend its summer sitting to allow the completion of the debate on free trade. As the issue once again dominated the headlines, John Crosbie, who had succeeded Pat Carney as minister of international trade at the end of March, was asked by reporters if he had read the agreement. He didn't have to read it, he explained, because the trade experts in his department had summarized and interpreted it for him. Turner couldn't believe what he was hearing. He thought it outrageous that a responsible minister of the Crown would not be master of his own brief, especially on such a critical file.

Turner continued to discuss the pros and cons of the Senate gambit with his advisers. They decided to take a sounding of public opinion. A poll published on May 28 had shown that 64 per cent of Canadians favoured an election on the free-trade issue. The Liberals commissioned Martin Goldfarb to conduct two more polls. One probed Canadians' attitudes toward current issues and a possible election. The other targeted Quebec, where support for the deal was highest. Respondents were asked whether an election on free trade should be held before it was passed and whether the Senate should block the bill to this end. The results indicated that two-thirds of Quebeckers looked favourably on having an election over the trade deal. A surprising number of those who supported the deal did not object to an election being called over it.

Turner saw the results of Goldfarb's polling on Tuesday, July 19. He convened a meeting at Stornoway to clear the plan with representatives of the party and caucus that evening. The next morning he explained it to caucus, then headed across the street for a news conference in the National Press Building at 150 Wellington Street. With the cameras rolling, he announced his resolve to have the Senate block the free-trade bill – and his democratic rationale for doing so. "Let the people decide," he concluded.[3]

The gamble paid off. The press applauded it as a masterful political stroke. Pundits agreed that it signalled principles and showed decisive leadership, easing Turner's enduring image problems. It also ensured that Turner, not

NDP leader Ed Broadbent, would be seen to lead the charge against free trade. Above all, it was a popular move, just as the Liberals' polling had predicted. In late August a Gallup poll showed that 52 per cent of Canadians thought he had done the right thing.[4] The manoeuvre dominated headlines and open-line radio shows in the days that followed. For the moment at least, Turner had captured the public's attention and put the government on the spot.

In an attempt to offer Quebeckers a free-trade alternative to the Mulroney deal, Turner devised a plan combining multilateral and bilateral sectoral trade initiatives and pitched it to Bourassa. But his peace overture was sabotaged by a subsidiary issue. In an attempt to show how the free-trade deal opened up Canadian financial practices to trade sanctions, Turner had suggested that it could jeopardize the Quebec stock savings plan. This popular provincial program allowed high-income earners to reduce their tax burden by investing in Quebec companies, thereby stimulating investment in the province. After a meeting with Mulroney, Bourassa assailed Turner's credibility by telling reporters that the Liberal leader was wrong. Turner responded that his comment was based on an interpretation of the agreement written for the White House. When Turner showed him the relevant passage, Bourassa muttered "merde" and agreed to appear at a press conference on August 16 to make a show of party unity. This was a strained affair because Bourassa was unwilling to stick his neck out too far for Turner. When asked about his relationship with Bourassa, Turner tried to dispel the tension by saying, "I don't know how I could get any closer to the premier without being indecent."[5] But the joke rang hollow.

The Lac St-Jean by-election earlier that summer had provided a better idea of what really moved Bourassa. The Conservative candidate was Lucien Bouchard, a law school chum of Mulroney who catered to the nationalist vote. Raymond Garneau and his campaign committee had a solid contingent of provincial Liberals at work in the riding, and their candidate was leading in the polls. Then Mulroney phoned Bourassa, told him that Bouchard would be a strong voice for Quebec in Ottawa, and mentioned, in passing, the benefits Quebec garnered from their relationship. Suddenly, half the Liberals working on the constituency campaign resigned, and Bouchard, in due course, was elected.

Anticipating an election call, Liberal strategists began to plan the main thrust of their campaign. Conventional wisdom holds that elections are lost and not won, which means that focusing a campaign on the shortcomings of the other guy is the best strategy. To this end, Goldfarb recommended making Brian Mulroney's trustworthiness the main issue of the campaign. Free trade would then become just one of many avenues of attack on Mulroney, along with his government's chequered record of patronage, scandal, and cozying up to the Yankees. No one wanted to make an issue of Meech Lake. Although opposition to it was growing, the three major parties all supported it, so raising it would risk unleashing demons with little electoral advantage to be gained. Turner could see the logic of the campaign strategy recommended by his advisers, but he had always been uncomfortable with personal attacks. Moreover, he knew from his contact with Canadians around the country that the trade issue could elicit a strong response.[6] He went along with the advisers for the time being, but he wasn't convinced.

The electoral brain trust also had to decide what to do with the forty-point platform that was the end result of the party's long policy process. Doug Kirkpatrick argued that it should be held in reserve. He thought that some policies needed to be thought through and costed more thoroughly. Strategically, he contended, it would be better to continue hammering away at the free-trade deal. Once Turner established his credibility on that central issue, they could roll out their policies to show he also had a constructive and credible platform. Kirby and Goldfarb, in contrast, thought they needed to announce the platform early and in its entirety in order to rebut the long-standing criticism that the Liberal Party had no vision. They won out. It was decided to release the platform in September whether or not an election was called.[7] Kirby and Goldfarb also pushed for adoption of a policy that would allow abortion up to the twenty-second week of pregnancy. Goldfarb's polling showed that this position would be popular among young urban women, whose votes could make the difference in many swing ridings. This proposal, however, was rejected. The Conservatives' response to Turner's Senate gambit was to delay calling the election until the fuss died down. After the free-trade bill passed the Commons, they tried to distract the public with a series of announcements of new government initiatives in other areas. A wide-ranging poll commissioned by the government with taxpayers' money gave an idea of what kind of pre-election goodies to offer. It indicated, for example, that the public was concerned about the environment, so Mulroney announced cleanups of Halifax harbour and the St. Lawrence River. The Tories' standing in the polls began to climb.

In late September the Conservatives decided that free trade had faded sufficiently in public consciousness that calling an election would be safe. They planned to present free trade during their campaign as just one of a range of Tory policies aimed at promoting economic growth. Criticisms of the deal would be dismissed as fear-mongering or, as John Crosbie put it in a speech to his riding association, "alarmist reasoning" from "CBC-type snivellers ... the self-appointed fakirs and philosophers of Hogtown."[8] The Conservative strategists planned to have the election turn on leadership, calculating that Mulroney would have a clear advantage on this ground.

On October 1 Mulroney called on Governor General Jeanne Sauvé and asked her to dissolve Parliament. Election day would be November 21, seven and a half weeks away. The Tories immediately rolled out more promises based on their reading of government polling data. Ed Broadbent arrogantly told the press that the campaign would confirm the death of the Liberal Party, leaving a refreshingly simple partisan landscape of Tories versus the NDP. If this pronouncement had any effect, it was to drive hesitant Liberals back to their party, just as NDP supporters, responding to Turner's position on free trade, began to contemplate the heresy of voting Liberal. Turner's opening salvo focused squarely on the trade deal. "For two months, I have been asking the Prime Minister to let the people decide; today he finally agreed," he told reporters. "The Liberal party is ready, our people are in place, we're set to go."[9] Thomas Walkom, one of the journalists who had been so cynical about Turner in 1984, was impressed by his sincerity, concluding, "He has found his issue."[10]

Turner embarked on his leader's tour, which promptly went awry in a fashion that recalled the 1984 campaign. On October 5 he arrived in Montreal to unveil a daycare policy that would create 400,000 new spaces for preschoolers. This measure was already outlined in the forty-point Liberal platform. The Montreal event was intended to flesh out details and publicize it. The announcement itself went smoothly until journalists began to question Turner and his retinue about the policy's cost. Poor communications between Turner's office and Lucie Pépin, the caucus lead on the issue, had left this salient point unspecified. Turner said it would cost $4 billion, Raymond Garneau said that it would be less, and Peter Connolly estimated $8-10 billion. Each pronouncement was captured on camera and edited into a comedic collage for the evening news. Three days later, after the media had a field day lampooning the Liberals' confusion, Turner called a press conference to announce that the cost of the 400,000 spaces would top $10.1 billion over seven years.

The media concluded that the Liberals, and their leader, continued to be inept. When the Liberals subsequently presented their other policy planks, they made little impression. All the painstaking policy work of the previous months seemed to have been for naught. Connolly took responsibility for the daycare botch-up to shield Turner, then further discredited himself by swearing at a reporter in the bar of Toronto's Royal York Hotel a few days later. Soon the rumour mill was saying that he would be replaced, again reviving memories of 1984, when Turner had switched his campaign chair in midstream.

Another knife blade sank into Turner's back on October 13, when Martin Goldfarb, the Trudeau pollster he had inherited, and Tom Axworthy, the former Trudeau aide, published *Marching to a Different Drummer: An Essay on the Liberals and Conservatives in Convention*. Equating the Liberal Party with the policies of Trudeau, the book made ominous predictions of its imminent demise under misguided leadership. Turner's support for Meech Lake "repudiated his party's intrinsic heritage," Goldfarb and Axworthy wrote. Why he did so "remains a mystery."[11] Moreover, Turner was a right winger who had abandoned the natural Liberal constituency of the poor, immigrants, women, and labour. The book's contents and its timing seemed yet another deliberate attempt to undermine Turner. Here was Goldfarb, the Liberals' pollster, publicly criticizing the party leader. A Goldfarb employee, Senator Michael Kirby, held a key position in the Liberal election campaign. In press interviews, Goldfarb and Axworthy said they had written the book a year earlier and that Turner had since redeemed himself by endorsing different policies. But why publish outdated criticisms in the middle of an election campaign? In any event, the damage was done. The incessant leadership gossip, sustained by the abortive August putsch, the

April coup attempt, and Greg Weston's *Reign of Error,* was reinvigorated. Turner's leadership, it seemed, was one damned mutiny after another.

Meanwhile, the Conservative campaign had begun its mechanized mobile assault on the nation. A carefully orchestrated exercise modelled on recent American presidential campaigns, it focused on staging positive images of the candidate for the television news. Tory tour coordinators with fat event-staging manuals fanned out across the land, scouting for appropriate backdrops and camera angles. The crowds who came to see Mulroney, and the journalists who followed him, were kept penned behind plastic chains at a safe distance from the leader. The media were fed selected sound bites and artfully arranged photo opportunities. At one such photo op in rural Saskatchewan, the crowd consisted of just a few curious locals. The control barrier came out regardless, looking quite incongruous on the open prairie. Once positioned for the cameras, Mulroney mouthed unctuous pieties about leadership. Everything was under control.

Turner, in contrast, had no choice but to run a go-for-broke campaign. Henry Comor had introduced him to the wireless microphone, which allowed him to walk about onstage instead of standing at a podium. That helped expend some of his nervous energy while adding a bit of show-biz razzmatazz to his appearances. Using their knowledge of their boss's strengths, his team put him in situations where they knew he performed well. But Turner was also far more comfortable than he had been in the previous campaign. He held press conferences almost daily to announce policies and answer questions. He mixed with journalists informally. He did open-line talk shows, waded into press scrums, and left himself exposed to chance encounters. This was open-field running, and he proved sure on his feet. Part of the credit for his performance was due to his belief in his mission. On free trade Turner was confident, sincere, and passionate – all qualities that played well on television.

Unfortunately, most journalists continued to report on the old John Turner. They had previously lambasted him for having no policies, but having a platform now did him little good. Television was, of course, notoriously poor at communicating the complexities of policy. Although Turner was being enthusiastically received at his campaign stops, his strong performance on the hustings was not making it onto the nightly news. The "bumbling leader" storyline still framed media reports. On October 12, for instance, he delivered a speech in Toronto. "He's limping! He's limping! Shoot that!" a television producer exclaimed as Turner tried to manage his back pain en route to the podium.[12] Ignoring this interjection, Turner proceeded to deliver a fiery, passionate speech against free trade to an audience of business people who favoured the deal. *CBC News* ran a clip of a point in the speech where he misspoke the word "birthright," making it sound like "birth rate."

Voters who had seen Turner on the campaign trail were angered by the way the media portrayed him. "I think it would be nice if the press started treating him like an honourable man instead of a bloody criminal," declared a woman in Thunder Bay who had just attended a Turner event. "The media certainly go on about his troubles in the party," said another. "He's not an actor like Mulroney," observed a Vancouver man. "I honestly think the news media have a lot to do with Turner's lack of popularity."[13] The Conservative campaign was also picking up on the gap between Turner's image and his performance. When it asked focus groups to rate the party leaders on nineteen leadership attributes, Turner initially scored the lowest by far. But after watching clips of him in recent campaign appearances, the participants became confused. The Turner they saw wasn't the Turner they remembered. Liberal strategists hoped that something would happen to make everyone take a second look.

One night, after a long day on the campaign trail in New Brunswick, journalist Graham Fraser asked Turner to elaborate on his opposition to free trade. Turner outlined his concerns about the deal and contextualized them within the history of Canada's trade policy and its struggles for national autonomy. "Was he getting frustrated trying to get his message across?" Fraser asked. Should he shift gears and look for something that might resonate more with the voters? "We're talking Canada here," Turner replied. "If people are fed up with talking Canada, then I will have fought the last Hurrah. But I will be able to look myself in the mirror for the rest of my life. I mean, there hasn't been a more important issue in terms of the direction of Canada since the war."[14] One of the problems in discussing the free-trade deal, he continued, was that the agreement was complex, and voters needed a basic knowledge of trade policy to understand his objections to it. Yet he had only a few seconds of air time to get his message across on television. He was still trying to hone his arguments and find the right catchphrases to convey them. "I've been accused of going at this issue too legally for the last year and a half, but I have done that deliberately to try to keep it on a rational basis," he explained. "What I will be doing now is converting it into more human, everyday terms with examples of how it will affect people."[15]

Turner was discovering that, if he cast his free-trade message in patriotic terms, saying that it spelled the end of Canada's independence, he got a response. If such a broad caricature were required, then so be it. Why should Canadians need to know the details of trade policy? They wanted their politicians to do the analysis and present them with the choices in the simplest terms. He began to find ways to convey his message. "It's not a trade deal – it's the 'Sale of Canada Act,'" he declared.[16] He would then elaborate:

> I will not let Brian Mulroney sell out our sovereignty. I will not let this great nation surrender its birthright. I will not let Brian Mulroney destroy a 120-year-old dream called Canada, and neither will Canadians ... I believe that on election day, November 21st, Canadians will understand that a vote for the Liberal Party is a vote for a stronger, fairer, more in-dependent and more sovereign Canada. I believe that Canadians are not going to vote for Brian Mulroney, a man who would be governor of a 51st state. They are going to vote for John Turner, a man who wants to be Prime Minister of Canada.[17]

During the previous free-trade elections of 1891 and 1911, opposition had been framed in just this way. Now Canadians would address the question again. Would their answer change?

It appeared so. An Environics poll conducted during the first week of the campaign and released on October 12 showed the Tories at 42 per cent, the NDP at 29 per cent, and the Liberals trailing with 25 per cent. As for the best leader, 40 per cent liked Mulroney, 29 per cent chose Broadbent, and only 15 per cent preferred Turner. The Liberals couldn't afford national polling, but they were tracking twelve bellwether ridings. Results in early October showed them behind in all but one, where they clung to a tenuous 1 per cent lead. If this situation prevailed, they would end up in third place with a dozen fewer seats than they currently held. The "strange death" of the Canadian Liberal Party once again seemed imminent. The Liberals' situation was depressing and still deteriorating, with a subsequent Gallup poll putting Turner's approval rating at 8 per cent.

As head of the party's strategy committee, Michael Kirby received the polling data in Ottawa, analyzed it, and passed it on to Turner with his commentary on his leader's tour. The committee, which also included Senator Al Graham and André Ouellet (the national campaign co-chairs), John Webster (the campaign director), and Michael Robinson (a lobbyist who was the party's director of finance), was rattled by this latest news. The prospect of losing again was, for all good Liberals, unthinkable. Either delusions of grandeur or a hyperactive but misguided sense of responsibility led them, with Kirby chairing, to discuss the possibility of switching leaders in mid-campaign.[18]

Ouellet hand delivered to Stornoway a memorandum from the committee, which Turner found waiting on his return to Ottawa on Friday, October 14. It began by saying that the poll numbers were bad, Turner's health was poor, and the campaign was not gaining momentum. Then it laid out a number of options. Without saying so specifically, it led to the obvious conclusion that Turner should quit.[19] He was astounded. He was confident that his bad luck couldn't last and that his message would eventually break through to the Canadian public. Besides, whoever thought the Liberals could replace their leader – even with the ever-popular Jean Chrétien – and win the election was dreaming. They would look like a clutch of mercenaries led by an opportunistic assassin with blood on his hands.

The same discussion occurred among other senior Liberals. Turner's friend Richard Alway began to receive "discreet" phone calls inquiring whether Turner would step down.[20] Ouellet buttonholed Connolly at a meeting in Ottawa on Saturday, October 15, to make the case. Kirby and Goldfarb took Kirkpatrick aside to deliver the same message. Connolly didn't know whether Ouellet was speaking for himself or for the committee and thought it best not to ask. From his perspective, Turner was doing quite well – they need only be patient and wait for Canadians to recognize it. He told Turner about the discussion. Ouellet later phoned Turner to talk about the polls but never broached the notion of a leadership change. Turner didn't help him out by saying that he knew what he was thinking. If another mutiny were in the works, he would not pre-approve it.[21]

That Sunday evening, Al Graham flew to Quebec City, where Turner was campaigning. Turner's aides thought he had been sent to deliver the message that Turner should step down but couldn't bring himself to go through with it. What he did say was that Chrétien should be more involved with the campaign. Everyone knew that the Chrétien forces had been dragging their heels, realizing that a victory would put the leadership beyond his reach for years. Turner nevertheless said that if Chrétien were willing to take the party line on Meech Lake and free trade, he was welcome to campaign. No such participation was forthcoming.

In the midst of all the rumours about leadership change came another campaign gaffe. On Monday, October 17, the *Toronto Star* published a story claiming that Turner would soon unveil the abortion policy that Kirby and Goldfarb had recommended unsuccessfully at the start of the campaign. Abortion had resurfaced on the political agenda the previous January. Dr. Henry Morgentaler, who ran an abortion clinic in Toronto, had been acquitted in the Ontario courts on charges of performing illegal abortions. The Supreme Court was asked to rule on the constitutionality of the abortion law, and in a majority ruling in January 1988 struck down the law Turner had introduced in 1969 on the grounds that restrictions on abortion violated the Charter of Rights. Turner held that the Liberals supported the Supreme Court judgment because they supported the Charter of Rights. The government promised to fill the legal vacuum and, in July, introduced a three-part proposal in the House to make abortion relatively accessible in the early stages of pregnancy and more difficult in the later stages. The motion and the amendments were defeated, leaving Canada with a de facto policy of abortion on demand. On September 2 Mulroney said he would wait for a Supreme Court decision on the constitutional rights of the unborn before moving ahead. That response effectively shelved the issue until after the election.

The abortion issue nevertheless remained highly volatile. At a Liberal rally in Vancouver Quadra, pro-choice and anti-abortion forces converged and derailed proceedings, jostling and yelling at each other with naked hostility. Stephen Hastings, the chief Turner aide on the scene, grew gravely concerned about Turner's personal safety.[22] Small wonder, then, that Liberal candidates were dumbfounded to hear through the *Toronto Star* that their party had announced a controversial new position on the issue. For those running in socially conservative ridings, it represented a serious threat to re-election. Peter Connolly was named as the source of the *Toronto Star* article, but although he had chatted with a number of reporters about campaign strategy, he could not remember ever mentioning abortion. Someone else had provided the story to the *Star,* which was the only paper to run it. Serious damage resulted, from both the proposed policy itself and the now familiar spectacle of the Liberals in disarray.[23]

Meanwhile, CBC-TV news was hot on the trail of the latest instalment in the saga of Liberal leadership intrigue. On October 19, the Wednesday of the campaign's third week, it reported on Turner's campaign in Vancouver Quadra, where he faced a second candidate named John Turner, a thirty-one-year-old unemployed carpenter who sported a diamond earring and was running for the Rhinoceros Party, pushing its commitment to repeal the law of gravity. Sheldon Turcotte, the acting anchorman for *CBC News,* then introduced regular anchorman Peter Mansbridge, dressed like a journalist in a trenchcoat. Mansbridge described the Liberal strategy meeting of the week before and reported that the committee members had considered pressuring Turner to quit, sent him a memo outlining the desperate condition of the Liberal campaign, and followed up with phone calls before backing off. A shot of what was supposed to be the memo Ouellet had delivered to Stornoway flashed up on the screen. In fact, the CBC didn't have the memo and was just showing a facsimile. When Turner, who was in Vancouver that night, learned that the story would be broadcast, he shrugged. "Well, we've got a speech to make," he said simply, and soldiered off to give it.[24]

Mansbridge's report involved some guesswork about what had really gone on. Even if the story were true and the CBC had got it right, whether a public broadcaster should have intervened so dramatically in an election was debatable. Pat Gossage, the media adviser travelling with Turner, called the CBC report "the most flagrant political intervention by a major news organization in a national campaign in the modern life of Canada."[25] Others agreed. Kirby and his committee members subsequently denied everything. They told reporters that, though many of the facts in the story were correct, the construction put on them was not. They had written a memo describing the polling data. And they had considered what to do if Turner quit, either because of his back pain or because he decided that a different leader would do better. But they had not attempted another coup.[26]

The effect of the Mansbridge report resonated in the days that followed as other networks presented it as news, overshadowing Turner's tour. Meanwhile, in Quebec, Liberal MPs spooked by the polls were doing exactly what Mansbridge had accused the strategy committee of doing – discussing how to overthrow their leader. The discussions ultimately fizzled, but not before Chrétien had been approached to see if he would step up. "He turned it down because it is not his agenda, the candidates are not his choices, the party has no money, and he doesn't want to destroy himself," a source reported.[27]

The discouraging polls, the rumours of another coup, and the inability of the Liberals to behave honourably when presented with the possibility of being out of power combined to devastate party morale in the middle of the election campaign. Some Quebec Liberal candidates tried to distance themselves from Turner by positioning themselves as independents. Turner, for his part, found himself in mid-campaign with senior advisers he could no longer trust. Chrétien, who was quoted in newspapers as telling Liberals he wanted this election to be "a stake through Turner's heart," was seeing his fondest hopes realized.[28]

By this point in the campaign, Turner had been tripped up, knocked about, and stabbed in the back to the point that he should, by rights, have staggered and pitched face-first into the turf. Yet he kept on running. Ahead, in week four of the campaign, lay the television debates, his best chance to speak directly to Canadians and, not incidentally, to make up for his "no option" debacle of 1984. The French debate was scheduled for Monday, October 24, with the English debate to follow the next day.

During the third week of October, Turner increasingly focused his attention on the debates. He had learned from 1984. Then he had been overstuffed with facts, figures, and advice, some of it contradictory. This time he would be rested, relaxed, and loose. Although he was exhausted from the exertions of the campaign and in continuous pain from his back, he spent long hours that week preparing. His aides put him through dry runs and worked up one-liners he could use to deliver points succinctly and colourfully. By this juncture in the campaign, however, he had been out on the hustings working crowds and giving speeches for weeks and had developed his own instinctual feel for how best to communicate his message.

André Morrow, a Montreal advertising and media consultant, took the lead in preparing Turner for the French debate. He cut off caffeine and alcohol for his charge and ruthlessly limited access to him. Morrow advised Turner to be aggressive throughout the debate and to look at Mulroney with a stern and disapproving gaze. This would send the message visually that Mulroney was not to be trusted and that Turner had the authority to judge. On the evening of the French debate, Peter Connolly arrived at Stornoway fifteen minutes early to take Turner to the studio. He found him pacing the driveway. "Let's go!" Turner told him. So off they went to the studios of the local CTV affiliate, CJOH, in suburban Ottawa. Turner entered the studio building hunched over as he tried to minimize the pain that shot through his back with every step. Once at the lectern, however, he stood erect and shut out the pain for the next three hours.

The debates were structured as a series of rotating one-on-one encounters between the three leaders. Turner's French was fluent, and he seemed at ease and in command of the issues. Against Mulroney, he took the offensive, attacking him on patronage with particularly devastating effect. Mulroney, who had planned to remain unflappably prime ministerial, was riled by Turner's accusations, went off-script, and ended up looking raffish. Turner, in contrast, appeared bemused by Mulroney's pompous evasions. When the reviews came in the next day, he was seen as the clear winner.

Bolstered by this success, Turner was primed for the English debate the next day, Tuesday, October 25. He was so pleased with the way the French debate had gone that he asked Morrow to prepare him for the English debate as well. Morrow advised a change of tactics. He should hold off, cultivate an image of calm and reason, then unload on Mulroney toward the end. When he arrived at the studio, Turner was cheered to see anti-free-trade demonstrators outside waving placards reading "Free Canada, Trade Mulroney."

When he squared off against Broadbent, Turner successfully distinguished the Liberals from the NDP by drawing attention to the NDP's promise to withdraw Canada from NORAD and NATO. While Turner was offstage waiting for his debate with Mulroney, the final pairing of the event, Scott Sheppard, his legislative assistant, told him that he'd failed to take advantage of the chances he'd had so far. Sheppard was deliberately trying to provoke Turner, and it worked. Turner got angry, but Sheppard kept after him as he went back to the stage, and Turner went into the last session riled up.[29]

In response to a question from Pamela Wallin about free trade's effect on employment for women, Turner noted that women were particularly vulnerable to job losses under the deal. He regretted not having had the chance to cover this and associated issues fully thus far in the debates. Mulroney, he asserted, had yet to address some fundamental questions. Why did he surrender energy policy, agriculture, and investment to the United States? Why hadn't he protected social and regional equality programs? Why didn't he pull out of the deal when he failed to get secure access to the American market? Turner suggested a separate debate on the free-trade agreement to address these issues.

Mulroney parried Turner's assertion that he had not been forthcoming, responding with, "There has been a most vigorous and I think probably unprecedented exchange of views."

"I think the issues happen to be so important for the future of Canada," countered Turner. "I happen to believe you've sold us out. I happen to believe that once you enter –"

"Just one second," Mulroney interjected, wagging his finger at Turner. "You do not have a monopoly on patriotism!"

"Once –"

"I resent the fact of your implication that only you are a Canadian!" Mulroney again interrupted.

"I'm saying –"

"I want to tell you that I come from a Canadian family, and I love Canada!"

"Once any –"

"And that is why I did it, to promote prosperity!"

"Once any country –"

"Don't you impugn my motives!"

"Once any country yields its economic levers –"

"Don't you impugn my motives or anyone else's!"

"Once a country yields its investments, once a country yields its energy –"

"We have not done it!"

"Once a country yields its agriculture –"

"Wrong again!"

"Once a country opens itself up to a subsidy war with the United States –"

"Wrong again!"

"– on terms of definition, then the political ability of this country to sustain the influence of the United States, to remain as an independent nation, that is lost forever, and that's the issue of this election."

Having fractured Turner's initial sally with repeated interruptions, Mulroney launched into his personal genealogy to display his credentials as a salt-of-the-earth Canadian:

> Mr Turner, let me tell you something, sir. This country is only about 120 years old, but my own father 55 years ago went himself, as a labourer, with hundreds of other Canadians, and with their own hands in north-eastern Quebec they built a little town, and schools and churches and they in their own way were nation building ... I today sir, as a Canadian, believe genuinely in what I am doing. I believe it is right for Canada. I believe that in my own modest way I am nation building.

With this last declaration, Mulroney seemed to have temporarily exhausted his lexicon of patriotic pieties. Turner got a chance to speak without being interrupted and, after declaring that his own ancestry was as Canadian as Mulroney's, blasted the prime minister with a withering outburst:

> You mentioned 120 years of history. We built a country east and west and north. We built it on an infrastructure that deliberately resisted the continental pressure of the United States. For 120 years we've done it. With one signature of a pen, you've reversed that, thrown us into the north-south influence of the United States and will reduce us ... to a colony of the United States, because when the economic levers go, the political independence is sure to follow.

Drawing on his rich innate understanding of Canada, Turner had invoked myths and fears at the core of its collective psyche with a few vivid phrases. The country he was defending was one he had lived in and loved since childhood, studied in university, and criss-crossed innumerable times on the nation's business. He knew Canada. It was an independent dominion built on an east-west backbone, not just a northern annex of the United States.

Mulroney was rattled by his adversary's certainty and began to contradict himself, first arguing that the agreement was critical to Canada's future and then that it was just a commercial document cancellable on six months' notice.

"Commercial document?" Turner protested. "It relates to every facet of our life!"

"Be serious," Mulroney scoffed.

"Well, I am serious," Turner answered. "I have never been more serious in my life."[30]

On CBC-TV, Peter Mansbridge talked to two undecided voters who had been watching in a Winnipeg studio. When they both said Turner had won, he commented that they should not "fall into the trap" of picking a winner.[31] But the interviewees knew better than the interviewer, for next morning politicians on the ground across the country found that Turner had broken through. Voters were now worried about free trade. It soon became clear that Turner had scored a dramatic and decisive victory.

More than seven million Canadians who watched the debate saw for the first time what the audiences at Turner campaign events had been seeing for weeks. Instead of the media's Turner-as-hapless-has-been, they saw a confident, knowledgeable, and patriotic Canadian with serious concerns that the prime minister evaded. His passion conveyed integrity and deep conviction. "By performing well in the debate," one commentator observed, "he far exceeded expectations and caused voters to reassess their opinion of him, which they did with a vengeance."[32] Now journalists began falling all over themselves to praise the man. The old lens was shattered. They saw a "new" John Turner, and this revelation gave them what they had always needed: a news story.

Ed Broadbent had started the campaign predicting that the Liberals would fall and the NDP rise in their place. He knew that the NDP had little chance of defeating the Conservatives – that was the task for the next election – but, with luck, it might sweep the Liberals aside except in a few regional pockets. But Broadbent and his advisers had misjudged the moment. The key to this election was not presenting a catch-all platform but taking a stand on free trade. Turner had seized the issue and run with it;

Broadbent missed out. The NDP's momentum sputtered, stalled, and would not recover.

And the Liberals had more. Their ad agency, Red Leaf, reinforced Turner's debate message with a memorable television ad that aired the day before the first debate. It showed US and Canadian negotiators facing each other across a table. "Since we're talking about the free-trade deal," the slightly sinister-looking American said, "there's one line I'd like to change." The camera shifted to a map of Canada and the United States, where a hand took an eraser and rubbed out the border between the two countries. The ad effectively conveyed Turner's message, as did the frequent replays on news and public affairs shows of his broadside against Mulroney during the debate. His free-trade stance was coming across simply yet dramatically on television.

Undecided voters swung toward Turner, and the Liberal Party soared in the polls. An Environics poll conducted immediately after the debate found that support for the Conservatives had fallen by 10 points, to leave them in a tie with the Liberals at 32 per cent. In another poll just a few days later, Environics found the Liberals leading the Conservatives 37 to 31 per cent.[33] An Insight Canada poll prepared for CTV gave the Liberals 40 per cent of the decided vote, the Conservatives 37 per cent, and the NDP 20 per cent.[34] For those who didn't see the debate itself, the poll results provided all the evidence they needed that Turner had won.

The Liberal campaign took off, with attendance at rallies soaring, donations flowing in, and volunteers flocking to join the campaign. Party workers were inspired by the prospect of victory. Even Jean Chrétien became more active on the hustings. On *Canada AM*, Michael Kirby joked that "This week's coup attempt has been delayed."[35] A few MPs and candidates grew so cocky that they began talking about Cabinet posts and other prospects of office. The media responded by reframing its coverage of Turner. Instead of showing him limping to symbolize his political condition, they now ran pictures of him being swarmed by friendly mobs. "Do television debates cure bad backs?" asked Charles Gordon of the *Ottawa Citizen*.[36]

Free trade shot to the top of voters' concerns. A November 7 Gallup poll showed that support for it had fallen to 26 per cent from 34 per cent two weeks earlier. By a two-to-one margin, Canadians told pollsters they believed Turner was genuine in his belief that the free-trade deal would be disastrous for Canada. The same poll put the Liberals at 43 per cent popular support, with the Tories down to 31 per cent and the NDP at 22 per cent. There had been a 19 per cent change in voters' intentions since the previous Gallup poll – the largest one-time shift recorded by the organization in its forty-one-year history. Turner was not at all happy to see these numbers. According to the Liberals' own polling, they had no more than a 6 per cent lead. When more accurate polls subsequently became public, they would encourage the perception that momentum was shifting back to the Tories.

By the time the full impact of the debate was apparent, it was early November, and just three weeks remained in the campaign. Turner had wrested control of the election agenda away from the Tories and made it a referendum on free trade. Allan Gotlieb, who was, as Canadian ambassador to the United States, heavily invested in the free-trade deal, fretted that "the Liberals seem to be organizing a systemic hatred of the United States."[37] Allan Gregg, the Conservative pollster, later told a journalist, "It was dire, it was black ... The election was en route to being lost."

Yet the well-financed Tory campaign had ample capacity to fight back. When Conservative strategists met to consider what they could do to reverse their plunge in the polls, Gregg maintained that the only way to save the situation was to attack Turner's character. Despite his recent resurrection in the eyes of voters, Gregg explained, Turner had a legacy of low approval ratings. They should revive latent suspicions about his leadership qualities. "We saw that the bridge that joined the growing fear of free trade and the growing support for the Liberal party was John Turner's credibility," he later explained. "So we had to get all the planes in the air and smash the bridge and blow it up."[38] The plan was simple: destroy Turner's reputation.

The Tories' first step was to instruct their most credible national figures to call Turner a liar. The first of the heavy cannon to be wheeled to the parapet was Finance Minister Michael Wilson. Arrangements were made to have him speak at a luncheon in Ottawa on October 31, just five days after the debate. "John Turner in the debate Tuesday night said [Mulroney] has agreed to let the Americans have a say in the future of our social programmes such as unemployment insurance and medicare," Wilson intoned. "I say to Mr. Turner, that is a lie ... Taking this lie into our senior citizens' homes is the cruellest form of campaigning that I've seen in 10 years in politics."[39]

Similar strong words of denunciation were scripted for Don Mazan-kowski and John Crosbie, the two other Conservative ministers who were seen to have integrity. The Conservatives coaxed eighty-nine-year-old Justice Emmett Hall, who had headed the royal commission that drafted national health care insurance in the 1960s, to make a statement that free trade presented no danger to medicare. Hall had, in an earlier life, been a Conservative and now returned to his roots. In Quebec they got Claude Castonguay, a prominent provincial Liberal and a key figure in the intro-duction of medicare in the province, to say the same. It was reasonable to conclude that he was a surrogate for Bourassa, his intervention yet another signal that the provincial Liberals had transferred their allegiance to the federal Progressive Conservatives. (Mulroney would later appoint Castonguay to the Senate, where he sat as a Conservative.) The Tories also put Simon Reisman on the road to repudiate the Liberals' claims about the trade deal he had negotiated. Warming to his topic, Reisman told an audience that Turner was worse than a liar – he was a traitor. Turner was used to politics taking a toll on personal relationships, but having an old friend turn on him in this way was truly hurtful.

The Tory assault was reinforced by the NDP. Seeing the Liberals in the lead, Broadbent joined the Conservatives in impugning Turner's motives for opposing the trade deal. He had strange bedfellows in Turner's former business associates and friends. Alf Powis, CEO of Noranda, said that Turner was "dead wrong" on the issue and that rejecting free trade would be a "national tragedy." Conrad Black floridly denounced Turner's "sulphur-ous falsehoods and banalities."[40] "No one anticipated that Turner would turn into such a mad dog," said Jack Fraser, vice-president of the Business Council on National Issues (BCNI). "It's one thing to want to be elected, but to screw your country in order to win, that's just disgusting."[41] The PMO then launched a whispering campaign against Turner. Journalists received anonymous calls suggesting that they interview Bill Lee and other disenchanted former Turnerites. Copies of documents of dubious veracity, purporting to show that the Liberal opposition to free trade was hypocritical opportunism, were put into circulation. Party workers were instructed to show up at Liberal gatherings and shout "Liar!" and "Traitor!" at Turner. In the face of this onslaught, Turner refused to reply in kind. "We should have called Mulroney a liar," recalled John Webster. "But he didn't want to do that."[42] Turner's Queensberry rules for political bouts left him fighting with one hand behind his back.

Next the Conservatives unleashed a barrage of negative advertising. They had more television advertising room than their opponents because electoral rules allotted time in proportion to a party's representation in the House of Commons. They also had bulging campaign coffers. Businesses, many of them American owned, donated some $10 million to the Conservative campaign. Given the capital-intensive nature of polling, advertising, public relations, and other modern electioneering techniques, that afforded them a considerable advantage over their rivals. The average viewer saw approximately twenty Tory television ads in the final week of the election, compared to ten or twelve for the Liberals and the NDP combined.[43]

Instead of scheduling their advertising around newscasts to reach those Canadians who followed public affairs, the Tories placed their attack ads on daytime television – around soap operas and other light entertainment. They focused on unsophisticated voters who were confused about free trade, a demographic Gregg identified as the poor, the uneducated, and youthful and aged urbanites. The message was simple: Turner had lied to Canadians about free trade. He was just trying to save his job. The ads included "streeters" – commercials in which actors, pretending to be average citizens, expressed deep distrust of Turner when they were questioned in the street. One, responding to the Liberal ad erasing the forty-ninth parallel, featured a hand drawing the border back in. A mock tabloid newspaper with a print-run of 5-6 million copies attacked Turner under the headline "The Ten Big Lies."

The Conservative campaign was reinforced by a huge onslaught of third-party advertising. In Canada's previous free-trade elections of 1891 and 1911, business interests had worked to keep the protection of high tariffs and were thus opposed to free trade. Now they wanted access to the vast American markets Mulroney promised them. The Business Council on National Issues, led by Thomas D'Acquino, had been lobbying for free trade for years. Its members – the CEOs of the 150 largest corporations in Canada – had plenty of resources to throw into the Conservative campaign. In 1987 BCNI had joined with other business groups to form the Canadian Alliance for Trade and Job Opportunities, a pro-free-trade coalition that had spent millions promoting free trade. Now it launched a $1.3 million blitz that placed multi-page ads in thirty-five newspapers across the country, predicting severe economic consequences for Canada if it rejected the deal. Estimates of the total amount spent by the private sector on pro-free trade advertising in the last three weeks of the campaign ranged between $4-5 million, whereas the total budget for the Pro-Canada network for the entire campaign was $750,000 – most of which had already been spent by this point. The Canadian Chamber of Commerce wrote to its 170,000 members, urging them to campaign for free trade. Business also tried to browbeat its employees into line. The Canadian Manufacturers' Association sent letters to its three thousand members, telling executives to instruct their workforces on where their interests lay. Many CEOs complied by warning employees that their jobs depended on the deal. The *Toronto Globe and Mail* joined the chorus with a series of articles and editorials outlining the dire economic consequences of rejecting free trade. "Big business, led by American multinationals, is now trying to buy this election," Turner warned.[44] But his voice was drowned out. Even the Alberta government got involved, sponsoring a $500,000 advertising campaign for free trade.

On November 17, with four days left in the campaign, President Ronald Reagan, then in the last few weeks of his second term, promoted the deal in a high-profile speech. It was, he opined, a fine example of solidarity between nations, a testament to the commitment of two governments to free-market principles and economic cooperation. Turner, who was appearing on a Quebec open-line radio show that day, described Reagan's remarks as "unprecedented interference" in Canadian domestic affairs and characterized them as "a case of a lame-duck trying to rescue a dead duck."[45] It was a good line that didn't get the air play it might have if he had uttered it on television. Meanwhile, Margaret Thatcher told the *Washington Post* that, if the free-trade deal were revoked, it would be "very difficult for any prime minister of Canada to negotiate another international agreement with another country." Thatcher, Turner said in French, was treating Canadians like "colons," which meant "colonials" but had connotations in French of ignorance, stupidity, and naïveté.[46]

Turner and his advisers tried desperately to think of some way to strike back. They agreed that it would be best to find a new issue with which to throw the Tories off-balance. Those who had advised holding the party's forty-point policy platform in reserve had just such a predicament in mind. But it was too late now – all that ammunition was spent. Martin Goldfarb revived the idea of a liberalized abortion policy, but Turner wouldn't unleash such a divisive issue merely for partisan advantage.[47] Goldfarb then suggested attacking the Tories' plan for a value-added tax, the GST. Turner again refused, because he thought it a good policy. He raised other issues but received scant media coverage. The Conservative advertising onslaught kept the focus on Turner's character.

With their superior resources, the Conservatives were able to poll, advertise, and massage the media on a scale that dwarfed their rivals' efforts. They were now enjoying a steady point-a-day climb in voter support. Whereas polls conducted immediately after the debates said that 55 per cent of people believed that Turner opposed free trade because of conviction, that percentage had now fallen to 27 per cent. In terms of voters' ratings of leadership qualities, Turner was driven back to third place among the party leaders. One week before the election, fully 40 per cent of the Canadian electorate said it feared the economic consequences of rejecting the deal.[48] For the first time since polling began, the electorate had executed a double reverse – shifting from majority government territory for one party to the other and then back again in the course of one election campaign. Character assassination and fear-mongering worked.

The weekend before election day, Turner toured Ontario, trying to consolidate support in ridings where the race was tight. The Liberals emptied their campaign war chest to place an ad in every major Canadian daily telling readers they should vote Liberal, not NDP, to block the free-trade deal. Turner remained convinced that he was right – and that his analysis of the deal would prove prophetic.

When the first results came in from Atlantic Canada on election night, the Liberals had tripled their seats in the region from 7 to 20. In Quebec, however, the combination of free trade, Meech Lake, federal spending, and Bourassa's support for Mulroney was too much to beat. The Liberals won 12 of the 75 seats, down from 17 in 1984. The Tories swept all the remaining 63 seats, including Raymond Garneau's riding. In Ontario, where they had Premier David Peterson's support, the Liberals netted 43 of the 99 seats, but it wasn't enough to make up for Quebec and Conservative strength in the West, where they took only 6 seats to the Tories' 48. When all the results were in, the Conservatives won the election with a reduced majority. With 170 of the 295 seats in Parliament, they had the votes needed to pass the trade deal.

Turner's Liberals more than doubled their seats to 82, and the NDP came out with 43. The Conservatives received 43 per cent of the popular vote; the Liberals, 31.9 per cent; and the NDP, 20.4 per cent, with fringe parties, including the new Reform Party out west, splitting the remainder. "I have promoted my vision of a strong, independent and sovereign Canada," Turner declared in his concession speech, "and I've done so with all my heart and all my strength and I have no regrets at all."[49]

If one were to read the 1988 federal election as a plebiscite on free trade, the deal was supported by only 43 per cent of voters. The New Democrats split the anti-free-trade vote with the Liberals, preventing a party of that conviction from gaining power. If the election were read as a choice between preserving a distinctive type of liberal democracy in the northern half of North America versus securing an American standard of living, most Canadian voters opted for identity and sovereignty over a prosperous junior partnership in the continental economic order.

Many commentators have argued that the election should not be read in either of these ways, because too many other factors were in play.[50] One of the biggest was the attack on Turner's character. "We had all those business guys coming out, guns blazing. Together, we were out to destroy Turner's credibility," a Tory insider recalled with satisfaction. "We did a damn good job."[51] With their counter-offensive, the Conservatives had changed the election issue from free trade to Turner's leadership. The question hanging over Turner for years was whether his image could be rehabilitated after the public mauling he sustained in 1984. Now the answer was in. The Tories had successfully evoked the 1984 Turner in their counter-attack of 1988. Had this factor been taken out of the electoral equation, the vote against free trade would have been much higher.

The Conservatives' attack on Turner was enabled by the Liberal Party itself. Its failure to close ranks behind Turner while in opposition was fatal. The media's negative assessment of him had been reinforced regularly by the Liberals themselves, often at the most inopportune moments. In the few short months leading up to the election, and even during the campaign, the damage inflicted on Turner by his own party was devastating. Inspired by a cause that he saw as central to his country's future, he came close to saving them from themselves, but he was undercut by incessant disloyalty within his party. The Liberals had behaved badly and deserved to lose. The tragedy was that their ignoble conduct had distracted voters from deciding on its merits an issue with profound implications for Canada's future.

LEGACIES AND MIGHT-HAVE-BEENS

W ith the election loss, there was again, inevitably, speculation about Turner's future as leader. One rumour had it that he was so encouraged by his temporary resurgence that he wanted to stay on to fight the next election. The smart money said it was time for him to go and that, if he tried to stay, he would lose the leadership review.

Turner had, in fact, had enough. He liked to think he could win the review, but he hadn't the stomach for it. Although he had won the previous contest, it hadn't stopped the backstabbing. He figured that Canadian political leaders got only two kicks at the can, and he'd now had both of his. It was difficult to turn over the party he had rebuilt to someone else, but he had done all he could with the job of leader. His sixtieth birthday was coming up that spring. It was time for new blood.

The race to replace him now surfaced into plain view. Jean Chrétien ramped up his public appearances, and his main competitor, Paul Martin Jr., played catch-up. Turner may have had little choice but to leave, but he had some control over the timing, so he played things out as long as he could to better Martin's chances.

According to the party constitution, the leadership review had to be held at the first party convention following an election. A convention scheduled for the fall of 1988 had been delayed because of the election and was now slated for the fall of 1989 in Calgary. Delegate selection would commence on May 1, so Turner could expect to be the target of resurgent sniping and skulduggery from that point forward. He didn't want to interfere with the

Newfoundland election in April, and he wanted to critique the government budget that was due that month. Early May, then, would be a good time to announce his departure.

On January 10 he had surgery to repair his back, then left for Jamaica to recuperate. He returned to attend a caucus retreat in St. John's, Newfoundland, on February 20. The operation was successful, he told his MPs – "All the knives were removed."[1] The *Toronto Sun* published an article claiming that he had asked for $500,000 to leave the leadership. Turner sued. "He was really badly shaken by that story," said a friend, "and he kept asking, 'Will it never stop?'"[2]

Turner discussed his resignation with his family over dinner at Stornoway the evening of Tuesday, May 2. The next morning he gathered his senior staff and told them, "We'll do it today." They faxed a prepared letter of resignation to party president Michel Robert and announced it to both caucus and the national media later that day. The press praised Turner in the elegiac tones reserved for golf pros and washed-up politicians. He was amused by all the accolades. Some of his most vicious enemies within the party were now lavishing him with praise. It was a bit much. "The goodbyes are far more generous and spontaneous than the hellos," he noted wryly.[3] His cynicism nonetheless masked a deep disappointment with how things had turned out. When a fellow MP read in the House from a 1984 speech in which Turner had outlined his plans as prime minister, those close to him noticed he was fighting back tears. The thought of what might have been was just too hurtful.

In response to Turner's announcement, the party leadership postponed the upcoming convention in Calgary by six months and transformed it into a full-blown leadership convention. The timing of the rescheduled convention – June 20-24, 1990 – was decidedly odd. The deadline for ratification of the Meech Lake Accord fell on June 23. It was also the weekend of St-Jean Baptiste Day celebrations in Quebec, and the first year since the rioting in 1968 that a parade was allowed. If Meech Lake died that weekend, ugliness in the streets of Quebec could well cast a shadow over proceedings at the Liberal convention.

Turner continued to serve as leader of the opposition until February, 1990, when he turned the job over to Herb Gray. This precipitated another round of fulsome eulogies. His friend Marjorie Nichols equated him with "straight dealing." He was exceptional in treating politics as "an honourable occupation of public service" and "played by Queensberry rules, even when his opponents were punching below the belt."[4] *Toronto Globe and Mail* columnist Jeffrey Simpson contrasted Turner's style with Mulroney's. Some Ontario municipalities, most notably Sault Ste. Marie, had recently declared themselves unilingual jurisdictions. In response, Turner had introduced a motion into the House affirming Canada's bilingual character. Mulroney took the opportunity to exploit the continuing divisions in opposition ranks by transforming Turner's resolution into an endorsement of the Meech Lake Accord. "At a time of linguistic tension in the country, concerned Canadians might properly look to Parliament for leadership," Simpson observed. "They found it this week in Mr. Turner, who, in contrast to Prime Minister Mulroney, put gamesmanship aside."[5]

By the time the convention rolled around, the ratification of Meech Lake had been held up by the protracted ambivalence of Newfoundland premier Clyde Wells and a legislative roadblock in Manitoba. The first ministers had twisted Wells' arm during a final round of negotiations that spring, and he had reluctantly agreed to go along. Then Mulroney made the mistake of crowing in a *Globe and Mail* interview that he had "rolled all the dice" and won. Wells was offended and began to reconsider. The continuing divisions in the Liberal Party over Meech were evident in alliances mimed before the television cameras at the leadership convention at the Calgary Saddledome. Jean Chrétien ostentatiously hugged both Wells and Manitoba Liberal leader Sharon Carstairs, who was anti-Meech, while David Peterson made a point of sitting with Turner.

In his speech on Thursday, June 21, Turner summed up everything he had fought for in his political career. Switching between English and French, he talked about the Liberals' commitment to fighting poverty and creating opportunities for all Canadians. He urged tolerance on Meech Lake while interpreting the passions the issue provoked as a healthy sign of Canadians' love for their country. He castigated Mulroney for deciding the fate of the nation behind closed doors in the Meech negotiations and called for a more open political process. In his stewardship of the Liberal Party, he explained, "My pledge was to open up this party to new ideas, new people, new approaches. I promised you a more open party. We are a more open party. I promised you a more democratic party. We are a more democratic party. I promised you a more accountable party. We are now more accountable. Our party again belongs to you. Make sure it stays that way!" Turner spoke of the beauty and majesty of the land, the diversity of its people, and the richness of life in Canada. Fighting free trade was the best thing he had ever done in public life, he declared, and he would do it all over again. He wound up with an inspiring invocation of the country's defining virtues:

> We have such a unique heritage, such boundless opportunity. Our limitless land, water, resources. Our northern frontier. The space to be alone when you want. Our two languages, many cultures. Our spirit of freedom and tolerance. Our respect for the law. Our faith in Parliamentary democracy.
>
> We want this nation to endure because millions of Canadians share my dream for a Canada that is strong, independent, sovereign and united.
>
> If I have helped concentrate the attention of Canadians on these issues, if I have helped focus our national purpose, if I have managed to encourage only a few others to become involved, then my time will have been well spent.[6]

The supporters of Paul Martin applauded enthusiastically; those in Jean Chrétien's camp politely. High up in the stands sat Pierre Trudeau, watching.

Meech Lake collapsed the following day when MLA Elijah Harper blocked a vote on it in the Manitoba legislature. At the Liberal convention, Chrétien won on the first ballot with 2,652 votes. Martin trailed with 1,176 delegates, whereas candidates Sheila Copps, John Nunziata, and Thomas Wappel won just handfuls of votes each. Chrétien made an attempt to acknowledge Turner in his acceptance speech. "Canadians will remember forever the fantastic fight he made for Canada in 1986," he declared, getting his years confused.[7]

In a perfect world, Turner would have returned to private life scarred but wreathed in honour. He would have been welcomed back to McMillan Binch and had his blue-chip directorships restored by a business community grateful for his years of public service. But his former colleagues didn't want him back. He had betrayed them by opposing free trade. Worse, he now had the image of a loser. Mulroney asked Conrad Black to offer Turner, on his behalf, the post of ambassador to the Vatican. Turner declined.[8] Ron Basford's law firm in Vancouver offered him a position, but he chose to return to Toronto. On March 1, 1990, he joined Miller Thomson, a mid-sized Toronto firm, and began to rebuild his legal career.

Turner would continue to sit in Parliament as a backbencher until the 1993 election. Early in 1991 the House of Commons was debating the government's decision to participate in the Gulf War. After Saddam Hussein had invaded Kuwait the previous August, the United Nations had authorized a military response, and an invasion was about to begin. Chrétien's position was that Canadian soldiers would remain in Kuwait solely in a peacekeeping role and should leave when fighting broke out. For Turner, this stand contravened the tradition of Canadian support for the UN dating back to Lester Pearson's Nobel Prize-winning days. He asked Chrétien's office for speaking time, was denied, then appealed to the Commons, and was granted it on January 16, 1991. "This Parliament and our country, Canada, are faced with a clear choice," he declared:

> We can continue to stand behind the United Nations and its resolutions for which we voted, and which told Iraq what it must do to avoid war.
>
> We can remain an integral part of the most determined demonstration of collective political will ever marshalled by the United Nations to stand up against aggression. In my view it is the choice which all our history and the long tradition of Canada's support for the United Nations oblige us to make today ...
>
> This is a crucial test for that international organization. This is a crucial test for the United Nations, and Canada must support it.[9]

Some observers judged this the best speech he had made in the House since his return to politics in 1984. That wasn't quite true, but it was the best speech that got notice. The newsworthiness of war meant that the media were, for once, paying attention to a parliamentary debate.

Turner's intervention was decisive: the Liberals subsequently changed their position and voted in favour of the motion. He was pleased with himself. He had intervened out of conviction, but it was nice to see he still had influence. There was some satisfaction, too, in giving Chrétien a taste of what it was like to have a rogue critic in the ranks.[10] Chrétien retaliated by moving him to a smaller office, and Turner found his caucus peers reluctant to sit with him in the House for fear of similar reprisals.

Brian Mulroney attempted to build a new constitutional settlement from the wreckage of Meech Lake, this time consulting widely and including women, aboriginals, ethnocultural groups, and other stakeholders. A tentative agreement, to be approved by national referendum, was struck at meetings in Charlottetown in August 1992. Turner supported the Charlottetown Accord and sat with former BC premier Bill Bennett on a task force that tried to sell the new deal to the electorate. They encountered deep resistance. Canadians were suffering from constitutional fatigue attended by resentment and suspicion of the politicians who had put them through the Meech ordeal. Turner detected anger in the electorate, and the Charlottetown Accord became the first casualty. He warned Conservative Cabinet minister Kim Campbell, who was touring with him in support of Charlottetown, that the public was in an ugly mood and she had better watch out.

After Campbell became Mulroney's successor in June 1993, Chrétien benefited from the voters' mood. In the fall 1993 election, he defeated her and won a majority government. Turner was *persona non grata* in party affairs throughout the Chrétien era. Stephen LeDrew once suggested to an influential Chrétien loyalist that Turner should be appointed governor general. "The former PM knew every nook of Canada, its people and its history," he said. "He's a national treasure."[11] It would never happen – for Chrétien, Turner continued to be the enemy. During a birthday party for Turner in Ottawa, Chrétien staffers sat in the parking lot outside, noting the Liberals who attended.

Only when Paul Martin Jr. became Liberal leader in 2003 did Turner receive recognition as a senior statesman of the party. In December 2004 Martin asked him to lead a five-hundred-person delegation to observe the presidential elections in the Ukraine. The following year, in November, Martin had Turner represent Canada at the tenth anniversary of the assassination of Yitzhak Rabin in Israel. Turner enjoyed these assignments and appreciated the recognition.

Turner's work with Miller Thomson paralleled his earlier career at McMillan Binch. The firm grew substantially, and he was a big part of its success. He knew prominent business figures, diplomats, and politicians from around the world, and when they were in Canada, he arranged lunches to which his firm invited bank chairmen and CEOs, helping to build its profile as a savvy player in a globalizing business world. When Miller Thomson merged with a Vancouver firm in 2000 and a Montreal firm in 2005, Turner's knowledge of the business and legal communities in those cities smoothed the way. He was particularly adept at developing business in the Kitchener-Waterloo area of Ontario, where Miller Thomson merged with a local firm in 2002, becoming one of the first big Canadian law firms with a presence in the region's fast-growing high-tech sector. Turner took particular pleasure in advising the young lawyers in the company.[12] He went to the office every day, even when his back problems returned, making it increasingly difficult for him to walk. "One of my earliest cases was against a 90-year-old lawyer who was sharp as a whip," he recalled. "That's the way to go."[13]

John Turner had two distinct political careers: the first, a glorious progress in which success crowned success; the second, a frustrating ordeal survived with dignity. In the early 1960s he was a leader in a new generation of Liberals in tune with changing times who revitalized the party and helped it regain power. He built the new department of Consumer and Corporate Affairs and, from this base, ran for the 1968 Liberal leadership on a reform platform. A high-powered Cabinet minister in Trudeau's regime, he matured into the anglophone half of a bicultural alliance of the type that, historically, has underpinned the most successful Canadian governments. He won acceptance across the country for the *Official Languages Act,* which redefined Canada as a bilingual nation. As minister of justice he did more than any of his colleagues to translate the reform spirit of the 1960s into substantial political change. He was a voice of moderation during the October Crisis. As finance minister he battled for fiscal responsibility in an era when government spending threatened to spiral out of control. Throughout this period he was the government's most effective emissary to the provinces and the United States, and he played a key role in the International Monetary Fund. As the leading anglophone Liberal in the Trudeau government, he gave English Canadians a stake in an administration that might otherwise have seemed to be dominated by French

Canadians. He commanded confidence nationwide and legitimized tolerance and cooperation in a period of sectional tensions. Without Turner, national unity and the public accounts would have been far worse in the 1970s.

Turner's second coming has long overshadowed his first in public memory. He didn't win power, which is the main objective of politics – particularly for Liberals – and by that measure he was a failure. The contrast between his second career and the first begs for explanation. How did the golden boy of the 1970s become "yesterday's man" of the 1980s? The answer lies in a tangle of character, circumstance, timing, and sheer bad luck.

Turner himself admitted he was rusty when he returned to politics. His political instincts had atrophied during his nine-year break, and whipping himself back into shape took a while. Yet rustiness was only part of the problem. Canadian politics had also changed significantly. Politics is a full-immersion experience in which participants unconsciously adjust to subtle alterations that, over time, make for a substantially different milieu. When Turner plunged back into politics in 1984, he spent a number of months not just rediscovering his political skills but also adapting to an unfamiliar environment.

During the 1980s he was dogged by organizational problems that had never beset him before. His 1984 election campaign was the most disastrous example, but his leadership bid had been similarly plagued, and, subsequently, his office was often blamed for problems with caucus and bungles such as the daycare announcement during the 1988 campaign. Had he lost his management skills somewhere along the way? He had always been a great networker and an effective chief executive officer. As a Cabinet minister he had successfully managed a number of government departments, and he had helped to build McMillan Binch into a leading national legal firm. A friend compared him to a talented quarterback, who, "with a good coach and strong team ... can look spectacular."[14] If Turner had been elected in 1984 or 1988, in all likelihood he would have been a successful prime minister. Leading a large and complex enterprise in a politicized context was the type of role to which he was accustomed and at which he excelled.

In each of the successful outings of his early career, Turner had assumed a lead role in a pre-existing, well-managed organization. In his second political career he had to build organizations from scratch – first his leadership campaign, then his election campaign, and finally the opposition leader's office.[15] All were start-ups trying to find their legs under pressurized circumstances, a situation that is challenging to manage even for those who have related experience. In each case problems arose with reporting relationships, communications, appointments, access to the leader, and effective delegation. Wires were crossed, messages garbled, commitments breached, and initiatives fumbled – all of which damaged his image and the loyalty of those affected.[16]

The chaos was partially attributable to the combination of a gutted party organization and a venomous caucus of still-recovering Trudeauites, emasculated power-brokers, wonky eccentrics, and plotting Chrétienites. Another contributing factor was that Turner was not the consummate political professional he had once been. In his first political career, he was attuned to shifting constellations of personalities, alliances, and interests. He made few mistakes and exploited most of the opportunities that came his way. When he returned to public life, he could be remarkably maladroit even after he had time to adjust to the new political environment. His personnel decisions were sometimes questionable, his political instincts less acute, and he didn't have the same passion for the game he had displayed as a younger man. That was most evident in the way he handled the vexed issue of Quebec and the constitution, both in the development of the resolution for the 1986 policy convention and in responding to Meech Lake. Meech was, granted, a tough sell, but in his first career he had excelled at pre-empting dissent and closing the deal. In round two, he failed to co-opt potential opponents.

Turner's saving grace was that, when challenged, he rose to the occasion and performed superbly. "Like certain, big, rangy, lazy but hugely talented hockey players," one journalist wrote, thinking of Frank Mahovlich, Turner "would get an elbow in the face, a knee to the groin, and suddenly wake up and put on a display so dazzling that, for a while, the critics would wonder if perhaps for once they had been completely wrong."[17] These heroics, though impressive, would not have been necessary had he remained as consistently sharp as he had once been. He was no longer the lean and hungry up-and-comer but an elder who felt he had paid his dues and deserved respect. Years of adulation in the private sector had reinforced this mindset, instilled habits of indulgence, and conditioned him to deference rather than dissent. Ironically, the post-1984 Turner seemed something of the "mellow man" the young Turner had warned against in 1968.

The mellowing would not have been such a problem if he had inherited a strong, unified party. Louis St. Laurent, for example, was a hands-off, chairman-of-the-board type of leader, and he was venerated. Instead, in the spring of 1984 Turner found himself head of a dysfunctional Liberal administration that faced formidable challenges as its popularity ebbed. The Liberals had been in office, with the exception of the short Clark interlude in 1979, for more than twenty years. They had grown self-satisfied and remote from the electorate, prompting critics to portray them as arrogant and out of touch. Parties that govern for long periods are blamed for everything that has gone wrong under their watch. Trudeau's last term saw frightening economic developments, with a deep recession, record unemployment, and interest rates peaking around 20 per cent as central banks tried to quash inflation. In the normal course of events, political parties get turned out of office on a regular basis purely for the sake of a change. The Liberals' return to power in 1980 was something of a fluke that only postponed the inevitable. In 1984 a Conservative government was long overdue, and voters needed a good reason not to vote one in.

Turner also had to contend with the ideological imprint that Trudeau left on the party. Trudeau streaked to power amid the formative nationalist fervour of the late 1960s, and many Canadians came to associate his policies with what it meant to be Canadian. The Trudeau vision of Canada hardened into an orthodoxy that inhibited Turner's ability to modify party policy in keeping with changing times and political circumstances. He encountered this problem when he talked about the deficit, suggested more cooperation with the provinces, or got technical about language policy. When journalists dismissed him as yesterday's man, they were suggesting he was out of touch because his views on these key issues deviated from those of the Trudeau regime. They did not consider the possibility that Trudeau was an aberration and that Turner in fact represented enduring verities in the *longue durée* of Canadian politics that were as valid in the present as they had been in the past.

The continuing influence of Trudeau both perplexed and annoyed Turner, who felt he had a better grasp of Canada and how to govern it. He thought Trudeau's rational approach to politics to be, for Canada, irrational. "You have to understand this country," he explained. "There's nothing symmetrical, nothing logical, nothing Cartesian, about Canada. This country makes no sense, geographically, economically, historically. What we have has been built by consensus and compromise. Canada is not a product of the mind, it's a product of the heart, of feelings. Unless that's understood, you cannot get this country to work."[18] Reason over passion made no sense when passion was a key factor in the equation. Apprenticed in the traditional Liberal craft of politics, Turner had learned to broker the country's divergent regional, ethnic, and linguistic interests through elite accommodation. He, not Trudeau, was the legitimate heir of a long-standing Canadian Liberal tradition.

Yet Turner's accommodating, gradualist, politics-as-usual style proved inadequate when Canadian politics became very unusual in the late 1980s. Neither Meech Lake nor free trade was amenable to consultation, conciliation, and compromise. Both were extraordinary issues that invoked fundamental principles and fiery emotions. With Meech, Turner discovered the extent to which Trudeau had succeeded in redefining Canada as a rational idealistic project in accord with his personal principles. Trudeau's interventions into the debate outflanked the political elites by taking the issue to the country and generating implacable opposition. With free trade, too, Turner's politics of negotiated incrementalism was displaced, though in this case it was he who became the principled and uncompromising defender of the status quo.

There was another significant way in which politics as usual no longer applied. During Turner's career, the Liberal Party sadly lost the genius for bicultural accommodation that had helped keep it in power and the country unified from the 1920s through the 1970s. As we have seen, this loss was largely attributable to leadership rivalries exacerbated by personality conflicts. Turner bore a share of the responsibility: his resignation and occasional sniping from the sidelines during his Toronto years poisoned relations with both Pierre Trudeau and Jean Chrétien. Yet, though Turner would happily have repaired these relationships, his predecessor and successor were unrelentingly spiteful and inflicted severe political damage on him with little regard for the cost to their party.

Trudeau made life difficult for Turner by clinging to power late into his last term of office, bequeathing him a party lacking the organization and resources to stage an immediate campaign, and sliming him with a stinking mass of patronage. As if this legacy weren't enough, Trudeau repeatedly intervened publicly to contradict his successor, with devastating effect on the unity of the Liberal Party and its electoral prospects. This intra-party factionalism would continue, with damaging consequences, for decades.

In retrospect, it is clear that Turner paid a huge price for failing to make Chrétien his right-hand man in the wake of the 1984 leadership contest. He would have had the most popular politician in Canada on his side and a strong foothold in the rural Quebec ridings in which Chrétien had currency. Even though he felt he couldn't trust Chrétien, he might better have heeded the old adage to keep your friends close and your enemies closer. Yet he had long been committed to a new deal for Quebec, and he had recruited Raymond Garneau with that in mind. Chrétien, in contrast, represented the Trudeauvian constitutional status quo, which Turner felt was both unfair and untenable. When Chrétien left caucus, his supporters waged a guerrilla war that undermined Turner's leadership and the party's electoral prospects. Turner's long-running leadership troubles were in this way connected to his commitment to a new deal for Quebec. He could not have expected to pay so high a price for this commitment. Before Chrétien, no Liberal leader aspirant had ever so consistently challenged the party's unspoken rule of loyalty to the leader.

Chrétien's insurgency was successful because Turner's image problems sapped his power. Many Liberals concluded he was not electable. The way in which his image worked to his advantage in the 1960s and early 1970s but became his biggest albatross in the 1980s was crucial to the different outcomes of his two political careers. In part Turner's bad image the second time around was a reflection of good character. Politicians' images are a result of organization and planning as well as their personalities. Part of the reason Turner made such a poor initial impression in 1984 was that ethical scruples had constrained him from organizing before Trudeau's announcement of his retirement.

Yet broad cultural changes also contributed to his image problems. Turner's sensibility was modern in that he believed in progress through the application of expertise to master a complex but tangible and ultimately comprehensible world. His brokerage style of political management can be seen as the application of this managerial rationalism to Canadian federal politics. As such, it constituted a kind of modern Liberal modus operandi. Yet from the late 1960s on, many of the epistemological certainties on which modern Canada had been constructed were destabilized. The mass media became all-pervasive purveyors of culture both popular and political, engendering postmodern skepticism about the reliability of their representations. Turner recognized that changes were afoot, reflecting in his speeches on how the electronic media personified politics, privileged image, and created a "leadership cult" that, among other things, made it possible for a charismatic neophyte to leapfrog into power.

And so it came to pass. Trudeau's 1968 ascension to the leadership was a triumph of image over the experience and organization of other candidates. The same approach worked for him in national elections – so well, in fact, that he had little need for the Liberal Party electoral machine in subsequent campaigns. Trudeau came across very well on television, not least because he displayed contempt for it. Turner was his generation's star apprentice in the Liberal art of managing a heterogeneous federal state through brokerage politics, but, as the celebrity figurehead of an imagined nation, Trudeau proved to be more electable. His vision of Canada, which puzzled Turner, was of a piece. Like Jean Baudrillard's simulacrum, it was a perfect copy of a non-existent original, yet no less influential for its detachment from reality.

There was yet another way in which the Trudeau legacy plagued Turner. Trudeau, a charismatic figure with a bold vision, established a model of leadership against which Turner compared poorly. The events of 1984 suggested that, though Canadians wished to get rid of Trudeau, they wanted to replace him with another Trudeau insofar as they sought a forceful, engaging television performer. Turner was not that type, although initially he was represented as that type. In the late 1970s and early 1980s, the media mythologized him as a suitable celebrity replacement for Trudeau. When it became evident on his return that the myth was inflated, the media blamed him rather than themselves for the gap between promise and performance. Some claimed that Turner's image problems were yet more proof that he was not the politician he used to be, but no reporters bothered to check old videotape. Had they done so, they would have seen that, in the early 1970s, Turner came across as dynamic but tightly wound, with all the mannerisms that later played poorly in the national media spotlight.

The difference was that television then had been less invasive and all-pervasive, and John Turner hadn't been at centre stage.

Curiously, Turner was also cursed by his good looks. A widespread suspicion of the establishment man in post-1960s popular culture underlay journalists' perception of Turner as a myth in need of debunking. The new cultural ideal was the anti-hero who projected an ironic tone, cynicism about traditional moral verities, and self-consciousness about role playing in a game. Turner looked the part of the modern hero, opening himself up to ridicule as a Roger Ramjet type in an era when Ratso Rizzo was seen as more authentic. The private Turner was self-aware with a rich sense of irony, but he took public service too seriously to show this side of himself on television. The importance of not being earnest was lost on him.

In time, Turner developed the necessary skills to fulfill the minimum performance requirements of the new media environment. Yet he still thought substance more important than image. He had always been a House of Commons man who saw it as the centre of the action. Although he valued good publicity, as his inveterate speechifying across the country demonstrated, he thought of it primarily in terms of a print media commenting on political action centred in Parliament. It never occurred to him that the media themselves could become the main forum in which national politics was conducted and that television would be their focal point. He reluctantly recognized that television mattered, but he could never accept that it mattered most. He continued to give well-researched and reasoned speeches in the House of Commons and across the country, but the mass audience wasn't tuned in.

In this context it is understandable that Turner's seemingly trivial bum patting in 1984 had such devastating effects. The gesture was broad enough to register with an audience distracted by the ceaseless stream of ephemeral media imagery. It was a potent symbol, invoking myriad intimations of a refugee from a past that was a foreign country. Most viewers, no matter how politically illiterate, were attuned sufficiently to the contemporary zeitgeist to feel superior and to laugh at him. In patting bums he made an ass of himself, becoming a stock comic character in the carnivalesque passing parade.

Image was the source of the problems Turner experienced in controlling his party. He was elected leader because he promised to deliver the Liberals back to power. When he failed to do so, and failed to convince others that he could do so in the future, he lost the ability to command loyalty. Chrétien, in contrast, had successfully established his "le petit gars de Shawinigan" image. It had the simple and compelling authenticity of a William Henry Drummond poem, sold well in the political marketplace, and made him a more electable political commodity.

With this attractive alternative always in mind, the main question for Liberals after the disastrous 1984 election was whether Turner's image could be rehabilitated sufficiently for him to regain power. Could a politician screw up so spectacularly in public and hope to recover? Turner nearly pulled it off. In the 1988 campaign he was a new politician: passionate, principled, inspiring. His media training yielded dividends as he began to deliver effective television performances. The Conservatives were taken by surprise, but Mulroney was still able to drag him down with base personal attacks invoking the old John Turner of 1984. "Almost" ended up being the answer to the question, but "almost" doesn't cut it in winner-takes-all politics.

With hindsight, it is easy to second-guess key decisions Turner made as Liberal leader. Meech Lake and free trade raised fundamental questions about Canada's future that would have been challenging to manage under the best of circumstances. The former caused a breach with Trudeau Liberals, and the latter with business Liberals, leaving most of the party disenchanted with Turner for one reason or another. It is tempting to imagine a remix of Turner's policy positions on the two great issues of the day that could have kept his party united and won the 1988 election. Had he adopted ambiguous stances on Meech Lake and free trade, and focused on Mulroney's trustworthiness, as his political strategists recommended, he might well have won in 1988. But he would not take that approach. He was uncomfortable with personal attacks and, more important, he took stands on issues based on conviction rather than political expediency. He had been committed to a new deal for Quebec for decades, and when presented with one, he felt bound to support it for the good of the country. He believed that the Mulroney free-trade agreement was deeply flawed, and his opposition to it was consistent with positions he had taken on trade and natural resource policy going back to the 1960s.

Despite his failure to win office, Turner could be proud of his achievements as Liberal leader. Chief among them was his rebuilding of the party.

Missionary work to the grassroots was well suited to his gregarious nature and romantic patriotism. He began with the smoking ruins of a party decimated by a historic electoral defeat in 1984 and, defying predictions of its imminent demise, built it back into a national political force. In the process he opened up its ranks to women, young people, and ethnic Canadians who infused it with a new vitality.

In the short term, his work paid off as the new rank and file supported him through the conspiracies and mutinies he endured from 1984 to 1988. In the long term, it established the organizational groundwork for a return to power. In 1993 the Liberals won the first of a series of elections that would produce majority governments for them for the next eleven years. Instead of the Liberals, Mulroney's Progressive Conservatives were on the road to extinction, dropping from 169 to a mere 2 seats in the 1993 election, then limping along for a decade before being absorbed into a new Conservative Party.

It is tempting to speculate what Canada would have been like if Turner had been prime minister in the 1970s or the 1980s. From the early 1970s on, he had been concerned about the economic viability of the Canadian welfare state. His opponents claimed that his apprehension about deficits evinced right-wing views. In fact, in keeping with his centrist Liberalism, Turner represented fiscal responsibility with a heart. As finance minister in the early 1970s, he oversaw a troubled economy labouring to support the new social programs introduced by the Pearson Liberals. He wanted to restore fiscal balance in order to consolidate Pearson's accomplishments and, with luck, develop the fiscal capacity to introduce new programs to continue building the welfare state.

On his return to politics, Turner encountered resistance to any mention of balancing the books. As opposition leader he had a left-wing caucus and no power with which to discipline it. As a result, he did not talk about deficits. When asked, he said the national debt was "still an albatross around the country's neck" and that the Tories were not distributing the burden of reducing it fairly, making the poorer regions and classes pay too much.[19] Mulroney, for his part, was reluctant to cut spending, because he wanted to take over traditional Liberal ground in the vote-rich centre of the political spectrum. As a Liberal, Turner may have been more free than Mulroney to implement deficit-reduction had he achieved power. It took another decade and a Liberal majority government to tackle the problem. By then Canada's fiscal situation had deteriorated to the point that far deeper cuts were required. Arguably, the fiscal base for Canadian social democracy would have been stronger and social programs better preserved under a Turner administration.

Perhaps, too, an accompanying ideological shift could have been mitigated. By the early 1990s, years of deficit discourse had eaten away at the social justice ethos that had sustained welfare-state building in the post-war era. When deficit cutting finally came, it was attended by a neo-liberal political philosophy that idealized smaller government and privileged the market, rather than liberal democratic principle, as the chief arbiter of public policy. In keeping with this new common sense, the federal government subsequently eschewed any thought of reinvesting in existing social programs and creating new ones. Such an ideological rationalization might not have transpired had national accounts been reconciled earlier.

On the issue of national unity, it is not hard to imagine a better outcome to the 1980s under Turner. He may not have been able to make the full constitutional deal with Quebec as set out in the Liberals' 1986 policy resolution, but he would have avoided the convulsions induced by Mulroney's dice rolling on Meech Lake and the ensuing Charlottetown debacle. Conceivably, the constitutional road-not-travelled under Turner would not have given rise to the Bloc Québécois, the close-run 1995 referendum, or the ensuing sponsorship scandal. Turner's Canada included not only Quebec but also the West, which generated its own regional protest party, Reform, on Mulroney's watch. The failure of the traditional brokerage system in the 1980s gave rise to two regional protest parties that fundamentally altered the Canadian political system for decades to come.

Finally, if Turner had been prime minister, Canada would not have ended up with its current free-trade arrangement with the United States. His assessment of the weaknesses of the free-trade deal proved accurate. Canada gave up control over significant parts of its economy and, in return, did not get the secure access to US markets that had been the original justification for the deal. This deficiency was illustrated by a series of trade disputes with the Americans that followed the signing of the free-trade agreement. In some cases, Canada's ability to protect its culture was assailed; in others, the provinces' ability to manage resources was at stake. The latter type of conflict was epitomized by the softwood lumber dispute, which dragged on for years, with Canada ultimately winning a favourable ruling from the World Trade Organization – only to have the US Congress, just as Turner predicted, unilaterally modify its trade law to suit itself. That prompted a remarkable turn of events in 2006 in which the original Canadian negotiators of the deal recanted their support for it.[20]

Denied power, Turner instead endured in opposition one of the roughest rides ever experienced by a Canadian party leader. He was publicly denounced by anonymous enemies and ambushed by mutinous caucus members. The fair-weather Bay Street friends who had pressured him to return to politics quickly faded into the woodwork. Former colleagues and aides fed journalists anecdotes that were used to concoct hatchet jobs. It was suggested on national television that he had a drinking problem. Across the country, comics could get a sure-fire laugh by exaggerating his untelegenic mannerisms.

Turner might well have been forgiven had he fled the field in rueful self-pity. Instead, he was philosophical about it all. He had been unlucky his second time around but was duty bound to fulfill his responsibilities to those who had elected him leader of the Liberal Party. He came from an era when men took their lumps and kept their own counsel. He would not be seen emoting to ingratiate himself with the masses or whining when he was rejected. Instead, he continued to urge Canadians, particularly the young, to consider public service as a way to make a difference in the world. In the wake of the 1986 leadership review, a journalist inquired how he could ask others to run for office given what he had been through. "Well, the job has to be [done] and the job is worth doing," he replied – despite his personal experience of lower pay, less time for his family, and critical media scrutiny. His only regret, he concluded, was that concrete results were difficult to achieve in politics.[21]

Turner's response to adversity suggests yet another way in which the "yesterday's man" label missed the point. Not only did it disregard the possibility that certain verities endure in Canadian political culture, it ignored the fact that some virtues are always desirable in democratic politicians. Turner was honest and conducted his political dealings honourably. He was, like most politicians, ambitious and competitive – part of what drove him was a love of the chase. Yet he had also entered public life due to a sense of duty, a love of country, and a desire to give something back. He had democratic sensibilities and the courage – if not foolhardiness – to run an open party. His code of conduct guided his political vocation with a consistency that belied the complexity of the man. He had exceptional talents, a middle-class upbringing with a taste of wealth, and the best education available, yet he wanted to pass as one of the guys. He was a man's man conditioned by 1940s gender conventions yet was influenced profoundly by the many strong women in his life. He was ambitious and driven yet caring and thoughtful of others, gregarious and fun loving yet private and self-sufficient. He was a small and large "l" liberal who was a buddy of both Duplessis and Diefenbaker. He could be ribald and profane yet was guided by an ethical compass oriented by Catholicism and theological reflection.

On a beautiful fall day in St. John's, Newfoundland, in the late 1980s, journalist Roy MacGregor bumped into John Turner as he was showing his daughter Elizabeth the city's harbour. Turner greeted him, then gestured out to sea. "He gave us a history lesson on the discovery of this cove, the settlement of St. John's and the entire story of Newfoundland right up until the vote to join Confederation," MacGregor recalled:

> He knew the explorers, the ships, the countries, the treaties, the politicians. His daughter and I stood there listening, her mesmerized by a man she knew was far more than Her Majesty's Leader of the Loyal Opposition, me listening, perhaps for the first time, to a man who was obviously far, far more than what he always insisted was true about himself.
>
> "What you see is what you get."
>
> Not at all.[22]

What Canadians did not get from the man who would be prime minister will likewise remain unknown, a past possibility forever lost to the passage of time.

NOTES

INTRODUCTION

1 The full text of the debate can be found in Library and Archives Canada (LAC), Ottawa, John Turner fonds, MG 26 (hereafter cited as JNTP), Q7-2, vol. 7, file 4, "Leaders' Debate, 25 October 1988."

2 "The *Playboy* Interview: Marshall McLuhan," *Playboy,* March 1969, http://www.digitallantern.net/.

3 Ron Graham, "The Politics of Nostalgia," *Saturday Night,* September 1984.

CHAPTER 1: THE MAKING OF AN EXTROVERT

1 Goldwin Smith, quoted in Robert M. Hamilton and Dorothy Shields, eds., *The Dictionary of Canadian Quotations and Phrases* (Toronto: McClelland and Stewart, 1979), 650.

2 John H. Taylor, *Ottawa: An Illustrated History* (Toronto: Lorimer, 1986), 154; Interview of John Taylor, Ottawa, May 17, 2006.

3 Jack Cahill, *John Turner: The Long Run* (Toronto: McClelland and Stewart, 1984), 37. The material on Turner's youth that follows draws extensively from Cahill, who in 1984 conducted numerous interviews with Turner covering this period.

4 Interview of Brenda Norris (née Turner), Montreal, April 7, 2005. Although Phyllis Gregory's mother came from a more privileged background than her husband, Brenda Norris believes that Phyllis's father encouraged her to do well at school.

5 "These Key Women at Ottawa," *Canadian Home Journal,* August 1942, 7, 10, 16; Kay Alsop, "Necessity Has Its Own Virtue," *UBC Alumni Chronicle* 30,2 (Summer 1975), 17-19; Doris Milligan, "The Four Lives of Phyllis Ross," *Vancouver Life,* April 1966, 39-42.

6 Certified copy of an entry of death, General Register Office, Registration District: Dartford, 1932, Subdistrict: Dartford and Farningham, County: Kent, No. 330, Leonard

Hugh Turner. The certificate reads "Acute Broncho Pneumonia. Acute Delirium. Thyroidectomy. Natural Causes. PM." and gives the date of death as November 18, 1932.

7 Valerie Gibson, "Born to Run," *Vancouver Magazine,* September 1988, 36-43, 119-20.

8 Norris interview.

9 Roy MacGregor, "'My Time Is Now!'" *Toronto Star,* June 17, 1984.

10 Gibson, "Born to Run."

11 Ibid.

12 J.L. Granatstein, *The Ottawa Men: The Civil Service Mandarins, 1935-1957,* 2nd ed. (Toronto: University of Toronto Press, 1998), 10-11. "The ethos that governed them," Granatstein speculated, "was probably attributable in part to the Oxford background of so many of them – Balliol and St. John's had for generations been the training-ground for Whitehall's mandarins." Ibid.

13 Cahill, *John Turner,* 39. The friend was Barbara Ann Scott, who would become an Olympic figure-skating champion in 1948. She lived around the corner from the Turners in Sandy Hill and was a playmate of the Turner children.

14 Ron Graham, *One-Eyed Kings: Promise and Illusion in Canadian Politics* (Toronto: Collins, 1986), 189.

15 Mungo James, "Shake the Hand That Ends the Arm That Once Held Princess Margaret," *Saturday Night,* May 1966, 33-35.

16 Norris interview.

17 Charles Lynch, *Race for the Rose: Election 1984* (Toronto: Methuen, 1984), 69.

18 Norris interview.

19 Interview of John Turner, Ottawa, July 25, 2005.

20 Pearson aide John de B. Payne believed that Turner was always looking for a father figure. See Cahill, *John Turner,* 209-10.

21 Ibid.; *Report of the Wartime Prices and Trade Board,* September 3, 1939, to March 31, 1943, 3, Records of the Wartime Prices and Trades Board, Library and Archives Canada (LAC), Ottawa, RG 64, vol. 51, *The Wartime Prices and Trade Board: History of the Oils and Fats Administration, 1939-1948,* index (archivist's description of the WPTB prefacing the LAC finding aid); "These Key Women," 10; "Science Aids War Effort: 25th Canadian Chemical Convention at Hamilton," *Canadian Chemistry and Process Industries,* June 1942, 329-38.

22 Interview of John Turner, Toronto, May 1, 2007.

23 Norris interview.

24 Eddie MacCabe, "St. Pat's Grads Re-knot Old School Ties," *Ottawa Journal,* May 24, 1973; John Grace, "An Address by John Grace on the Occasion of the Celebration of John Turner's 75th Birthday at the York Club," Toronto, June 7, 2004 (a copy of this speech was provided to the author by Mr. Grace).

25 MacCabe, "St. Pat's."

26 Interview of John Grace, Ottawa, July 25, 2005.

27 Peter B. Sievenpiper, "A Second Rhodes Scholar," *Beta Theta Pi,* March 1949.

28 Interview of Jacques Monet, SJ, Toronto, June 27, 2005. Monet observes that the education offered at St. Patrick's College and similar institutions run by other Catholic orders

had much in common with Jesuit education, whose distinctiveness he believes has been overdrawn.

29 Grace, "An Address."

30 Interview of John Turner, Ottawa, July 25, 2005.

31 Monet interview.

32 The quotation from St. Augustine reads, "If then your merits are God's gifts, God does not crown your merits as your merits, but as His gifts." St. Augustine, "A Treatise on Grace and Free Will," in *A Select Library of the Nicene and Post-Nicene Fathers of the Christian Church,* vol. 5, *St. Augustine: Anti-Pelagian Writings,* ed. Philip Schaff (New York: Christian Literature, 1887), 450. The Biblical verse is Luke 12:48.

33 Gary Mason, "The Even Couple: John Turner," *Vancouver Magazine,* December 1984, 33-34, 141-42.

34 Ibid.

35 In 1960 Phyllis Turner Ross was appointed chancellor of UBC, the first female university chancellor in the Commonwealth.

36 Cahill, *John Turner,* 53.

37 Ibid., 56.

38 Donald Ferguson, "Brock Hall to Parliament Hill," *UBC Alumni Chronicle* 38,3 (Fall 1984): 11. The examples of Turner's writing style are from the following *Ubyssey* articles under the "Chick Turner" byline: "Gym Club Brightens Campus Sport," January 9, 1947; "Scribe Enjoys Confab with Harlem," January 23, 1947; "Annual Intramural Swimming Meet at Crystal Pool Headlines Gala Sport Card for Fans This Weekend," January 30, 1947; "Record Swim Entry Marks Intramural Meet Tonight," February 1, 1947; "Jokers Take Intramural Swim Meet," February 4, 1947.

39 Martin Cleary, "Unable to Hurdle Red Tape: Turner Missed '52 Olympics," *Ottawa Citizen,* June 17, 1984.

40 Allan Fotheringham, "The Chivas in the Liberal Mix," *Maclean's,* March 12, 1984; Interview of John Turner, Toronto, December 9, 2008.

41 Interview of John Dobson, Montreal, May 26, 2005.

42 Mason, "The Even Couple."

43 Ron Haggart, "This Is the Way I Remember Him in His UBC Days," *Toronto Star,* January 18, 1968.

44 Mason, "The Even Couple."

45 Vancouver filmmaker Morton Klenman, quoted in Edison Stewart, "Leaders' Futures Hinge on Sept. 4th," *Toronto Star,* July 11, 1984.

46 Cahill, *John Turner,* 55.

47 Mason, "The Even Couple."

48 Photo caption, *Ubyssey,* September 24, 1948.

49 Fred Rowell, "Around the Track," *Ubyssey,* January 27, 1949; "UBC Trackmen Prep Daily in Hopes of New Title," *Ubyssey,* March 18, 1949.

50 He would eventually revise the paper for publication as John Turner, "The Senate of Canada – Political Conundrum," in *Canadian Issues: Essays in Honour of Henry F. Angus,* ed. Robert M. Clark (Toronto: University of Toronto Press, 1961), 57-80.

51 Cahill, *John Turner,* 51.

52 Haggart, "This Is the Way."

53 Cahill, *John Turner*, 51.

54 Ibid., 58.

55 Ibid., 66.

56 John Turner to Phyllis Ross, October 11, 1950, private correspondence of Brenda Norris (loaned to the author by Brenda Norris).

57 John Turner to Brenda Turner, April 5, 1952, Norris correspondence.

58 Ibid., January 21, 1951.

59 Ibid., April 5, 1952.

60 Hedley Burrell, "John Turner Topples Egan Chambers by 2,000 Votes," *Montreal Gazette,* June 19, 1962.

61 Diana (Gill) Kirkwood, quoted in Cahill, *John Turner,* 65.

62 Norris interview.

63 Interview of John Turner, Toronto, December 18, 2008.

64 Graham, *One-Eyed Kings,* 196.

CHAPTER 2: CIRCLING HOME

1 Richard Pound, *Stikeman Elliott: The First Fifty Years* (Montreal/Kingston: McGill-Queen's University Press, 2002), 34.

2 Jack Cahill, *John Turner: The Long Run* (Toronto: McClelland and Stewart, 1984), 69.

3 Interview of John Turner, Toronto, December 9, 2008.

4 Cahill, *John Turner,* 78.

5 Interview of James Robb, Montreal, April 6, 2005.

6 Interview of Mel Rothman, Montreal, May 26, 2005.

7 Cahill, *John Turner,* 71.

8 Turner recognized that "the Quiet Revolution of Jean Lesage was a natural aftermath of Duplessis's type of paternalistic government," but he thought "one has to concede that he [Duplessis] ran a good government. This is not to say that there wasn't a share of influence peddling [but] no one has ever attached any corruption to Duplessis himself." Cahill, *John Turner,* 72.

9 Paul Rutherford, "Designing Culture: Reflections on a Post/Modern Project," in *Media, Policy, National Identity and Citizenry in Changing Democratic Societies: The Case of Canada,* ed. J. Smith (Durham, NC: Canadian Studies Center, Duke University, 1998), 184.

10 Christopher Dummitt, *The Manly Modern: Masculinity in Postwar Canada* (Vancouver: UBC Press, 2007), 2.

11 Brenda Norris recalls that they both "lit up" when they met. Her brother never discussed the relationship with her afterward. Interview of Brenda Norris, Montreal, April 7, 2005.

12 John Turner, "The Senate of Canada – Political Conundrum," in *Canadian Issues: Essays in Honour of Henry F. Angus,* ed. Robert M. Clark (Toronto: University of Toronto Press, 1961), 57-80.

13 A file in the Turner papers contains a typed list of names, headed "Distribution of Senate Article." Two names were added in pencil at the bottom of this list, one of them being P.E. Trudeau. Library and Archives Canada (LAC), Ottawa, MG 26 (hereafter cited as JNTP), Q13-1, vol. 1, file 1, "Article on the Senate of Canada" (file 1 of 3).

14 Rothman interview.

15 Cahill, *John Turner*, 84.

16 Mitchell Sharp, *Which Reminds Me: A Memoir* (Toronto: University of Toronto Press, 1994), 90; J.W. Pickersgill, *Seeing Canada Whole: A Memoir* (Toronto: Fitzhenry and Whiteside, 1994), 536.

17 Norris interview.

18 Cahill, *John Turner*, 69.

19 Mungo James, "Shake the Hand That Ends the Arm That Once Held Princess Margaret," *Saturday Night,* May 1966, 33-35. Interview of Dino Constantinou, Montreal, April 7, 2005; Robb interview; Interview of John Claxton, Montreal, April 6, 2005. The previous incumbents in the riding were Charles Colquhoun Ballantyne, Government (Unionist), 1917-21; Herbert Meredith Marler, Liberal, 1921-25; Charles Hazlitt Cahan, Conservative, 1925-40; Brooke Claxton, Liberal, 1940-54; and Claude Richardson, Liberal, 1954-58.

20 Interview of John Grace, Ottawa, July 25, 2005.

21 Claxton interview.

22 Telephone interview of Emmett Kierans, February 12, 2005.

23 Robb interview; Claxton interview; Joseph Wearing, *The L-Shaped Party: The Liberal Party of Canada, 1958-1980* (Toronto: McGraw Hill Ryerson, 1981), 27-28; John English, *The Worldly Years: The Life of Lester Pearson,* vol. 2, *1949-1972* (Toronto: Knopf Canada, 1992), 232.

24 "Liberals Nominate Turner," *Montreal Star,* May 2, 1962. See also JNTP, Q8-2, vol. 1, file 4, "Candidate for the Liberal Convention, St. Lawrence–St. George, John N. Turner"; JNTP, Q8-2, vol. 1, file 6, "Election Campaign, 1962 and 1963 – Publicity Material, n.d., 1962-1963."

25 Claxton interview. Pierre Trudeau was listed in campaign planning materials as a speech writer, but no one remembered him participating in the campaign. "Publicity," JNTP, Q8-2, vol. 1, file 2.

26 J.M. Davey, "A Report on the Research and Analysis Work Carried Out in the St. Lawrence–St. George Election Campaign of John Turner, Federal Election of 1962," September 1962, JNTP, Q8-2, vol. 1, file 3, "Election Campaign, 1962 – Scrapbook" (file 2 of 2).

27 Constantinou interview.

28 Claxton interview.

29 *Going My Way? My Way Is the Liberal Way* (Turner campaign brochure), n.d., JNTP, Q8-2, vol. 1, file 6, "Election Campaign, 1962 and 1963 – Publicity Material, n.d., 1962-63."

30 Turner often tells this story. Bill Pothitos, a Montreal restauranteur, was with him at the time and remembers the incident. James Robb to the author, Memo, December 14, 2007.

31 Frank McGee, "Turner as PM? He'd Probably Shake Up the Establishment," *Toronto Star,* January 18, 1968.

32 "Role of Youth in Politics Stressed," *Montreal Star,* May 9, 1962.

33 Peter Gzowski, "Man to Watch: Politician in the New Frontier Style," *Maclean's,* August 11, 1962.

34 "Memorandum on the Erection of a Tent," n.d., JNTP, Q8-2, vol. 1, file 3.
35 "Report Concerning Turner-Pearson Motorcade, June 12, 1962," JNTP, Q8-2, vol. 1, file 3.
36 "Survey Analysis," June 12, 1962, JNTP, Q8-2, vol. 1, file 3.
37 James, "Shake the Hand."
38 Gzowski, "Man to Watch."

CHAPTER 3: GETTING AHEAD IN CANADIAN POLITICS

1 Mungo James, "Shake the Hand That Ends the Arm That Once Held Princess Margaret," *Saturday Night*, May 1966, 33-35.
2 "The Concerns of a Liberal," notes taken from "Three Challenges for Contemporary Liberalism," remarks by John Turner to the Alberta Liberal Association, November 17, 1962, in John Turner, *Politics of Purpose* (Toronto: McClelland and Stewart, 1968), 14.
3 Harold Innis, "Great Britain, the United States, and Canada," in *Essays in Canadian Economic History*, ed. Mary Quayle Innis (Toronto: University of Toronto Press, 1956), 405.
4 John Turner to Selma Robinson of *McCall's* magazine, December 12, 1966, Library and Archives Canada (LAC), Ottawa, MG 26 (hereafter cited as JNTP), Q13-1, vol. 7, file 5, "Minister – Personal" (file 1 of 2).
5 Robert Bothwell and William Kilbourn, *C.D. Howe: A Biography* (Toronto: McClelland and Stewart, 1979), 320.
6 Tom Saunders, "In Winnipeg South: A New Voice from the East," *Winnipeg Free Press*, February 19, 1963.
7 Interview of Cam Avery, Vancouver, September 16, 2008.
8 Interview of James Robb, April 6, 2005. Payne had his own consulting company, which did fundraising for Montreal hospitals and represented, among other clients, big tobacco in Ottawa and Washington.
9 Russell Gilliece, "Happy Days Return to Reform Club," *Montreal Gazette*, April 9, 1963.
10 Christopher Young, *Ottawa Citizen*, November 16, 1963, quoted in Jack Cahill, *John Turner: The Long Run* (Toronto: McClelland and Stewart, 1984), 92.
11 John Turner, "The Member of Parliament," reprint of a speech, "The Role of an M.P." as delivered to McGill University, January 29, 1964, in Turner, *Politics of Purpose*, 18.
12 Ibid., 18-19.
13 Cahill, *John Turner*, 92.
14 Allan Levine, *Scrum Wars: The Prime Ministers and the Media* (Toronto: Dundurn, 1993), 312; Patrick Brennan, *Reporting the Nation's Business: Press-Government Relations during the Liberal Years, 1935-1957* (Toronto: University of Toronto Press, 1994), x. Brennan, who covers an earlier period than that currently under discussion, thinks that the relationship was becoming more adversarial by the 1960s.
15 Erik Nielsen, *The House Is Not a Home* (Toronto: Macmillan, 1989), 159.
16 Interview of John Turner, Toronto, December 9, 2008; Interview of Geills Turner, Toronto, January 22, 2009; Sean O'Sullivan, *Both My Houses: From Politics to Priesthood* (Toronto: Key Porter, 1986), 52.

17 Turner, who favoured the new flag, was dismayed by the bitter debate in Parliament. He advised Pearson to switch his emphasis from the flag itself and to make Diefenbaker's obstructionism the political issue. In a letter to Joseph Coyle, September 11, 1964, Turner did not hide his exasperation, writing, "The Conservative filibuster has become a victory for Mr. Diefenbaker instead of an issue on which we could, in the long run, have rallied public opinion." JNTP, Q13-1, vol. 2, file 3, "Canadian Flag – Speech Material, 1964."

18 "Turner Defends English Quebecers," *Montreal Star,* March 2, 1964. See also "Separatism Means Isolation," *Montreal Gazette,* March 3, 1964. Turner continued to make similar speeches on Quebec as the decade progressed. See, for example, "Liberalism: Formula for the Future," excerpts of a speech given to the Western Canadian Young Liberal Policy Convention, Calgary, February 25, 1967, and "Options for Unity," excerpts of a speech given to the Montreal Reform Club, October 16, 1967, in Turner, *Politics of Purpose,* 1-8, 32-46.

19 Excerpts from a speech, "Off the Couch and Back to the Drawing Board," Vancouver, BC, October 21, 1964, in Elizabeth McIninch and Arthur Milnes, eds., *Politics of Purpose: 40th Anniversary Edition* (Montreal/Kingston: McGill-Queen's University Press, 2009), 84.

20 "Turner Defends English Quebecers."

21 The Inuit were the responsibility of Northern Affairs and National Resources rather than Indian Affairs – revisions to the *Indian Act* in 1960 had excluded the Inuit simply because they hadn't made treaties with the Crown. Morris Zaslow, *The Northward Expansion of Canada, 1914-1967* (Toronto: McClelland and Stewart, 1988), 301.

22 "Eskimos' Future Subject of Talk," *Montreal Star,* April 15, 1964; JNTP, Q1, vol. 7, file 2, "Nouveau-Quebec/William Eccles"; Michael Gillan, "Turner: The Man in the Middle of the Liberal Race," *Toronto Globe and Mail,* March 29, 1968; G.E. Mortimore, "Cold War in New Quebec," *Globe Magazine,* April 24, 1965.

23 G.W. Rowley, "Quebec's Inuit Today," *Polar Record* 16, 10 (1972): 203.

24 See, for example, John Turner, "Education of Eskimos in Nouveau Quebec," September 16, 1963, JNTP, Q10-1, vol. 1, file 6; Speech to the Franklin Society, McGill University, February 27, 1965, JNTP, Q1, vol. 4, file 9, "Franklin Society, McGill University, 1965"; Speech on the launching of the M.S. *Frank H. Brown,* April 22, 1965, JNTP, Q10-1, vol. 2, files 3-4, "Launching of M.S. 'Frank H. Brown' at the Georges P. Vanier Drydock."

25 John Turner, "Voice across the Border," based on notes from "A New Look at Canada," a speech given to the Canadian Club of New York, January 15, 1964, in Turner, *Politics of Purpose,* 174-75.

26 Cahill, *John Turner,* 99.

27 See, for example, JNTP, Q1, vol. 1, file 1, "Arctic Institute, 1963-1969," and file 2, "Arctic Institute Speech, July 15, 1965"; "Journey into Siberia: Lessons for Canada," speech to Rotary Club of Montreal, Queen Elizabeth Hotel, October 5, 1965, JNTP, Q10-1, vol. 2, file 11; Speech to the Franklin Society, February 23, 1966, JNTP, Q10-1, vol. 2, file 21, "Franklin Society, Montreal, Feb. 23, 1966"; "The Canadian and Soviet Norths – A Common Frontier," speech to the Toronto Branch of the Engineering Institute of Canada, Toronto, February 3, 1966, JNTP, Q10-1, vol. 2, file 18.

28 Arthur Laing to Paul Martin, November 21, 1963, JNTP, Q1, vol. 2, file 9, "Columbia River – Confidential." Turner hired an expert in the field, Maxwell Cohen, dean of the McGill Law School and chairman of the Research Committee of the Canadian branch of the International Law Association, to write a background brief on the issue.

29 John Turner, "The Diplomacy of Water," notes based on a speech given in Washington to the National Water Conference of the Chamber of Commerce of the United States, December 9, 1965, in Turner, *Politics of Purpose,* 176.

30 Peter C. Newman, "Workable Ideas, Not Grand Ideologies," *Toronto Star,* November 29, 1966.

31 John Turner to Lester Pearson, September 17, 1965, JNTP, Q1, vol. 9, file 7, "Priority for Canada/Resource Policy."

32 John Turner to Lester Pearson, October 25, 1965; John Turner, "Priorities for Canada," notes of a speech to the Women's Canadian Club of London, Ontario, March 16, 1965; Anthony Westell, "Liberals Declare 5 Major Issues in Election Fight" (newspaper clipping), n.d.: JNTP, Q1, vol. 7, file 7, "Priority for Canada/Resource Policy."

33 Turner to Pearson, September 17, 1965.

CHAPTER 4: SHOALS OF CANDIDACY

1 Christopher Young, "Some Curious Casting in the Cabinet Drama," *Ottawa Citizen,* December 18, 1965; Blair Fraser, "Backstage at Ottawa: John Turner's a Minister without a Portfolio but with a Bright Future," *Maclean's,* January 22, 1966.

2 Peter Newman, "John Turner: Tempting to Compare Him with JFK," *Ottawa Journal,* December 22, 1965.

3 "Marine Safety on the St. Lawrence River," *Seaports and the Transport World,* April 1966. After this system was implemented, no more major accidents occurred – it was one of those improvements that no one ever hears about, because there were no problems with it. Interview of John Turner by Elizabeth McIninch, January 10, 1995, Library and Archives Canada (LAC), Ottawa, MG 26 (hereafter cited as JNTP), acc. no. 240670, consultation copy no. V1-2008-08-0009.

4 John Turner, *Politics of Purpose* (Toronto: McClelland and Stewart, 1968), ix.

5 Interview of Jerry Grafstein, Toronto, April 30, 2009.

6 John Turner, "The Political Challenge of Change," address to the Toronto Kiwanis Club, Royal York Hotel, June 15, 1966, JNTP, Q10-1, vol. 3, file 1, "The Political Challenge of Change."

7 Interview of John Turner by Elizabeth McIninch, January 10, 1995, JNTP, acc. no. 240670, consultation copy no. V1-2008-08-0009.

8 "The Young Contenders," *Twenty Million Questions,* March 30, 1967, Canadian Broadcasting Corporation (CBC) Television, CBOT Film Library, CBC Archives, ISN 215115.

9 Jack Cahill, *John Turner: The Long Run* (Toronto: McClelland and Stewart, 1984), 106.

10 John Turner, "A National Resource Policy," excerpts of a speech, "A Second Canada: The Reach for Resources," to the B.C. Weekly Newspapers Association, October 28, 1966, in Turner, *Politics of Purpose,* 150-55.

NOTES TO PAGES 66-70

11 Turner, *Politics of Purpose*, xiii-xiv. Turner's "A Second Canada" platform was also informed by the work of Michael Harrington, an American political activist with socialist leanings, whose recently published *Accidental Century* warned that progress was outpacing society's ability to adapt. Turner identified with him as a fellow Catholic whose perspective on public policy issues was informed by his faith, and he adapted many of his ideas to the Canadian political context. Harrington's earlier book on poverty, *The Other America*, had influenced both the Kennedy and the Johnson administrations. Turner cited this aspect of Harrington's work in "A Separate Nation: The Troubled Consumer," notes from "The Troubled Consumer in an Affluent Society," a speech delivered to the Ottawa-Carleton Liberal Association, November 15, 1967, in Turner, *Politics of Purpose*, 76.

12 Turner, "The Political Challenge of Change."

13 Paul Rush, "John Turner and the Voice of Youth," *Weekend Magazine*, June 3, 1967.

14 "A Second Canada – Law Reform and Lawyers: The Changing Order and Static Law," speech delivered at Osgoode Hall Law School, Toronto, February 2, 1967, in Turner, *Politics of Purpose*, 68-76.

15 Gordon Robertson, Memo, December 19, 1966, JNTP, Q3, vol. 1, file 3, "Organization and Structure of the Department of Consumer and Corporate Affairs"; Hansard, January 18, 1966, 8.

16 Stephen Azzi, *Walter Gordon and the Rise of Canadian Nationalism* (Montreal/Kingston: McGill-Queen's University Press, 1999), 143.

17 Peter C. Newman, "Workable Ideas, Not Grand Ideologies," *Toronto Star*, November 29, 1966; Cahill, *John Turner*, 111.

18 JNTP, Q10-1, vol. 4, file 9, "The Pierre Berton Show, March 22, 1967."

19 Cahill, *John Turner*, 123.

20 Woodrow Wilson, *Congressional Government: A Study in American Politics* (1885; repr., Baltimore: Johns Hopkins University Press, 1981), 47-48.

21 Bruce Hutchison, "Mr. Turner and the Taxpayers," *Winnipeg Free Press*, May 28, 1967.

22 Lester Pearson to John Deutsch, May 25, 1966, LAC, Pearson Papers, MG 26, N4, vol. 146, file 352/R337 Conf. At Pearson's request, Gordon Robertson had written earlier (February 3, 1966) to Deutsch on this matter. LAC, MG 26, Q3, vol. 1, file 3, "Organization and Structure of the Department of Consumer and Corporate Affairs, 1966-1976" (file 1 of 2).

23 JNTP, Q3, vol. 4, file 1, "Consumer Policy, 1967-1968." There was also discussion about the name for the new department. Pearson favoured the Department of Consumer and Corporate Affairs. This Pearson-Turner correspondence is in JNTP, Q3, vol. 1, file 4, "Organization and Structure of the Department of Consumer and Corporate Affairs, 1966-1976" (file 2 of 2).

24 Interview of Jerry Grafstein, Toronto, April 30, 2009.

25 JNTP, Q3, vol. 1, file 1, "Department of Registrar General." Bélanger, Ouellette et Associés, a consulting firm, was hired in May to "explore the operational features" of the new department. It was to report to Turner's executive assistant, Jerry Grafstein.

26 JNTP, Q3, vol. 4, file 1, "Consumer Policy, 1967-1968."

27 JNTP, Q3, vol. 4, file 5, "Consumer Program – News Releases, 1967-1968"; Hansard, October 13, 1967, 3067.

28 Walter Gray, "Consumer Watchdog Turner's Big Chance," *Toronto Star,* May 10, 1967.

29 John Turner to Cabinet, Memo, August 4, 1967, JNTP, Q3, vol. 4, file 8, "Consumer Protection, 1967-1968" (file 2 of 2).

30 Lloyd Axworthy, *Navigating a New World: Canada's Global Future* (Toronto: Vintage, 2004), 34-35.

31 JNTP, Q3, vol. 6, file 1. On his last day as minister of consumer and corporate affairs – July 5, 1968 – Turner addressed a memo to Cabinet, "Proposed Action to Reduce the Price of Drugs," which summarized developments to date on this file and recommended that the government proceed with Bill C-190 – with a few revisions. JNTP, Q3, vol. 6, file 6, "Drug Bill – Reference Material."

32 John Turner, September 22, 1967, quoted in "Here's What the Candidate Says ..." *Toronto Star,* January 18, 1968.

33 Tim Creery, "Trudeau and Turner," *Edmonton Journal,* March 22, 1968.

34 Gordon Pape, "Can You Imagine This Montreal Man Becoming Canada's Prime Minister?" *Montreal Gazette,* March 25, 1967.

35 Peter C. Newman, "Ottawa's Action Generation," *Monetary Times,* April 1967, 21-24. Turner, prepared for the media's slippery tactics by John de B. Payne, was remarkably consistent in delivering his answer to this kind of question. To another such query, he said, "Sure I'm ambitious. I'm ambitious for cauooo. There are a lot of things I want to see done in this country – and I want to be in a position to get them done." Mungo James, "Shake the Hand That Ends the Arm That Once Held Princess Margaret," *Saturday Night,* May 1966, 33-35.

36 Douglas Fisher and Harry Crowe, "The Man Who Danced with a Princess," *Toronto Telegram,* December 6, 1967.

CHAPTER 5: CLOSE TO POWER

1 J.L. Granatstein, *Canada, 1957-1967: The Years of Uncertainty and Innovation* (Toronto: McClelland and Stewart, 1986), 306-7.

2 Ben Malkin, "Turner's Young and Dashing, Which Could Be His Problem," *Ottawa Citizen,* January 19, 1968.

3 Interview of David Smith, Toronto, April 26, 2005. Smith had first met Turner when he was a student at Carleton University and had invited both Turner and Jean Chrétien to speak to campus Liberals. He later went on to work as an executive assistant on the Hill, first for Pearson, then for Walter Gordon. As Gordon anticipated leaving politics, he advised Smith to move to someone else. With his cross-country network of Young Liberals, Smith was an important catch. He had been courted by Paul Martin and by Paul Hellyer but opted for Turner in the fall of 1967 because he felt most comfortable with him.

4 Malkin, "Turner's Young."

5 Dino Constantinou busied himself collecting and analyzing data, Jerry Grafstein handled PR and convention organization (tracking delegates and organizing demonstrations), and Vic Chapman, who had coordinated a highly publicized voyageur canoe pageant during the Centennial, was appointed tour coordinator. They also hired pollster Peter Regenstreif, who had worked for the Liberal Party and the NDP. In major cities,

Turner supporters organized groups of businessmen to canvass for donations toward the campaign. "The Turner Machine," *Montreal Gazette,* April 5, 1968; Interview of Dino Constantinou, Montreal, April 7, 2005; Claire Hoy, *Margin of Error* (Toronto: Key Porter Books, 1989), 29; Interview of John Claxton, Montreal, April 6, 2005; Library and Archives Canada (Ottawa), Alastair Gillespie fonds, Liberal Party Series, vol. 6, file 27, "John Turner Campaign 1968: Lists of Potential Donors, List of Donations, and File Folder, All with Extensive Marginalia, 1967?/Early 1968."

6 Keith Davey, *The Rainmaker: A Passion for Politics* (Toronto: Stoddart, 1986), 200-1.

7 "Mr. Turner is Right-Handy," *Toronto Telegram,* April 10, 1968.

8 Ibid.

9 John English, *The Worldly Years: The Life of Lester Pearson,* vol. 2, *1949-1972* (Toronto: Knopf Canada, 1992), 381-82.

10 Roy MacGregor, "'My Time Is Now!'" *Toronto Star,* June 17, 1984.

11 John Turner, "The Political Challenge of Change," address to the Toronto Kiwanis Club, Royal York Hotel, June 15, 1966, LAC, MG 26 (hereafter cited as JNTP), Q10-1, vol. 3, file 1, "The Political Challenge of Change."

12 One reporter commented that Turner was "in the curious position of appearing less hip to some young Liberals than Justice Minister Pierre Trudeau, who is eight years older, and less experienced or mature than other major contenders." Michael Gillan, "Turner: The Man in the Middle of the Liberal Race," *Toronto Globe and Mail,* March 29, 1968.

13 Allan Fotheringham, "Turner's Biggest Problem Is to Convince Delegates," *Vancouver Sun,* March 25, 1968.

14 Charles Lynch, "John Turner: Yes, He Does Sweat and Swear," *Executive,* April 1972.

15 Christopher Young, "Turner in Action," *Ottawa Citizen,* March 16, 1968.

16 JNTP, Q3, vol. 7, file 4, "Prairie Royal Commission on Consumer Prices and Inflation, 1968"; "Charges of Monopoly under Study – Turner," *Saskatoon Star Phoenix,* March 3, 1968.

17 The drug bill would not be passed until after the leadership race and the general election in June. It was passed into law and would keep Canadian prescription costs low until pharmaceutical companies persuaded the Mulroney government to reverse it in the 1980s.

18 Hansard, February 12, 1968, 6620. The Turner papers contain many drafts of this speech. JNTP, Q-3, vol. 6, file 3, "Drugs – Drug Bill – Drafts of Minister's Speech, 1967-1968."

19 "Text of a Statement by the Hon. John N. Turner, Minister of Consumer and Corporate Affairs, Made in Montreal, Thursday, March 28, 1968, 8:30 p.m.," JNTP, Q3, vol. 6, file 2, "Drugs – Drug Bill, 1967-1968" (file 5 of 5).

20 "Telephone Turner," *Vancouver Sun,* March 23, 1968.

21 Sally Barnes, "Turner Campaigns 15 Hours Non-Stop," *Toronto Star,* March 11, 1968.

22 Young, "Turner in Action."

23 Martin Sullivan, *Mandate '68: The Year of Pierre Elliott Trudeau* (Toronto: Doubleday, 1968), 286.

24 Fotheringham, "Turner's Biggest Problem."

25 Gillan, "Turner."

26 W.R. Wright to John Turner, February 22, 1968, JNTP, Q8-1, vol. 1, file 10, "Election Campaign – Ottawa Carleton – Strategy, 1968" (file 4 of 4).

27 Paul Rush, "John Turner and the Voice of Youth," *Weekend Magazine,* June 3, 1967.

28 John Turner to W.R. Wright, February 26, 1968, JNTP, Q8-1, vol. 1, file 10, "Election Campaign – Ottawa Carleton – Strategy, 1968" (file 4 of 4).

29 "John Turner," *Ottawa Journal,* March 20, 1968.

30 Gillan, "Turner."

31 Elizabeth McIninch and Arthur Milnes, eds., *Politics of Purpose: 40th Anniversary Edition* (Montreal/Kingston: McGill-Queen's University Press, 2009), 87. "There developed among my contemporaries the feelings of very strong nationalism – of wanting to be masters in their own house," he later recalled. "When you get six or seven million people living in a territory where they form a majority, where they've had a connection with the geography for almost four centuries, where they've got their own language, where in those days they had a common religion, where they have their own system of law, which is quite distinct in many areas, quite different from the Common Law tradition, where they have their own sense of humour, where television arrived and gave them a collective identity, because they're a great verbal people: when you get this group of people in these circumstances with a common history and common feeling of purpose, then it is inevitable that the heart is going to struggle with reason." Jack Cahill, *John Turner: The Long Run* (Toronto: McClelland and Stewart, 1984), 73.

32 Interview of John Turner, Toronto, June 13, 2005.

33 JNTP, Q8-1, vol. 3, file 1, "Leadership Campaign: Convention, Speech, April 5 (Drafts)"; JNTP, Q8-1, vol. 6, file 5, "Leadership Campaign – National Liberal Convention – 1968 – Transcript of Proceedings."

34 Ibid.

35 Sullivan, *Mandate '68,* 348.

36 Maurice Western, *Winnipeg Free Press,* April 4, 1968, quoted in Paul Rutherford, *When Television Was Young* (Toronto: University of Toronto Press, 1990), 432; Peter C. Newman, *A Nation Divided: Canada and the Coming of Pierre Trudeau* (New York: Knopf, 1969), 458-59.

37 Sally Barnes, "Turner Goes Down with 'Guns Blazing,'" *Toronto Star,* April 8, 1968.

38 John Sawatsky, *The Insiders: Government, Business, and the Lobbyists* (Toronto: McClelland and Stewart, 1987), 28.

39 Barnes, "Turner Goes Down."

40 Michael Gillan, "Political Puzzle Remains: Why Did Turner Stay In?" *Toronto Globe and Mail,* April 8, 1968.

41 Cahill, *John Turner,* 128.

42 Telephone interview of Tex Enemark, November 28, 2008.

43 Paul Martin Jr. in a video screened for John Turner's seventy-eighth birthday, National Club, Toronto, June 13, 2007.

44 John Turner to D.J. Wright, May 7, 1968, JNTP, Q8-1, vol. 4, file 1, "Leadership Campaign – Correspondence – General" (file 3 of 3).

45 Christina McCall-Newman, "Turner: The Once and Future Contender," *Maclean's,* May 1971.

46 "Basford's Swing-in Draws over 900 to the Commodore," *Vancouver Sun*, May 30, 1968.

47 Sullivan, *Mandate '68*, 2.

48 The olive branches extended to Turner's camp included the appointment of Ron Basford to Turner's old portfolio of Consumer and Corporate Affairs. JNTP, Q5, vol. 20, file 1, "Mr. Turner's Confidential Notes, 1968-1969-1970-1971." The BC Liberal Party, anticipating the end of W.A.C. Bennett's Social Credit dynasty, tried to recruit Turner as leader, but he politely declined the offer.

CHAPTER 6: DRIVING THE OMNIBUS

1 Peter Newman, *Toronto Daily Star*, April 25, 1967, quoted in John English, *Citizen of the World* (Toronto: Knopf, 2006), 440.

2 Telephone interview of Allan Gotlieb, January 21, 2010; Richard Pound, *Chief Justice W.R. Jackett: By the Law of the Land* (Montreal/Kingston: McGill-Queen's University Press, 1999).

3 Catherine Gidney, *A Long Eclipse: The Liberal Protestant Establishment and the Canadian University, 1920-1970* (Montreal/Kingston: McGill-Queen's University Press, 2004), xxv, 142; Gary R. Miedema, *For Canada's Sake: Public Religion, Centennial Celebrations, and the Re-making of Canada in the 1960s* (Montreal/Kingston: McGill-Queen's University Press, 2005), 202.

4 Martin L. Friedland, *My Life in Crime and Other Academic Adventures* (Toronto: University of Toronto Press for the Osgoode Society for Canadian Legal History, 2007), 32.

5 Ibid., 72.

6 Donald Maxwell had drafted the new *Divorce Act* with the assistance of his former boss, Wilbur Jackett, now the president of the Exchequer Court.

7 "Turner May Expand Criminal Code Bill," *Toronto Globe and Mail*, July 17, 1968.

8 "A Stanfield Win?" *Toronto Globe and Mail*, July 9, 1968; "Turner to Argue Split Bill Ideas," *Ottawa Journal*, July 19, 1968.

9 *The Criminal Code, 1953-54 (Can.), Ch. 51, as Amended to 1965* (Toronto: Carswell, 1965). The precedent for abortion went back to *Rex v. Bourne*, a 1939 case in England that had made the mother's health a legitimate defence for abortion.

10 "Abortion Statistics 'Utterly Fantastic,'" *Ottawa Journal*, July 19, 1968.

11 Joseph Dunlop, "John Turner, Pierre Trudeau and the Canadian Bishops: Catholic Involvement in the Federal Legal Reforms of 1967-68" (undergraduate research essay, University of Toronto, 2008).

12 According to Turner, he referred the issue to John O'Brien of O'Brien, Holm, Nolan in Montreal; Jack Weir of Weir & Foulds in Toronto; and C. Francis Murphy of Farris, Vaughn, Wills & Murphy in Vancouver. Murphy was legal adviser to Archbishop Carney in British Columbia, and Jack Weir was an adviser to Archbishop Pocock of Toronto. John Turner, "Faith and Politics," in *The Hidden Pierre Elliott Trudeau: The Faith behind the Politics*, ed. John English, Richard Gwyn, and P. Whitney Lackenbauer (Ottawa: Novalis, 2004), 112.

13 Robert W. Crooker to John Turner, August 26, 1968, Library and Archives Canada (LAC), Ottawa, MG 26 (hereafter cited as JNTP), Q4, vol. 1, file 1, "Abortion" (file 1 of 6). Turner received a detailed letter setting out objections to the abortion reform from Senator John J. Connolly, another English Catholic Liberal and a mentor he had often consulted on issues of the day. Connolly spelled out the conservative Catholic position on abortion, emphasizing that a fetus is potentially human from the moment of conception, and cited *Humanae Vitae* to back up his arguments. John J. Connolly to John Turner, February 11, 1969, JNTP, Q4, vol. 1, file 2, "Abortion" (file 2 of 6).

14 The name of the Laval priest is not known. In 1975 Turner tried to get a copy of the letter for his Cabinet colleague, Secretary of State Hugh Faulkner, but was unable to find it. John Turner to Hugh Faulkner, May 19, 1975, JNTP, Q4, vol. 1, file 6, "Abortion" (file 6 of 6).

15 "Statement of the Catholic Bishops of Canada on Abortion," February 7, 1968, JNTP, Q4, vol. 1, file 1, "Abortion" (file 1 of 6).

16 Turner, "Faith and Politics," 115-16.

17 Dunlop, "John Turner, Pierre Trudeau and the Canadian Bishops." Turner would later provide the rationalization that "the legislation ... had been the Church's last and best defence on the abortion issue," as demonstrated by the Supreme Court's later decision to strike it down under the Charter of Rights and Freedoms, thereby ushering in abortion on demand. Turner, "Faith and Politics," 113. See also Bernard Daly, "Trudeau and the Bedrooms of the Nation: The Canadian Bishops' Involvement," in English, Gwyn, and Lackenbauer, *The Hidden Pierre Elliott Trudeau*, 137.

18 This provision in the original legislation had prompted Trudeau's famous remark on national television in the fall of 1967 that "the state has no place in the bedrooms of the nation." See Sylvain Larocque, *Gay Marriage: The Story of a Canadian Social Revolution* (Toronto: James Lorimer, 2006), 11-12, for a journalistic account of the background to this legislation. As an example of the problem with the existing law, both Trudeau and Turner referred to a Saskatchewan case in which one Everett Klippert was charged in 1966 with gross indecency for homosexual acts and sentenced as a dangerous sexual offender to an indeterminate sentence that could extend to life in prison. See "Man Who Spurred Homosexual Law Still Jailed," *Ottawa Citizen*, February 12, 1971. It was on this case that the Supreme Court had ruled. See *Klippert v. The Queen*, [1967] S.C.R. 822. Some students of the issue argue that homosexuality was legalized in 1969 because of a growing consensus in society that it was a treatable medical problem. See David Kimmel and Daniel J. Robinson, "Sex, Crime, Pathology: Homosexuality and Criminal Code Reform in Canada, 1949-1969," *Canadian Journal of Law and Society* 16,1 (2001): 147-65.

19 See Turner's handwritten notes, n.d., JNTP, Q4, vol. 10, file 11, "Homosexuality."

20 Turner, "Faith and Politics," 116; Interview of Turner by Elizabeth McIninch, January 10, 1995, JNTP, acc. no. 240670, consultation copy no. V1-2008-08-0009. The heckler was George Muir (PC, Cape Breton–The Sydneys).

21 Hansard, April 17, 1969, 7633, 4, 5. See also CBC Digital Archives, "Second Go-Round for the Omnibus Bill," Broadcast date April 20, 1969, http://archives.cbc.ca/ for a radio interview of Turner on the subject.

22 In 1986 Turner would advocate revision of the *Canadian Human Rights Act* to prohibit discrimination on the basis of sexual orientation. JNTP, Q9-3, vol. 16, file 13.
23 J.A. Scollin to the deputy minister of justice, Memo, September 17, 1968, JNTP, Q4, vol. 9, file 6.
24 JNTP, Q4, vol. 9, file 6, "Firearms." This file contains a full list of organizations that presented submissions on the firearms changes.
25 Patrick Boyer, *A Passion for Justice: The Legacy of James Chalmers McRuer* (Toronto: University of Toronto Press for the Osgoode Society for Canadian Legal History, 1994), 280.
26 JNTP, Q4, vol. 13, file 13, "Lotteries."
27 Department of Transport News bulletin, November 14, 1969, Breathalyzer Publicity Campaign, JNTP, Q4, vol. 3, file 4, "Breathalyzer Publicity Campaign" (file 1 of 4).
28 "Quote, Unquote," *Financial Post* (Toronto), September 19, 1970.
29 JNTP, Q4, vol. 1, file 1, "Abortion" (file 1 of 6).
30 Gordon Pape, "The Omnibus Bill: The Clash of Ideals Goes On," *Montreal Gazette*, February 25, 1969.
31 JNTP, Q4, vol. 1, file 3, "Abortion" (file 3 of 6).
32 Press release, April 6, 1970, JNTP, Q4, vol. 8, file 3, "Drinking and Driving – General" (file 1 of 3).
33 JNTP, Q4, vol. 8, file 5, "Drinking and Driving – General" (file 3 of 3). For the Supreme Court of Canada decision, see *Criminal Law Amendment Act, Reference,* [1970] S.C.R. 777.

CHAPTER 7: IMPLEMENTING THE JUST SOCIETY

1 John Turner, inaugural lecture in the George M. Duck Lecture Series at the University of Windsor, March 4, 1970, published as John N. Turner, "Law for the Seventies: A Manifesto for Law Reform," *McGill Law Journal* 17, 1 (1971): 1-10. Gerard McNeill, "Turner to 'Dramatize Law as Reform,'" *Ottawa Citizen,* July 21, 1968.
2 John Turner to Pierre Trudeau, November 12, 1968, Library and Archives Canada (LAC), Ottawa, MG 26 (hereafter cited as JNTP), Q4, vol. 7, file 12, "Dept. of Justice – Priorities, Planning and Philosophy." The list also included professional education programs for judges and a law reform commission, measures that will be considered below as part of his attempt at systemic reform of the justice system. Later that year, he added to the list computerization of case-law data. Douglas Marshall, "*Maclean's* Interviews: Justice Minister John Turner," *Maclean's,* October 1968; Keith Bradbury, "Turner Tells Vancouver Lawyers: Law Treatment Not Equal," *Vancouver Sun,* December 4, 1969; John Turner, Speech to Vancouver Bar Association, December 3, 1969, JNTP, Q10-1, vol. 10, file 6.
3 John English, *Just Watch Me: The Life of Pierre Elliott Trudeau, 1968-2000* (Toronto: Knopf Canada, 2009), 110.
4 Martin L. Friedland, *My Life in Crime and Other Academic Adventures* (Toronto: University of Toronto Press for the Osgoode Society for Canadian Legal History, 2007), 75. Many of the prominent legal reformers of the era were Jewish. Despite the emerging rights discourse, leading Toronto clubs and law firms in the early 1960s still

did not accept Jews as members. As members of a minority group that continued to be subject to discrimination, these Jewish lawyers tended to be more sensitive to rights issues than were their WASP counterparts. This group included Jerry Grafstein, Martin Friedland, and Irwin Cotler, who was soon to become Turner's speechwriter. Turner also relied on the advice of Maxwell Cohen, dean of the McGill Law School.

5 Jerry S. Grafstein to John Turner, "Justice, Man. What's That?" memo, October 15, 1968, JNTP, Q4, vol. 7, file 12, "Department of Justice – Priorities, Planning and Philosophy." See also Confidential memo, August 21, 1968, same file; J.S. Grafstein to John N. Turner, "On Developing a Philosophy for the Department of Justice or Somebody Has Got to Care!" May 1, 1969, same file; and Richard Hayes to John Turner re: Memo from J.G. on Television Interview – Question Period – Sunday, April 20, 1969, same file. (The date of the television program was April 20, 1969; Hayes's memo is dated May 12, 1969.)

6 J.C. McRuer had served on the Archambault Commission, a federal royal commission of inquiry into conditions in Canada's prisons, 1936-38. The commission's report had called for more humane treatment of prisoners and recommended a complete revision of the Criminal Code that would include gun control and legal aid. Patrick Boyer, *A Passion for Justice: The Legacy of James Chalmers McRuer* (Toronto: University of Toronto Press for the Osgoode Society for Canadian Legal History, 1994), 305.

7 Friedland, *My Life in Crime*, 96-97.

8 JNTP, Q4, vol. 1, file 12, "Bail Reform, Bill C-220."

9 "A Dramatic Advance in Criminal Law," *Montreal Star*, June 13, 1970. Friedland was one of the team, including Cotler, that did the drafting. The new act set out a series of steps that justices of the peace should take in determining whether a person should be released. Friedland, *My Life in Crime*, 102-3.

10 Hansard, October 16, 1968, 1238; Press release, May 23, 1969, 1, JNTP, Q4, vol. 8, file 9; Press release, June 7, 1970, same file.

11 "Smoothing Path of Justice," *Montreal Gazette*, March 5, 1970. See also "Memorandum to the Cabinet, Re: Revision of the Exchequer Court Act and the Admiralty Act," December 19, 1968, signed by John Turner, Minister of Justice, JNTP, Q4, vol. 12, file 8, "Justice – Memos to Cabinet." This bill also removed an archaic restriction that prevented a citizen from suing the Crown without the Crown's consent. See Ian Bushnell, *The Federal Court of Canada: A History, 1875-1992* (Toronto: University of Toronto Press, 1992), 157-67; Richard Pound, *Chief Justice W.R. Jackett: By the Law of the Land* (Montreal/Kingston: McGill Queen's University Press, 1999), 213; Boyer, *A Passion for Justice*, 317.

12 John Turner, "Twin Freedoms: The Right to Privacy and the Right to Know," notes for an address to the Canadian Bar Association Annual Meeting in Ottawa, September 2, 1969, JNTP, Q4, vol. 15, file 13, "Protection of Privacy" (file 1 of 4).

13 Donald Stainsby, "Computer Seen as Threat to Citizen Right to Privacy," *Vancouver Sun*, June 1, 1970. The privacy legislation would pass third reading on December 4, 1973 (Hansard, December 4, 1973, 8419), and receive royal assent on January 14, 1974 (Hansard, January 14, 1974, 9303).

14 "Protection of Privacy Act," press release, Office of the Minister of Justice, June 28, 1971, JNTP, Q4, vol. 15, file 13, "Protection of Privacy" (file 2 of 4).

15 Robert Hull, "Turner's 'Open Government,'" *Windsor Star,* July 13, 1971.
16 Friedland, *My Life in Crime,* 114. In 1963 the US Supreme Court ruled that indigent defendants had a right to counsel in state courts (a right previously operative only in federal courts). A woefully underfunded and inadequate legal aid program had been running in Ontario since 1951. In 1965 a joint committee of the bar association and the attorney general in Ontario recommended a new comprehensive legal aid scheme to be administered by the Law Society, but nothing had come of it.
17 JNTP, Q4, vol. 13, file 6, "Legal Aid, 1970-72" (file 1 of 3).
18 In August 1971 the Justice Department launched a comprehensive legal aid plan for the Northwest Territories. Press release, August 17, 1971, JNTP, Q4, vol. 13, file 10, "Legal Aid – Yellowknife, N.W.T."
19 One example was changes he made to the *Canada Evidence Act.* Among the measures that failed were proposals for compensation for victims of violent crime, legalization of off-track betting, weekend sentences for some minor offences, civilian boards to oversee police forces, and expunging criminal records for all offenders who completed five crime-free years after the end of their prison term.
20 A memo from the Department of the Solicitor General to Turner said, "This Report (if adopted) makes law enforcement of the Narcotics Control Act impossible." Observations by the Department of Solicitor General on the report, June 16, 1970, JNTP, Q4, vol. 13, file 4, "Le Dain Commission." See also John Turner to Pierre Trudeau, June 17, 1970, 2, same file.
21 "Turner Sees More Flexible Law to Avoid 'Tomorrow's Oppression,'" *Toronto Star,* September 17, 1970. See Marcel Martel, *Not This Time: Canadians, Public Policy and the Marijuana Question, 1961-1975* (Toronto: University of Toronto Press, 2006), 121-56.
22 Rae Corelli, "Turner Says Law Won't Work Unless the People Believe in It," *Toronto Star,* May 8, 1971.
23 Marshall, "*Maclean's* Interviews."
24 Richard Hayes was a lawyer who hailed from Vancouver. He was succeeded by Michael Hunter, another Vancouver lawyer, in the summer of 1970. Hébert was succeeded in August 1970 by Toronto lawyer Peter Vivian.
25 Interview of John Turner by Elizabeth McIninch, May 3, 1995, JNTP, acc. no. 240674, consultation copy no. unavailable; Interview of Irwin Cotler, September 25, 2008.
26 "Thoughts on the Montebello Week-End," Jerry Grafstein to John N. Turner, June 30, 1969, JNTP, Q4, vol. 7, file 12, "Dept. of Justice – Priorities, Planning and Philosophy, 1968-1972." La Forest would become the first head of the Canadian Law Reform Commission and then a Supreme Court judge. Le Dain would head up the federal Commission of Inquiry on the Non-Medical Use of Drugs and later became a Supreme Court judge as well.
27 Marshall, "*Maclean's* Interviews," 14.
28 From July 15 to 17, 1970, Turner met in Halifax with the provincial attorneys general to discuss the issues they had in common. It was only the second such meeting in Canadian history and the first to be held outside Ottawa. Turner's provincial counterparts were usually supportive of his policies.
29 Christina Newman, "Turner: The Once and Future Contender," *Maclean's,* May 1971.

30 Friedland, *My Life in Crime,* 167.
31 "Law Reform: In Search of Credibility," *Time,* October 5, 1970; "How the Computer Is Used in Justice Dept.," *Canadian Printer and Publisher,* July 30, 1970.
32 Peter C. Newman, "Turner: Doing Justice to the Justice Department," *Ottawa Journal,* December 7, 1968. Attracting young legal talent to the department was a problem because private-sector legal jobs now paid significantly more, even at junior levels. Turner campaigned to increase his lawyers' salaries, only to run into roadblocks from cost-cutters and Cabinet colleagues. He also stepped up recruitment efforts, sending senior managers to law schools to recruit young graduates who were motivated less by money than by the chance to make a difference in society.
33 Jeffrey Simpson, *Spoils of Power: The Politics of Patronage* (Toronto: Collins, 1988), 307.
34 JNTP, Q10, vol. 11, file 8, "Judicial Appointments – Confidential" (file 2 of 2); "Judicial Appointments since 1968," JNTP, Q4, vol. 17, file 8, "Turner, John N. – Personal Career in the Department of Justice."
35 Frances Russell, "Ottawa Considering Naming Women Judges," *Toronto Globe and Mail,* January 28, 1969.
36 JNTP, Q4, vol. 14, file 9, "National Conference on the Law – Announcement, 1971."
37 JNTP, Q10-1, vol. 7, file 1, "'Frontiers of Law and Lawyership,' October 17-18, 1968, Convocation, Osgoode Hall, Toronto" (file 1 of 2).
38 Turner would subsequently deliver many similar speeches. In December 1969, for example, when he addressed the North American Judges Association in San Francisco, he said that some laws, such as those for vagrancy, "have made it virtually a crime to be poor in public." John Turner, "Justice for the Poor: The Courts, the Poor and the Administration of Justice," JNTP, Q10-1, vol. 10, file 5, "December 1, 1969 – 'Justice for the Poor,' International Conference, North American Judges, San Francisco, California."
39 JNTP, Q4, vol. 14, file 9, "National Conference on the Law – Announcement, 1971."
40 Press release, February 16, 1970, JNTP, Q4, vol. 13, file 1, "Law Reform" (file 2 of 2).
41 "Young Tigers," *Ottawa Citizen,* February 17, 1970. At the Montebello Conference the following June, the commission's mandate and composition were major topics of discussion.
42 W.A. Wilson, "Weakness of the Government," *Montreal Star,* April 2, 1970.
43 "Public Rates Job Being Done by Kierans, Turner, Greene," *Toronto Star,* September 16, 1970. Turner got a 62 per cent approval rating in Quebec.

CHAPTER 8: APPREHENDED INSURRECTION

1 Under the "aid to the civil power" provision of the *National Defence Act,* provinces had the power to call out the army. They had done so in the past to quell disturbances such as strikes, demonstrations, and prison riots.
2 "Abduction of the British Trade Commissioner," October 6, 1970, 2-3, Cabinet Conclusions, Library and Archives Canada (LAC), Ottawa, RG 2, Privy Council Office, Series A-5-a, vol. 6359. See also "Kidnapping of British Trade Commissioner," October 7, 1970, Cabinet Conclusions, LAC, RG 2, Privy Council Office, Series A-5-a, vol. 6359.
3 "Front de Libération du Québec, Manifeste," LAC, MG 26 (hereafter cited as JNTP), Q4, vol. 10, file 6, "F.L.Q. – Front de Libération du Québec."

4 The army was not experienced in executing such duties. While it guarded the house and Turner, his wife and children went about their daily routines unescorted. Interview of Geills Turner, Toronto, January 22, 2009.

5 William Tetley, *The October Crisis, 1970: An Insider's View* (Montreal/Kingston: McGill-Queen's University Press, 2006), 120-27; Carole de Vault, with William Johnson, *The Informer: Confessions of an Ex-Terrorist* (Toronto: Fleet Books, 1982), 94. Tetley, then a Cabinet minister in Quebec, recalls that there was solidarity in the Bourassa Cabinet and that rumours of its instability were unfounded. See Tetley, *The October Crisis*, 134-37.

6 Cabinet Committee on Security and Intelligence, Minutes, October 14, 1970 (Morning Meeting), 1-5, Privy Council Office, 176-009. (This material was obtained by an access to information request from the Privy Council Office and, at the time of publication was not available at Library and Archives Canada.)

7 Cabinet Committee on Security and Intelligence, Minutes, October 14, 1970 (Evening Meeting) 11, Privy Council Office, 176-009.

8 "The FLQ Situation," Cabinet meeting, October 15, 1970, 9:00 a.m., 4, 6, Cabinet Conclusions, LAC, RG 2, Privy Council Office, Series A-5-a, vol. 6359.

9 Eric Kierans, with Walter Stewart, *Remembering* (Toronto: Stoddart, 2001), 181.

10 "The FLQ Situation," 9:00 a.m., 6, 8. The comments of various Cabinet ministers at this meeting suggest that, in addition to Turner, the following ministers fell into the cautious camp: Mitchell Sharp, Bud Drury, Ron Basford, Herb Gray, Joe Greene, George McIlraith, and Allan MacEachen. Members of the alarmist camp included Trudeau, Bryce Mackasey (who twice spoke about the possibility of civil war during this meeting), Eric Kierans, and Bud Olsen (who advocated immediate decisive action).

11 These rumours affected French Canadian members of Cabinet more than they did their colleagues. From past decades of political infighting in Quebec, they were familiar with most of the players in the drama. "Trudeau knew his enemies well," notes his biographer. "Many had formerly been his friends." John English, *Just Watch Me: The Life of Pierre Elliott Trudeau, 1968-2000* (Toronto: Knopf Canada, 2009), 75. See also Christina McCall-Newman, *Grits: An Intimate Portrait of the Liberal Party* (Toronto: Macmillan of Canada, 1982), 282-85. Ryan's talk of reinforcing the provincial administration fed rumours that a plot was afoot to replace the elected government. Trudeau and his circle took the possibility seriously and fretted that democracy was threatened in Quebec. "I acted on information I've been accumulating since I was three years old," Trudeau told Peter Newman. Newman, *Here Be Dragons: Telling the Tales of People, Passion and Power* (Toronto: McClelland and Stewart, 2004), 310.

12 Gérard Pelletier, *The October Crisis*, trans. Joyce Marshall (Toronto: McClelland and Stewart, 1971), 14, 113. "What the terrorists are seeking," Pelletier later commented, "is Goebbels's old strategy, a strategy which is also described in great detail in Malaparte's *Technique du coup d'État*. They provoked repression deliberately, in the belief that the resulting deterioration of the social climate can in the long run only further the cause of 'worker power.'" Ibid., 177.

13 Ibid., 115.

14 "The FLQ Situation," 9:00 a.m., 5.

15 Ibid.

16 Ibid., 7-8. George McIlraith, the solicitor general, "indicated that he had a figure of 240 people reported to be the 'hard core' of the F.L.Q. and he was really wondering where the figure of 1,000 had come from. He indicated that using too large a figure could result in innocent people being involved." "The FLQ Situation," Cabinet meeting, October 15, 1970, 2:30 p.m., 4, Cabinet Conclusions, LAC, RG 2, Privy Council Office, Series A-5-a, vol. 6359. Pelletier would later estimate that the FLQ consisted, at most, of fifty hard-core extremists, a smaller group of propagandists, three hundred active sympathizers, and three thousand passive sympathizers. Pelletier, *The October Crisis,* 51.

17 "Would have preferred to bring in special legislation instead of WMAB, but urgency, speed and surprise essential," Turner wrote on one of his index cards on December 23, 1971. JNTP, Q5, vol. 20, "Mr. Turner's Confidential Notes, 1968-1969-1970-1971."

18 "The FLQ Situation," 2:30 p.m., 5. In this afternoon session, Cabinet also discussed Bourassa's wish to parole some of the prisoners whose release the FLQ kidnappers had demanded. Marchand wanted to help Bourassa negotiate with the FLQ. If things went badly in Montreal, he rationalized, the government should be in a position to say it had done everything possible to solve the problem. Turner objected that this concession would "be tantamount to bargaining with criminals." Ibid., 3. Cabinet decided to ask the parole board to accelerate its hearings of the requests for parole of those FLQ members currently serving sentences. Ibid., 9.

19 The government insisted on receiving a formal written request from Premier Bourassa both for the army and for special police powers. Cabinet Committee on Security and Intelligence, Minutes, October 14, 1970 (Evening Meeting) 6, Privy Council Office, 176-009.

20 Hansard, October 16, 1970, 210. Marchand continued to claim that the FLQ had infiltrated official organizations in Quebec and even federal institutions such as the CBC. He said that the government feared that anarchy would convulse Montreal and spread throughout Quebec and all of Canada. There was a link between the FLQ and the Black Panthers in the United States, he claimed, and evidence that FLQ members were receiving training in foreign countries. "Quebec Kidnappings: GOC Minister's Statement Causes Furor," American Embassy, Washington, to Secretary of State, Washington, October 22, 1970, National Archives and Records Administration (NARA), College Park, MD, RG 59, box 2162, POL 23 Can.

21 Approval was high among both French and English Canadians. A Gallup poll published on December 12 showed that those who supported the introduction of the *War Measures Act* numbered 89 per cent of English Canadians and 86 per cent of French Canadians. Tetley, *The October Crisis,* 188.

22 "The government continued to enjoy support of vast majority of Canadians for its actions in Quebec crisis," noted a senior official in the American Embassy, "but some seeds of confusion and doubt are being sown." Department of State, "GOC Minister's Statement Creates Furor."

23 Hansard, October 28, 1970, 652.

24 Press release, November 2, 1970, JNTP, Q4, vol. 16, file 3, "Public Order Act."

25 Turner misquoted Sanford and credited him with being chief justice, a position he never occupied. James Eayrs, "Did John Turner Have His Quotes Right?" *Toronto Star,* November 17, 1970.

26 "Brief for the Minister" in Turner's files, dated December 3, 1970, describes the state of the Cross investigation as the police closed in on the apartment in which Cross was being held. Turner's papers include notes on the subsequent negotiations. "L'affaire Cross, 3/xii/70," JNTP, Q4, vol. 7, file 15, "Dept. of the Solicitor General" (file 2 of 2).

27 John Burns, "Cross Is 'Well, Joyful and Relieved,' Trudeau Says after Call," *Toronto Globe and Mail,* December 4, 1970.

28 McCall-Newman, *Grits,* 285. "Turner's personal power was demonstrated during the FLQ crisis," McCall-Newman continues, "when Trudeau looked to Turner almost hourly for advice. The two men became closer friends as a result of the long sleepless hours they spent together." This is an exaggeration. Turner's relationship with Trudeau was correct and cordial, but the crisis did not substantially alter it. They socialized occasionally, but these outings were usually initiated by their wives. Interview of John Turner, Toronto, January 19, 2009; Geills Turner interview.

29 The first suggestion that the FLQ crisis was less than it appeared came on November 9 with the testimony of Bernard Lortie at the inquest into Pierre Laporte's death. John Burns, "The Anti-Terrorist Bill: A Dilemma for All MPs," *Toronto Globe and Mail,* November 23, 1970.

30 John Turner to Huntly Sinclair, October 27, 1970, JNTP, Q4, vol. 12, file 10, "Kidnapping – General."

31 Hansard, November 4, 1970, 878-84. Turner also explained that the government had felt it necessary to declare the FLQ an illegal organization because, although the criminal law deals with treason and sedition, it addresses both crimes as acts of individuals. It had no provisions for dealing with an organization dedicated to the use of force to effect political change. Another reason it was necessary to outlaw the FLQ was that some of its aims (such as concern for the underprivileged) were legitimate, and people might donate funds to it without realizing their money would be used for violent ends. Hansard, November 4, 1970, 878-84.

32 Edna Hampton, "Critics Missed Extent of FLQ Crisis: Turner," *Toronto Globe and Mail,* March 12, 1971. See also a speech Turner delivered to the Yale Political Union explaining the reasons for invoking the *War Measures Act.* JNTP, Q10-1, vol. 14, file 13, "Yale Political Union, New Haven, Connecticut, April 22, 1971."

33 "Minister Silenced at Chaotic Meeting," *UBC Reports,* March 11, 1971. Turner was very concerned about protecting his reputation as a civil libertarian. In a speech at the Beth Shalom Synagogue in Toronto on May 5, where he was being honoured with an award, he called for an entrenched Canadian bill of rights – something he had been advocating since the mid-1960s and one of the federal government's major objectives in constitutional negotiations.

34 "Emergency Legislation," April 8, 1971, 9, Cabinet Conclusions, LAC, RG 2, Privy Council Office, Series A-5-a, vol. 6381. See also Cabinet discussions under the same heading, 1971/03/25, 1971/04/01, 1971/04/22, 1971/04/28, 1971/05/06 in ibid.

35 Rae Corelli, "Turner Says Law Won't Work Unless the People Believe in It," *Toronto Star,* May 8, 1971. Corelli added, "A Quebec lawyer who has known Turner for many years says, 'one thing that's interesting is why did [Premier Robert] Bourassa attack Turner personally for letting the Public Order Act expire and not Trudeau? Why not attack the federal government rather than just a member of it? To me the reason is

obvious – Trudeau must have supported Bourassa's demand that the law be extended, and Turner threw a monkey-wrench into the deal.' An Ontario Liberal MP estimates that more than a dozen of his colleagues would have fled the party and crossed the floor of the Commons if a replacement bill had gone through." Ibid. A letter from Bourassa to Trudeau indicates that the Quebec government wanted permanent legislation to provide for special powers in the case of another emergency. Robert Bourassa to Pierre Trudeau, April 2, 1971, JNTP, Q4, vol. 10, file 6, "F.L.Q. – Front de Libération du Québec" (file 1 of 2). See also Jack Cahill, *John Turner: The Long Run* (Toronto: McClelland and Stewart, 1984), 148, and Douglas Fisher, "John Turner and the Rumours," *Toronto Telegram*, May 6, 1971.

36 Stan McDowell, "Trudeau-Turner Rift Reported on Replacing Public Order Act," *Toronto Star*, May 3, 1971. Two weeks later, Turner moved a motion in the House that a Special Joint Committee of the Senate and Commons be set up to study the type of legislation required to deal with any future crisis similar to the one of the previous October. As time passed and the crisis faded in memory, however, nothing came of this initiative. Hansard, May 13, 1971, 5778.

37 "Minister of Justice: 'Some Day the Full Details Will Show the Reason Why,'" *Ottawa Journal*, October 17, 1970.

38 Cahill, *John Turner*, 148. Choquette announced that Quebec was considering requiring all residents to carry ID cards showing their photo and fingerprints. Turner stated that this scheme might not be legal and that the federal government had no plans to introduce such a measure. He was not prepared to limit civil liberties on a permanent basis.

CHAPTER 9: INTRANATIONAL DIPLOMACY

1 Hansard, April 6, 1966, 3915-16.

2 W.A.C. Bennett, "Opening Statement of the Province of British Columbia to the Constitutional Conference," 5-6, Library and Archives Canada (LAC), Ottawa, MG 26 (hereafter cited as JNTP), Q4, vol. 15, file 4. The issues were summarized in remarks Bennett prepared for the federal-provincial conference on the subject. "Official Languages – Minister's Briefing Book, 1969," JNTP, Q4, vol. 15, file 4.

3 "I write to you," Trudeau said, "to see if you would be willing to collaborate with Mr. Pelletier on this issue. I am sure that together you could manage this very delicate task quite well." ("Je vous écris donc pour vous demander si vous seriez disposé à collaborer avec monsieur Pelletier à ce sujet. Je suis sûr qu'ensemble vous sauriez mener à bien cette tâche très délicate.") Pierre Trudeau to John Turner, January 24, 1969, JNTP, Q5, vol. 20, file 6. Pelletier was "getting clobbered" in the House, Turner recalled to Jack Cahill. "This is a complicated country, you know, and this black-and-white approach, this ultra logical approach, this Cartesian approach of the Prime Minister's of course caused us problems in western Canada." Jack Cahill, *John Turner: The Long Run* (Toronto: McClelland and Stewart, 1984), 134.

4 "Turner Visits Weir to Give Ottawa View," *Winnipeg Free Press*, February 4, 1969.

5 Interview of John Turner by Elizabeth McIninch, May 3, 1995, JNTP, acc. no. 240674, consultation copy number unavailable.

6   Derik Hodgson, "Languages Bill Crucial: Turner," *Winnipeg Free Press*, February 5, 1969.

7   John Turner to Pierre Trudeau, February 5, 1969, JNTP, Q4, vol. 5, file 11; John Turner to Jean-Jacques Bertrand, February 14, 1969, JNTP, Q4, vol. 8, file 17.

8   See W.A. Wilson, "Ottawa Firm on Official Language Bill," *Montreal Star*, February 12, 1969; "Success at the Mini-Summit," *Victoria Times*, February 12, 1969; "Turner agira comme conciliateur," *Le Droit* (Ottawa), February 12, 1969.

9   Wilson, "Ottawa Firm"; "Meeting with Provincial Attorneys General (Victoria – 17/2/69), Draft Reply for Minister to Question in House," JNTP, Q4, vol. 15, file 3.

10 A number of documents in the Turner papers illustrate this point, including "Notes re: 'Official Languages Bill,'" February 10, 1969 (partly typed, and partly in Turner's handwriting), and his notes on points to raise with Premier J.J. Bertrand of Quebec concerning bilingual districts, March 7, 1969, JNTP, Q4, vol. 15, file 2.

11 Bob Bell, "Turner Promises Detailed Changes to Languages Bill," *Edmonton Journal*, April 9, 1969.

12 John Turner to Cabinet, Memo re: official languages, May 6, 1969, JNTP, Q4, vol. 12, file 8.

13 Hansard, May 20, 1969, 8836-38.

14 Ibid., July 3, 1969, 10819.

15 John Harman to John Turner, October 30, 1969, JNTP, Q4, vol. 2, file 3.

16 Appeal of John Harman, April 30, 1970, JNTP, Q4, vol. 2, file 11.

17 John Turner to John Carson, May 11, 1970, JNTP, Q4, vol. 2, file 3, "Bilingualism in the Public Service, 1968-1971" (file 1 of 10); John Carson to John Turner, May 19, 1970, JNTP, Q4, vol. 3, file 1; John Turner to Gérard Pelletier, June 18, 1970; John Turner to Pierre Trudeau, July 23, 1970, JNTP, Q4, vol. 15, file 3, "Official Languages – General, 1968-1971."

18 Unsigned notes, July 8, 1970, JNTP, Q4, vol. 2, file 11.

19 William Morris, "Is Civil Service Bilingual Policy on Collision Course?" *Toronto Globe and Mail*, July 15, 1970; William Morris, "Interpreting the Plan for Bilingualism," *Toronto Globe and Mail*, July 16, 1970. Also on July 16, the *Toronto Globe and Mail* printed an editorial on the issue entitled "Ignoring Parliament's Intent."

20 Turner would still be fighting the same battle to humanize the implementation of bilingualism years later. See, for example, his letter to Trudeau about the creation of bilingual districts. John Turner to Pierre Trudeau, January 25, 1972, JNTP, Q4, vol. 1, file 13. In 1974 he wrote to Jean Chrétien, president of the Treasury Board, to express his concern about the high rate of failure of anglophones trying to learn French. He asked for understanding of their situation and suggested less stringent requirements for civil servants who were middle-aged or older. John Turner to Jean Chrétien, November 12, 1974, JNTP, Q5, vol. 1, file 12.

21 Transcript of Opening Remarks ... December 8, 1969, JNTP, Q4, vol. 6, file 7, "Constitutional Conference, Ottawa, December 1969" (file 1 of 3); Statement of Conclusions, February 17, 1970, 1, JNTP, Q4, vol. 9, file 1, "Fed.-Prov. Conference – Feb. 1970."

22 Gordon Robertson, *Memoirs of a Very Civil Servant* (Toronto: University of Toronto Press, 2000), 274.

23 Interview of Michael Hunter, Vancouver, September 16, 2008.

24 JNTP, Q4, vol. 6, file 4. Turner suspects that the arrangements made for patriation in 1982 were based on his 1971 work. Interview of John Turner by Elizabeth McIninch, January 30, 1995, JNTP, acc. no. 240671, consultation copy number V1-2008-08-0010; Robertson, *Memoirs,* 276.

25 Robertson, *Memoirs,* 281.

26 John Turner to George Cumming, June 30, 1971, JNTP, Q4, vol. 6, file 11, "Constitutional Conference, Victoria, June 1971" (file 1 of 2).

27 John Turner, Notes, June 15, 1971, JNTP, Q5, vol. 20, file 1, "Turner, John N. – Confidential Notes, 1968-71"; John Turner, "Constitution – June 24, 1971," same file.

28 "Regrets – But Little Surprise," *Ottawa Citizen,* June 23, 1971. In later years Turner would come to see the failure of the Victoria Charter as a missed opportunity even more significant than he had recognized at the time. For all its underlying diversity, Canada was still viewed as a product of two founding peoples. Aboriginal and multicultural groups subsequently won recognition as legitimate constituent parts of Canada, and constitutional negotiations would never again be so simple. The fate of the Meech Lake Accord would inform his judgment on this matter (see Chapter 20).

29 Rae Corelli, "Turner Says Law Won't Work Unless the People Believe in It," *Toronto Star,* May 8, 1971.

30 Ibid.

31 John Turner, "Faith and Politics," in *The Hidden Pierre Elliott Trudeau: The Faith behind the Politics,* ed. John English, Richard Gwyn, and P. Whitney Lackenbauer (Ottawa: Novalis, 2004), 111; Interview of Geills Turner, Toronto, January 22, 2009.

32 Christina Newman, "Turner: The Once and Future Contender," *Maclean's,* May 1971. According to Irwin Cotler, the label originated with Maxwell Cohen, dean of the McGill Law School. Interview of John Turner by Elizabeth McIninch, May 3, 1995, JNTP, acc. no. 240674, consultation copy number unavailable.

33 Roy MacGregor, "'My Time Is Now!'" *Toronto Star,* June 17, 1984.

34 Ibid. Alastair Gillespie and Turner would sometimes excuse themselves from Cabinet meetings to play squash at the Skyline Hotel. Interview of Alastair Gillespie, Toronto, January 2010.

35 "John Turner Brings a New Style to Finance," *Toronto Star,* May 13, 1972.

36 Interview of Barney Danson, Toronto, January 21, 2005.

37 Interview of Cam Avery, Vancouver, September 16, 2008; Mary Trueman, "If There Really Is a 195 Club, Will the Members Please Stand Up?" *Toronto Globe and Mail,* December 13, 1978; Interview of Alastair Gillespie, Toronto, January 19, 2005.

38 Cahill, *John Turner,* 8. The Belvedere Hotel mentioned by Cahill was probably the Belle Clair Hotel on Queen Street in Ottawa.

CHAPTER 10: *SHOKKU*

1 "Politics, 13/viii/71" (handwritten notes), Library and Archives Canada (LAC), Ottawa, MG 26 (hereafter cited as JNTP), Q5, vol. 20, file 1, "Turner, John N. – Confidential Notes, 1968-1971."

2 Michael A. Bernstein, "Understanding American Economic Decline: The Contours of Late-Twentieth-Century Experience," in *Understanding American Economic Decline,*

ed. Michael A. Bernstein and David E. Adler (Cambridge: Cambridge University Press, 1994), 17.

3 Robert Bothwell, *Alliance and Illusion: Canada and the World, 1945-1984* (Vancouver: UBC Press, 2007), 321.

4 Another of Turner's terms was the freedom to get a new deputy minister. He knew the incumbent, Simon Reisman, could be difficult and thought he might have to replace him. As things turned out, however, they got on well together, so nothing came of this condition. John Turner, "For Dinner with PM, Nov. 12/71" (file card notes), JNTP, Q5, vol. 20, file 1, "Turner, John N. – Confidential Notes, 1968-1971."

5 Peter Vivian to John Turner, Memo, April 17, 1972, JNTP, Q5, vol. 20, "Turner, John N. – (PERSONAL) 1972-1975."

6 "Plain Talk," notes for an address to the Empire Club, November 18, 1971, Michael Hunter private papers.

7 Peter Dempson, "Will the Jinx Escape John Turner?" *Halifax Chronicle-Herald,* June 6, 1972.

8 Michael Lavoie, "12 Changes Made as Trudeau Picks Election Cabinet," *Toronto Star,* January 29, 1972; Dempson, "Will the Jinx."

9 Charles Lynch, *Race for the Rose: Election 1984* (Toronto: Methuen, 1984), 7.

10 Robert Hull, "Why Trudeau Needs John Turner," *Windsor Star,* February 26, 1972.

11 "Just Keep Cool," *Winnipeg Free Press,* June 20, 1972.

12 George Bain, "Budgets and Elections," *Toronto Globe and Mail,* April 28, 1972.

13 "A real concern for human values is right, and is generally thought to be lacking in this Government," John de B. Payne advised. "You should, I think, come down clearly and strongly on the side of concern for human misery from unemployment as the basic philosophy of your ministry. It is not only right but politically wise to do so." This thrust carried over from Turner's empathy for the "little guy" in Justice. As subthemes, Payne recommended that Turner ameliorate the residual ill-will from Benson's tax reforms by simplifying and clarifying the new tax measures, making the administration of the tax system more efficient, and displaying a willingness to work with the provinces on taxation policy. He also suggested a rebate on income taxes for the middle class, and, for corporations, extra depreciation for new capital investment and an accelerated implementation of cuts in corporate tax rates. John de B. Payne, "Random Notes for J," March 26, 1972, JNTP, Q5, vol. 2, file 5, "Budget 1972" (file 3 of 3).

14 "The Temptation Faced by a Finance Minister ...," *Toronto Globe and Mail,* May 9, 1972.

15 Douglas Fisher, "Turner as Budget Writer: 'It Either Floats or It Bombs,'" *Executive,* January 1975.

16 W.A. Wilson, "An Attack of Confidence," *Montreal Star,* June 28, 1972.

17 Charles Lynch, "Canada-U.S. 'Partnership' Is Ended; We're Now 'Foreign Like the Others,'" *Ottawa Citizen,* April 11, 1972.

18 Kenneth Norrie and Douglas Owram, *A History of the Canadian Economy* (Toronto: Harcourt Brace, 1991) 575; John Saywell, ed., *Canadian Annual Review of Politics and Public Affairs, 1971* (Toronto: University of Toronto Press, 1972), 314.

19 "Hopes of Canadian Finance Minister Turner for Private Meeting with Treasury Secretary Connally," American Embassy, Ottawa to Secretary of State, Washington, April 1972, NARA, RG 59, box 2164, file POL Can-US.

20 Interview of John Coleman, Ottawa, March 2, 2006. Coleman, who was chief of international organizations, International Finance Division in the Department of Finance, provided valuable background information about IMF negotiations.

21 Samuel Rosenberg, *American Economic Development since 1945: Growth, Decline and Rejuvenation* (New York: Palgrave Macmillan, 2003), 195-97; Bothwell, *Alliance and Illusion*, 324.

22 SDRs were to be issued to IMF members to supplement gold and the US dollar as foreign exchange reserve assets if global liquidity seemed to be threatened. They had a value pegged to a set amount of gold and could be used to borrow funds to purchase a currency in foreign exchange markets when a country was trying to shore up its currency's value. See "Turner Pushes Reform," *Vancouver Sun,* September 25, 1973.

23 "Canadian Representation at the Commonwealth Finance Ministers' Meeting in Dar-es-Salaam, Tanzania, September 17-20 – And the Annual Meetings of the International Monetary Fund, IMF – And the International Bank for Reconstruction and Development, IBRD – In Nairobi, Kenya, September 24-28, 1973," September 13, 1973, Cabinet Conclusions, LAC, RG 2, Privy Council Office, Series A-5-a, vol. 6422.

24 JNT confidential memo re: meeting with Shultz, November 8, 1972, 4-5, JNTP, Q5, vol. 14, file 6, "Michelin."

25 George Shultz to John Turner, April 12, 1973, JNTP, Q5, vol. 5, file 12, "Committee of Twenty, Washington, March 26-27, 1973."

26 See, for example, "Canada-United States Trade Negotiations," August 1, 1973, Cabinet Conclusions, LAC, RG 2, Privy Council Office, Series A-5-a, vol. 6436.

27 Simon Enoch, "Changing the Ideological Fabric? A Brief History of (Canadian) Neoliberalism," *State of Nature* 5 (Autumn 2007), http://www.stateofnature.org/; David Harvey, *A Brief History of Neoliberalism* (Oxford: Oxford University Press, 2005), 22, 39-63.

28 John English, *Just Watch Me: The Life of Pierre Elliott Trudeau, 1968-2000* (Toronto: Knopf Canada, 2009), 213.

29 Jack Cahill, "A New Pattern of Political Power Emerges in Ottawa," *Toronto Star,* August 26, 1972.

30 Peter Desbarats, "John Turner Faces a Tough Campaign," *Toronto Star,* September 9, 1972.

31 Peter Desbarats, "Cabinet Team to Campaign," *Saint John Telegraph-Journal,* August 31, 1972.

32 Quoted in Douglas Fisher, "Where Have Turner's 195 Gone ...?" *Toronto Sun,* November 22, 1972.

33 W.A. Wilson, "Pitfalls Threaten Turner," *Montreal Star,* September 15, 1972.

34 Peter Desbarats, "John Turner Has a Delicate Job," *Toronto Star,* October 14, 1972; Interview of Michael Hunter, Vancouver, September 16, 2008. Turner was away at the International Monetary Fund meetings in London and in Washington for his first talks with George Shultz.

35 John Saywell, ed., *Canadian Annual Review of Politics and Public Affairs, 1972* (Toronto: University of Toronto Press, 1974), 52.

36 Ibid.

37 John Meisel, *Working Papers on Canadian Politics* (Montreal/Kingston: McGill-Queen's University Press, 1973), 228.

38 John Turner, "Cabinet 1/x/72," JNTP, Q5, vol. 20, file 2, "Turner, John N., Personal – Confidential Notes and Cards, 1976" (despite its title, cards from various years appear in this file).

39 "MP Urges Trudeau Call Leadership Convention," *Toronto Globe and Mail*, November 2, 1972. One of Turner's index cards, dated November 6, 1972, has notes titled "Lalonde," which read, "i) never doubted my loyalty, ii) I'm the only guy if Trudeau fails. Expression of loyalty." JNTP, Q5, vol. 20, file 2, "Turner, John N., Personal – Confidential Notes and Cards, 1976."

40 John Sawatsky, *The Insiders: Government, Business, and the Lobbyists* (Toronto: McClelland and Stewart, 1987), 56.

41 Jack Cahill, *John Turner: The Long Run* (Toronto: McClelland and Stewart, 1984), 125-26.

CHAPTER 11: THE PRICE OF GAS

1 Barbara Frum, "How They Get It All Together – John Turner, Minister of Finance," *Maclean's*, August 1973.

2 Interview of Michael Hunter, Vancouver, September 16, 2008.

3 Frum, "How They Get It All Together."

4 Richard Gwyn, *The Northern Magus: Pierre Trudeau and Canadians* (Toronto: McClelland and Stewart, 1980), 185.

5 Frum, "How They Get It All Together."

6 Telephone interview of John Coleman, January 17, 2006.

7 Ron Graham, *One-Eyed Kings: Promise and Illusion in Canadian Politics* (Toronto: Collins, 1986), 188.

8 Walter Stewart, "The Natural," *Toronto Life*, June 1983. The staff member was Finance official John Coleman. Coleman interview.

9 Richard Gwyn, "The Aitken Formula: John Turner's Way Out?" *Ottawa Journal*, May 22, 1975.

10 Charles Lynch, "John Turner: Yes, He Does Sweat and Swear," *Executive*, April 1972.

11 "John Turner Brings a New Style to Finance," *Toronto Star*, May 13, 1972.

12 Sean O'Sullivan, *Both My Houses: From Politics to Priesthood* (Toronto: Key Porter, 1986), 81-82.

13 James Ferrabee, "The Turner Phenomenon," *Montreal Gazette*, October 9, 1975.

14 Gwyn, "The Aitken Formula."

15 Jack Cahill, *John Turner: The Long Run* (Toronto: McClelland and Stewart, 1984), 173.

16 M.W. H., "Note to the Minister," July 13, 1973, Michael Hunter private papers.

17 Interview of Sandra Kaiser, Vaughan, August 26, 2008. A few minutes later, Hunter got another phone call from Reisman asking him to come by his office for a drink and a chat. They worked out an accommodation. Reisman realized that he would not be able to control Turner as he might have liked.

18 John Gray, "The View from Ottawa," *Maclean's*, July 1972.

19 Hunter interview.

20 Gray, "The View." John Swift, Turner's executive assistant in his later Finance years, confirmed this modus operandi. Interview of John Swift, Vancouver, September 17, 2008.

21 Pierre Trudeau to John Turner, February 16, 1972; Simon Reisman to John Turner re reply, March 23, 1972; John Turner to Pierre Trudeau, March 24, 1972; and receipt from Trudeau's office, March 29, 1972: Library and Archives Canada (LAC), Ottawa, MG 26 (hereafter cited as JNTP), Q5, vol. 20, file 6, "Turner, John N. – Personal, 1972-1975."

22 Simon Reisman to John Turner, "Prime Minister's Letter to You on Work of the Department," March 23, 1972, JNTP, Q5, vol. 20, file 6, "Turner, John N. – Personal, 1972-1975."

23 John Turner to Pierre Trudeau, March 24, 1972, JNTP, Q5, vol. 20, file 6, "Turner, John N. – Personal, 1972-1975."

24 John English, *Just Watch Me: The Life of Pierre Elliott Trudeau, 1968-2000* (Toronto: Knopf Canada, 2009), 194-95.

25 John Saywell, ed., *Canadian Annual Review of Politics and Public Affairs, 1973* (Toronto: University of Toronto Press, 1974), 9.

26 "Budget Discussion (Previous Reference February 13)," February 15, 1973, Cabinet Conclusions, LAC, RG 2, Privy Council Office, Series A-5-a, vol. 6422.

27 "Diary 16/2/73 – a.m."; "Feb 16, JNT – Payne," Michael Hunter private papers. See also "May 1972 Budget Bills," 1973/01/25, "Budget Discussion," 1973/02/13, "Budget Discussion," 1973/02/15, Cabinet Conclusions, LAC, RG 2, Privy Council Office, Series A-5-a, vol. 6422.

28 John Turner, "PM-(JNT?) before Budget, 19/02/73," JNTP, Q5, vol. 20, file 3, "Turner, John N. – Confidential Cards and Notes, 1973."

29 "Diary 16/2/73 – a.m."; "Feb 16, JNT-Payne," Michael Hunter private papers.

30 "Budget Discussions," February 13, 1973, and "Budget Discussions," February 15, 1973, Cabinet Conclusions, LAC, RG 2, Privy Council Office, Series A-5-a, vol. 6422.

31 JNTP, Q5, vol. 2, file 6, "Budget, 1973" (file 1 of 2); "Budget Speech Delivered by the Honourable John N. Turner, Minister of Finance and Member of Parliament for Ottawa-Carleton, in the House of Commons, Monday, February 19, 1973," JNTP, Q10-1, vol. 17, file 21. The wage and price controls introduced in the United States as part of Nixon's New Economic Policy were still in force and would continue in various iterations until 1974.

32 JNTP, Q5, vol. 24, file 1, "Amendments to Bill C-193, Income Tax Act"; "Corporate Tax Cuts and Government Longevity," American Embassy, Ottawa, to Secretary of State, Washington, June 1973, NARA, RG 59, box 859, file FN 9.

33 Terrance Wills, "Turner Onstage, PM in Wings," *Toronto Globe and Mail*, March 29, 1973.

34 *Western Economic Opportunities Conference* (Ottawa: Minister of Supply and Services Canada, 1977), 154.

35 Interview of Cam Avery, Vancouver, September 16, 2008.

36 For context, see G. Bruce Doern and Glen Toner, *The Politics of Energy: The Development and Implementation of the NEP* (Toronto: Methuen, 1985), 91-93.

37 Simon Reisman (actually signed by Tommy Shoyama on behalf of Reisman) to John Turner, "Re Phased Increases in the Price of Western Canadian Crude Oil," memo, October 31, 1973, JNTP, Q5, vol. 7, file 5, "Energy" (file 1 of 3).

38 "Forthcoming Federal-Provincial Negotiations on Oil and Gas," JNTP, Q5, vol. 1, file 1, "Alberta – Negotiations with Alberta"; "Oil and Natural Gas Pricing, Taxing and Revenue Sharing," memo, January 15, 1974, para. 16, JNTP, Q5, vol. 9, file 3, "Federal-Provincial First Ministers' Conference on Energy, Jan. 1974" (file 3 of 3).

39 Pierre Trudeau to John Turner, April 3, 1974; John Turner to Pierre Trudeau, April 18, 1974: JNTP, Q5, vol. 16, file 10, "Parliamentary – Prime Minister."

40 JNTP, Q5, vol. 14, file 3, "Memoranda – JNT – Important, 1974"; JNTP, Q5, vol. 13, file 6, "Meeting with Provincial Premiers, Ottawa, October 30, 1974" (file 2 of 2); JNTP, Q5, vol. 3, file 2, "Budget 1974" (file 3 of 4).

41 Alan G. Green, "Twentieth-Century Canadian Economic History," in *The Cambridge Economic History of the United States,* vol. 3, *The Twentieth Century,* ed. Stanley L. Engerman and Robert E. Gallman (Cambridge: Cambridge University Press, 2000), 232, 241.

42 W.C. Hood to John Turner, Memo, July 16, 1973, JNTP, Q5, vol. 25, file 1, section E, pt. 1, "Committee of Twenty (Board of Governors Committee on Reform of the International Monetary System and Related Issues), Washington, July 30-31, 1973."

43 "Notes for Press Conference, 9/10/74," typed, but with many notes in Turner's writing, JNTP, Q5, vol. 12, file 1; Memorandum of a conversation between Chancellor Schmidt and Mr. Turner, September 18, 1974, JNTP, Q5, vol. 14, file 4, "Memoranda, Important – JNT 1974."

44 JNTP, Q5, vol. 19, file 4, "Trip to Middle East, April–May 1975."

45 "Telegram to PMO Ottawa," April 20, 1975, JNTP, Q5, vol. 20, "Correspondence with P.M. and P.C."; E.P. Neufeld to the minister, "Reports on Your Trip to OPEC Countries," May 9, 1975, JNTP, Q5, vol. 14, file 4, "Memoranda, Important – JNT 1974."

46 Interview of John Turner by Elizabeth McIninch, January 30, 1995, JNTP, acc. no. 240671, consultation copy no. V1-2008-08-0010; Coleman interview.

47 Simon Reisman to John Turner, Memo, September 13, 1973, JNTP, Q5, vol. 14, "Memoranda, Important – JNT – 1973-74"; Simon Reisman to John Turner, March 22, 1974, JNTP, Q5, vol. 14, file 4, "Memoranda – Important – JNT – 1974"; John Turner to Pierre Trudeau, March 1, 1974, JNTP, Q5, vol. 1, file 1, "Alberta – Negotiations with Alberta."

48 Douglas Fisher, "Turner as Budget Writer: 'It Either Floats or It Bombs,'" *Executive,* January 1975.

49 Pierre Trudeau, *Memoirs* (Toronto: McClelland and Stewart, 1993), 176-77.

50 Keith Davey, *The Rainmaker: A Passion for Politics* (Toronto: Stoddart, 1986), 164-65.

51 Roy MacGregor, "'My Time Is Now!'" *Toronto Star,* June 17, 1984. "[Turner] was *key* to that campaign," said another Liberal insider. "It's never been recognized. You think that wouldn't make you bitter?" Ibid.

52 Gwyn, *The Northern Magus,* 159.

53 Interview of Marc Lalonde, Montreal, July 5, 2005.

54 MacGregor, "'My Time Is Now!'"

CHAPTER 12: STALKING STAGFLATION

1 Its members were mostly academic economists, including Albert Breton (University of Toronto), whose economic views Trudeau had long relied on; Carl Beigie (executive director, C.D. Howe Research Institute); Thomas Wilson (University of Toronto, director of the Institute for Policy Analysis); and Grant Reuber (University of Western Ontario, chairman of the Ontario Economic Council).

2 Speaking notes for the minister, February 13, 1974, Library and Archives Canada (LAC), Ottawa, MG 26 (hereafter cited as JNTP), Q5, vol. 14, "Memoranda, Important – JNT – 1973-74."

3 John Turner to Richard Gwyn, July 9, 1975, JNTP, Q13-1, vol. 9, file 1, "Personal – Correspondence, 1973-1975" (file 2 of 2).

4 "A Conversation with Finance Minister Turner," *Executive,* July-August 1972.

5 "Interview with Mr. Turner, September 12, 1974," JNTP, Q5, vol. 14, file 2, "Memoranda, Important – JNT, 1974" (file 1 of 3).

6 "Secret. Recommendations Proposed by the Minister of Finance," JNTP, Q5, vol. 14, file 2, "Memoranda – Important – JNT, 1974" (file 1 of 3).

7 "The Social Security Review: Income Support and Supplementation," January 30, 1975, Cabinet Conclusions, LAC, RG 2, Privy Council Office, Series A 5 a, vol. 6436.

8 Stephen Clarkson and Christina McCall, *Trudeau and Our Times,* vol. 2, *The Heroic Delusion* (Toronto: McClelland and Stewart, 1994), 111-13. Rodney S. Haddow, *Poverty Reform in Canada, 1958-1978* (Montreal/Kingston: McGill-Queen's University, 1993), 107-10, 124-29; Dennis Guest, *Emergence of Social Security in Canada* (Vancouver: UBC Press, 1980), ch 12; Rick Van Loon, "Reforming Welfare in Canada," *Public Policy* 27,4 (Fall 1979): 469–504; John Saywell, ed., *Canadian Annual Review of Politics and Public Affairs, 1973* (Toronto: University of Toronto Press, 1974), 13-17; W. Irwin Gillespie, *Tax, Borrow, and Spend: Financing Federal Spending in Canada, 1867-1990* (Ottawa: Carleton University Press, 1991), 192-93.

9 John Turner to Richard Gwyn, July 9, 1975, JNTP, Q13-1, vol. 9, file 1, "Personal – Correspondence, 1973-1975" (file 2 of 2).

10 "JNT 15/vii/74," JNTP, Q5, vol. 20, file 4, "Mr. Turner's Confidential Cards 1974."

11 "Evolving Thoughts of a Finance Minister," *Toronto Star,* May 15, 1975.

12 Quoted in Douglas Fisher, "Turner as Budget Writer: 'It Either Floats or It Bombs,'" *Executive,* January 1975.

13 Clive Baxter, "PM's Outside Advisers Crux of Ottawa Ruckus," *Financial Post* (Toronto), January 25, 1975; Richard Gwyn, *The Northern Magus: Pierre Trudeau and Canadians* (Toronto: McClelland and Stewart, 1980), 187.

14 The full list read as follows: "2/i/75 New Career 1. PM set for duration. 2. No other challenges. 3. Lack of stimulus at cabinet table. 4. Family. 5. Finances. 6. Am[?] right for new start. 7. Uncertainty of Quebec." JNTP, Q5, vol. 20, file 5, "Mr. Turner's Personal Cards, 1975."

15 Christina McCall-Newman, *Grits: An Intimate Portrait of the Liberal Party* (Toronto: Macmillan of Canada, 1982), 270.

16 Michael Hunter to John Turner, February 5, 1975, JNTP, Q13-1, vol. 6, file 1, "Confidential – Notes from Mike Hunter."

17 Charles Lynch, "Talking Sense to Canadians," *Ottawa Citizen,* January 29, 1975; Victor Mackie, "John Turner's Future," *Winnipeg Free Press,* February 3, 1975; Paul Hellyer, "Time for John to Go?" *Ottawa Citizen,* January 29, 1975.

18 On February 11, 1975, Claude Isbister, a former Ottawa mandarin who was now an executive director of the World Bank, asked Turner if he was interested in the position. Claude Isbister to John Turner, February 11, 1975, JNTP, Q5, vol. 20, file 6, "Turner, John N. – Personal, 1972-1975" (file 1 of 5).

19 John English, *Just Watch Me: The Life of Pierre Elliott Trudeau, 1968-2000* (Toronto: Knopf Canada, 2009), 278.

20 John Turner, "Reflections on the Retirement of a Deputy Minister," *Ottawa Journal,* March 31, 1975, JNTP, Q5, vol. 17, file 8, "Reisman, Simon."

21 Gwyn, *The Northern Magus,* 181-83.

22 "Politics 3/v/75," JNTP, Q5, vol. 20, "Mr. Turner's Confidential Cards 1975."

23 "Evolving Thoughts"; Peter Cook, "Worry Grows over Turner's Consensus-by-Crisis," *Financial Times of Canada,* May 19, 1975.

24 Interview of John Swift, Vancouver, September 17, 2008.

25 John Turner to Pierre Trudeau, June 6, 1975, JNTP, Q5, vol. 4, file 1, "Budget – 1975."

26 "Budget Proposals and Expenditure Reductions – 1975-76," June 19, 1975, Cabinet Conclusions, LAC, RG 2, Privy Council Office, Series A-5-a, vol. 6456.

27 Hansard, June 23, 1975, 7024.

28 Richard Gwyn, "Ottawa Knows Budget Hurts but Says It's Time to Pay the Bills," *Toronto Star,* June 24, 1975.

29 "Confidential – Meetings and Correspondence with the Prime Minister," JNTP, Q13-1, vol. 5, file 9.

30 "Options, 20/viii/75," JNTP, Q5, vol. 20, file 1, "Mr. Turner's Confidential Notes, 1968-1969-1970-1971."

31 JNTP, Q13-1, vol. 10, file 11, "Retirement from Government Service, 1975-1976." The index card in Turner's pocket read,

> PM Sept. 10/75.
> 1. Non-negotiable.
> 2. His to announce.
> 3. Any leak, I'm [indecipherable].
> 4. I'm having no press conference.
> 5. Resign riding at my option.

JNTP, Q13-1, vol. 5, file 9, "Confidential – Meetings and Correspondence with the Prime Minister, 1967-1976."

32 JNTP, Q5, vol. 20, file 11, "Correspondence with P.M. and P.C., 1972-1975." Turner also resigned as chairman of the IMF's Interim Committee, but he remained a member of parliament.

33 See, for example, Gwyn, *The Northern Magus,* 188; Charles Lynch, *Race for the Rose: Election 1984* (Toronto: Methuen, 1984), 11; Ron Graham, *One-Eyed Kings: Promise and Illusion in Canadian Politics* (Toronto: Collins, 1986); McCall-Newman, *Grits,* 229-30. Turner would later flesh out the two-ships-passing-in-the-night interpretation: "The guy is a Cartesian logician and I'm an empiric guy. I'm an Anglo Saxon. I'm not

for codes and all that. I'm for working it out. I can't speculate, but if Mr. Pearson had been in a similar circumstance I would still be in government." Jack Cahill, *John Turner: The Long Run* (Toronto: McClelland and Stewart, 1984), 182.

34 "Note to Mr. Turner," September 15, 1975, JNTP, Q13-1, vol. 10, file 11. According to Jean Chrétien, Turner had agreed to see Trudeau again. Jean Chrétien, *Straight from the Heart* (1985; repr., Toronto: Key Porter Books, 1994), 78. See also Richard Gwyn, "Lawyer or Leader? Turner Must Choose," *Toronto Star*, November 22, 1975.

35 Interview of John Turner, Ottawa, July 25, 2005. Alastair Gillespie, a Rockcliffe Park neighbour, remembers Turner dropping by his house after he resigned. He told Gillespie that he had informed Trudeau that he couldn't carry on, because he didn't agree with mandatory controls. There would have to be a new minister. Interview of Alastair Gillespie, Toronto, January 19, 2005.

36 Pierre Trudeau to John Turner, September 11, 1975, JNTP, Q5, vol. 20, file 11, "Correspondence with P.M. and P.C., 1972-1975."

37 Roger Croft, "Criticism over Interest Rates Pushed Turner," *Toronto Star*, September 12, 1975.

38 "Note to Mr. Turner," September 15, 1975, JNTP, Q13-1, vol. 10, file 11, "Retirement from Government Service." The note was from John Swift, who had talked to John de B. Payne about the Coutts initiative.

39 Bruce Hutchison, "A Misjudgement of Politics," *Winnipeg Free Press*, September 19, 1975.

40 "Mr. Turner's Resignation," *Ottawa Journal*, September 12, 1975; "There Is Still a Need for Mr. Turner's Advocacy," *Toronto Globe and Mail*, September 12, 1975.

41 Peter Lloyd, "Turner a Tory? Don't Rule It Out Say Leading PCs," *Toronto Star*, September 13, 1975.

42 "Answer by John Turner to a Reporter in Saskatoon," JNTP, Q13-1, vol. 6, file 8, "Diefenbaker's 80th Birthday – Saskatoon, Sept. 1975."

43 Turner later claimed that forty Conservative MPs approached him in November 1975 and asked him to run for the Conservative leadership. "Turner Says He Was Asked to Seek Tory Leadership in '75," *Toronto Star*, June 14, 1985.

44 "Budget Proposals and Expenditure Reductions – 1975-76," June 19, 1975, Cabinet Conclusions, LAC, RG 2, Privy Council Office, Series A-5-a, vol. 6456.

45 JNTP, Q5, vol. 2, file 6, "Budget 1973" (file 1 of 2). Kenneth Norrie and Douglas Owram, *A History of the Canadian Economy* (Toronto: Harcourt Brace, 1991), 603; Mitchell Sharp, *Which Reminds Me: A Memoir* (Toronto: University of Toronto Press, 1994), 132; Gillespie interview.

46 Haddow, *Poverty Reform in Canada*, 128; Clarkson and McCall, *Trudeau and Our Times*, 113.

47 Richard Gwyn, "The Aitken Formula: John Turner's Way Out?" *Ottawa Journal*, May 22, 1975.

48 Turner's successors as minister of finance proved ineffective in addressing the deficits and the mounting national debt. In 1975 the deficit reached $5.7 billion, up from $2.0 billion the year before, and $2.0 billion more than Turner had predicted in his budget. But that was just a drop in the bucket. It would reach $15.0 billion in 1981 and $38.0 billion in 1984 during Trudeau's last term in office.

49 Hutchison, "A Misjudgement of Politics."
50 Victor Mackie, "Why Turner Resigned," *Ottawa Journal,* September 30, 1975; Cahill, *John Turner,* 184; English, *Just Watch Me,* 690n8.

CHAPTER 13: CITIZEN TURNER

1 Roy MacGregor, "'My Time Is Now!'" *Toronto Star,* June 17, 1984. See also Graham Fraser, *Playing for Keeps: The Making of the Prime Minister, 1988* (Toronto: McClelland and Stewart, 1989), 79.
2 His old seat, Ottawa-Carleton, was to be filled via a by-election set for October 18, 1976. A relatively weak Liberal candidate, Henri L. Rocque, was running against Conservative Jean Pigott, the head of a family baking business in Ottawa and one of the few female CEOs in the country. Pigott won by a sixteen-thousand-vote margin. The loss of this Liberal stronghold, which had been Liberal for more than ninety years, was seen as a sharp rebuke for the government – especially from its large number of public servants.
3 "Reflections and Perspectives," speech to the Ontario Economic Council, March 15, 1976, Library and Archives Canada (LAC), Ottawa, MG 26 (hereafter cited as JNTP), Q10-1, vol. 21, file 39.
4 In his study of the rise and fall of Keynesianism in Canada, Robert Malcolm Campbell sees 1975 as the year in which ongoing intransigent economic problems finally pushed policy-makers to abandon established techniques and to experiment with new solutions. Robert Malcolm Campbell, *Grand Illusions: The Politics of the Keynesian Experience in Canada, 1945-1975* (Toronto: Broadview Press, 1987), 6.
5 Jack Cahill, *John Turner: The Long Run* (Toronto: McClelland and Stewart, 1984), 8.
6 John Sawatsky, *The Insiders: Government, Business, and the Lobbyists* (Toronto: McClelland and Stewart, 1987), 190-91.
7 Richard Gwyn, "Turner: Ready to Run If Called, Ready to Serve If Elected," *Windsor Star,* September 16, 1976.
8 Ibid. Of course, awaiting the call could also be good politics. Trudeau's seeming reluctance had worked to his advantage in 1968.
9 John English, *Just Watch Me: The Life of Pierre Elliott Trudeau, 1968-2000* (Toronto: Knopf Canada, 2009), 329-56.
10 Dick Chapman, "Turner Hammers PM for Not Doing Enough to Rescue Quebec," *Toronto Star,* November 19, 1976.
11 The Primrose incident wasn't the only one of its type. "I don't think the status quo is any longer a realistic option," Turner told a Vancouver audience in March 1977. He thought that powers should be devolved to all the provinces, not just to Quebec under some form of special status. Cahill, *John Turner,* 192.
12 Richard Gwyn, *The Northern Magus: Pierre Trudeau and Canadians* (Toronto: McClelland and Stewart, 1980), 189.
13 Robert Lewis, "The Turner Campaign," *Maclean's,* March 21, 1977.
14 Richard Gwyn, "John Turner May Be Back – To Save Us All," *Toronto Star,* June 27, 1977; John Sawatsky, "The Big Fight," *Canadian Review,* April 1977.

15 W.A. Macdonald and J.N. Turner, "Federal Election and Budget," March 31, 1978, LAC, Alastair Gillespie fonds, R1526, Minister's Personal Papers Series – Correspondence Sub-series, vol. 363, file 17, "Turner, John – Criticisms of the Trudeau Government, 1978."

16 W.A. Macdonald and J.N. Turner, "Political Interregnum," June 30, 1978; W.A. Macdonald and J.N. Turner, (no title) July 14, 1978, LAC, Alastair Gillespie fonds, R1526, Minister's Personal Papers Series – Correspondence Sub-series, vol. 363, file 17, "Turner, John – Criticisms of the Trudeau Government, 1978."

17 John Turner to Alastair Gillespie, September 5, 1978, LAC, Alastair Gillespie fonds, R1526, Minister's Personal Papers Series – Correspondence Sub-series, vol. 363, file 17, "Turner, John – Criticisms of the Trudeau Government, 1978."

18 Interview of Alastair Gillespie, Toronto, January 19, 2005; Interview of David Smith, Toronto, April 26, 2005; Walter Stewart, "The Natural," *Toronto Life,* June 1983. John de B. Payne was rumoured to have penned most of the newsletters. Interview of John Swift, Vancouver, September 17, 2008.

19 Interview of Barney Danson, Toronto, January 21, 2005.

20 Lawrence Martin, *Chrétien,* vol. 1, *The Will to Win* (Toronto: Lester, 1995), 325-26.

21 They included York University, the Institute for International Economics in Washington, DC, the Canadian Council of Christians and Jews, the Metro Toronto Advisory Board of the Salvation Army, the Toronto Branch of the Ludwig Institute for Cancer Research, the Toronto School of Theology, and St. Michael's College at the University of Toronto. At St. Michael's he was a director of the Pontifical Institute of Mediaeval Studies. The institute's board, which included Conrad Black, managed the investment of its endowment.

22 Diane Francis, "Bay St. Years Have Been Good for Turner," *Toronto Star,* April 19, 1984.

23 Bechtel was an irresistible target for conspiracy theorists because of its private ownership, international operations, and political connections. The nature of its business – megaprojects such as dams, factories, nuclear reactors, and mines – politicized its activities. Among Bechtel's alumni were George Shultz, the US secretary of state; Caspar Weinberger, the US defense secretary; Philip Habib, President Reagan's special Mideast emissary; and Kenneth Davis, the US deputy secretary of energy.

24 Allan Fotheringham, "When Blue Chips Down, Blue-Eyes Chose Safety," *Vancouver Sun,* December 13, 1979.

25 Diane Francis, "Bay St. Years Have Been Good for Turner," *Toronto Star,* April 19, 1984.

26 Val Sears, "Waiting for Turner," *Montreal Gazette,* December 16, 1978.

27 Mary Trueman, "If There Really Is a 195 Club, Will the Members Please Stand Up?" *Toronto Globe and Mail,* December 13, 1978. See also Sears, "Waiting for Turner."

28 Charles Lynch, *Race for the Rose: Election 1984* (Toronto: Methuen, 1984), 3-4.

29 Lewis, "The Turner Campaign."

30 Peter Regenstreif, "Turner Could Put 'Liberals in Front,'" *Toronto Star,* December 9, 1978.

31 JNTP, Q13-2, vol. 1, file 2, "Correspondence – Miscellaneous – Political, 1978."

32 S.W. Proudfoot to John Turner, September 27, 1978, JNTP, Q13-2, vol. 1, file 2, "Correspondence – Miscellaneous Political, 1978."

33 David Smith to John Turner, November 26, 1979, JNTP, Q8-2, vol. 5, file 13, "Campaign Material – Turner – Personal/Leadership, 1979-1984."
34 "Addison 26/xi/79," JNTP, Q8-1, vol. 14, file 15, "JNT Notes – 1979."
35 JNTP, Q8-1, vol. 14, file 15, "JNT B Political – JNT Statements, 1979-1980"; Joe O'Donnell, "Going for It!" *Toronto Star,* June 26, 1982; Richard Gwyn, "Liberal Slogan Might Be, 'Time for a Westerner,'" *Toronto Star,* January 17, 1984.
36 Lewis, "The Turner Campaign."

CHAPTER 14: A MYTH AND A MUDDLE

1 Stephen Clarkson and Christina McCall, *Trudeau and Our Times,* vol. 2, *The Heroic Delusion* (Toronto: McClelland and Stewart, 1994), 169; John English, *Just Watch Me: The Life of Pierre Elliott Trudeau, 1968-2000* (Toronto: Knopf Canada, 2009), 433-37.
2 Weston was among those who offered financial support if Turner decided to re-enter politics. Galen Weston to John Turner, April 16, 1982, Library and Archives Canada (LAC), Ottawa, MG 26 (hereafter cited as JNTP), Q13-2, vol. 1, file 6, "Correspondence, Jan.-Aug. 1982."
3 Val Sears, "John Turner: Armored and Ready," *Toronto Star,* November 22, 1986.
4 Walter Stewart, "The Natural," *Toronto Life,* June 1983.
5 Terrance Wills, "Turner Greeted Like Long-Lost Prince," *Montreal Gazette,* February 7 [or 8], 1982.
6 "Clark Would Lose in Race against Turner, Gallup Suggests," *Toronto Globe and Mail,* January 20, 1983. Turner would, however, lose if the Conservatives had Peter Lougheed or Bill Davis as leader.
7 Jeffrey Simpson, "Liberal Ruins Offer Clues to Party's Collapse," *Toronto Globe and Mail,* September 6, 1984.
8 Douglas Fisher, "Glitter Fades," *Toronto Sun,* June 13, 1983.
9 Stewart, "The Natural."
10 Senior RCMP officers told the McDonald Commission (the Royal Commission of Inquiry into Certain Activities of the Royal Canadian Mounted Police) that their political masters had known about their illegal activities. Turner appeared before the commission in 1981 and testified that he had had no knowledge of any wrongdoing. Ultimately, the commission found no proof of the accusations against him. His only other brush with impropriety was his peripheral involvement with the Hal Banks affair. Banks, an American thug, had been imported to rid the Seafarers' International Union (SIU) of communists. The SIU had donated money to Turner's election campaigns in St. Lawrence–St. George during the early 1960s. When the RCMP questioned Turner about these donations, he denied knowing about them. JNTP, Q13-2, vol. 2, file 4; JNTP, Q13-2, vol. 2, file 2. Later, criminal charges were laid against Banks, including conspiracy to assault. He jumped bail and went to the United States, was arrested in New York City in August 1967, and was subsequently ordered extradited to Canada. In March 1968 the US secretary of state decided not to proceed with the extradition. William Kaplan, *Everything That Floats: Pat Sullivan, Hal Banks, and the Seamen's Union of Canada* (Toronto: University of Toronto Press, 1987). There were allegations that the Liberal government did not want Banks brought back for fear of embarrassment

if he revealed it had sanctioned his illegal activities. As minister of justice, Turner made several statements in the House of Commons denying these charges. See Hansard, May 10, 1965, 1097; Donald Christie to deputy minister, November 18, 1968, JNTP, Q4, vol. 8, file 11. For insinuations that Turner was somehow covering up corruption, see Bob MacDonald, "Darker Side of Turner," *Toronto Sun,* October 1, 1985.

11 Turner personally lost his $35,000 investment in CFI. He had also invested in Infinitum Growth Fund, a venture capital firm that had made a lot of bad investments, but such firms made high risk investments, so in this case the losses were not as controversial.

12 John Ferguson, "Voters' Mood Is for a Change of Government," *Ottawa Citizen,* September 10, 1983.

13 Bruce Hutchison, "Trudeau's Problem: A Tight Timeframe," *Vancouver Sun,* November 24, 1983.

14 Richard Gwyn, "Parliamentary System Has Become Presidential," *Toronto Star,* February 7, 1984.

15 Allan Fotheringham, "Word's out Turner's In," *Toronto Sun,* October 26, 1983. The comment that he would stay on and rebuild the party as opposition leader appeared in the press during the late fall and early winter. See, for example, Richard Gwyn, "Liberal Slogan Might Be, 'Time for a Westerner,'" *Toronto Star,* January 17, 1984. It might be dismissed as the type of leak calculated to counter portrayals of Turner as power-hungry, yet a period in opposition was a very real prospect.

16 Roy MacGregor, "'My Time Is Now!'" *Toronto Star,* June 17, 1984.

17 "Addenda – Policy Agenda," November 7, 1983, JNTP, Q8-2, vol. 5, file 13, "Campaign Material – JNT – Personal/Leadership, 1979-1984"; John Swift to John Turner, December 13, 1983, same file. Payne had already been briefing Turner for a year.

18 Angus Reid to John Turner, November 28, 1983, JNTP, Q8-1, vol. 15, file 15, "Planning for Leadership Race, 1979-1984."

19 There was some controversy among Turner's other advisers about the six-figure salaries that Swift and Foulkes arranged. By not organizing sooner, however, Turner had no choice but to go with the people at hand, and these numbers were among their conditions. John Sawatsky, *The Insiders: Government, Business, and the Lobbyists* (Toronto: McClelland and Stewart, 1987), 197.

20 H.E. Karpus to J.N. Turner, Memo, January 3, 1984, JNTP, Q8-2, vol. 8, file 10, "Survey of Voters' Attitudes, Dec. 1983." A Gallup poll released in February had the Conservatives even higher, at 63 per cent of the popular vote, and the Liberals still around 22 per cent. Lawrence Martin, "PM Leaving New Leader Too Little Time, Turner Friends Say," *Toronto Globe and Mail,* January 26, 1984.

21 MacGregor, "'My Time Is Now!'"

22 Ibid.

23 Jeffrey Simpson, "They're Off: Who's Leading the Leadership Race?" *Toronto Globe and Mail,* March 1, 1984.

24 Interview of Howard Brown, Toronto, October 19, 2007.

25 Stewart, "The Natural."

26 Val Sears, "Turner Eager to Join Race, Friends Say," *Toronto Star,* March 9, 1984.

27 MacGregor, "'My Time Is Now!'"

28 Ibid.

29 "Statement, 11/iii/84," in Turner's handwriting, attached by a paper clip to a typed memo entitled "First Response," JNTP, Q8-2, vol. 5, file 14, "Campaign Material – Turner – Personal/Leadership, 1984."
30 J.L. Granatstein and Norman Hillmer, *Prime Ministers: Ranking Canada's Leaders* (Toronto: Harper Collins, 1999), 182.
31 Jack Cahill, *John Turner: The Long Run* (Toronto: McClelland and Stewart, 1984), 206-7.
32 Allan Fotheringham, "Berths on the Tory Train," *Toronto Sun,* November 27, 1983.

CHAPTER 15: OILING THE TINMAN

1 Ron Graham, *One Eyed-Kings: Promise and Illusion in Canadian Politics* (Toronto: Collins, 1986), 243.
2 "Announcement of Candidacy, John N. Turner, Friday, March 16, 1984," Library and Archives Canada (LAC), Ottawa, MG 26 (hereafter cited as JNTP), Q8-2, vol. 5, file 14. John de B. Payne helped to draft his announcement speech.
3 James Rusk, "Turner Plays Down Right-Wing Stance in Leadership Bid," *Toronto Globe and Mail,* March 17, 1984. In a column otherwise critical of Turner, Jeffrey Simpson wrote that he handled himself with aplomb and wit. Jeffrey Simpson, "Forward into the Past," *Toronto Globe and Mail,* March 17, 1984.
4 Turner announcement, video, March 16, 1984, LAC, acc. no. 201963, consultation copy no. VI 2007-04-0004.
5 Bob Hepburn, "Turner Vows 'Bright Future' for Jobless," *Toronto Star,* March 17, 1984.
6 Anthony Wilson-Smith, "Quebec Reacts to the Manitoba Issue," *Maclean's,* April 2, 1984.
7 Carol Goar, "The New Politics of Language," *Maclean's,* April 2, 1984.
8 James Rusk, "Chrétien Launches Campaign Surrounded by MPs, Senators," *Toronto Globe and Mail,* March 21, 1984.
9 R.B. Byers, ed., *Canadian Annual Review of Politics and Public Affairs, 1984* (Toronto: University of Toronto Press, 1987), 86.
10 Goar, "The New Politics."
11 "Statement: John N. Turner – March 21, 1984," JNTP, Q8-1, vol. 15, file 2.
12 John de B. Payne to John Turner, March 30, 1984, JNTP, Q8-2, vol. 5, file 14.
13 John de B. Payne, "Leadership Campaign Memorandum no. 1," April 4, 1984, JNTP, Q8-1, vol. 15, file 12, "Payne Papers, 1984."
14 Graham, *One-Eyed Kings,* 217.
15 Roy MacGregor, "'My Time Is Now!'" *Toronto Star,* June 17, 1984.
16 Thomas Walkom, "Veteran Organizer Is Reluctant Rescuer of Turner Campaign," *Toronto Globe and Mail,* June 14, 1984.
17 John Sawatsky, *The Insiders: Government, Business, and the Lobbyists* (Toronto: McClelland and Stewart, 1987), 206.
18 MacGregor, "'My Time Is Now!'"
19 Organizational issues would continue to plague Turner's campaign. In late May, Lloyd Axworthy, one of the campaign co-chairs, blasted Turner for leaving him out of the loop. Lloyd Axworthy to John Turner, May 25, 1984, JNTP, Q8-2, vol. 5, file 14.

20 Norman Snider, *The Changing of the Guard* (Toronto: Lester and Orpen Dennys, 1985), 58; Lawrence Martin. *Chrétien,* vol. 1, *The Will to Win* (Toronto: Lester, 1995), 326-30.
21 Val Sears, "Turner's Rusty but It's All Coming Back," *Toronto Star,* April 7, 1984. The "rusty" label was first applied by Jeff Sallott of the *Toronto Globe and Mail* after the first policy forum in Toronto. Sears, who covered that event as well, had not used it then.
22 Frances Russell, "Axworthy Marks Time in Slow Turner March," *Winnipeg Free Press,* April 4, 1984. This criticism echoed an earlier assessment of Turner by Christina McCall-Newman: "I see him as an anachronistic figure ... stuck in the mind-set of 1957, stuck in seeing C.D. Howe as the ideal political man. He thinks you can manage Canadian society as if it is a men's club, and I'm not sure you can anymore." Mary Janigan, "Revelations from the Corridors of Power," *Maclean's,* November 15, 1982. "An endless succession of biographies in print," wrote Charles Lynch, "speculated that ... [Turner] was a naturally shy man who had assumed an activist personality as a cover-up, that he was nervous with people and the press, that he was running on his reflexes, and that they were the reflexes of another age." Charles Lynch, *Race for the Rose: Election 1984* (Toronto: Methuen, 1984), 65.
23 Graham, *One-Eyed Kings,* 213.
24 Jerry Grafstein to John Turner, Position Paper no. 1, March 23, 1984, JNTP, Q8-1, vol. 14, file 10, "Input from Others, 1984."
25 Lawrence Martin, "Turner Backs Quebec Law on Language," *Toronto Globe and Mail,* April, 12, 1984; Robert Mackenzie, "Turner Backs PQ's Bill 101 'in Principle,'" *Toronto Star,* April 12, 1984.
26 Sawatsky, *The Insiders,* 200.
27 Derek Hodgson, "Welcome to the '80s, Mr. Turner," *Toronto Sun,* April 15, 1984.
28 Peter Newman, *The Canadian Revolution* (Toronto: Viking, 1995), 256.
29 Mary Janigan, "Turner's Days of Decision," *Maclean's,* June 26, 1984.
30 *The National,* May 3, 1984, LAC, Television News Digest: John Turner, 1985/05/03, Privy Council Collection, acc. no. 1989-0292, IDC no. 208888.
31 Bruce Ward, "Candidate Turner Uses Two Separate Styles of Handshake," *Toronto Star,* May 27, 1984.
32 "Mr. Turner on Trust," *Toronto Globe and Mail,* June 9, 1984.
33 Henry Karpus to John Turner, March 26, 1984, JNTP, Q8-2, vol. 5, file 13, "Campaign Material – JNT – Personal/Leadership, 1979-1984."
34 MacGregor, "'My Time Is Now!'"
35 Turner didn't resign his directorships until the end of the second quarter, June 30, 1984, the day he was sworn in as prime minister.
36 "Briefing Material. Turner – Questions and Answers. Second Draft. 1984," JNTP, Q8-2, vol. 10, file 11. Bill Lee advised this response, and Turner agreed.
37 Thomas Walkom, "Investment Climate Is Top Priority: Turner," *Toronto Globe and Mail,* May 10, 1984.
38 Byers, *Canadian Annual Review,* 14.
39 Allan Fotheringham, "Ho-Hum Leadership Race," *Toronto Sun,* April 18, 1984.
40 Jeffrey Simpson called it "an unprecedented intervention by an outgoing leader in the succession fight." Jeffrey Simpson, "Mr. Trudeau's Rebuttal," *Toronto Globe and Mail,* May 12, 1984.

41 John de B. Payne to John Turner, May 14, 1984, JNTP, Q8-2, vol. 5, file 14.
42 Jack Cahill, *John Turner: The Long Run* (Toronto: McClelland and Stewart, 1984), 215. Retired Canadian Labour Congress president Joe Morris supported Turner's version of events, saying that progress was being made but that Trudeau didn't support Turner, because he favoured legislation.
43 Graham, *One-Eyed Kings,* 200.
44 MacGregor, "'My Time Is Now!'"
45 Val Sears, "Turner Booming along in the Home Stretch," *Toronto Star,* June 8, 1984.
46 Lawrence Martin, "Trudeau Bids Party Goodbye in Emotional Extravaganza," *Toronto Globe and Mail,* June 15, 1984.
47 Ross Howard, "Turner, Chretien Soar in Pitch for Key Votes," *Globe and Mail*, June 16, 1984; Graham, *One-Eyed Kings,* 251; Excerpts from a Speech to the Liberal Leadership Convention, Ottawa, 15 June 1984, in Elizabeth McIninch and Arthur Milnes, eds., *Politics of Purpose: 40th Anniversary Edition* (Montreal/Kingston: McGill-Queen's University Press, 2009), 10-11; John Gray, "The Surprise Was Delivered by Bay Street," *Globe and Mail*, June 16, 1984. Keith Davey claimed to have coined the phrase "let's pretend Liberal" and passed it on to Bill Lee. Keith Davey, *The Rainmaker: A Passion for Politics* (Toronto: Stoddart, 1986), 325.

CHAPTER 16: PRIME MINISTER FOR A DAY

1 As Lawrence Martin put it, "No one was proud of the way Jean Chrétien behaved after the convention ... He became convinced that a grave injustice had been perpetrated." Lawrence Martin, *Chrétien,* vol. 1, *The Will to Win* (Toronto: Lester, 1995), 339.
2 Interview of James Robb, Montreal, May 26, 2005.
3 John Sawatsky, *The Insiders: Government, Business, and the Lobbyists* (Toronto: McClelland and Stewart, 1987), 217.
4 "Turner Cuts Some, Chrétien Still a Holdout," *Ottawa Citizen,* June 27, 1984; Allan Fotheringham, "Media Star Chrétien Almost Overplayed Hand," *Ottawa Citizen,* June 28, 1984. Fotheringham cited columnist Douglas Fisher as his source.
5 "To: JNT From: Bill Lee Re: Timing of the General Election Date: June 4, 1984," Library and Archives Canada (LAC), Ottawa, MG 26 (hereafter cited as JNTP), Q8-2, vol. 5, file 14. The Liberals were usually in power, so they could choose when to call an election and did so when their support was peaking, which explained why they usually lost support over the course of an election campaign.
6 Sawatsky, *The Insiders,* 225.
7 Bill Lee to prime minister, August 3, 1984, JNTP, Q8-2, vol. 11, file 16.
8 Marc Lalonde and Tom Axworthy had been heading up an election planning committee that had produced new policies, speech materials, and campaign manuals. They had planned to make use of Martin Goldfarb's polling firm to track public opinion nationally, regionally, and even locally, and to respond with policies at each level. These plans fell between the two stools of the old and new regimes. On the one hand, they were premised on Trudeau running again on a typical Trudeau platform; on the other, they were not appreciated by the new regime, which was suspicious of everything Trudeauvian.

9 "Tom Axworthy," Lee continued, "made it clear that if Mr. Trudeau had decided to go again, he (Tom) would have run it entirely out of the P.M.O. – simply because there was nothing at 102." JNTP, Q8-2, vol. 11, file 16, "To: Prime Minister From: Bill Lee August 3, 1984"; Sawatsky, *The Insiders*, 227-28. What happened to the Axworthy-Lalonde system during the transfer of power to Turner was a matter of controversy, with Trudeauites and Turnerites blaming each other for fumbling the passing of the baton. Keith Davey, *The Rainmaker: A Passion for Politics* (Toronto: Stoddart, 1986), 330-34; Greg Weston, *Reign of Error* (Toronto: McGraw-Hill Ryerson, 1988), 72; Stephen Clarkson, "The Dauphin and the Doomed: John Turner and the Liberal Party's Debacle," in *Canada at the Polls, 1984,* ed. Howard Penniman (Durham, NC: Duke University Press, 1988), 106.

10 Jeffrey Simpson, "Liberal Ruins Offer Clues to Party's Collapse," *Toronto Globe and Mail,* September 6, 1984. Turner received the list of the remaining patronage positions that Trudeau wanted on Tuesday, June 26.

11 Turner sent Chrétien a letter confirming his terms the next day. John N. Turner to Jean Chrétien, June 29, 1984, JNTP, Q10-2, vol. 2, file 38.

12 Carol Goar and Mary Janigan, "Turner's Muted Ascension," *Maclean's,* July 9, 1984.

13 G.F. Osbaldeston to the prime minister, Memo, June 28, 1984, JNTP, Q6-2, vol. 1, file 2.

14 Pierre Trudeau to John Turner, June 29, 1984, JNTP, Q6-2, vol. 1, file 1

15 John Turner to Pierre Trudeau, June 29, 1984, JNTP, Q6-2, vol. 1, file 1.

16 Jamie Lamb, "John Turner's Transformation," *Vancouver Sun,* July 3, 1984.

17 Charles Lynch, "Turner's Bay Street Talk Puts Best Possible Face on Liberal Mess," *Montreal Gazette,* July 3, 1984. Lynch recalled that Trudeau had ignored Pearson's suggested patronage appointments when he had succeeded him and speculated that Keith Davey, remembering this lapse, had probably recommended to Trudeau that he get a commitment from Turner in writing. Charles Lynch, "Trudeau Appointments Hurt Turner the Most," *Ottawa Citizen,* September 4, 1985.

18 Charlotte Montgomery, "Turner Launches Campaign to Sell 'New Era' to Voters," *Toronto Globe and Mail,* July 2, 1984.

19 Hugh Winsor, "Two Rookie Leaders Learned Hard Reality of Press Relations," *Toronto Globe and Mail,* September 4, 1984.

20 Lamb, "John Turner's Transformation."

21 Goar and Janigan, "Turner's Muted Accession."

22 Angus Reid Associates Inc., "Canadians' Voting Intentions, the Perceptions of Political Leaders and Attitudes towards Selected National Issues," June 1984, JNTP, Q7-2, vol. 16, file 38, "Polls."

23 "Talking Points for the Prime Minister, Priorities and Planning," July 3, 1984, JNTP, Q6-2, vol. 2, file 8, "Finance Meeting."

24 "Speaking Notes for the Minister of Finance, Priorities and Planning – July 4," June 29, 1984, JNTP, Q6-2, vol. 2, file 8, "Finance Meeting."

25 Nigel Hawkes, "The Queen Is Not Amused by Canada's Election Date," *London Observer,* July 8, 1984.

26 Bob Hepburn, "Turner Calls Election on Sept. 4 'I Sense People Want a Choice,'" *Toronto Star,* July 10, 1984.

27 Richard Gwyn, "Let's Not Place Too Much Trust in the Polls," *Toronto Star,* July 7, 1984.

28 Interview of James Robb, Montreal, April 6, 2005.

CHAPTER 17: THINGS FALL APART

1 Bill Lee to John Turner, June 28, 1984, Library and Archives Canada (LAC), Ottawa, MG 26 (hereafter cited as JNTP), Q8-2, vol. 11, file 16; John Rae to John Turner, July 4, 1984, JNTP, Q8-2, vol. 11, file 16.
2 John Meisel, "The Boob-Tube Election: Three Aspects of the 1984 Landslide," in *The Canadian House of Commons: Essays in Honour of Norman Ward,* ed. John C. Courtney (Calgary: University of Calgary Press, 1985), 341-72.
3 David Vienneau, "'Jackass Bonehead' Gave Advice to PM on Patronage, Forsey Says," *Toronto Star,* July 11, 1984.
4 "Final Insult," *Toronto Sun,* July 11, 1984; Charlotte Montgomery, "Turner Stands by Raft of Postings, but Half-Heartedly," *Toronto Globe and Mail,* July 13, 1984.
5 Bruce Ward, "Patronage Plums Passed Out to 17 Longtime Liberal MPs," *Toronto Star,* July 10, 1984.
6 "Confidential, Memorandum for the Prime Minister – Appointments – Cabinet Meeting of July 9," JNTP, Q8-2, vol. 5, file 14. One of the six was a routine diplomatic posting. Charles Bédard, a career foreign service officer then serving on the International Joint Commission, was appointed as consul general to Strasbourg, France. Another was Paul Cosgrove, a Toronto MP who had earlier turned down an appointment, then changed his mind. Chrétien supported the Cosgrove appointment. He had also backed those of Whelan; of Maurice Dupras, MP (Labelle), as consul general in Bordeaux, France; and of Léonce Mercier, who had quit his job as the Liberals' director general for Quebec to work on Chrétien's campaign, as a citizenship judge. The one appointment Turner thought of as his own was that of Arthur Portelance, the Liberal MP for the Montreal riding of Gamelin, who was named to the Canadian Aviation Safety Board to make way for a female candidate, Lise Thibault.
7 Carol Goar, "The Race for Sussex Drive," *Maclean's,* July 23, 1984.
8 Philippe Gigantès to André Masse, July 21, 1984, JNTP, Q7-2, vol. 16, file 3. Aides advised Turner to rescind the Mackasey appointment, which was responsible for most of the flak, but he refused on the grounds that Mackasey was innocent of the corruption charges against him until proven guilty.
9 Jeff Sallot, "Mulroney Trips over 'Jokes' on Patronage," *Toronto Globe and Mail,* July 17, 1984.
10 Interview of Michael Hunter, Vancouver, September 16, 2008.
11 "Confidential, Memorandum for the Prime Minister – Appointments – Cabinet Meeting of July 9."
12 Keith Davey, *The Rainmaker: A Passion for Politics* (Toronto: Stoddart, 1986), 325; Stephen Clarkson, "The Dauphin and the Doomed: John Turner and the Liberal Party's Debacle," in *Canada at the Polls, 1984,* ed. Howard Penniman (Durham, NC: Duke University Press, 1988), 108; Interview of Michael Marzolini, Toronto, June 2, 2005.
13 Interview of John Swift, Vancouver, September 17, 2008.

14 L. Ian MacDonald, *Mulroney: The Making of the Prime Minister* (Toronto: McClelland and Stewart, 1984), 253-54; Interview of James Robb, Montreal, December 3, 2008; Interview of Raymond Garneau, Montreal, December 4, 2008.

15 Linda Diebel, "Lalonde Led Plot to Topple Turner in '84 Election, Papers Show," *Ottawa Citizen,* November 28, 1986.

16 Michael Hunter recalled that Turner was punning in a self-deprecating manner by saying, "I've been a perfect ass." Interview of Michael Hunter, Vancouver, September 16, 2008. One observer saw an "undercurrent of hostility" in the exchange. Norman Snider, *The Changing of the Guard* (Toronto: Lester and Orpen Dennys, 1985), 123.

17 John Sawatsky, *The Insiders: Government, Business, and the Lobbyists* (Toronto: McClelland and Stewart, 1987), 239; Interview of Sandra Kaiser, Vaughan, August 26, 2008.

18 "Turner Says Posterior-Patting Is Part of His Political Style," *Toronto Globe and Mail,* July 21, 1984; JNTP, Q8-2, vol. 5, file 14. Turner eventually apologized for his bum patting but not until August 13, just before the television debate on women's issues, by which time it was too late.

19 Michel Gratton, *So, What Are the Boys Saying?* (Toronto: McGraw-Hill Ryerson, 1987), 35-37; MacDonald, *Mulroney,* 287-90; Transcript of the French debate, July 24, 1984, JNTP, Q8-2, vol. 11, file 13.

20 "Debate (English), Transcript of the Televised Debate between the Leaders of the Three Major Federal Political Parties," July 25, 1984, JNTP, Q8-2, vol. 11, file 12, "Debate (English), 1984."

21 Hunter interview.

22 Marc Lalonde to John Turner, July 27, 1984, JNTP, Q8-2, vol. 11, file 16.

23 Thomas Walkom, "Myths Belied the Real John Turner," *Toronto Globe and Mail,* September 10, 1984; James Rusk, "Liberals Regroup after Losing Lee," *Toronto Globe and Mail,* August 6, 1984.

24 Val Sears, "Turner's Campaign: A Lot of Flapping but Little Lift," *Toronto Star,* July 30, 1984.

25 Bob Hepburn, "Turner Vows to Wipe Out Discrimination," *Toronto Star,* July 28, 1984.

26 Peter Desbarats, "'New Journalism' in Flower," *Financial Post* (Toronto), September 29, 1984.

27 Stephen LeDrew to Bill Lee, August 3, 1984, JNTP, Q8-2, vol. 11, file 16.

28 Bill Lee to prime minister, August 3, 1984, JNTP, Q8-2, vol. 11, file 16.

29 Ibid.

30 Val Sears, "A Month Ago John Turner Admitted: 'I've Screwed Up,'" *Toronto Star,* September 6, 1984. Lee was mortified and enraged by the turn of events. Michael Hunter took notes of a telephone call with Lee in which he blamed Turner for the problems with the election campaign. Notes of a telephone call from Bill Lee, August 5, 7:45 p.m., Michael Hunter private papers. Thereafter, Lee became a major source for journalists critical of Turner.

31 "Polls actually outranked leadership in overall issue salience. This is the first time we have known this to happen," concluded one study of the election. "What now may be influencing voting decisions is less where parties stand on substantive matters than

whether they are deemed likely to win or lose." Walter C. Soderlund et al., *Media and Elections in Canada* (Toronto: Holt, Rinehart and Winston of Canada, 1984), 126.

32 "There's no question that there's evidence, huge evidence, of bandwagon voting in those campaigns," Gregg concluded. John Laschinger and Geoffrey Stevens, eds., *Leaders and Lesser Mortals* (Toronto: Key Porter, 1992), 97. For similar opinions, see also Frederick J. Fletcher, "The Media and the 1984 Landslide," in Penniman, *Canada at the Polls, 1984*, 171-72; Jeffrey Simpson, "Liberal Ruins Offer Clues to Party's Collapse," *Toronto Globe and Mail*, September 6, 1984. The argument against the strategic voting thesis would be that Turner continued to make mistakes that cost him support. Angus Reid, for example, reported a seven-point drop in Liberal support in the days following the announcement that Keith Davey was joining the campaign.

33 R.B. Byers, ed., *Canadian Annual Review of Politics and Public Affairs, 1984* (Toronto: University of Toronto Press, 1987), 24.

34 Gratton, *So, What Are the Boys Saying?* 49.

35 Val Sears, "Merlins of Image Making," *Toronto Star*, February 28, 1987.

36 Hugh Winsor, "Liberal Survey Said Strategy Would Fail," *Toronto Globe and Mail*, September 1, 1984.

37 Turner in the *Toronto Globe and Mail*, August 24, 1984, quoted in Byers, *Canadian Annual Review*, 200.

38 In 1958 the Conservatives under John Diefenbaker won 208 seats, when the House of Commons consisted of 265 seats. This number represented 78 per cent of the seats in the House. When Mulroney won 211 seats, the House consisted of 282 seats, so the Conservatives had 74 per cent of them.

39 "Transcript of Remarks by PM, Bayshore Hotel, Vancouver, British Columbia, Sept. 4, 1984," JNTP, Q10-2, vol. 5, file 8; "Transcript of Remarks by PM, Vancouver Quadra Headquarters, Vancouver, British Columbia, Sept. 4, 1984," JNTP, Q10-2, vol. 5, file 9.

40 Lawrence LeDuc, "The Flexible Canadian Electorate," in Penniman, *Canada at the Polls, 1984*, 51; Allan Levine, *Scrum Wars: The Prime Ministers and the Media* (Toronto: Dundurn, 1993), 323.

41 See Marjorie Nichols, "Gallup Gamble: PM Has Taken a Very Big Risk," *Ottawa Citizen*, October 3, 1988. The polling Turner commissioned from Peter Hart the previous December had reported that, though the Liberals were then lagging far behind the Conservatives, they were the party of preference for 52 per cent of Canadians. Sawatsky, *The Insiders*, 194.

42 Levine, *Scrum Wars*, 323.

43 Fletcher, "The Media," 183.

44 Quoted in Alan Frizzell and Anthony Westell, "Who Shot J.T.? – The Media Coverage," in Alan Frizzell and Anthony Westell, *The Canadian General Election of 1984: Politicians, Parties, Press and Polls* (Ottawa: Carleton University Press, 1984), 55, 69. See also Meisel, "The Boob-Tube Election," 173-94; R.H. Wagenberg et al., "Note: Campaigns, Images and Polls – Mass Media Coverage of the 1984 Canadian Election," *Canadian Journal of Political Science* 12, 1 (March 1988): 117-29.

45 Here Turner was the victim of a cruel twist of fate. In some ways, the economy looked pretty good during the first half of 1984. Building on a strong recovery the year before, it was growing at the rate of 5.8 per cent. Leading indicators such as productivity,

output, and corporate profits were up, and inflation was down. These good signs had been offset, however, by a disturbing rise in interest rates and unemployment during the first half of the year. Undetectable at the time of Lalonde's February budget, they were trending ominously by June. On July 11, after weeks of steady decline, the Canadian dollar fell below the symbolic level of 75.00 cents US, hitting a historic low of 74.86 cents. Short-term interest rates, which had gone down to 9.5 per cent in 1983, now shot up to 11.45 per cent. Yet as it turned out, this was as bad as things got. The dollar recovered somewhat in the third and fourth quarters, and short-term rates peaked at 12.45 per cent before falling back to 10.94 per cent in the third quarter. Meanwhile, the overall positive indicators, such as economic growth, continued to trend positively. The economy was in fact leaving the recession far behind. The sad irony was that, had Turner waited and run in the fall, the economic indicators would uniformly have been trending favourably. Michael Hawes, "The National Economy," in Byers, *Canadian Annual Review*, 100-20.

46 Martin Myers, creative director of Miller, Myers & Bruce, quoted in Roy MacGregor, "The Selling of a Leader: Do TV Ads Work?" *Toronto Star*, September 1, 1984.

CHAPTER 18: THE ROAD BACK

1 Jeffrey Simpson, "The Party's Bleak Future," *Toronto Globe and Mail*, January 3, 1985.
2 John Turner to Brenda Norris, September 17, 1984, Library and Archives Canada (LAC), Ottawa, MG 26 (hereafter cited as JNTP), Q13-3, vol. 1, file 6, "Correspondence, June-September 1984."
3 Walter Gordon to John Turner, September 6, 1984, JNTP, Q7-2, vol. 22, file 9.
4 L.C. Audette to John Turner, September 11, 1984, JNTP, Q6-2, vol. 2, file 2-23, "Support and Encouragement." There was even a note of condolence and support from Bill Lee.
5 Richard Stanbury to John Turner, November 22, 1984, JNTP, Q7-2, vol. 12, file 9.
6 Peter Newman, "Paving a Long Road Back," *Maclean's*, November 19, 1984.
7 Transcript of interview of Pierre Trudeau by Craig Oliver, November 15, 1984, JNTP, Q7-2, vol. 21, file 11; Lawrence Martin, "Turner Tries to Make Up to Trudeau," *Toronto Globe and Mail*, January 10, 1985.
8 JNTP, Q11-2, vol. 1, file 4; JNTP, Q7-2, vol. 21, file 5.
9 Hansard, November 7, 1984, 32.
10 Interview of Doug Frith, Toronto, November 27, 2008.
11 Ron Graham, *One Eyed-Kings: Promise and Illusion in Canadian Politics* (Toronto: Collins, 1986), 424.
12 Newman, "Paving."
13 Jamie Lamb, "A Resurgent Opposition Leader," *Vancouver Sun*, September 12, 1985; Don McGillvray, "Turner's Agenda Worth Watching," *Ottawa Citizen*, November 8, 1985.
14 Greg Weston, *Reign of Error* (Toronto: McGraw-Hill Ryerson, 1988), 159.
15 Telephone interviews with Alex Graham, Toronto, January 11 and 12, 2011.
16 Brooke Jeffrey, *Divided Loyalties: The Liberal Party of Canada, 1984-2008* (Toronto: University of Toronto Press, 2010), 44-45.
17 Interview of Stephen Hastings, Toronto, January 31, 2011.

18 Malcolm Curtis, "Turner Relaxed, Confident in New Role," *Ottawa Citizen,* July 6, 1985.
19 Interview of Scott Sheppard, Ottawa, July 26, 2005.
20 Curtis, "Turner Relaxed."
21 Jamie Lamb, "John Turner Relishing Challenge on Comeback Trail," *Vancouver Sun,* June 21, 1985. See also Sheila Copps, *Nobody's Baby: A Woman's Survival Guide to Politics* (Toronto: Deneau, 1986), 72-73; Joseph Wearing, *Strained Relations: Canadian Parties and Voters* (Toronto: McClelland and Stewart, 1988), 168. The Rat Pack's name had a familiar ring because it had been applied in the 1960s to the Frank Sinatra–Sammy Davis Jr. crowd of American celebrities. Interview of Jack Cahill, Mississauga, January 20, 2005; Interview of John Nunziata, Toronto, May 21, 2005; Interview of Donald Boudria, Ottawa, August 8, 2005.
22 John Nunziata organized the rally and invited Turner to be the keynote speaker. John Nunziata to John Turner, June 18, 1985, JNTP, Q7-2, vol. 16, file 22, "Nunziata, John"; John Turner, Douglas Frith, and Jean-Claude Malépart to "Dear Citizens," JNTP, Q7-2, vol. 18, file 1, "Press releases, 1985."
23 Copps, *Nobody's Baby,* 158; JNTP, Q7-2, vol. 8, file 12, "LPC – Caucus Letters, 1985-1986."
24 Interview of John Turner, Ottawa, July 25, 2005.
25 Val Sears, "How the Liberal Opposition Conspires against the Tories," *Toronto Star,* February 9, 1986.
26 Terry Hargreaves, "A Lonely Journey back from Defeat," *Maclean's,* June 10, 1985.
27 Hyman Solomon, "Turner's Taken Firm Hold in Rebuilding the Party," *Financial Post* (Toronto), February 2, 1985.
28 Ian Mulgrew, "Turner on Road to Recovery from Stumbles in Campaign," *Toronto Globe and Mail,* February 16, 1985.
29 Jeffrey Simpson, "Beyond the Civility," *Toronto Globe and Mail,* October 17, 1985; R.B. Byers, ed., *Canadian Annual Review of Politics and Public Affairs, 1985* (Toronto: University of Toronto Press, 1988), 38-39.
30 Bob Hepburn, "Author Chrétien May Be Our Most Popular Politician," *Toronto Sunday Star,* November 3, 1985.
31 Aileen McCabe, "Turner 'Absolutely Finished' in Quebec, Critics Say," *Montreal Gazette,* October 25, 1985.
32 Michael Hart, Bill Dymond, and Colin Robertson, *Decision at Midnight: Inside the Canada-US Free-Trade Negotiations* (Vancouver: UBC Press, 1994), 123.
33 Interview of John Turner by Barbara Frum, March 16, 1984, JNTP, Q10-2, vol. 1, file 3, "Interview – The Journal, CBC."
34 "Plain Talk," notes for an address to the Empire Club, November 18, 1971, Michael Hunter private papers.
35 G. Bruce Doern and Brian W. Tomlin, *Faith and Fear: The Free Trade Story* (Toronto: Stoddart, 1991), 230-31.
36 "The Right Honourable John N. Turner, Response to the Government's Announcement on Free Trade," September 26, 1985, JNTP, Q7-2, vol. 4, file 35, "Free Trade, 1985."
37 Doug Richardson to John Turner, November 14, 1985, JNTP, Q7-2, vol. 16, file 39, "Polls"; "Voters Believe Turner Is Doing as Good a Job as PM, Poll Suggests," *Montreal Gazette,* November 14, 1985.

38 Peter Maser, "Turner Turn-On: Leader's Speech Rekindles Liberal Love Affair," *Vancouver Sun,* November 12, 1985; Elizabeth McIninch and Arthur Milnes, eds., *Politics of Purpose: 40th Anniversary Edition* (Montreal/Kingston: McGill-Queen's University Press, 2009), 13-15.

39 Maser, "Turner Turn-On."

40 Carol Goar, "Teary Delegates Shed Defeatism to Hail Turner," *Toronto Star,* November 11, 1985.

CHAPTER 19: PARTICIPATORY DEMOCRACY

1 Turner sent a letter to Liberal Party members on January 23, 1986, inviting them to concentrate on three policy themes: "the growing gap between rich and poor, job creation, and Canadian sovereignty." Library and Archives Canada (LAC), Ottawa, MG 26 (hereafter cited as JNTP), Q7-2, vol. 5, file 11; JNTP, Q7-2, vol. 11, file 6, "LPC – National Caucus, 1984-1986."

2 In the party's May newsletter, he disinterred the idea of a guaranteed annual income, urging fellow Liberals to consider it seriously. He also attended the various regional policy conferences and spoke about issues such as regional disparity, the tax system, unemployment, homelessness, the elderly, education, and child care

3 "Transcript of a Televised Address by the Right Honourable John N. Turner on the Free Trade Initiative of the Mulroney Government, Ottawa – June 16, 1986," JNTP, Q12, vol. 46.

4 Mary Janigan, "The Liberals Starting Over," *Maclean's,* February 25, 1985.

5 Val Sears, "John Turner: Armored and Ready," *Toronto Star,* November 22, 1986.

6 In the summer, Turner often went on a wilderness canoe trip and spent vacation time at the family cottage; in the winter, he always took a break in the Caribbean.

7 Val Sears, "How the Liberal Opposition Conspires against the Tories," *Toronto Star,* February 9, 1986.

8 Interview of Doug Kirkpatrick, Ottawa, May 25, 2009; Interview of Scott Sheppard, Ottawa, July 26, 2005.

9 Robert McKenzie, "Behind the Scenes: Quebec Liberals Debate Turner-Chrétien Power Play," *Toronto Star,* February 21, 1986. Fox had been in Ottawa earlier that day, and Turner had tried unsuccessfully to meet him. He waited until Fox was home to call him that evening, after his dinner with Chrétien.

10 Richard Cleroux, "Chrétien Quits: Enough Is Enough," *Toronto Globe and Mail,* February 28, 1986.

11 Lawrence Martin, *Chrétien,* vol. 1, *The Will to Win* (Toronto: Lester, 1995), 359.

12 McKenzie, "Behind the Scenes"; Interview of James Robb, Montreal, December 3, 2008.

13 The team included Garneau; Serge Joyal, a former secretary of state and co-chairman of the Special Joint Committee on the Constitution in 1980-81; Michel Robert, a prominent constitutional lawyer (and a Trudeau supporter on matters constitutional); Eric Maldoff, a Montreal lawyer and former head of an English-language rights group, Alliance Quebec; and Michèle Tremblay, Turner's communications director.

14 Bernard Descoteaux and Pierre O'Neill, "Oui aux conditions du Québec," *Le Devoir* (Montreal), June 13, 1986.

15 Roy MacGregor, "Turner Policy on Quebec Unleashes P.E.T. Threat," *Ottawa Citizen*, September 17, 1986. Donald Johnston was angered that he had not been consulted while the new constitutional policy was being developed. Although Michèle Tremblay, a Turner adviser on the committee, maintained that all Quebec MPs had access to the drafts, Turner hadn't advertised the process to caucus. Worried that the initiative would be hijacked by caucus, he elected instead to develop a coherent plan, win endorsement for it in Quebec, and present it as a *fait accompli* with political support that would make it more difficult to oppose.

16 For Turner's preparation for this meeting, see "Quebec and the Constitution: Background Document, for Discussion Only. September 1986," JNTP, Q7-2, vol. 13, file 12, "L.P.C. – Special Caucus – Ottawa – 4-5 Sept. 1986."

17 Greg Weston, *Reign of Error* (Toronto: McGraw-Hill Ryerson, 1988), 195. JNTP, Q7-2, vol. 6, file 18.

18 Hugh Winsor and Graham Fraser, "Turner Friends Gather a Network of 107 Key Supporters," *Toronto Globe and Mail*, November 8, 1986; Interview of Geills Turner, Toronto, January 22, 2009.

19 Weston, *Reign of Error*, 194.

20 Carol Goar, "Three Weeks That Shattered Liberal Calm," *Toronto Star*, September 25, 1986.

21 Ibid.

22 Ibid.

23 Sandro Contenta, "Fight John Turner out in the Open MP Tells Davey," *Toronto Star*, September 18, 1986.

24 "An Open Letter to the Hon. Iona Campagnolo, October 28, 1986," JNTP, Q7-2, vol. 11, file 2; Iona Campagnolo to Senator Pierre De Bané, Gerry McCauley, and co-signers of the "Open Letter," October 30, 1986, same file.

25 Joel Ruimy, "Turner Asks for 'Clear Mandate,'" *Toronto Star*, November 30, 1986; 1986 National Convention, Liberal Party of Canada, "Policy Resolutions Passed by the Plenary Session at the 1986 National Convention," JNTP, Q7-2, vol. 16, file 1.

26 Val Sears, "Turner Polishes Final Plea for Support," *Toronto Star*, November 29, 1986.

27 Marc Lalonde to "Dear Delegate," November 11, 1986, JNTP, Q7-2, vol. 15, file 28.

28 "Communiqué," November 17, 1986, JNTP, Q7-2, vol. 10, file 2, "L.P.C. – Internal Business, n.d., 1985-1987."

29 John Turner, "My Vision of Our Future: Opportunities and Growth," *John Turner News*, April 1984, Howard Brown papers (private papers lent to the author by Liberal Party member Howard Brown).

30 Sheila Copps, David Herle, Jean Lapierre, and Brian Tobin to delegates, November 25, 1986, Howard Brown papers.

31 John Nichol, Richard Stanbury, Gildas Molgat, Al Graham, and Norman McLeod, "Former Liberal Party Presidents Endorse Rt. Hon. John N. Turner, November 21, 1986," Howard Brown papers.

32 JNTP, Q7-2, vol. 16, file 9. See also "LPC – Memos – Iona Campagnolo," JNTP, Q7-2, vol. 11, file 2.

33 Carol Goar, "Turner," *Toronto Star,* November 29, 1986.

34 Peter Stoler, "A Former 'Patter's' Return," *Time,* December 15, 1986.

35 Val Sears, "76% of Liberal Delegates Tell Turner He's the Boss," *Toronto Star,* December 1, 1986; Val Sears, "Renewal: An Old Tune Gets Played by Liberals," *Toronto Star,* December 6, 1986.

CHAPTER 20: CREATURE FROM THE BLACK LAGOON

1 Lawrence Martin, *Iron Man: The Defiant Reign of Jean Chrétien* (Toronto: Viking, 2003), 11.

2 "Secretary General to Leave Post," press release, March 18, 1987, Library and Archives Canada (LAC), Ottawa, MG 26 (hereafter cited as JNTP), Q7-2, vol. 7, file 11.

3 Interview of Jean Lapierre, Montreal, December 5, 2008. See also Greg Weston, *Reign of Error* (Toronto: McGraw-Hill Ryerson, 1988), 212.

4 E-mail communication from Doug Frith, December 5, 2008.

5 George Perlin, *The Tory Syndrome* (Montreal/Kingston: McGill-Queen's University Press, 1980).

6 Ross Howard, "Liberals Say Party Can't Sustain Election," *Toronto Globe and Mail,* April 11, 1987.

7 Peter Maser, "Former Staunch Supporters Admit Turner Has Failed to Ignite Liberals," *Ottawa Citizen,* May 30, 1987.

8 The Meech Lake Accord formalized an existing agreement between Ottawa and Quebec regarding the selection of immigrants coming into the province and provided for the negotiation of similar agreements with the other provinces. It recognized the federal government's right to fund shared-cost programs in areas of exclusive provincial jurisdiction while permitting provinces to opt out and still receive funding, provided they created programs with similar objectives. In addition to stipulating that future Supreme Court justices would be selected from lists of candidates provided by the provinces, it formalized the long-standing practice of having three of the nine justices appointed to the Supreme Court from Quebec. Senate appointments would also be made from lists provided by the provinces, enhancing that body's chances of fulfilling its theoretical role as a regional counterbalance against the power that central Canada, the most populous region of the country, exercised in the House of Commons. It also increased the number of parts of the constitution that could be amended only by unanimous consent of the provinces and the federal government.

9 Interview of David Peterson, Toronto, December 12, 2008. Peterson was an MPP in the late 1970s when he first met Bourassa, who by then was the former leader of the Quebec Liberals. They kept in touch over the years.

10 Andrew Cohen, *A Deal Undone: The Making and Breaking of the Meech Lake Accord* (Toronto: Douglas and McIntyre, 1990), 144.

11 Ibid., 143.

12 Marc Lalonde, who could live with the provisions of Meech itself, objected to it for this reason. Interview of Marc Lalonde, Montreal, July 5, 2005.

13 Michael Kirby to John Turner, "The Constitutional Issue," May 28, 1987, JNTP, Q7-2, vol. 20, file 1, "Senators – Michael Kirby, 1986-1987."

14 Interview of Douglas Richardson, Saskatoon, May 29, 2007.
15 Joel Ruimy, "Constitutional Deal Puts Nation in 'Straightjacket,' Turner Says," *Toronto Star,* May 5, 1987.
16 Kirby to Turner, "The Constitutional Issue," May 28, 1987.
17 The passion Meech aroused and the uncompromising divisions it engendered were illustrated by the fact that Turner's sister, Brenda Norris, who lived in Johnston's Westmount riding and had served on his local constituency organization, opposed her brother on the issue. Interview of Brenda Norris, Montreal, April 7, 2005.
18 Pierre Trudeau, "P.E. Trudeau: 'Say Goodbye to the Dream of One Canada,'" *Toronto Star,* May 27, 1987.
19 Transcripts of three press interviews with Trudeau about Meech Lake on May 29, 1987, two in English and one in French, are in JNTP, Q7-2, vol. 21, file 12.
20 Kirby to Turner, "The Constitutional Issue," May 28, 1987.
21 Cohen, *A Deal Undone,* 99-117.
22 JNTP, Q10-2, vol. 13, file 15, "Televised Address on the 1987 Constitutional Accord, 4 June 1987." This file contains drafts of Turner's speech, some annotated in his handwriting, and drafts of the amendments the Liberals were recommending.
23 "Transcript of the Right Honourable John N. Turner, Leader of the Opposition, Following a Meeting with the National Liberal Caucus, Ottawa, June 3, 1987," JNTP, Q10-2, vol. 13, file 14, "Press Conference – Ottawa, 3 June 1987."
24 Hugh Winsor, "PM and Turner Both Getting Burned by Meech Lake Fallout," *Toronto Globe and Mail,* June 6, 1987. On June 8, 1987, the management committee of the Liberal Party sent a memo to caucus members that summarized concerns about Meech. JNTP, Q7-2, vol. 7, file 11. Two days later, Michael Kirby informed Turner that he would vote against the deal if it were not amended before it reached the Senate. Michael Kirby to John Turner, June 10, 1987, JNTP, Q7-2, vol. 20, file 1.
25 Brooke Jeffrey, *Divided Loyalties: The Liberal Party of Canada, 1984-2008* (Toronto: University of Toronto Press, 2010), 100.
26 Joe O'Donnell, "Turner Scores Leadership Points with Gutsy Defence of Accord," *Toronto Star,* June 21, 1987. See also JNTP, Q10-2, vol. 13, file 22.
27 Graham Fraser, "Liberals Made Accord Possible, Says Turner to Cheers in Ontario," *Toronto Globe and Mail,* June 22, 1987. Some of Turner's correspondence related to Meech Lake is in JNTP, Q9-3, vol. 30, file 60 and JNTP, Q9-3, vol. 3, file 34.
28 Michael Kirby to John Turner, "Assessment of Current Situation and Suggestions for Future Action," August 24, 1987, JNTP, Q7-2, vol. 20, file 1, "Senators – Michael Kirby, 1986-1987."
29 Interview of Michael Marzolini, Toronto, June 2, 2005.
30 Douglas Richardson to John Turner, "Unity within the Party and Caucus/Other Matters," August 10, 1987, JNTP, Q7-2, vol. 18, file 12, "Principal Secretary, 1987"; Interview of Doug Frith, Toronto, November 27, 2008.
31 Marjorie Nichols, "Meech Deal Discord Marks End of Turner's Tenure," *Ottawa Citizen,* June 6 1987.
32 "Turner Shrugs Off Aides' Defections, Criticism," *Toronto Star,* August 16, 1987.
33 Cameron, "Liberals Hunt Ways."

34 Stevie Cameron, "Liberals Hunt Ways to Replace Turner Gently," *Toronto Globe and Mail,* August 22, 1987.

35 Carol Goar, "Sink or Swim Time for Turner," *Toronto Star,* August 29, 1987.

36 Jeffrey, *Divided Loyalties,* 107.

37 Garol Goar, "Liberals Finally Look at Turner Honestly," *Toronto Star,* September 1, 1987.

38 Hilary Mackenzie, "Hoisted on My Own Petard," *Maclean's,* September 14, 1987.

39 Val Sears, "Liberals Said Ready to Demand Major Change in Meech Lake Accord," *Toronto Star,* September 2, 1987.

40 Goar, "Liberals Finally Look."

41 Joan Forsey, "Turner Faces the Acid Test in Unruly Party," *Toronto Globe and Mail,* September 1, 1987.

42 Cohen, *A Deal Undone,* 176.

43 Carol Goar, "Turner Can Perform, When He Wants To," *Toronto Star,* April 30, 1987.

CHAPTER 21: IMAGE, SUBSTANCE, AND SUBVERSION

1 Michael Kirby to John Turner, "Assessment of Current Situation and Suggestions for Future Action," August 24, 1987, Library and Archives Canada (LAC), Ottawa, MG 26 (hereafter cited as JNTP), Q7-2, vol. 20, file 1, "Senators – Michael Kirby, 1986-1987."

2 Joe O'Donnell, "Turner Blames Self for Party Slide, Cites Row over Accord," *Toronto Star,* July 28, 1987.

3 Ibid.

4 Val Sears, "Merlins of Image Making," *Toronto Star,* February 28, 1987.

5 Peter Maser, "Dr. Death Smooths Turner," *Ottawa Citizen,* July 7 1988; David Taras, *The Newsmakers* (Scarborough, ON: Nelson, 1990), 168.

6 Interview of John Turner, Toronto, September 18, 2008.

7 Pamela Wallin, *Since You Asked* (Toronto: Random House Canada, 1998), 222-23. In Deborah Downing, "Questions on Turner Drinking Rumours Prompt Privacy Plea from Broadbent," *Ottawa Citizen,* January 18, 1988, Bill Lee was quoted as saying that in the eighteen years he had known Turner, he had never encountered a situation in which drinking had affected his work. Jack Cahill, who was on the Hill in the seventies as a parliamentary bureau chief and who later wrote a biography of Turner, said the same, as did John Swift. Interview of Jack Cahill, Mississauga, January 20, 2005; Interview of John Swift, Vancouver, September 16, 2008.

8 E.B. Biggar, *Anecdotal Life of Sir John Macdonald* (Montreal: John Lovell, 1891), 194.

9 Graham Fraser, "Turner Still Feeling Way in High-Tech Politics," *Toronto Globe and Mail,* April 13, 1987.

10 Carol Goar, "Turner Can Perform, When He Wants To," *Toronto Star,* April 30, 1987.

11 Interview of John Turner by Elizabeth McIninch, September 25, 1995, JNTP, acc. no. 240677, consultation copy number unavailable; Christopher Waddell, "U.S. Senators Support Free-Trade Deal," *Toronto Globe and Mail,* December 10, 1986. Garneau was at this meeting, too, and is convinced that it profoundly affected Turner's thinking on free trade. Interview of Raymond Garneau, Montreal, December 4, 2008.

12 "Raymond Heard to John Turner," and "Comments of Sunday, August 30, 1987," August 31, 1987, JNTP, Q7-2, vol. 6, file 7, "Heard, Raymond."

13 Turner's handwritten notes in response to a government press release, "Statement by the Prime Minister of Canada/USA Trade Negotiations," JNTP, Q7-2, vol. 5, file 5; Val Sears, "PM Made Colossal Trade Blunder, Turner Says," *Toronto Star,* September 29, 1986.

14 Hansard, October 5, 1987, 9633.

15 "Turner's Stance Could Reverse Slide in Fortunes," *Toronto Star,* October 8, 1987.

16 Hansard, December 11, 1987, 11723; Hansard, December 15, 1987, 11789; Hansard, December 18, 1987, 11954-60. Turner's challenge to Mulroney to call an election is on page 11959. A draft of this speech, annotated in Turner's handwriting, is in JNTP, Q10-2, vol. 14, file 23, "Debate on Legal Text of the Trade Deal – House of Commons, December 18, 1987." See also JNTP, Q10-2, vol. 14, file 10.

17 Interview of Doug Kirkpatrick, Ottawa, May 25, 2009.

18 Graham Fraser, *Playing for Keeps: The Making of the Prime Minister, 1988* (Toronto: McClelland and Stewart, 1989), 201. This excellent account of the 1988 election was used for background information throughout this chapter and the next. The Turner-Axworthy exchange is also related in Lloyd Axworthy, *Navigating a New World: Canada's Global Future* (Toronto: Vintage, 2004), 85.

19 Garneau interview.

20 Robert McKenzie, "Bourassa's Praise for Mulroney Splits Liberals, Angry MP Says," *Toronto Star,* February 2, 1988.

21 Andrew Cohen, *A Deal Undone: The Making and Breaking of the Meech Lake Accord* (Vancouver: Douglas and McIntyre, 1990), 175.

22 Robert Jackson, a Carleton University political scientist, became the new senior policy adviser.

23 Kirkpatrick interview.

24 Bruce Wallace, "The Long Fight Back," *Maclean's,* May 16, 1988. Some of the breakdowns in communication were inexcusable. Doug Frith, one of Turner's staunchest supporters, read in the newspaper that he was no longer going to run the 1988 campaign. He sat three seats over from Turner in the House, so he passed him a note suggesting that he was owed an explanation. Turner met him in the stairwell behind the curtain but couldn't give him satisfactory reasons. Frith decided not to run again.

25 Wallin, *Since You Asked,* 223.

26 JNTP, Q10-2, vol. 14, file 29, "Interview with Pamela Wallin, CTV News, January 17, 1988."

27 Terrance Wills, "Turner Wants to Be Remembered as a Man with Guts," *Montreal Gazette,* December 23, 1989. In 2002 Chrétien would appoint Wallin Canada's consul-general in New York; she later became a Conservative senator.

28 Lawrence Martin, *Iron Man: The Defiant Reign of Jean Chrétien* (Toronto: Viking, 2003), 372.

29 Carol Goar, "Turner up the Creek with a Paddle," *Toronto Star,* April 16, 1988.

30 Cohen, *A Deal Undone,* 155. Various reports indicate that the following MPs signed: David Berger, Charles Caccia, Roland de Corneille, David Dingwall, Sheila Finestone, Douglas Frith, George Henderson, Gaston Isabelle, Alfonso Gagliano, Gilles Grondin,

Thérèse Killens, Jean Lapierre, Russell MacLellan, Sergio Marchi, John Nunziata, Keith Penner, Lucie Pépin, Fernand Robichaud, Carlo Rossi, and Alain Tardif.

31 Ibid.

32 Interview of James Robb, Montreal, December 3, 2008; Kirkpatrick interview; Interview of André Ouellet, Ottawa, March 30, 2009.

33 Graham Fraser, "Crisis over, but It Hurt, Leader Says," *Toronto Globe and Mail,* May 2, 1988.

34 Duncan McMonagle, "Move by MPs 'Politically Stupid,' Potential Turner Successor Says," *Toronto Globe and Mail,* April 28, 1988.

35 JNTP, Q7-5, vol. 6, file 78, "Release: Statement on Rizzuto's Departure, May 2, 1988."

36 John Laschinger and Geoffrey Stevens, eds., *Leaders and Lesser Mortals* (Toronto: Key Porter, 1992), 9.

37 Don McGillvray, "Turner Shines at Press Gallery Dinner," *Ottawa Citizen,* May 3, 1988.

38 Paul Gessell, "Off the Ropes: Turner Turns Caucus Revolt to His Advantage," *Ottawa Citizen,* June 4, 1988.

39 Don McGillvray, "Turner Must Confound His Critics," *Ottawa Citizen,* September 9, 1988.

40 Mike Duffy, "Turner Deserves His Own Chapter," *Ottawa Sun,* February 11, 1990.

CHAPTER 22: MAD DOG AND BUSINESSMEN

1 Library and Archives Canada (LAC), Ottawa, MG 26 (hereafter cited as JNTP), Q7-2, vol. 20, file 1, "Senators – Michael Kirby, 1986-1987."

2 Martin Cohn, "Thatcher Causes a Furor with Free Trade 'Meddling,'" *Toronto Star,* June 23, 1988.

3 Graham Fraser, *Playing for Keeps: The Making of the Prime Minister, 1988* (Toronto: McClelland and Stewart, 1989), 98.

4 Claire Hoy, *Margin of Error* (Toronto: Key Porter Books, 1989), 2.

5 Heather Bird, "Turner's Advances Rebuffed – Bourassa Stays Neutral," *Toronto Star,* August 17, 1988.

6 Fraser, *Playing for Keeps,* 103.

7 Doug Kirkpatrick recalled that he favoured holding it back, whereas Kirby and Goldfarb wanted to put it out early. Interview of Doug Kirkpatrick, Ottawa, May 25, 2009.

8 David Leyton-Brown, ed., *Canadian Annual Review of Politics and Public Affairs, 1988* (Toronto: University of Toronto Press, 1995), 18.

9 Fraser, *Playing for Keeps,* 199.

10 Thomas Walkom, "Finally, the Sound of Sincerity," *Toronto Globe and Mail,* October 3, 1988.

11 Martin Goldfarb and Thomas Axworthy, *Marching to a Different Drummer: An Essay on the Liberals and Conservatives in Convention* (Toronto: Stoddart, 1988), 127-28.
12 Fraser, *Playing for Keeps*, 232.
13 Joan Bryden, "Turner 'in Person' Is Making a Hit," *Ottawa Citizen*, October 22, 1988.
14 Fraser, *Playing for Keeps*, 69.
15 Carol Goar, "Adversity Hardens Turner for Power," *Toronto Star*, September 18, 1988.
16 Paul Kemp, director/writer/producer, *John Turner: In His Own Words* (Toronto: Stornoway Productions, 2006), film documentary.
17 JNTP, Q10-2, vol. 17, file 15, "Caraquet, N.B., Oct. 10, 1988."
18 Kirby had earlier shown a similar propensity to second-guess the leader. In May 1987, during a regular appearance on a CTV *Canada AM* panel of political pundits, he had declared that Turner must have been misquoted or mistaken about the party's Meech Lake position. Michael Kirby to John Turner, "The Constitutional Issue," memo, May 28, 1987, JNTP, Q7-2, vol. 20, file 1.
19 Kirkpatrick interview.
20 Telephone interview of Richard Alway, January 30, 2009.
21 Fraser, *Playing for Keeps*, 240; E-mail communication from Doug Kirkpatrick, March 31, 2011.
22 Interview of Stephen Hastings, Toronto, January 31, 2011.
23 Martin Goldfarb was more interested in issues that could swing votes than in big issues such as free trade or Meech Lake on which he thought public opinion irrevocably polarized. In 1988 he looked at his polling numbers and decided that, if Turner announced a liberalized abortion policy, he could win a lot of votes from women as well as substantial support in urban Quebec. There was potential for a 3 per cent swing in Turner's favour, enough to carry the election. But Turner would not go for it. Interview of Martin Goldfarb, Toronto, June 21, 2005. Turner aide Scott Sheppard attributed Turner's refusal not to his Catholicism but to his view that Mulroney's position was reasonable and to his reluctance to play politics with such a divisive issue. Interview of Scott Sheppard, Ottawa, July 26, 2005.
24 Fraser, *Playing for Keeps*, 254.
25 Alan Frizzell and Anthony Westell, "The Media and the Campaign," in Alan Frizzell, Jon H. Pammett, and Anthony Westell, *The Canadian General Election of 1988* (Ottawa: Carleton University Press, 1989), 83; Marjorie Nichols, "Turner Is Another Victim of Lazy Pack Journalism," *Ottawa Citizen*, October 22, 1988.
26 Gerald Caplan, Michael Kirby, and Hugh Segal, *Election: The Issues, the Strategies, the Aftermath* (Scarborough: Prentice-Hall, 1989), 131-44.
27 Fraser, *Playing for Keeps*, 261.
28 Lawrence Martin, *Chrétien*, vol. 1, *The Will to Win* (Toronto: Lester, 1995), 366.
29 Interview of Stephen Hastings, Toronto, January 31, 2011.
30 This account of the exchange is reconstructed from CBC Digital Archives, "1988 Leaders' Debate, Broadcast Date: Oct. 25, 1988," http://archives.cbc.ca. For a videotape, see "Party Leaders' Debate CBC via Satellite Coll.," October 25, 1988, acc. no. 1988-0442, IDC no. 106827. The full text of the debate can be found in JNTP, Q7-2, vol. 7, file 4, "Leaders' Debate, 25 October 1988." Turner had been using similar language to attack the free-trade agreement for months. See, for instance, "Free Market Forces and Canadian

Sovereignty," speech to the Victoria Chamber of Commerce Luncheon, March 15, 1988, in his constituency brochure, "John Turner, M.P. Vancouver Quadra, April 1988 Special Report Canada-United States Trade Agreement," JNTP, Q7-2, vol. 5, file 7.

31 Hoy, *Margin of Error,* 71.

32 Peter Maser, "On the Hustings," in *The Canadian General Election of 1988,* ed. Alan Frizzell, Jon Pammett, and Anthony Westell (Ottawa: Carleton University Press, 1989), 64.

33 Harry Anderson, "You Have Sold Us Out," *Newsweek,* November 14, 1988.

34 Bruce Wallace and Teresa Tedesco, "Straight to the Heart," *Maclean's,* November 14, 1988.

35 Heather Bird, "Turner Vaults from Zero to Hero," *Toronto Star,* October 30, 1988.

36 Charles Gordon, "Networks Adopt New Look for Turner," *Ottawa Citizen,* October 31, 1988.

37 Allan Gotlieb, *Washington Diaries, 1981-1989* (Toronto: McClelland and Stewart, 2006), 602.

38 David Taras, *The Newsmakers* (Scarborough, ON: Nelson, 1990), 222.

39 Maser, "On the Hustings," 67.

40 Peter Newman, *The Canadian Revolution* (Toronto: Viking, 1995), 275.

41 Ibid. Fraser was president and CEO of Federal Industries of Winnipeg.

42 Hoy, *Margin of Error,* 67-68.

43 Taras, *The Newsmakers,* 209-10.

44 Wallace and Tedesco, "Straight to the Heart."

45 Fraser, *Playing for Keeps,* 429.

46 Ibid.

47 Goldfarb interview; Interview of John Turner, Toronto, February 26, 2009.

48 Janine Brodie, "The 'Free Trade' Election," *Studies in Political Economy* 28 (Spring 1989): 176.

49 David Vienneau, "No Regrets in Campaign Fought 'with All My Heart,' Turner Says," *Toronto Star,* November 22, 1988; JNTP, Q10-2, vol. 18, file 12, "Majorité PC – Conservative Majority (Nov. 1988)."

50 G. Bruce Doern and Brian W. Tomlin, *Faith and Fear: The Free Trade Story* (Toronto: Stoddart, 1991), 232-33.

51 Hoy, *Margin of Error,* 76.

CONCLUSION

1 Library and Archives Canada (LAC), Ottawa, MG 26 (hereafter cited as JNTP), Q10-2, vol. 18, file 19, "Clive Wells Reception, Feb. 21, 1989."

2 Val Sears, "Final Decision to Quit Made at Family Meal," *Toronto Star,* May 4, 1989.

3 "Turner: A White Knight Whose Mission Failed," *Montreal Gazette,* May 4, 1989.

4 Marjorie Nichols, "Grits Will Sorely Miss Turner's Basic Decency," *Ottawa Citizen,* February 8, 1990.

5 Jeffrey Simpson, "The Style of John Turner," *Toronto Globe and Mail,* February 8, 1990.

6 "Transcript of Speech by the Right Honourable John N. Turner," JNTP, Q10-2, vol. 20, file 32, "Liberal Leadership Convention, 21 June 1990."

7 CBC Digital Archives, "'Yesterday's Man' Voted Today's Liberal Leader," June 22, 1990, http://archives.cbc.ca.

8 Conrad Black, *A Life in Progress* (Toronto: Key Porter, 1993), 395.

9 Hansard, January 16, 1991, 17132.

10 JNTP, Q10-2, vol. 21, file 1; Interview of Lisa Haley, Ottawa, May 13, 2005; Interview of John Grace, Ottawa, July 25, 2005.

11 Mary Janigan, "The Renaissance Man," *Maclean's*, February 14, 2005.

12 Telephone interview of Judd Whiteside, May 29, 2009.

13 Anthony Wilson-Smith, "I Would Do It Again," *Maclean's*, July 1, 2004.

14 Carol Goar, "John Turner Has What It Takes," *Toronto Star*, November 19, 1988.

15 His work in putting together the Department of Consumer and Corporate Affairs was the most notable exception to this generalization. One could argue that it entailed combining pre-existing organizations rather than building a new department and that the timetable was less strenuous, yet it involved the same skill set that is at issue here.

16 Turner's high-level personnel problems offer evidence of this point. Heather Peterson was appointed campaign director during the 1984 leadership campaign, but Bill Lee soon took over. That summer, Lee was replaced in spectacular fashion by Keith Davey in the middle of the election campaign. Two years later Davey was eased out in favour of Michael Kirby, who proved to be an unreliable lieutenant. Doug Frith was understanding during the 1984 election about having his co-chairmanship position taken away without prior consultation, but when the same thing happened in 1988, he quit politics. This kind of incident occurred frequently during the party's vicious internecine warfare in Quebec, as contending factions regularly installed their people in key positions, only to see them bounced out when opposing forces came to the fore (Pietro Rizzuto was just one example). Turner went through three principal secretaries and several other key aides in the 1984-88 period. High turnover among political staff is common, but the rate in Turner's office was higher than most.

17 Roy MacGregor, "Remembering the Good Times of John Napier Turner," *Ottawa Citizen*, May 5, 1989.

18 Richard Gwyn, "Turner: Ready to Run If Called, Ready to Serve If Elected," *Windsor Star*, September 16, 1976.

19 Nicole Parton, "Turner Battles On against All Odds," *Vancouver Sun*, June 21, 1988.

20 The United States was a "schoolyard bully," concluded Derek Burney, Mulroney's one-time chief of staff. "Jackboot negotiators," was former minister of international trade Pat Carney's equally negative description. "When you're dealing with a bully, and the bully punches you, you should punch him back," declared Gordon Ritchie, who had been the deputy chief free-trade negotiator. John Ibbitson, "'Betrayed' over Free Trade: Trading with the 'Schoolyard Bully,'" *Toronto Globe and Mail*, August 20, 2005.

21 Carol Goar, "Turner: Sunshine after Cloudy Days," *Toronto Star*, December 20, 1986.

22 MacGregor, "Remembering the Good Times."

SELECTED BIBLIOGRAPHY

The main sources for this study have been the John Turner fonds at Library and Archives Canada (LAC), interviews, and political journalism covering Turner's career. I am indebted to Mr. Turner for providing access to his papers for the author and his researchers. The John Turner fonds, which are under the designation MG 26-Q at LAC, have for the sake of brevity been listed in the notes under the heading JNTP (John Napier Turner Papers). Interviews were conducted with friends, family, and colleagues of Turner. The interview subjects are listed alphabetically below; the dates and locations of the interviews can be found in the notes. In many cases, journalism was used to reconstruct events and issues, but it was most valuable as a source for tracking how perceptions of Turner's image in the media changed over time.

Other records consulted include the Lester B. Pearson fonds (LAC), the Alastair Gillespie fonds (LAC) (I am grateful to Mr. Gillespie for granting me special permission to consult his papers), Cabinet Conclusions (LAC), the Wartime Prices and Trade Board (LAC), the Liberal Party of Canada fonds (LAC), the minutes of the Cabinet Committee on Security and Intelligence (Privy Council Office), Bryn Mawr College Archives (Bryn Mawr, Pennsylvania), the Phyllis Turner fonds (City of Vancouver Archives), the General Register Office for England and Wales, the records of the Department of State (US National Archives and Records Administration), and personal papers provided by Brenda Norris of Montreal, Michael Hunter of Vancouver, and Howard Brown of Toronto.

INTERVIEWS

Alway, Richard
Anderson, Nancy
Avery, Cam
Axworthy, Lloyd
Axworthy, Tom
Boudria, Donald
Brown, Howard
Cahill, Jack
Campagnolo, Iona
Claxton, John
Coates, Daniel
Coleman, John
Constantinou, Dino
Cotler, Irwin
Danson, Barney
Dobson, John
Doran, Burke
Enemark, Tex
Ezrin, Hershell

Fotheringham, Allan
Frith, Doug
Garneau, Raymond
Gillespie, Alastair
Goldfarb, Martin
Gotlieb, Allan
Grace, John
Grafstein, Jerry
Graham, Alex
Gray, Herb
Haley, Lisa
Hastings, Stephen
Hunter, Michael
Kaiser, Sandra
Kierans, Emmett
Kirkpatrick, Doug
Lalonde, Marc
Lapierre, Jean
Mahoney, Richard

Marzolini, Michael
Monet, Jacques
Norris, Brenda
Nunziata, John
Ouellet, André
Payne, Walyssa
Peterson, David
Pratt, Dorothy
Richardson, Douglas
Robb, James
Rothman, Mel
Sheppard, Scott
Smith, David
Swift, John
Taylor, John
Turner, Geills
Turner, John
Weston, Greg
Whiteside, Judd

BOOKS AND ARTICLES

Aberbach, David. *Charisma in Politics, Religion, and the Media: Private Trauma, Public Ideals.* Houndsmills: Macmillan, 1996.

Axworthy, Lloyd. *Navigating a New World: Canada's Global Future.* Toronto: Vintage, 2004.

Axworthy, Thomas S., and Pierre Elliott Trudeau, eds. *Towards a Just Society: The Trudeau Years.* Markham, ON: Viking, 1990.

Azzi, Stephen. *Walter Gordon and the Rise of Canadian Nationalism.* Montreal/Kingston: McGill-Queen's University Press, 1999.

Banting, Keith G. *The Welfare State and Canadian Federalism.* Montreal/Kingston: McGill-Queen's University Press, 1987.

Barber, Clarence L., and John C.P. McCallum. *Controlling Inflation: Learning from Experience in Canada, Europe and Japan.* Ottawa: Canadian Institute for Economic Policy, 1982.

Beck, J. Murray. *Pendulum of Power: Canada's Federal Elections.* Scarborough, ON: Prentice-Hall, 1968.

Berkowitz, Edward D. *Something Happened: A Political and Cultural Overview of the Seventies.* New York: Columbia University Press, 2006.

Bernstein, Michael A., and David E. Adler, eds. *Understanding American Economic Decline.* Cambridge: Cambridge University Press, 1994.

Biggar, E.B. *Anecdotal Life of Sir John Macdonald.* Montreal: John Lovell, 1891.

Black, Conrad. *A Life in Progress.* Toronto: Key Porter, 1993.

Bothwell, Robert. *Alliance and Illusion: Canada and the World, 1945-1984.* Vancouver: UBC Press, 2007.

Bothwell, Robert, and William Kilbourn. *C.D. Howe: A Biography.* Toronto: McClelland and Stewart, 1979.

Boyer, Patrick. *A Passion for Justice: The Legacy of James Chalmers McRuer.* Toronto: University of Toronto Press for the Osgoode Society for Canadian Legal History, 1994.

Brennan, Patrick. *Reporting the Nation's Business: Press-Government Relations during the Liberal Years, 1935-1957.* Toronto: University of Toronto Press, 1994.

Brodie, Janine. "The 'Free Trade' Election." *Studies in Political Economy* 28 (Spring 1989): 175-82.

Bushnell, Ian. *The Federal Court of Canada: A History, 1875-1992.* Toronto: University of Toronto Press, 1992.

Byers, R.B., ed. *Canadian Annual Review of Politics and Public Affairs, 1984.* Toronto: University of Toronto Press, 1987.

Cahill, Jack. *John Turner: The Long Run.* Toronto: McClelland and Stewart, 1984.

Campbell, Robert Malcolm. *Grand Illusions: The Politics of the Keynesian Experience in Canada, 1945-1975.* Toronto: Broadview Press, 1987.

–. "Post-Mortem on the Free Trade Election." *Journal of Canadian Studies* 24, 1 (1989). 3-4, 163-65.

Caplan, Gerald, Michael Kirby, and Hugh Segal. *Election: The Issues, the Strategies, the Aftermath.* Scarborough, ON: Prentice-Hall, 1989.

Carisse, Jean-Marc. *Privileged Access with Trudeau, Turner, and Chrétien.* Toronto: Warwick, 2000.

Chrétien, Jean. *Straight from the Heart.* 1985. Reprint, Toronto: Key Porter Books, 1994.

Clarke, Harold D. *Absent Mandate: Interpreting Change in Canadian Elections.* Toronto: Gage Educational, 1991.

Clarkson, Stephen. "Charisma and Contradictions: The Legacy of Pierre Elliott Trudeau." *University of Toronto Bulletin,* October 16, 2000.

Clarkson, Stephen, and Christina McCall. *Trudeau and Our Times.* Vol. 2, *The Heroic Delusion.* Toronto: McClelland and Stewart, 1994.

Cohen, Andrew. *A Deal Undone: The Making and Breaking of the Meech Lake Accord.* Vancouver: Douglas and McIntyre, 1990.

Comber, Mary Anne, and Robert S. Mayne. *The Newsmongers: How the Media Distort the Political News.* Toronto: McClelland and Stewart, 1986.

Copps, Sheila. *Nobody's Baby: A Woman's Survival Guide to Politics.* Toronto: Deneau, 1986.

Crosbie, John C. *No Holds Barred: My Life in Politics.* Toronto: McClelland and Stewart, 1997.

Danson, Barney, with Curtis Fahey. *Not Bad for a Sergeant: The Memoirs of Barney Danson.* Toronto: Dundurn, 2002.

Davey, Keith. *The Rainmaker: A Passion for Politics.* Toronto: Stoddart, 1986.

de Vault, Carole, with William Johnson. *The Informer: Confessions of an Ex-Terrorist.* Toronto: Fleet Books, 1982.

Doern, G. Bruce, and Brian W. Tomlin. *Faith and Fear: The Free Trade Story.* Toronto: Stoddart, 1991.

Doern, G. Bruce, and Glen Toner. *The Politics of Energy: The Development and Implementation of the NEP.* Toronto: Methuen, 1985.

Duffy, John. *Fights of Our Lives: Elections, Leadership, and the Making of Canada.* Toronto: Harper-Collins, 2002.

Dummitt, Christopher. *The Manly Modern: Masculinity in Postwar Canada.* Vancouver: UBC Press, 2007.

Engerman, Stanley L., and Robert E. Gallman, eds. *The Cambridge Economic History of the United States.* Vol. 3, *The Twentieth Century.* Cambridge: Cambridge University Press, 2000.

English, John. *Just Watch Me: The Life of Pierre Elliott Trudeau, 1968-2000.* Toronto: Knopf Canada, 2009.

–. *The Worldly Years: The Life of Lester Pearson.* Vol. 2, *1949-1972.* Toronto: Knopf Canada, 1992.

English, John, Richard Gwyn, and P. Whitney Lackenbauer, eds. *The Hidden Pierre Elliott Trudeau: The Faith behind the Politics.* Ottawa: Novalis, 2004.

Enoch, Simon. "Changing the Ideological Fabric? A Brief History of (Canadian) Neoliberalism." *State of Nature* 5 (Autumn 2007). http://www.stateofnature.org.

Fraser, Graham. *Playing for Keeps: The Making of the Prime Minister, 1988.* Toronto: McClelland and Stewart, 1989.

Friedland, Martin L. *My Life in Crime and Other Academic Adventures.* Toronto: University of Toronto Press for the Osgoode Society for Canadian Legal History, 2007.

Frizzell, Alan, Jon Pammett, and Anthony Westell, eds. *The Canadian General Election of 1988.* Ottawa: Carleton University Press, 1989.

Gidney, Catherine. *A Long Eclipse: The Liberal Protestant Establishment and the Canadian University, 1920-1970.* Montreal/Kingston: McGill-Queen's University Press, 2004.

Gillespie, W. Irwin. *Tax, Borrow, and Spend: Financing Federal Spending in Canada, 1867-1990.* Ottawa: Carleton University Press, 1991.

Goldfarb, Martin, and Thomas Axworthy. *Marching to a Different Drummer: An Essay on the Liberals and Conservatives in Convention.* Toronto: Stoddart, 1988.

Gotlieb, Allan. *Washington Diaries, 1981-1989.* Toronto: McClelland and Stewart, 2006.

Graham, Ron. *One-Eyed Kings: Promise and Illusion in Canadian Politics.* Toronto: Collins, 1986.

Granatstein, J.L. *Canada, 1957-1967: The Years of Uncertainty and Innovation.* Toronto: McClelland and Stewart, 1986.

Granatstein, J.L., and Norman Hillmer. *Prime Ministers: Ranking Canada's Leaders.* Toronto: Harper Collins, 1999.

Gratton, Michel. *So, What Are the Boys Saying?* Toronto: McGraw-Hill Ryerson, 1987.

Green, Alan G. "Twentieth-Century Canadian Economic History." In *The Cambridge Economic History of the United States.* Vol. 3, *The Twentieth Century,* ed. Stanley L. Engerman and Robert E. Gallman, 191-247. Cambridge: Cambridge University Press, 2000.

Gwyn, Richard. *The Northern Magus: Pierre Trudeau and Canadians.* Toronto: McClelland and Stewart, 1980.

Hamilton, Robert M., and Dorothy Shields, eds. *The Dictionary of Canadian Quotations and Phrases.* Toronto: McClelland and Stewart, 1979.

Hart, Michael, Bill Dymond, and Colin Robertson. *Decision at Midnight: Inside the Canada-US Free-Trade Negotiations.* Vancouver: UBC Press, 1994.

Harvey, David. *A Brief History of Neoliberalism.* Oxford: Oxford University Press, 2005.

Heinmiller, B. Timothy. "Harmonization through Emulation: Canadian Federalism and Water Export Policy." *Canadian Public Administration* 46,4 (Winter 2003): 495-513.

Hoy, Claire. *Margin of Error.* Toronto: Key Porter Books, 1989.

Innis, Harold. "Great Britain, the United States, and Canada." In *Essays in Canadian Economic History,* ed. Mary Quayle Innis, 394-412. Toronto: University of Toronto Press, 1956.

Jeffrey, Brooke. *Divided Loyalties: The Liberal Party of Canada, 1984-2008.* Toronto: University of Toronto Press, 2010.

Johnston, Donald. *Up the Hill.* Montreal: Optimum, 1986.

Kent, Tom. *A Public Purpose: An Experience of Liberal Opposition and Canadian Government.* Montreal/Kingston: McGill-Queen's University Press, 1988.

Kierans, Eric, with Walter Stewart. *Remembering.* Toronto: Stoddart, 2001.

Kimmel, David, and Daniel J. Robinson. "Sex, Crime, Pathology: Homosexuality and Criminal Code Reform in Canada, 1949-1969." *Canadian Journal of Law and Society* 16,1 (2001): 147-65.

Larocque, Sylvain. *Gay Marriage: The Story of a Canadian Social Revolution.* Toronto: James Lorimer, 2006.

Laschinger, John, and Geoffrey Stevens, eds. *Leaders and Lesser Mortals.* Toronto: Key Porter, 1992.

Levine, Allan. *Scrum Wars: The Prime Ministers and the Media.* Toronto: Dundurn, 1993.

Leyton-Brown, David, ed. *Canadian Annual Review of Politics and Public Affairs, 1988.* Toronto: University of Toronto Press, 1995.

Litt, Paul. "Trudeaumania: Participatory Democracy in the Mass-Mediated Nation." *Canadian Historical Review* 89, 1 (March 2008): 27-53.

Lynch, Charles. *Race for the Rose: Election 1984.* Toronto: Methuen, 1984.

MacDonald, L. Ian. *Mulroney: The Making of the Prime Minister.* Toronto: McClelland and Stewart, 1984.

MacLeod, Alex. *The Fearsome Dilemma: Simultaneous Inflation and Unemployment.* Stratford, ON: Mercury Press, 1994.

Mann, W.E. *Poverty and Social Policy in Canada.* Toronto: Copp Clark, 1970.

Martel, Marcel. *Not This Time: Canadians, Public Policy and the Marijuana Question, 1961-1975.* Toronto: University of Toronto Press, 2006.

Martin, Lawrence. *Chrétien.* Vol. 1, *The Will to Win.* Toronto: Lester, 1995.

–. *Iron Man: The Defiant Reign of Jean Chrétien.* Toronto: Viking, 2003.

Martin, Paul. *A Very Public Life.* Vol. 2, *So Many Worlds.* Toronto: Deneau, 1985.

Maslove, Alan M., and Gene Swimmer. *Wage Controls in Canada, 1975-78: A Study of Public Decisionmaking.* Montreal: Institute for Research on Public Policy, 1980.

McCall-Newman, Christina. *Grits: An Intimate Portrait of the Liberal Party.* Toronto: Macmillan of Canada, 1982.

McIninch, Elizabeth, and Arthur Milnes, eds. *Politics of Purpose: 40th Anniversary Edition.* Montreal/Kingston: McGill-Queen's University Press, 2009.

McLaren, Angus, and Arlene Tigar McLaren. *The Bedroom and the State: The Changing Practices and Politics of Contraception and Abortion in Canada, in 1880-1980.* Toronto: McClelland and Stewart, 1986.

Meisel, John. "The Boob-Tube Election: Three Aspects of the 1984 Landslide." In *The Canadian House of Commons: Essays in Honour of Norman Ward,* ed. John C. Courtney, 341-72. Calgary: University of Calgary Press, 1985.

–. *Working Papers on Canadian Politics.* Montreal/Kingston: McGill-Queen's University Press, 1973.

Miedema, Gary R. *For Canada's Sake: Public Religion, Centennial Celebrations, and the Re-making of Canada in the 1960s.* Montreal/Kingston: McGill-Queen's University Press, 2005.

Newman, Peter. *The Canadian Revolution.* Toronto: Viking, 1995.

–. *Here Be Dragons: Telling the Tales of People, Passion and Power.* Toronto: McClelland and Stewart, 2004.

Nichols, Marjorie. *Mark My Words: The Memoirs of a Very Political Reporter.* Toronto: Douglas and McIntyre, 1992.

Nielsen, Erik. *The House Is Not a Home.* Toronto: Macmillan, 1989.

Norrie, Kenneth, and Douglas Owram. *A History of the Canadian Economy.* Toronto: Harcourt Brace, 1991.

O'Leary, Grattan. *Recollections of People, Press and Politics.* Toronto: Macmillan, 1977.

O'Sullivan, Sean. *Both My Houses: From Politics to Priesthood.* Toronto: Key Porter, 1986.

Owram, Douglas. *The Government Generation: Canadian Intellectuals and the State, 1900-1945.* Toronto: University of Toronto Press, 1986.

Pelletier, Gérard. *The October Crisis.* Trans. Joyce Marshall. Toronto: McClelland and Stewart, 1971.

Penniman, Howard, ed. *Canada at the Polls, 1984.* Durham, NC: Duke University Press, 1988.

Perlin, George. *The Tory Syndrome.* Montreal/Kingston: McGill-Queen's University Press, 1980.

Pickersgill, J.W. *Seeing Canada Whole: A Memoir.* Toronto: Fitzhenry and Whiteside, 1994.

Pound, Richard. *Chief Justice W.R. Jackett: By the Law of the Land.* Montreal/Kingston: McGill-Queen's University Press, 1999.

–. *Stikeman Elliott: The First Fifty Years.* Montreal/Kingston: McGill-Queen's University Press, 2002.

Riddell, W. Craig. *Dealing with Inflation and Unemployment in Canada.* Toronto: University of Toronto Press, 1986.

Robertson, Gordon. *Memoirs of a Very Civil Servant.* Toronto: University of Toronto Press, 2000.

Royal Commission on Canada's Economic Prospects. *Final Report.* Ottawa: Queen's Printer, 1958.

Rutherford, Paul. "Designing Culture: Reflections on a Post/Modern Project." In *Media, Policy, National Identity and Citizenry in Changing Democratic Societies: The Case of Canada,* ed. J. Smith, 184-94. Durham, NC: Canadian Studies Center, Duke University, 1998.

–. *When Television Was Young.* Toronto: University of Toronto Press, 1990.

Sawatsky, John. *The Insiders: Government, Business, and the Lobbyists.* Toronto: McClelland and Stewart, 1987.

Saywell, John, ed. *Canadian Annual Review of Politics and Public Affairs, 1971.* Toronto: University of Toronto Press, 1972.

–. *Canadian Annual Review of Politics and Public Affairs, 1973.* Toronto: University of Toronto Press, 1974.

Schaff, Philip, ed. *A Select Library of the Nicene and Post-Nicene Fathers of the Christian Church.* Vol. 5, *St. Augustine: Anti-Pelagian Writings.* New York: Christian Literature, 1887.

Sharp, Mitchell. *Which Reminds Me: A Memoir.* Toronto: University of Toronto Press, 1994.

Simpson, Jeffrey. *Spoils of Power: The Politics of Patronage.* Toronto: Collins, 1988.

Smith, David. *The Regional Decline of a National Party: Liberals on the Prairies.* Toronto: University of Toronto Press, 1981.

Snider, Norman. *The Changing of the Guard.* Toronto: Lester and Orpen Dennys, 1985.

Soderlund, Walter C., E. Donald Briggs, Walter I. Romanow, and Ronald H. Wagenberg. *Media and Elections in Canada.* Toronto: Holt, Rinehart and Winston of Canada, 1984.

Sullivan, Martin. *Mandate '68: The Year of Pierre Elliott Trudeau.* Toronto: Doubleday, 1968.

Swainson, Neil A. *Conflict over the Columbia: The Canadian Background to an Historic Treaty.* Montreal/Kingston: McGill-Queen's University Press, 1979.

Swift, Jamie. *Odd Man Out: The Life and Times of Eric Kierans.* Toronto: Douglas and McIntyre, 1988.

Taras, David. *The Newsmakers.* Scarborough, ON: Nelson, 1990.

Taylor, John H. *Ottawa: An Illustrated History.* Toronto: Lorimer, 1986.

Tetley, William. *The October Crisis, 1970: An Insider's View.* Montreal/Kingston: McGill-Queen's University Press, 2006.

Trudeau, Pierre. *Memoirs.* Toronto: McClelland and Stewart, 1993.

Turner, John. *Politics of Purpose.* Toronto: McClelland and Stewart, 1968.

–. "The Senate of Canada – Political Conundrum." In *Canadian Issues: Essays in Honour of Henry F. Angus,* ed. Robert M. Clark, 57-80. Toronto: University of Toronto Press, 1961.

Van Loon, Rick. "Reforming Welfare in Canada." *Public Policy* 27, 4 (Fall 1979): 469-504.

Wagenberg, R.H., W.C. Soderlund, W.I. Romanow, and E.D. Briggs. "Note: Campaigns, Images and Polls: Mass Media Coverage of the 1984 Canadian Election." *Canadian Journal of Political Science* 21, 1 (March 1988): 117-129.

Walker, Michael, ed. *Which Way Ahead? Canada after Wage and Price Control.* Vancouver: Fraser Institute, 1977.

Wallin, Pamela. *Since You Asked.* Toronto: Random House Canada, 1998.

Waterfield, Donald. *Continental Waterboy: The Columbia River Controversy.* Toronto: Clark, Irwin, 1970.

Wearing, J., ed. *The Ballot and Its Message: Voting in Canada.* Toronto: Copp Clark Pittman, 1991.

Wearing, Joseph. *The L-Shaped Party: The Liberal Party of Canada, 1958-1980.* Toronto: McGraw Hill Ryerson, 1981.

–. *Strained Relations: Canadian Parties and Voters.* Toronto: McClelland and Stewart, 1988.

Weston, Greg. *Reign of Error.* Toronto: McGraw-Hill Ryerson, 1988.

Whitaker, Reginald. *The Government Party: Organizing and Financing the Liberal Party of Canada, 1930-1958.* Toronto: University of Toronto Press, 1977.

Wilson, Woodrow. *Congressional Government: A Study in American Politics.* 1885. Reprint, Baltimore: Johns Hopkins University Press, 1981.

Zaslow, Morris. *The Northward Expansion of Canada, 1914-1967.* Toronto: McClelland and Stewart, 1988.

ACKNOWLEDGMENTS

A rchivist and historian Grace Hyam has been a partner in this project from its innocent beginnings and saw it through to the bitter end. She knows the Turner papers at Library and Archives Canada (LAC) inside out, prepared thorough background notes on events and dramatis personae, checked and double-checked niggling details, and advised on issues of interpretation. Resourceful, cheerful, and tolerant of the author's many failings (his memory and note-taking accuracy in particular), she was always a pleasure to work with and deserves a large portion of the credit for the final product.

Elizabeth McIninch conducted several interviews with Mr. Turner on videotape in 1995 that are now part of the Turner papers at LAC and wrote background reports on significant aspects of Turner's career for this study. An author in her own right, in 2009 she published (with co-editor Arthur Milnes) a collection of Turner's speeches that commemorated the fortieth anniversary of his 1968 volume, *Politics of Purpose*. At one point, Milnes was working on Brian Mulroney's memoirs in an office across the hall from the Turner project in the West Memorial Building in Ottawa, and Turner versus Mulroney was frequently reprised by McIninch versus Milnes during coffee breaks.

A number of other researchers dug up information on particular aspects of Turner's career. Beatrice Orchard mined secondary sources for context and specific references to Turner. Ryan Shackleton surveyed newspaper coverage of Turner, summarizing the highlights and selecting illuminating examples, and then inventoried videotapes of Turner speeches, press conferences, and other television appearances for the author to consult at LAC. In England, Enid Hunt tracked down Turner family records, and in Washington, Jake

Hirsch-Allen combed the records of the secretary of state for perspectives on Turner from south of the border. Joseph Dunlop conducted research on the abortion issue in the late 1960s, in the process clarifying many murky dimensions of the issue.

Throughout the intensive phase of research in the LAC Turner papers, Peter DeLottinville (director, Political and Social Division) and Maureen Hoogenraad (archivist, Political Archives Section) were generous hosts, good neighbours, and indispensable liaisons with the rest of the archives. Alix McEwen of LAC Reference Services cut through many procedural tangles and always bailed me out when I was caught inside the archives without credentials. Andrew Rodger (photo archivist) helped with the photo records, and Jim Burant (manager, Art and Photography Division) and Guy Tessier (photo archivist) went out of their way to resolve a photo-scanning crisis.

Several interview subjects offered more than just an interview. John Turner himself was extraordinarily generous with his time – getting to know him was one of the great pleasures of this project. I enjoyed extended discussions on numerous occasions with Turner's friends Jim Robb, the late John Grace, and Richard Alway. The late Jack Cahill was an invaluable resource, and a lunch we had with Turner generated some wonderful reminiscences. John Coleman took it upon himself to tutor me in the intricacies of international monetary reform in the early 1970s. Sandra Kaiser and Lisa Haley not only gave me informative interviews, they opened up doors that put me in touch with other important interview subjects. Brenda Ross, Michael Hunter, and Howard Brown lent me papers that shed light on unknown dimensions of my subject. Hunter, Grace, Coleman, and Robb also read and commented on portions of the manuscript covering aspects of Turner's career with which they were familiar, as did interviewees Doug Kirkpatrick and Stephen Hastings.

Geills Turner supported this project from the start and played a critical role in applying one of the finishing touches. Over the years she has collected a remarkable photo archive documenting her husband's career. Under tight timelines she offered up a trove of images and, given her expertise in photography, provided them in digital files of publishable quality. The photographs that appear here are a fine testament to her work.

Robert Bothwell, who doesn't suffer fools gladly, read successive drafts and suffered greatly. His numerous corrections and enhancements much improved the manuscript. John English also read the book in draft form, pointing out errors and weaknesses in interpretation. The opportunities we had to compare notes on Trudeau and Turner were both diverting and instructive. Barry

Wright kindly read over sections relating to his expertise in Canadian legal history and provided corrections and clarifications. I am also obliged to two anonymous readers for UBC Press who noted errors and offered stimulating commentary.

Rosemary Shipton conducted a thorough edit of the manuscript – and then had to do it again, cutting twenty thousand words to trim it to the publisher's specified length. An engaged critic as well as an editor, she made many suggestions that greatly improved the book. At UBC Press, Melissa Pitts good-naturedly and resiliently oversaw a project that at times mirrored the experience of its subject in the 1980s, and production manager Holly Keller was both resourceful and unflappable. Copy editor Deborah Kerr did an incredibly thorough job, delving into the deepest darkest corners of the endnotes to ferret out inconsistencies and omissions. And publishing intern Jane Hope was resolute in tracking down permissions for the illustrations.

Geoff Seaborn has my deep appreciation for handling many of the administrative aspects of the project with professionalism, good cheer, and, above all, endurance. Finally, I appreciate the infinite patience of my wife and family, whom I expect will soon be parading about the house singing a Harold Arlen requiem from a Judy Garland musical.

As these acknowledgments testify, I have been fortunate to have had the support of many generous and talented people in the writing of this book. Despite their help and my own best efforts, I am sure that I've blundered on matters of both interpretation and fact, and apologize in advance for the failings that are a hallmark of my work.

ILLUSTRATION CREDITS

A reasonable attempt has been made to secure permission to reproduce all material used. If there are errors or omissions they are wholly unintentional and the publisher would be grateful to learn of them.

SECTION 1 (AFTER PAGE 50)

1 John Turner's father, Leonard Turner. Turner family collection, photographer unknown.
2 The Turner family in Rossland, BC. Turner family collection, photographer unknown.
3 Turner as a boy. Turner family collection, photographer unknown.
4 Turner preparing to sprint. Photographer unknown.
5 Phyllis Turner. Used with permission of *Maclean's*.
6 Turner and Chataway at Helsinki Olympics. Photographer unknown.
7 Front page of *Toronto Star*, August 5, 1958. The Toronto Star/GetStock. com.
8 Turner the bachelor. Turner family collection, photographer unknown.
9 Turner's campaign tent. Photographer unknown.
10 Turner, 1962 election. Photographer unknown.
11 Turner, Phyllis Ross, Geills Kilgour, and Brenda Norris. Photographer unknown.
12 Diefenbaker and Turner on beach. Used with permission, photographer Geills M. Turner.

13 Pearson with new cabinet ministers. Photographer unknown.
14 Trudeau, Turner, Pearson, and Chrétien. The Canadian Press, photographer Chuck Mitchell.
15 Turner greeting delegates. Photographer unknown.
16 Turner, 1968 Liberal leadership convention. The Canadian Press, photographer Peter Bregg.

SECTION 2 (AFTER PAGE 146)

17 Turner at Rideau Hall, 1968. The Canadian Press, photographer Doug Ball.
18 Turner with breathalyzer, 1969. The Canadian Press, photographer Peter Bregg.
19 Turner walking to Parliament Hill, 1970. The Canadian Press, photographer Peter Bregg.
20 Trudeau and Turner, October 18, 1970. Photographer unknown.
21 Turner family in 1972. Photographer unknown
22 Victoria conference with Trudeau and Robarts. The Canadian Press Images, photographer Boris Spremo.
23 Turner and Trudeau, May 8, 1972. The Canadian Press, photographer Peter Bregg.
24 Turner and George Shultz. Photographer unknown.
25 Turner and Simon Reisman at a parliamentary committee. Photographer unknown.
26 Turner negotiating with Peter Lougheed. Glenbow Archives, NA-2864-23512.
27 "Jumping Ship" by Duncan Macpherson. © Estate of Duncan Macpherson. Reprinted with permission of Torstar Syndication Services.
28 John and Geills Turner at Toronto press conference. *Toronto Star*, photographer Jeff Goode.

SECTION 3 (AFTER PAGE 274)

29 Turner on the cover of *Toronto Life*. Courtesy of Arnaud Maggs.
30 Turner with supporters outside the Peace Tower. Reproduced with permission, photographer Jean-Marc Carisse.
31 John and Geills Turner, 1984 Liberal leadership convention. The Canadian Press, photographer Ron Poling.

32 Front page of *Globe and Mail*, August 25, 1984. Used with permission of the *Globe and Mail*, photographer Tibor Kolley.
33 Turner in profile. The Canadian Press, photographer Ron Poling.
34 Turner at microphone. CORBIS Images.
35 Turner with Rat Pack. The Canadian Press, photographer Ron Poling.
36 Turner and Raymond Garneau. Reproduced with permission, photographer Jean-Marc Carisse.
37 Turner at Liberal convention, Ottawa, 1986. Photographer unknown.
38 Turner celebrates winning leadership review. The Canadian Press Images, photographer Boris Spremo.
39 *Toronto Sun* political cartoon. Sun Media Inc./Andy Donato.
40 Turner at House of Commons. Library and Archives Canada/Robert Cooper/Office of the Prime Minister Collection, PA-152412.
41 Turner and Brian Mulroney. The Canadian Press, photographer Fred Chartrand.

INDEX

Macdonald, Bill, 205, 210, 215

Macdonald, Donald, 46, 179, 214-16, 219, 227, 229, 302, 304

Macdonald, John A., 12, 349-50

Macdonald Commission. *See* Royal Commission on the Economic Union and Development Prospects for Canada

MacEachen, Allan: budget, 80, 221; leadership candidate, 76, 86-87, 229; and NDP, 173, 182; in Senate, 290, 297; and Trudeau, 219; and Turner, 39, 245, 257; view of FLQ, 426n10

MacGuigan, Mark, 229, 235, 246, 251, 257; delegate votes, 248

Mackasey, Bryce, 160, 256, 268-69, 290, 426n10, 448n8

Maclean's, 45, 47, 116, 166, 234, 239, 289

Manitoba, 133, 277, 278, 335, 391; French-language rights in, 233

Manning, Preston, 328

Mansbridge, Peter, 360, 375-76, 380

Maple Leaf flag, 53, 414n17

Marchand, Jean, 38, 77-78, 176, 183, 426n20; on FLQ question, 124-25, 126, 127, 426n18

Marchi, Sergio, 291, 315, 343, 359, 458n30

Martin, Paul, Jr., 325, 351, 389, 394; delegate votes, 392

Martin, Paul, Sr., 39, 60, 77, 82, 88-89, 299, 417n3; delegate votes, 86

Masse, Marcel, 310

Maxwell, Donald, 96, 114, 420n6

Mazankowski, Don, 383

McCall-Newman, Christina, 223, 445n22

McDonald Commission. *See* Royal Commission of Inquiry into Certain Activities of the Royal Canadian Mounted Police

McGuinty, Dalton J., 102

McIlraith, George, 129, 426n10

McKenna, Frank, 361

McMillan Binch, 396; expansion, 204-5, 220; newsletters, 210-11

McNaughton, Andrew, 59, 60

McRuer, James C., 109, 423n6

McRuer Commission. *See* Royal Commission Inquiry into Civil Rights (Ontario) media: contradictions, 344; criticisms of Turner, 73-74, 235, 237-41; and image creation, 70, 223-24, 230, 299-300, 401, 417n35; lampoons, 282, 285, 351, 362-63, 369-71; and Meech Lake Accord, 330-31; and Mulroney, 223; PC and, 386; portrayals of Turner *vs.* rivals, 83, 161-63, 241; praise of Turner, 380, 381-82; sensationalism, 125; slippery tactics, 234, 417n35; wolfpack journalism, 238-39, 285. *See also* press coverage

medicare, 54, 187-88, 197; free trade and, 383

Meech Lake Accord, 328, 332, 335; amendments, Liberals, 333-35, 337-38, 343; amendments, Senate, 358; and Charter, 332-33; collapsed, 392; emotional issue, 345, 399, 456n17; parallels with Victoria Charter, 329, 336; and Quebec conditions, 328; ratification, 337, 344, 390-91; substance of, 455n8

members of parliament (MPs): free votes, 98-99; role, 51-52. *See also* individual members of parliament

Michelin plant, 156-57, 159

Miller Thomson, 393, 394-95

minority groups: Jewish, 422n4; in judiciary, 117; language rights of, 233-34; in and outside Quebec, 133; treatment of, 108

modernity: and Canadian economy, 157; dangers of, 66; prosperity and, 34, 35; in Quebec, 34, 38, 134; and social justice, 54, 67, 71, 73

Montebello conferences, 115-16, 291, 292-94, 425n41

Montreal, 30; bombing, 121-22, 124; legal community, 30-32; Old Montreal, 30, 31; social unrest in (*see* October Crisis); St. Lawrence-St. George riding, 39, 40-41, 43, 49, 89, 412n19

oil industry: export taxes, 177, 178-79; pipelines, 177, 178; and price of oil, 177-78, 179, 221; tax exemptions, 179-81

oil shock. *See* energy issues

Olympics, 24, 27

omnibus bill, 78, 96, 102-5, 109-10, 116

195 Club, 88, 148, 213

Ontario, 109, 110, 188, 335, 424n16

open government, 112, 232, 260, 391-92; and disorganization, 328

Orange Paper. *See* Working Paper on Social Security in Canada

Organization of Petroleum Exporting Countries (OPEC), 177, 178; and IMF oil facility, 180

organized labour, 189, 191

Osbaldeston, Gordon, 251, 256, 258-59

Osgoode Hall Law School, 67

O'Sullivan, Sean, 169

Ottawa: neighbourhoods, 11-12, 15, 50, 409n13; Ottawa-Carleton riding, 89-90, 102, 440n2; power brokers, 14-15, 161-62, 409n12; schools, 12

Ottawa Citizen, 51, 146, 269

Ottawa Journal, 37, 83

Ouellet, André: Cabinet duties, 257; and constitution, 338; and Garneau, 291; and Johnston, 332-33; on patronage, 270; Quebec organizer, 236, 252, 256-57, 273, 295, 311, 354; and Turner, 373, 375

Ouimet Committee, 109-10

Oxford University, 25-27

Parti Québécois, 134, 145, 209, 238, 272

party discipline, 52, 326-27, 342, 361, 402-4

patent protection, 72, 354-55

patriation of constitution, 137, 220; agreement in principle, 144; Turner's role in, 431n24

patriotism, and free trade, 371-72, 379

patronage, 117; as corruption, 267-69; Mulroney appointments, 309-10;

Pearson appointments, 447n17; rescinded appointments, 290; Trudeau appointments, 255-56, 258-60, 264, 447n10; Turner appointments, 448n6

Payne, John de B.: consultant, 413n8; and election campaign, 280; on press corps, 235-36; on Turner, 409n20; Turner adviser, 41, 49, 215, 224, 236, 244, 296, 326, 417n35, 432n13; and Turner nomination, 40-41, 89, 228-30

Pearson, Lester B. (Mike): and bilingualism in public service, 135; cabinet choices, 50-51, 68; commission on price spreads, 70; elections, 42, 45, 50, 61-62; leadership style, 5, 38, 51, 59, 63; and non-confidence vote, 80; parallels with Turner, 292, 293; patronage appointments, 447n17; and Phyllis Turner, 16; in polls, 42; reform agenda, 53-54, 59, 414n17; resignation, 75; and Trudeau, 78-79; and Turner, 37, 165

Pelletier, Gérard, 38, 126-27, 135-36, 141, 143, 336, 426n12, 429n3

Penner, Keith, 343, 458n30

Pépin, Lucie, 315, 318, 369, 458n30

personality: and image, 5-6, 16, 409n20; for politics, 39; Turner *vs.* Trudeau, 78

Peterson, David, 300, 320, 330, 361, 386, 391

Peterson, Heather, 227, 230, 462n16

Peterson, Leslie, 140

petrodollars, recycling of, 180, 181

Pickersgill, Jack, 37, 63-64, 168, 299

Pitfield, Michael, 193, 194

policy development: on constitutional deal, 313-16; grassroots role, 293-94, 307-8, 322-23, 453n2; in open party, 340; and platform, 356, 367; thinkers' conference, 337; three themes, 453n1

policy differences: Chrétien *vs.* Turner, 241-42, 400; Trudeau *vs.* Turner, 80, 83-84, 199-200, 231-32, 243-44, 247, 313-14, 398-99, 446n42. *See also* political rivalries

political capital, 194, 195, 344
political centre, 160, 225
political cultures, 230, 239, 347-48, 400-1, 445n22
political interventions: in election campaign, 375-76, 385; in leadership campaign, 243-44, 445n40; in Meech Lake, 336
political rivalries: Chrétien vs. Turner, 240-42, 245-46, 251-53, 310-12, 323, 393-94, 453n19; Trudeau vs. Turner, 171-74, 208-10, 215, 243-44, 249, 258-59, 283
political styles: Trudeau, 172-73; Trudeau vs. Turner, 147-49, 429n3; Turner, 168-69
politics: in cabinet, 64; in caucus, 51-52; federal, 37-45; of image, 286; in legal community, 36-37; Liberal Party, 72-73; on Parliament Hill, 46; university, 22-24
Politics of Purpose, 83
Pontifical Institute of Mediaeval Studies, 101
Pope Leo XIII, 206-7
Pope Paul VI, 99
Popowich, Terry, 317-18
pork-barrel system. *See* patronage
power: bilateral agreements and, 308, 351; Canada vs. US, 60-61; economic vs. political, 221-22; federal vs. provincial, 56, 145, 313-14; fragility of, 287; Liberal addiction to, 320; locus of, 297-98; and party unity, 324, 327; of PMO, 193, 254-55; of the state, 107-8, 111, 423n11; transition from Trudeau, 251, 258, 446n9; of younger generation, 66, 69
prescription drug prices, 71-72, 81, 354-55, 417n31, 418n17
press coverage: of budget, 156, 197; of bum patting, 274; of finance minister appointment, 153-54; of language issues, 233-34; of leaders' debates, 276-77; of leadership issue, 213, 375-76; of

Liberal platform, 368-69; of Meech Lake Accord, 330-31, 334; of October Crisis, 123, 125, 128; polls and, 281; of Senate embargo, 365-66; of Turner Cabinet, 260-61; of Turner campaign, 267, 269; of Turner resignation, 200, 243; of Turner's critiques of Trudeau, 211; of water issues, 60, 61. *See also* media
Prices and Incomes Commission, 190
Prime Minister's Office (PMO): assaults on Turner, 198-200, 383-84; and elections, 254-55, 270, 279; and Liberal Party, 289; and patronage, 309; self-sufficiency, 171, 186, 193, 208, 437n1, 446n8
Primrose Club incident, 209, 440n11
Princess Margaret, 35-36, 411n11
privacy legislation, 107, 111-12, 423n13
private sector. *See* business
Privy Council Office, 208
Pro-Canada Network, 353, 385
Progressive Conservative Party, 42, 60; campaigns, 266-67, 384-86; in elections, 2, 49, 183, 214, 219, 404; financial stewardship of, 300-1; fundraising, 266, 308; leadership, 204, 223, 269, 442n6; Liberal aid to, 366, 383, 387-88; nepotism, 310; offer to Turner, 200-1, 439n43; in opposition, 172; in polls, 2, 227, 243, 264, 279, 281, 304, 306, 312, 338, 368, 372, 381-82, 443n20, 450n41; in Quebec, 273, 275; response to Senate embargo, 367-68; scandals, 298, 301, 310, 328. *See also* House of Commons, seats (Tory)
protectionism, 152, 180, 302, 304, 352, 384
Public Order (Temporary Measures) Act, 128-29, 130
public service: bilingual, 142; French Canadians in, 133-34, 135; politicization of, 193
Public Service Commission, 70, 142-43

Quebec: civil law, 31; and constitution, 144-46, 272, 291, 313-16, 328 (*see also* Charlottetown Accord; Meech Lake Accord); electorate, 271-72; *vs.* English Canada, 134; federal spending in, 252; and free trade, 366; language issues, 121, 135, 238 (*see also Official Languages Act*); modernization, 34, 38, 54-55, 134; nationalism/separatism, 6, 34, 38, 54-55, 76, 209, 219-20, 419n31; opting out, 187; special status, 79, 138, 140; Turner *vs.* Trudeau approaches to, 80, 83-84

Quebec lieutenant, 40, 252, 256-57, 260-61, 313, 355

Question Period, 296-98

Quiet Revolution, 38, 54-55, 134, 411n8

rainmakers pledge, 232, 254, 278

Rat Pack, 292, 297-98, 309-10, 452n21

Reagan, Ronald, 225, 266, 290, 305, 364-65, 385

Red Leaf Communications, 278, 381

reform ethos, 113-14, 115-16. *See also* legal reform

Reform Party, 328, 387, 405

Registered Home Ownership Savings Plan, 182

Reid, Angus, 225, 227, 236, 254, 262, 270, 290-91, 338, 358-59, 450n32

Reisman, Simon, 169-72, 186, 194, 251, 302, 383, 432n4, 434n17

reputation: advertising blitz and, 384-86; assassination of, 300, 340, 349, 362-63, 382, 458n30; attacks on, 387, 390; Cabinet positions and, 189, 194, 203, 225, 428n33; as civil libertarian, 130, 428n33, 429n38; McDonald Commission and, 224-25, 442n10, 443n11; plan to destroy, 382-83; and private sector, 205, 207, 211

Rex v. Bourne, 420n9

Rhodes Scholarship, 25, 27

Richardson, Claude, 40, 412n19

Richardson, Doug, 316, 317, 327, 332, 339, 356, 363

Ricoeur, Paul, 100

right to counsel. *See* legal aid

rights discourse, 108, 422n4

Rizzuto, Pietro, 317, 342, 359, 361, 462n16

Robb, Jim, 31-32, 41, 227, 265

Robert, Michel, 323, 325, 341-42, 360-61, 390, 453n13

Roberts, John, 235, 246, 248, 257, 358

Robertson, Norman, 14, 16

Roman Catholic Church. *See* Catholicism

Ross, Frank, 19-22, 28, 35-36, 39

Ross, Phyllis Turner. *See* Turner, Phyllis Gregory

Rossland, 12, 244

Royal Commission Inquiry into Civil Rights (Ontario), 109-10

Royal Commission of Inquiry into Certain Activities of the Royal Canadian Mounted Police, 224-25, 442n10 Royal Commission on Bilingualism and Biculturalism, 54, 76, 135, 336

Royal Commission on Canada's Economic Prospects, 47

Royal Commission on the Economic Union and Development Prospects for Canada, 302, 304

Royal Commission on Taxation, 151

Ryan, Claude, 84, 123, 146, 426n11

Saint-Martin Tremblay, Lise, 232, 270, 274, 341

Saskatchewan, 66, 278

Saturday Night, 168

Sauvé, Jeanne, 38, 260, 264

Sauvé, Maurice, 38, 46

Schollar, Sharon, 295, 338-39

Schwartz, Gerry, 325, 357

Scott, F.R., 116

Sears, Val, 237, 245, 282, 445n21

"A Second Canada," 66, 416n12

Printed and bound in Canada by Friesens

Set in Alternate Gothic, Perpetua Titling, and Minion
by Artegraphica Design Co. Ltd.

Text design: Irma Rodriguez

Copy editor: Deborah Kerr

Proofreader and indexer: Dianne Tiefensee